C. De
7118 Bokute

Jehl
Yale

Maysville Rd

Yale

Bokute

Social Problems

Social Problems

William Kornblum
City University of New York, Graduate School and University Center

Joseph Julian
San Francisco State University

In collaboration with
Carolyn D. Smith

Prentice Hall, Englewood Cliffs, New Jersey 07632

Library of Congress Cataloging-in-Publication Data

Kornblum, William.
    Social problems / William Kornblum, Joseph Julian, in
collaboration with Carolyn D. Smith.—8th ed.
      p.   cm.
    Includes bibliographical references and index.
    ISBN 0-13-101148-0
    1. Sociology.   2. Social problems.   3. United States—Social
conditions.   I. Julian, Joseph.   II. Smith, Carolyn D.   III. Title.
HM51.K657 1995
361.1—dc20   94-18152
                                             CIP

Editorial Director: Charlyce Jones Owen
Editor-in-Chief and Acquisitions Editor: Nancy Roberts
Project Manager: Marina Harrison
Copy Editor: Linda Pawelchak
Cover and Interior Designer: Jeannette Jacobs
Design Director: Anne Bonanno Nieglos
Buyer: Mary Ann Gloriande
Editorial Assistant: Pat Naturale
Photo Researcher: Melinda Reo
Cover art: John Marin. *Lower Manhattan* (Composing Derived from Top of Woolworth). 1922
       Watercolor and charcoal with paper cutout attached with thread, on paper.
       21 5/8 3 26 7/8 ″. Acquired through the Lillie P. Bliss Bequest.
       The Museum of Modern Art, New York.

Social Problems, 8/e
William Kornblum/Joseph Julian

© 1995, 1992, 1989, 1986, 1983, 1980, 1977, 1974 by Prentice-Hall, Inc.
A Simon & Schuster Company
Englewood Cliffs, New Jersey 07632

Printed in the United States of America
10 9 8 7 6 5 4 3 2

ISBN 0-13-101148-0

Prentice-Hall International (UK) Limited, *London*
Prentice-Hall of Australia Pty. Limited, *Sydney*
Prentice-Hall Canada Inc., *Toronto*
Prentice-Hall Hispanoamericana, S.A., *Mexico*
Prentice-Hall of India Private Limited, *New Delhi*
Prentice-Hall of Japan, Inc., *Tokyo*
Simon & Schuster Asia Pte. Ltd., *Singapore*
Editora Prentice-Hall do Brasil, Ltda., *Rio de Janeiro*

Contents

Chris

18. *War and Terrorism* *529*

Preface

As this 8th edition of *Social Problems* goes to press, the world seems an increasingly dangerous and difficult environment for human development. A comprehensive social problems textbook may seem discouraging at times. After all, each chapter describes one or more of the may serious challenges facing our society, if not our species. But readers of this book will also find that it is a testimony to the human ability to innovate and to improve social conditions.

For every major social problem confronting Americans and citizens of other nations, there are groups of people dedicated to seeking a solution. Some of those groups are composed of experts on particular social problems, like the members of the medical professions who each day confront the tragedy of AIDS, or the law enforcement professionals who cope with crime and violence. Others are made up of nonprofessionals. Often they are composed of citizens who have decided to devote themselves to doing something about a particular situation or problem. Among these activists are people who have experienced the condition they seek to improve—women who have experienced sexual abuse, people who understand what it is to be homeless, drug and alcohol abusers who seek to help themselves and others, neighbors confronted with dumping of toxic wastes. Such groups may include elected officials and other political leaders who are expected to formulate sound social policies to address social problems.

Even when a problem that was thought to be improving, such as poverty and homelessness, is actually worsening—as is happening now in some parts of the United States—more and more people are organizing to do something about it. This book is written in an effort to make their work more effective and in the hope that some readers will be moved to take up their cause. We dedicate it to the citizens of the world who devote some of their precious time on earth to helping others.

ORGANIZATION OF THE BOOK

The early chapters of this book focus on relatively individual behaviors, such as drug use and crime. The social institutions and other factors affecting these behaviors are noted and described. The middle chapters focus on inequality and discrimination in discussing such topics as poverty, prejudice, sexism, and ageism. Every attempt has been made to indicate the effects of large-scale discrimination on individuals as well as to deal with the concept of institutionalized inequalities. Later chapters discuss problems that are common to many societies, such as those related to family life and work. The final chapters, those on the problems of cities, environmental pollution, and war and terrorism, focus on matters of global significance. It seemed best to discuss each subject in a separate chapter in order to deal with it comprehensively and in depth. Throughout the book, however, an attempt has been made to indicate how the different problems overlap and are interrelated.

PEDAGOGICAL DEVICES

Social Problems has been designed to be as helpful as possible to both students and teachers. Each problem is discussed in a well-organized and readable manner. As much as possible, unnecessary terminology has been avoided. The treatment of each problem is analytical as well as descriptive, and includes the most up-to-date findings available.

Each chapter begins with an outline and a set of significant facts, and ends with a summary that lists the important concepts presented in the chapter. There is also an annotated list of suggested readings. Important terms in each chapter are italicized; definitions of those terms are included in a glossary at the end of the book. In addition, boxed discussions in each chapter deal with current controversies or unintended consequences of efforts to alleviate social problems.

CHANGES IN THE EIGHTH EDITION

The reception given to previous editions of *Social Problems* by both colleagues and students has been encouraging, and many of their suggestions and criticisms have been incorporated in subsequent revisions. This edition represents a continuing effort to create a comprehensive, up-to-date text. To this end, the text has been thoroughly revised. Our aim has been to retain the book's emphasis on the sociological analysis of social problems, as well as the policies designed to alleviate or eliminate them. Although policies change continually, we have attempted to update the discussions of policy to reflect the most recent thinking about solutions to social problems.

In the preparation of this edition, certain areas of the text have received special attention. Chapter 2 ("Problems of Physical Health") has been extensively revised in light of the Clinton administration's health care reform proposals. Chapter 5 ("Alcohol and Other Drugs") includes a thorough discussion of the study of patterns of drug use in the U.S. population and subgroups within it, along with the potential for misinterpretation of the findings. The chapters on crime and violence include more discussion of corporate crime, rape, gangs, and gun control. Chapter 9 ("Prejudice and Discrimination") includes expanded discussions of residential segregation and the link between continuing school segregation and the failure to enforce fair-housing legislation.

Later chapters include new material on topics that are receiving increased attention from both researchers and policy makers: sexual harassment (Chapter 10); elder abuse (Chapter 11); stepfamilies, gay and lesbian parents, child care by fathers (Chapter 12); corporate downsizing, mergers and takeovers (Chapter 14); shelter poverty, homelessness, and neighborhood distress (Chapter 15); China's "missing" female infants (Chapter 16); and the impact of ethnic and tribal conflicts on prospects for world peace (Chapter 18).

Throughout the text, statistical material, figures, and tables have been updated wherever possible, and recent research has been cited throughout. The Social Policy sections incorporate the Clinton administration's programs and proposals.

SUPPLEMENTS

The text is accompanied by an instructor's edition, a test item file, PH Test Manager gradebook software, telephone test preparation service, a study guide, transparencies, The New York Times *Themes of The Times,* and the ABC News/Prentice Hall Video Library for Social Problems. The instructor's edition, the student version of the text with the instructor's manual bound into the front of the book, provides chapter overviews, teaching objectives, teaching suggestions, discussion questions, class exercises, essay questions, and a list of audiovisual resources. The test item file contains multiple choice and essay questions. PH Test Manager, free upon adoption, provides the test item file on disk, available for either the IBM or the Macintosh, and allows the instructor to edit existing Prentice Hall questions, create and edit additional questions, and delete questions. The gradebook software, also free upon adoption, is a program for the IBM that allows instructors to keep class records, assign grades, average grades, compute class statistics, print graphs of individual test grades and final grades, and sort by student name or grade. The telephone test preparation service, free to adopters, allows the instructor to select up to 200 questions from the test item file and call Prentice Hall, toll free, to prepare a test (and an alternate version if requested). The test is prepared on bond paper or a ditto master and within 24 hours is mailed together, with a separate answer key, directly to the instructor. The study guide provides chapter summaries, learning objectives, chapter outlines, key terms and definitions, self-tests (multiple choice and essay), and an answer key for self-tests that provides questions to be considered in answering the essays.

ABC News/Prentice Hall Video Library for Sociology, Series I, II, III (Issues in Sociology), and IV (Global Culturalism)

Video is the most dynamic supplement you can use to enhance a class. But the quality of the video material and how well it relates to your course still make all the difference. Prentice Hall and ABC News are now working together to bring you the best and most comprehensive video ancillaries available in the college market.

Through its wide variety of award-winning programs—*Nightline, Business World, On Business, This Week with David Brinkley, World News Tonight,* and *The Health Show*—ABC offers a resource for feature and documentary-style videos related to the chapters in *Social Problems,* Eighth Edition. The programs have extremely high production quality, present substantial content, and are hosted by well-versed, well-known anchors.

Prentice Hall and its authors and editors provide the benefit of having selected videos and topics that will work well with this course and text and include notes on how to use them in the classroom. An excellent video guide in the *Data File* carefully and completely integrates the videos into your lecture. The guide has a synopsis of each video showing its relation to the chapter and discussion questions to help students focus on how concepts and theories apply to real-life situations.

The New York Times Supplement

The New York Times and Prentice Hall are sponsoring *Themes of The Times,* a program designed to enhance student access to current information of relevance in the classroom.

Through this program, the core subject matter provided in the text is supplemented by a collection of time-sensitive articles from one of the world's most distinguished newspapers, *The New York Times.* These articles demonstrate the vital, ongoing connection between what is learned in the classroom and what is happening in the world around us.

To enable the students to enjoy the wealth of information of *The New York Times* daily, a reduced subscription rate is available. For information, call toll-free: 1-800-631-1222.

Prentice Hall and *The New York Times* are proud to co-sponsor *Themes of the Times*. We hope it will make the reading of both textbooks and newspapers a more dynamic, involving process.

ACKNOWLEDGMENTS

Revising and updating a social problems textbook is a formidable task. Social problems is a far-ranging field with a myriad of findings and concepts that accumulate rapidly and are often changed. This edition has benefited from the reviews of many sociologists, all of whom have contributed useful comments and suggestions. We are happy to number among them the following: Nancy Bartkowski, Northern Michigan University; Susan L. Blackwell, Delgado Community College; Verghese J. Chirayath, John Carroll University; William M. Cross, Illinois College; Phillip W. Davis, Georgia State University; Julia Hall, Drexel University; Daniel J. Klenow, North Dakota State University; Linda Mooney, East Carolina University; Robert Perrucci, Purdue University; Edward G. Stockwell, Bowling Green State University; and Kevin Thompson, North Dakota State University.

To the following, whose suggestions have enriched all seven previous editions, a special thank-you: Mark Abrahamson, University of Connecticut; Howard Bahr, Brigham Young University; Nancy Bartowski, Northern Michigan University; William Bielby, University of California–Santa Barbara; Edwin Boling, Wittenberg University; Carol E. Chandler, McHenry County College; William T. Clute, University of Nebraska–Omaha; William Cockerham, University of Illinois–Urbana–Champaign; William L. Collins, Asheville-Buncombe Technical Community College; Paul L. Crook, San Diego Mesa College; John Farley, Southern Illinois University; Michael P. Farrell, State University of New York–Buffalo; William Feigelman, Nassau Community College; Morris A. Forslund, University of Wyoming; Sidney Forsythe, Wheaton College; John Galliher, University of Missouri; Harry Gold, Oakland University; Erich Goode, State University of New York–Stony Brook; Norman Goodman, State University of New York–Stony Brook; Marshall Graney, Wayne State University; James Greenley, University of Wisconsin; Julia Hall, Drexel University; John Hedderson, University of Texas–El Paso; John Hendricks, University of Kentucky; Mary R. Holley, Montclair State College; Nils Hovik, Lehigh County Community College; Gary Jensen, University of Arizona; Richard I. Jolliff, El Camino College; Russell I. Johnson, Washington University; Louis Kriesberg, Syracuse University; Patricia Lengermann, George Washington University; and Betty Levine, Indiana University.

Also, Peter Maida, University of Maryland; Wilfred Marston, University of Michigan–Flint; Edward J. McCabe, Eastern Michigan University; Robert G. Miller, Baker University; George C. Myers, Duke University; Charles Nam, Florida State University; Steven Nock, University of Virgina; Donald Noel, University of Wisconsin; Donald Olmsted, Michigan State University; Barry Perlman, Community College of Philadelphia; Karen Predow, formerly of Rutgers University; Robert Rothman, University of North Carolina; Nora Roy, Tennessee University; Earl R. Schaeffer, Columbus State Community College; David Schulz, University of Delaware; Mary Sellers, Northampton County Area Community College; John W. Shepard, Jr., Baylor University; Edward G. Stockwell, Bowling Green State University; Russell Stone, State University of New York–Buffalo; Ann Sundgren, Tacoma Community College; Miriam G. Vosburgh, Villanova University; William Waegel, Villanova University; Ruth Wallace, George Washington University; and Irving Zola, Brandeis University.

Finally, thanks are due to the many skilled publishing specialists who contributed their talents to this edition. Much of the research on which the revision is based was provided by Michael McSpedon. Administrative aspects of the project were skillfully handled by acquisitions editor Nancy Roberts. Designer Jeannette Jacobs created pleasing cover and interior designs. Marina Harrison, the production editor, did an enormous amount of work to get the book out on time. Melinda Reo took charge of rounding up the photographs that complement the text, and Mary Ann Gloriande was responsible for the manufacturing process. The book owes much to the efforts, creativity, and perseverance of each of them.

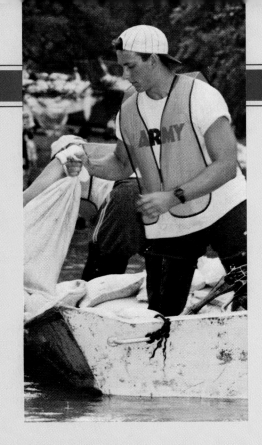

Sociological Perspectives on Social Problems

Chapter Outline

Peter Canavan is a nurse on the AIDS floor of a large public hospital. After earning his M.A. in sociology during the early 1980s, he became committed to taking action against the AIDS epidemic. He chose a career in nursing and now must deal every day of his working life with the suffering of AIDS patients and the immense difficulty of treating their multifaceted illnesses. Although he remains dedicated to the fight against this insidious disease, he is increasingly frustrated by the lack of services for indigent AIDS patients, especially those who are members of minority groups and have no homes or families. Canavan is only one of a growing number of health-care professionals who are lending their voices to the protest against official policies on AIDS.

Charles Keating once was riding high as the director of a large savings and loan association in the Southwest. Now he is serving a ten-year sentence for defrauding the public. During the deregulation of the banking industry in the 1980s, he maneuvered his corporation into extremely risky real estate ventures, knowing that if his gambles failed, the government would guarantee the bad debts at the taxpayers' expense. He didn't expect the investments to go bad, but they did. Many people lost large portions of their savings, and in the early 1990s the American taxpayers realized that this and other savings and loan scams were going to cost them untold billions of dollars. Upon closer investigation it turned out that many other S&L officials besides Keating had engaged in fraudulent business dealings, and some of them, but by no means all, will be serving time along with this notorious "white-collar" criminal.

Alfonso Morales works for a small electronics manufacturer in the Midwest. For many years during the 1980s the town where the Morales family lives was losing manufacturing jobs, so the state and the town worked together to attract manufacturing firms that would hire the unemployed machine operators. But in order to attract the cost-conscious new firms, the state government had to agree to less stringent rules regarding employee benefits. As a result, many of the new businesses, including the factory where Morales works, do not offer pensions to their workers. This means that when Morales and his wife retire, they will not have anything to live on besides their federal social security payments. The proportion of American workers who are not covered by pension plans increased from 51 percent in 1979 to 57 percent in 1992, a signal of economic distress for older Americans early in the next century.

57%

In 1994 the rate of AIDS infection through heterosexual transmission surpassed the rate of transmission via homosexual contact. In consequence, participants in demonstrations for increased funding for AIDS research and treatment are more representative of the general population than was true in the past.

WHAT IS A SOCIAL PROBLEM?

Most readers will no doubt agree that these brief but all too common episodes from daily life are examples of social problems. We can readily identify AIDS, crime, and reduced employee benefits as some of our society's most pressing problems. Of course, we might mention others, such as drugs, poverty, violence, racism and sexism, environmental pollution, and homelessness. Our final list would depend to a large extent on what part of the nation we live in and what issues affect our lives most immediately.

For any one of the problems just mentioned, debates may arise over its nature. Some might argue, for example, that people who are sexually promiscuous or use drugs intravenously bring their troubles upon themselves. But others might point out that the consequences of AIDS and other illnesses are problems that should concern everyone. These and similar arguments deal not only with the causes of social problems but also with what should be done about them. Most people will agree that AIDS is a problem that society must somehow address. And this is true for all the other issues mentioned earlier: Most members of society agree that they are conditions that ought to be remedied.

Of course, agreement that remedies are necessary does not imply that people agree on what the remedies should be. In the aftermath of the historic Mississippi Valley floods of 1993, for example, many people in the immediate flood area believed that more government funds should be made available to rebuild levees and flood protection systems. Others, who were less directly affected by the flooding, were more likely to argue that the river should be allowed to periodically flood a larger plain and that the government should no longer subsidize flood insurance for people in flood-prone areas. Thus, while all agree that the problems of destruction of communities and loss of livelihood caused by flooding are social problems that need to be addressed, there is conflict over how best to solve these problems. In short, recognition that a social problem exists is far different from arriving at a consensus about what to do about the problem.

When most people in a society agree that a condition exists that threatens the quality of their lives and their most cherished values, and also agree that something should be done to remedy that condition, sociologists say that the society has defined that condition as a social problem. In other words, the society's members have reached a broad consensus that a condition that affects some members of the population is a problem for the entire society, not just for those who are directly affected.

The importance of this definition will become clearer if we consider one or two examples. In China before the Communist revolution of the mid-twentieth century, opium use and addiction were widespread. In Shanghai alone there were an estimated 400,000 opium addicts in the late 1940s. Everyone knew that the condition existed, and many responsible public figures deplored it; but few outside the revolutionary parties believed that the society should intervene in any way. After all, many of the society's richest and most powerful members had made their fortunes in the opium trade. The Chinese Communists believed that society should take responsibility for eradicating opium addiction, and when they took power they did so, often through drastic and violent means. What had previously been seen as a social condition had been redefined as a social problem that had to be solved.

To take an example from our own society, before 1920 women in the United States did not have the right to vote. Many women objected to this condition and opposed it whenever possible, but most men and many women valued the traditional pattern of male dominance and female subservience. To them, there was nothing unusual about women's status as second-class citizens. It took many years of painstaking organization, persuasion, and demonstration by the leaders of the women's suffrage movement to convince significant numbers of Americans that women's lack of voting rights was a social problem that the society should remedy through revision of its laws. We will see later in the book, and especially in Chapter 10, that the conditions that affect women's lives continue to be viewed by some members of society as natural and inevitable and by others as problems that require action by the society as a whole (Goldberg, 1972).

It is worth noting that the idea that a society should intervene to remedy conditions affecting the lives of its citizens is a fairly recent innovation. Until the eighteenth century, for example, most people worked at exhausting tasks under poor conditions for long hours; they suffered from severe deprivation all their lives, and they often died young, sometimes of terrible diseases. But no one thought of these things as problems to be solved. They were accepted as natural, inevitable conditions of life. It was not until the so-called "enlightenment" of the late eighteenth century that philosophers began to argue that poverty is not inevitable but is a result of an unjust social system. As such, it could be alleviated through intentional change in the system itself, through such means as redistribution of wealth and elimination of inherited social status.

The founders of the American nation applied these principles in creating a form of government that was designed to "establish justice, insure domestic tranquility . . . promote the general welfare . . . and secure the blessings of liberty." The U.S. Constitution guaranteed the rights of individual citizens and established the legal basis for remedying conditions that are harmful to the society's members. Moreover, through the system of representative government that it also created, the Constitution established a means by which citizens could define a condition like poverty as one that society should attempt to remedy. Later in this chapter and at many points throughout the book, we will see how this process is carried out and the effects it has had and continues to have on American society.

We will also see many instances of the interconnections among social problems. This interconnectedness is already evident from the brief examples given at the beginning of the chapter. In the case of AIDS, for example, we see a direct link to the rising costs of medical care. In the case of Alfonso Morales, the decline in manufacturing is linked to the increasing economic hardships facing American workers, especially those just entering or leaving the workforce. Very often, therefore, when governmental leaders seek solutions to social problems they must consider multifaceted approaches that address entire sets of problems rather than a single problem by itself, a situation that makes the formulation of effective social policy quite difficult.

SOCIOLOGICAL PERSPECTIVES ON SOCIAL PROBLEMS

Everybody has opinions about the causes of social problems and what should be done about them. Some people will argue, for example, that the problems of a homeless single mother are her own fault. She may be morally loose or mentally unsound, not very bright, or not motivated to work hard and lift herself and her family out of poverty. These are all familiar explanations of individual misfortune. At worst, they blame the individual for his or her situation. At best, they explain individual troubles in terms of traits that the person cannot control. In fact, for this one unfortunate woman any of these simple explanations might be true. But even if they are true for particular individuals, none of them tells us why the same pattern is repeated for entire groups of people.

Why are increasing numbers of women becoming single mothers, and why are an increasing number of these women becoming homeless as well? Why does it seem that women who are born into poor and minority families are more likely to become single mothers, and possibly heads of homeless families, than women who are born into middle-class families of any racial or ethnic group? And what about the experience of being homeless? Does that experience inflict hardships on women and children that make it more difficult for them to perform productive roles in society and attain the "good life"?

These are sociological questions. They ask why a condition like homelessness exists. They ask how the condition is distributed in society and whether some people are more at risk than others. They are questions about the social rather than the individual aspects of a problem. And they are not important merely from an academic or social-scientific viewpoint. Answers to these questions are a prerequisite for effective action to eliminate social problems. Note, however, that research on these issues is not limited to sociology. Other social-scientific approaches to the study of social problems are described in Box 1–1 on page 6.

Contemporary sociology is founded on three basic perspectives, or sets of ideas, that offer theories about why societies hang together and how and why they change. These perspectives are not the only sociological approaches to social problems, but they can be extremely powerful tools for understanding such problems. Each of these perspectives—functionalism, conflict theory, and interactionism—gives rise to a number of distinctive approaches to the study of social problems. (See Table 1–1.) We will explore several of those approaches in the following sections, devoting special attention to how they seek to explain one of society's most pressing problems: criminal deviance.

TABLE 1–1 MAJOR PERSPECTIVES ON SOCIAL PROBLEMS

PERSPECTIVE	VIEW OF SOCIETY AND SOCIAL PROBLEMS	ORIGINS OF SOCIAL PROBLEMS	PROPOSED SOLUTIONS
Functionalist	Views society as a vast organism whose parts are interrelated; social problems are disruptions of this system. Also holds that problems of social institutions produce patterns of deviance or that institutions must address such patterns through strategic social change.	Social expectations fail, creating normlessness, culture conflict, and breakdown. Social problems also result from the impersonal operations of existing institutions, both now and in the past.	Engage in research and active intervention to improve social institutions.
Conflict	Views society as marked by conflicts due to inequalities of class, race, ethnicity, gender, age, and other major divisions. These often produce conflicting values. Defines social problems as conditions that do not conform to society's values.	Groups with different values and differing amounts of power meet and compete.	Build stronger social movements among groups with grievances. The conflicting groups may then engage in negotiations and reach mutual accommodations.
Interactionist	Holds that definitions of deviance or social problems are subjective; separates deviant and nondeviant people not by what they do but by how society reacts to what they do.	Society becomes aware that certain behaviors exist and labels them as social problems.	"Resocialize" deviants by increasing their contacts with accepted patterns of behavior; make the social system less rigid. Change the definition of what is considered deviant.

BOX 1–1   OTHER APPROACHES TO THE STUDY OF SOCIAL PROBLEMS

In addition to sociology, other disciplines within the social sciences are concerned with the analysis of human behavior. Sociologists often draw upon the results of research in these disciplines. The work of historians, for example, is vital to an understanding of the origins of many social problems. The research of anthropologists on nonindustrial and tribal societies offers contrasting views of how humans have learned to cope with various kinds of social problems. Perhaps the greatest overlap is between sociology and political science, both of which are concerned with the processes by which policies deal with social problems that arise in different societies. Following are brief descriptions of several social-scientific disciplines whose research has a bearing on the study of social problems.

HISTORY

History is the study of the past. However, historical data can be used by sociologists to understand present social problems. In studying homelessness, for example, historians would focus on changes in how people obtained shelter in a society and what groups or individuals tended to be without shelter in different historical periods.

CULTURAL ANTHROPOLOGY

Cultural anthropologists study the social organization and development of smaller, nonindustrial societies, both past and present. Since cultural anthropology is closely related to sociology, many of the same techniques can be used in both fields, and the findings of cultural anthropologists regarding primitive and traditional cultures shed light on related phenomena in more complex modern societies. An anthropological study of homelessness would be likely to look very closely at one or a few groups of homeless persons. The anthropologist might be interested in how the homeless and others in their communities seek to understand their situation and what might be done about it.

PSYCHOLOGY AND SOCIAL PSYCHOLOGY

Psychology deals with human mental and emotional processes, focusing primarily on individual experience. Rooted in biology, it is more experimental than the other social sciences. An understanding of the psychological pressures underlying individual responses can illuminate social attitudes and behavior. Thus, a psychologist would tend to study the influences of homelessness on the individual's state of mind or, conversely, how the individual's personality and ways of looking at life might have contributed to his or her situation of homelessness.

Social psychology, the study of how psychological processes, behavior, and personalities of individuals influence, or are influenced by, social processes and social settings, is of particular value for the study of social problems. A social psychologist would be likely to study how life on the streets damages the individual in various ways.

ECONOMICS

Economists study the levels of income in a society and the distribution of income among the society's members. To understand how the resources of society—its people and their talents, its land and other natural resources—can be allocated for the maximum benefit of that society, economists also study the relationship between the supply of those resources and the demand for them. Confronted with the problem of homelessness, an economist would tend to study how the supply and demand for housing of different types influences the number of homeless people in a given housing market.

POLITICAL SCIENCE

Political scientists study the workings of government at every level of society. As Harold Lasswell, a leading American political scientist, put it, "Politics is the study of who gets what, when, and how." A political scientist, therefore, would be likely to see homelessness as a problem resulting from the relative powerlessness of the homeless to influence the larger society to respond to their needs. The political scientist would tend to focus on ways in which the homeless could mobilize other political interest groups to urge legislators to deal with the problem.

They don't have any money!

The Functionalist Perspective

From the day we are born until the day we die, all of us hold positions, or *statuses*, in a variety of groups and organizations. In a hospital, for example, the patient, the nurse, the doctor, and the orderly are all members of a social group that is concerned with health care. Each of these individuals has a status that requires the performance of a certain set of behaviors, known as a *role*. Taken together, the statuses and roles of the members of this medical team and other teams in hospitals throughout the country make up the social institution known as the health-care system. An *institution* is a more or less stable structure of statuses and roles devoted to meeting the basic needs of people in a society. The health-care system is an institution; hospitals, insurance companies, and private medical practices are examples of organizations within that institution.

The functionalist perspective looks at the way major social institutions like the family, the military, the health-care system, and the police and courts actually operate. According to this perspective, the role behavior associated with any given status has evolved as a means of allowing a particular social institution to fulfill its function in society. Thus, the nurse's role requires specific knowledge and behaviors that involve treatment of the patient's immediate needs and administration of care according to the doctor's orders. The patient, in turn, is expected to cooperate in the administration of the treatment. When all members of the group perform their roles correctly, the group is said to be functioning well.

In a well-functioning group there is general agreement about how roles are to be performed by each member of the group. These expectations are reinforced by the society's basic values, from which are derived rules about how people should and should not behave toward each other in different situations. The Ten Commandments, the Golden Rule, the Bill of Rights, and the teachings of all the world's religions are examples of sets of rules that specify how people should behave in different social roles.

But if society is composed of groups in which people know their roles and adhere to the underlying values, why do we have social problems like crime and warfare, and why does it seem so difficult to make social organizations function effectively? From the functionalist perspective, the main reason for the existence of social problems is that societies are always changing and having to adapt to new conditions; failure to adapt successfully leads to social problems. *failure to adapt results in social problem*

The French social theorist Émile Durkheim observed that changes in a society can drastically alter the goals and functions of human groups and organizations. As a society undergoes a major change—say, from agricultural to industrial production—the statuses people assume and the roles they play also change, with far-reaching consequences. Thus, for example, the tendency for men and women from rural backgrounds to have many children, which was functional in agrarian societies because it produced much-needed farmhands, can become a liability in an urban-industrial society, where housing space is limited and the types of jobs available are constantly changing. From the standpoint of society's smooth functioning, it can be said that the roles of the father and mother in the rural setting, which stresses long periods of childbearing and many children, become "dysfunctional" in an industrial setting.

Wars, colonial conquest, disease and famine, population increases, changing technologies of production or communication or health care—all these major social forces can change societies and thereby change the roles their members are expected to perform. As social groups strive to adapt to the new conditions, people in those groups may feel set adrift, unsure of how to act, or troubled by conflict over how to perform as parents or wage earners or citizens. They may question the values they learned as children and wonder what to teach their own children. This condition of social disequilibrium can lead to an increase in social problems like crime and mental illness as individuals seek their own, often antisocial, solutions to the dilemmas they face.

Criminal Deviance: A Functionalist View   From the functionalist perspective, all societies produce their own unique forms of crime and their own ways of responding to them. All sociologists recognize that there are causes within the individual that help explain why one person becomes a criminal while another, who

note

may have experienced the same conditions, does not. But for the sociologist, especially one who applies the functionalist perspective, the question of why particular crimes are committed and punished in some societies and not in others is an important research topic. Why is it that until quite recently a black man who was suspected of having made advances to a white woman was often punished more severely than one who was suspected of stealing? Why was the theft of a horse punishable by immediate death on the western frontier? Why was witchcraft considered such a heinous crime in the Puritan settlements of colonial New England? And why is it that these crimes occurred at all when those who committed them were punished so severely?

The functionalist answer is that societies fear most the crimes that seem to threaten their members' most cherished values, and individuals who dare to challenge those values will receive the most severe punishments. Thus, the freedom to allow one's horses to graze on common land was an essential aspect of western frontier society that was threatened by the theft of horses. The possibility that a white woman could entice a black man, and that their affair could be interpreted as anything other than rape, threatened the foundations of the American racial caste system, which held that blacks were inferior to whites. In both cases immediate, sometimes brutal punishment was used to reinforce the central values of the society.

Social Problems as Social Pathology   The functionalist perspective on problems like criminal deviance has changed considerably since the nineteenth century. In the late 1800s and early 1900s, functionalist theorists regarded such behavior as a form of "social disease" or *social pathology*. This view was rooted in the organic analogy that was popular at the time. Human society was seen as analogous to a vast organism, all of whose complex, interrelated parts function together to maintain the health and stability of the whole. Social problems arise when either individuals or social institutions fail to keep pace with changing conditions and thereby disrupt the healthy operation of the social organization; such individuals or institutions are considered to be "sick" (hence the term *social pathology*). In this view, for example, European immigrants who failed to adjust to American urban life were considered to be a source of "illness," at least insofar as they affected the health of their adopted society. Underlying this concept was a set of moral expectations; social problems violated the expectations of social order and progress.

Although many people who comment on social problems today are tempted to use the organic analogy and the disease concept, most sociologists reject this notion. The social-pathology approach is not very useful in generating empirical research; its concepts of sickness and morality are too subjective to be meaningful to many sociologists. Moreover, it attempts to apply a biological analogy to social conditions even when there is no empirical justification for doing so. More important, it is associated with the idea that the poor and other "deviant" groups are less fit to survive from an evolutionary perspective and hence should not be encouraged to reproduce. The social-pathology approach therefore has been largely discredited. Modern functionalists do not focus on the behaviors and problems of individuals; instead, they see social problems as arising out of the failure of institutions like the family, the schools, and the economy to adapt to changing social conditions.

Social-Disorganization Theory   Rates of immigration, urbanization, and industrialization increased rapidly after World War I. Many newcomers to the cities failed to adapt to urban life. European immigrants, rural whites, and southern blacks were often crowded together in degrading slums and had trouble learning the language, manners, and norms of the dominant urban culture. Many of those who managed to adjust to the city were discriminated against because of their religion or race, while others lost their jobs because technological advances made their skills obsolete. Because of these conditions, many groups formed their own subcultures or devised other means of coping. Alcoholism, drug addiction, mental illness, crime, and delinquency rates rose drastically. Some sociologists believed that the social-pathology viewpoint could not adequately explain the widespread existence of these social problems. They developed a new concept that eventually became known as social-disorganization theory.

This theory viewed society as being organized by a set of expectations or rules. *Social disorganization* results when those expectations fail, and it is manifested in three major ways: (1) *normlessness,* which arises when people have no rules that tell them how to behave; (2) *culture conflict,* which occurs when people feel trapped by contradictory rules; and (3) *breakdown,* which takes place when obedience to a set of rules is not rewarded or is punished. Rapid social change, for example, might make traditional standards of behavior obsolete without providing new standards, thereby giving rise to normlessness. The children of immigrants might feel trapped between the expectations of their parents and those of their new society—an example of culture conflict. And the expectations of blacks might be frustrated when they do well in school but encounter job discrimination; their frustration, in turn, might lead to breakdown.

The stress experienced by victims of social disorganization may result in a form of personal disorganization such as drug addiction or crime. The social system as a whole also feels the force of disorganization. It may respond by changing its rules, keeping contradictory rules in force, or breaking down. Disorganization can be halted or reversed if its causes are isolated and corrected.

Modern Functionalism: Building Institutions In this book we will see many instances in which social-disorganization theory has been used to explain social problems. However, this approach is not widely used today. A more modern version of the functionalist perspective attempts to show how people reorganize their lives to cope with new conditions. Often the result is new kinds of organizations and, sometimes, whole new institutions. This research focus is known as the *institutional* or *institution-building approach* (Janowitz, 1971, 1978). Research on how to improve the organization of public schools to meet new educational demands is an example of this approach.

school meet new ed. demands

The Conflict Perspective

By no means do all sociologists accept the functionalist view of society and social problems. There is an alternative set of theories, often known as the *conflict perspective,* that rejects the idea that social problems can be corrected by reforming institutions that are not functioning well. The conflict perspective is based on the belief that social problems arise out of major contradictions in the way societies are organized, contradictions that lead to large-scale conflict between those who have access to the "good life" and those who do not. This perspective owes much to the writings of Karl Marx (1818–1883), the German social theorist who developed many of the central ideas of modern socialism.

In *The Communist Manifesto* (1848), *Capital* (1867), and other works, Marx attempted to prove that social problems like unemployment, poverty, crime, corruption, and warfare are not usually the fault of individuals or of poorly functioning organizations. Instead, he argued, their origins may be found in the way societies organize access to wealth and power. According to Marx, the social problems of modern societies arise from capitalism. An inevitable outcome of capitalism is class conflict, especially conflict between those who own the means of production (factories, land, and the like) and those who sell their labor for wages. In such a system

how society organizes access to wealth & power

The helicopter shown in this arrest scene symbolizes the increasing visibility and cost of efforts to control crime and other social problems.

workers are exploited by their bosses, for whom the desire to make profits out-weighs any humanitarian impulse to take care of their employees.

In the capitalist system as Marx described it, the capitalist is driven by the profit motive to find ways to reduce labor costs—for example, through the purchase of new machinery that can do the work of several people, or by building factories in places where people will work for less money. These actions continually threaten the livelihood of workers. Often they lose their jobs, and sometimes they resort to crime or even begin revolutions that seek to overturn the system in which they are the have-nots and the owners of capital are the haves. In sum, for Marx and modern Marxian sociologists, social problems may be attributed to the ways in which wealth and power come to be concentrated in the hands of a few people, and to the many forms of conflict engendered by these inequalities.

Marxian conflict theory can be a powerful tool in the analysis of contemporary social problems. To illustrate this point, let us look at how Marxian conflict theorists explain criminal deviance in societies like that of the United States.

Deviance: A Marxian Conflict View   Marxian students of crime and deviance believe that situations like those described at the beginning of the chapter do not occur merely because organizations like the police and the courts function in certain ways or do not function as they were intended to. Instead, they believe that such situations are a result of differences in the power of different groups or classes in society. Top organized-crime figures, for example, have the money and power to influence law enforcement officials or to hire the best attorneys when they are arrested. Street drug dealers, on the other hand, are relatively powerless to resist arrest. Moreover, they serve as convenient targets for an official show of force against drug trafficking. From the Marxian conflict perspective, the rich and powerful are able to determine what kinds of behaviors are defined as social problems because they control major institutions like the government, the schools, and the courts. They are also able to shift the blame for the conditions that produce those problems to groups in society that are less able to defend themselves, namely, the poor and the working class (Balbus, 1978; Quinney, 1978; Turk, 1978).

Scholars who adopt a Marxian conflict perspective tend to be critical of proposals to reform existing institutions. Since they attribute most social problems to underlying patterns of class conflict, they do not believe that existing institutions such as prisons and courts can address the basic causes of those problems. Usually, therefore, their research looks at the ways in which the material conditions of society, such as inequalities of wealth and power, seem to account for the distribution of social problems in a population. Or they conduct research on social movements among the poor and the working class in an attempt to understand how those movements might mobilize large numbers of people into a force that could bring about major changes in the way society is organized (Piven & Cloward, 1977, 1982).

Value Conflict Theory   The Marxian theory of class conflict cannot explain all the kinds of conflict that occur around us every day. In families, for example, we see conflicts that may range from seemingly trivial arguments over television programs to intense disputes over issues like drinking or drug use; in neighborhoods we may see conflict between landlords and tenants, between parents and school administrators, or between groups of parents who differ on matters of educational policy such as sex education or the rights of female athletes. Such conflict often focuses not on deep-seated class antagonisms but on differences in values. For most feminist groups, for example, abortion is a social problem if women cannot freely terminate a pregnancy within some reasonable time. In contrast, many religious groups define legal abortion as a social problem. The debate over the legalization versus criminalization of abortion reflects the conflicting values of important groups in society.

Value conflict theorists define social problems as "conditions that are incompatible with group values" (Rubington & Weinberg, 1971, p. 86). Such problems are normal, they add, since in a complex society there are many groups whose interests and values are bound to differ. According to value conflict theory, social problems occur when groups with different values meet and compete. To return to the example of criminal deviance, value conflict theorists would say that deviance from society's rules results from the fact that some groups do not agree with those rules and therefore feel free to break them if they can. For example, whenever a society prohibits substances like alcohol or drugs there will be some groups that will break the rules to obtain the banned substance. This stimulates the development of criminal organizations that employ gangsters and street peddlers to supply the needs of those who deviate. The underlying cause of the problem is conflicting values regarding the use of particular substances.

From the value conflict viewpoint, many social problems need to be understood in terms of which groups hold which values and have the power to enforce them against the wishes of other groups. Once this has been determined, the value conflict approach leads to suggestions regarding adjustments, settlements, negotiations, and compromises that will alleviate the problem. These, in turn, may result in new policies such as civilian review boards, arbitration of disputes, open hearings on issues, and changes in existing laws to reflect a diversity of opinions (Gusfield, 1966, 1981).

The Interactionist Perspective

Why do certain people resort to criminal deviance while the vast majority seek legitimate means to survive? A functionalist would point out that individuals who do not adhere to the society's core values or have been uprooted by social change are most likely to become criminals. When they are caught, their punishment reinforces the desire of the majority to conform. But this explanation does not help us understand why a particular individual or group deviates.

Conflict theorists explain deviance as resulting from conflict over access to wealth and power (in the Marxian version) or over values (in the non-Marxian version). But how is that conflict channeled into deviant behavior? Why do some groups that experience value conflict act against the larger society while others do not? Why, for example, do some homosexuals "come out" publicly while others hide their sexual preference? Presumably both groups know that their sexual values conflict with those of the larger society, but what explains the difference in behavior? The conflict perspective cannot provide an adequate answer to this question.

The interactionist perspective offers an explanation that gets us closer to the individual level of behavior. Research based on this perspective looks at the *processes* whereby different people become part of a situation that the larger society defines as a social problem. The interactionist approach focuses on the ways in which people actually take on the values of the group of which they are members. It also explores how different groups define their situation and in so doing "construct" a version of life that promotes certain values and behaviors and discourages others.

A key insight of the interactionist perspective originated in the research of W. I. Thomas and his colleagues in the early decades of this century. In their classic study of the problems of immigrants in the rapidly growing and changing city of Chicago, these pioneering sociologists found that some groups of Polish immigrant men believed that it would be easier to rob banks than to survive in the mills and factories where other immigrants worked long hours under dangerous conditions. The sociologists discovered that the uneducated young immigrants often did not realize how little chance they had of carrying out a successful bank robbery. They defined their situation in a particular way and acted accordingly. "Situations people define as real," Thomas stated, "are real in their consequences." From the interactionist perspective, thus, an individual or group's definition of the situation is central to understanding the actions of that individual or group.

Another early line of interactionist research was associated with Charles Horton Cooley and George Herbert Mead. Cooley, Mead, and others realized that although we learn our basic values and ways of behaving early in life, especially in our families, we also participate throughout our lives in groups of people like ourselves, known as peer groups. From these groups we draw much of our identity, our sense of who we are, and within these groups we learn many of our behaviors and values. Through our interactions in peer groups, be they teams, adolescent friendship groups, or work groups, we may be taught to act in ways that are different from those our parents taught us. Thus, when interactionists study social problems like crime, they focus on the ways in which people are recruited by criminal groups and learn to conform to the "rules" of those groups.

Labeling: An Interactionist View of Deviance Labeling theory is an application of the interactionist perspective that offers an explanation for certain kinds of social deviance. Labeling theorists feel that the label "deviant" reveals more about the society applying it than about the act or person being labeled. In certain societies, for example, homosexuality is far more accepted than it is in the United States. Labeling theorists suggest that there are groups and organizations in American society that benefit from labeling homosexuals as deviant—religious and military institutions, for example. Similarly, deviant acts are not always judged in the same way—prison sentences for black offenders, for example, tend to be longer than sentences for white offenders who commit the same crimes. In the view of labeling theorists, this difference has to do with the way power is distributed in our society. In short, labeling theory separates deviant and nondeviant people not by what they do but by how society reacts to what they do.

According to labeling theorists, social problems are conditions under which certain behaviors or situations become defined as social problems. The cause of a social problem is simply society's awareness that a certain behavior or situation exists. A behavior or situation becomes a social problem when someone can profit in some way by applying the label "problematic" or "deviant" to it. Such labeling causes society to suffer in two ways. First, one group unfairly achieves power over another— "deviants" are repressed through discrimination, prejudice, or force. Second, those who are labeled as deviant may accept this definition of themselves, and the label may become a self-fulfilling prophecy. The number and variety of deviant acts may be increased in order to reinforce the new role of deviant. A person who is labeled as a drug addict, for example, may adopt elements of what is popularly viewed as a drug addict's lifestyle: resisting employment or treatment, engaging in crime, and so on. Sociologists term this *secondary deviance*.

According to labeling theory, the way to solve social problems is to change the definition of what is considered deviant (Rubington & Weinberg, 1971). It is thought that accepting a greater variety of acts and situations as normal would automatically eliminate concern about those acts or situations. (Decriminalization of the possession of small amounts of marijuana for personal use is an example of this approach. Note, however, that many people would consider marijuana use a social problem even if it were decriminalized.) At the same time, discouraging the tendency to impose labels for gain would reduce the prevalence of labeling and cause former problems to become less significant. Communism, for example, was a matter of great concern to Americans in the 1950s; many people won popularity or power by applying the label "communist" to others. When it became clear that the label was being misapplied and that the fear it generated was unjustified, the communist label lost its significance and the "social problem" of internal communist influence largely disappeared.

Labeling theory is only one of numerous applications of the interactionist perspective to social problems. Another common approach focuses on the processes of socialization that occur in groups and explores the possibility of *re*socialization through group interaction—as occurs, for example, in groups like Alcoholics Anonymous. At many points in this book we will encounter situations in which intentional resocialization has been used in efforts to address social problems.

ASSUMPTIONS ABOUT SOCIAL PROBLEMS

Regardless of the basic perspective from which they approach the study of social problems, sociologists make certain assumptions about why things happen the way they do. These assumptions, or premises, are a starting point for studying some very complicated problems. Among those premises are the following:

1. Social problems are, to some extent, a result of indirect and unexpected effects of acceptable patterns of behavior. There are numerous examples of this phenomenon. Consider the rapid growth of the world population. In many societies, having a large number of children has been valued for a long time, and for most of that time this value was also a necessity, since so many children died in infancy. Now, because of improved health care and sanitation, many countries have more people than they can adequately support. The population problem is more than a question of food supply, although severe malnutrition is widespread in overcrowded countries; clean air, adequate housing, education, employment, and quality of life are also involved. Consequently, having many children, once a fundamental value, has become a social problem.

Consider also the use of insecticides. These chemicals were once considered a boon to farmers and consumers; they destroyed insects and helped preserve crops. Farmers could produce more food for more people at less cost than before. However, ecologists have demonstrated that some insecticides destroy the soil, damage

One unintended consequence of our high demand for energy and manufactured goods is air pollution, which causes acid rain and severe damage to the environment.

plants, and may be harmful to people who eat foods prepared from those plants. Insecticides have therefore created new problems—for the farmers who now depend on them to protect their crops, for the consumers who eat the foods affected by them, for the government agencies that must decide whether or not to restrict their use, and for the scientists who must find new substances to replace them and ways to undo whatever harm they have caused. Thus, insecticides, formerly viewed as a beneficial innovation, have created new and unexpected problems.

These examples should provide an idea of how some social problems may arise—not because of bad deeds, bad people, or bad luck, but as the unintended consequences of accepted ways of doing things, especially when seen in the light of later technological changes. Although many religions and philosophies hold that conditions like crime and poverty are a result of human wickedness or frailty, this explanation is no longer adequate.

Far from being caused by people with evil intentions, social problems may even be caused by well-intentioned actions. For example, Prohibition (a set of laws banning the sale of alcoholic beverages) went into effect in 1919 to protect people from the "evil" of alcohol. But in effect it promoted bootlegging—the illegal production and distribution of liquor—and contributed to the rise of modern organized crime. Boxed features in later chapters present other examples of how policies directed at solving social problems can have unintended consequences.

Why do people with good intentions tend to create social problems or indirectly cause others to create such problems? The answer gives us our second premise:

2. A certain social structure and culture induce most people to conform but can cause some to deviate. This premise can be illustrated by the example of property rights, a major element in the social structure of the United States. We regard ownership of land, money, or other goods as legitimate, and we believe that ownership confers the right to keep the property or dispose of it as we choose, subject to certain socially determined limitations. Many ways of acquiring property are socially approved—working to earn money, buying a car from a dealer, growing vegetables on one's own land, writing a book and copyrighting it, and so on. Other ways of acquiring property, such as stealing or fraud, are considered deviant.

Most Americans conform to the established pattern regarding property rights. They may bend the rules sometimes—a little deceit, an occasional "liberation" of company property—but not beyond the limits society will tolerate. The average wage earner wants to own a house; is willing to work at a steady job and pay interest on a mortgage; and claims the right to remodel, enlarge, or sell the house after buying it. Some people, however, are unable or unwilling to acquire property by approved means. They may be unable to find a job with an adequate salary, or they may have many children, high medical bills, unwise investments, or other expenses that eat up their earnings. These people may resort to deviant means to obtain money and goods. Thus we have the shoplifter, the embezzler, the burglar, the mugger, and the armed robber—all deviate from cultural norms, yet in a sense all are created by them.

In this connection it is worth noting that behavior that is deviant in the eyes of one group within a society may be approved, or at least tolerated, by another group. What middle-class merchants call stealing may be "taking" to lower-class children who reason that they need the object more than the merchant does.

This leads to a third premise:

3. Every society is composed of different categories of people who are similar in income, education, and occupation; these various groups constitute "strata," or layers. People in different strata experience the same problems differently and therefore are likely to understand them differently. People's attitudes are influenced by their background, education, income, occupation, and personal experience. Since a person may occupy more than one position in society (e.g., a middle-class Catholic lawyer or an upper-class Protestant executive), attitudes are seldom determined by any single factor. Chances are that a person who earns over $100,000 a year and lives in an affluent suburb will react differently to the problems of ghetto life than a person who lives in a ghetto. A Jewish corporation president, on the other hand, may have the same views on Israel as a Jewish secretary.

One's attitude toward a particular social problem may change when one moves from one social position to another. For example, in their study of Poles in Chicago, W. I. Thomas and Florian Znaniecki (1922) pointed out that most Chicago residents considered the Poles (most of whom were poorly paid immigrants) a threat to law, order, and middle-class morality because they had unusually high rates of delinquency and crime. Later, when these same Poles had acquired well-paying jobs, suburban homes, and social respectability, they, in turn, were hostile toward the poor blacks who had taken their place in the ghetto areas. The same thing has happened with other ethnic groups—Italians, Irish, and Russians—some of whose members react to black and Hispanic ghetto residents in much the same way that Anglo-Saxon Protestants once reacted to them and their parents.

To assess people's attitudes toward social problems, therefore, one should consider their social background and previous experiences. These factors not only influence their understanding of a particular problem but also influence the solutions they propose. This leads to our fourth major premise:

4. People in different social strata propose different solutions to social problems. Since those solutions usually favor their own interests and values, it is often difficult to reach agreement on a solution to a given problem, or to implement agreed-upon solutions. Any number of events that are common in today's world illustrate this premise. If the problem is one of improved housing for the poor, it is likely that the poor will favor public financing and dispersal of public housing in middle-class neighborhoods. Residents of those neighborhoods, fearful of increased crime, new taxes, and declining property values, will advocate private financing and rebuilding of slum areas. Similarly, minority groups may demand open admission to a college, regardless of academic qualifications, as a means of improving their social status. The college's administrators, on the other hand, may maintain that the same purpose will be accomplished by holding minority students to the same standards as everyone else.

In some situations groups may prefer that certain problems not be solved, since they may actually benefit from the existence of those problems. Many landlords, for example, profit from housing shortages among the poor and the middle class, since a shortage allows them to impose high rents without providing adequate services.

These premises imply two important points. First, every social structure can generate social problems, thereby also creating new forms of deviance. Second, people's behaviors, perceptions, and attitudes are influenced largely by their social position. The social background and environment of the groups involved, therefore, is a significant factor in both the origin and the solution of social problems.

RESEARCH ON SOCIAL PROBLEMS

William J. Wilson and his colleagues and students at the University of Chicago are engaged in an important study of the causes of persistent poverty among some segments of the city's white, black, and Hispanic populations. Their research is funded by foundations devoted to the study of the underlying causes and consequences of poverty. As part of their study, Wilson and his colleagues are conducting interviews in many Chicago neighborhoods. Their research design requires that they select the people to be interviewed at random and then find those individuals and interview them. In poor neighborhoods, where people are often forced to move around in search of shelter, this can be a very difficult and expensive proposition.

Lyn Lofland and her students at the University of California at Irvine are conducting research on the way women and men cope with the pressures and problems of urban living. They are particularly interested in the way gender influences people's experiences on city streets. Through careful observation of the street life of cities like San Francisco, the researchers hope to help urban planners find ways to enable members of both sexes to feel safe in public places.

Yale University sociologist Kai Erikson is investigating the effects of a local bank failure on migrant farm workers and sharecroppers in rural Florida. Erikson was asked to conduct this research by the law firm representing the people who lost their savings as a result of the bank failure. The firm's attorneys learned about him through his famous study of the effects of the dam rupture at Buffalo Creek, West Virginia, in 1972. Erikson's book about the Buffalo Creek flood, *Everything in Its Path*, won a National Book Award for social research and helped make lawmakers more sensitive to the human costs of major natural and economic disasters.

These three examples illustrate some of the ways in which sociological research is brought to bear on social problems. We could add many more. When the media seek an expert to comment on changes in crime rates from one year to the next, they often call upon criminologists such as Hans Zeisel, whose work we will encounter in Chapter 6. When members of Congress debate the merits of different proposals for reforming the welfare system, they often turn to the work of sociologists such as Assistant Secretary of Health and Human Services Mary Jo Bane, an expert on trends in welfare dependency, or they may consult Sheldon Danziger and his colleagues at the University of Washington's Institute for Research on Poverty. In these

A scene of the devastation caused by the earthquake that shook San Francisco in 1989. The effects of natural disasters like this earthquake and the even more severe one that occurred in Los Angeles in 1994 are an increasingly important aspect of the study of social problems such as homelessness.

and countless other areas, sociologists are asked to conduct empirical research and to supply information that can be referred to in debates on these issues.

In this age of rapid social change, information about social problems is in ever-increasing demand. Even if you do not go on to a career that requires expertise in social research, as an informed citizen you will benefit from the ability to evaluate the findings of such research. In this section, therefore, we will briefly introduce the most frequently used research methods: demographic studies, survey research, field observation, and social experiments.

Demographic Studies

Demography is the subfield of sociology that studies how social conditions are distributed in human populations and how those populations are changing. When we ask how many people are affected by a particular condition or problem—for example, when we want to know how many people are affected by crime or unemployment—we are asking a demographic question. The answers to such questions consist of numerical data about the people affected compared to those who are not affected. Demographers frequently supply data about the *incidence* of a social phenomenon, that is, how many people are affected and to what extent. Incidence can be given in absolute numbers; for example, in 1991 there were 2,482 persons under the death sentence in the United States, of whom 1,464 were white and 1,018 were nonwhite (*Statistical Abstract,* 1993). The incidence of a phenomenon can also be expressed as a rate. In 1986, for example, the rate of reported cases of child abuse was 328 per 10,000 children in the U.S. population, compared to 101 per 10,000 in 1976 (*Statistical Abstract,* 1992). Rates are often more useful than absolute numbers because they are not affected by changes in population size. Thus, in the example just given, the increase in reported cases of child abuse is not due to the growth of the population during the period covered but must have some other cause.

Survey Research

We often take for granted the availability of statistics about social conditions and problems. Every month we see reports on the latest unemployment figures or crime rates or trends in the cost of housing, and we are given statistics on what people think about these and other issues. Political campaigns rely heavily on measures of public opinion, both on the issues and on the popularity of the candidates. All this information, including the basic information about the U.S. population derived from the national census, is obtained through a sociological method known as *survey research*.

Survey research was developed earlier in this century as a way of gathering information from a number of people, known as a *sample*, who represent the behavior and attitudes of the larger population from which they are selected. Today survey research is a major industry in much of the world. The techniques of sampling and interviewing are used routinely by market research firms; political polling organizations; media corporations of all types; university research centers; and many other organizations, including the Census Bureau and other government agencies. Whenever we encounter statistics about what people in a society believe about a problem or how different groups within a population behave, there is a good chance that those statistics are based on the results of a sample survey.

In a survey, people speak to interviewers, either in person, on the telephone, or by mail, and provide them with information. That information is aggregated and converted into numerical data. When looking at survey data, therefore, be sure to ask who was interviewed and for what reasons. You should also ask whether the survey reports the results of a "wave" of questions asked about conditions prevailing at one time or whether matched samples were interviewed on more than one occasion. A questionnaire that is given to a sample on a single occasion yields what sociologists call a *cross section* of behavior and opinion at a particular time. Comparisons of matched samples over time yield *longitudinal* survey data, which tell us what changes have occurred in a particular social condition over a specific period.

Field Observation

When sociologists seek to understand the processes that occur among the people who are directly involved in a social problem, they may attempt to observe social behavior as it is actually taking place. This often requires that the sociologist participate directly in the social life of the individuals or groups in question, a technique known as *participant observation or field research.* (The term *field* refers to the social settings in which the observed behavior occurs.) Neighborhoods, communities, organizations like police headquarters or hospital emergency rooms or prisons or schools—all are examples of field settings. The technique of participant observation requires skill in gaining and keeping the trust of the people whose behavior is being observed, together with practice in careful observation and recording of the behaviors in question and skill at conducting interviews that may range over many issues, some of which may be highly personal or controversial.

Research based on participant observation usually seeks to discover how the processes of human interaction contribute to particular social conditions or problems. Thus, field research frequently, though not always, applies the interactionist perspective. This approach is illustrated in the following example of field research on marijuana use.

In a classic study of how people become drug users, sociologist Howard Becker spent time interacting with groups of musicians and other people who were likely to use marijuana. A jazz musician himself, Becker was readily accepted in the groups whose behavior he wished to observe. As he watched first-time users take their first puffs on a joint, he noted that they often claimed not to feel any effect, even when

Sociologist William Kornblum interviews a respondent in a boxing gym as part of his ongoing research on value conflict and social change in New York City's Times Square area.

Becker himself observed changes in their behavior. But when more experienced users explained to the novice what the "proper" feelings were, the new smoker began to feel the sensation of being high. Becker concluded that to some extent the experience of using marijuana is a social construction; the drug may have certain physiological effects on everyone, but social interaction must occur for the new smoker to define what the appropriate feelings are and then experience them.

Becker's famous research paper, "Becoming a Marijuana User" (1963), was among the first empirical descriptions of the degree to which the experience and extent of drug use are determined by users' definitions of the situation. It is an excellent example of the way sociologists can discover important aspects of behavior through observation in the field. In the chapters to come, whenever we refer to a field research study or to participant observation research, remember that the researcher has actually observed the behavior in question firsthand. Also, since the research describes the behavior of real people, note how careful the researcher has been to disguise the identities of the individuals who were observed and interviewed.

Social Experiments

There are times when it is possible for a sociologist or other social scientist to apply experimental methods to the study of a social problem. In an experiment, the investigator attempts to systematically vary the conditions that are of interest in order to determine their effects. In a controlled experiment, the investigator applies a "treatment" to one group—that is, exposes its members to a certain condition, to which they must respond somehow—but does not apply the treatment to a second group that is identical to the first in every other way. The subjects who receive the treatment are known as the *experimental group;* those who do not are the *control group.* When the investigator compares the experiences of the experimental and control groups, it can be assumed that any differences between them are due to the effects of the treatment.

We will have occasion in later chapters to describe controlled experiments that have applied this model to human subjects in order to study social problems. Here we will briefly present two examples of social experiments. One of them was able to use both experimental and control groups; the other could establish only an experimental group.

In order to study the influence of jobs on ex-offenders, the Vera Institute of Justice undertook the Wildcat experiment, in which individuals serving jail terms were allowed to take part in various forms of "supported work." Instead of being placed individually in unfamiliar jobs, Wildcat workers were assigned to jobs in groups of three to seven and received guidance and evaluation while they were working. Other prisoners were assigned to individual jobs under traditional work-release arrangements; they constituted a control group. The results of the experiment were mixed: Although the Wildcat workers earned more, had more stable jobs, and were less likely to become dependent on welfare than members of the control group, they were also more likely to be arrested and returned to prison (Friedman, 1978).

In sharp contrast to the Wildcat experiment is the famous "prison" study conducted by Philip Zimbardo. Zimbardo and his colleagues created a simulated prison in the basement of a building at Stanford University. Twenty-four students who had volunteered to take part in the experiment were divided into two groups: "prisoners" and "guards." The prisoners were confined to the simulated prison, and the guards were instructed in their duties and responsibilities. In this experiment it was not possible to form a control group; in fact, the experiment itself was canceled after six days. In that brief time both the guards and the prisoners had become unable to distinguish between the experiment and reality, with the result that "human values were suspended, self-concepts were challenged, and the ugliest, most base, pathological side of human nature surfaced" (Zimbardo, 1972, p. 243).

As informative as experimental studies like these may be, they raise major questions about the ethical limits of social research. Sociologists and other social scientists realize that they must not infringe on the basic rights of human subjects. Under the rules of professional associations like the American Sociological Association and the guidelines of government agencies like the National Institute of Mental Health, people who conduct research using human subjects must guarantee the following rights:

1. *Privacy*—"the right of the individual to define for himself, with only extraordinary exceptions in the interest of society, when and on what terms his acts should be revealed to the general public" (Westin, 1967, p. 373).
2. *Confidentiality*—ensuring that information supplied by a subject or respondent will not be passed on to anyone else in a form that could be traced to that respondent.
3. *Informed consent*—informing subjects and respondents beforehand about what they are being asked and how the information they supply will be used.

SOCIAL PROBLEMS AND SOCIAL POLICY

Much of the research conducted by sociologists is designed to provide information to be used in formulating social policies as well as in evaluating existing policies and suggesting improvements and new directions. *Social policies* are formal procedures designed to remedy a social problem. Generally they are designed by officials of government at the local, state, or federal level, but they can also be initiated by private citizens in voluntary associations, by corporations, and by nonprofit foundations.

There is generally a good deal of debate about any proposed social policy. Much of the debate consists of discussion and analysis of how well a proposed policy appears to address the problem. Such analysis tends to be considered "technical" in the sense that there is general agreement on the need to address the problem; the technical debate hinges on the adequacy of the proposed means to achieve the agreed-upon ends. Increasingly, however, we are witnessing policy debates that

During her first two years as part of the Clinton administration, Hillary Rodham Clinton was committed to learning about the problems of the nation's health-care system and defining them as a social problem that should be addressed through public policy.

are ideological rather than technical, and in the United States such debates frequently pit conservatives against liberals or socialists.

Conservatives usually seek to limit the involvement of government in the solution of social problems. They believe that private firms, governed by the need to compete in markets and make profits, are the best type of organization for coping with the problems of prisons, schools, and the like. Liberals and socialists reject the dominance of the market (and, hence, the profit motive) in social-welfare institutions. However, the policies they propose tend to expand government bureaucracies without always delivering adequate services to the populations that need them.

Throughout this century the government's role in attempting to solve social problems has increased steadily, despite the ideological stands of various administrations. America's role as a world military power, for example, has required the continual expenditure of public funds on military goods and services. These costs have increased dramatically with every war and every major change in military technology. Similarly, the fight against drug commerce has added greatly to the cost of maintaining the society's judicial and penal institutions.

Every function of government has a similar history of escalating costs due to increases in the scale of the society or the scope of the problem. During the 1980s, for example, the Reagan administration sought to decrease the cost of government involvement in regulating economic institutions such as airlines, banks, and financial markets. Among other measures taken were those designed to decrease the regulation of the banking industry. Banks and savings and loan associations were allowed to operate in markets that had previously been barred to them because of the risks associated with investments in those markets. At the same time, personnel cuts were made in the federal bank regulatory agencies. The risk to depositors was held to a minimum by the continued existence of government guarantees in the form of deposit insurance. The combination of deregulation and deposit insurance, along with regional recessions in the oil-producing states, caused many savings and loan associations to become insolvent, exposing the often corrupt practices of their directors. Amid escalating costs to the government and American taxpayers—estimated in the hundreds of billions of dollars—Congress is once again seeking to increase its regulation of the banking industry and to prevent future financial disasters of such magnitude.

Policy decisions of similar scope are responsible for unemployment insurance, social security, community mental-health systems, and numerous other benefits that Americans have come to view as "entitlements" of citizenship. But these benefits are costly. They require the transfer (via taxation) of funds from the well-off to the less well-off. As the overall cost of government has increased, so has the tax burden on individual citizens. This increase in the cost of government comes from policies that serve specific segments of the population as well as from those designed to benefit the entire population. For example, organized labor has consistently promoted policies that regulate industry in the interests of workers, whereas industrialists claim that any regulations that increase their costs of doing business will hurt their ability to compete in domestic or world markets.

This conflict is typical of many current controversies over the best ways to handle social issues, with conservatives stressing private or market solutions and liberals calling for public or governmental actions. Some of the conflicting approaches to the solution of various social problems that have been proposed by conservatives, liberals, and others will be discussed in the Social Policy sections that conclude each chapter of this book, as well as in boxed features focusing on particular controversies.

The "Natural History" of Social Problems

To readers of daily newspapers and faithful watchers of television news, social problems may often resemble fads. We hear a great deal about a particular problem for a while, and then it fades from public attention, perhaps to reappear some time later if there are new developments in its incidence or control. With AIDS, crack cocaine, DWI, serial killers, financial scandals, racial violence, and so many other problems demanding attention, it is little wonder that the attention devoted to any given subject by the press and the public tends to last only a few days or weeks.

To a large extent, the short attention span of the media can be explained by the need to attract large numbers of viewers or readers; the media can be expected to be rather fickle and to constantly go after stories that will capture the attention of the reading or viewing public. However, sociologists distinguish between the nature of media coverage of a social problem and the way a problem is perceived by the public and political leaders. They have devoted considerable study to the question of how social problems develop from underlying conditions into publicly defined problems that engender social policies and sustained social movements. This subject is often referred to as the "natural history" of social problems.

Early in this century sociologists recognized that social problems often seemed to develop in a series of phases or stages. They called the study of this process the "natural history" approach because their effort was analogous to the work of biologists who study the development of a great many individual organisms to chart the stages of development of a species (Edwards, 1927; Park, 1955; Shaw, 1931; Wirth, 1927). But while sociologists recognize that social problems often follow certain regular stages of development, they also know that there are many deviations from the usual sequence of stages.

In a useful formulation of the natural history approach, Malcolm Spector and John Kitsuse (1987) outlined the following major stages that most social problems seem to go through:

> Stage 1—*Problem definition.* Groups in society attempt to gain recognition by a wider population (and the press and government) that some social condition is "offensive, harmful, or otherwise undesirable." These groups publicize their claims and attempt to turn the matter into a political issue.

> Stage 2—*Legitimacy.* When the groups pressing their claims are considered credible and their assertions are accepted by official organizations, agencies, or

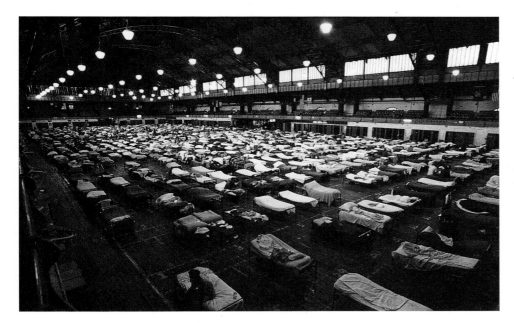

As homelessness has come to be recognized as a major social problem, efforts have been made to provide shelters for homeless people, including a growing number of children. Vast "congregate shelters" like the one shown here are unable to cope effectively with the complex mental and physical problems of many homeless people.

institutions, there may be investigations, proposals for reform, and even new agencies created to respond to claims and demands.

Stage 3—Reemergence of demands. Usually the original groups are not satisfied with the steps taken by official agencies; they demand stronger measures, more funding for enforcement, speedier handling of claims, and so on. They renew their appeals to the wider public and the press.

Stage 4—Rejection and institution building. The complainant groups usually decide that official responses to their demands are inadequate. They seek to develop their own organizations or counterinstitutions to press their claims and enact reforms.

Let us briefly apply this natural history model to the development of the idea that environmental degradation is a social problem. In the early 1960s many relatively small groups, such as the Sierra Club and the Audubon Society, renewed their efforts to get the general public to see that environmental degradation in its many forms was a major social problem. This activity culminated in the first national Earth Day demonstration in 1970. The U.S. Congress and many state legislatures responded to the growing strength of environmental groups by passing much new legislation, including the Clean Air Act, the National Environmental Policy Act of 1972 (which created the federal Council on the Environment), and many others.

Later in the 1970s the environmental groups began to believe that reforms were not being enforced adequately. They became convinced of this in the early 1980s as the government began to relax environmental regulations. In recent years the environmental movement has gained new strength and is seeking even stronger legal controls while adapting its strategies to make greater use of the courts and legal challenges.

Similar natural history analyses could be made for problems like DWI, AIDS, the drug epidemic of the late 1980s, and many others. Figure 1–1 on page 24 shows how quickly the public's perception of the severity of such problems can change. When questioned in September 1989, over 60 percent of respondents named drugs as the nation's number one problem. By July 1990, drugs had slipped below the federal budget deficit as the nation's "worst" problem. Less than a month later both of these problems had faded in the minds of most Americans as they worried about the

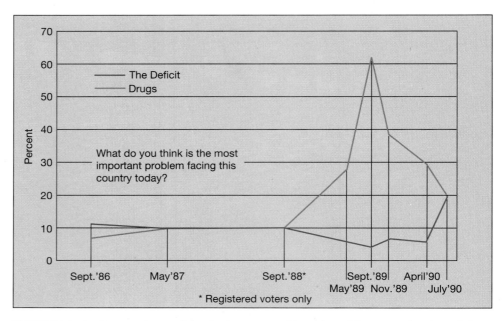

FIGURE 1–1 Perceptions of the Seriousness of Social Problems on the Eve of the Persian Gulf Crisis of 1990–1991

Source: Gallup Polls.

chances of a deadly war with Iraq. In 1993, as a result of the floods in the Midwest and devastating winter storms along the East Coast, many Americans began to see environmental problems as dominant. Such changes in the perception of social problems will continue as conditions around the world change.

SUMMARY

1. When most people in a society agree that a condition exists that threatens the quality of their lives and their most cherished values, and also agree that something should be done to remedy that condition, sociologists say that the society has defined that condition as a social problem.

2. Sociologists who study social problems ask questions about the social rather than the individual aspects of a problem. The primary sociological approaches to the study of social problems are the functionalist, conflict, and interactionist perspectives.

3. The functionalist perspective looks at the way major social institutions actually operate. From this perspective, the main reason for the existence of social problems is that societies are always changing; failure to adapt successfully to change leads to social problems.

4. In the early 1900s, functionalist theorists regarded social problems such as criminal deviance as a form of

social pathology. Later they tended to emphasize the effects of immigration, urbanization, and industrialization; this emphasis formed the basis of *social-disorganization theory.* Modern functionalists often conduct *institutional* research designed to show how people and societies reorganize their lives and institutions to cope with new conditions.

5. The conflict perspective is based on the belief that social problems arise out of major contradictions in the way societies are organized, which lead to large-scale conflict. This perspective owes a great deal to the writings of the German social theorist Karl Marx.

6. Marxian conflict theory attributes most social problems to underlying patterns of class conflict. A broader view is taken by *value conflict* theorists, who believe that social problems occur when groups with different values meet and compete.

7. Research based on the interactionist perspective looks at the processes whereby different people become part of a situation that the larger society defines as a social problem. It focuses on the ways in which people actually take on the values of the group of which they are members.

8. According to *labeling theory,* social problems are conditions under which certain behaviors or situations become defined as problems. In this view, the cause of a social problem is simply society's awareness that a certain behavior or situation exists. The labels applied to certain behaviors act as self-fulfilling prophecies because people who are labeled accept society's definition of themselves and behave accordingly.

9. Regardless of the basic perspective from which they approach the study of social problems, sociologists make the following assumptions: (a) Social problems are, to some extent, a result of indirect and unexpected effects of acceptable patterns of behavior; (b) a certain social structure and culture induce most people to conform but can cause some to deviate; (c) people in different social strata experience the same problems differently and therefore are likely to understand them

differently; and (d) people in different social strata propose different solutions to social problems.

10. The most frequently used research methods in the study of social problems are demographic studies, survey research, field observation, and social experiments. People who conduct research with human subjects must guarantee the rights of privacy, confidentiality, and informed consent.

11. *Social policies* are formal procedures designed to remedy a social problem. They are formulated by officials of governments at all levels as well as by voluntary associations, corporations, and nonprofit foundations. Much of the research conducted by sociologists is designed to provide information to be used in formulating and evaluating social policies.

12. The "natural history" approach to the analysis of social problems focuses on public perception of conditions that come to be defined as problems. In this view, there are four stages in the development of a social problem: problem definition, legitimacy, reemergence of demands, and rejection and institution building.

SUGGESTED READINGS

BECKER, HOWARD S. *The Outsiders: Studies in the Sociology of Deviance.* New York: Free Press, 1963. One of the first sociological statements, based on empirical research, about deviance and deviant subcultures in the United States.

EDWARDS, RICHARD C., MICHAEL REICH, AND THOMAS E. WEISSKOPF. *The Capitalist System: A Radical Analysis of American Society,* 3rd ed. Englewood Cliffs, NJ: Prentice Hall, 1986. A collection of original essays and research reports that traces the origins of social problems in the United States and other advanced nations to the way capitalist economies operate.

MAZUR, ALAN. *Global Social Problems.* Englewood Cliffs, NJ: Prentice Hall, 1992. A brief but highly valuable overview of the key social problems affecting large regions of the earth. Provides a comparative perspective on how social problems are dealt with in other nations and focuses on problems common to all societies.

MILLS, C. WRIGHT. *The Sociological Imagination.* New York: Oxford University Press, 1959. Perhaps the seminal statement of the differences between sociology and other social-scientific approaches to social problems; a classic in critical sociology.

RACHELS, JAMES. *The Elements of Moral Philosophy.* New York: Random House, 1986. A well-written, concise analysis of the ways in which different moral philosophies view contemporary social problems.

RUBINGTON, EARL, AND MARTIN W. WEINBERG. *Deviance: The Interactionist Perspective,* 5th ed. New York: Macmillan, 1987. A collection of classic and contemporary readings that presents issues in deviance and social problems from a close-up, interactionist perspective.

SMITH, CAROLYN D., AND WILLIAM KORNBLUM. *In the Field: Readings on the Field Research Experience.* New York: Praeger, 1989. A selection of personal accounts by a group of noted ethnographic researchers.

SPECTOR, MALCOLM, AND JOHN I. KITSUSE. *Constructing Social Problems.* Hawthorne, NY: Aldine de Gruyter, 1987. The essential volume for the "social constructionist" approach to social problems.

Statistical Abstract of the United States. Washington, DC: Government Printing Office, annual. An indispensable source of quantitative facts about the population of the United States.

WILSON, JAMES Q. *Thinking About Crime.* New York: Vintage, 1977. A good example by a political scientist of how social-policy recommendations are related to social-scientific knowledge more generally.

Problems of Physical Health

Chapter Outline

- The health-care industry in the United States employs more than 8 million people and accounts for about 13 percent of the gross domestic product.
- In Uganda a person can expect to live only 38.4 years. In the United States, a person can expect to live 75.8 years.
- Of each dollar spent by individuals on health care in 1991, almost 24 cents was spent for physicians' services.
- Almost 29 million Americans have orthopedic impairments; about 31 million have visual or hearing impairments.
- Since AIDS first appeared in the United States in 1981, approximately 245,000 Americans have contracted it; of these, more than 166,000 have died.

Americans are spending more on health care each year. Increasingly, however, they feel that they are getting less care and more worry in return for their dollars. Little wonder that health-care issues are becoming ever more important in voters' ratings of political candidates. And the problems associated with reforming the health-care system are vastly complicated by specific health problems that affect many Americans. The spread of AIDS, babies born with fetal alcohol syndrome or drug addiction, new strains of virulent diseases like tuberculosis, the moral dilemmas of prolonging or terminating life—these and other developments that we will discuss in this chapter are all serious problems in themselves. But from a sociological standpoint the most significant problems are those that stem from the inadequacies of the existing health-care system or from the growing social inequalities that produce increasingly unequal access to health care.

Americans believe that illness and its prevention and treatment are conditions that society as a whole should be concerned with; they expect society to create institutions and policies designed to improve the quality of health care and to increase equality of access to such care. AIDS is only the most recent in a long series of challenges to the institutions that deliver health care. But increasingly Americans are looking at the experiences of other nations, among them nearby Canada, that have similar health-care problems but seem to be dealing with them more effectively and at a lower cost. In consequence, more and more Americans both in and out of government are calling for fundamental reforms in the health-care system in the United States.

HEALTH CARE AS A SOCIAL PROBLEM

The health-services industry in the United States employs more than 8 million people, and spending on health care accounts for 13.2 percent of the gross domestic product (*Statistical Abstract,* 1993). But if the efforts of so many people and so large an investment of the nation's wealth are channeled into health care, how can health care be considered a social problem? One answer can be found in comparative indicators of how well a society is doing in providing health care for its population. Among those indicators are life expectancy and infant mortality. Table 2–1 presents statistics on life expectancy and infant mortality for a representative set of low-income and industrial nations.

Life expectancy is highly correlated with the quality of health care in a society. As a population's health improves as a result of better medical care and improved living conditions, the average age to which its members live (i.e., the life expectancy of the population) rises dramatically. For example, Table 2–1 indicates that a person

TABLE 2–1   LIFE EXPECTANCY AND INFANT MORTALITY RATES: SELECTED COUNTRIES, 1993, AND PROJECTIONS, 2000

Country	Expectation of Life at Birth (Years)		Infant Mortality Rate[a]	
	1993	2000	1993	2000
Afghanistan	44.4	47.8	158.9	137.5
Australia	77.4	78.7	7.4	6.4
Austria	76.4	78.0	7.3	6.2
Bangladesh	54.7	57.5	109.2	93.0
Belgium	76.7	78.2	7.4	6.3
Canada	78.0	79.1	7.0	6.2
China, Mainland	67.7	70.2	52.1	38.7
Denmark	75.5	77.4	7.1	6.1
Dominican Republic	68.0	70.4	53.6	40.8
Ethiopia	52.2	55.4	108.8	92.1
France	78.0	79.2	6.8	5.9
Germany	76.1	77.8	6.6	5.7
Ghana	55.2	57.5	84.5	74.8
Haiti	45.5	43.9	109.5	102.2
India	58.1	61.4	80.5	65.8
Italy	77.4	78.7	7.8	6.6
Japan	79.2	80.0	4.3	4.1
Kenya	54.1	46.4	74.7	72.3
Nepal	52.0	55.9	85.8	70.1
Netherlands	77.6	78.8	6.2	5.5
Pakistan	57.1	59.7	103.6	90.3
Senegal	56.0	59.9	77.8	63.5
Spain	77.5	78.8	7.0	6.1
Sri Lanka	71.5	73.0	22.8	19.1
Sweden	78.1	79.2	5.8	5.2
Switzerland	78.0	79.1	6.6	5.8
Tanzania	44.0	38.4	110.4	104.3
Uganda	38.4	33.6	112.1	106.8
United Kingdom	76.5	78.1	7.4	6.3
United States	75.8	77.8	8.4	6.6
Zaire	47.3	48.4	113.2	97.9

[a]Number of deaths of children under 1 year of age per 1,000 live births in a calendar year.

Source: Statistical Abstract, 1993.

born in Uganda in 1993 can expect to live only a little over thirty-eight years. In the United States, in contrast, a person born in 1993 can expect to live more than seventy-five years.

Differences in life expectancy between developed and less developed nations are due largely to the increasing chance that people in more developed nations will survive the childhood diseases and parasites that cause such high death rates in less developed nations. Table 2–1 shows the wide gap between the industrial and low-income countries in infant mortality rates, the most important comparative indicator of health. In Afghanistan the infant mortality rate is 158.9, about three times the rate in the Dominican Republic, nineteen times the rate in the United States, and twenty-seven times the rate in Sweden.

Table 2–1 also indicates that health care is less effective in the United States than in other highly developed countries. The infant mortality rate is higher in the United States than in the United Kingdom and the Scandinavian nations.

Infant mortality rates are highly correlated with the number of health-care professionals in a society, which serves as a measure of the quality of the health care available to its members. Table 2–2 presents comparative figures on the number of people per physician and per nursing person in low-income and industrial

TABLE 2–2 HEALTH-REALATED INDICATORS IN SELECTED LOW-INCOME AND HIGH-INCOME ECONOMIES

| | Population per | | | | Births Attended by Health Staff (percent) | Daily Calorie Supply (per capita) | |
| | Physician | | Nursing Person | | | | |
	1965	1984	1965	1984	1985	1965	1986
Low-Income Economies	9,760	5,580	6,101	2,200	—	1,993	2,384
Ethiopia	70,190	78,970	5,970	5,400	58	1,824	1,749
Tanzania	21,700	26,200	2,100	8,130	74	1,832	2,192
Bangladesh	8,100	6,730	—	8,980	—	1,971	1,927
Zaire	34,740	—	—	—	—	2,187	2,163
Nepal	46,180	32,710	87,650	4,680	10	1,901	2,052
China	1,600	1,000	3,000	1,710	—	1,926	2,630
India	4,880	2,520	6,500	1,700	33	2,111	2,238
Pakistan	—	2,910	9,910	4,900	24	1,761	2,315
Kenya	13,280	9,970	1,930	950	—	2,289	2,060
Haiti	14,000	7,180	12,890	2,290	20	2,000	1,902
Ghana	13,740	14,890	3,730	640	73	1,950	1,759
Sri Lanka	5,820	5,520	3,220	1,290	87	2,153	2,400
High-Income Economies	940	470	470	140	—	3,083	3,376
Spain	800	320	1,220	260	96	2,822	3,359
Ireland	950	680	170	140	—	3,546	3,632
New Zealand	820	580	570	80	99	3,237	3,463
Australia	720	440	150	110	99	3,118	3,326
United Kingdom	870	—	200	120	98	3,353	3,256
Italy	1,850	230	790	—	—	3,091	3,523
Belgium	700	330	590	110	100	—	—
Netherlands	860	450	270	170	—	3,108	3,326
Austria	720	390	350	180	—	3,231	3,428
France	830	320	380	110	—	3,217	3,336
Canada	770	510	190	120	99	3,212	3,462
Denmark	740	400	190	60	—	3,395	3,633
Germany, Fed. Rep.	640	380	500	230	—	3,102	3,528
Finland	1,300	440	180	60	—	3,111	3,122
Sweden	910	390	310	100	100	2,888	3,064
United States	670	470	310	70	100	3,224	3,645
Norway	790	450	340	60	100	3,032	3,223
Japan	970	660	410	180	100	2,687	2,864
Switzerland	710	700	270	130	—	3,412	3,437

Source: Adapted from World Bank, *World Development Report 1990*. New York: Oxford University Press, 1990. Reprinted with permission.

economies. It shows that the United States is well endowed with health-care professionals when compared with the less developed nations, but not when compared with other highly developed nations such as Switzerland, Sweden, and Belgium.

Other factors besides availability of health-care professionals may affect the health of a population. In our society, our comparatively poor health is due largely to the way we live. Sedentary occupations; fattening, nonnutritious foods; and lack of proper exercise contribute to the high incidence of heart disease and other ailments. Environmental pollution and cigarette smoking contribute to the high incidence of cancer. There can be little doubt, however, that many of our health problems are aggravated by the kind of medical care that is—or is not—available.

Medical sociology is the subfield of sociology that specializes in research on the health-care system and its impact on the public, especially the question of access to health care (Cockerham, 1992; Mechanic, 1986, 1989) and the evolution of health-care institutions (Anderson, 1991; Starr, 1982). In describing problems of physical health, sociologists are particularly interested in learning how a person's social class, as measured by income, education, and occupation, influences his or her access to medical care and the outcome of that care. Sociologists also work with economists and health-care planners in assessing the costs of different types of health-care delivery systems (Bergthold, 1990; Gibson, 1983; Yanick, 1983).

Medical sociologists often point out that health-care institutions themselves are the source of many of the problems we associate with health in the United States. They emphasize that the health-care system has evolved in such a way that doctors maintain private practices while society supports the hospitals and insurance systems that allow them to function (Starr, 1982). In other words, American health care never developed as a competitive industry. Instead, it became a complex institution composed of many private and public organizations.

As great strides were made in the ability to treat illnesses—especially through the use of antibiotics—and to prevent them through improved public-health practices, doctors began to develop narrow specialties and to refer patients to hospitals with special facilities. This created a situation in which doctors and hospital personnel became highly interdependent and developed a need to "assert their long-run collective interests over their short-run individual interests" (Starr, 1982, p. 230). All efforts to change our health-care system, to make it less costly or more efficient or more humane, must deal with the power of doctors and other health-care providers, which derives not from their wealth or their ownership of health-care facilities but from their mode of relating to each other and to the public (Anderson, 1989). This is a subject that will become clearer once we have discussed some of the specific problems of health care in American society.

THE SCOPE OF HEALTH-CARE PROBLEMS IN AMERICA

The range of situations in which health care can be viewed as a social problem is extremely wide. At the micro, or individual, level, where people whom we know and love are affected, we think of such problems as whether to terminate life support systems or whether the correct medical treatment is being applied or whether an elderly parent should be placed in a nursing home. But people's experiences at the micro level are influenced by larger forces that act throughout the society and touch the lives of millions of people. These are the macro problems of health care. At the micro level we may worry about elderly loved ones, but at the macro level the issue is how effectively health care is distributed among all elderly people and what can be done to improve the delivery of needed medical services.

Health care is distributed very unevenly in the United States. Indeed, the national debate over health care during the 1992 presidential campaign was largely motivated by the fact that almost 39 million citizens have no health insurance and millions more have inadequate coverage. The poor, the near-poor, members of racial and ethnic minority groups, and residents of depressed rural areas are most likely to fall into the uninsured category. Economic class and race are also correlated with the risk of becoming seriously ill. For example, industrial workers are more likely to contract certain forms of cancer and respiratory diseases than other population groups, and lack of prenatal care is a serious problem in minority ghetto communities (Daniels, 1985). Thus, to a large extent health care as a social problem can be viewed in terms of inequality of access to health-care services.

Recent research confirms that to be black and poor places one at greatest risk of not receiving adequate health care or emergency treatment. In a study of patients at U.S. hospitals, medical researchers found that only 47 percent of very sick black and poor patients were put in intensive-care units. Seventy percent of white poor Medicare patients were put into intensive care. And even in federal V.A. hospitals, where care is supposedly more uniformly distributed, blacks were less likely than whites to receive more costly medical procedures like catheterization of the heart in cases of blocked arteries (Blakeslee, 1994).

The issue of access to health care implies two further questions: access for whom? and access to what? (Daniels, 1985; Waltzer, 1983). Most of us would say that access to health care should be based on need, not on extraneous factors like social class, race, ethnicity, age, gender, or geographic location. But we do not expect other goods and services, such as automobiles and appliances, to be distributed on the basis of individual need. What is different about health care? Social policy on health care in the United States and other countries is based on the assumption that health care involves a set of special needs that must be met if the society as a whole is to function effectively. Health, in other words, is so fundamental to individual well-being, which in turn is necessary for the well-being of the society as a whole, that society is obligated to help individuals who cannot afford adequate care.

Health-care policy must also deal with the question of what constitutes adequate health care. Most of us would identify competent doctors and the ability to obtain the care they provide as elements of adequate care. But for a society health involves much more than good medical care.

Comparative measures of a population's overall health, such as those presented in Tables 2–1 and 2–2, reflect differences in all these dimensions. Especially important are adequate nutrition for pregnant women and the society's general level of sanitation. We will deal with some of these aspects of social health in the chapters on poverty and working conditions. In this chapter we will focus primarily on one major dimension of social health: availability of and equality of access to medical services.

Unequal Access to Health Services

The use and availability of medical care are directly related to socioeconomic class and race. The racial aspect is most directly illustrated by a comparison of life expectancy for whites and nonwhites: On the average, the life expectancy for white males is about eight years longer than that for black males, and the life expectancy for white females is about seven years longer than that for black females. In addition, the infant mortality rate for blacks is more than twice that for whites: 17.0 per 1,000 live births, compared to 7.7 (*Statistical Abstract*, 1993); this discrepancy increased during the 1980s despite a downward trend (i.e., an improvement) in the national rate. Nonwhites suffer proportionately more from almost every illness than do whites; and because they are less likely to have been immunized, nonwhites suffer higher rates of death from infectious diseases. Such differences cannot be ascribed to income differences alone, since even in cases in which income is the same, death rates remain higher for nonwhites.

From a socioeconomic point of view, there is a strong relationship between membership in a lower class and a higher rate of illness. People in the lower classes tend to feel sicker and have higher rates of untreated illness than people in the middle and upper classes. They also tend to be disabled more frequently and for longer periods. Moreover, mortality rates for almost all diseases are higher among the lower classes. For example, although top executives have a high rate of heart disease, caused in part by stressful jobs, the highest rate of heart disease actually occurs among workers with the lowest salaries. Quite often low-income workers experience high levels of stress in their jobs, along with the stress that comes with severe concerns about money.

Low income affects the health of the poor from birth. The high rate of infant mortality among the poor is due to a number of factors associated with poverty. Inadequate nutrition appears to account for the high death rates among the newborn children of low-income mothers. The babies most at risk are those with a low birthweight. Among the causes of low birth weight are the low nutritional value of the mother's diet, smoking or other drug use by the mother during pregnancy, and lack of prenatal care. After the neonatal period (the first three months), the higher rate of infant death among the poor is linked with a greater incidence of infectious diseases. Such diseases, in turn, are associated with poor sanitation and lack of access to high-quality medical care as well as, in some cases, drug use.

Since the introduction of Medicaid (health insurance for low-income households) in 1965, the poor have increased their consumption of medical services dramatically. Of all income groups, the poor used physicians least in 1930, but by the 1980s they had the highest rate of physician visits. Improved access to doctors has not led to a proportional improvement in the health care received by poor people, however; the quality of the health-care services received has often remained low. Not only are some segments of the poor unable to afford proper care, but in some neighborhoods adequate care is not available. Rural areas, for example, suffer from a chronic shortage of physicians and medical services. As a result, patients from rural areas are often sent to hospitals in urban centers (Cockerham, 1995; Hatten & Connerton, 1986).

The High Cost of Health Care

As noted in the preceding section, unequal access to health care is related to its cost. In recent decades that cost has been very high. In fact, because of the rapid rates of increase in the cost of medical care in recent years, the American health-care system is often said to be "in crisis." Expenditures on health care in the United States amounted to $2,566 per capita in 1990, an increase of about 150 percent over the 1980 level of $1,055 per capita (Farnsworth, 1992). It is true that all the highly developed nations have been experiencing rapid increases in health-care spending, as can be seen in Figure 2–1 on page 34. Nevertheless, the United States has seen the highest increases in these expenditures.

Runaway health-care costs began to be a serious social problem in the United States during the 1970s and 1980s. Before that time, medical costs as a share of gross domestic product were not out of line with those in other highly developed Western nations. Why have health-care costs risen so sharply in the United States, and why have they proven so difficult to control? The consensus among medical sociologists is that one answer may be found in the third-party "fee-for-services" system that resulted from the expansion of medical insurance in the 1960s. As the cost of health care was increasingly separated from the patient's household budget through coverage by "third parties" (public and private insurers), more people were receiving more medical services, but at a greater cost to the third parties, which paid doctors and hospitals "fees for services." Thus, as Paul Starr (1982) explains, "Since under fee-for-services, doctors and hospitals make more money the more services they provide, they have an incentive to maximize the volume of services. Third-party, fee-for-service payment was the central mechanism of medical inflation" (p. 385). The clearest example of this problem is hospital costs.

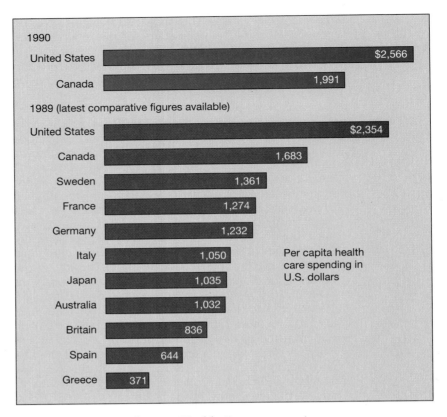

1990

United States — $2,566

Canada — 1,991

1989 (latest comparative figures available)

United States — $2,354

Canada — 1,683

Sweden — 1,361

France — 1,274

Germany — 1,232

Italy — 1,050

Japan — 1,035

Australia — 1,032

Britain — 836

Spain — 644

Greece — 371

Per capita health care spending in U.S. dollars

FIGURE 2–1   Spending on Health Care

Source: U.S. and Canadian governments, 1990; Health Officers newsletter, 1989.

Hospitals   Spending for personal health care accounts for slightly under 90 percent of total national health-care expenditures, and hospital charges account for about 56 cents of every dollar spent on personal health care. In addition, the cost of nursing home care has increased from 2 percent of total personal health-care expenditures in 1960 to almost 9 percent in 1990. As the population continues to age, the costs of nursing home care and related services will continue to escalate. These trends combine to make health-care reform and control of health-care expenditures an urgent national priority (HHS, 1993; White House Domestic Policy Council, 1993).

Until the mid-1980s hospital costs rose at a dramatic pace, primarily because hospitals had little incentive to keep costs down. Both patients and physicians were often discouraged from using hospitals on an outpatient basis, and hospitals offered few self-care facilities for patients who can look after themselves. This situation was aggravated by health insurance programs like Blue Cross, which enabled hospitals to raise their fees almost at will. Expensive medical technologies are another important factor in the increase in hospital costs, as is the aging of the population, which increases the demand for hospital services.

In recent years the rate of increase in hospital costs has slowed somewhat, largely as a result of improvements in the efficiency of hospital administration. Among the techniques that have been used to reduce the level of hospital costs are preadmission testing in outpatient departments and physicians' offices and a reduction in the average length of hospital stays. In addition, many procedures that formerly were performed on an inpatient basis have been moved to outpatient and office settings. Other factors in the reduction of the overall level of hospital care are the increased use of second opinions and an increase in care by nonhospital providers such as nursing homes and home health agencies (Waldo, Levit, & Lazenby, 1986).

Unfortunately, these various measures to control costs have not been fully successful. Between 1991 and 1992 hospital costs rose about 12 percent, a figure roughly four times the average annual inflation rate for the same period. And as more patients are treated outside hospitals or stay in hospitals for shorter periods, the costs of home care of the ill have begun to mount rapidly, increasing by about 30 percent between 1991 and 1992 (Pear, 1993). Another problem is that severe measures to reduce hospital costs have a disproportionate impact on the poor and the elderly, who are more likely to suffer from chronic illnesses that may require hospitalization. These and similar situations illustrate the tendency of cost control efforts in one area to result in higher costs elsewhere, and they provide an argument for comprehensive reform of the nation's health-care system. As we will see in the Social Policy section of this chapter, the Clinton administration is attempting to avoid piecemeal reforms that are likely to produce problems elsewhere in the system. (See Figure 2–2.)

Physicians   Another factor in the high cost of health care is the fees charged by physicians. Of each dollar spent by individuals on health care in 1991, almost 24 cents was spent for physicians' services. Moreover, the cost of physicians' services has increased more rapidly than the costs of other goods and services: In 1983, the mean net income of practicing physicians was $85,400; in 1990, it was $150,000. This seven-year increase represents a gain of about 57 percent (*Statistical Abstract,* 1993).

During much of the twentieth century a shortage of physicians, together with increasing demand for medical services, helped doctors command high fees. In 1950, for example, there were about 109 physicians for every 100,000 people in the United

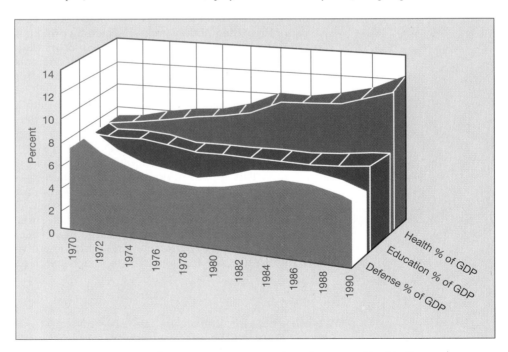

FIGURE 2–2   Percent of Gross Domestic Product Spent on Health Care, Education, and Defense, 1970–1990

Source: Data from *Statistical Abstract,* 1992.

States; in 1990 there were about 215. However, the growth in the supply of doctors has not necessarily led to improved access to medical care, or to lower costs. A look at the distribution of physicians will indicate why. People living in cities and suburbs can afford high-cost, specialized medical care. These places also tend to be more attractive than rural locales to physicians. As a result, physicians who engage in private patient care tend to be clustered in metropolitan areas, producing shortages elsewhere. Even in densely settled urban areas, poor sections may have too few practicing physicians. On the other hand, it should be noted that rural areas have small populations that cannot support major institutions like teaching hospitals, where many physicians practice and conduct research.

Another cause of the increase in the cost of physicians' services is specialization. At the turn of the century, the majority of the nation's doctors were general practitioners; by 1990, only 10.5 percent were. One reason for the high degree of specialization is the rapid increase in medical knowledge, which means that physicians can become competent only in limited areas. Another reason is that high-quality medical care often requires the availability of specialists. The fact remains, however, that specialists command more income than doctors who engage in primary care. A specialist, for example, can make up to one and one-half times what a general practitioner earns. Specialization also increases costs in another way: Patients must consult several physicians for a variety of ailments instead of one physician for all of them. Visiting several different physicians multiplies the cost of treatment many times.

A major factor in the high cost of physicians' services is the cost of malpractice insurance. Malpractice litigation has become more frequent, for several reasons. Ineffective insurance programs play a significant role. If more people were adequately covered, they would be less likely to go to court to recover their health-care costs. The increasing sophistication of medical technology also plays a part in the rise of malpractice litigation. Although recent advances enable doctors to perform treatments that once would have seemed miraculous, the treatments can be more hazardous for the patient if they are performed incorrectly or without sufficient skill and care. Public expectations about the powers of modern medicine also increase the likelihood of malpractice suits. When the new technology fails, people tend to feel angry and frustrated and blame the most available representatives of medical science—their physicians. Although many experts believe that the cost of malpractice suits accounts for less than 2 percent of total health-care costs, this proportion is huge in dollar terms. In consequence, the Health Security Act proposes a full revamping of the malpractice system, starting with special hearings about each case before litigation begins (White House Domestic Policy Council, 1993).

Still another factor that contributes to the high cost of medical care is unnecessary surgery. This applies not only to cosmetic surgery such as "nose jobs" and face-lifts but also to large numbers of hysterectomies and tonsillectomies. Although the individuals who undergo unnecessary surgery usually can pay for the operation, society as a whole pays a price. For one thing, such surgery increases the demand for surgeons' services, enabling them to charge higher fees. For another, it causes surgeons to spend a disproportionate amount of time caring for affluent patients, with the result that they are less available to patients with less money.

Inadequate Protection

We often hear it said that "an ounce of prevention is worth a pound of cure." It is certainly true that the heavy burden on the American health-care system would be alleviated if greater emphasis were placed on the prevention as well as the cure of illness. (This will become especially clear in the discussion of AIDS later in the chapter.) In an ideal society all citizens would have comprehensive health insurance that would encourage preventive measures as well as the treatment of disease and injury.

But if prevention is not possible, at least there should be some form of protection. Given the fact that both as individuals and as a society we seem to be unable to prevent a wide variety of illnesses and chronically disabling conditions, there is clearly a need for some means of protecting citizens against the potentially devastating economic impact of major health-care expenditures.

Every year approximately 34 million people are admitted to hospitals for an average stay of one week, and there are approximately 300 million outpatient visits to hospitals (White House Domestic Policy Council, 1993). Clearly, the ability to afford medical care for oneself and one's family is a matter of great concern to Americans. Nevertheless, surprising as it may seem, the system of health insurance in which a third party, the employer or the government in most cases, pays the majority of insurance costs is relatively new. For much of the nation's history, individuals paid for their own health care, or if they had insurance they paid for it themselves. As a result, the poor and the near-poor often received medical care only in the most extreme emergencies.

Along with the New Deal legislation of the 1930s—which included the establishment of social security, the extension of pension benefits for employed Americans, and other social-welfare legislation—the United States began to establish a system of health insurance whose costs were shared by employers, individuals, and government. There are now four categories of health insurance: commercial insurance companies selling both individual and group policies; public insurance (Blue Cross and Blue Shield); independent prepaid groups, or HMOs (which will be discussed later in the chapter); and public insurance. Public insurance includes two programs designed to help the medically needy—Medicare and Medicaid—which were enacted by Congress in 1965. *Medicare* is paid for by social security taxes. It is designed to cover some of the medical expenses of people age 65 and over. Those over 65 who are ineligible for Medicare may voluntarily enroll in the program by paying premiums. *Medicaid*, an assistance program financed from tax revenues, is designed to pay for the medical costs of people who cannot afford even basic health care.

The introduction of public insurance for the poor and the elderly improved their access to medical care to such an extent that by 1970 poor and old people who did not have private health insurance policies were almost as likely to use hospital facilities as people with private insurance. Medicare and Medicaid also affected another indicator of access to health care: visits to physicians. These programs enabled a larger proportion of the elderly, the poor, and nonwhites to visit doctors. In addition, low-income and minority members not only visited physicians in large numbers but also visited them more often than they had before the mid-1960s (Andersen & Anderson, 1979).

The Uninsured Despite the existence of public insurance programs, there remain large numbers of Americans who are not covered by health insurance—an estimated 38.9 million. And contrary to what many people in the United States believe, the majority of the uninsured are full-time and part-time workers and their children. The very poor who are out of the labor force qualify for Medicaid, and the elderly are eligible for Medicare. Young people who are subject to frequent periods of unemployment, and minority workers who are employed at jobs with no health benefits, are especially likely to be uninsured. (See Figures 2–3 and 2–4 on page 38.)

This situation is especially serious for families who experience unemployment, often resulting from declines in the industries on which they depend for jobs. Between 1970 and 1983, for example, the steel industry closed scores of factories throughout the nation. A study by the Steelworkers Research Project (1985) found that between 1979 and 1983, 81 percent of Chicago steelworkers lost their health insurance coverage as a result of layoffs in the steel industry; at the time of the study, 44 percent had no health insurance at all. Sudden loss of medical insurance is a common occurrence in a rapidly changing economy. An influential study by

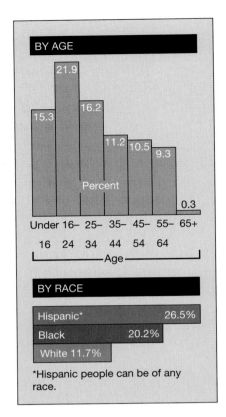

FIGURE 2–3 Persons Lacking Medical Insurance in the United States, by Age and Race

Source: Data from Census Bureau.

Families USA, a Washington-based research center, found that each month almost 2 million families lose their benefits, some for extended periods (Eckholm, 1993). In consequence, the Clinton administration's health plan attempts to provide a health insurance system that will allow benefits to continue for the unemployed and people who are out of the labor force. (See the discussion in the Social Policy section.)

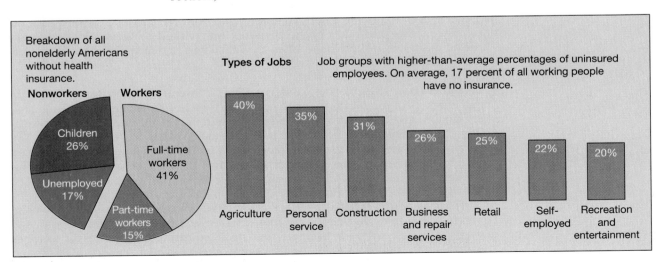

FIGURE 2–4 Persons in the Labor Force without Medical Insurance, United States, 1993

Source: Data from Employment Benefit Research Institute.

Another group that lacks sufficient health insurance is the elderly population. Many older people believe, incorrectly, that Medicare and other insurance programs will cover the cost of long-term care in nursing homes. As a result, elderly people whose families are unable to care for them may find their savings exhausted after less than a year in a nursing home (Freudenheim, 1987).

Insurance companies also attempt to increase premiums for categories of people who they believe will create a financial burden in the future, such as people who have been infected with HIV or families with disabled children. This is accomplished through the practice known as "policy churning," in which the insurance company raises its rates each year and invites some policyholders to reapply for an attractive low rate—but denies that rate to people who are ill or fall into other high-risk categories (Kolata, 1992).

Medicaid and Medicare have been helpful to many Americans, but a number of ills plague these programs. First, there is inequity in the distribution of services. The poorest people continue to receive the fewest services, despite their increased frequency of clinic visits. There are also inequities in geographic distribution. In addition, a number of factors have caused the Medicare program to fall short of its goal of providing full access to health care for the elderly. Among them is the requirement of deductible payments and coinsurance (additional insurance policies that must be purchased to ensure complete medical coverage). People who are financially secure can meet this requirement, and the poor can turn to Medicaid for this portion of their expenses. But the near-poor aged still must go without the care they need because they cannot pay for it and are not eligible for Medicaid.

Another problem with Medicare and Medicaid is their cost to the public and their impact on health-care costs in general. Both programs have been criticized for waste and abuse by administrators and physicians, who have no incentive to keep costs down and few auditing controls to keep them ethical. Hospitals, for example, have used Medicare funds to construct new buildings, purchase superfluous equipment, and hire nonmedical personnel such as public-relations directors. Some physicians operate "Medicaid mills"—clinics that serve the poor—often carrying out unnecessary tests and treatments. Many physicians refuse to treat patients under Medicaid because of the paperwork and regulations involved, and since many doctors' offices are inaccessible to the poor, the Medicaid mills often are their only source of health care.

Recent research has revealed that the volume of care received by patients in hospitals is directly related to their ability to pay, and that ability to pay has a significant effect on whether patients are given procedures to diagnose or treat heart disease. One study found that patients who are privately insured have an 80 percent greater chance of receiving an angiography (a test for clogged arteries), are 40 percent more likely to undergo coronary bypass surgery, and are 28 percent more likely to be given angioplasty (a procedure in which tiny balloons are used to open diseased arteries) than patients who lack insurance. It is not entirely clear why these discrepancies exist, but one possible explanation is that doctors are more likely to order unnecessary procedures when they know that the tests will be covered by insurance (Wenneker, Weissman, & Epstein, 1990). Other research has shown that the burden of paying for the treatment of AIDS is rapidly shifting from private insurance to Medicaid. Many AIDS patients once had private insurance, but they lost it when they lost their jobs (either because of illness or because of discrimination); joblessness and the high cost of treating AIDS combine to produce poverty, and the patient eventually qualifies for Medicaid (Green & Arno, 1990).

In sum, although insurance plans, both public and private, were originally intended to solve many of the problems and inequities of the American health-care system, in many ways these plans have compounded existing difficulties. Not only do they add to the cost of health care but they leave control of the system in the hands of health-care practitioners: Physicians and hospitals decide what and how much treatment each patient needs.

Women and Health Care

Since the late 1960s some of the strongest criticisms of the health-care system have come from the women's movement. Feminists argue that in American society women are forced to play subordinate roles in every social institution, including health care. As part of an effort to enhance the power of women, they have campaigned for the legal right to terminate unwanted pregnancies through safe, nonexploitive abortions, as well as for more control over their own medical care, especially in the areas of obstetrics and gynecology. This activism has had some influence on the delivery of health care to women, but the permanence of these gains is far from assured.

One of the first issues around which the women's movement was able to mobilize mass support was abortion. Although the majority of the American public opposed the procedure during the 1960s, increased publicity about birth defects (notably those caused by the use of thalidomide, a tranquilizer, during pregnancy) helped change many people's attitudes. In the late 1960s, as state legislatures began to liberalize restrictions on abortion, a number of women's groups demonstrated and lobbied aggressively, not merely for a loosening of restrictions but for outright repeal of all limitations on access to abortion. In 1973, in the case of *Roe* v. *Wade,* the United States Supreme Court affirmed the right of all women to obtain abortions early in pregnancy. Since then, however, opponents of abortion have succeeded in gaining the passage of legislation restricting federal funding of abortion.

In 1990 a number of decisions on abortion seemed to pave the way toward a reversal of the *Roe* decision. In particular, the decision in *Webster* v. *Reproductive Health Services* allows states to ban the use of public funds for counseling or encouraging women to have an abortion, and to prohibit abortions in publicly owned hospitals and by doctors paid with public funds. According to Chief Justice William Rehnquist, the *Webster* decision would not return the states to the "dark ages" in which abortion was outlawed; it merely "allows more governmental regulation of abortion than was permissible before." A key issue in the 1992 presidential election campaign, the "freedom of choice" view gained influence with the election of Bill Clinton and his appointment of Ruth Bader Ginsberg to the Supreme Court. Despite these developments, however, the controversy over abortion will almost certainly continue. Few medical issues so divide the American people, as well as those in other societies. (The abortion issue is discussed further in Chapter 10.)

The controversy over abortion awakened many women to larger problems in the health-care system, and the women's movement has continued its efforts to make medical personnel more sensitive to the physical and psychological needs of women. Feminists point out that in many ways health-care organizations have placed their own interests ahead of the needs and preferences of their clients. In the case of childbirth, in most states infants must be delivered by an M.D. Because the birthing process usually occurs in a hospital with the participation of a number of specialists, mothers lack the supportive presence of one person from the beginning of labor until the birth of the infant. Moreover, until recently the hospital setting was dominated by high-status male physicians who retained exclusive command of relevant medical knowledge, making it difficult for women to challenge established procedures (Katz Rothman, 1982; Shaw, 1974). Thus, efforts to win acceptance of midwives, who perform deliveries in the home and are present throughout the childbirth process, have been only moderately successful. The work of "nurse midwives," for example, is usually limited to hospitals and performed under medical supervision, whereas that of "lay midwives," who practice outside of medical control, is not fully legal in all states (Conrad & Kern, 1981).

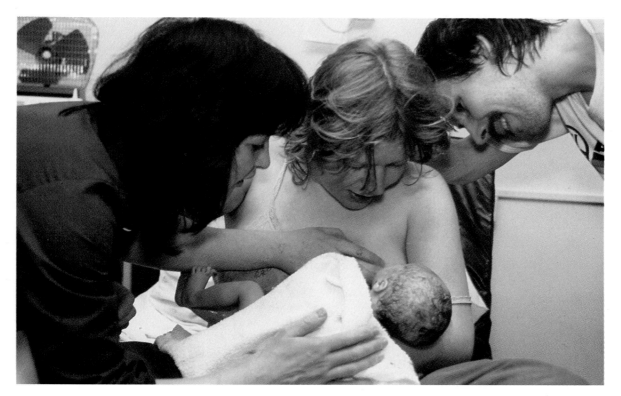

A growing minority of women are choosing to have their babies with the help of a midwife because they feel that the midwife can be more responsive to their needs during labor and delivery.

Other critics of the health-care system as it relates to women have called for less intervention in the birth process itself. Anesthesia, induced labor, and surgical practices such as caesarian sections and the use of forceps have come under attack. Some of these forms of intervention not only can cause harm to both mother and infant but also inflate the cost of delivery. As a result of these criticisms, classes in "prepared childbirth" taught by nurse practitioners have become widespread. Such classes prepare a woman (and often her partner as well) for the experience of childbirth by describing the process in detail and teaching a variety of techniques for reducing or eliminating pain during labor and delivery. These techniques not only make it possible to avoid excessive use of anesthetics but also greatly reduce the woman's fear and anxiety about giving birth. Some hospitals are also granting women a greater say in decisions affecting their deliveries, including the choice of having a mate or friend present in the delivery room.

Women's groups have also criticized the nature of gynecological care in the United States. It is argued that the simple fact of being female has been "medicalized"; that is, certain conditions, such as pregnancy and menstruation, have been defined in terms of health and illness (Ehrenreich & English, 1979). This has permitted "experts," especially gynecologists and psychiatrists (see Chapter 3), to achieve professional dominance over women, with results that not only are economically beneficial to physicians but also contribute to women's relative lack of power in society (Riessman, 1983).

While many politically active women concern themselves with issues of reproductive care and abortion, medical researchers and health administrators point out that women and their needs are vastly underrepresented in medical research. Eighty percent of health-care workers are women, yet women are virtually absent from the leadership ranks of medicine (Brooks, 1990). The National Institutes of Health, the most important source of funds for medical research, spend less than 20 percent of their research budget on women's health issues, yet breast cancer alone claims the lives of about 40,000 women a year. Most of the studies of heart disease and smoking use only male subjects, and again the possible unique needs of women go unresearched.

In 1990, in response to the latter criticism, the National Institutes of Health created an Office of Research on Women's Health. The office provides funds for studies designed to fill gaps in scientific knowledge resulting from the exclusion of women from past experiments. In addition, proposals for studies using only male subjects must be justified on scientific grounds.

The Disabled and Handicapped

Another important population from the standpoint of health-care needs consists of people who are disabled or handicapped, usually as a result of automobile accidents and accidents occurring in industrial settings. Automobile accidents are a major cause of paralysis and other permanent disabilities, in addition to serious injuries that often require hospitalization and costly surgery. Until recently the disabled and handicapped were literally a forgotten people. They were excluded from work, school, and society both by active discrimination and by barriers imposed by a world designed for the able-bodied. Steps, curbs, narrow doorways and aisles—impassable obstacles to many disabled people—are only a few of the aspects of everyday life that still impede the physically disabled. Although the situation has improved since the 1960s as a result of the political organization of the disabled themselves, many problems remain.

The disabled suffer from extremely high unemployment rates. Of the 13.3 million people with a work disability, 33.6 percent are in the labor force and 15.6 percent are unemployed (Kraus & Stoddard, 1989). (The comparable figures for the nondisabled are 78.5 percent and 6.8 percent.) In addition, many handicapped peo-

Today disabled people refuse to be denied active and productive roles in society.

ple are underemployed—assigned to low-level, low-paying jobs because employers are afraid to offer them challenges. In many instances social security regulations contribute to the problem by limiting the amount of money a handicapped person can earn and still receive benefits. For all these reasons, the majority of the handicapped are poor.

Numerous studies have shown that when disabled people are hired, they usually dispel all the negative myths that surround them. An overwhelming majority prove to be dedicated, capable workers; they have only a slightly higher than average absentee rate, and their turnover rate is well below average. The disabled are neither slower nor less productive than other workers and have excellent safety records.

Almost 29 million Americans have deformities or orthopedic impairments; about 31 million have visual or hearing impairments (*Statistical Abstract,* 1993). In addition, advances in medical science have made it possible for many people to survive serious accidents, usually with handicaps. Technology is also making it possible for many disabled people, who would have been bedridden or housebound in the past, to be mobile and to acquire new skills. Improved health care and prevention of disease have meant that more people than ever before are living to old age and incurring the disabilities that often accompany advanced age.

The disabled and handicapped have emerged as a recognized minority group. Like women and blacks, they are demanding an end to the discrimination that keeps them out of jobs and out of the mainstream of life. They oppose efforts to place them in special programs or schools, except during the necessary phases of rehabilitation or therapy. Special programs, they claim, are the ghettos of the handicapped. As we will see in the Social Policy section, in the past two decades some legislation has been enacted in an attempt to address the problems of the disabled and handicapped.

Ethical Issues

As medical technology has improved and life-prolonging procedures have become more available and dependable, a number of complex ethical issues have arisen. Some of the new medical technologies, such as heart transplants, are extremely costly and cannot be provided to all patients who might benefit from them. Thus, the question arises of how to choose the patients who will undergo these procedures (Callahan, 1994). (See Box 2–1 on page 58.)

The availability of life-prolonging equipment and procedures has also given rise to questions about the meaning of life and death. State legislatures across the country have found themselves debating the question of whether death occurs when the heart stops beating or when the brain stops functioning. Courts have been required to decide whether patients should be given the right to die by having life-prolonging treatments stopped. The latter issue, known as euthanasia or mercy killing, is a subject of widespread controversy in the United States today.

In recent years a related issue, assisted suicide, has come to the fore. In one case Michigan doctor Jack Kevorkian helped a 54-year-old woman with Alzheimer's disease kill herself, using an intravenous device that allowed the patient to receive a lethal drug by pressing a button. The doctor was arrested and charged with first-degree murder; later the charges were dropped, but the doctor was ordered to refrain from using the suicide device in the future. Although many doctors and health authorities condemn the practice, Kevorkian has assisted other terminally ill individuals who wished to end their lives, bringing the "right to die" issue to national attention.

Some court decisions have upheld the right to die. For example, in 1990 a Las Vegas judge granted the request of a 31-year-old quadriplegic that he be allowed to end his life by being disconnected from a respirator. In another case, a Missouri court allowed the family of a comatose woman to stop having chemical nutrition and water pumped into her stomach; the decision was based on evidence that the young woman, if she had been mentally able, would have wished to have life-support measures terminated.

One attempt to cope with the dilemma of "mercy killing" is the concept of the "living will." Individuals who are suffering from a terminal illness and wish to spare both themselves and their relatives the pain and expense of a slow, lingering death can request that doctors do nothing to prolong their lives artificially. Although this concept is rapidly gaining social acceptance, the idea of a right to die remains highly controversial.

The issues raised by advances in medical technology have been aptly summed up by Robert E. Cranford, a neurologist:

> We are beginning to realize that our wonderful medical advances enable us to prolong the dying process. The first question is, Should we? And then come all the others: Who lives? Who dies? How do you decide? . . . Who decides? . . . Machines give us more choices. But the more choices there are, the more dilemmas there are. (quoted in Malcolm, 1984)

AIDS—A MODERN PLAGUE

The social problems related to health care became especially acute in the mid-1980s with the spread of a previously unknown disease: acquired immune deficiency syndrome, or AIDS. AIDS is caused by a virus known as HIV (human immunodeficiency virus), which attacks the body's immune system. An unusual feature of HIV is the long period of latency—up to ten years—between the time of infection and the appearance of the disease. During this period there may be no visible symptoms. Once it has been rendered ineffective by the virus, however, the immune system is unable to combat other diseases that routinely infect humans, such as pneumonia, cancer viruses, and tuberculosis, and death is almost inevitable. But not all people who carry the HIV virus in their bloodstreams actually develop AIDS. It appears that between 25 and 50 percent of individuals who are infected by HIV will develop AIDS within two to five years. Approximately 25 percent will develop AIDS-related complex (ARC), which many health scientists believe is an earlier stage of AIDS. The remaining 25 percent of those who carry the virus in their blood may never develop AIDS or ARC, yet they may transmit it to others (Kreiger & Appelman, 1986).

AIDS is a global epidemic—cases have been reported to the World Health Organization from more than 100 countries. More than 850,000 cases of AIDS have been reported, and an estimated 15 million people are infected with the HIV virus, two thirds of them in Africa. In parts of the developing world, up to 20 percent of sexually active people are infected by the virus.

Since AIDS first appeared in the United States in 1981, approximately 245,000 people have contracted it; of these, more than 166,000 have died (*Statistical Abstract*, 1993). It is not known how many more people may be infected with the virus but are not actually becoming ill. AIDS has been particularly destructive for blacks and Hispanics. Blacks, for example, make up 12 percent of the population but account for almost 30 percent of reported AIDS cases in the United States (Centers for Disease Control, 1990).

We do not fully understand why the rate of AIDS infection is rising so rapidly among blacks—especially black women—in the United States. Many researchers and community health workers believe that the causes are closely related to increasing poverty in some black and Latino communities. Increasing poverty is closely associated with higher rates of intravenous drug use and unprotected sexual contact (Dugger, 1992). Although there is a history of resistance to condom use in some minority communities, especially those in which rates of AIDS infection are rising, a recent New York Times /CBS News poll found that knowledge about how AIDS is transmitted and how to practice safe sex is spreading especially rapidly among African Americans (Kagay, 1993).

AIDS is transmitted through the exchange of body fluids, that is, directly from an infected person's blood, semen, or vaginal secretions into another person's bloodstream. Transmission can occur through sexual activity that leads to the tearing of membranes; through blood transfusions, sharing of hypodermic needles, and other means; or from an infected mother to her unborn or newborn infant. The disease is not transmitted by mere contact with skin—by a handshake or a hug, for example—or through the air as a result of a sneeze or cough. It is not transmitted by the sharing of meals, bathrooms, and beds with infected individuals or by casual contact in the home, school, or workplace. The primary means of transmission are sexual intercourse, especially anal intercourse, and sharing of needles by drug users.

AIDS is sometimes referred to as a "gay disease" because in the United States it first appeared in male homosexuals between the ages of 20 and 49, and the majority of deaths from the disease have occurred among this population. But the disease is by no means limited to homosexuals. The data in Table 2–3 on page 46 show that users of intravenous drugs are also infected by the virus in large numbers.

AIDS has spread among heterosexual individuals in a variety of ways. One of those ways is prostitution: The Centers for Disease Control have found that over half of all prostitutes in the United States are serum positive; that is, they have been infected by HIV even if they are not yet showing outward symptoms of the disease. However, the primary bridge between homosexual and heterosexual transmitters is intravenous drug users, who transmit the disease to their sexual partners and to others with whom they share needles. Intravenous drug users and their mates, as well as their babies, now account for more than 25 percent of AIDS cases in the United States.

Most people want to know whether AIDS is going to become widespread among heterosexuals, as it seems to have done in some segments of the population in Africa and Brazil. "The answer," says Thomas C. Quinn, an AIDS researcher at the National Institute of Allergy and Infectious Diseases, "is not a yes or a no. Heterosexuals will get infected, but they will not be your everyday person. It will be the people already at risk for syphilis, gonorrhea, chlamydia, and with life styles that include risky sexual partners. Among those, it will be an epidemic" (quoted in Hilts, 1990, p. C1). The epidemic will also affect the children of some AIDS victims. An estimated 100,000 orphans will have been produced by the disease by the year 2000.

Quinn and his colleagues studied almost 5,000 patients in two inner-city clinics that treat sexually transmitted diseases. They found that non-IV-drug-using heterosexuals with syphilis were seven to nine times more likely to have AIDS than other patients at the clinics, suggesting that heterosexual intercourse played a role in transmitting both syphilis and AIDS to those patients. Similar conditions have been found among IV drug and crack users and their partners: Promiscuity occurs in combination with untreated disease. The realization that non-IV drugs like crack are implicated in the AIDS epidemic (because women and men in crack houses engage in sex with many partners, thereby greatly increasing their risk of infection) emerged in part from the pioneering research by sociologist Claire Sterk (1988), who spent hundreds of hours interviewing street women about their drug and sexual behavior.

For AIDS victims and their families, the impact of the disease is devastating. Not only must they deal with fear and grief, but they must also cope with feelings of shame. Because AIDS is associated with homosexuality and drug abuse, relatives and close friends of the patients feel stigmatized. They may become angry at the patient and blame themselves for failing to rescue him or her from drug use or homosexuality (Ayala, 1994). "Having AIDS is a little bit like being treated as if you're a leper," says a therapist who works with AIDS patients and family members (quoted in Walker, 1987).

Although certain drugs, such as AZT, may slow the onset of AIDS symptoms, to

TABLE 2-3 AIDS CASES BY AGE GROUP, EXPOSURE CATEGORY, AND RACE/ETHNICITY, UNITED STATES

ADULT/ADOLESCENT EXPOSURE CATEGORY	WHITE, NOT HISPANIC		BLACK, NOT HISPANIC		HISPANIC		ASIAN/PACIFIC ISLANDER		AMERICAN INDIAN/ ALASKAN NATIVE		TOTAL	
	No.	(%)	No.	(%)	No.	(%)	No.	(%)	No.	(%)	No.	(%)
Male homosexual/bisexual contact	63,669	(76)	15,043	(36)	9,445	(41)	692	(74)	116	(54)	89,155	(60)
Intravenous (IV) drug use (female and heterosexual male)	6,541	(8)	16,180	(39)	9,375	(40)	39	(4)	36	(17)	32,257	(22)
Male homosexual/bisexual contact and IV drug use	5,848	(7)	2,713	(7)	1,437	(6)	19	(2)	28	(13)	10,058	(7)
Hemophilia/coagulation disorder	1,106	(1)	87	(0)	102	(0)	16	(2)	8	(4)	1,323	(1)
Heterosexual contact:	1,652	(2)	4,712	(11)	1,357	(6)	34	(4)	10	(5)	7,785	(5)
Sex with IV drug user	909		2,083		1,067		14		7		4,090	
Sex with bisexual male	254		148		53		8		1		465	
Sex with person with hemophilia	66		6		2		1		—		75	
Sex with transfusion recipient with HIV infection	90		21		21		1		—		135	
Sex with HIV-infected person, risk not specified	288		438		195		6		2		929	
Recipient of blood transfusion, blood components, or tissue	2,480	(3)	591	(1)	357	(2)	70	(8)	3	(1)	3,512	(2)
Other/undetermined	2,009	(2)	2,080	(5)	1,195	(5)	61	(7)	12	(6)	5,408	(4)
Adult/adolescent subtotal	83,260	(100)	39,390	(100)	23,249	(100)	927	(100)	213	(100)	147,407	(100)

Source: Centers for Disease Control, 1990.

date there is no cure for AIDS. The only defense against it is prevention. At present, therefore, behavioral changes are the only means of stopping the spread of the virus. Indeed, AIDS is different from most other diseases in that individuals can, at least in theory, *choose* to avoid infection. The battle against the AIDS epidemic, thus, is a social as well as a biological one: While scientists conduct research in an effort to find a cure, educators, social scientists, and policy makers are attempting to influence the behavior of large numbers of people. But efforts to control behavior— especially sexual behavior—raise a variety of moral and ethical issues: Should people be required to undergo testing for the presence of the HIV virus? Should they be required to reveal the names of individuals with whom they have had sexual contacts? Should drug addicts be given clean needles? Should condoms be distributed in public schools? Just how controversial this subject is will become clear in discussions of AIDS-related issues at several points in this book.

AIDS is having a major impact not only on individuals and their loved ones but also on the health-care system itself. HIV infection can be detected almost as soon as it occurs, and in most cases months or years go by before severe symptoms appear.

PROCEED WITH CONDOMS

The more sexual partners you have, the greater your risk of contracting AIDS. Use condoms and limit your sexual partners.

As medical researchers strive to find a cure for AIDS, educators and policy makers use posters like this one to make people more aware of the need to engage in "safer" forms of sexual behavior.

Therefore, there is ample time for medical intervention. But treatment for AIDS is complex and prolonged. Because it destroys the body's ability to fight disease, the presence of AIDS is signaled by the onset of many different illnesses, ranging from pneumonia to various forms of cancer. In the terminal stages of the disease, the patient often suffers from acute illnesses like meningitis. Thus, treatment for the illnesses associated with AIDS is complex and usually requires long periods of hospitalization and intensive care. The health-care system, already overburdened, is severely strained by the need to provide expensive care for hundreds of thousands of AIDS patients. Health insurance costs are also increasing as more AIDS cases develop.

A key factor in the problems facing the health-care system is the slowness of its response to the AIDS epidemic. According to activists in groups like ACT-UP, one reason for this slow response is the reluctance of the scientific community—and government agencies concerned with health care—to tackle a disease that was initially thought to affect primarily gay men (Krieger & Appelman, 1986). Another reason is conflict over such issues as who will pay the costs of research on AIDS, who will profit from any drugs or vaccines that may be developed in the course of that research, and who should be tested for the presence of HIV and under what conditions. These and related issues of insurance and prevention will be discussed further in the Social Policy section.

Clearly, AIDS is a great deal more than a serious illness. It can, in fact, be viewed as three epidemics rolled into one: the spread of the HIV virus; the epidemic of the disease AIDS; and the social, political, psychological, and ethical reactions to the disease and those who suffer from it (Mann, 1987). AIDS has had a profound effect on American society—on its ways of living and dying and on its debates over health care, sex education, drug abuse, and social justice. It has had an especially dramatic effect on sexual behavior; to put it succinctly, "People are putting on the sexual brakes" (Dimen, 1987, p. 14). There has been a resurgence of traditional sexual mores and values, not only among the groups most at risk but throughout the population. These changes will be discussed more fully in Chapter 4, which deals with sex-related social problems.

EXPLANATIONS OF HEALTH-CARE PROBLEMS

Why do we have such difficulty improving the quality of health-care services and providing more equal access to those services? The explanations offered by medical sociologists depend to a large extent on the perspective from which they view the problem. Conflict theorists, for example, tend to view the problem as a feature of capitalism: The poor get less medical care because they get less of everything in American society. Those who approach this question from a functionalist perspective have sought the answers in medicine's development into a complex and costly social institution. And from an interactionist perspective many of the problems of health care in the United States and other highly developed nations can be traced to cultural factors, including the way people are taught to interact with one another. In this section we will briefly discuss each of these approaches to the explanation of health-care problems.

Class and Class Conflict

Sociologists often point out that social class, measured by the income and wealth a household has at its disposal, goes a long way toward explaining the types of illnesses experienced by members of that household and the kinds of health care they receive. We have already suggested that lack of access to good medical care causes higher rates of illness and death among the poor. Until the early twentieth century, the ill health of the poor was caused largely by infectious diseases. Today medical science is able to control and cure such diseases much more effectively, with the result that by themselves they no longer account for tremendous differences in health between the poor and the nonpoor. Instead,

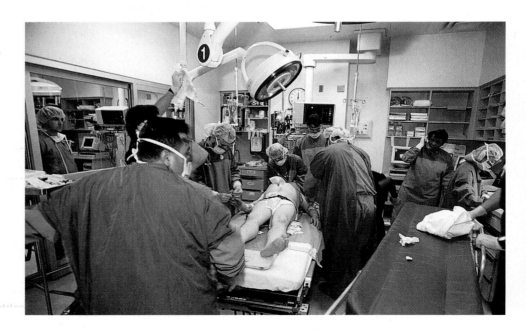

Crowding in hospital emergency rooms is often a result of the tendency of people who lack medical insurance to seek primary care at an emergency room in lieu of visiting a private physician.

access to good medical care, preventive medical action, health knowledge, and limitation of delay in seeking treatment have become increasingly important in combating mortality, as chronic diseases have become the chief health enemy in the developed world. In these areas, lower class people may well be at a disadvantage. (Antonovsky, 1974, p. 178; see also Cockerham, 1995)

In fact, as control of chronic diseases like cancer becomes more important, the differences between the health of the poor and that of the nonpoor is likely to increase; that is, the poor will still have higher rates of illness and death than the nonpoor because of their relative lack of access to high-quality medical care.

In an analysis of the relationship between social class and ill health, Lee Rainwater (1974) suggested that lack of access to medical care is not the only factor that affects the health of the poor: Just being poor promotes poor health. The poor, for example, cannot afford to eat properly, so they are likely to be weak. They often live in the most polluted areas and hence are susceptible to respiratory diseases. Because they cannot afford proper housing, they are exposed to disease-carrying refuse and rodents. Perhaps most important, their lives are filled with stress—they are always worried about getting enough money to pay for necessities. Such long-term stress can cause both physical and mental illness. It also makes it difficult to react to minor signs of ill health. A cough is likely to be dismissed if one does not have enough to eat; only a much worse cough will prompt a visit to a clinic, and by then it may be too late. The poor also seem to feel middle-aged earlier than the nonpoor. As a result, they are likely to accept illness and disability as somehow natural—even in their thirties.

Another issue that has been studied by conflict theorists is overmedication and iatrogenic illness. (*Iatrogenic* means "physician generated," that is, caused by medical treatments, especially the administration of incorrect drug doses.) This is an extremely controversial issue. Some writers on the subject claim that our society is seriously overmedicated and that adverse reactions to drug therapies are commonplace; in hospitals, for example, "2 to 8 percent of all drug doses given . . . are in error—wrong drug, wrong dose . . . wrong patient, or failure to give the prescribed drug" (Silverman & Lee, 1974, p. 262). One study found that 36 percent of over 800 patients at a university hospital had iatrogenic diseases (Steel et al., 1981).

In response to such findings, members of the medical community have accused researchers and reporters of sensationalism and of playing a "numbers game." Nevertheless, many pharmacists view drug iatrogenesis as serious and preventable and have taken steps to create a new role for themselves as "clinical pharmacists" responsible not only for the safe storage and accurate dispensing of drugs prescribed by physicians but also as "drug consultants" and providers of information to physicians and patients (Broadhead & Facchinetti, 1986).

Social scientists who view health-care problems from a conflict perspective often explain the outcomes of conflicts over medical policy in terms of conflict between classes. For example, in a study of the social, political, and psychological impact of AIDS in America, Dennis Altman (1987) showed that as long as AIDS was perceived as a disease of homosexuals and intravenous drug users, members of the middle and upper classes did not put pressure on the government to invest heavily in its treatment and cure. Altman and others have pointed out that because AIDS strikes disproportionately at less advantaged citizens and members of minority groups, it is often thought of as "their" disease.

Institutions and Health Care

Functionalist explanations of health-care problems focus on features of health-care institutions themselves. Sociologists with this institutional orientation point out that every society is faced with the problem of distributing health-care services among its members. The United States uses a marketplace approach, which views health care as a commodity that is subject to the demands and spending power of consumers. Canada, by contrast, views health care as an entitlement of citizenship and extends full coverage to all its legal residents.

Since health-care costs are lower in Canada and many medical professionals feel that the quality of care in that nation is at least equal to the quality of care in the United States, there are many advocates for a comparable "universal and single payer" insurance system in the United States (Sidney Wolfe, personal communication, 1993). Opponents of the Canadian system point out, however, that it deprives the well-off of the higher-quality health care they can afford. The broad sociological issue here is how to improve health-care institutions so as to provide the best possible care for the greatest number of people. Most medical sociologists do not agree that health care should be treated as a commodity available in higher amounts and quality to those most able to afford it. But this does not mean that they believe the Canadian model could be imported to the United States without a great deal of compromise.

There are a number of functionalist arguments for why a service that has come to be viewed as a basic human right should not be treated as a commodity:

- *Information*—a consumer is not in a position to shop for medical treatment in the same way that one shops for other products or services, since the need for such treatment cannot be evaluated by the consumer.
- *Product uncertainty*—the consumer does not have sufficient knowledge to judge the effectiveness of sophisticated treatments.
- *Norms of treatment*—medical care is performed under the control of a physician. A patient does not direct his or her own treatment.
- *Lack of price competition*—prices for doctors' services are not advertised and are not subject to true competition.
- *Restricted entry*—there are numerous barriers to entry to medical school. Many qualified applicants are turned down because of a limited number of places.
- *Professional dominance*—many health-care services that are restricted to physicians could be performed by trained technicians. This restriction has created a monopoly.
- *Misallocated supply*—an abundance of specialists encourages the use of expensive and sophisticated treatments when simpler ones would be just as effective (Mechanic, 1978).

The drawbacks of the American system in its present form are illustrated by the role of the American Medical Association (AMA) in limiting the number of physicians. During the first half of the twentieth century, stringent licensing requirements and strict standards for medical school admissions reduced the doctor-to-population ratio to a critical low. The scarcity of doctors allowed physicians to raise their fees whenever they wished. Recently the scarcity problem has been alleviated, although medical schools still limit the number of places open to applicants. Minority group members, women, and people from disadvantaged backgrounds, who might work as doctors among poorly served segments of society, continue to be underrepresented in medical schools despite some improvement in recent years. In addition, the AMA has been active in establishing legal and licensing barriers that restrict the activities of other health-care practitioners, such as nurse midwives (Freddi & Bjorkman, 1989; Mechanic, 1978).

This situation is made worse by the fact that few states have an agency where incompetence can be reported and investigated. Moreover, since patients rarely know that they are being poorly treated, the responsibility for reporting incompetence lies with other physicians—yet most physicians are reluctant to report on their colleagues, even when they know that patients' lives are endangered (Millman,

1977). In a study of how doctors control errors among colleagues, sociologist Charles Bosk (1979) spent eighteen months observing the operations of two surgical services in an elite teaching hospital. He followed surgeons through their daily activities, becoming aware of their shared worldview, the way they judge themselves and others, and their attitudes toward patients. In the course of this research he documented the norms under which surgeons forgive technical errors and punish mistakes that they believe are due to moral lapses (e.g., carelessness or laxity). These norms result in a system of professional social control that is not often subject to outside authorities.

Health and Social Interaction

The relatively poor health of Americans is due in part to features of our lifestyle, including sedentary occupations, nonnutritious diets, lack of proper exercise, environmental pollution, and cigarette smoking. But if activities like smoking are detrimental to health, why do people engage in such behaviors? Interactionist explanations of social problems related to health care often draw upon studies of patterns of sociability (i.e., interaction among people in groups) and the ways in which people are socialized in different societies and communities. Features of a society's lifestyle, such as smoking, drinking, and diet, are deeply ingrained in the way people interact with one another. Very often we eat, drink, or smoke as much to be sociable as to sustain ourselves. Advertising reinforces these patterns by associating consumption with sociability, as you can see by completing the following phrases: "It's _____ Time"; "Welcome to _____ Country."

Excessive eating, leading to obesity, and high rates of alcohol consumption are among the health problems related to patterns of sociability in an affluent society. But the most pervasive and serious of these problems are those created by smoking. Despite the efforts of health professionals both in and out of government, 50 million Americans continue to smoke cigarettes. Each year thousands of adolescents ignore warnings about the health risks associated with smoking. In addition, women often expose unborn infants to the negative effects of smoking, especially low birth weight. One thousand deaths a day and a greater number of serious illnesses are directly attributable to cigarette smoking, and recent research has shown that passive smoking (breathing air that contains cigarette smoke) is a serious environmental hazard.

Interactionist perspectives on issues like smoking and health typically focus on the way communications (e.g., advertising images and messages) seek to connect the use of tobacco with particular lifestyles. They may also take a more explicitly critical look at the way tobacco companies directly or indirectly influence those communications. For example, a study by Kenneth E. Warner at the University of Michigan found that "the higher the percentage of cigarette advertising revenues, the lower the likelihood that a magazine will publish an article on the dangers of smoking" (quoted in Carmody, 1992, p. D22).

Interactionist explanations of health problems do not end with observations about lifestyle and patterns of sociability, however. The interactionist perspective is often applied to problems that stem from doctor–patient relations. One study of this problem found that the primary cause of malpractice suits is failures of communication between patients and doctors. Patients apparently feel intimidated by physicians and believe that their doctors will not listen to their complaints and concerns. As a result, they avoid confrontation until the situation is completely out of hand, at which point they may feel compelled to bring a malpractice suit (May, 1986).

It is helpful to think of the major sociological perspectives as conceptual tools to use in analyzing a complex social problem like the prevention and treatment of physical illnesses. No single perspective explains all the important issues, but together they go a long way toward providing a full explanation. The functionalist view is most helpful in pointing out how social institutions like hospitals should function, why they do not function effectively, and how they could be improved. The conflict perspective allows for more insight into the influence of inequalities of wealth, education, and power on access to and quality of medical care. The interactionist perspective points to the way differences in people's perception of social conditions such as the AIDS epidemic influence their behavior toward others, both in health-care institutions and in community settings.

SOCIAL POLICY

We have seen throughout this chapter that health-care services in the United States have not attained the levels of quality and availability that prevail in other advanced industrial societies. We have also seen that almost 39 million Americans lack medical insurance coverage. In the case of AIDS, we are faced with a modern plague that is severely taxing the capabilities of the existing health-care system and has the potential to overwhelm it. What, then, are the prospects for improvement in health-care institutions and, thus, for the overall health of the American population?

In 1993, under the leadership of President Clinton and Hillary Rodham Clinton, the United States embarked upon a far-reaching debate over health-care policy. In Hillary Clinton's view, the core of the debate is the issue of how to bring more security to the nation's citizens. As she observes, "Each time someone loses health coverage or is denied insurance, their experience becomes another chapter in a growing national tragedy" (White House Domestic Policy Council, 1993, p. ii). The Clinton health plan rejects extensive single-payer medical systems, such as those in Canada and England, as well as the purely market-driven systems in which high-quality medical care is available only to those who can afford it. Instead, it calls for a "health security system" in which every person in the system would receive a "health security card" that guarantees a comprehensive benefit package that can never be taken away. The benefit package would be offered by different insurance systems rather than by a single federal bureaucracy, but the federal government would guarantee coverage to all citizens by requiring all health insurance providers to include the comprehensive package in their plans and to conform to new regulations designed to maintain health security.

At this writing, Congress is beginning to consider the complex and ambitious health plan known as the Health Security Act of 1994. While innumerable surveys show that the American public is committed to widespread health-care reform, there is also strong opposition to the plan by interest groups that believe their revenues would be reduced or that choice and quality of health care may be diminished. Clearly, a great deal of compromise will be necessary. Therefore, in this discussion of social policy related to health care we will look at some of the fundamental issues underlying the debate and at how the proposed plan would address them.

Medical sociologists have been deeply involved in evaluating proposed and existing health-care policies. And as the merits of various approaches to health-care delivery have been debated, medical sociologists have increasingly engaged in research designed to supply empirical data on prevention and care systems of all kinds. This has usually involved providing data on what classes of people benefit from a given policy and in what ways, and on how those benefits or losses compare to the situation that existed before the new policy was implemented.

The findings of medical sociology regarding widespread reforms such as those proposed during the 1990s also suggest the inevitability of compromise and improvisation. After a thorough review of the evolution of health-care systems in many of the world's advanced democratic nations—including Great Britain, Sweden, Canada, West Germany, France, and the United States—medical sociologist Odin W. Anderson concluded that none of these nations has a central "blueprint" for how its health-care system should develop or how costs could be controlled. Although all of the nations studied have developed highly complex systems with a wide array of trained specialists, Anderson observes, they now "are wondering how to manage multiple chronic illnesses in an aging population" (1989, p. 160).

Although the Clinton health plan is a major blueprint for change in U.S. health-care policies, it is by no means a radical departure from existing practices. The basic expenses of the system would continue to be paid by employers, with a proposed 20 percent of insurance costs to be paid by employees. The elderly, the poor, and the disabled would continue to be covered by insurance plans subsidized by the federal government. People with more money would still be able to buy higher-quality health care for some purposes. But above all, everyone would be covered by the basic, comprehensive benefit package. Of at least equal importance, the reform plan places heavy emphasis on reducing the soaring costs of medical care through measures to enhance preventive health behavior.

Focusing on Prevention

One way of reducing the cost of health care is to prevent serious illnesses and other conditions that require hospitalization and surgery. *Health maintenance organizations* (HMOs), or prepaid group practices, constitute an attempt to shift the empha-

As health-care reforms place a greater emphasis on prevention, the cost and effectiveness of immunization programs have become subjects of controversy.

sis from treatment to prevention. They provide complete medical services to subscribers in a specific region for a monthly fee. Members are entitled to all the medical services provided by the HMO, which may, depending on the plan, include everything from vaccinations to major surgery. Since members' fees are the HMO's only source of income, the HMO has a strong incentive to keep its members healthy. HMOs stress ambulatory care rather than hospitalization, and generic drugs rather than expensive name brands. General practitioners, rather than more expensive specialists, are the primary providers of care. Physical examinations, early detection and treatment, and inoculations are emphasized.

The first HMOs were established in the 1930s. In 1973 the concept received a boost from the Health Maintenance Act, which provided funds for establishing new HMOs, gave employees the right to choose HMOs over group insurance plans, and abolished numerous state restrictions on these programs. In the early 1980s they received further support from the Reagan administration because they encourage economy in health-care spending. Between 1980 and 1990 total enrollment in HMOs increased from about 9 million members to more than 33 million (*Statistical Abstract*, 1993). Enrollment continues to grow, but at a far lower rate than during the 1980s (Meier, 1990).

Passage of a Health Security Act would spur a rapid increase in HMO membership, since employers that are required to fund health-care plans are likely to select HMOs to offer their employees. On the other hand, the findings of recent studies suggest that patients in HMOs often believe that they are treated in an impersonal fashion in comparison with private, "fee-for-service" doctors. Health-care policy makers are seeking ways to improve patients' satisfaction with HMO services (Freudenheim, 1993).

Principles of Reform in the Clinton Plan

The reason HMOs are so central to debates over how to prevent illness and reduce health-care costs is that they provide comprehensive services for all their members. In consequence, many of the features of HMO operation are incorporated in the basic principles of the Health Security Act. The act is based on six fundamental principles: security, simplicity, savings, quality, choice, and responsibility (White House Domestic Policy Council, 1993).

- *Security:* The act guarantees comprehensive benefits to all Americans and ensures that those benefits cannot be taken away. It bars insurance companies from denying coverage to seriously ill people or from charging higher premiums to the elderly or people with serious illnesses like AIDS.
- *Simplicity:* The act requires all health-care plans to adopt a standard claim form. It also creates a uniform package of benefits and standardizes billing procedures.
- *Savings:* By forcing health-care plans to compete, the act gives them an incentive to control costs. It also creates "health alliances" that can obtain lower prices for insurance coverage than consumers and small businesses could obtain on their own. It reduces administrative costs and places limits on premium increases.
- *Quality:* The act provides for research on prevention, treatment, and cure. It pays for preventive services and encourages the training of primary-care doctors and nurses.
- *Choice:* Patients can choose among several types of health-care plans.
- *Responsibility:* The act asks drug companies to maintain reasonable prices and includes measures to discourage frivolous malpractice suits.

There is widespread agreement on the need for far-ranging change in the American system of health care (Callahan, 1989). But as the debate on the Health Security Act indicates, there is little consensus on what changes should be made. As sociologist Paul Starr, one of the key health-care planners in the Clinton administration, has pointed out in numerous articles, the complexity of the existing system and the lack of consensus about the desirability of a more centralized, single-payer model have forced planners to develop an approach to health-care reform that seeks to maintain much of the existing system while also seeking to implement the principles of reform just listed. From a sociological standpoint, the most relevant aspects of these efforts are the mix of medical-care strategies contained in the Clinton plan, the plan's attempt to control the administrative costs of health care and reduce the amount of paperwork involved, and perhaps most important, its proposals for paying for the new system of health security.

Managing the Mix of Medical Care A central idea in the Clinton plan is "managed competition." "Bringing competition to health care will give consumers the same buying clout in health care they've always had in other areas," claim the sponsors of the Health Security Act (White House Domestic Policy Council, 1993, p. 54). Essentially, the managed-competition approach would allow consumers to choose among existing health-care provider systems: fee-for-service plans (with "private" doctors), preferred-provider organizations (networks of doctors and other health-care professionals who join together to offer services and reduce costs), and health maintenance organizations. Individuals enrolled in Medicare (for the elderly) or Medicaid (for the poor) would have improved coverage as well, but different groups of health-care professionals would compete on a regional basis to serve these large populations.

The Clinton health plan would manage competition through a system of non-profit organizations known as health-care alliances, which would combine the buying power of their members to ensure quality, reduce costs, and share administrative expenses. The alliances would enable small businesses to afford health insurance for their employees. Often too small to be eligible for the lower-cost group insurance rates available to larger firms, and fearing the high costs of catastrophic illnesses, many small businesses do not offer health insurance to their employees. The alliances would give such businesses a chance to buy lower-cost insurance. They would act as intermediaries, collecting premiums from private employers and the federal and state governments and passing them on to the health plans.

The proposal to create a system of regional alliances has become one of the plan's most controversial aspects. Critics on the right fear that the alliances will become rigid bureaucracies that exert far too much regulatory power. Critics on the left argue that political pressures would result in the drawing of boundaries in such a way that richer suburbs would be separate from poorer central-city areas, thereby preserving the inequities of health-care distribution found in the existing system (Toner, 1993).

A somewhat less controversial aspect of the Clinton plan is the attempt to change the mix of medical services by increasing the number of primary-care physicians relative to specialists and health administrators. The planners of the Health Security Act point out that over the last decade the number of administrators in hospitals and insurance companies increased sixteen times as fast as the number of doctors, while the number of specialists in training in American hospitals rose even faster. These imbalances, which create shortages of primary-care physicians in such areas as pediatrics, would be corrected by policies that encourage medical students to enter primary-care fields—policies such as scholarship incentives, the formation of a medical corps to supply doctors to underserved areas, and funding for medical schools that recruit and train primary-care physicians.

The Clinton plan proposes to reduce the rate of increase in the number of hospital administrators by reducing the amount of hospital paperwork. This would be done through a system of simplified insurance forms and more computerization of medical records. Each citizen and legal resident would receive a "health security card" that would authorize access to insurance information and records and streamline the payment of benefits.

Paying for Health Security At the heart of the debate over health-care reform is the question of how to pay for the changes. The authors of the Clinton plan note that by extending medical insurance coverage to the 38.9 million people who are uninsured, they can save roughly $25 billion in annual costs. In addition, the Clinton plan proposes a 75-cents-a-pack tax on cigarettes; a 1 percent payroll tax for corporations with more than 1,000 employees; payment of a share of insurance costs by small employers; and a sliding scale for Medicare recipients in which retired people earning more than $100,000 per year in interest, pension, and other income would pay a larger share of their medical costs.

In addition to providing for direct funding through the tax on cigarettes, the Clinton plan would produce enormous long-term savings due to decreases in smoking, resulting not only from the tax but also from intensified antismoking campaigns. Specifically, the civilian population of cigarette smokers age 25 and over will incur an estimated $187 billion in expenses every five years to pay for the medical care required for the additional diseases they suffer compared to nonsmokers (Hodgson, 1992). Clearly, the continued campaign against smoking is a vital part of the health-care reform movement. Additional measures to control the cost of prescription drugs and to reduce the costs of billing fraud and malpractice insurance promise to reduce the cost of medical care. In the longer run large savings can be expected from the increased level of health among the nation's citizens.

The Disabled and Handicapped

The first significant measure affecting the disabled and handicapped was the Rehabilitation Act of 1973, which prohibited government agencies and contractors from discriminating against the handicapped and mandated affirmative-action plans for their hiring and promotion. The act was strengthened in 1977, when the Department of Health and Human Services issued regulations requiring all recipients of HHS funds to provide the handicapped with equal access to their employment or services—or lose their subsidies. The new regulations extended the term *handicapped* to include people who are disfigured, retarded, mentally ill, emotionally disabled, or drug or alcohol addicted, as well as people with histories of cancer and heart disease.

In practical terms, the HHS rulings meant that new buildings constructed with HHS grants must be equipped with such features as ramps and elevators. Old buildings had to be remodeled. Employers had to provide assistance for handicapped employees or potential employees, such as braille literature, telephone amplifiers, and special parking or furniture.

A related act, the Education for All Handicapped Children Act of 1975, required that handicapped children be provided with a "free appropriate public education" in the least restrictive environment appropriate to their needs—often an ordinary classroom in a public school. This policy is sometimes called *mainstreaming*. Critics of this act pointed out that it costs twice as much to educate a handicapped child in the public school system as it does to educate a nonhandicapped child; supporters of the act emphasized the substantial reduction in Medicaid and disability costs that it would achieve.

The 1975 act poses complex problems beyond the question of who will pay the added costs of educating handicapped children in the public school system. Critics suggest that mainstreaming harms both the handicapped and the able-bodied. The handicapped, they maintain, do not get the attention they need from teachers who are not trained to cope with their special problems. The critics feel that this is particularly true in the case of emotionally disturbed, learning-disabled, or retarded children. Nonhandicapped students, they contend, suffer because the pace of learning has to be slower to accommodate the handicapped. However, in schools where the act has been implemented, the results are encouraging. Teachers say that both handicapped and nonhandicapped children have benefited from the experience.

The most far-reaching legislation affecting people with physical and mental disabilities is the Americans with Disabilities Act, which was passed in 1990. This act bars discrimination against the disabled in employment, transportation, public accommodations, and telecommunications. It requires employers that receive federal funds to provide equal opportunity for employment and for participation in programs and services to otherwise qualified people with disabilities. Employers must make reasonable accommodations to the disabilities of those individuals—that is, they must make facilities physically accessible; restructure job duties and modify work schedules; purchase or modify equipment; and provide readers, interpreters, or other support services. In addition, public accommodations and transportation facilities must be made accessible to people in wheelchairs, and telephone companies must provide relay services allowing hearing- or voice-impaired people to place and receive calls.

Social Policy and AIDS

The effort to control the AIDS epidemic has raised some extremely serious policy issues. At the heart of the problem is the fact that AIDS is transmitted through the most personal and private of acts. Ironically, at a time when the right of privacy has gained greater recognition in American society (and has been supported in numerous Supreme Court rulings), it has become necessary to attempt to control private acts for the sake of public welfare (Bayer, 1986).

As we saw earlier in the chapter, the main way to protect against HIV infection is by taking great care in one's sexual behavior. Thus, the only effective public health strategy for limiting the spread of HIV is to promote changes in the behavior of millions of men and women. But this concept raises the specter of "Big Brother"—of large-scale governmental intervention in people's private lives. The most extreme version of governmental intervention would take the form of mass quarantine of infected individuals to keep the infection from spreading. But even if such a policy were socially acceptable, it would be impossible in practical terms. Somewhat more tolerable is the concept of mandatory screening of high-risk individuals for the presence of HIV. However, since it is impossible to know who is in fact a member of a high-risk group, this policy would in effect require universal screening—which, in turn, would require registration of the entire population and a system for tracking the movements of individuals for repeated testing (Bayer, 1986).

Even though it is impractical or impossible to engage in mass screening, some experts advocate testing on a voluntary basis. They caution that testing must be anonymous, or at least confidential, and must be accompanied by a policy of uninterrupted access to health care for those who test positive (Hunter, 1987). A related policy issue is *contact notification,* or informing the sexual partners of infected individuals that they are at risk. There is considerable controversy over whether such notification may be made without the consent of the infected individual. The American Civil Liberties Union is opposed to any policy of involuntary disclosure, but it can be argued that individuals who have unknowingly been infected by HIV have a right to such knowledge and that public health departments have a duty to provide appropriate warnings (Bayer, 1987).

Opponents of "intrusive" measures like those just described believe that a more appropriate strategy is to undertake campaigns to teach members of high-risk groups how to avoid infecting others and to educate the general public about ways of avoiding infection. In a major report by the National Commission on AIDS (1990), the government was urged to act more forcefully in developing a set of policies for AIDS education and for emergency relief to areas of the nation that have been hit hardest by the disease. The commission was critical of the government's lack of action to date. In particular, it called attention to the policy that requires that government-sponsored sex-education materials be approved by local panels composed mostly of persons for whom the communications are not intended.

In order to avoid arousing the anger of conservative groups, the government has been careful not to issue AIDS brochures and materials that seem to promote sexuality or are offensive to the general population. The AIDS Commission pointed out that this restriction actually serves to prolong the epidemic. Many groups at risk of contracting AIDS need very straightforward verbal and pictorial descriptions of the kinds of behavior they must avoid. They need plain language and blunt warnings. But pictures of people shooting drugs and engaging in sexual contact are not likely to gain the approval of local panels. The commission strongly urged policies that would reduce the power of local panels and permit the creation of more effective communications to target populations.

There are numerous other policy issues related to the AIDS epidemic. One area of controversy is how to prevent AIDS among intravenous drug users and their sex partners. Proposals include increasing the availability of treatment for drug users,

---

BOX 2–1   UNINTENDED CONSEQUENCES OF LIFE-SAVING TECHNOLOGIES

In September 1989 a Superior Court judge in Georgia ruled that a quadriplegic, paralyzed from the neck down as a result of a motorcycle accident, could be allowed to end his life by refusing to remain connected to a respirator (breathing machine). The 33-year-old victim had let his family know that he did not want to receive the medical care that was keeping him alive. The judge ruled in his favor because existing laws make it clear that people have the right to decide what level of medical care they wish to receive. It is for this reason that many people are writing "living wills," indicating the circumstances under which they do *not* wish to receive heroic medical treatments.

All medical policies and technologies have both intended and unintended consequences. In this case the new life-saving technologies also create situations in which people who wish to die can do so by refusing treatment. Policies and laws designed to protect people's rights can also become a means of protecting their right to die. But the new medical technologies are also posing even more difficult challenges.

Medical researcher Daniel Callahan is one of a growing number of health-care experts who believe that new policies will have to be established to determine who has access to many life-saving medical procedures. In his view, priority should be given to preventive medicine and to the needs of groups that are particularly at risk—for example, providing prenatal care for the poor—rather than to high-cost efforts to save the lives of individuals whose chances of surviving and leading a comfortable life are minimal. Every person should have the right to humane care, not cure, he believes; expensive medical resources should not be devoted to marginal cases such as 18-ounce babies or quadriplegic teenage victims of automobile accidents.

Callahan and other researchers and policy makers have yet to agree on an equitable system for rationing expensive medical treatments. However, this failure does not deny the importance of the issue so much as it points to the immense political and ethical difficulties involved.

providing for "safer" injection, and preventing people from starting to inject drugs (Des Jarlais, 1987). Programs in which addicts exchange old needles for new, sterile needles have proven to be extremely controversial. They have been initiated in some American cities on a demonstration basis but have not yet received adequate support to increase their scope, as they have in Holland and some other European nations.

Another area of concern is how to speed up the production, testing, and distribution of medicines that can prolong the lives of AIDS patients. The Department of Health and Human Services has done relatively little to expedite this process, nor has action been taken to make existing AIDS medications available to patients who cannot afford them. However, late in 1990 the federal Food and Drug Administration approved a vastly accelerated process for testing and emergency administration of two somewhat promising AIDS drugs, and a number of pharmaceutical companies that produce the medicines have agreed to make them available at lower prices to indigent patients. Both developments may signal an increased resolve to move more quickly in response to the continuing spread of AIDS, especially among the very poor.

Since the incidence of AIDS in the United States is increasing most rapidly among very poor people, especially members of minority groups, many AIDS activists believe that there is a danger that the disease will become a neglected issue (Ayala, 1994). President Clinton addressed this concern in forceful language in his speech on International AIDS Awareness Day in 1993, in which he agreed to redouble the efforts of his administration to combat the disease.

SUMMARY

1. Health care is considered a social problem when members of a society have unequal access to health-care institutions and the quality of the care provided is low relative to its cost.

2. Health care is distributed very unequally in the United States. The use and availability of medical care are directly related to socioeconomic class and race. People in the lower classes tend to have higher rates of untreated illness and disability and higher mortality rates for most diseases than people in the middle and upper classes.

3. Unequal access to health care is related to the cost of obtaining it. The rate of increase in health-care costs is well above the overall inflation rate. Hospital charges are a major factor in the high cost of health care in the United States, as are the fees charged by physicians. Among the factors contributing to high fees are specialization, malpractice litigation, and unnecessary surgery.

4. Many Americans lack adequate health insurance. Public insurance programs (Medicaid and Medicare) have helped the poor and the elderly obtain greater access to health care, but despite the existence of such programs there remain large numbers of people who are not covered by health insurance, either public or private.

5. The controversy over legalized abortion has awakened many women to problems in the treatment of women by the medical establishment and has led to efforts to make medical personnel more sensitive to the physical and psychological needs of women. These include efforts to win acceptance of midwives, efforts to decrease medical intervention in the birth process, and pressure to increase funding of research on women's health issues.

6. The disabled and handicapped encounter special problems related to their condition. They suffer high unemployment rates, and the majority are poor.

7. The social problems related to health care have become especially acute as a result of the AIDS epidemic. The disease is especially prevalent among homosexuals and intravenous drug users, but it is also spreading among the heterosexual population. There is no cure for it, and at present behavioral changes are the only defense against the spread of the virus.

8. Conflict theorists believe that social class goes a long way toward explaining the types of illnesses experienced by members of a household and the kinds of health care they receive. They also believe that differences in power between physicians and patients lead to overmedication and iatrogenic illness.

9. Functionalist explanations of health-care problems focus on features of health-care institutions themselves, such as the marketplace approach to health care in the United States.

10. The interactionist perspective on health-care problems points to the role of lifestyle features such as poor diet, lack of exercise, and smoking, including passive smoking, or breathing air containing cigarette smoke. Interactionists also study problems that stem from doctor–patient relations, such as malpractice litigation.

11. One way of reducing the cost of health care is to prevent serious illnesses and other conditions that require hospitalization and surgery. Health maintenance organizations, or prepaid group practices, attempt to shift the emphasis from treatment to prevention. They provide complete medical services to subscribers in a specific region, who pay a monthly fee.

12. The Clinton administration has proposed a health-care plan that calls for a health security system in which every citizen would receive a health security card that guarantees a comprehensive benefit package that can never be taken away. The package would be offered by different insurance systems, but the federal government would guarantee coverage to all by requiring insurance providers to include the comprehensive package in their plans and conform to new regulations. The reform plan places heavy emphasis on reducing the costs of medical care by means of measures to enhance preventive health behavior. Many of the features of health maintenance organizations are incorporated in the Health Security Act.

13. Policy measures affecting the disabled and handicapped include the Education for All Handicapped Children Act of 1975, which required that handicapped children be provided with free public education in the least restrictive environment appropriate to their needs, and the Americans with Disabilities Act of 1990, which bars discrimination against the disabled in employment, public accomodations, and other areas.

14. Policy issues related to the AIDS epidemic include the question of who should be tested for the presence of the virus, whether sexual partners of infected individuals should be informed that they are at risk, and how to educate the general public about ways of avoiding infection.

SUGGESTED READINGS

ALTMAN, DENNIS. *AIDS in the Mind of America.* Garden City, NY: Doubleday/Anchor, 1987. A study of the social, political, and psychological impact of AIDS.

ANDERSON, ODIN. *The Health Services Continuum in Democratic States.* Ann Arbor, MI: Health Administration Press, 1989. An excellent comparative study of the way health-care systems have developed in the world's major industrial democracies.

BOSK, CHARLES L. *Forgive and Remember: Managing Medical Failure.* Chicago: University of Chicago Press, 1979. A study of the nature of professional social control and deviance and professional socialization, based on field research in an elite training hospital.

CALLAHAN, DANIEL. *What Kind of Life: The Limits of Medical Progress.* New York: Simon & Schuster, 1989. A controversial exploration of the ways in which medical technology poses ethical and financial problems that ultimately may require that limits be set on modern medical procedures.

KORNBLUM, WILLIAM, AND CAROLYN D. SMITH, EDS. *The Healing Experience: Readings on the Social Context of Health Care.* Englewood Cliffs, NJ: Prentice Hall, 1994. A collection of original essays and summaries of important studies that provide a background to the current health-care reform movement and also remind the reader that health professionals are above all committed to preventing and healing illness.

MECHANIC, DAVID. *From Advocacy to Allocation: The Evolving American Health Care System.* New York: Free Press, 1986. A comprehensive look at the successes and remaining serious problems of the American health-care system by one of the nation's leading medical sociologists.

STARR, PAUL. *The Social Transformation of American*

Medicine. New York: Basic Books, 1982. The definitive sociological analysis of the evolution of the American health-care industry.

White House Domestic Policy Council. *Health Security: The President's Report to the American People.* New York: Simon & Schuster, 1993. "Must" reading for every student of social problems, not so much for the details of the Clinton plan, which are better analyzed in more thorough sources, as for its highly accessible manner of presentation and brilliant organization of facts and examples.

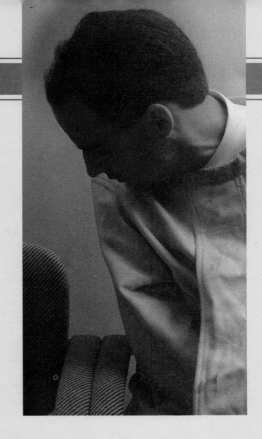

Mental Illness

Chapter Outline

- Mental Illness as a Social Problem
- The Social Construction of Mental Illness
  Defining Mental Illness
  Classification of Mental Disorders
  Diagnosis or Label?
- Inequality, Conflict, and Mental Illness
  Social Class and Mental Disorder
  Mental Disorder and Urban Life
  Other Factors
- Institutional Problems of Treatment
  and Care

Methods of Treatment
Changes in Mental-Health Professions
Treatment Institutions
Deinstitutionalization and Homelessness
- Social Policy

■ One out of every four Americans experiences some form of mental disorder at some point during any given year.

■ Approximately 3.3 million individuals in the noninstitutionalized population, or 18.2 adults per 1,000 persons, suffer from a serious mental illness within a 12-month period.

■ Although overall rates of mental illness are about the same for men and women, women are more likely than men to suffer from depression, anxieties, and phobias.

■ The costs of treating alcohol and drug problems and mental illness are by far the most rapidly increasing portion of health-care expenditures in the United States.

Approximately one out of every four Americans experiences some form of mental disorder in a given year. These disorders range from mild depression and anxiety to severely debilitating psychoses like schizophrenia and manic depression (Regier, 1993, cited in Goleman, 1993; Kraus & Stoddard, 1989). The National Institute of Mental Health estimates that there are between 4 and 5 million seriously mentally ill persons in the adult population of the United States (National Center for Health Statistics, 1992). Among the population under age 18 (one-quarter of the U.S. population), at least 12 percent have a diagnosable mental illness (HHS, 1990).

Each year millions of Americans are treated for mental disorders. Many of them are hospitalized in either mental or general hospitals. Of these, most are discharged after a brief stay, but many are long-term patients with chronic disorders, and some will be hospitalized until they die. Many other patients are treated in outpatient clinics or by family doctors, psychologists, or psychiatrists in private practice. In addition, millions of Americans who are not under treatment suffer from some degree of mental disorder, often unrecognized as such.

MENTAL ILLNESS AS A SOCIAL PROBLEM

The terms *mental disorder* and *mental illness* are often used interchangeably (Gallagher, 1987), and that is how they are used here. However, in formal social-scientific writing *mental illness* is usually reserved for mental disorders that require hospitalization or for which close medical supervision would normally be recommended. Most people who seek help from mental-health institutions are unlikely ever to be hospitalized.

Until the mid-twentieth century a large proportion of people who were classified as mentally ill and admitted to mental hospitals were actually suffering from physical ailments like epilepsy and brain tumors (Grob, 1985). Today researchers are learning about the biological origins of many mental illnesses, including schizophrenia, autism, and alcoholism (Goleman, 1987). As we discover the biological bases of some mental illnesses, we also gain information about the social conditions, such as physical abuse, neglect, and severe stress, that may bring on the mental breakdowns that cause people to cease functioning "normally."

The specific relationships between biological factors and certain types of mental illness are considered in detail in psychology and genetics courses. For our purposes here it is enough to be aware that mental illness, whatever its causes, is a source of serious social problems, not only in terms of the number of people affected but also in terms of the extent to which social institutions are strained by efforts to care for the mentally ill.

The mental disorders that cause severe social problems are the most extreme forms of mental illness. Of these, the most sensational are the ones that threaten the social order itself. Examples include the derangement that causes a person to become a mass murderer, or episodes of "mass psychosis" such as the case of the Branch Davidians in Waco, Texas, in which an entire community surrendered itself to a paranoid religious leader who led them into a fatal confrontation with federal authorities in the spring of 1993. The number of individuals with such disorders may be small, but they constitute an especially serious social problem because they are so violent and irrational.

Less threatening to public safety and perceptions of security, but far more widespread as a social problem, are severely ill individuals (often diagnosed as psychotic) who cannot care for themselves without specialized attention. For the mentally ill as individuals, their problem is a terrible affliction. They experience such symptoms as unimaginable fear, uncontrollable hallucinations, panic, crushing feelings of sadness, wild elation, and roller-coaster mood swings. For society as a whole, their illness presents a range of social problems: stress in family life, heavy demands on health-care institutions, moral and ethical problems (e.g., whether to permit the plea of insanity in criminal cases), the cost of treatment to society, and so on. All of these can be aggravated by the social stigma attached to mental illness. It can be said that the mentally ill suffer twice: They suffer from the illness itself; and they also suffer rejection, as if their illness were their own fault. This is not nearly as true in the case of physical illnesses, and this factor alone marks off mental illness for special consideration in the study of social problems.

In the United States, phobias—severe fears such as fear of going outside, fear of heights, or fear of being in an enclosed space—are the most common form of mental illness, affecting an estimated 20 million Americans. In any given year another 18 million Americans suffer from depression, including manic depression, major depression, and minor depression. Alcoholism, classified as a mental illness, has been diagnosed in approximately 14 million people. To complicate matters, about 6 million Americans have a substance abuse disorder along with one or more severe or relatively severe mental disorders such as schizophrenia. These individuals are often referred to as mentally ill chemical abusers (MICA) and are a particularly problematic population in major urban centers (Regier, 1991).

A distressing aspect of the general problem of mental illness is the social impact

Mentally ill patients like this woman experience a degree of anguish that is difficult for the non-mentally ill to comprehend.

of *deinstitutionalization*, or discharging patients from mental hospitals directly into the community. Some of these patients are not able to function as "normal" members of society, and the consequences can be painful both for them and for those who come into contact with them. Others may suffer from less severe, but also debilitating, problems caused by rejection and stigma. As we will see later in the chapter, it has been difficult to develop (or consistently fund) effective means of treating such individuals in settings outside mental hospitals.

Policy makers at every level of society look to sociologists and other social scientists for basic research on the causes of mental illness and on the effects of major policy initiatives like deinstitutionalization or community treatment, as well as recommendations on how to deal with trends in mental illness. Thus, in addition to sponsoring research on medical approaches to treatment and rehabilitation, the National Institute of Mental Health funds studies of the social epidemiology of mental illness—by which we mean not simply its distribution in the population but also its impact on families and communities and welfare institutions, and the associated problems of homelessness and social dependency.

In studying social problems related to mental illness, the basic sociological perspectives can help clarify the relevant issues and explain some aspects of the origins of mental disorders. The interactionist perspective focuses on the "social construction" of mental illness, that is, on how our definitions of "normal" and "deviant" behavior in social situations lead to definitions of mental disorders. To a large extent, the definition of mental illness is the province of psychologists and psychiatrists. Their diagnoses result in labels like "schizophrenic" or "depressed." Research by sociologists who have studied the interactions among people who are thought of as mentally ill suggests that simply labeling a person as mentally ill may cause the person to define himself or herself as ill and to behave in ways that confirm that self-definition.

Conflict theorists tend to focus on how mental illness may be associated with deprivation and inequality, including unequal access to appropriate care. For example, race and sex are associated with inequality of wealth, power, and other social values and hence are often associated with stress and with some mental disorders. Research by conflict theorists suggests that in treatment institutions people with less of what is valued in the larger society often receive less adequate care after symptoms of mental illness appear. Also, the mentally ill may themselves become a subject of conflict as they are shunted from one place to another outside of mental institutions.

From a functionalist perspective, mental illnesses constitute a social problem because they challenge our ability to provide effective treatment. This is especially true in societies that are marked by rapid social change, in which people do not have long-standing attachments to others in their immediate social surroundings or are often separated from their families, or in which systems of treatment have been changing rapidly and it is not clear how people with mental disorders should be helped (Meyer, 1985).

THE SOCIAL CONSTRUCTION OF MENTAL ILLNESS

Defining Mental Illness

When social scientists say that mental illness is "socially constructed," they are highlighting aspects of those illnesses that help define how both the mentally ill and "normal" people behave. The usefulness of this approach will become clearer if we consider some alternative views of mental illness. In this section we will look briefly at three different explanations of mental illness: (1) the medical model, which asserts that mental illness is a disease with physiological causes; (2) the deviance approach, which asserts that mental illness results from the way people who are considered mentally ill are treated; and (3) the controversial argument that mental illness is not a disease but a way governments have of defining certain people as needing isolation and "treatment."

The Medical Model   The most familiar school of thought holds that a mental disorder should be viewed as a disease with biological causes. That is, a mental disorder is primarily a disturbance of the normal personality that is analogous to the physiological disturbance caused by physical disease. It can be remedied primarily by treating the patient. Once this has been done, the patient will be able to function adequately.

Research in the biological sciences, especially genetics, has uncovered strong evidence to support biological explanations of mental illnesses like schizophrenia, manic depression, childhood autism, senility, and even alcoholism (to which we will return in Chapter 5). In addition to disorders that are classified as mental illnesses, many of which have been found to have somatic causes, there are a host of mental disabilities that usually appear at birth, such as Down's syndrome, cerebral palsy, and brain damage due to birth trauma; such disorders present unusual and difficult challenges to those who experience them.

Research on the medical model of mental disorder arose in reaction to the older notion that mentally disturbed people are mad or "possessed" and should be locked up, beaten, or killed. It made possible serious investigation of the causes and cures of mental disorder and was responsible for the development of virtually all the systems of mental-health care and therapeutic treatment in existence today—systems that are still largely in the hands of medically oriented personnel. It has helped to reduce the stigma and shame of mental disorder, since, after all, "illness can happen to anyone."

Nevertheless, the concept of mental disorder as a disease has certain disadvantages. Because it concentrates on individuals and their immediate environment (often their childhood environment), it tends to disregard the wider social environment as a possible source of the problem. In addition, especially for hospitalized patients, the medical model can lead to impractical criteria of "recovery"—people may have gained considerable insight into their inner tensions but may still be unable to function adequately when they return to the outer tensions of home, job, or society. It is also true that many mental illnesses, which may or may not be caused by an individual's physiology, may be brought on, alleviated, or made worse by conditions in that person's social environment.

Mental Illness as Deviance   Neither social nor biological scientists know precisely what kinds of interactions among the multitude of physical and social conditions that affect human beings may cause mental illness in some cases or lead to remission or recovery in others. We do know, however, that the way a mentally ill person is treated once the illness has been diagnosed can have a lasting impact on that person's behavior and on his or her chances of leading a happy and productive life.

The concept of mental disorder as a disease holds that something about a person is abnormal and that the fundamental problem lies in his or her emotional makeup, which was twisted, repressed, or otherwise wrongly developed as a result of genetic or chemical factors or events early in life. Although this theory seems to explain some mental disorders, many observers believe that other factors need to be taken into account, especially the constant pressure exerted by modern society. Out of this has developed the view that mental disorder represents a departure from certain expectations of society—that it is a form of social deviance.

In this connection the idea of *residual deviance* is useful. According to Thomas Scheff (1963), who formulated the concept, most social conventions are recognized as such, and violation of those conventions carries fairly clear labels: People who steal wallets are thieves; people who act haughtily toward the poor are snobs; and so on. But there is a large residual area of social convention that is so completely

taken for granted that it is assumed to be part of human nature. To use Scheff's example, it seems natural for people holding a conversation to face each other rather than to look away. Violation of this norm seems contrary to human nature.

Scheff suggests that residual deviance occurs in most people at one time or another and usually passes without treatment. What causes it to become a mental disorder in some cases is that *society decides to label it as such.* When this happens, the *role* of "mentally ill person" is offered to the deviant individual. Since such people are often confused and frightened by their own behavior during a time of stress—as well as by other people's reactions to their behavior—they are likely to be particularly impressionable and may accept the role that is offered to them. Once this happens, it becomes difficult for them to change their behavior and return to their "normal" role.

If this is so, mental disorder may actually be caused by some of the attempts to cure it. By treating a patient in a separate treatment institution, the mental-health profession certifies that the individual is indeed a patient and that he or she is mentally ill (Levine & Levine, 1970). The point of the concept of mental disorder as deviance, thus, is that the disorder may be a function not only of certain individuals' inability to comply with societal expectations but also of the label attached to those who deviate (Scull, 1988).

Problems in Living A third approach to understanding mental disorder has been offered by Thomas Szasz, a psychiatrist who has generated considerable controversy by contending that mental illness is a myth. Although this is not a widely accepted view, it does call attention to the relationship between diagnosis and repression. Szasz does not claim that the social and psychological disturbances referred to as mental illness do not exist; rather, he argues that it is dangerously misleading to call them illnesses. Instead, he believes, they should be regarded as manifestations of unresolved problems in living.

The significance of Szasz's basic argument is that it concerns justice and individual freedom. As he sees it, a diagnosis of mental disorder involves a value judgment based on the behavioral norms held by psychiatrists. Referring to certain behaviors as illnesses allows doctors to use medicine to correct what are essentially social, ethical, or legal deviations. Not only is this logically absurd, Szasz contends, but it is dangerous.

Szasz draws a distinction between the "legal state" and the "therapeutic state." The business of the legal state is "the maintenance of peace through a system of just laws justly administered" (1970, p. 439). The legal state has no claim on its citizens beyond what is set down in the law; whatever else citizens do is none of the state's business. In the therapeutic state, by contrast,

> *Conflict among individuals, and especially between the individual and the State, is invariably seen as a symptom of "illness" or psychopathology, and the primary function of the State is accordingly the removal of such conflict by "therapy"—"therapy" imposed by force, if necessary. It is not difficult to recognize in this imagery of the Therapeutic State the old Inquisitorial, or the more recent Totalitarian, concept of the State, now clothed in the garb of psychiatric treatment. (1970, p. 439)*

In short, Szasz believes that liberty can be unwittingly sacrificed through too great a concern for the "cure" of "mental illness." This issue has come to the fore in connection with the forcible removal of homeless individuals from city streets. The presence of these people, who are often shabby and dirty and may behave in bizarre ways, offends "normal" citizens. As we will see later in the chapter, the interpretation of this lifestyle as a sign of mental illness has been used to justify the involuntary placement of homeless people in shelters or hospitals, where they are out of sight.

When sociologists speak of the "social construction" of mental illness, they incorporate all the approaches just described into their explanations. They recognize that there is often a biological basis for mental illness, and that just as often the disease is aggravated by the fact that mentally ill people are treated as social deviants. They also recognize and study instances in which the label of mental illness is a convenient way of ridding society of people who are troublesome. (The nations of the former Soviet Union were notorious for this technique, but it has been used in societies all over the world at one time or another.) Most important, sociologists recognize that the classification of mental illnesses and decisions about how they should be treated are determined by how we think about the causes, consequences, and possibilities of treating mental disorders. Even the diagnosis of mental illness requires the emergence of a common set of perceptions among mental-health professionals, a point that will become clearer if we look in more detail at the problems of diagnosis.

Classification of Mental Disorders

Clinicians and researchers need a common language with which to discuss mental disorders. It is impossible to plan a consistent program of treatment for a patient without an accurate diagnosis, and it is impossible to evaluate the effectiveness of various forms of treatment if patient groups are not described using clearly defined diagnostic terms.

In 1973, in an effort to deal with these problems, the American Psychiatric Association (APA) embarked on a controversial and ambitious revision of its manual of mental disorders. The new manual, released in 1980 and referred to as the *Diagnostic and Statistical Manual of Mental Disorders*, Third Edition, or simply as *DSM-III*, represents the work of hundreds of scientists and professionals in the field of mental-health care. A revised edition, *DSM-IV*, was published in 1994.

Widely regarded as a major advance in the scientific description and classification of mental disorders, *DSM-III* had a significant impact on the treatment of mental disorders. Among other things, it made an important contribution to the separation of mental disorders from behaviors, such as homosexuality, that deviate from societal norms but are not necessarily a result of mental illness.

Although, as we will see shortly, labeling theorists continue to believe that the diagnostic categories of psychiatrists reflect the biases of the people who make them up, *DSM-III* resolved some of the more controversial issues in the classification of mental disorders. In general, however, the manual continues to represent the illness model of mental disorder. To a large extent it seeks to attribute mental dysfunctions to physiological, biochemical, genetic, or profound internal psychological causes. The major categories of the illness model, as presented in *DSM-IV*, are shown in Figure 3–1.

A number of familiar terms are not used in *DSM-IV*. Chief among these is *neurosis*, the older term for a wide range of disorders in which the individual suffers from severe anxiety but continues to attempt to function in the everyday world, usually through a variety of subterfuges or by means of defense mechanisms such as denial of problems or projection of one's own problems onto another person (e.g., perceiving others as hostile or angry rather than acknowledging these traits in oneself). The new classification system replaces this term with more specific ones such as *affective disorder, anxiety disorder, somatoform disorder,* and *psychosexual disorder.* In everyday usage, however, the term *neurosis* continues to appear with some frequency.

Diagnosis or Label?

Just as some physical illnesses may be culturally defined, so may certain mental disorders. The medical model assumes that patients present symptoms that can be classified into diagnosable categories of mental illness. But there is a growing belief that at least some psychiatric diagnoses are pigeonholes into which certain behaviors are placed arbitrarily. The diagnosis of schizophrenia has, according to labeling theorists, been especially subject to misuse. Although there is little agreement about its origins, causes, and symptoms, it is the most commonly used diagnosis for severe mental illness. To labeling theorists, this suggests that diagnoses of mental illnesses tend to reflect cultural values, not scientific analysis. People are not "schizophrenic" in the sense that they manifest definite symptoms; instead, their behavior violates society's norms and expectations. For example, a person who sees visions might be considered perfectly normal, even admirable, in many cultures, although in the United States such a person would probably be regarded as disturbed.

The problem with labeling people as mentally ill is threefold: It makes us perceive certain behaviors as "sick," something to be eliminated rather than understood; it gives public agencies the right to incarcerate people against their will simply for not conforming; and it causes those people to define themselves as rule breakers and undesirables and allows them to fulfill that image. Despite the undeniable influence of labeling on the diagnosis and treatment of mental illness, recent large-scale research has shown that interviewers with basic training in the diagnosis of mental illness can spot people with serious mental disorders like schizophrenia and severe depression quite accurately. Such research is vital to our knowledge of the extent of mental illness in a population (Goleman, 1993; Regier, 1993).

Many studies have demonstrated the influence of societal factors on the diagnosis of mental illness, as well as the vagueness of such diagnoses. Rosenhan (1973), in a study that will be described more fully later in the chapter, found that psychologists and psychiatrists on the staffs of several mental hospitals were unable to determine accurately which of the people they interviewed were mentally healthy and which ones were mentally ill. Greenley (1972) found that the attitudes of the families of patients in a mental hospital were a critical factor in how the patients' illnesses were defined. If the family insisted that the patient be released, the psychiatrist in charge would generally agree. Upon being discharged, the patient would be

DISORDERS EVIDENT IN INFANCY, CHILDHOOD, OR ADOLESCENCE

These disorders that begin prior to adulthood include mental retardation, attention-deficit hyperactivity, anorexia nervosa, bulimia nervosa, stuttering, sleepwalking, and bedwetting.

ORGANIC MENTAL DISORDERS

Psychological or behavioral abnormalities associated with temporary or permanent dysfunction of the brain resulting from aging, disease, or drugs; include delirium and dementia.

PSYCHOACTIVE SUBSTANCE USE DISORDER

Disorders resulting from excessive and persistent use of mind-altering substances like alcohol, barbiturates, cocaine, or amphetamines.

SCHIZOPHRENIA

Characterized by symptoms such as delusions or hallucinations and deterioration from a previous level of functioning, with symptoms existing for more than six months. Examples include catatonic schizophrenia and paranoid schizophrenia.

DELUSIONAL DISORDERS

The key feature is the presence of a delusion (e. g., belief that one is being persecuted). It is often difficult to clearly differentiate delusional disorders from paranoid schizophrenia.

MOOD DISORDERS

These disorders, also known as affective disorders, involve extremes in emotion; they include major depression and bipolar (manic-depressive) disorder.

ANXIETY DISORDERS

The key symptom, anxiety, is manifest in phobias, generalized anxiety disorder, panic attacks, or obsessive-compulsive disorder.

SOMATOFORM DISORDERS

The presentation of physical symptoms such as paralysis without medical explanation. Examples include somatization disorder, hypochondriasis, and conversion disorder.

DISSOCIATIVE DISORDER

Involves a splitting or dissociation of normal consciousness. Includes psychogenic amnesia, psychogenic fugue, and multiple personality.

PSYCHOSEXUAL DISORDERS

Disorders characterized by sexual arousal by unusual objects or situations (fetishism) or by sexual dysfunctions such as inhibition of sexual desire.

PERSONALITY DISORDERS

Chronic, inflexible, and maladaptive personality patterns that are generally resistant to treatment, such as the antisocial personality disorder.

DISORDERS OF IMPULSE CONTROL

These include kleptomania, pyromania, and pathological gambling.

FIGURE 3–1   Categories of Psychological Disorders Listed in the *Diagnostic and Statistical Manual of Mental Disorders*, Fourth Edition

Source: Adapted from American Psychiatric Association (1994).

defined, both in the doctor's conversations and in official records, as being well enough to leave. When there was no pressure for a patient to be released, the patient generally was defined as being too sick to leave the hospital.

In a fascinating episode in the history of psychiatry, a group of people who had long been considered mentally ill successfully challenged their label and convinced the APA to remove it from *DSM*. For a number of years homosexuals had demonstrated at psychiatric conventions, demanding that homosexuality no longer be considered a mental disorder. In 1973, after several years of heated controversy, the Board of Trustees of the APA voted to strike homosexuality from its official list of mental diseases. But this decision infuriated large numbers of conservative psychiatrists, who viewed homosexuality not as a label applied to a deviant group by a dominant group but as an illness that requires treatment and, if possible, cure. They insisted that the question be considered in a referendum by the entire membership of the APA. After intensive maneuvering that resembled the efforts of factions to garner support at political conventions, the medical model was voted down and the label "mental disorder" was no longer officially applied to homosexuality by psychiatrists (Bayer, 1987).

Incidents like the one just described serve to remind us that the members of a society, especially mental-health professionals and political leaders, are continually negotiating the definitions and, thus, the possible treatments of mental disorders. We will see in the next section that a large number of factors—including whether people are rich or poor, live in a central city or a suburb or a rural area, are black or white or Hispanic, male or female—can affect how, or even if, their illnesses are diagnosed and treated.

INEQUALITY, CONFLICT, AND MENTAL ILLNESS

According to the National Institute of Mental Health, "Both the prevalence of SMI [serious mental illness] and resulting disability are clearly related to poverty status. SMI [is] over 2½ times as likely among adults in poverty than among those not in poverty, and proportionally more poor than nonpoor adults with SMI [have] resulting disability" (National Center for Health Statistics, 1992, p. 4). Sociologists are interested in the relationship between social factors like poverty and the incidence of mental disorders. Is mental disorder associated with social class and with conflicts over the distribution of social rewards? Does it occur more frequently in urban centers than in rural areas or suburbs? In what population groups is it most prevalent? Would changes in social conditions prevent or alleviate certain mental disorders? The study of such relationships is complicated by the difficulty of ascertaining the prevalence of mental disorders. We can count the number of patients in mental hospitals and, somewhat less accurately, those receiving treatment in clinics and other outpatient facilities. It is far more difficult to obtain reliable statistics on the number being treated in private practice. Moreover, any number of people who would qualify as emotionally disturbed are not under treatment at all and therefore do not appear in most estimates of the incidence of mental disorders. Consequently, any statistics on treated mental disorders must be regarded as providing only a very rough estimate of the total number of people suffering from such problems.

Despite these difficulties, sociologists have reached several tentative conclusions about the relationship between mental disorders and patterns of inequality in a society. It should be noted that research on the impact of inequality is often conducted from a conflict perspective. Conflict theorists call attention to the ways in which inequalities of wealth and power produce inequalities in access to effective treatment for mental disorders. Underlying these inequalities is class conflict: The poor demand more services and better care from public institutions, while those who are better off believe that the poor bring their troubles on themselves and do not deserve expensive care facilities and treatment programs. Conflict theorists also emphasize that poverty itself is a social problem that can produce severe stress in those who experience it. Life in poverty is associated with higher exposure to crime and violence, which adds to the stress of everyday life. In some individuals such extreme stress can precipitate mental illness (Kozol, 1988; Snow, Baker, & Anderson, 1988).

Social Class and Mental Disorder

Long before sociologists began to make systematic studies of social conditions and mental disorders, the connection between the two had been recognized. It was only in the 1930s, however, that serious sociological study of this relationship began, and although the results are not in perfect agreement, they offer some useful information.

One pioneering study (Faris & Dunham, 1938) investigated the residential patterns of 35,000 hospitalized mental patients in the Chicago area. The highest rates of mental disorder were found near the center of the city, where the population was poor, of very mixed ethnic and racial background, and highly mobile. Although this number included many cases of organic psychosis due to syphilis and alcoholism in the "skid row" districts, it also included a significantly high rate of schizophrenia throughout the area. Conversely, the lowest rates of mental disorder were found in stable, higher-status residential areas.

We now know that the early research was somewhat misleading in suggesting that psychoses are more likely to occur among people who are poor and live in run-down areas. It has been shown that schizophrenia and people with drug-induced organic disorders tend to inhabit the poorer areas of cities, partly because they usually have limited incomes and also because they feel more comfortable where there are people like themselves.

A later study sought to determine the relationship between social class and treated mental illness in New Haven, Connecticut (Hollingshead & Redlich, 1958). Whereas the Chicago study included only hospitalized patients, the New Haven researchers obtained reasonably complete data on clinic and private patients as well. Using a socioeconomic scale running from class I (highest) to class V (lowest), they determined that the *incidence* (rate of occurrence of new cases in a year) and *prevalence* (number of cases existing on a given date) of psychosis were significantly higher in class V than in the other four classes. Schizophrenia was the most common psychosis in all classes, but it was especially prevalent in class V. The study also revealed that the types of treatment and opportunities for rehabilitation available to the lower classes were much less satisfactory than those for the upper classes, situations that may have contributed to the greater frequency of schizophrenia in class V. Another possible factor is the tendency for the same symptoms to be perceived as more severe in working-class patients than in middle-class patients. Such inconsistencies in diagnosis could have inflated the figures for class V.

A study by William Rushing (1969), which tended to confirm the relationship between mental disorder and social class, included a relatively large number of cases occurring over an extended period. Rushing studied 4,650 males who were admitted for the first time to mental hospitals in Washington, D.C., between 1954 and 1956. He found that the rate of hospitalization for lower-class males was higher than that for all others; that hospitalization varied inversely with class; and that although the rate increased steadily with each drop in social class, the increase from the next-to-lowest to the lowest class was disproportionately large. Rushing believed that the high incidence in the lowest class might be explained by the frequent contact that members of this class have with the courts, welfare workers, and other officials who can refer them for hospitalization; moreover, members of the lower class are less likely to be protected, tolerated, or supported financially by their families, to whom they have become a burden. From this perspective, lower-class status is associated with a greater likelihood of being identified or labeled as mentally ill.

The Midtown Manhattan Study went beyond treatment to include a random sample of 1,660 adult residents of Manhattan's midtown area (Srole et al., 1978). The researchers found that almost 23 percent were significantly impaired in mental functioning, including many people who were not under treatment. One of the factors investigated was socioeconomic status, not only that of the subjects but also that of their parents. Among subjects who were considered seriously impaired in their mental functioning, the percentage with lower-class parents was twice the percentage with upper-class parents. This finding suggests that socioeconomic status has a strong influence on the mental health of children.

A similar study of a nonhospitalized population was conducted among residents of rural Sterling County in Nova Scotia (Leighton et al., 1963). Like the Midtown Manhattan Study, this study found high rates of untreated mental disorder. More recent research confirms this finding; for example, a study carried out in New Haven, Baltimore, and St. Louis reported that between 29 and 38 percent of the sample had experienced symptoms of mental illness (Robins et al., 1984).

It should be kept in mind that studies like those just cited tend to come up with widely divergent estimates of the proportion of mentally ill individuals in various populations. Some of these differences are due to the use of different data-collection techniques and different definitions of mental illness. The studies are consistent, however, in reporting that only a minority of the cases observed have ever received treatment (Barker, Manderscheid, & Gendershot, 1992; Gallagher, 1987).

The Drift Hypothesis   All the studies just described agree that psychosis in general and schizophrenia in particular are much more common at the lowest socioeconomic level than at higher levels. They do not indicate, however, whether most schizophrenic individuals were originally in the lowest class or whether they drifted down to it as the disorder worsened. In other words, they fail to make clear whether low socioeconomic status is primarily a cause or an effect of serious mental disorder.

Some researchers reject the social-stress hypothesis as an explanation of the preponderance of mental illness in the lower classes. Instead, they propose the *social-selection* or *drift* hypothesis, which holds that social class is not a cause but a consequence of mental disorder. In this view, mentally disordered people tend to be

Most cities have rundown areas where troubled people from other neighborhoods and outlying areas congregate. Often suffering from the consequences of multiple problems (poverty, homelessness, mental illness, alcoholism), these individuals may feel less deviant in these areas than in more "respectable" parts of the city.

found in the lower classes because their illness has prevented them from functioning at a higher class level and they have "drifted" downward to a lower class. This interpretation is partially supported by a study of a population of over 16,000 individuals in southern Appalachia (Harkey, Miles, & Rushing, 1976), which found that the primary effect of psychological disorder is to retard upward mobility (although it does not necessarily contribute to downward mobility). A study of Dutch schizophrenics also supported the social-selection theory (WHO, 1983).

Studies like those just cited, though not conclusive, provide evidence that low social class does not cause mental illness. Instead, a low social-class position is associated with mental disorders, most likely as a result of a process in which the mentally ill drift downward in society.

Mental Disorder and Urban Life

Whatever the precise relationship between mental illness and social class, there is no doubt that people who live in lower-class communities or neighborhoods, especially in central cities, experience high levels of stress. This aspect of their social environment can bring on bouts of mental illness. The presence of high rates of mental illness in urban settings leads many people to assume that there is a connection between city life and mental disorder. However, since there has been little research on mental disorder that compared urban and nonurban areas, no conclusive test of this assumption is available. Investigation is made more difficult by the fact that mental disorder is more likely to be diagnosed and treated in areas where facilities are readily accessible—which usually means in and around cities. Studies of treated mental disorder, therefore, are of limited usefulness in making urban–rural comparisons.

Studies of the incidence of mental illness are also fraught with methodological problems. The findings of such studies need to be interpreted with caution, especially when different studies are being compared. Studies that compare mental illness in different societies or different parts of the United States on the basis of hospitalization rates are particularly misleading because there are no universal criteria for hospital admission, the availability of facilities varies widely, and people who undergo treatment are only part of the population of individuals with mental-health problems (Gallagher, 1987).

The best studies of the rates of mental illness and impairment in society are conducted by means of random samples of members of the nonhospitalized population. In analyzing the results of more than sixty such studies conducted throughout the world, Bruce P. Dohrenwend and Barbara S. Dohrenwend found that rates of reported psychiatric disorder varied from as low as 1 percent to over 50 percent. Within the United States there was more consistency among the methods used to measure mental disorders. In reviewing twelve studies conducted in urban areas and twelve studies conducted in rural communities, the Dohrenwends found that the median percentage of psychiatric disorder in the cities was 21.0, compared to 17.3 in the rural communities (Dohrenwend & Dohrenwend, 1974). These results confirm the somewhat higher incidence of mental disorder in urban areas but also suggest that the rather small differences could well be due to the "drift" of people with such disorders to urban areas where their deviance is not as burdensome to them.

The Midtown Manhattan Study, the major urban study dealing with how mental disorder is distributed in a general population, revealed a high percentage of disturbance among adults. Only about 18 percent of the respondents were rated as "well"; roughly 60 percent showed mild to moderate symptoms of disorder; and slightly over 20 percent were significantly impaired in their functioning. However, a study of the rural Hutterite communities of Montana, the Dakotas, and Canada found a similar incidence of mental illness (Eaton & Weil, 1955). According to the researchers, the Hutterites differed from the usual urban sample in that they had a higher proportion of manic-depressive than of schizophrenic individuals and usually kept the mentally ill at home rather than in hospitals. Other studies lend additional support to the theory that it is not urban life per se but the deteriorated quality of life that often develops in cities—the dirt, noise, transportation problems, inadequate housing, and so on—that creates a high level of mental disorder (Freeman, 1972; Snow et al., 1988).

A feature of urban life that has received particular attention in studies of the causes of mental illness is crowding in the home. Research on this subject has generated considerable controversy. A survey of Chicago residents (Gove, Hughes, & Galle, 1979) measured both objective crowding (number of persons per room) and subjective crowding (excessive social demands, lack of privacy). The results indicated that household crowding has a number of adverse consequences, including poor mental health. However, this conclusion has been challenged by critics who contend that complaints of lack of privacy and excessive demands by others may themselves be signs of mental disorder (Booth, Johnson, & Edwards, 1980).

Like much other research on the conditions associated with mental illness, the studies of crowding are inconclusive. In general, however, research on the relationship between urban life and mental disorder tends to support the drift hypothesis discussed earlier. It appears that urban life does not actually cause mental illness but that people with mental disorders like schizophrenia often come to cities, where they can live among people like themselves and where they may be able to choose among a wider variety of treatment options. This interpretation is supported by a review of five major studies of rural and urban rates of mental disorder (Eaton, 1980), which found that schizophrenia is treated more often in urban populations but also that treatment facilities are more common in cities than in rural areas. Probably the true rates of schizophrenia are similar in both areas but city people have much greater access to treatment, a fact that increases the number of reported cases among urban dwellers (Davidson, 1982; Dohrenwend & Dohrenwend, 1969; Gallagher, 1987).

Other Factors

A variety of other factors have been investigated in an attempt to discover their relationship to mental disorder. Among these are race and sex.

Race Race does not appear to be a significant variable by itself. Instead, racial differences in mental health can be explained in terms of social class. Poor people, of whom a large proportion are black, are much more likely to be seen as requiring hospitalization than members of the middle and upper classes, most of whom are white. The latter are more likely to be seen as needing outpatient psychotherapy. The poor are also much more likely to deal with public agencies, including mental-health centers, and to live in deteriorated urban environments.

Sex Although overall rates of mental illness are about the same for men and women (Regier et al., 1984), women are more likely than men to suffer from depression, anxieties, and phobias. Phyllis Chesler (1972) has suggested that the nature and incidence of mental disorder among women are a reflection of women's secondary status and restricted roles. Women are expected to conform to rigidly defined standards of behavior—to be passive, dependent, and emotional, for example, in accordance with traditional feminine roles. Since mental-health professionals are predominantly male, women who behave in nontraditional ways are more likely to be defined as mentally ill.

Chesler cites a study in which mental-health clinicians were asked to identify healthy male traits and healthy female traits. The researchers found that the standards of mental health for men and women differed according to traditional sex-role stereotypes. Thus, healthy women were considered to be unaggressive, submissive,

As more women enter traditionally male occupations, they face an increased risk of occupational hazards and illnesses, which in turn increases the level of stress in their lives.

excitable, and vain. Other studies cited by Chesler confirm that such attitudes do indeed serve as a basis for the decisions of mental-health professionals. For example, the major difference between female ex-mental patients who were rehospitalized and those who were not was that the rehospitalized patients had refused to perform their domestic "duties"—cleaning, cooking, and the like. Females were also more likely to be called schizophrenics when they behaved in ways that are considered acceptable in men.

In a study of depression among middle-aged women, Bart (1971) found that women who accepted their traditional roles became depressed when those roles were no longer useful—for example, when their children grew up and left home. Other studies, however, have found that women who have more demanding roles are more likely to be rehospitalized, partly because of the greater pressure associated with those roles (Angrist et al., 1968; Freeman & Simmons, 1963).

The question of whether men and women have different rates of psychosis has not been fully resolved. Men are thought to be more susceptible than women to schizophrenia; however, in a review of existing research Dohrenwend and Dohrenwend (1975) found that half of the studies they investigated reported schizophrenia to be more prevalent among men while the other half found it to occur more frequently among women. On the other hand, a study based on the criteria listed in *DSM-III* found significantly more men than women among schizophrenic patients (Lewine, Burbach, & Meltzer, 1984).

Although the evidence on schizophrenia, the most serious mental illness, is contradictory, there is widespread agreement among researchers that women tend to experience significantly higher rates of depression than men and that men exhibit significantly higher rates of personality disorders. Women who are single parents and in the labor force experience the highest rates of depression (Cockerham, 1988; Mirowsky, 1985).

INSTITUTIONAL PROBLEMS OF TREATMENT AND CARE

The treatment of people with mental disorders has undergone enormous changes in the past century and remains one of the most controversial aspects of mental health in all societies. In this section we will review the major approaches to the treatment of mental illness as well as changes in mental-health institutions. We will see that although there has been a great deal of progress in treating mental illness, many problems remain, especially in creating and maintaining effective institutions for the treatment and care of the mentally ill (Dial et al., 1992).

Methods of Treatment

The two major approaches to the treatment of mental disorders are psychotherapy (sometimes called insight therapy) and medical treatment in the form of psychotropic drugs or electroconvulsive therapy. Although these approaches are sometimes used simultaneously, they involve different groups of mental-health professionals, who often have difficulty coordinating the diagnosis and treatment of their patients. The problem of coordination will be discussed more fully in the Social Policy section of the chapter. In this section we will briefly review the most important methods of treatment.

Nonmedical Forms of Treatment   Patients who undergo psychotherapy are helped to understand the underlying reasons for their problems so that they can try to work out solutions. The process involves some form of interaction between the patient and the therapist or among patients in groups. Among the major forms of psychotherapy are psychoanalysis, client-centered therapy, and various types of therapy and support groups.

Developed by Sigmund Freud in the late nineteenth century, psychoanalysis seeks to uncover unconscious motives, memories, and fears that prevent the patient from functioning normally. Patients may use various methods of exploration and discovery, including dreams and free association. Client-centered therapy was developed by Carl Rogers in the 1940s. This approach emphasizes current problems rather than unconscious motives and past experiences. The patient sets the course of the therapy, while the therapist provides support. In therapy and support groups, people attempt to solve their problems through interaction with one another. Therapy groups are led by professionals; support groups are organized by people who have experienced the same problems as the other participants. Examples of the latter type are Alcoholics Anonymous, Weight Watchers, and Gamblers Anonymous. Another important type of group therapy is family therapy, in which family members work with the help of a trained professional to overcome their difficulties.

Still another nonmedical approach, hypnosis, can help patients recall deeply repressed but significant memories that may be blocking their progress toward understanding and dealing with their problems. Hypnosis is often used successfully in the treatment of neurotic patients but has not had a major impact on the treatment of psychoses.

Medical Approaches to Treatment   Medical treatments, particularly chemotherapy and shock treatment, are applied to the most severe mental illnesses, such as schizophrenia and manic depression. Control over these treatments is in the hands of medical or clinical psychiatrists, whereas insight therapies are practiced by other professionals, including licensed psychologists, clinically trained social workers, and lay therapists. None of the latter are authorized to prescribe drugs, shock treatment, or hospitalization.

Before the late 1930s severe psychosis was treated in a variety of ways: by confining the patient in a straitjacket; by administering sedatives; by wrapping the patient in moist, cool sheets; or by immersing patients in "continuous flow tubs" of water for hours at a time (Sheehan, 1982). Then a more drastic treatment was introduced: electroconvulsive therapy, in which an electric shock produces a convulsion and brief unconsciousness. This frightening and dangerous treatment has produced dramatic results with deeply depressed patients and some schizophrenics. However, the effects tend to be temporary, and it is not clear how much brain damage the treatment causes. Moreover, it often results in long-term memory loss.

In the 1940s and early 1950s shock treatment was used extensively, sometimes in coercive and excessive ways (Squire, 1987). The procedure was modified in the mid-1950s and made somewhat safer, but in the 1960s and 1970s it fell into disfavor as drug therapies became increasingly popular. Recently interest in this form of treatment has revived, partly because drug therapies have turned out to be less effective than anticipated.

The other important medical approach to treatment, chemotherapy, involves treating patients with a variety of drugs, ranging from mild tranquilizers to antidepressants and antipsychotic agents. The development of the antipsychotic drugs has made it possible to control the most incapacitating aspects of schizophrenia and paranoia. This, in turn, often permits the patient to return to the commuity, with occasional periods of hospitalization when stress or other problems cause more severe symptoms of the disorder to recur. But these powerful drugs cause side effects when they are administered over long periods.

Chemotherapy is also used in the treatment of anxiety. This usually involves the use of mild tranquilizers such as Valium and Xanax, the most frequently prescribed drugs today. It is generally believed that chemotherapy should be used in conjunction with some other form of therapy, since drugs alone can rarely bring about significant long-term changes in behavior.

Changes in Mental-Health Professions

In the largest survey of mental-health needs and access to medical care in many decades, researchers at the National Institute of Mental Health contacted more than 20,000 Americans, who were interviewed about their recent history of mental disorders and asked what they did when they had symptoms of mental illness and distress. The study showed that mental illness goes untreated in seven out of ten cases. Of people who did go to doctors or other mental-health professionals for treatment of mental distress, those with severe mental illnesses were likely to be treated by psychiatrists and other highly trained mental-health professionals, while people with milder but often quite troubling mental-health problems (43 percent of this group) most often consulted their family physicians, who did not necessarily have special training in mental-health care. About 40 percent of those who sought medical help for mental illness said that they visited mental-health professionals, including psychiatrists, who can dispense psychotropic drugs, and psychologists and clinical social workers, who cannot dispense such drugs. Another 18 percent said that they visited a family friend, a member of the clergy, or a self-help group (Regier, 1993). These findings suggest that there is an urgent need for more research to find better ways to identify and treat individuals with severe untreated mental illnesses. They also indicate that family physicians require more training in dealing with mental-health issues.

In treating patients who seek professional help for mental disorders, psychiatrists increasingly find themselves in direct competition for patients with therapists who rely on insight methods or "talking cures." The latter include clinical psychologists, clinical social workers, and marriage and family counselors. These professions are growing far more rapidly than psychiatry, despite the fact that only psychiatrists with an M.D. degree are legally permitted to write drug prescriptions and only psychiatrists can supervise the treatment of hospitalized patients. The services of clinically trained social workers and psychologists cost less than two-thirds of what psychiatric care costs, and insurance companies would rather pay these lower fees. Also, many insurance companies have reduced the number of therapy visits they will cover. When patients have to pay some of the fees, they too are more likely to choose the less costly form of treatment as long as their disorder does not involve symptoms that require drug therapy. Figure 3–2 shows the consequences of these trends; the number of clinical social workers and psychologists has more than tripled since 1975, while the number of psychiatrists has leveled off at about 36,000.

Treatment Institutions

The forms of treatment described earlier are carried out in a variety of settings. Psychotherapy and other nonmedical forms of treatment generally occur in nonhospital settings such as psychologists' offices. Medical treatments, on the other hand, often require hospitalization. In addition, some patients are so seriously ill that they cannot be cared for outside a hospital or asylum. In this section we will discuss issues related to the care of the mentally ill in hospitals and other institutions.

Mental Hospitals   In the late nineteenth and early twentieth centuries, mental-health care meant, in practice, mental hospitals. During this period the ties among members of extended families were being weakened as a result of increased mobility. The smaller nuclear family was less well equipped to care for its disabled mem-

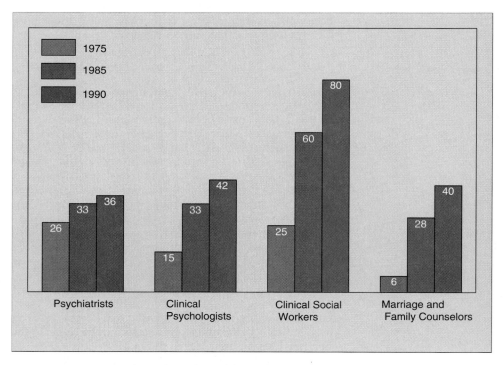

FIGURE 3–2   Growth in Mental Health Professions (in thousands)

Source: Data from American Psychiatric Association; American Psychological Association; National Association of Social Workers; 200 American Association of Marriage and Family Therapists.

Increasingly, medical professionals like this psychiatric social worker feel the need to leave their clinics and reach out to troubled populations in the streets and elsewhere.

bers and began to look to the state for assistance (Curtis, 1986). Institutions such as mental hospitals developed to meet this need. In such institutions the insane were to be sheltered from a hostile world, kept from harming themselves or others, and given help and treatment. Hospitals were built in secluded spots and surrounded by high walls and locked gates. Within the walls, all the patient's needs were to be met. But the purpose of the hospital was not merely to protect patients from society and, if possible, cure them; it was also to protect society from the patients. The old stereotype of the "raving lunatic" persisted, and gradually security came to be considered more important than therapy.

In the interest of economy and efficiency, the present system of enormous hospitals developed, each housing several thousand patients and staffed largely by aides whose main job is to keep things quiet on as low a budget as a state legislature can decently supply. Staffing these hospitals is a perennial problem. Salaries are usually low; working conditions are often unattractive or discouraging; and professionally trained personnel are almost irresistibly tempted by private hospitals, clinics, or private practice, where the rewards, both monetary and in terms of visible therapeutic achievement, are much greater. Consequently, public institutions must depend heavily on partially trained personnel, particularly in the case of the attendants or nursing aides. These attendants, though not fully qualified, are the people who have the most contact with patients, and typically they control most aspects of the patients' daily lives, including access to doctors.

There is evidence that hospitalization may not always be the best solution to problems of mental health, even in good hospitals. Long-term studies have shown that patients who do not improve enough to be discharged within a short period are likely to remain hospitalized for a very long time, if not indefinitely. This effect is due in part to the inadequacies of the hospital. It also seems to be a consequence of hospitalization itself. This is the position taken by Erving Goffman (1961). Goffman developed the concept of the *total institution*, which may be defined as "a place of residence and work where a large number of like-situated individuals, cut off from the wider society for an appreciable period of time, together lead an enclosed, formally administered round of life" (p. xiii).

Goffman regarded the mental hospital as a prime example of a total institution. His field research and experiences working in mental hospitals convinced him that because inmates are constantly subject to its control, the hospital profoundly shapes their sense of self. In general, mental hospitals downgrade patients' desire for self-esteem and emphasize their failures and inadequacies. Uniform clothing and furniture, a regimented routine, and the custodial atmosphere of the hospital make patients docile and unassertive. Since the psychiatric approach requires cooperation, staff members often encourage patients to view themselves as sick and in need of help. Any act of self-assertion or rebellion will probably be interpreted as further evidence of illness, and patients will be expected to take that view of themselves. Release from the hospital is often contingent on the patient's accepting, or appearing to accept, the official interpretation of his or her hospital and prehospital life. Goffman concluded that in most cases there is a high probability that hospitalization will do more harm than good.

In recent years Goffman's research has come in for some heavy criticism. In particular, he is faulted for not having conducted enough empirical research on enough hospitals to determine whether all mental hospitals could be labeled as total institutions. Moreover, although Goffman's idea has had a great influence on the way people think about mental hospitals (and jails), he is accused of having himself been influenced by the literary power of his ideas and images rather than by the force of empirical data (McEwen, 1988; Scull, 1988).

The Rosenhan (1973) study mentioned earlier illustrates the conditions prevailing in many mental hospitals. This research project involved eight normal people, or pseudopatients, who were admitted to a mental hospital and diagnosed as schizophrenics. Their only symptom was a fabricated one: They said that they had heard voices on one occasion. Although the pseudopatients spent some time in the institution and were recognized as normal by their fellow inmates, the staff continued to think of them as schizophrenic. Some were released with the diagnosis of "schizophrenia in remission," and none was ever thought to be cured. In a follow-up study, a hospital that had heard of these findings was informed that over a period of three months some pseudopatients would attempt to gain admission to the hospital, and staff members were asked to judge which applicants were faking illness. Over the three-month period at least forty-one patients were judged to be pseudopatients. In fact, none of those patients was faking.

The results of this study were widely cited as supporting the labeling theory, in that the diagnosis of illness—or health—was applied regardless of the actual condition of the patient. But here we are interested in what the pseudopatients observed while in the hospital. As much as possible, staff members were separated from patients by a glass enclosure; psychiatrists, in particular, almost never appeared on the wards. When pseudopatients approached staff members with questions, the most common response by the latter was to ignore the questions or mumble something—avoiding eye contact with the patient—and quickly move on. Patients were sometimes punished excessively for misbehavior, and in one case a patient was beaten. In sum, the atmosphere was one of powerlessness and depersonalization.

Community Psychology   The increased use of chemotherapy in the treatment of mental disorders caused a revolution in mental-health care. It began in the hospitals in the 1950s. As a result of the introduction of psychotropic drugs,

> *thousands of patients who had been assaultive became docile. Many who had spent their days screaming subsided into talking to themselves. The decor of the wards could be improved: Chairs replaced wooden benches, curtains were hung on the windows. Razors and matches, once properly regarded as lethal, were given to patients who now were capable of shaving themselves and lighting their own cigarettes without injuring themselves or others or burning the hospital down. (Sheehan, 1982, p. 10)*

But the revolution went far beyond hospital care. The new "wonder drugs" made it possible to release hundreds of thousands of hospitalized patients. Those patients were supposed to receive outpatient treatment in their own communities.

Outpatient treatment for mental disorders is far from new, but until the 1960s it was confined largely to less severe disorders and to the upper and middle classes. With the passage of the Community Mental Health Centers Construction Act in 1963, the idea of easily accessible, locally controlled facilities that could care for people in their own communities—*community psychology*—was established.

The community psychology movement arose from two basic sources: (1) awareness that social conditions and institutions must be taken into account in dealing with individual mental-health problems, and (2) the idea that psychologists or psychiatrists should be able to contribute to the understanding and solution of social problems. The guidelines laid down for the centers provided for a wide range of mental-health care within the community and for coordination with, and consultative assistance to, other community agencies. Other nations, particularly Belgium and France, had had great success in developing residential treatment facilities for mentally ill individuals who were able to live among people who were not suffering from mental illnesses.

The Community Mental Health Centers Construction Act set up a sophisticated support system to aid newly released patients, many of whom need considerable help in relearning the skills of everyday life and social interaction. The cornerstone of this system is the *halfway house*, a small, privately run residential community, usually located in an urban area, in which ex-patients are helped to make the transition from the hospital to normal life. They may receive therapy from a psychiatrist; they may be trained for a job and helped to obtain or keep one; and they are able to practice fitting into a community in which behavior is not subject to hospital regulations.

Under optimal conditions halfway houses are capable of providing high-quality care; however, a variety of obstacles have prevented them from meeting the needs of many discharged mental patients. Operating almost in a vacuum—with no working relationship with the state mental hospitals from which they receive patients— many halfway houses soon found themselves with far more patients than they had staff or facilities to handle. This problem was exacerbated as hospitals rushed to reduce their patient loads long before community support systems were in place. In addition, halfway houses and other community mental-health centers faced the enormous problem of lack of funds. The insurance coverage of mentally ill patients tended to favor hospital care, and the coverage for mental problems was inferior to that available for physical illnesses. As a result, halfway houses, nursing homes, and other community mental-health facilities found it difficult to meet the growing demand for services.

In addition to the problems of caring for released patients, the community psychology movement has given rise to a number of issues related to the civil rights of patients. Are released mental patients entitled to the full rights of citizenship, even when this allows them to behave irrationally in public? Is there any justification for the *re*hospitalization of mental patients who have joined the homeless population? These issues will be discussed more fully in the Social Policy section. But first we need to examine the situation of released mental patients in some detail, especially as it relates to the serious problem of homelessness.

Deinstitutionalization and Homelessness

We noted in the preceding section that beginning in the mid-1950s large numbers of mental patients were *deinstitutionalized*, or released from mental hospitals. As the prominent medical sociologist David Mechanic notes, in the United States "we have emptied out mental institutions, reducing the number of public mental hospital beds from a peak of 559,000 in 1955 to 110,000 today, but have not developed effective systems of community care" (1990, p. 9). As Figure 3–3 on page 84 shows, deinstitutionalization reversed a trend that had extended throughout the early twentieth century, in which the population of state mental hospitals increased fourfold. During that time

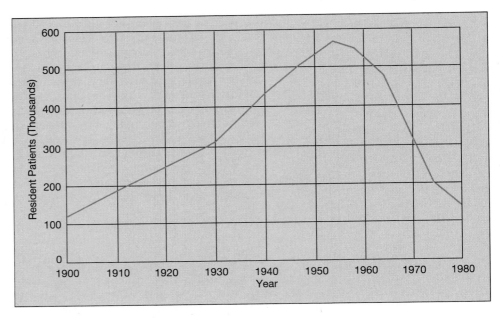

FIGURE 3–3   The Impact of Deinstitutionalization

mental hospitals were subjected to intense criticism, but the solutions proposed involved increasing the funding of hospitals, not the wholesale release of their inmates.

The trend toward deinstitutionalization is generally attributed to the introduction of psychotropic drugs; such drugs greatly reduced the disruptive behavior of patients and made it possible to treat them outside of hospital settings. However, some experts on mental-health care believe that other factors besides the "drug revolution" played a role in deinstitutionalization. One such factor was the expansion of federal health and welfare programs, which resulted in "the emergence of a new philosophy regarding what was possible and desirable in the provision of mental health care for the seriously mentally ill" (Gronfein, 1985, p. 450). In other words, although the advent of psychotropic drugs certainly played an important role in deinstitutionalization, they were not the *cause* of large-scale discharges of patients. It would be more accurate to say that the use of psychotropic drugs reinforced a trend that began at about the same time in response to a combination of factors, including not only expanded federal welfare programs but also the fiscal crises that were developing in many states, as well as growing demands for protection of the rights of the mentally ill (Gronfein, 1985).

Throughout the 1960s and 1970s it was hoped that reductions in the hospital population would be accompanied by equivalent reductions in the incidence of mental disorders. This hope proved vain. Far from decreasing, the incidence of mental disorders increased. At the same time, funding of community mental-health care was cut back. Of the 2,000 community mental-health centers planned in 1963, fewer than 1,000 have been established. As a result, hospital emergency rooms are often crowded with psychiatric patients. In addition, large numbers of former patients are homeless (Isaac & Armat, 1990; Johnson, 1990).

The presence of deinstitutionalized mental patients among the homeless is due partly to the tendency of these individuals to congregate in central-city neighborhoods, which are unable to provide the services they need. It has also been caused, in part, by the passage of laws designed to protect the rights of the mentally ill. Because only patients who are demonstrably dangerous may be involuntarily committed to mental hospitals, most mentally ill patients receive only brief, episodic care (Bassuk, 1984). Chronically disturbed people who are not dangerous to themselves or others are released "into the community." Some find housing in single-room occupancy (SRO) hotels or cheap rooming houses, but these forms of housing are far less available today than they were in the 1950s and 1960s because landlords have either abandoned them or converted them into condominiums. As a result, mentally ill people often end up on the streets.

The presence of mentally ill individuals among the homeless is highly visible and has contributed to the widespread impression that a large proportion of homeless people have mental disorders. It has been estimated that between 30 and 60 percent of the homeless are seriously mentally ill. Social-scientific research has found, however, that the majority of the homeless are individuals who have been "caught in a cycle of low-paying, dead-end jobs that fail to provide the means to get off and stay off the streets" (Snow, Baker, & Anderson, 1986, p. 407). In one study, 164 homeless people in Austin, Texas, were tracked over a twenty-month period. Approximately 10 percent were found to have psychiatric problems of varying degrees of severity. Even among this group, more than 50 percent registered for job referrals at the Texas Employment Commission at least once. The researchers concluded that the erroneous notion that the homeless are predominantly mentally ill is explained by four interconnected factors: undue emphasis on the causal role of deinstitutionalization; the medicalization of homelessness (i. e., viewing it as an illness instead of a social condition); the high visibility of the homeless mentally ill; and the difficulty of assessing the mental status of the homeless (Snow et al., 1986).

The fourth factor just mentioned was emphasized by a New York State judge in a case involving a homeless woman who had been involuntarily hospitalized under a program to remove seriously disturbed people from New York City streets. The judge ordered the woman released on the ground that the city had failed to prove that she was mentally ill. (The ruling was subsequently reversed by a court of appeals.) "The issue for most homeless people," he said, "is not whether they are mentally ill, but housing" (quoted in Barbanel, 1987). The crisis in housing for low-income individuals and families will be discussed further in Chapters 8, 12, and 15.

Even though the proportion of mentally ill individuals among the homeless may have been exaggerated, there is no doubt that a frequent outcome of untreated mental disorder is rejection and homelessness. Homelessness usually is the final stage in a long series of crises and missed opportunities, the end result of a gradual process of disengagement from supportive relationships and institutions. The situation is especially severe for the mentally ill. They are isolated. Family members and friends have become tired and discouraged or are unable to help. Social workers are overburdened and cannot give them the attention they need, and the mentally ill themselves cannot communicate their needs adequately (Bassuk, 1984). In addition, the mentally ill encounter hostility from other residents of the urban communities in which they try to exist.

As a result of experiences like these, the homeless, especially those who are mentally disturbed, tend to be extremely afraid of strangers. This is one explanation for the fact that they often reject offers of shelter and efforts to help them. The fear experienced by some homeless people is so great that it can be overcome only with effort and patience. However, much of the assistance offered to these individuals is perfunctory and uncaring, serving only to further isolate them from society.

It should be pointed out that mental illness can be a consequence of homelessness as well as a factor leading to social isolation (Institute of Medicine, 1988). People who lose their homes suffer severe stress. They experience hunger, lack of sleep, and physical illnesses ranging from asthma to tuberculosis. In addition, they are "disorganized, depressed, disordered . . . immobilized by pain and traumatized by fear" (Kozol, 1988). To the uninformed observer, such individuals resemble the former mental patients who have also ended up on the streets, and their disordered appearance helps perpetuate the belief that all homeless people are crazy.

The passage of the Community Mental Health Centers Construction Act in 1963 ushered in a new era of treatment for the mentally ill. As noted earlier, however, the community mental-health facilities that took over the role of the large custodial institutions were unable to cope with their new responsibilities. Among the problems they faced were insufficient funding, poor community relations, the difficulty of providing follow-up care, and uncertainty about proper medical care for released mental patients. (See Box 3–1.)

In September 1984 the American Psychiatric Association released its first comprehensive report on the homeless mentally ill, in which it declared that the practice of releasing mental patients into ill-prepared communities was a failure and "a major societal tragedy" (quoted in Boffey, 1984). The report also stated that the APA continues to support deinstitutionalization when adequate alternative services are provided, noting that patients who have been fortunate enough to receive those services are often better off than those remaining in institutions. However, the number of patients who have succeeded in making the transition from the hospital to the community is extremely small.

A study of homelessness and health commissioned by the U.S. Congress in 1985 and conducted by the National Academy of Sciences concluded that "deinstitutionalization and noninstitutionalization have become increasingly difficult to implement successfully because they depend heavily on the availability of housing and supportive community services. In reality, few communities have established adequate networks of services for the deinstitutionalized mentally ill" (Institute of Medicine, 1988, p. 29).

For the most part, state and municipal governments have been unwilling to assume the burden of caring for the mentally ill. Some have provided shelters for the homeless, but these cannot hope to replace the mental hospital or the halfway house. Shelters offer minimal medical, psychological, and social services. Generally understaffed, they are open only at night and cannot provide the supervision and support needed by disturbed individuals.

Some *re*institutionalization has occurred as a result of the public outcry over the plight of the homeless mentally ill. This is especially true of patients under constant medication, who need careful monitoring because their tolerance of and need for psychotropic drugs are constantly changing. If they receive adequate treatment outside as well as inside the hospital, this "revolving door" system is reasonably effective. However, such situations are rare.

In the absence of adequate shelter and other support, homeless mentally ill persons wander the streets of many cities and often spend much of their time being shuttled back and forth between jails and shelters. The Los Angeles County Jail houses the nation's largest concentration of severely mentally ill persons, with up to 3,600 per night swelling its inmate rolls (Public Citizen Health Research Group, 1990).

An important factor in problems of caring for the mentally ill is the lack of coordination of treatment. Because of the division of mental-health care between insight therapists and medical practitioners, there is a widespread tendency to see psychotherapy and medical treatment as mutually exclusive. Yet a patient who is on medication needs to have enough insight to be able to take the medicine in the prescribed dosage at the correct intervals. It follows that there must be a high level of coordination of treatment between social workers and others in the patient's social world, on the one hand, and the clinical personnel who prescribe medication and decide whether patients should be hospitalized, on the other.

Problems of treatment and supervision of nonhospitalized patients stem in part from certain characteristics of the organization of mental-health institutions. According to John W. Meyer (1985), the mental-health care system lacks integration or

Although social scientists who conduct research on homelessness generally agree that only about 30 percent of the homeless are mentally ill, this segment of the homeless population presents special problems for policy makers. In an era of public debt and reluctance to promote new initiatives to build low-cost housing, homelessness is likely to remain a severe problem for the foreseeable future. But even if there were a crash program to build more adequate housing for homeless people, some critics argue that the mentally ill homeless would not avail themselves of it. Many think they would continue to wander the streets and sleep in railway stations, bus terminals, and alleys even if better shelters or housing were available.

In reviewing most of the available research on this question, as well as the broader issue of how to improve the situation of homeless mentally ill persons, the Committee on Health Care of the National Academy of Sciences noted that "there are no known studies that prove that if affordable housing were provided to homeless people they would use it" (1988, p. 144). But the committee also reviewed reports from many American cities that show that temporary shelters for the homeless are, with few exceptions, filled to capacity or so heavily used that many more people are discouraged from using them. This is strong indirect evidence that if more and better shelters were provided they would be highly sought after.

In addition, in the existing shelters it is often the persons with histories of mental illness or alcohol and drug addiction—those who are hallucinating or high or who otherwise act in a somewhat bizarre fashion—who either discourage others from using the shelters or are themselves most frequently victimized. Most recommendations in this area of social policy, therefore, insist on the need to provide special shelters and housing units for the homeless mentally ill. Ideally these would be places where there could also be a concentration of health ser-

vices, occupational therapy programs, and supported workshops (where people can work under conditions that tolerate their differences and support their individual needs). Where these types of community-based and comprehensive programs have been instituted, they have tended to be very successful. One of the major obstacles to their growth, however, is the resistance of communities and neighborhoods to the location of such programs in their midst. Known as the NIMBY (Not In My Back Yard) phenomenon, this is a serious obstacle to many types of social programs designed to address severe problems, but shelters and programs for the homeless mentally ill are especially vulnerable to such resistance.

NIMBY responses frequently delay the implementation of programs to address social problems like homelessness among the mentally ill. People who claim that they want to see such problems addressed but do not want to make any sacrifices themselves usually need to be confronted by neighbors who are willing to do their share. But the latter also need to feel that the demands being placed on them are fair. Very often shelters and low-income housing for special populations are proposed for poor or moderate-income neighborhoods, and even sympathetic residents come to feel that too much is asked of them while not enough is asked of more affluent residents elsewhere in the community or city. In the more affluent communities, on the other hand, people tend to feel that they have "more to lose" in terms of property values and status, and they justify their resistance on those grounds. It takes long hours of persuasion, carefully designed programs, firm leadership that is committed to action, and adequate funding to overcome NIMBY problems. In the meantime the combination of local resistance and inadequate funding impedes progress toward providing housing and supportive programs for the homeless mentally ill.

structure. The various types of organizations that provide mental-health services differ greatly in the types of cases they handle, the way they are staffed and funded, the way they relate to other mental-health organizations, and many other respects. In addition, they are constantly changing, and they are continually under attack for failures both real and imagined. There is a need for what Meyer terms *institutional coordination* such as exists in education. Educational institutions also differ greatly, but they are held together by shared definitions of the nature of education, the requirements for teaching, the meaning of degrees and credit, and so on. Similar agreements are needed in the field of mental-health care—for example, agreements on the definition of treatable problems, appropriate professionals, funding responsibilities, and the like.

The health-care reform proposals of the Clinton administration would have far-reaching effects on the system for caring for mentally ill persons in the United States. Those proposals address the foremost problems of mental illness: lack of adequate insurance coverage for mental illness, lack of responsibility for care of the mentally ill, and lack of adequate funding for the treatment of the mentally ill. Under the vast majority of private medical insurance policies, mental-health problems are treated as far less important than problems of physical illness. The Clinton plan addresses this problem by insisting that mental illnesses be covered in the Health Security Act and covered more adequately in insurance plans, both private and public. These measures will eventually increase access to mental-health care. However, there will remain large gaps in funding for community mental-health centers and related institutions, especially those that treat the indigent, the homeless, and the chronically unemployed. In consequence, despite the hope of major improvements in access to mental-health care, much mental illness will continue to go untreated (Pear, 1993).

Recent research on the annual cost of mental depression shows that it ranks as high as heart disease as a drain on national resources. As knowledge about the economic impact of mental-health problems accumulates, there are likely to be further improvements in social policies to deal with these serious illnesses.

SUMMARY

1. The mental disorders that cause severe social problems are the most extreme forms of mental illness, in which individuals become violent and irrational. Less threatening, but more widespread as a social problem, are severely ill individuals who cannot care for themselves without specialized attention.

2. There are three different explanations of mental illness: (a) the medical model, which simply asserts that mental illness is a disease with physiological causes; (b) the deviance approach, which asserts that mental illness results from the way people who are considered mentally ill are treated; and (c) the argument that mental illness is not a disease but a way of defining certain people as being in need of isolation and "treatment." When sociologists speak of the "social construction" of mental illness, they incorporate all three approaches into their explanations.

3. The American Psychiatric Association's *Diagnostic and Statistical Manual of Mental Disorders* has gone a long way toward standardizing the diagnosis of mental illness. However, many researchers believe that psychiatric diagnoses are arbitrary and amount to labels describing behavior that is contrary to accepted social and psychological norms.

4. Poverty is associated with high exposure to crime and violence, which create stresses that can precipitate

mental illness. In addition, lower social-class status is associated with a greater likelihood of being selected or labeled as mentally ill. Researchers have also found high rates of untreated mental disorder among lower-class populations.

5. According to the *social-selection* or *drift* hypothesis, low social-class status is not a cause but a consequence of mental disorder. Mentally disordered people tend to be found in the lower classes because their illness has prevented them from functioning at a higher class level.

6. Research on the correlation between mental illness and such factors as urban life and crowding in the home has not produced conclusive results. Race also does not appear to be a significant variable by itself, but there are differences in the types of mental illnesses suffered by men and women.

7. The two major approaches to the treatment of mental disorders are psychotherapy and medical treatment. The major forms of psychotherapy are psychoanalysis, client-centered therapy, and therapy and support groups. Medical treatments such as chemotherapy and shock treatment are applied to the most severe mental illnesses.

8. Increasingly psychiatrists find themselves competing for patients with therapists who rely on insight methods. The services of the latter cost less and therefore are favored by insurance companies and many patients. As a result, the number of clinical social workers and psychologists has increased dramatically while the number of psychiatrists has leveled off.

9. Medical treatments often require hospitalization. Until the mid-twentieth century, this usually meant care in mental hospitals or asylums. However, long-term studies have shown that patients who do not improve enough to be discharged within a short period are likely to remain in the hospital indefinitely.

10. The community psychology movement arose in the 1950s, partly as a result of the increased use of chemotherapy in the treatment of mental disorders. Many patients were released from mental hospitals to be cared for in community mental-health centers or *halfway houses*. The large-scale deinstitutionalization of mental patients led to a variety of problems, including the tendency of deinstitutionalized patients to end up among the homeless population.

11. The plight of the homeless mentally ill has given rise to calls for reinstitutionalization, especially for patients under constant medication. Treatment of patients both within and outside mental-health institutions is difficult to achieve, however, because of the lack of coordination of medical and nonmedical treatment. The Clinton administration's health-care reform proposals attempt to address the problems of lack of adequate insurance coverage for mental illness, lack of responsibility for care of the mentally ill, and lack of adequate funding for treating mental illness.

SUGGESTED READINGS

Asylums: Essays on the Social Situation of Mental Patients and Other Inmates. Garden City, NY: Doubleday, 1961. A classic study of social control and labeling in a state mental hospital.

DOHRENWEND, BRUCE P., ET AL. *Mental Illness in the United States: Epidemiological Estimates*. New York: Praeger, 1980. An attempt to assess the magnitude and distribution of problems of mental illness in the United States.

GALLAGHER, BERNARD J., III. *The Sociology of Mental Illness,* 2nd ed. Englewood Cliffs, NJ: Prentice Hall, 1987. A comprehensive text that provides in-depth coverage of many of the issues raised in this chapter.

GARY, LAWRENCE E., ED. *Mental Health: A Challenge to the Black Community*. Philadelphia: Dorrance, 1978. A collection of essays that addresses the role of racism in the mental health of African Americans.

HOPE, MARJORIE, AND JAMES YOUNG. *The Faces of Homelessness*. Lexington, MA: D. C. Heath/Lexington Books, 1986. Covers many of the controversies related to homelessness and mental illness, with a well-researched analysis of the previously institutionalized and never-institutionalized mentally ill components of the homeless population.

JENCKS, CHRISTOPHER. *Homelessness*. Cambridge, MA: Harvard University Press, 1994. An incisive look at the facts of homelessness on a thorough reading and critique of the latest U.S. literature on the subject. Ends with an argument for more investment in low-cost housing.

SHEEHAN, SUSAN. *Is There No Place on Earth for Me?* New York: Scribner's, 1982. A sensitive, in-depth study of a schizophrenic woman's career in and out of mental institutions and drug therapies.

Sex-Related Social Problems

Chapter Outline

■ The average age of male heterosexual sex offenders is under 40.

■ In recent polls between 1 and 4 percent of men indicated that they had had homosexual relations in the year prior to the survey.

■ About 40 percent of street prostitutes have been exposed to AIDS.

■ A majority of American adults have been exposed to some kind of explicit sexual material, and up to one-quarter of the male population has somewhat regular experience with such material.

Until fairly recently—that is, until about thirty years ago—Americans' attitudes toward sexual behavior seemed fairly traditional and easy to define: Normal sex was that which led to the bearing of children within a socially legitimate family. Premarital intercourse might come within the narrowly defined range of acceptable behaviors, but only if it led to marriage fairly quickly. All other sexual acts, such as any act between consenting adults of the same sex, were condemned and prohibited. The possibility of allowing for variations in sexual tastes, or even the idea that such differences might be legitimate reflections of human individuality, was ignored. While many people pursued sexual adventures and found pleasure in sexual behaviors that differed from the generally accepted norms, those differences were not recognized as legitimate and their behavior was condemned.

Today attitudes toward sex are much more ambivalent and inconsistent, although sexual matters are discussed more openly. On the one hand, a variety of sexual behaviors are portrayed in the media and elsewhere. On the other hand, many people are strongly opposed to greater sexual freedom, considering it abnormal or even degenerate. Many citizens oppose even basic sex education in schools. And in most states laws continue to prohibit not only nonheterosexual or nonmarital sexual acts but even some sex acts between husband and wife.

Although attitudes toward sex may be ambivalent, there can be no doubt that the past 50 years have seen immense changes in sexual behavior in the United States. To take just one example, between 1938 and 1976 the proportion of 19-year-

U.S. Surgeon General Dr. Joycelyn Elders is a strong advocate of health and sex education as well as universal driver education. "We taught them what to do in the front seat of a car. Now it's time to teach them what to do in the back seat," she says.

Sex education is one means of addressing sexual ignorance, but to be effective such education must be more explicit than some parents consider acceptable.

old girls in one midwestern community who had had premarital intercourse increased from 18.0 percent to 55.8 percent (Kinsey, Pomeroy, & Martin, 1953; Zelnik, Young, & Kantner, 1979). Increases have also been reported in such previously frowned-upon behaviors as oral and anal intercourse.

Despite these developments, many traditional attitudes are still present—not only in our laws but also in our behavior. For example, although more Americans are permissive regarding premarital, oral, and anal sex, they still prefer that such practices occur within the context of close and affectional relationships (Blumstein & Schwartz, 1983; Schur, 1988; Weinberg & Williams, 1980). Couples who live together in what amount to trial marriages have "firm emotional ties, conventional standards regarding fidelity, and a definite social identity as a couple" (Hunt, 1974, p. 153). The role of traditional values has become especially pronounced in recent years as a result of the AIDS epidemic. Psychiatrists, public health workers, and law enforcement officials agree that there has been a significant decrease in casual or promiscuous sexual activity. Many gay men are limiting their sexual encounters, and "straight" men and women are avoiding one-night stands. Women carry condoms for their dates to use when and if they have sex, and some dating services require their members to undergo regular testing for the presence of the HIV virus (Dimen, 1987).

In addition to the AIDS epidemic, the shift toward generally more conservative attitudes among Americans has slowed the trend toward more permissive sexual norms. The efforts of government agencies, religious groups, and other organizations to prevent women from obtaining abortions and to discourage sexuality among teenagers are further indications that the liberalization of sexual norms has come to a halt. According to one writer on the subject, a sexual counterrevolution is under way, "a reaffirmation of monogamy over promiscuity, the nuclear family over sexual and domestic experiment, work over sensual pleasure" (Dimen, 1987, p. 14).

The changes in sexual attitudes and behaviors that have occurred in recent decades are not in themselves a social problem. The problem is that the resulting diversity leads to a great deal of conflict over how society should address issues related to sexual behavior. Among those issues are how to understand and respond to sexual behaviors that deviate from widely held norms, particularly homosexuality and prostitution, and how to cope with the most severe sex-related social problem of modern times: AIDS.

The spread of AIDS and the increased prevalence of other sexually transmitted diseases (e.g., herpes and syphilis), as well as the continuing problem of adolescent pregnancy, point up another problem associated with sexuality: the absence of "sexual literacy." In 1990 the Kinsey Institute and the Roper Organization asked 1,974 randomly selected adult Americans a series of 18 questions designed to test their basic knowledge about sex and human reproduction. The majority of those questioned answered 10 or more of the questions incorrectly (Reinisch, 1990). (See Figure 4–1.) The sexual ignorance revealed by this survey is itself a problem because of its consequences. But as the questions in Figure 4–1 indicate, the main problem with sexual illiteracy is that it prevents the nation's citizens from engaging in healthy

---

A survey by the Kinsey Institute and the Roper Organization found gaps in Americans' knowledge about sex. These are 5 of the 18 questions. The answers appear below with the percentage of people who answered correctly.

1. Nowadays, what do you think is the age at which the average or typical American first has sexual intercourse?

a. 11 or younger b. 12 c. 13 d. 14 e. 15 f. 16 g. 17 h. 18 i. 19
j. 20 k. 21 or older l. Don't know

2. Of every 10 married American men, how many would you estimate have had an extramarital affair—that is, have been sexually unfaithful to their wives?

a. Fewer than 1 of 10 b. One c. Two d. Three e. Four f. Five
g. Six h. Seven i. Eight j. Nine k. More than 9 of 10 l. Don't know

3. Of every 10 American women, how many would you estimate have had anal (rectal) intercourse?

a. Fewer than 1 of 10 b. One c. Two d. Three e. Four f. Five
g. Six h. Seven i. Eight j. Nine k. More than nine l. Don't know

4. More than one of four (25 percent) of American men have had a sexual experience with another male during their teen or adult years.

True   False   Don't know

5. A woman or teen-age girl can get pregnant during her menstrual flow (her "period").

True   False   Don't know

ANSWERS

1. f or g	Percentage correct: 24%	
2. d or e	Percentage correct: 25%	
3. d or e	Percentage correct: 21%	
4. True	Percentage correct: 21%	
5. True	Percentage correct: 51%	

FIGURE 4–1   Selected Questions from the Kinsey-Roper Survey on Sexual Literacy

Source: Copyright © 1990 by the New York Times Company. Reprinted by permission.

and responsible sexual behavior and leads to ignorance about even more difficult social and biological issues.

SEX AS A SOCIAL PROBLEM

We saw in Chapter 1 that a social condition becomes a social problem when many people in a society agree that it threatens the quality of their lives and their most cherished values, and that something should be done about it. In the case of sexual behavior, a social condition—liberal attitudes toward sexual experimentation—has been identified as a social problem because it is associated with other problems such as sexually transmitted diseases. However, it is difficult to state precisely the nature of sex as a social problem. Even before the "sexual revolution" there was a great difference between the stated norms of our society and people's actual behavior. Today it has become even more difficult to define sex-related social problems. Sexual behavior that was once condemned is now considered acceptable by most people. Not long ago, for example, oral intercourse was considered immoral; today the majority of young people have engaged in it. Until recently masturbation was considered sinful and unhealthy; today it is widely assumed that masturbation is not only normal but beneficial to sexual development, although Catholics, Mormons, and other religious groups preach against it.

Nevertheless, there are still sex-related acts or conditions that many people have difficulty accepting; among these are homosexuality, prostitution, and pornography. In the past such behavior was labeled "deviant," but we now avoid this term whenever possible because it implies that there is a normal and therefore proper form of sexual expression, and also because it entails the same stigma as "degenerate," "perverted," or "sick." We prefer instead to refer to these acts or conditions as sex-related social problems.

A useful classification of sex-related social problems is that of Gagnon and Simon (1967), who classify such problems into three categories. We will use our own names for these categories: tolerated sex variance, asocial sex variance, and structured sex variance.

Tolerated Sex Variance

Tolerated sex variance includes such acts as heterosexual oral-genital contact, masturbation, and premarital intercourse. These acts "are generally disapproved, but . . . either serve a socially useful purpose and/or occur so often among a population with such low social visibility that only a small number are ever actually sanctioned for engaging in [them]" (Gagnon & Simon, 1967, p. 8). Except for premarital intercourse among teenagers, which has resulted in the current high rate of teenage pregnancy, these acts arouse little special interest, and outside of certain religious organizations there is little pressure for policies regulating such behavior. The Church of Latter Day Saints (Mormons), the most rapidly growing religious group in the United States, condemns masturbation, and conservatives support bans on heterosexual "sodomy" of all kinds. In 1986, in *Bowers* v. *Hardwick,* the Supreme Court upheld Georgia's antisodomy laws, which apply to heterosexuals as well as to homosexuals. Nevertheless, it is likely that over time these behaviors will become socially acceptable and cease to be regarded as social problems.

Asocial Sex Variance

Asocial sex variance includes incest, child molestation, rape, exhibitionism, and voyeurism. These acts are usually committed by a lone individual or at most a small number of people. Although there are social influences on the incidence of such acts, they must be understood primarily from a psychological or social-psychological viewpoint. People who engage in such behavior do not have a social structure that recruits, socializes, and provides social support for these acts. Major forms of asocial sex variance—incest, rape, and child molestation—elicit widespread and strong disapproval even among other lawbreakers.

Incest   *Incest*, or sexual relations between individuals who are so closely related that they are forbidden to marry by law or custom, is almost universally prohibited. "The incest taboo is universal in human culture. . . . All cultures, including our own, regard violations of the taboo with horror and dread. Death has not been considered too extreme a punishment in many societies. In our laws, some states punish incest with up to twenty years' imprisonment" (Herman & Hirschman, 1977, p. 735).

Weinberg (1955) found that in cases of father–daughter incest (i.e., in most cases of incest), the family is likely to be characterized by paternal dominance, with the father intimidating and controlling the other family members. When incest occurs between siblings, the parents are not dominant and do not prevent the children from engaging in sex play. In cases of mother–son incest, the family is characterized by maternal dominance, with the father either absent or extremely subservient. In all cases, Weinberg found, incest causes confusion in family roles and creates rivalries within the family. It also generates conflict within the child or children involved and disturbs other family members who may be only subliminally aware of what is happening. Even when they are aware of what is happening, family members keep the behavior a secret. Indeed, according to one expert "the essence of incest is secrecy. Anything that breaks the silence . . . makes it more possible for victims and others to speak out" (Dr. Judith L. Herman, quoted in Kleiman, 1987, pp. A1, B5).

Research findings suggest that the common belief that incest occurs more frequently among people of low socioeconomic status is incorrect. Hunt (1974) found that incestuous acts are more common at higher socioeconomic levels. A study by Diana E. H. Russell (1986) also found that incest is more frequent in high-income families than in low-income ones. Higher rates of incest are reported for lower socioeconomic groups because "the poor, the ignorant, and the incompetent come to official attention, while people of higher socioeconomic status are able either to keep their acts hidden or, if discovered, to keep the discovery from becoming part of the official record" (Hunt, 1974, p. 347).

Child Molestation   In most societies, including our own, child molestation is feared and deplored and results in humiliation and loss of status for the adult involved. Contrary to popular belief, heterosexual child molestation is far more common than homosexual child molestation. Most child molesters do not fit the stereotype of the "dirty old man"; the average age of male heterosexual sexual offenders is under 40. Nor do child molesters fit the image of the lurking stranger: Most young girls who are molested know the man. [Sixteen percent of the women in Russell's (1986) sample had been sexually abused by a relative before reaching the age of 18.] Offenders may be wealthy or poor, educated or uneducated, a member of any ethnic group or occupation. We can say with confidence, however, that most child abusers capitalize on the society's system of male dominance and female submission, which explains why most offenders are male and most victims are female (Herman, 1981). Often offenders are people to whom the care of children is entrusted (Collins, 1982).

Child molestation in preschools and day-care centers is an ominous recent development in this area of sexual abuse. Arrests of workers in early-childhood care institutions in Los Angeles, New York, and other cities have caused governments at all levels to review their standards for evaluating these programs and their personnel. However, while charges of sexual abuse in day-care centers have generated much hysteria, so far there is little real evidence of widespread abuse. In the highly publicized case of the Los Angeles child-care workers accused of sexual abuse, the state dropped its charges against five of the seven defendants; and after the longest trial in American history, the two remaining defendants were acquitted of all charges. Still, such charges are serious because child abuse in day-care settings would represent a glaring misuse of child and parental trust and would threaten the future of a vital institution of childhood socialization.

Rape *Forcible rape*—coercive coitus with another person—is a violent crime. As such, it will be discussed more fully in Chapters 6 and 7. Our concern here is with some of the psychosocial factors involved.

Many studies have found that rapists are usually young and unmarried; some studies also suggest that a disproportionate number of convicted rapists are physically handicapped in some way (Chappell et al., 1971). Ostensibly, then, sexual deprivation is a key factor in rape. Most analysts believe, however, that the desire for sexual gratification is at most a secondary motive. In this view, rape is an act of aggression or sadism engaged in by males to bolster a weak self-image and to feel powerful (Guttemacher, 1951; Russell, 1984; Warr, 1985).

In recent years increasing attention has been focused on acquaintance or "date rape." Also termed *paraphyllic rapism*, it has been proposed to the American Psychiatric Association as a diagnosis for men who can achieve sexual pleasure only in the context of rape and coercion. Women's rights groups oppose the use of the latter term because it might be used to exonerate men who have been formally charged with forcible rape (Bayer, 1987). Those groups have also sponsored publicity campaigns to make women more aware of the danger of being raped by men who are known to them (Parrot & Bechhofer, 1991).

Various theories attempt to explain the relationship between rape rates and the social climate. One, suggested by Merton's theory of anomie (see Chapter 6), is that when heterosexual contact is valued but access to such contact is restricted, the rape rate will be higher. According to this hypothesis, the more sexually permissive a society is, the lower its rape rate will be. Another theory, advanced by feminists, holds that rape is a result of the patriarchal structure of American society, in which heterosexual love is expressed through male dominance and female submission.

Peggy Reeves Sanday (1984) studied patterns of rape in 186 tribal societies and found that cultures marked by high levels of male dominance and high levels of interpersonal violence had a high incidence of rape. These cultural traits may also help explain the high incidence of rape in the United States. Edwin Schur (1988) suggests that the extent to which sex is made into a desirable commercial commodity and viewed as an abstract pleasure (rather than part of an intimate relationship) also helps explain the incidence of rape.

Exhibitionism and Voyeurism Minor forms of asocial sex variance are exhibitionism (deliberate exposure of one's sex organs) and voyeurism (watching people undressing or performing a sexual act). "Flashers" and "peeping Toms" may be annoying, but perhaps because they are not usually very threatening, their behaviors have not received much analysis.

Structured Sex Variance

Behaviors that are classified as *structured sex variance* are associated with relatively well-defined roles and social institutions. Although they are engaged in by large numbers of people, these behaviors run counter to prevailing norms and legal statutes and therefore are often perceived as problems that threaten the social order. Such behaviors are also associated with the development of unique subcultures. Three examples of this type of sex variance that we will examine in some detail are

In the 1990s date or aquaintance rape has become a major concern on many university campuses and in other communities across the nation.

Rape Prevention Education Program

Women don't cause acquaintance rape. Rapists do.

But there are things you can do to reduce the risks of being raped by someone you know.

1 STAY away from men who: put you down a lot, talk negatively about women, think that "girls who get drunk should know what to expect," drink or use drugs heavily, are physically violent, don't respect you or your decisions.

2 SET sexual limits and intentions. Communicate them early and firmly.

3 DON'T pretend you don't want to have sex if you really do.

4 STAY sober.

5 DON'T make men guess what you want. Tell them.

6 REMAIN in control. Pay your own way. Make some of the decisons.

7 LISTEN to your feelings.

8 FORGET about being a "nice girl" as soon as you feel threatened.

9 LEARN self-defense. Know how to yell. Take assertiveness training.

10 TAKE care of yourself. Don't assume others will.

*For more information, please phone 893-3778
A service of the Women's Center and Police Department, University of California, Santa Barbara*

homosexuality, prostitution, and pornography. Of course, these are not the only sexual behaviors that are regarded as social problems, but it can be argued that they are the most visible and controversial sex-related social problems in our society.

HOMOSEXUALITY

Homosexuality is a sexual preference for members of one's own sex. Some people are exclusively homosexual; others may engage in homosexual behavior only under special circumstances, such as imprisonment; still others have both homosexual and heterosexual experiences. Both males and females may be homosexual; female homosexuals are usually referred to as *lesbians*. Much more research has been done on male homosexuality than on lesbianism.

It is difficult to determine the number of homosexuals in the United States. An often-cited estimate based on the original research of Alfred Kinsey (Kinsey, Pomeroy, & Martin, 1948), which included 17,000 interviews, places the proportion of homosexual or lesbian Americans at 10 percent. Kinsey found that 37 percent of the male population had had physical contact to the point of orgasm with other men at some time between adolescence and old age. The extent to which respondents had engaged in homosexual behavior varied, with 10 percent of the sample reporting that they had been more or less exclusively homosexual for at least three years.

The most recent surveys of sexual behavior in the United States and other Western societies have found lower percentages, varying between 1 and 4 percent, of men who indicated that they had had homosexual relations in the year prior to the survey (Alan Guttmacher Institute, cited in Barringer, 1993). Gay rights activists and survey research experts agree that while the Kinsey figures may be high estimates, the fluctuations in recent survey data suggest that sensitive questions about sexual behavior are subject to rather high levels of error because respondents may not feel comfortable about answering truthfully (Barringer, 1993).

In our society homosexuality has alternately been regarded either as a sin or as the effect of some physical or mental disturbance; until the rise of the gay liberation movement in recent decades it was considered too shameful and indecent to be spoken of openly. Although society has become more tolerant of open discussions of homosexuality today, many prejudices still prevail. Surveys consistently show increasing public tolerance of homosexuality, but almost half of all Americans believe that homosexuals should be barred from certain jobs for which they may be qualified, particularly jobs involving young people (Harris, 1977). Thus, homosexuality is a social problem not only because many people consider it a threat to their values but also because homosexuals are discriminated against in many occupations.

Social-Scientific Perspectives on Homosexuality

In the early decades of this century, social scientists generally viewed homosexuality as a form of social pathology brought on by the disorganization of families and communities experiencing the effects of rapid urbanization and industrialization. Sociologists tended to regard homosexuality, along with prostitution, as an individual response to the disorganization of family life. Psychologists attempted to treat it as an illness with physiological causes.

Sigmund Freud and other founders of the psychoanalytic movement realized that many homosexuals are well-adjusted, productive adults. Freud also believed that homosexuality is a stage that all people pass through on the way to developing heterosexual desires. Homosexuals, in his view, have been "arrested" and have failed to develop further. The Freudian perspective on homosexuality did not become a dominant viewpoint, however. The majority of American social scientists continued to view homosexuality as an illness that should be cured through some kind of therapy.

Kinsey's study of the sexual behavior of American males (Kinsey et al., 1948) marked a turning point in the understanding of homosexuality from both a scientific and a popular point of view. Kinsey's work was extraordinary because it was based on interviews with thousands of ordinary Americans rather than people who had requested psychiatric treatment. Kinsey's work revealed a wide gap between sexual norms and actual behavior.

Despite the torrent of criticism that greeted Kinsey's studies when they first appeared, other social scientists soon published findings that supported his conclusion that homosexuals cannot be distinguished from nonhomosexuals in psychological terms. The most famous of these studies were conducted by psychologist Evelyn Hooker during the 1950s. Hooker showed that it is not possible to distinguish homosexuals from nonhomosexuals using any of the standard projective tests available in clinical psychology. She went on to show that alleged homosexual obsessions (with anonymous sex, for example), where they exist, are caused not by homosexuality itself but by the experience of stigmatization and rejection. If homosexuals are a deviant group in society, she reasoned, they are so not because of any inherent feature of homosexuality but because of their experience of rejection by the larger society (Hooker, 1966).

Thomas Szasz—who, as we have seen, was one of the founders of labeling theory—carried this perspective a step further. He argued that psychiatrists and others who labeled homosexuality as an illness were merely taking the place of the church in identifying homosexuals and punishing them for their deviant sexual behavior. The gay rights movement of the 1960s and 1970s drew upon this perspective with great effectiveness.

Most recent social-scientific research on homosexuality has focused on its collective features. Research on the correlates (psychological and sociological variables) associated with homosexuality continues, but social scientists are increasingly turning to questions about the institutions of gay life and the problematic interactions between homosexuals and heterosexuals. Bayer's (1987) study of the conflict between gay activists and the American Psychiatric Association, discussed in Chapter 3, illustrates this trend. This study showed how the victory of the activists contributed to a new pride among homosexuals and reinforced the growing tendency of gays to assert the right to equal treatment. We will have more to say about these developments later in this section.

New trends in social-scientific research do not necessarily replace older research. Thus, social scientists who study behavior that deviates from major social norms continue to investigate such questions as who becomes homosexual and what factors are associated with higher rates of homosexuality in some groups. Researchers who apply labeling theory to the study of sexual behavior continue to demonstrate the effects of stigmatization on homosexuals. And social scientists who study the institutions and conflicts that shape our perceptions of social problems tend to focus on the ongoing conflicts that occur over such issues as acceptance of homosexuality in the military and other social institutions.

Who Becomes a Homosexual?

People have always wondered what causes someone to be a homosexual, but no one has yet found a definite answer. Some authorities have suggested that homosexuality has a biological cause; studies with identical twins suggest a genetic or inherited hormonal determinant. W. S. Schlegel (1962), for example, found that in 95 percent of cases in which one identical twin was homosexual the other twin also was homosexual, whereas among fraternal twins the figure was only 5 percent. Biological studies have been inconclusive, however, and the twin studies are confounded by envi-

TABLE 4–1   HOW DO GAY MEN DEFINE THE TERM *COMING OUT*?

	Responses	
	%	NO.
To admit to oneself a homosexual preference, or decide that one is, essentially, homosexual	31	77
To admit to oneself a homosexual preference *and* to begin to practice homosexual activity	27	41
To start actively seeking out other males as sexual partners	9	13
First homosexual experience as a young adult (i.e., after middle teens)	8	12
A homosexual experience that triggers self-designation as homosexual	1	2
Other	3	5
	99	150

*Informants were asked to define what the term *coming out* meant to them—that is, how they would use the term.

Source: Reprinted with permission of Macmillan Publishing Company from *Deviance: The Interactionist Perspective,* 5th Edition by Earl Rubington and Martin S. Weinberg. Copyright © 1987 by Macmillan Publishing Company.

ronmental factors. To date there is no strong evidence that homosexuality is biologically determined (Burr, 1993)—although a large proportion of homosexuals believe that it is. Sociobiologists, who seek the origins of social behavior in the genetic makeup of the individual, believe that they will find a physiological explanation for homosexuality, but so far they have been unable to do so (Konner, 1989).

Sociologists, psychiatrists, and anthropologists argue that the social environment in which a person grows up plays a greater role in producing homosexuality than any biological factor. They emphasize that human sexual behavior is learned behavior. Human beings may or may not have a basic need for sex, but its expression is shaped by experience. Psychiatrists and psychologists have not succeeded in identifying any early experiences that result in homosexuality. Certain situations do seem to be frequent in the case histories of homosexuals: The family often includes a dominant or seductive mother and a weak, detached, or overly critical father—factors that discourage the male child from identifying with male role models. Yet it is not clear why homosexuality develops only in some children who are reared under these conditions; many researchers, in fact, question whether homosexuality is caused by a pathological family situation at all.

One study of the process by which an individual becomes a homosexual (Troiden, 1987) emphasized the importance of labeling. The process of gaining a homosexual identity was divided into four stages: (1) sensitization, (2) dissociation and signification,* (3) coming out, and (4) commitment. In this model the gay identity is subject to modification at each stage, and the later stages do not inevitably follow the earlier ones. The third stage, coming out, marks the point at which the individual defines himself or herself as homosexual and becomes involved in the homosexual subculture. The specific means through which this occurs may vary, as Table 4–1 indicates.

*These terms refer to the mental processes by which sexual feelings and/or activity are distinguished from sexual identity.

Whatever the factors that contribute to homosexuality, one point is clear: There is no single form of homosexual expression or identity. One of the most common misconceptions about homosexuals is that they are easy to identify. The "typical" male homosexual is thought to be effeminate in manner, dress, and speech and to work in the creative arts. In reality there is as wide a divergence among homosexuals as among heterosexuals, and homosexuals can be found in all kinds of occupations, even stereotypically masculine ones. It has been estimated that only about 15 percent of all homosexuals conform in appearance or manner to the commonly held stereotype (Tripp, 1975). Many may do so only for a brief period, when they have recently acknowledged their homosexuality and feel compelled to act out the stereotype (Simon & Gagnon, 1967).

In addition, homosexuals do not share any evident pattern of personality characteristics. As noted earlier, Hooker (1957, 1958) showed that clinical projective tests do not distinguish reliably between homosexuals and heterosexuals. The one thing that homosexuals have in common is their sexual preference and the resulting social and psychological strains imposed by a society that strongly disapproves of it. The ways in which they satisfy their desires and cope with the attendant problems vary—to some extent along socioeconomic lines (Bell & Weinberg, 1978).

One important difference among homosexuals involves their willingness to "come out" and live their homosexuality openly. Some are completely candid about it. They may have relatively low-status and/or low-visibility jobs, which they are unlikely to lose because of their homosexuality. Or they may work in fields in which homosexuality is frequently taken for granted, such as the arts. Some are young people who have not yet made family and career commitments and believe that their sexual, psychological, and emotional needs are more important than their job or social position. Such individuals are likely to be most committed to a homosexual lifestyle. Many homosexuals, however, lead conventional lives that are simply homosexual counterparts of conventional heterosexual patterns: They have steady jobs and regular social lives that may center on groups of homosexual friends. These individuals generally avoid public settings like gay bars (Bell & Weinberg, 1978).

Some married homosexuals enjoy intercourse with their wives; a few are genuinely bisexual, enjoying the sex act with either male or female partners. Most are more comfortable in homosexual relationships but are married for the sake of domestic stability, companionship, and respectability. Barry M. Dank (1971) studied fifteen marriages in which the husband was homosexual. He found that whereas all the men had been homosexually oriented before marriage and most had had homosexual relations, 80 percent refused to consider themselves homosexual at the time that they were married. Some expected to outgrow their homosexual desires with age, and others had married explicitly to escape them. Their refusal to accept their own homosexuality stemmed primarily from abhorrence at being identified with a socially outcast minority. Although more than half of these men were able to function sexually with their wives, most continued to have sex with other men while they were married, and only one of the marriages survived the wife's discovery of her husband's homosexuality.

Although some male homosexuals have many sexual partners, most seek and achieve a stable relationship with one other male. A study by Saghir and Robins (1973) showed that 61 percent established a deep emotional relationship with one other male for a relatively long time. These relationships often adopt the traditions and symbols of heterosexual marriages. Homosexuals may exchange rings, celebrate wedding anniversaries, and dream of raising a child. However, contrary to popular belief, it appears that roles within homosexual marriages are not clearly divided into "masculine" and "feminine" or dominant and submissive (Harry & DeVall, 1978).

A special category of homosexuality is situational, that is, homosexual activity that takes place in circumstances in which heterosexual contact is virtually impossible. Such behavior is common in prisons, for example, where some of it can only be characterized as rape. Another form of situational, transitory homosexuality is that of delinquent youths who engage in homosexual prostitution with adult males. A. J. Reiss, Jr. (1964) found that some lower-class boys in large cities are taught this behavior by a peer group or gang whose older members know how to locate potential clients. These encounters occur at specific locations, such as certain street corners, parks, public toilets, or movie houses. A boy who engages in such behavior must belong to a group that accepts and encourages it; the group must indoctrinate him into it; and he must participate strictly for the money and never for sexual gratification. Only oral-genital fellatio, with the adult client acting as fellator, is permitted. The boy and/or his peer group will resort to violence if the adult does not conform to the established customs for such transactions. As long as the boy also conforms, he will not be defined as a homosexual and will not define himself as one.

The Gay Identity

The phenomenon of "coming out" was the focus of the study by Dank (1971) mentioned earlier. Dank found that most people do not identify themselves as homosexual for some time after they become aware of homosexual desires. The average interval is six years, but it may be considerably longer. Usually this lag occurs because society has provided no meaning for the term *homosexual* that meshes with the person's own experience. As one of Dank's subjects said, "I really didn't know what a homosexual was. In the back of my mind, my definition of a homosexual or queer was someone who wore girls' clothes and women's shoes, 'cause my brother said this was so, and I knew I wasn't" (p. 182). Consequently, some people may carry on homosexual relationships for years without admitting to themselves or oth-

Homosexual men and women who engage in public demonstrations are asserting the legitimacy of their gay identity and their claim to the full rights of citizenship.

ers that they are homosexuals. This stage is equivalent to the period of "dissociation and signification" referred to earlier (Troiden, 1987).

Generally, coming out takes place as a result of contact with admitted homosexuals. Gay bars, public toilets, and one-sex environments such as prisons, mental hospitals, the military, and some schools are frequent settings for this experience. Whatever the setting, the significant fact is that homosexuals encounter a concept of their homosexuality with which they can identify, unlike the highly negative concept usually instilled in them by straight society. For nearly all homosexuals this discovery comes as a great relief. As one of Dank's subjects described it,

I knew that there were homosexuals, queers, and what not; I had read some books, and I was resigned to the fact that I was a foul, dirty person, but I wasn't actually calling myself a homosexual yet. . . . The time I really caught myself coming out is the time I walked into this bar and saw a whole crowd of groovy, groovy guys. And I said to myself, there was the realization, that not all gay men are dirty old men or idiots, silly queens, but there are some just normal-looking and acting people, as far as I could see. I saw gay society and I said, "Wow, I'm home." (1971, p. 187)

In view of the increasingly free circulation of positive and objective information about homosexuality and the increasing visibility of the homosexual community, Dank hypothesized that more men would be able to identify themselves as homosexuals than in the past, and at an earlier age. This, in turn, would make it easier for homosexuality to be regarded as a way of life rather than as a crime or a mental illness, leading to greater integration of homosexuals into the general society. However, the trend toward increasing acceptance of homosexuality slowed in the mid-1980s as a result of widespread fear of AIDS. Homosexuals found that society at large became less receptive to attempts to protect them against discrimination, and incidents of violence against homosexual individuals became more frequent. Attitudes toward homosexuality in general became more negative. In addition, the AIDS crisis diverted the energy of the gay rights movement toward efforts to persuade the government to become more involved in research on AIDS and care of AIDS patients.

Polls taken during government debates over acceptance of homosexuals in the military show the nation to be rather evenly split on the issue. Further, slightly over 50 percent of Americans believe that homosexuality is a feature of one's identity that cannot be changed, while about 30 percent feel that it is a voluntary "lifestyle choice" (with the remainder "not sure"). Those who believe that homosexuality is not a choice or mere preference but a deep-seated sexual orientation tend to be far more tolerant of the civil rights of homosexuals than do those who believe that it is a voluntary choice (Schmalz, 1993).

Lesbianism

It is even harder to estimate the number of lesbians in the United States than it is to estimate the number of male homosexuals. Lesbians are less conspicuous; they are generally less publicly active and have fewer sex partners than do male homosexuals; they are less likely to "cruise" or to frequent bars; and they are less likely to be arrested. In addition, social norms make it easier to conceal female homosexuality. A single women who does not date men is usually assumed to be uninterested in or afraid of sex rather than being suspected of lesbianism. Also, it is considered more acceptable for women to share an apartment or to kiss or touch in public than it is for men (Goode & Troiden, 1974). Finally, laws against homosexuality usually are concerned primarily with the activities of males.

Although as individuals female homosexuals are as diverse as male homosexuals, there are some general differences between the ways in which males and females manage homosexuality. Many of these differences appear to arise from differences in socialization. Homosexuals, as much as heterosexuals, are affected by society's expectations about the kinds of behavior that are appropriate for members of each sex. Well before a girl begins to experience homosexual tendencies, she is absorbing society's assumptions about how females should act—for example, that they should be less aggressive than males and that sex is permissible only as part of a lasting emotional relationship. Moreover, sexual experience usually begins later for females than for males. A boy is likely to have sexual experience to the point of orgasm—usually through masturbation—relatively early in adolescence, whereas for a girl the corresponding experience is likely to occur in late adolescence or early adulthood (Arafat & Cotton, 1974). It is therefore likely that a girl will learn to think in terms of emotional attachment and permanent love relationships before she develops any strong sexual commitment; when that commitment appears, whether heterosexual or homosexual, it does so in the context of love. Thus, for most of the lesbians studied by Gagnon and Simon (1973), the first actual sexual experience came late, during an intense emotional involvement.

These differences in development and socialization underlie many of the subsequent differences in the behavior of male and female homosexuals. The lower level of sexual activity among lesbians, for example, parallels the behavior of women in general. Lesbians typically come out at a later age than male homosexuals. When a lesbian does come out, she usually looks for one partner and remains with her as long as the relationship is satisfying. When she lacks a partner, she is less likely than a male to look for one-night stands and hence spends less time in the gay bars and other gathering places that are so important to male homosexuals.

As in the case of male homosexuality, a special category of lesbianism is found in prisons. Many women who are in prison have experienced severe abuse by male partners or parents and feel angry and estranged from men. In prison they form friendships that may lead to sexual relations, a pattern that may endure later in life (Miller, 1986).

The Homosexual Subculture

When we speak of the homosexual subculture, we are referring to the visible institutions of the gay community. An undetermined proportion of homosexuals remain "in the closet"; that is, they do not participate openly in the life of the gay community. It is the declared homosexuals who create the gay subculture and have mobilized to bring about changes in laws and social norms that would create a more tolerant climate for all homosexuals.

The homosexual subculture may be found in most large cities in the United States, which have large homosexual populations in certain neighborhoods. The term *gay ghetto* is often used to define such an area. According to Levine (1979), a gay ghetto "must contain gay institutions in number, a conspicuous and locally dominant gay subculture that is socially isolated from the larger community, and a residential population that is substantially gay" (p. 185). Two of the largest gay ghettos are in Greenwich Village in New York City and the Castro Valley district in San Francisco. Gay institutions in these neighborhoods, which provide services and serve as meeting places for homosexuals, include certain parks, restrooms, movie theaters, public bathhouses, gyms, and bars. Cities with large gay populations also support businesses—restaurants, boutiques, barbershops, bookstores, travel agencies, and repair shops—that cater primarily to a gay clientele. Certain doctors, dentists, and lawyers also have largely gay clienteles. The growth of such businesses has fostered a sense of community among homosexuals. In New York and San Francisco, for example, it is possible for a homosexual to live, work, shop, and be entertained in a largely gay milieu.

Increasingly in the 1990s, as homosexuals have had to defend their identity in communities outside major metropolitan centers, they have had to demonstrate that

The AIDS quilt is a strategy designed to capture public attention and remind citizens that anyone can be afflicted by the disease.

they exist in significant numbers even outside the publicly known "gay ghettos." In 1993, for example, the arts commission of Cobb County, a suburb of Atlanta, Georgia, bowed to conservative pressure and declined to fund a theater group that had presented a play about AIDS that also dealt with homosexuality. The region's gay population, normally reluctant to call attention to itself, staged demonstrations to protest the decision. The purpose of such demonstrations is to show not only that homosexuals demand fair treatment but also that they are a subculture that is not isolated in a few major urban centers.

A major function of the homosexual subculture is to provide its members with a way of understanding and accepting their sexual orientation. This function is performed not only by gay bars and similar meeting places but also by some homosexual organizations. These groups work to abolish laws that discriminate against homosexuals and to persuade homosexuals themselves and society in general that there is nothing shameful or harmful about being homosexual. Since the advent of the AIDS epidemic they have also worked to propagate knowledge about "safe sex" and to lend support to those stricken by the disease.

The Impact of AIDS   The AIDS epidemic has had a profound effect on the homosexual subculture. As it became increasingly evident that the dreaded virus can be transmitted through sexual intercourse and that certain sexual activities, such as anal intercourse, are particularly risky, many gay men felt compelled to modify their lifestyle.

It has been argued that the risk of contracting AIDS would be eliminated if homosexuals would simply stick to one sexual partner. However, this notion ignores both medical and emotional realities (Altman, 1987). From a medical standpoint, many thousands of people have already been exposed to the HIV virus, with its long incubation period, so the chances are high that any given sex partner is already infected. From an emotional standpoint, it is often difficult to find the "right" partner, one who can satisfy both physical and emotional needs; this is true whether one is gay or straight. Nevertheless, homosexuals have come under a great deal of pressure to limit their sexual activity.

In the face of the tragedy of AIDS, large numbers of gay men have sought to establish monogamous relationships. They have not always succeeded, however, and the outcome for many has been "an increase in sexual misery and frustration" (Altman, 1987, p. 160). Others have become less interested in sex and have attempted to find other outlets for their feelings and desires. Still others have lent their support to the concept of "safe sex"; this approach to the AIDS crisis is discussed in the Social Policy section of the chapter.

Prostitution can be defined as sexual relations on a promiscuous and mercenary basis with no emotional attachment; prostitutes make a living by selling sexual favors to anyone who will pay for them. Although most prostitutes are female, there are also male prostitutes. Both groups cater to a male clientele.

Prostitution has existed since the dawn of history—it is sometimes referred to as the oldest profession—but its place in society and the prevailing attitudes toward it have varied. In early societies it was often associated with religious rituals. Occasionally secularized prostitution has been legitimatized (somewhat reluctantly), as it is today in some parts of Nevada. The usual rationale for this is the belief that no matter what society attempts to do about prostitution there will be prostitutes and men will patronize them, and therefore it is better to have the practice out in the open where it can be supervised to some extent. More often, especially during the past century, prostitution has been banned (with varying degrees of enforcement) and the female prostitute has been considered a fallen woman, degraded and disreputable.

Social-Scientific Perspectives on Prostitution

Early American sociologists tended to study prostitution in association with the disruption of family and community life brought about by immigration and rapid urbanization. For example, W. I. Thomas's (1923) pioneering study *The Unadjusted Girl* conceived of prostitution as an outcome of parental neglect combined with the need for young girls to adjust to a competitive social environment. In the 1940s and 1950s social scientists increasingly studied prostitution as a form of deviance from the dominant normative order. Sociologist Kingsley Davis, whose research we will consider in some detail shortly, suggested that prostitution exists because in many situations in which men need sexual release and women need money, prostitution may appear preferable to the more difficult seduction process.

More recent research takes the interactionist perspective. Jennifer James's (1977) research on prostitution in Seattle showed that over half of the women interviewed who were prostitutes at the time of the study had been raped or otherwise sexually abused before becoming prostitutes. This finding and others similar to it suggest that once women have been sexually abused, they are more likely to be labeled or to label themselves as morally degraded, and that this condition is a likely precursor to self-identification as a prostitute.

Functionalist research on prostitution tends to look at the roles, statuses, and types of conflict that are typical of the prostitute's world. For example, in her research on how prostitutes learn their trade in brothels, Barbara Heyl (1978) has shown that a madam who is talented as a trainer of prostitutes can establish a status for herself in "the life" (as the world of prostitution is called) in which she functions as a teacher. This research, along with that of Christina and Richard Milner (1973), describes the actions of prostitutes, madams, pimps, their customers ("tricks" or "Johns"), the police, and the courts as forming an interrelated set of social institutions that create "the life." These researchers tend to see prostitution as a social problem because of the degree of conflict it generates over such issues as the impact of prostitution on certain parts of cities, the use of scarce law enforcement and judicial resources to arrest and try prostitutes, and related problems stemming from prostitution.

Table 4–2 on page 108 presents various social-scientific perspectives on prostitution.

Norms of Prostitution

Prostitutes are not a homogeneous group. There are several fairly well-defined levels of prostitution, with typical differences in education, fees, methods of attracting customers, and types of customers served. Fees for services vary not only according

TABLE 4–2 SOCIAL-SCIENTIFIC PERSPECTIVES ON PROSTITUTION

PERSPECTIVE	REASONS FOR PROSTITUTION	WHY PROSTITUTION IS A SOCIAL PROBLEM
Functionalist	Exists because it is useful in societies as a way of coping with male sexuality.	Actually fills social needs, but is a problem because many segments of society see it as a threat.
Conflict	Exists because women are oppressed and poor women especially are attracted to "the life" as a means of survival.	Perpetuates or increases gender conflict and represents another form of exploitation.
Interactionist	Exists because once they become part of the prostitute subculture, women base their identity and social life on that subculture.	Prostitutes become stigmatized and cannot leave "the life" without great difficulty.

to the "class" of the prostitute but also according to the community or neighborhood in which the prostitution occurs, as well as other factors such as inflation.

The aristocrats among prostitutes are the call girls and call boys. They are the best educated, best dressed, and most attractive prostitutes, and they may work part time in modeling or the theater. This type of prostitute never solicits; clients come through personal references, and arrangements are usually made by telephone. The cost of the prostitute's services ranges from $200 to much more for an evening, which may include dinner at an expensive restaurant. The clients come from the upper-middle and upper classes. Often, as in the recent case of the prostitution business operated by Hollywood madam Heidi Fleis, the clients may be well known in their communities and hence also subject to blackmail and extortion. Both call boys and call girls consider themselves totally distinct from other prostitutes and in fact never refer to themselves as prostitutes.

Like call girls, female hustlers are attractive and place a high value on the status symbols, such as good clothes, that separate them from other types of prostitutes. Unlike call girls, however, hustlers solicit directly, working out of night clubs and bars. They are also paid less than call girls, receiving between $100 and $150 for "turning a trick." They may have several clients each night.

A house girl works in a brothel and is an employee of the madam who runs the house. She must accept any client the madam assigns to her and is allowed to keep half of the fee ($100–$200) for each trick.

Looked down upon somewhat by all other prostitutes is the streetwalker, who solicits customers wherever she can find them and charges about $20 a trick (typically fellatio). In small towns, under highly competitive conditions, or if she is desperate, a woman may charge less.

Prostitutes at these various levels have little to do with one another; they work in different places and attract different clients. The only movement between the groups is generally downward: When a call girl begins to lose her looks and is in less demand, she may be forced to solicit directly; hustlers and house girls may eventually be reduced to walking the streets. On the other hand, a sizable but undetermined proportion of prostitutes eventually leave "the life," establish themselves in legitimate careers, and have families.

There is a similar hierarchy among male prostitutes, although there are fewer types. The most visible male prostitute is the hustler. Typically he wears a "masculine" uniform—Levis, a leather jacket, and boots. To most of his clients, or "scores,"

Like most occupations, prostitution has various levels of prestige, with high-priced call girls at the top and the far more visible and lower-paid street prostitutes at the lower levels.

it is important to believe that the hustler is heterosexual—and in fact research has shown that the majority of hustlers are straight.

Researchers have found that sexual self-definition is extremely important to the male prostitute, whether he is a call boy, a hustler, a delinquent youth out to make a quick buck, or a "chicken" (child or teenage prostitute) (Benjamin & Masters, 1964; Elifson, Boles, & Sweat, 1993). Some male prostitutes have no difficulty accepting their homosexuality. But those to whom a heterosexual self-image is necessary follow a clearly defined set of rules to maintain that image. The first rule relates to motivation: The goal must be monetary; to seek sexual gratification would be to admit to homosexuality. The second rule relates to "masculinity": Although many male prostitutes, both straight and gay, will perform any sexual act for the right price, many straight hustlers set limits on what they will do with a client and perform only in the traditional masculine role.

Another form of prostitution occurs in massage parlors. In these establishments a man can pay not only to be stimulated to ejaculation (a procedure known as a local) but also to obtain more extensive sexual services. Velarde and Warwick (1973) studied owners, masseuses, and customers in a suburban West Coast community. Virtually all the workers were young and unskilled females who had taken the job to earn money. They had to become licensed masseuses first and were instructed in the local solicitation laws, which make it illegal for the worker to solicit. She had to become expert both in getting the customer to ask for her services and in detecting undercover police officers.

In the face of the AIDS epidemic, prostitutes are under a great deal of pressure from law enforcement authorities and public health officials to practice safe sex, which usually means use of condoms and avoidance of anal intercourse. Research indicates that prostitutes are increasingly insisting on the use of condoms but that they are often pressured by tricks who are unwilling to do so (Centers for Disease Control, 1989; Sterk, 1989).

Prostitution as Functional Deviance

A classic study of prostitution as an institution was conducted by Kingsley Davis in 1937. Davis related prostitution to several aspects of human physical nature and human society. First, unlike most female animals, which have well-defined periods of fertility that correspond to sexual responsiveness, human females can be sexually receptive at any time. Second, it takes a relatively long time to rear and socialize human young. Given these facts, Davis considered it imperative that human society control the sex drive and make it compatible with the nurturing of children; otherwise society could not perpetuate itself. As he put it, "Erotic gratification is made dependent on, and subservient to, certain cooperative performances inherently necessary to societal continuity" (1937, p. 746).

Most societies control the sex drive primarily through the family unit, making sexual gratification permissible chiefly within the family, in which the young are reared. Sexual expression that contributes to the family's existence or cohesion is approved and recommended; to the extent that it fails to do so, it is disapproved.

The mercenary and impersonal nature of prostitution, which makes it contrary to the stated values and norms of society, also makes it functional. Many people feel unable to satisfy their sexual needs within the family structure. Not only do unmarried men and widowers have no legally recognized outlet within this framework, but some married men want more (or more varied) sexual satisfaction than their wives can or want to supply. Others, such as members of the armed forces or salespeople whose work entails much traveling, may be absent from their families for extended periods. Such men may be unable or unwilling, because of possible complications, to have a permanent liaison with any one women, and a brief, impersonal, nonobligating relationship with a prostitute meets their immediate needs. There are those, too, who have a desire for unconventional forms of sexual activity that they hesitate to reveal to their wives or friends, or who suffer from physical deformities that lead them to suppose that they must buy sex. For such men, anonymity is highly valuable. A prostitute is quickly available; she is knowledgeable enough to provide a variety of sexual satisfactions; and when the business is done she can be paid and forgotten. Emotional complications and possible pregnancy are her concern, not the customer's.

The functionalist view does not imply that prostitution has no dysfunctional aspects. There is a good deal of suffering associated with prostitution, especially among women; they may suffer violence, sexually transmitted disease, and unwanted pregnancies, for example. But the fact that prostitution is so universal—it is found in cultures throughout the world—is a sign that it continues to serve a purpose or function in society. This may be seen in many African nations today. Many African males are migrant workers or cannot afford to marry and settle down; for them prostitution seems to serve a positive function. But the dysfunctions of prostitution surely outweigh its functions, since the spread of AIDS through the heterosexual population is associated with prostitution. For African societies in which AIDS is spreading rapidly, prostitution without safe sex measures is deadly and devastating.

Why Do People Become Prostitutes?

If society considers prostitution unacceptable and degrading, why do people become prostitutes? It is usually assumed that because of society's disapproval, asking why someone becomes a prostitute is different from asking why someone becomes a lawyer. Robert Bell (1971) has suggested, however, that the answers to the two questions may not be so different and that more attention should be paid to the answers prostitutes give when they are asked why they entered their line of work. If good pay and association with glamorous people are acceptable reasons for becoming an administrator, why should they not apply to becoming a prostitute? Kingsley Davis (1937) noted that one might legitimately ask why more people do *not* become prostitutes—why so many people stick to such tedious jobs as secretary or clerk when they could make more money in less time as prostitutes. Evidently society's norms against prostitution work very strongly for most women, just as norms against prostitution and homosexuality work very strongly for most men.

Some studies approach the question from a psychological perspective. They consider two things: the unique life history and psyche of an individual (to see what factors might predispose him or her to become a prostitute) and the psychological defenses or mechanisms the individual develops after becoming a prostitute to maintain an acceptable self-image.

Many investigators have related early sexual abuse to later prostitution. In studies of female prostitutes carried out during the 1970s, Jennifer James and Jane Meyerding (1977) found that a disproportionately high number of prostitutes had been raped as children. Fifty-seven percent of the prostitutes in their earlier study and 65 percent of those in their later study had been raped. In addition, many of the prostitutes in these sample populations (23 percent and 12 percent) had been sexually abused by their fathers. James and Meyerding concluded that although rape and incest cannot be viewed as the cause of female prostitution, they may play a part in its development. "To be used sexually at an early age in a way that produces guilt, shame, and loss of self-esteem on the part of the victim would be likely to lessen someone's resistance to viewing oneself as a saleable commodity" (1977, p. 41).

In a study of teenagers from low-income families in four American cities, Williams and Kornblum (1985) found that young women who live in communities characterized by severe poverty and the visible presence of prostitutes tend to regard part-time prostitution as a means of obtaining money for clothes and entertainment. In another study fifteen female prostitutes, all streetwalkers, were interviewed (Jackman, O'Toole, & Geis, 1963). The researchers identified certain common background characteristics: The women generally were alienated from their parents and usually had broken totally with their fathers, toward whom they expressed hostility. Before becoming prostitutes they had felt that they were isolated in an urban society, without any real friends. Similar findings were reported by Nanette Davis (1971) in another study of streetwalkers. Most of Davis's subjects had felt since early childhood that they were considered "bad," "slow," "troublemakers," or "different" by their families and teachers. Davis concluded that this early negative labeling contributed to the later emergence of an identity as a prostitute. Studies of male prostitutes have revealed similar characteristics—a high percentage of broken homes and a feeling of being either unwanted or misunderstood (Ginzburg, 1977).

Some of the conditions that can lead to prostitution are illustrated by the tragic case of Lisa McElhaney of Columbus, Ohio. Nicknamed "Red" for her auburn hair, Lisa was an unwanted child of a mentally ill mother and an alcoholic father. She grew up in poverty, was raped as a child, became pregnant and miscarried at 15, and was abandoned to the streets, where she drifted into a life of prostitution, drug addiction, and child pornography. Early in 1987 Red, who was not yet 16, was murdered by a 34-year-old truck driver with a record of attacking prostitutes.

Eleanor Miller (1986) has studied the recruitment of young women from black, Hispanic, and white families into a deviant lifestyle that includes prostitution. A factor that Miller identifies as particularly important for black women is a familial structure known as the *domestic network* (Stack, 1974). In such a network a number of households are linked together by ties based on kinship, pseudokinship, and reciprocal personal and economic obligations. Domestic networks evolve out of numerous intersecting attempts to achieve financial and emotional security; they have no obvious nucleus or defined boundary. For this reason, it is relatively easy to recruit younger members of the network to engage in various illegal activities. (Although parents and guardians usually disapprove of such behavior on the part of their children, other members of the network who may engage in such activities—for example, step-siblings, young aunts or uncles, or friends of these relatives—often have enough influence to counteract the parents' efforts.)

In the case of Hispanic women, Miller finds that the most frequent route to prostitution is membership in peer groups in which drug use is common. Prostitution serves as a means of obtaining the money to buy drugs. Running away from home—often to escape from an incestuous relationship—also frequently leads to prostitution, regardless of the young woman's race, ethnicity, or social class. Miller points out that these routes to prostitution are not mutually exclusive and in fact often overlap; however, a dominant influence can usually be identified.

It should be noted that there is no evidence for a causal link between drug abuse and prostitution. However, there is a high correlation between the two conditions. In one study, 87 percent of female and 65 percent of male prostitutes had used drugs other than alcohol and tobacco in the past year (Marshall & Handtlass, 1986). There is a strong tendency for street prostitutes to use illicit drugs more than other prostitutes, thereby conveying the impression of a causal relationship.

Becoming a Prostitute Nanette Davis (1971) interviewed thirty prostitutes in correctional institutions. She found that her subjects typically had progressed through three stages: casual promiscuity, a transitional phase, and full-fledged prostitution. Her findings led her to conclude that the crucial influences in this process are those that lead a woman to identify herself as a person who has departed from the values and norms of society and to organize her behavior accordingly.

The first stage in the process, a period of gradual drift from promiscuity to the first act of prostitution, might take several years but typically begins at an early age. Nineteen of Davis's subjects had had intercourse by age 13. The mean age for the first act of prostitution was 17.3, but the earliest age was 14. In the three cases in which sexual intercourse did not occur until age 17 or 18, the girls' families were very strict, with strong control and a rigid attitude toward sex; sexuality became an act of rebellion. But most of the subjects' families were highly permissive, exercising little or no supervision, and peer group norms favored early sexuality. As a result, both opportunities for and encouragement of promiscuity were present in the girls' social environment.

During adolescence and even earlier, most of the girls were already considered "bad" by their parents and others. In most cases their family life was unstable, and more than half the girls had spent part of their childhood separated from their families. Twenty-three had been sentenced to correctional institutions during adolescence for truancy, sexual delinquency, or other reasons. At the institutions they met more experienced inmates who made prostitution seem prestigious. Since the girls were usually confused about their own identities, they were glad to learn a new and attractive role.

The girls who were not institutionalized generally experienced peer pressure to engage in prostitution—"everybody's doing it." Some of the girls were encouraged by pimps, who provided clients and, apparently, the kind of secure relationship that the girls badly needed; this was the precipitating factor in their choice of prostitution as a career. The girls who came from overly strict families reacted by doing what their suspicious parents apparently believed they were already doing.

During the second stage, which Davis labeled "transitional deviance," the girl learns the skills of prostitution, engaging in prostitution on an occasional basis but not yet thinking of herself as a prostitute. She usually retains some commitments to the straight world—a job, marriage, and/or nonprostitute friends. Economic motivation becomes more important, together with loneliness or entrapment by the pimp.

Eventually this stage culminates in some situation, such as arrest, that forces the girl to perceive herself unequivocally as a prostitute.

Professionalization is the final stage. Labeled as a prostitute by society and perceiving herself as one, the girl makes sex her vocation and shapes her life around it. Most of Davis's subjects claimed that they would not want to go back to the "square" life, although some maintained that their prostitution was a transition to another career such as modeling or dancing. Only a few succeeded in maintaining a home with children, and they had to keep their "respectable" and "unrespectable" lives and associates strictly separate.

In sum, it appears that the low-status prostitute typically drifts into her profession through a combination of circumstances, social conditions, and internalization of the label of prostitute. Rarely has she set out deliberately, through free choice, to become a prostitute.

High-Status Prostitutes   The situation of the higher-status prostitute is somewhat different. Historical studies show that for well over a century most call girls have gotten their start as a result of personal contact with someone else in the field, by approaching a known call girl directly, or by associating with a pimp. Before going out on their own, most girls go through a period of training or apprenticeship that usually lasts two or three months. The training may be provided by the pimp or by an experienced call girl; in the latter case the trainee usually lives in the other call girl's apartment. During this time she is taught certain attitudes toward prostitution and toward her customers. For example, she is taught that males are exploitive and that it is right to exploit them in return. Such values create an *esprit de corps* among call girls, along with contempt for the rest of the world. The training also covers practical matters such as how to converse with a client or negotiate a fee. Very little is taught about sexual techniques. The chief function of the apprenticeship is to help the novice call girl develop a clientele. Once she has done so, she goes out on her own.

In contrast, in a study of the training of house girls Barbara Heyl (1978) found that the madam ("Ann") has two goals: to train the girls in sexual and hustling techniques so that they are ready to work in a house of prostitution, and to teach a set of work standards and practices. Clients are customers of the house, not of a particular girl.

Ann's training sessions for novice prostitutes include lectures, discussions, and role-playing activities such as "Learning the Hustling Rap." In these sessions, after essential sexual techniques and principles of physical and legal self-protection have been taught, certain codes of behavior are explained. These include rules designed to preserve a peaceful and profitable atmosphere (e.g., not talking in the lineup or giving clients free sexual favors); subtly aggressive hustling skills designed to get clients to spend as much money as possible; and the ethic of loyalty to the "racket world" and its values, as well as alienation from the "square world" that the prostitute must leave behind.

The Prostitute Subculture

Like members of other subcultures, prostitutes usually develop their own specialized knowledge, language, folklore, and network of relationships, in this case with other prostitutes, pimps, customers, and the police. Becoming a prostitute means more than selling sex for money; it means becoming part of a distinct, well-defined world.

A major part of the prostitute subculture involves the roles of those who participate in it. One important role, obviously, is that of the customer.* The prostitute

---

*An insightful and often amusing account of a sociologist's first visit to a brothel is provided in Steward, "On First Being a John" (1972).

learns to see the customer in strictly economic terms, as her source of income. This is facilitated by the attitude that the customer is basically corrupt—a belief that prostitutes adopt as a way of maintaining their self-image.

Another subculture figure who is important to many prostitutes is the pimp. A pimp lives off the earnings of one or more prostitutes and serves as manager, protector, and companion/lover. Virtually all streetwalkers have a pimp, who may be their husband or boyfriend and is usually referred to as "my man." Although in the past pimps often acquired customers for their girls, today their responsibilities are primarily financial, and they almost never appear on the street except to check up on their women.

A study by two anthropologists (Milner & Milner, 1973) found that part of the attraction of pimping is the pimp's delight in exercising total control over women, who, he believes, should be completely subservient to men. This feeling might have been enhanced by the fact that many of the pimps studied were black and many of their prostitutes were white. Another considerable attraction, of course, is the chance to make a great deal of money while doing virtually nothing. The study found that pimps put great value on material possessions, lavish parties, expensive jewelry and clothing, and an elegant life free from strain and drudgery.

Although pimps exploit their prostitutes, it is clear that the women derive something from the relationship. A streetwalker's status in the subculture is derived from that of her pimp—how good-looking and well dressed he is and whether he drives an expensive car. The pimp takes care of business matters—paying bills, arranging bail and lawyers' fees when necessary, and so on. Without a pimp, the streetwalker is an "outlaw" and is likely to be harassed or threatened with assault and robbery. The pimp also provides his prostitutes with a sense of family and a feeling of being taken care of. It has been pointed out that the relationship between a pimp and a prostitute is similar to the traditional husband–wife relationship, with the economic roles reversed. The prostitute makes money, and the pimp gives her a sense of security and family.

Miller (1986) describes the everyday life of street women as "characterized by alternating periods of hustling and partying; lying low, running, and furtive hustling; ill health or frequent court appearances and institutional confinement; and hustling as outlaw women, independent of street networks" (p. 139). During periods of "hustlin' and partyin'," street women feel a sense of "mastery, independence, individual accomplishment, and immediate reward" (p. 140). The fast life sometimes leads a woman to take exceptional risks, however, and she may find herself "runnin'" or "sittin'." Depending on the seriousness of the crime she has committed, she may run to another state, often accompanied by her man, or just lie low for a while. During such periods the woman may feel "victimized, hopeless, vulnerable, and disillusioned" (p. 142).

"Sittin'" refers to temporary withdrawal from street life because of ill health or incarceration and may have the effect of enlarging the woman's contacts with other members of the deviant network—including, sometimes, a new man. Finally, in some situations a street woman may attempt to hustle as an outlaw, that is, independently of a man. Periods of outlaw hustling tend to be short-lived, however, partly because "men" interfere and partly because the woman has difficulty reconciling solo street hustling with care of her children.

The Impact of AIDS

We noted in Chapter 2 that prostitution is one of the means by which AIDS has spread among the heterosexual population. A study commissioned by the Centers for Disease Control has found that about 40 percent of street prostitutes have been exposed to AIDS (usually because their lovers are intravenous drug users); in contrast, fewer than 20 percent of call girls are AIDS carriers (Sterk, 1989). Rates of infection for male prostitutes are lower than for female street prostitutes, but risks increase dramatically with age (Elifson, Boles, & Sweat, 1993; Elifson & Sterk-Elifson, 1992).

The presence of AIDS among prostitutes poses numerous problems both for the individual and for society. When a prostitute discovers that she has been infected by the HIV virus, she may be reluctant to seek medical and social assistance for fear of being arrested and imprisoned. Because she still needs to support herself, she may continue to hustle, thereby transmitting the virus to her customers. Although many prostitutes supply their clients with condoms, this practice is by no means universal and does not entirely eliminate the risk of transmission.

Part of the difficulty of limiting the spread of AIDS through prostitution stems from the attitudes of prostitutes and their customers. According to one streetwalker, "You can just as easy get it at home or on the streets. . . . There's no one-woman men or one-man women any more" (quoted in Winerip, 1988, p. B1). As for the customers, recent research indicates that there may be an increasing number of HIV-positive men who continue to frequent prostitutes, especially streetwalkers (Ayala, 1991).

PORNOGRAPHY

A third sex-related social problem is *pornography*, which may be defined as the depiction of sexual behavior in such a way as to excite the viewer sexually. Pornography has existed for centuries, but in recent decades it has come to be considered a social problem in many communities. The vast increase and unprecedented openness of its distribution, and its tendency to become concentrated in particular areas and thereby adversely affect whole neighborhoods, have caused serious disagreement both about what actually constitutes pornography and about the wisdom of permitting or suppressing it.

As was pointed out at the beginning of the chapter, sexual attitudes and behavior are learned. Among the things we learn is that anything "pornographic" is something other than an appropriate sex object that has the capacity to arouse us. This belief in the power of pornography is related to the view of sex as innate, overwhelming, and instinctual. Pornography is thought to be able to release the sexual beast in all of us (especially males) and to have "a magical capacity to push men into overt sexual action" (Gagnon & Simon, 1973, p. 261).

According to Gagnon and Simon (1973), pornography deals with illicit sex; it does not describe conventional sexual activity that occurs within a marital relationship: "The rule is: If the activity is conventional, the context is not (the relationship, the motives, etc.); if the context is conventional, the activity is not" (p. 263). It is this illicit emphasis that makes pornography controversial.

An aspect of pornography that almost everyone agrees is a serious social problem is the exploitation of children in the production of pornographic materials. There are no reliable estimates of how many children are affected by sexual abuse connected with the production of pornographic books and films, but even a casual inspection of the materials available in a large city's pornography market will convince the reader that children are being photographed and filmed in sexual acts that clearly constitute abusive behavior. Advocates of legalized pornography claim that they are being victimized by allusions to crimes that involve only a small portion of their industry, but in the public mind the exploitation of children is the most serious charge against the pornography industry (Sherman, 1980). Women who are active in antipornography campaigns argue that much commercial pornography expresses violence against their sex, but this argument has not had nearly as great an impact on the courts or the media as the issue of exploitation of children.

Pornography is often associated with central-city "combat zones," but as this photo shows, it can appear in rural settlements as well.

Social-Scientific Perspectives on Pornography

Social scientists generally find that pornography is a subjective matter—that it is often perceived as a social problem not only because it offends conventional sexual norms but also because it may have negative effects on neighborhoods in which it is sold. (As happens with many retail goods, the distributors of pornography and commercial sex tend to cluster in a market neighborhood. Such neighborhoods are often referred to as "combat zones" because of police officers' belief that they are dangerous areas.)

Conflict theorists are interested in pornography as an issue that reveals a great deal about changing moral values in the United States. The degree to which the law is used in instances in which the value issue is unclear is a primary concern:

> When law becomes a vehicle to enforce a particular moral philosophy, there is the continual danger of its abuse, since the law does not reflect a consensus as to the appropriate social policy for the society, but the power of a particular group engaged in status politics. (Rist, 1975, p. 12)

The functionalist perspective on pornography is illustrated by the research of William Kornblum, Charles Winick, and Terry Williams in New York City's West 42nd Street area (CUNY, 1978; Williams and Kornblum, 1994). Here the concentration of commercial sex establishments, adult bookstores, peep shows, topless bars, and adult movies creates a de facto (i.e., not legal but tolerated) combat zone. This sex neighborhood discourages the development of other businesses and forms of entertainment; from the perspective of those who wish to build up the city's economy, pornography is a form of urban blight.

Another perspective on pornography is that of feminists, who have organized to protest the distribution of pornographic materials in many cities. In New York City, a group called Woman Against Pornography has taken the lead in organizing demonstrations and other protests against the concentration of pornography in the Times Square area. Led by feminist writers like Susan Brownmiller, such groups assert that most pornography is aimed at a male audience that can only be negatively affected by the obvious violence directed against women in pornographic materials. According to feminists, pornography degrades and "objectifies" women; that is, women's bodies are treated as things rather than as parts of whole human beings. The feminist perspective generally does not seek to infringe on First Amendment rights; instead, its goal is to regulate the concentration of pornography outlets and to formulate advertising codes that protect the rights of people who do not want to see displays of pornography. In this regard the feminists are allied with many church and neighborhood groups in cities where combat zones exist.

Pornography and Censorship

Any discussion of pornography must take into account the issue of censorship and, in the United States, the rights guaranteed by the First Amendment. Today this is a particularly sensitive issue. Serious arguments both for and against the suppression of pornographic material can be made. The arguments against limiting pornography include the following:

1. Censorship is damaging to artistic and literary efforts, since experience has shown that works of sound artistic value are likely to be considered pornographic or obscene if they contain any explicit sexual material.
2. The vagueness of existing legal definitions of pornography gives too much latitude to judges and other authorities, enabling them to suppress material because they personally consider it offensive.
3. The reading or viewing of pornographic material is a private act that does no harm to society and therefore cannot legitimately be prohibited by society.
4. If pornography is freely available, sophisticated people with good judgment will soon become bored with it and turn to more worthwhile entertainment.

Those who argue against pornography claim that habitual exposure to pornographic materials is indeed harmful, particularly to young people and, therefore, to the society of which they are a part. They believe that when pornography becomes so widespread that people (presumably a majority) who want to avoid it find it extremely difficult to do so, it is legitimate for society to attempt to control it. This argument has prompted several attempts by the Supreme Court to define and control pornography. In 1976 the Court ruled that it is constitutional for municipalities to restrict the proliferation of pornographic theaters and bookstores through zoning regulations; such regulations must be based on "community standards" regarding what types of materials are considered obscene. In 1987, however, the Court ruled that judges and juries deciding whether sexually explicit material is legally obscene must assess the social value of the material from the standpoint of a "reasonable person."

Research on Pornography

Unfortunately for the objectivity of these arguments, until recently very little empirical research has been done on either the effects of pornography or the extent of exposure to it. A few studies have been carried out, notably in connection with the work of the U.S. Commission on Obscenity and Pornography, reported in 1970. On the basis of those studies, the commission concluded (though not unanimously) that no social or individual harm can be traced directly to exposure to pornographic material. For example, there is no connection between pornography and street crime (aggravated assault, forcible rape, mugging), although it is linked with organized crime. On the basis of these findings the commission recommended that most existing restrictions on pornography be relaxed. The rejection of the commission's findings and recommendations, both in the government and elsewhere, suggests the extent to which empirical study in this area must contend with deeply ingrained fears.

What exactly have studies of pornography revealed? For one thing, they have shown that some degree of exposure to pornographic material is quite common in our society and apparently has been for a long time. A study by Abelson and associates (1970), conducted under the auspices of the Commission on Obscenity, found that in a nationwide representative sample of 2,486 adults, 84 percent of the men and 69 percent of the women had been exposed to some kind of explicit sexual material. Other studies have yielded similar results. Younger adults and people with some college education are more likely than older adults and people with only a high school education to have encountered sexual materials. Among men, but not women, geographic location makes a difference: The greatest exposure occurs in large metropolitan areas in the Northeast; the least exposure occurs in the north central states.

The number of people who report extensive experience with erotic materials is relatively small. Of Abelson's subjects, only 14 percent of the men and 5 percent of the women reported having seen specific types of sexual pictures as often as five times in a two-year period. Because of the design of the study, it is likely that this figure is somewhat low; the commission concluded that probably "around one-fifth or one-quarter of the male population in the United States has somewhat regular experience with sexual materials as explicit as intercourse" (Commission on Obscenity and Pornography, 1970, p. 122), and a somewhat smaller number have regular experience with depictions of oral-genital or sadomasochistic activities.

How early does this exposure begin? In the study by Abelson and his colleagues (1970), 74 percent of the men and 51 percent of the women had encountered explicit sexual materials before age 21; 54 and 44 percent before age 18; and 30 and 17 percent before age 15. Other studies have tended to confirm this pattern. The findings suggest that early exposure is more common among young adults than among older people. However, the commission pointed out that this may not be a reliable difference, since older people often have trouble recalling the exact year when a given event took place.

Apparently neither adults nor teenagers generally see pornographic material in an "adult" bookstore. Most report having obtained the material through friends and having viewed it with them. Those who do patronize the bookstores are likely to be white middle-class males between the ages of 26 and 55 who are married and are shopping alone. The typical patron of sexual movies is similar, except that he may be somewhat more likely to attend with companions (Abelson et al., 1979; Finkelstein, 1970; Nawy, 1970; Winick, 1970).

Two relatively new technologies—videotape and disk—as well as private cable television systems have extended the consumption of explicitly sexual materials more widely than ever. The availability of such materials in the home has reduced the demand for many of the products and services provided in combat zones. According to Vernon Boggs, a sociologist who has conducted extensive research on the pornography establishments in the Times Square area of New York City, there has been a dramatic decline in the patronage of sex establishments there (cited in *The New York Times*, October 5, 1986). At the same time, as new forms of pornography become more accepted there is likely to be an increase in the demand for related items such as paraphernalia and live sex shows. In fact, pornography has been referred to as a "growth industry," with estimated revenues of $7 billion a year (Elshtain, 1984). One very controversial new market for pornography is developing through the 900 commercial telephone network. Millions of dollars for erotic phone calls are being billed over the private telephone network, but the local operating companies are under intense pressure to limit this business.

Why people want pornographic materials is an unresolved question. Many of the adult-movie patrons surveyed by Nawy (1970) said that such movies enable them to enhance their (largely heterosexual) sex life. Many others claimed that they simply enjoy the viewing. A large proportion of the subjects interviewed by Abelson and his co-workers (1970) said that pornographic material excites them sexually, provides entertainment and information, and in some cases improves their marital relations. These may be true effects of experience with pornography, or they may be rationalizations that enable people to justify such experience to themselves; the question remains open.

Pornography and Public Opinion

The public has a complex and seemingly contradictory view of pornography. According to surveys conducted from 1978 to 1986 (NORC, 1987), most Americans appreciate the role of pornography as an outlet for bottled-up sexual impulses. However, at the same time they fear that pornography may lead to rape and other crimes, even though the evidence does not prove anything of the sort. In a survey of the major studies of pornography and crime, W. Cody Wilson (1971) pointed out that most sex crime offenders had significantly less experience with pornographic materials, and later introduction to such materials, in their youth than the control groups. Less information is available about sex crimes among juveniles, but from 1960 to 1969, when sexual materials became far more widely available than they had been before, juvenile arrests for sex crimes decreased (Wilson, 1971).

In 1990 the issue of pornography, and especially of what constitutes child pornography, spread to the art world. The highly controversial photographs of Robert Mapplethorpe, a homosexual artist and photographer who died of AIDS in 1989, became the subject of a precedent-setting trial in Cincinnati. The director of the Cincinnati Contemporary Arts Center was accused of the crime of obscenity for including in the Mapplethorpe exhibit photographs that depicted homosexual sex and nude children. Actually, seven photographs out of a total of 175 drew the criminal charges against the director. The director was acquitted of all charges in an emotional trial that had far-reaching implications for social policy, but at this writing the controversy continues, with conservative critics like Sen. Jesse Helms of North Carolina arguing that taxpayers' money should not be used (through the National Endowment for the Arts and other public agencies) to support art that some people find obscene and offensive.

SOCIAL POLICY

Efforts to combat homosexuality, prostitution, and pornography often resemble what Joseph Gusfield (1963) terms *symbolic crusades*. Debates over whether these behaviors should be permitted become struggles for status among different subcultures in American society. Like the controversies over abortion and birth control, efforts to force legislators to permit or to ban these behaviors often serve the larger purposes of people involved in conservative, liberal, or feminist movements.

From a functionalist perspective these battles prove that there is a great deal of dissension about sex-related social problems. All the parties are attempting to influence government to intervene because the norms and institutions that formerly controlled these behaviors have broken down. Interactionists argue, however, that each side is struggling to define the situation—that is, to have its version of reality become the dominant one, which in turn will lead to social policies that are favorable to its position. Conflict theorists argue that the struggles are inevitable, since the various parties hold irreconcilable views. In recent years these debates have intensified as a result of the AIDS epidemic, focusing on issues of sexual morality and practical questions such as contact notification. (See Chapter 2.) Nevertheless, to a large extent they remain symbolic crusades with little promise of resolution.

Homosexuality

The furor during the first year of the Clinton administration over acceptance of avowed homosexuals in the armed forces shows how divided the society is on this issue. The administration succeeded in bringing about a compromise in which military officials will not ask recruits about their sexual orientation, nor will recruits announce their orientation. Nevertheless, homosexuality remains a controversial issue. Despite much more open discussion of homosexuality in recent years, society has continued to repress it through laws and employment practices. In many states homosexual behavior is illegal both in public and in private; in some, penalties range from ten years to life imprisonment. Only one state—Wisconsin—has enacted a gay rights law, although the cities of San Francisco and New York have enacted guarantees of gay rights.

Laws like those just mentioned have come under attack as violating constitutional rights and attempting to legislate private morality. Those who support such laws usually argue that they are necessary to protect young boys from seduction. They believe that legalizing homosexual behavior will encourage more people to become homosexual. Against this view must be set the loss suffered by society when homosexuals are legally or informally prevented from pursuing certain careers because of their sexual preference, together with the cost of the suffering imposed on them and their families by society's rejection of them.

A 1976 decision by the United States Supreme Court in effect held that states may prosecute and imprison people who commit private homosexual acts, even when both parties are consenting adults. Although the Court's ruling did not require states to enact or reinstate sodomy prohibitions, the decision reduced the pressure on states to repeal such laws and slowed the movement for homosexual rights in employment, housing, and other areas. (See Box 4–1.)

Some careers, notably in medicine, law, teaching, and the military, have been virtually out of the question for acknowledged homosexuals, although medical and law schools now accept homosexual applicants. People who are discovered to be homosexual or to participate in homosexual acts are separated from the armed forces, usually with an "undesirable" discharge, which does not entitle them to certain benefits and may deter potential employers from hiring them. Moreover, homosexuals often have difficulty obtaining insurance because they are considered insurance risks; they also can be evicted from privately owned housing and usually are unable to obtain security clearances in either government or industry (for fear of blackmail).

Nowhere is homosexuality itself a crime; only certain acts, usually referred to as sodomy and including both oral-genital and anal-genital contact, are defined as crimes. These laws have been invoked primarily against male homosexuals. In 1973 the American Bar Association called for the repeal of all state laws defining any form

---

BOX 4–1   CURRENT CONTROVERSIES: HOMOSEXUALITY AND CHILD CUSTODY

In 1993, in an immensely controversial decision, a state court in Virginia ruled that a two-year-old boy must be removed from the custody of his mother, a lesbian, and given to his grandmother for rearing. "The mother's conduct is illegal and immoral and renders her an unfit parent," the judge stated. The ruling was based on an earlier decision by the Virginia Supreme Court holding that a parent's homosexuality is a legitimate reason for losing custody of a child, but other issues were involved as well. Among these were the child's best interests and the rights of parents, whether gay or straight.

The charges in the case were originally brought by the grandmother, who believed that the behavior of her daughter was damaging the health of the child. The authorities could intervene because in Virginia, as in about half of the states, oral sex between adults is a punishable offense. The grandmother also believed that the child would be emotionally confused throughout his life by the relationship between his mother and her female companion, whom he occasionally referred to as "Da Da."

Conservative groups were immensely pleased by the decision, believing it to be "fully in keeping with the historical norms and laws and mores of Western civilization" (quoted in Ayres, 1993, p. A16). Gay rights advocates were outraged, however, claiming that the ruling violated the right of any parent, gay or straight, to raise his or her child. They pointed out that there was no evidence that the mother's lesbian relationship was having a detrimental effect on her child. Moreover, there is no reputable study showing that children raised by homosexual parents are more likely to become homosexuals themselves than children raised by heterosexual parents.

There have been several cases in which a heterosexual parent, after divorce from a homosexual partner, sued for custody of a child; those cases have been decided in various ways. The ruling just described was overturned by the Virginia Court of Appeals, providing further evidence that the law in this area is in considerable flux. Nevertheless, it seems clear that despite some progress on issues such as acceptance of homosexuals in the military, there remain major areas of conflict over the right of gay people to live their lives as they wish.

of private noncommercial sex between consenting adults as criminal (Stencel, 1974). Peter Fisher (1972) has pointed out that only a few nations (including Russia, China, and Cuba as well as the United States) punish homosexuals. He also notes that numerous Western nations, including Mexico, Switzerland, Great Britain, Canada, and all other countries whose legal systems are based on the Napoleonic Code, do not consider homosexual acts a crime, nor do they include private homosexual acts between consenting adults in their penal codes.

There is some danger that the increasingly negative attitudes toward homosexuals that have resulted from the AIDS epidemic will create a backlash in the form of more restrictive policies. Conservative groups such as Moral Majority have campaigned against greater social tolerance in sexual matters and demanded action against homosexual carriers of AIDS; some have even called for the incarceration of homosexuals "until and unless they can be cleansed of their medical problems" (quoted in *The New York Times*, August 7, 1983). The Catholic Church and the Church of Latter Day Saints (Mormons) have also affirmed their strong stance against homosexuality, the former despite forceful protests by gay Catholics.

In the opinion of most gay social scientists, the only effective way to limit the spread of AIDS is through public education aimed at reducing high-risk sex, that is, through "safe sex" campaigns. This approach runs the risk of creating even more negative attitudes toward homosexuals by publicizing their sexual activities and appearing to condemn them. Some communities and gay organizations have managed to publish guidelines for less risky sex without being either moralistic or judgmental. In contrast, governments at all levels have been unwilling to become involved in education about high-risk sex (Altman, 1987).

Even with the continuing menace of AIDS, this reluctance to take a firm stand continues. In 1990 New York City Schools Chancellor Joseph Fernandez ordered secondary school administrators to prepare to dispense condoms to high school students. This policy and his avowed tolerance for homosexual themes in the school curriculum led to his dismissal in 1993. While public service announcements about safe sex and condom use are more visible and widespread each year, the United States continues to lag far behind other affluent and highly literate societies in its acceptance of sex education and explicit discussion of AIDS and related problems (Bennett et al., 1993).

One problem with "safe sex" campaigns is that to be effective they must reach a broader audience than the gay community; however, efforts to educate the general public about certain sexual behaviors tend to elicit angry reactions. There is also the danger that education will lead to control—that is, that demands for the dissemination of information will lead to demands for the enforcement of certain standards (as in San Francisco's decision to close gay bathhouses). Finally, it must be recognized that "safe sex," even when it is equated with the correct use of condoms, does not guarantee safety. In the words of one commentator, "The only foolproof way to avoid contracting the AIDS virus through sex is not to have sex" (Wofsy, 1987, p. 7). With the Catholic hierarchy and many other church organizations opposed to measures that seem to encourage extramarital sex, this admonishment takes on a far more political meaning than its author intended.

Prostitution

Prostitution is illegal everywhere in the United States except in some counties of Nevada. Although there is little pressure on other states to follow Nevada's example, many arguments have been offered in support of legalization. It is claimed that prostitution will continue to exist regardless of the law and that recognizing this fact will bring many benefits: Legalization would make prostitutes' incomes taxable; it could eliminate or reduce the frequent connection of prostitution with crime and governmental corruption; and health regulations for prostitutes could be enacted and enforced, reducing the incidence of venereal disease. It has been suggested that legalization of brothels would result in a reduction of streetwalking and public solicitation, which disturb residents of the neighborhoods where they occur.

Many advocates of legalization point to class differences in the enforcement of the laws. Unless they are very indiscreet, call girls and their upper-middle-class customers are seldom targets of police action. It is the lower-class prostitutes, with their lower-class customers, who bear the brunt of antisolicitation laws.

It has also been pointed out that prostitution is usually a victimless crime, since the customer participates willingly and generally has few complaints. Because most laws against prostitution and solicitation require specific evidence of an offer to exchange sexual favors for money, a major means of curbing prostitution is entrapment by plainclothes officers posing as customers. This method is objected to as unjust in that it singles out only one partner in the crime; if a prostitute commits a crime, so does her customer. A few states and cities now have laws stating that a man can be jailed for as much a year and fined up to $1,000 for offering to pay for sexual services.

Entrapment of participants of either sex is protested by civil libertarians, who argue that it is a violation of the right to privacy. They favor legalization on the ground that sex for a fee is a private matter between consenting adults. Supporters of legalization argue that it is harmful to the social order to have laws on the books that are routinely flouted; since laws against prostitution are not enforced effectively, it would be better not to have them at all.

Still another reason why it might be worthwhile to legalize prostitution is that prostitutes would no longer be labeled as lawbreakers. This change in status might go a long way toward reducing the tension and stress experienced by most prostitutes. Legally at least, they would no longer have to define themselves negatively; moreover, they would no longer be constantly in fear of arrest, even though by other norms prostitution would still be regarded as a social problem.

Some experts, such as criminologist James Q. Wilson and urban sociologist Vernon Boggs, continue to argue against legalization. They believe that society is the ultimate victim of prostitution and that legalization would not necessarily remove the prostitute from exploitation by pimps or organized crime figures. Moreover, it might encourage more young women to enter "the life." They therefore question whether any benefits would acrrue from legalization.

Pornography

As noted earlier, the market for pornography is growing rapidly among members of both sexes. Cable television, TV recordings, and the ease of videotaping are making adult films featuring explicit sex available to a wider audience than ever before. At the same time, there is continued pressure for stricter laws against pornography.

Insofar as the case for suppression of pornography rests on the supposed relationship between pornography and crime, it lacks a firm foundation. But a number of thoughtful writers wonder whether pornography, or at least the wide and open dissemination of it, may result in more subtle forms of harm. For example, sociologist Edwin M. Schur believes that most pornography is protected by the First Amendment but warns that this does not mean we should take a positive attitude toward the material itself. Pornography, he argues, "may not only signal but also strengthen some socially unhealthy aspects of how we think about sex. This use of objectifying imagery reinforces the devaluation of women in our society. It encourages heterosexual males to associate sexual excitement with such devaluation." He believes that use of pornography by homosexuals also has the effect of devaluing intimacy and highly personal sexual responses. "Surely," he continues,

> there is something wrong when sexual excitement, or the most enjoyable sexual climax, requires images of rape, bondage, violent assault, or humiliation. Nor is its dependence even on imagery of unrealistic sexual icons [e.g., enormous genitals and breasts] a sign of personal or social health. (1988, pp. 126–127)

It is foolish to claim that frequent exposure to pornography will have no effect on a person's tastes and outlook. This would be equivalent to saying that no experience or encounter affects human development—that no learning is possible. The question, then, is whether pornography has harmful effects—whether society has a legitimate interest in preventing people from being exposed to it.

Several counterarguments support the unhindered distribution of pornography. First, as already indicated, it is impossible to prove that pornography has a negative social impact. The danger of censorship, however, is clear and real; therefore, the burden of proof should be on those who wish to censor pornography. They should be required to demonstrate conclusively that it has a significant negative impact. Second, censorship of sexually explicit materials has sometimes led to censorship of great literature and art. Today we laugh at the idea of adding fig leaves to nude Greek and Roman statues or shadows to Breughel's paintings, yet in some parts of the United States books are routinely banned for being too sexually explicit. Sexually explicit films, whatever their merit, are rated with an *X*, a symbol with strong negative connotations. Censorship directed at works of art may also lead to censorship of unpopular ideas, thereby threatening the foundations of democracy.

In the late 1980s public policy regarding pornography focused on law enforcement efforts. In 1986 a federal advisory commission, the Attorney General's Commission on Pornography, called for a national assault on the pornography industry through a combination of more vigorous law enforcement and increased vigilance by citizens' groups. Stating that intensified enforcement should focus on child pornography and materials showing sexual violence, the commission recommended that "knowing possession of child pornography" should be made a felony under state law. In 1990 the Supreme Court ruled that sale or possession of what a local court deems to be child pornography can be declared illegal in that community or jurisdiction. In its majority opinion the Court held that the states are justified in passing such laws in order to "destroy a market for the exploitative use of children" and to protect the victims of child pornography.

Law enforcement officials have long maintained that the pornography industry has links to organized crime, and the commission arrived at the same conclusion: "Significant portions of the pornographic magazine industry, the peep show industry, and the pornographic film industry are either directly operated or closely controlled by [organized crime] members or very close associates" (Attorney General's Commission on Pornography, 1986). Accordingly, in 1988 the Justice Department began seeking racketeering indictments against major distributors of pornographic materials.

In 1987 a controversy erupted over the ethics of a "sting" operation conducted by the U. S. Department of Justice. The department mailed samples of child pornography to individuals who had previously subscribed to pornographic mailing lists. The recipients were surveyed regarding their interest in the illegal production of child pornography, and over 100 individuals were subsequently indicted on charges of child sexual abuse. The issue in this instance is whether a government agency has the right to entice potential or actual child sex abusers in order to remove them from society.

In recent years community groups have focused on the tendency of pornography and other adult sex establishments to concentrate in older central-city areas. The Supreme Court's decision in *Roth* v. *United States* (1975) called for the application of "community standards" to this market, and city zoning laws permit restrictions on the concentration of businesses in certain areas. In combination, these standards and restrictions make possible two strategies for dealing with a pornography and vice district. One of these has been applied in Boston, where a small area was declared the only place in the city where such establishments would be permitted. This policy created one of the few de jure pornography and live-sex districts in an American city. Before redevelopment and new building drove the pornography business out, the area had become identified as a dangerous one, to the detriment of other forms of entertainment, such as theaters, that may also cluster there.

The second strategy was applied in Detroit in the early 1970s. A city ordinance requires that pornography and adult sex establishments be at least half a mile apart. This "dispersal" strategy may prevent the emergence of a garish sex district, but it suburbanizes the combat zone by creating an incentive for such establishments to cluster just beyond the city line (CUNY, 1978; Shlay & Rossi, 1981).

In the 1980s, at the urging of feminists and others, lawmakers in Minneapolis and Indianapolis passed far more stringent measures designed to ban the sale of all types of pornography. Judges in both states found these measures to be an unconstitutional violation of freedom of speech. In the Indiana case, federal judge Sarah Evans Barker refused to overturn a lower-court ruling against the ban and wrote that "to deny free speech, in order to engineer social change in the name of accomplishing a greater good for one sector of our society, erodes the freedoms of all and as such threatens tyranny and injustice for those subjected to the rule of such law" (quoted in Schur, 1988, p. 133). This opinion was upheld on appeal, and the Supreme Court continues to apply this reasoning in all its deliberations on pornography.

The problem of pornography, in sum, is a complex one that involves not only issues of morality and freedom of speech but also such questions as how to prevent further deterioration of the quality of life in American cities. And it is no closer to a solution today than it has been at any time in the past twenty years. As is so often true in the formulation of policy on social problems, there is a need for more research, not only on the consumption and effects of pornographic materials but on sexual behavior in general. The need for further research on sexuality becomes especially urgent as society struggles to combat the AIDS epidemic.

SUMMARY

1. Social problems related to sex arise largely from changes and conflicts in attitudes toward human sexuality. Such problems are basically deviations from widely held norms of a particular society. In the United States there is a striking lack of "sexual literacy," which is itself a social problem because it prevents citizens from engaging in healthy and responsible sexual behavior.

2. Sex-related social problems may be grouped into three categories: tolerated sex variance (masturbation, premarital intercourse, etc.), asocial sex variance (incest, child molestation, etc.), and structured sex variance (homosexuality, prostitution, and pornography).

3. Homosexuality is a sexual preference for members of one's own sex. Sociologists have viewed homosexuality as a product of social disorganization, as an illness with physiological or psychological causes, as a product of societal labeling, and as a set of institutions in conflict with the institutions of "straight" society.

4. It is not known what causes people to become homosexual. An important factor may be the social environment in which a person grows up. Recent research has emphasized the importance of the labeling of the individual as homosexual.

5. Homosexuals differ greatly in the ways in which they satisfy their sexual desires and cope with the attendant problems, in their willingness to "come out," in their ties to the straight world, and in their marital status.

6. Lesbians are less conspicuous than male homosexuals and find it easier to conceal their sexual preference. They are more likely to view their relationships in terms of emotional attachment and tend to come out at a later age than male homosexuals.

7. Gay institutions and businesses are concentrated in areas with a large homosexual population. These provide homosexuals with the means of understanding and accepting their sexual orientation.

8. The AIDS epidemic has had a profound effect on the homosexual subculture. Homosexuals have come under a great deal of pressure to limit their sexual activity and to establish monogamous relationships.

9. Prostitution is defined as sexual relations on a promiscuous and mercenary basis with no emotional attachment. In the past century prostitution has generally been banned in the United States. There are several fairly well-defined types of prostitution, ranging from expensive call girls to streetwalkers who solicit customers wherever they can find them.

10. Psychological studies of the reasons that people become prostitutes focus on the individual's life history and psyche. Many investigators relate early sexual abuse to later prostitution. People who become prostitutes often come from broken homes and feel that they were unwanted or misunderstood as children.

11. Women who become prostitutes typically progress through three stages: casual promiscuity, transitional deviance, and professionalization. High-status prostitutes are trained by pimps or experienced call girls, whereas house girls are trained by madams.

12. Prostitutes have a subculture with its own language, folklore, and network of relationships. An important figure in this subculture is the pimp, who lives off the earnings of one or more prostitutes and serves as manager, protector, and lover.

13. Prostitution is one of the means by which AIDS has spread among the heterosexual population. Infected prostitutes may continue to seek clients because they need to support themselves. Prostitutes are under a great deal of pressure to practice safe sex, but tricks are often unwilling to do so.

14. Pornography may be defined as the depiction of sexual acts in such a way as to excite the viewer sexually. It is often perceived as a social problem not only because it offends conventional norms but also because it may have negative effects on neighborhoods in which it is sold.

15. A major issue in connection with pornography is censorship. It is argued that censorship of pornography is damaging to artistic and literary efforts and that vague legal definitions give too much latitude to judges. Recent trials on charges of obscenity have shown that juries of conservative citizens are able to apply "community standards" in determining whether material that is sexually disturbing nevertheless has artistic merit.

16. Research has shown that exposure to pornography is common in American society, often beginning at an early age, and that no social or individual harm can be traced directly to pornographic materials.

17. Public policy regarding sex-related social problems remains generally restrictive. Although attitudes toward homosexuality have become more accepting, there is some danger of a "backlash" as a result of widespread fear of AIDS, leading to more restrictive policies in some areas. Prostitution is illegal almost everywhere in the United States, although there are many advocates of legalization. With respect to pornography, policy has focused on efforts to prevent the exploitation of children in the creation of such materials.

SUGGESTED READINGS

BELL, ALLEN P., AND MARTIN S. WEINBERG. *Homosexualities: A Study of Diversity Among Men and Women.* New York: Simon & Schuster, 1978. A comprehensive study of the diversity of homosexual lifestyles.

BULLOUGH, VERN L., AND BONNIE BULLOUGH. *Sin, Sickness, and Sanity: A History of Sexual Attitudes.* New York: Garland, 1977. An attempt to show the extent to which many sexual attitudes and values are rooted in historical meanings and conditions.

ETTORRE, E. M. *Lesbians, Women and Society.* Boston: Routledge & Kegan Paul, 1980. An account of how lesbians live and a discussion of the implications of homosexuality for the status of women.

MILLER, ELEANOR. *Street Woman.* Philadelphia: Temple University Press, 1986. A study of the world of street prostitutes and their involvement in drug use and crime.

MORLEY, JOHN DAVID. *Pictures from the Water Trade.* New York: Harper & Row, 1986. A fascinating journey through the world of Japanese sexual deviance and the pleasure underground known in Japanese as *mizu-shobai,* the water trade.

NASS, GILBERT D., ROGER W. LIBBY, AND MARY PAT FISHER. *Sexual Choices: An Introduction to Human Sexuality.* Monterey, CA: Wadsworth, 1981. A positive treatment of sexuality that explores "sexual scripts" and "sexual careers" and covers "minority" points of view.

PLUMMER, KENNETH, ED. *The Making of the Modern Homosexual.* Totowa, NJ: Barnes & Noble, 1981. An examination of the ways in which changes in the nature of homosexuality are tied to changes in the wider society, beginning with the eighteenth century and continuing to the present.

RIST, RAY C., ED. *The Pornography Controversy: Changing Moral Standards in American Life.* New Brunswick, NJ: Transaction Books, 1975. A comprehensive set of readings dealing with the legal, sociological, and cultural aspects of pornography.

SCHUR, EDWIN M. *The Americanization of Sex.* Philadelphia: Temple University Press, 1988. An excellent overview of sexuality and the problems associated with it in American society.

SHERMAN, WILLIAM. *Times Square.* New York: Bantam Books, 1980. A firsthand account by a Pulitzer Prize–winning journalist of the pornography scene in New York's Times Square and the sad fate of a police officer who attempts to crusade against the industry.

Alcohol and Other Drugs

Chapter Outline

■ Surveys of American adults find that drinkers outnumber abstainers by three to one.

■ Heavy drinking among men is most common between the ages of 21 and 30; among women it occurs most frequently between the ages of 31 and 50.

■ In 1990 there were 23,351 traffic fatalities in which the driver was legally drunk.

■ The use of illicit drugs other than crack cocaine either remained stable or declined between 1982 and 1992.

■ Nicotine causes the deaths of some 360,000 Americans each year.

Ours is a drug-using society—we use drugs to ease pain, increase alertness, relax tension, lose weight, gain strength, fight depression, and prevent pregnancy. Americans of all ages and at all socioeconomic levels consume vast quantities of chemical substances every year. Most of these drugs are socially acceptable, and most people use them for socially acceptable purposes. Alcohol is a drug, as are caffeine and nicotine; these are commonly and widely used as aids to sociability and ordinary activity. But some drugs, and some users of other drugs, are socially defined as unacceptable, and it is these drugs and users that constitute the "drug problem."

The uses and abuses of alcohol and other drugs are discussed together in this chapter for a number of reasons. For one thing, through its personal and social effects alcohol abuse is at least as harmful as the abuse of less socially accepted drugs. Moreover, many drugs, including alcohol, offer satisfactions that make them attractive to many people, but they can be habit forming, sometimes with destructive consequences to users as well as to nonusers, and there are controversies over the causes, consequences, and moral implications of their use.

The rationale for the acceptability of any drug is highly subjective. Frequently a drug that is favored by the dominant culture is approved while one that is associated with a subculture is outlawed. Frederick H. Meyers (1970) pointed out that

> the effects of marijuana, both operationally and in its mechanism of action, correspond . . . to those of other sedatives and anesthetics, especially alcohol. . . . One is driven to the conclusion that the differences between the dominant attitudes and consequent laws toward marijuana and alcohol are unrelated to the pharmacological effects of the drugs but are due to a conflict between the mores of the dominant culture and one or more of the subcultures of the country. (p. 39)

Surveys of American adults find that drinkers outnumber abstainers by three to one, and over 30 percent of Americans admit that they sometimes drink more than they should. Yet the same surveys find that a large majority believe that more should be done to combat the use of drugs other than alcohol.

Other observers have noted that increased drug use in the 1960s and 1970s coincided with a period of social and political ferment that was especially prevalent among young people. Increasingly, adults in the dominant culture viewed young people as a separate cultural subgroup; and while alcohol use was interpreted as "part of growing up, as an act of socialization," some drug use was viewed as "growing away" rather than growing up (Gusfield, 1975, p. 9).

It should be kept in mind, however, that no matter what society thinks about certain drugs, many drugs are dangerous to the user when consumed in steady doses over time. In addition, many drugs (especially alcohol, the opiates, and cocaine) are associated with antisocial behaviors. Thus, illness, crime, and interpersonal violence are significant aspects of the social problem of alcohol and drug abuse that must be dealt with regardless of how any particular drug is viewed at any given time.

THE NATURE OF THE PROBLEM

From a pharmacological viewpoint, a *drug* is any substance, other than food, that chemically alters the structure or function of a living organism. So inclusive a definition, however, encompasses everything from vitamins and hormones to laxatives, snake and mosquito venom, antiperspirants, insecticides, and air pollutants. Obviously, this definition is too broad to be of practical value. Definitions that depend on context are more useful. In a medical context, for example, a drug may be any substance that is prescribed by a physician or manufactured expressly to relieve pain or to treat and prevent disease. In a sociological context, the term *drug* denotes any habit-forming substance that directly affects the brain or nervous system. More precisely, it refers to any chemical substance that affects physiological functions, mood, perception, or consciousness; has the potential for misuse; and may be harmful to the user or to society. In addition to the illicit drugs that attract so much attention, many pharmaceutical drugs are abused as narcotics.

Although the last definition is more satisfactory for our purposes than the original, much broader one, it omits the social bias that has traditionally determined what substances are labeled as drugs. When the members of a society have used a habit-forming substance for centuries, that substance may not be classified as a drug in that society even if it has been proven to be harmful. Alcohol and tobacco (nicotine) are examples of such substances.

Drug Abuse

We can define *drug abuse* as the use of unacceptable drugs and/or the excessive or inappropriate use of acceptable drugs in ways that can lead to physical, psychological, or social harm. (See the discussion of drug dependence later in this section.) Using this definition, there can be little question that the abuse of both legal and illegal drugs is a social problem.

Like so many other social problems, the issue of drug use has both objective and subjective dimensions. The objective aspect of drug use is the degree to which a given substance causes physiological, psychological, or social problems for the individual or the social group—the family, the community, or the entire society. The subjective aspect is how people perceive the consequences of drug use and how their perceptions result in social action with regard to drug use (norms, policies, laws, programs, etc.). Of course, these subjective perceptions may be based on objective evidence, but very often perceptions are based on past practices and combinations of scientific and folk wisdom about a given substance. Aspirin, for example, is one of the most widely used drugs in America. From an objective standpoint we know that aspirin is often taken in excessive dosages for every real or imagined physical or mental discomfort. Aspirin can cause ulcers, gastrointestinal bleeding, and other ailments. But most Americans believe—this is the subjective aspect—that aspirin is a harmless drug that is dangerous only when taken in massive doses. Thus, aspirin use is part of our overall drug problem in objective terms but not in subjective terms. For many Americans, the same failure to allow objective facts to shape subjective perceptions is true in the case of alcohol, as we will see presently.

Other drugs are part of the social problem of drug use because they are perceived as problems even if the way they are used by certain people is not problematic in objective terms. Marijuana use is an example. Objectively, there is little evidence that marijuana users damage themselves psychologically or physiologically, although researchers believe that marijuana may decrease the user's motivation to concentrate and learn complex material. Yet the subjective view of many Americans, expecially those in policy-making positions, is that marijuana is a dangerous drug. This subjective viewpoint is incorporated in laws against marijuana use, and these laws, in turn, foster the illegal traffic in marijuana (Van Dyke & Byck, 1982).

The discrepancy between the subjective viewpoint and objective reality comes to prominence quite often in American political affairs. In 1987, for example, President Reagan was forced to withdraw the nomination of Judge Douglas H. Ginsburg to the Supreme Court because of the publicity surrounding Ginsburg's admission that he had smoked marijuana in the past. In 1992, candidate Bill Clinton's admission that he had tried marijuana as a student, but had not inhaled, became the subject of innumerable jokes during the presidential election campaign. In the meantime, thousands of Americans are in prison for possession of marijuana. Facing a backlash from an important segment of voters, only the bravest or most secure legislators would seriously consider supporting a bill to legalize or decriminalize the substance (Skolnick, 1992).

Other examples of this type of discrepancy could be added. The point is that drugs such as marijuana are treated as social problems within our society's dominant system of norms and institutions. Other drugs, such as alcohol and nicotine, are much less sharply defined as problems even though in objective terms their harmful consequences have been fully documented. In the past fifteen or twenty years, as the harmful effects of smoking tobacco and heavy consumption of alcohol have been documented and have become a target of policies aimed at prevention and control, these behaviors have also begun to be defined as social problems. Nevertheless, these substances remain legal and continue to be sanctioned in many social settings.

Abuse, Addiction, and Dependence

The difficulty of separating the subjective and objective dimensions of drug use causes a great many problems of definition for experts in the field. The term *drug abuse* is widely used to refer to the objectively harmful consumption of drugs that are subjectively approved of, such as alcohol and tranquilizers. The term also refers to the use—in any amount—of drugs that are subjectively disapproved of, such as cocaine and marijuana, even if the objective facts regarding their effects in certain dosages do not indicate that they are harmful. Of course, almost all strongly addicting drugs, such as heroin, are harmful both to the user and to society at any level of use. But many other drugs whose use is considered abusive do not appear to be harmful when they are used sparingly or in small doses. Despite this ambiguity, the National Institute on Drug Abuse continues to support the use of the term, and we will use it in this chapter—except that we define drug abuse as *the use of a drug to an extent that causes harm to the user.*

Like the term *drug,* the term *addiction* is used rather loosely to denote any habitual or frequent use of a drug, with or without dependence. In fact, addiction is a complex phenomenon involving the drug user's physical and psychological condition, the type of drug used, and the amount and frequency of use. Similarly, precise degrees of dependence are difficult to define because of the physiological and psychological complexity of drug use. Nevertheless, a limited consensus has developed among some experts, and certain definitions are considered acceptable: Physical dependence occurs when the body has adjusted to the presence of a drug and will suffer pain, discomfort, or illness—the symptoms of withdrawal—if its use is discontinued. The word *addiction* is used to describe physical dependence; *psychological dependence* occurs when a user needs a drug for the feeling of well-being that it produces. The word *habituation* is sometimes used to mean psychological dependence.

Other experts prefer not to make a distinction between physical and psychological dependence, since these are so often interrelated and since words like *ad-*

Drug problems are by no means limited to the United States or other modern societies. In prerevolutionary China, for example, opium addiction seriously weakened the society by depriving it of hundreds of thousands of productive workers.

diction have come to connote something alien or evil. These experts prefer to characterize the compulsion to use a drug simply as *drug dependence*, without attempting to define its physical and psychological components.

It is important to note that not all drug use is considered drug abuse in the sense that it impairs health. A person who is suffering from an illness that requires treatment with morphine, for example, might be addicted but would not be considered an abuser. However, there can be no doubt that some drugs are not only physically addicting but also dangerous to society. This is so because they compel their users to seek ever-larger quantities in order to maintain their "high." These highly addictive drugs can be a major social problem in that thousands of otherwise productive people may disappear from the labor market or become involved in an underground drug economy. The classic example is the city of Shanghai before the Chinese Communist Revolution of 1949. It has been estimated that almost 500,000 residents of Shanghai were addicted to opium and had to spend hours in the smoking dens each day. In North America today, cocaine is a popular drug that is used in moderation by some people. But its more powerful smoking form, known as crack, creates an intense desire for more of the drug and can be extremely addicting. As we will see later in the chapter, addiction to crack has reached alarming proportions.

However one defines abuse and addiction, mere knowledge of patterns of use in the general population at a given moment and over time is an essential starting point. This is where social-scientific data play an important role. Monitoring the drug use of persons who are arrested; large-scale surveys in which people report on their alcohol and drug use; and national surveys of the incidence of mental illness, including drug- and alcohol-related disorders, are designed and carried out by professional social scientists. At their most basic level these surveys establish the prevalence of use of alcohol, tobacco, and illicit drugs in the general population, as

TABLE 5–1 LIFETIME PREVALENCE RATES OF THE USE OF DIFFERENT DRUGS IN 1990 AMONG HIGH SCHOOL SENIORS AND THE GENERAL U.S. POPULATION AGED 12 AND OVER

	EVER USING DRUGS (%)	
SUBSTANCE	SENIORS	GENERAL POPULATION
Alcohol	89.5	83.2
Cigarettes	64.4	73.2
Marijuana	40.7	33.1
Stimulants	17.5	6.9
Inhalants	18.5	5.1
Cocaine	9.4	11.3
Crack	3.5	1.4
Hallucinogens	9.4	7.6
Analgesics	8.3	5.7
Tranquilizers	7.2	4.3
Sedatives	5.3	3.7
Heroin	1.3	0.8
Any illicit drug	47.9	37.0
Total (N)	(15,200)	(9,259)

Source: Kandel, 1991.

shown in Table 5–1. *Prevalence* refers to the extent to which a behavior appears in the population to any degree at all; in other words, Table 5–1 shows the proportion of the population (high school seniors in this case) that has ever used the substance, regardless of frequency of use.

ALCOHOL USE AND ABUSE

American adults consume an average of 33.2 gallons of beer, 2.7 gallons of wine, and 2.0 gallons of distilled spirits a year (*Statistical Abstract,* 1993). Despite these high rates of consumption, the problems associated with alcohol abuse—chronic inebriation, vagrancy, drunken driving—arouse less interest and concern than the abuse, or even the use, of other drugs. In contrast to other drugs, alcohol is thoroughly integrated into Western culture. It may also be better adapted to our complex lifestyle, since besides relieving tension and reducing sexual and aggressive inhibitions, alcohol seems to facilitate interpersonal relations, at least superficially, whereas other drug experiences, even in groups, are often highly private.

In our society people have mixed feelings about alcohol. On the one hand, alcohol creates warmth and high spirits—it promotes interpersonal harmony and agreement ("Let's drink to that"). It has long been used in informal rituals (Christmas eggnog) and formal rites (wine as the blood of Christ) and has been important to the economies of many nations. The growing and harvesting of grapes, grain, and other crops used to produce alcoholic beverages, as well as the brewing, fermenting, distilling, and sale of alcoholic beverages, provide employment, trade, and tax revenues. On the other hand, the problems created by the abuse of alcohol are staggering. They include public drunkenness and disorderly behavior; traffic and industrial accidents; poor social functioning; broken marriages; and aggravation of existing conditions such as poverty, mental and physical illness, and crime.

The perception of alcohol as a social problem changes with changes in American culture and developments in knowledge about the effects of alcohol use. According to some sociologists, in the early decades of this century alcohol itself was a symbol that masked the larger social conflict between the working class, with its large immigrant component, and the upper class, which sought to control the workers and increase their productivity (Gusfield, 1963; Szasz, 1992). In recent years the American public has become more aware of the dangers associated with drinking—for example, the damage it can cause to an unborn fetus and the high correlation between highway accidents and driving while intoxicated. Alcohol is implicated in over half of all fatal highway accidents in the United States and approximately one-third of all homicides, drownings, and boating deaths (HHS, 1990). These problems have led to crusades against excessive drinking rather than against alcohol itself. In 1990 both the Highway Safety Council and the Council for Accident Prevention reported significant declines in traffic deaths due to drinking and in home accidents associated with alcohol consumption. These decreases seem to indicate that crusades against excess drinking are having an impact, and their success will surely reinforce efforts to educate the public about the risks of excessive alcohol consumption.

Problem Drinkers and Alcoholics

The U.S. Department of Health and Human Services estimates that 15.1 million Americans are suffering from alcoholism or alcohol dependence (cited in *Washington Post,* April 2, 1990). This figure represents 9.2 percent of the nation's population—12.5 percent of men and 5.1 percent of women.

The terms *problem drinker* and *alcoholic* are hard to define. According to sociologist Robert Straus (1971), a distinction should be made between addiction and nonaddiction to alcohol. Problem drinkers drink in order to achieve relief and relaxation; they may drink until they are stupefied, and their frequent intoxication may interfere with their health, interpersonal relationships, and economic functioning, but they are not addicted to alcohol. In contrast, alcohol addicts, or alcoholics, have an uncontrollable need to achieve intoxication, and if this need is frustrated they will develop acute withdrawal symptoms like those of narcotics addicts—uncontrollable trembling, nausea, rapid heartbeat, and heavy perspiration. Some alcohol addicts have physiological symptoms after abstaining for only one day; in fact, alcohol withdrawal is even more likely to be fatal than narcotics withdrawal.

Alcoholism may develop after ten or more years of problem drinking; however, many alcoholics go directly from total abstinence to chronic alcoholism. Such cases are believed to involve a complex set of physiological, psychological, and social factors.

Recent research on alcoholism has focused on the possibility that the tendency to become an alcoholic may be an inherited trait. It has been found, for example, that college-age sons of alcoholics tend to have better eye-hand coordination and muscular control when they drink. Another group of researchers has shown that college-age daughters of alcoholics exhibit the same traits as the sons (Kolata, 1987). Although this research does not prove that the tendency toward alcoholism is inherited, there is considerable evidence for a genetic link. Studies of adopted children of alcoholics have found that 30 to 40 percent become alcoholics themselves, regardless of the behavior of their adoptive parents (Kolata, 1987). On the other hand, Ralph E. Tarter and Kathleen L. Edwards (1987) point out that "a genetic susceptibility must be shaped by environmental forces to create the pathological condition" (p. 67). They note that individuals who abuse alcohol tend to exhibit a set of traits including high emotionality and activity level, low attention span, and low sociability, and they suggest that specific environmental conditions (e.g., heavy drinking in the child's home) determine whether an individual with these traits actually becomes an alcoholic.

Who Drinks?

Obviously, people are not alike in their drinking habits. Several factors seem to be related to whether, how much, and in what ways an individual uses alcohol. Among these are socioeconomic factors, sex, age, religion, and cultural influences.

Socioeconomic Factors Drinking appears to be most frequent among younger men at higher socioeconomic levels and least frequent among older women at lower levels. Members of the higher socioeconomic classes drink to excess less often; heavier drinking is found at lower socioeconomic levels and among young people (Kandel, 1992). When drinking is analyzed by occupation, however, a different pattern emerges: Business and professional men are most likely to be heavy drinkers, whereas farmers are least likely to drink heavily. Among women, service workers drink most heavily.

Sex Recent decades have seen a dramatic increase in alcoholism among adult women. There are several possible explanations for this, but recent research has focused on the differences between female and male alcoholics. For both sexes, social factors—the presence of alcoholism in the family, childhood unhappiness, and trauma—are important influences. But for women increasing rates of alcoholism seem to be related to their entry into the labor force in large numbers. One study found that married working women are more likely to become alcoholics than homemakers or single working women. Yet the statistics on female alcoholism may be misleading. As women have become more visible in society, their drinking patterns have become more noticeable. Perhaps researchers are only now learning to identify the female alcoholic, and many women may still be hiding their drinking problems at home. Moreover, even if there has been an increase in alcoholism among women, it remains true that women have far fewer drinking problems than men do (Ferrence, 1980).

Age Heavy drinking among men is most common at ages 21–30; among women, it occurs at ages 31–50. In general, older people are less likely than younger people to drink, even if they were drinkers in their youth. (Drinking among young people is discussed more fully in the next section.) Drinking among the elderly is a hidden social problem, however, especially because statistics on alcohol use suggest that drinking diminishes with age. As a larger portion of the population is elderly, the absolute number of problem drinkers in this segment of the population increases even if the proportion of heavy drinkers (five or more drinks per day) is lower than in other age groups.

Religion Regular churchgoers drink less than nonchurchgoers. However, within the former group, Episcopalians drink most heavily and conservative and fundamentalist Protestants drink most lightly. More Catholics than members of other religions are heavy drinkers. On the other hand, a low proportion of Jews are heavy drinkers. One study linked the low rate of problem drinking among Jews with informal processes of social control such as association of alcohol abuse with non-Jews and a set of techniques for avoiding excess drinking under social pressure (Glassner & Berg, 1980).

Cultural Influences Among some groups, alcoholic beverages are normally drunk in moderate amounts at meals. Members of other groups drink after meals or on other occasions, sometimes to the point of drunkenness. It is the latter custom

It is estimated that 3 million people 14–17 years old have problems related to the use of alcohol.

that seems to promote alcoholism, as is illustrated by a comparison of American Jews and Italian Americans, who customarily drink with meals and in the home, and Irish Americans, who are more likely to drink outside the home and/or not at meals. Among the Jews and Italians most adults use alcohol and report having done so since childhood, but the rate of alcoholism is quite low; among the Irish, childhood drinking is less likely and alcoholism rates are much higher. One study (Vaillant, 1983) found that Irish Americans are seven times as likely as those of Mediterranean descent (e.g., Italians and Greeks) to be alcoholics.

The correlation between familial drinking patterns and alcoholism has been found to hold true for other groups as well. In ethnic groups in which drinking habits are established by cultural custom, alcohol abuse is rare. But in groups with ambivalent attitudes toward alcohol, including American Protestants and Native Americans, alcoholism rates are high; in particular, drinkers from groups in which alcohol is seldom used are most likely to encounter problems (Chafetz, 1972). In general, when children grow up with routine, comfortable exposure to alcohol within the family, they are very unlikely to become excessive drinkers when they become adults. Indeed, "the power of the group to inspire moderation of consumption is perhaps the most consistent finding in the study of addictive behavior" (Peele, 1987, p. 189).

Recently there has been a marked decline in drinking, especially of hard liquor, in many segments of the American public. This is especially true among upwardly mobile members of the middle class. The consumption of distilled spirits declined dramatically during the 1980s, and the consumption of beer also fell. Despite these significant declines, however, rates of alcohol consumption in the United States remain extremely high, and newer products like wine coolers and specially promoted malt liquors threaten to diminish the downward trend in alcohol consumption.

Marketers of alcoholic beverages have attempted to address the problems associated with alcohol consumption by sponsoring advertising that promotes "moderate" or "responsible" drinking. However, a recent study identified a number of problems with such advertising (Dejong, Atkin, & Wallack, 1992). Slogans like "Know When to Say When" and "Drink Safely" tend to ignore or gloss over the fact that no level of alcohol consumption is completely risk free; moreover, they do not place sufficient emphasis on the need for some people—drivers, pregnant or nursing women, people using other drugs—to abstain totally. The ads themselves often undermine the message they are trying to convey; for example, they reinforce the idea that beer consumption is a reward for hard work, a form of escape, a means of promoting romance, and a way of obtaining comradeship, acceptance, and a social identity (Kilbourne, 1991; Postman et al., 1987). They also seem to imply that abstinence is not socially acceptable.

Drinking Among Young People

In the 1970s and 1980s there was a marked increase in alcohol consumption among teenagers and young adults. As early as 1974 Morris Chafetz noted that "the switch is on. Youths are moving from a wide range of other drugs to the most devastating drug—the one most widely misused of all—alcohol" (quoted in *Time*, April 22, 1974, p. 75). Today teenage and preteenage drinking is widespread; in fact, alcohol is the most widely used drug among youth.

Recent national data demonstrate that 46.4 percent of Americans between the ages of 12 and 17 have used alcohol; the proportion of 12- to 17-year-olds reporting current alcohol use (at least once within the past month) stood at 20.3 percent in 1991 (*Statistical Abstract*, 1993).

Teenagers who are defined as problem drinkers include those who have had confrontations with teachers or the police because of their drinking. Of these, only a relatively small percentage can be defined as chronically alcoholic. Alcoholic teenagers differ from other adolescent drinkers in that they drink more often and consume greater quantities, often with the intention of getting drunk; they are also more likely to drink alone, to display aggressive or destructive behavior, and to have severe emotional problems (HHS, 1990; Stencel, 1973).

The popularity of alcohol among young people is attributed to many factors, including the difficulty, expense, and danger of obtaining other drugs; low legal drinking ages; and the manufacture and advertisement of products that are especially appealing to the young, such as sweet wines and alcoholic beverages that resemble milkshakes. In recent years, alarmed at the increase in traffic fatalities caused by young drunk drivers, many states have passed laws raising the minimum age for the purchase of alcoholic beverages.

Drinking among young people can also be construed as a rebellion against the adult world—an attempt to assert independence and imitate adult behavior. Some authorities believe that strict regulations on drinking only make it more appealing. Moreover, prohibition of drinking among youth is extremely difficult in a society in which alcohol is widely used and relatively easy to procure.

Many young people turn to alcohol for the same reasons that their parents do: to have a good time, to escape from the stress of everyday life, and to conform to social norms. As one expert has pointed out,

> *Both their peer group and the adult society that they are being socialized to enter encourage and reward drinking behavior. Learning to drink for the adolescent is but present and anticipatory socialization. . . . The major influences on whether or not an individual drinks are the principal agents of socialization in his life, his parents and his peers. (Albrecht, 1973, pp. 30–31)*

Alcohol-Related Social Problems

The social problems related to excessive alcohol use are many and varied. They run the gamut from poor health to complete alienation from society. In this section we will briefly describe a few of those problems.

Health   On the average, alcholics can expect to live ten to twelve fewer years than nonalcoholics. There are several reasons for this shortened lifespan. First, alcohol contains a high number of calories and no vital nutrients. Thus, alcoholics generally have a reduced appetite for nutritious food and inevitably suffer from vitamin deficiencies; as a result, their resistance to infectious disease is lowered. Second, over a long period large amounts of alcohol destroy liver cells and cause them to be replaced by scar tissue; this condition, called cirrhosis of the liver, is the eighth most frequent cause of death (almost 25,000 a year) in the United States (*Statistical Abstract,* 1993). Heavy drinking also contributes to heart ailments, and there is some evidence that alcohol contributes to the incidence of cancer. And finally, alcohol is implicated in thousands of suicides every year (Centers for Disease Control, cited in *Washington Post,* April 2, 1990).

Drinking and Driving   Tests of the amount of alcohol in the blood of drivers involved in accidents have found a significant connection between alcohol and vehicular accidents. According to the National Highway Traffic Safety Administration, in 1992 drinking by either a driver, a passenger, or a pedestrian was a factor in 45 percent of all fatal accidents. The relationship between alcohol use and accident rates at different times of the day and week is portrayed in Figure 5–1.

Alcohol and Arrest Rates   In 1991, 1,074,000 arrests, or about 13 percent of all nonserious crimes, involved drunkenness or an offense related to violations of the liquor laws (*Statistical Abstract,* 1993). These criminal acts were minor, involving breaches of the peace, disorderly conduct, vagrancy, and so on. In arrests for major crimes, drunkenness generally does not appear in the charges, yet alcohol often contributes to crime. In many homicide cases alcohol is found in either the victim, the offender, or both; each year thousands of homicides are linked to alcohol use (Centers for Disease Control, cited in *Washington Post,* April 2, 1990). Among male sex offenders, a significant percentage are chronic alcoholics or were drinking at the time of the offense. The rates for drinking in relation to skilled property crimes, such

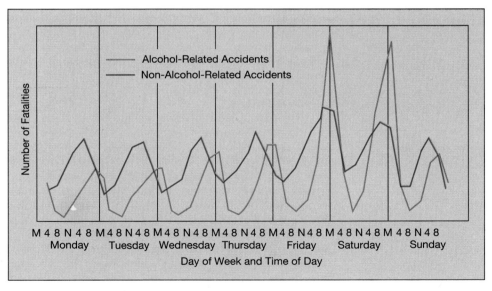

FIGURE 5–1   Number of Fatalities by Day of Week, Time of Day, and Alcohol Involvement

Note: Although the number of fatalities related to alcohol and not related to alcohol decreased slowly during the 1980s, the same proportional relationships by day of the week and time of day held into the early 1990s.

Source: DHHS, 1983b, Courtesy National Institute on Drug Abuse.

as forgery, appear to be somewhat lower than the rates for violent and sex-related crimes.

The reasons for the high correlation of drinking with arrests for serious crimes are not fully understood. It has been pointed out that alcohol, by removing some inhibitions, may lead people to behave in unaccustomed ways. Likewise, as with other drugs, the need to obtain the substance may lead to theft or other property crimes and sometimes to violent crimes like armed robbery. Since chronic alcoholics may be unable to hold steady jobs, their financial difficulties are compounded, perhaps increasing the temptation to commit crimes. Also, the values and self-image of chronic heavy drinkers tend to change as their condition worsens. They are more likely to associate with delinquents or criminals, which may lead them to commit criminal acts themselves.

In addition to its link with serious crimes, alcoholism creates another problem: It places a major strain on the law enforcement system, which must process large numbers of petty offenders. Arrests, trials, and incarceration of offenders cost taxpayers billions of dollars each year. And many of these arrests involve a small segment of the community—the neighborhood drunk or derelict who may be repeatedly arrested and imprisoned briefly during the course of a year.

Effects on the Family   If the only victims of alcoholism were the alcoholics themselves, the social effects would be serious enough; but other people, especially the families of alcoholics, also suffer. The emotional effect, which is part of any family crisis, is heightened when the crisis itself is socially defined as shameful. The effects of "acts of God" such as fire, illness, and accident on a family elicit sympathy, but those of alcoholism produce negative reactions. The children of an alcoholic parent frequently develop severe physical and emotional illnesses, and marriage to an alcoholic often ends in divorce or desertion. Finally, since alcoholics often are unable to hold jobs, the outcome may be poverty for their families.

Families of alcoholics often cease to function well because of a pattern known as *co-dependency*. The spouse of the problem drinker, and often the children as well, frequently participate in a pattern of interactions designed to excuse the problematic behavior. Without thinking about it, they may aid the drinker in his or her behavior—even helping to supply the drinks—in an effort to reduce conflict or ease pain. As a result of these activities, they may themselves become dependent on alcohol, despite its negative effects on the family. In many instances they too become problem drinkers.

If the families of alcoholics stand by them and attempt to help them overcome their condition, certain typical stages of adjustment are likely to occur. These stages were examined by Joan K. Jackson (1956) in a study of the families of alcoholic men. The first stage is denial, by everyone concerned, that the problem even exists—an attempt to pretend that excessive drinking is normal. When denial is no longer possible, there are various attempts to eliminate the problem, followed by progressive family disorganization. At some point the wife begins to take over the husband's roles, and gradually a reorganization takes place, with the alcoholic husband largely excluded. Eventually it may become necessary to exclude the husband even more, and a further reorganization occurs. Finally, if the husband obtains help and succeeds in controlling his alcoholism, he is reintegrated into the family, with a redefinition of family roles and an attempt to reestablish mutual trust and confidence. Not all families complete this cycle, and even in those that do there may be permanent scars (Vaillant, 1983).

Alcoholism and Homelessness   Contrary to popular belief, only about 5 percent of all alcoholics and problem drinkers are homeless vagrants; most have jobs and families. Several theories have been advanced to explain the differences between the alcoholics who end up homeless and those who do not. Homeless alcoholics often want to separate themselves from their past as well as to drink. Lack of social affiliation, a feeling that usually exists for a long time before the person finally becomes a derelict, is another likely cause. Homeless alcoholics have a strong need to escape from the realities of social life—an escape that is provided by chronic drinking (Rossi, 1989).

Additional evidence suggests that in some cases alcoholism itself helps produce homelessness. In a 1987 study of homeless male alcoholics in Baltimore, 59 percent of those interviewed said that drinking itself had led them to become homeless (Shandler & Shipley, 1987). Many other homeless men and women are alcoholics who formerly lived in single-room occupancy hotels; when the hotels were closed by urban redevelopment, they were cast out onto the streets (Kasinitz, 1984).

Treatment of Alcoholism

Rehabilitation   Alcoholism is increasingly viewed as an illness with a variety of psychological and physiological components; therefore, it is possible to rehabilitate, though not completely cure, many alcoholics. A variety of nonpunitive attempts have been made to assist alcoholics in overcoming their addiction or habituation and to help alcoholism-prone individuals handle disturbing emotions and anxieties. The Comprehensive Alcohol Abuse and Alcoholism Prevention, Treatment and Rehabilitation Act of 1970 created the National Institute on Alcohol Abuse and Alcoholism (to coordinate federal government activities) and the National Advisory Council on Alcohol Abuse and Alcoholism (to recommend national policies). The act also provided grants to states to use in developing comprehensive programs for alcoholism, grants and contracts for specific prevention and treatment projects, and incentives for private hospitals that admit patients with alcohol-related problems.

Traditionally hospitals offered little beyond "drying out" and release of alcoholic patients; they might treat a specific medical problem caused by alcohol but not alcoholism itself. The American Hospital Association now advocates hospital alco-

Film actor Drew Barrymore ("E.T."), an alcoholic in her early teenage years, is an outspoken advocate of treatment for adolescent drinking problems.

holism programs and is attempting to utilize the resources of general hospitals in community treatment programs.

Alcoholics Anonymous   The most impressive successes in coping with alcoholism have been achieved by Alcoholics Anonymous (AA). The effectiveness of this group in helping individual alcoholics is based on what amounts to a conversion. Alcoholics are led to this experience through fellowship with others like themselves, some of whom have already mastered their problem while others are in the process of doing so.

AA insists that drinkers face up to their shortcomings and the realities of life and, when possible, make amends to people whom they have hurt in the past. The movement also concentrates on building up alcoholics' self-esteem and reassuring them of their basic worth as human beings. Since its founding in 1935, the group has evolved a technique in which recovered alcoholics support and comfort drinkers who are undergoing rehabilitation. This support is also available during crises, when a relapse seems likely, and on a year-round basis through meetings that the alcoholic may attend as often as necessary.

AA has created special groups to deal with teenage and young adult drinkers. It has also established programs to aid nonalcoholic spouses and the children of alcoholics. The alcoholic family member need not be a member of AA for relatives to participate in these offshoot programs, which developed out of the recognition that an entire family is psychologically involved in the alcohol-related problems of any of its members.

AA appears to be the most successful large-scale program for dealing with alcoholism. According to the AA credo, it is essential for addicts to acknowledge their lack of control over alcohol use and to abstain from all alcoholic beverages for the rest of their lives. This approach sees alcoholism as an "allergy" in which even one drink can produce an intolerable craving for more. Although precise figures are not available, it seems that more than half the individuals who join AA with a strong motivation to cure themselves are rehabilitated (Chafetz & Demone, 1972). The voluntary nature of the program probably contributes to its success; however, it is unlikely that this approach, with its insistence on total abstinence, could be applied successfully to all alcoholics. This is especially true of alcoholics who reject the spiritual tenets of AA, which teach the recovering alcoholic to seek help from a "higher power," whatever that may mean to the individual. Alcoholics who are unwilling to accept these tenets can often find programs that are related to the twelve steps of the AA program but eliminate the program's spiritual aspects.

Antabuse Programs   Antabuse is a prescription drug that sensitizes the patient in such a way that consuming even a small quantity of alcohol causes strong and uncomfortable physical symptoms. Drinkers become intensely flushed; their pulse quickens; and they feel nauseated.

Before beginning treatment with Antabuse, the alcoholic is detoxified (kept off alcohol until none shows in blood samples). Then the drug is administered to the patient along with doses of alcohol for several consecutive days. The patient continues to take the drug for several more days, and at the close of the period another dose of alcohol is administered. The trial doses of alcohol condition the patient to recognize the relationship between drinking and the unpleasant symptoms. (Similar treatment programs depend on different nausea-producing drugs, or electric shock, to condition the patient against alcohol; this process is known as aversion therapy or behavior conditioning.)

Antabuse (or Disulfiram) has gained only limited acceptance in the treatment of alcoholics. Critics claim that its effect is too narrow and that this approach neglects the personality problems of the drinker. They also maintain that the drug does not work for people who are suspicious of treatment or have psychotic tendencies.

Other Programs A problem drinker or alcoholic who receives help while remaining in the family and on the job usually responds better than one who is institutionalized. Community care programs treat these problem drinkers and their families in an effort to improve the drinker's self-image and enhance his or her sense of security within the family.

Employee assistance programs are a relatively new development that has demonstrated considerable effectiveness in treating problem drinkers in the workplace (Schreier, Kane, & Reed, 1980). The success of such programs depends on their being available on a scheduled basis and during crises; on the maintenance of absolute confidentiality; and on the development of rapport between the counselor and the patient as they explore underlying psychological problems such as loneliness, alienation, and poor self-image. Also important is the patient's desire to remain in the community and continue working (Chafetz & Demone, 1972).

Research on the relationship between various work-related factors and alcoholism has not yielded conclusive results. Research on job-related stress, for example, is complicated by the difficulty of measuring the degree of stress people experience on the job. On the other hand, many studies have found that workers with drinking problems are also likely to mix alcohol with other drugs and to experience mental disorders. It is not clear which of these factors are causes and which are effects (Kasl, 1981; Price, 1984).

ILLEGAL DRUG USE AND ABUSE

Commonly Abused Drugs

The major categories of illegal drugs are constantly changing as culture and customs change. In eighteenth-century England the use of tobacco was forbidden; anyone found guilty of consuming it could be punished by such extreme measures as amputation or splitting of the nose. In the United States, cocaine was introduced to the

Marijuana is often the first illegal drug that young people experiment with.

public early in the twentieth century as an additive to a new commercial soft drink, Coca-Cola. Today the use of illegal drugs embraces an extremely diverse set of behaviors, ranging from recreational use of marijuana to heroin addiction. The most commonly used drugs today, in addition to alcohol, are marijuana, cocaine, the opiates (including heroin and morphine), hallucinogens, amphetamines, and barbiturates. Marijuana use was so widespread in the 1980s that the U.S. Department of Agriculture estimated that in some states the plant ranked among the top five cash crops. The use of cocaine has increased dramatically in recent years, and heroin continues to find a ready market in the United States. The spread of the smokable form of cocaine known as "crack" is the latest in the series of drug epidemics that have swept North America since World War II. As the crack epidemic wanes, there are indications that heroin use may be increasing among former cocaine addicts, and some young people are turning again to experimenting with psychedelic drugs like LSD and XTC. In short, trends in drug use change quite rapidly, but the most serious social problems associated with illegal drug use have always stemmed from drugs that cause severe psychological and physiological addictions, especially the opiates, cocaine, and amphetamines.

Marijuana Like alcohol, marijuana is a "social" drug, one that is often used in social gatherings because it is thought to ease or enhance interaction. This accounts for its popularity among the young, who in the 1960s considered it the hallmark of rebellion, as well as among many members of the middle and upper classes. Because the use of marijuana is widespread and there is little evidence that it has detrimental long-term effects or leads to the use of stronger drugs, the federal government has shifted its enforcement efforts to the more clearly addicting drugs. At the same time, the eradication of marijuana crops in the western United States and interdiction of bulk shipments from the Caribbean and Mexico have had the effect of reducing supplies of the drug, and some dealers have turned to trafficking in more dangerous but less bulky drug products like crack.

Cocaine Cocaine, which produces a sense of greater strength and endurance and a feeling of increased intellectual power, can cause paranoid psychoses when taken in large quantities over time. Until recently the high street price of cocaine caused it to be viewed as an upper-class indulgence, a pastime of celebrities like actor John

Increasing use of the smokable form of cocaine known as crack led to a high frequency of neurological disorders and seizures among chronic users in the late 1980s and early 1990s.

Belushi (who died as a result of excessive cocaine use). However, in recent years cocaine use has become more prevalent in the middle and working classes.

Crack is a form of cocaine that can be smoked rather than ingested through the nasal passages. Commercial cocaine is "cooked" with ether or bicarbonate of soda to form a "rock" of crack. When it is smoked, crack produces an instant and extremely powerful "rush" that tends to last only about fifteen minutes and to cause a strong desire for another rush. This form of cocaine therefore is highly addicting.

Crack is more expensive than cocaine in its powder form, and its use is often associated with an expensive lifestyle. Perhaps for this reason, some athletes and movie stars (as well as politicians such as Mayor Marion Barry of Washington) who previously used cocaine have become addicted to crack, with disastrous consequences in some cases. At this writing there is evidence that the crack epidemic has peaked, but the violence associated with the distribution and sale of crack continues. In addition, the birth of sickly, low-weight babies with cocaine addictions formed in utero is a serious problem in communities where the effects of the crack epidemic are still being felt.

Heroin   Most heroin users experience a sudden, intense feeling of pleasure; others may feel greater self-esteem and composure. But because heroin slows brain functions, after the initial euphoria the addict becomes lethargic. The acknowledged relationship between crime and heroin addiction results not from the influence of the drug but from the suffering caused by the lack of it: Withdrawal symptoms are avoided at all costs. Since addicts are seldom employable and a single day's supply of heroin may cost more than $100, most of an addict's day is usually devoted to crime, especially property crimes.

The typical lower-class heroin addict is under 30, lives in an urban area, has serious health problems, and has a greatly reduced life expectancy. The addict frequently suffers from malnutrition as well as from hepatitis, AIDS, and other infections caused by intravenous injection of the drug. In communities where heroin addicts are numerous and visible, there is often conflict over the advisability of providing free needles to addicts so that they will not be forced to share illegally purchased hypodermics with their companions and risk the mixing of blood that may contain the HIV virus.

Hallucinogens   Hallucinogens, such as lysergic acid diethylamide (LSD), distort the user's perceptions. Despite frequent warnings about "bad trips," studies indicate that long-term adverse reactions to LSD occur only when the user has preexisting mental problems (Ashley, 1975). There are no data to indicate that the drug can cause either physical or emotional dependence.

Amphetamines   Amphetamines—called "uppers" because of their stimulating effect—are legal when prescribed by a physician, and many people become addicted to them through medical use. In some cases an overdose of one of these drugs can cause coma, with possible brain damage or even death. "Amphetamine psychosis" is likely to occur when amphetamines are used in high doses over a long period, and abrupt withdrawal may cause suicidal depression in a heavy user.

Barbiturates   Barbiturates depress the central nervous system. Prolonged barbiturate use and high dosages can cause physical dependence, with symptoms similar to those of heroin addiction. Indeed, many drug experts believe that barbiturate addiction is even more dangerous, and more resistant to treatment and cure, than heroin addiction.

Barbiturate overdose can cause poisoning, convulsions, coma, and sometimes death. In fact, in the United States barbiturates are a leading cause of accidental death by poisoning, largely because they tend to heighten the effect of alcohol.

Taken in moderate doses, barbiturates, like alcohol, have a mildly disinhibiting effect; however, other personality changes show no consistent pattern. The barbiturate user may be calmed and relaxed—reactions that are normally associated with a depressant—or may become lively and convivial.

People frequently develop a habit of using both amphetamines and barbiturates, either together or alternately. Combined amphetamine-barbiturate use makes the normal rhythm of life, the alternation of rest and wakefulness, meaningless. It is replaced by the chemical cycling of consciousness through "ups" produced by amphetamines and "downs" produced by barbiturates. Such chemical regulation of activity, if prolonged, causes severe physical and psychological deterioration.

Patterns of Drug Abuse

Who Uses Drugs?   The *opportunity* to use drugs is among the most important factors leading to illicit drug use. The National Institute on Drug Abuse (1980) reports that acquaintance with a user precedes the first experience with drugs. Although most people who take drugs are likely to pass up the first opportunity to do so, they take advantage of subsequent opportunities. Among professionals, doctors are most likely to use drugs and to become addicted to them because they have the most knowledge about these substances as well as access to them. For the general public, the opportunity structure and lifetime experience with drugs (more than one or two "experiments") are strongly related to age. Older teenagers and young adults are more likely to use drugs than older adults, and the younger a person is at the time of the first opportunity, the more likely he or she is to eventually try the drug.

The study of drug use in the U.S. population is a social-scientific undertaking of great magnitude. Two primary data sources are used in studying patterns of drug use. The first is reports from public and private agencies dealing with arrest, hospitalization, treatment, or legal matters. These data offer important evidence about trends in drug use among individuals arrested for crimes or admitted to hospital emergency rooms. But the data do not tell us very much about the distribution of drug use in the general population. To obtain those data, social scientists conduct large-scale national surveys about people's experience with drug, alcohol, and tobacco use.

In an annual survey, Monitoring the Future, conducted by the Institute of Survey Research at the University of Michigan, more than 16,000 high school seniors are given a self-administered questionnaire (to encourage honesty) about their substance use. Conducted annually since 1975, this survey is an essential barometer of drug use among young Americans. Like all surveys, however, it has its limitations; in particular, it does not sample young people who have dropped out of school, an important population in the study of drug use.

Another important survey providing data on patterns of drug use is the National Household Survey on Drug Abuse, which is sponsored by the National Institute on Drug Abuse. Other surveys that collect information on various aspects of substance use and abuse are quite common, but the two just described allow us to track patterns of use from year to year.

Data gathered by the annual surveys on drug use are presented in Table 5–2. They show that illicit drug use by young people and adults peaked in the early or mid-1980s. Note that experimentation by teenagers with any illicit drug declined from 26 percent in 1979 to just under 16 percent in 1990. This decline is highly significant, since experimentation in the teenage years tends to produce higher levels of illicit drug use in the young adult years. The table also shows, however, that as marijuana experimentation or use declined among teenagers, alcohol use remained quite high, far higher than use of illicit drugs. Recent declines in alcohol use among teenagers are encouraging, but the extremely high prevalence of alcohol in the young-adult cohort suggests that continuing high rates of teenage experimentation

AGE GROUP AND DRUG CLASS		1974 (%)	1976 (%)	1977 (%)	1979 (%)	1982 (%)	1985 (%)	1988 (%)	1990 (%)
Youth (age 12–17)	N =	(952)	(986)	(1,272)	(2,165)	(1,581)	(2,246)	(3,095)	(2,177)
Marijuana		18.5	18.4	22.3	24.1	20.6	19.7	12.6	11.3
Cocaine		2.7	2.3	2.6	4.2	4.1	4.0	2.9	2.2
Alcohol		51.0	49.3	47.5	53.6	52.4	51.7	44.6	41.0
Cigarettes[a]		—[b]	—[b]	—[b]	13.3	24.8	25.8	22.8	22.2
Any illicit use		—[b]	—[b]	—[b]	26.0	22.0	23.7	16.8	15.9
Young adults (age 18–25)	N =	(849)	(882)	(1,500)	(2,044)	(1,283)	(1,813)	(1,505)	(2,052)
Marijuana		34.2	35.0	38.7	46.9	40.4	36.9	27.9	24.6
Cocaine		8.1	7.0	10.2	19.6	18.8	16.3	12.1	7.5
Alcohol		77.1	77.9	79.8	86.6	87.1	87.2	81.7	80.2
Cigarettes[a]		—[b]	—[b]	—[b]	46.7	47.2	44.3	44.7	39.7
Any illicit use		—[b]	—[b]	—[b]	49.4	43.4	42.6	32.0	28.7
Older adults (age 26+)	N =	(2,221)	(1,708)	(1,822)	(3,015)	(2,760)	(3,979)	(4,214)	(7,385)
Marijuana		3.8	5.4	6.4	9.0	10.6	9.5	6.9	7.3
Cocaine		—[c]	0.6	0.9	2.0	3.8	4.2	2.7	2.4
Alcohol		62.7	64.2	65.8	72.4	72.0	73.6	68.6	66.6
Cigarettes[a]		—[b]	—[b]	—[b]	39.7	38.2	36.0	33.7	31.9
Any illicit use		—[b]	—[b]	—[b]	10.0	11.8	13.3	10.2	10.0

[a]Includes only persons who ever smoked at least five packs.
[b]Estimate not available.
[c]Low precision. No estimate reported.

Source: NIDA, 1991.

with alcohol are likely to produce continuing high rates of alcohol use as these individuals become young adults. Moreover, the most recent data from the University of Michigan suggest that marijuana use increased sharply between 1989 and 1993, a trend that could indicate a revival of drug use among teenagers (Treaster, 1994).

The figures on cocaine use, in which young adults were, and remain, the heaviest users, show quite clearly that a drug epidemic has its greatest influence on the cohort who are in their teenage and young-adult years at the time that the fad of using a particular drug reaches epidemic proportions. The table also shows that tobacco use among teenagers increased somewhat during the mid-1980s and then began to decline, but by 1990 it had not reached nearly the low level reported in 1979. Finally, the effects of marketing cigarettes to young people are reflected in these figures.

Surveys of drug use over time also provide information about the distribution of drug use by gender, socioeconomic status, and racial or ethnic background. Table 5–3, on page 146, for example, clearly shows the higher prevalence of drug experimentation and use by men than by women (except among people with higher incomes, for whom levels of use by men and women are more similar). We can see in the table that people with lower incomes have a higher prevalence of illicit drug use as well as use of marijuana and cocaine. Other studies, however, have found opposite trends. A survey by Denise Kandel and her associates (Kandel & Davis, 1991) shows that affluent teenage students are substantially more likely to experiment with and use illicit drugs than those from modest and poor backgrounds. These differences in findings point to the difficulty of judging trends in illicit drug use from a

TABLE 5–3 PREVALENCE RATES OF THE USE OF SELECTED DRUGS AMONG FULL-TIME EMPLOYED MEN AND WOMEN AGED 18 TO 40 IN THE GENERAL POPULATION, BY SEX AND PERSONAL INCOME

ANNUAL PERSONAL INCOME	Past month use of any illicit drug (%)		Past month use of marijuana (%)		Past month use of cocaine (%)	
	MALE	FEMALE	MALE	FEMALE	MALE	FEMALE
Less than $12,000	24.8	8.4	22.8	7.7	13.9	5.8
$12,000 to $19,999	19.6	9.3	18.9	7.4	10.0	7.3
$20,000 to 29,999	15.2	4.3	12.0	3.6	12.5	4.7
$30,000 or over	8.6	10.8	8.1	5.6	9.4	7.8

Source: Kopstein and Gfroerter, n.d.

particular survey, especially where students are concerned, since student surveys miss many people who are out of school and, possibly, in the labor force.

Surveys on drug use by members of various racial and ethnic groups show that the prevalence of drug use is higher among whites than among blacks, with Hispanics falling somewhere between the two on this measure. Table 5–4, which presents data on cocaine use by ethnic groups, shows these trends quite clearly for most age groups. The figures on annual use and use in the past month reveal that more white than black teenagers are probably frequent users, but this situation is reversed among older age groups. Among adults aged 26 to 34, for example, frequent cocaine users are a far smaller proportion of the population than individuals who have ever used the drug. And among blacks in this age group 4.2 percent had used cocaine in the past month while 1.3 percent of whites admitted having used the drug. These proportions correspond to the experience of people in black communities, for whom the presence of cocaine addicts is perceived as a far more serious problem than it is in white or Hispanic communities. But since there are so many more whites, these proportions indicate that the number of frequent cocaine users is far higher among whites than among blacks or Hispanics.

There is a great deal of evidence from these surveys, as well as from agency reports, that frequent use of addictive drugs has been declining since the 1980s. The decline is encouraging and suggests that education and treatment programs are having a significant effect. However, the number of people using highly addictive drugs like crack and heroin is not necessarily decreasing as fast as the number of people who have ever tried an illicit drug. Also, drug use among teenagers can fluctuate rather widely, depending on fads in popular culture or changes in the labor market for youth. The history of drug epidemics and the large number of people who continue to use the most dangerous drugs attest to the need for strong social policies to deal with the nation's drug and alcohol problems.

How Does Drug Use Spread? Most sociologists and social psychologists agree that drug use is a learned behavior that spreads through groups of peers who influence one another. In the pioneering study described in Chapter 1, Howard S. Becker (1963) traced the career of a marijuana user, showing that the user must learn how to smoke the drug and identify his or her reaction to it as pleasurable. If the user is unable to make this identification, he or she stops using the drug. The user also gradually learns that the social controls working against marijuana use—limited supplies, the need to maintain secrecy, and the definition of drug use as immoral—either do not apply within the peer group or can be circumvented.

TABLE 5–4 LIFETIME, PAST YEAR, AND PAST MONTH PREVALENCE RATES OF THE USE OF COCAINE, BY ETHNICITY IN THE GENERAL POPULATION, IN 1990

AGE/ETHNICITY	EVER USED (%)	PAST YEAR (%)	PAST MONTH (%)	TOTAL (N)
Age 12–17				
White	2.7	2.3	0.4	(1,136)
Black	2.0	1.7	—	(448)
Hispanic	3.2	3.1	—	(526)
Age 18–25				
White	21.0	7.2	1.9	(1,126)
Black	12.3	7.3	3.6	(414)
Hispanic	18.7	9.7	3.1	(448)
Age 26–34				
White	27.7	6.4	1.3	(1,359)
Black	20.3	9.7	4.2	(460)
Hispanic	20.4	8.6	2.5	(462)
Age 35+				
White	5.9	0.8	—	(1,620)
Black	7.1	1.0	—	(520)
Hispanic	6.1	2.0	—	(479)
Total white	11.7	2.8	0.6	(5,241)
Total black	10.0	4.0	1.7	(1,842)
Total Hispanic	11.5	5.2	1.9	(1,915)

Source: NIDA, 1991.

The popular view that marijuana use is a stepping-stone to stronger drugs is not supported by research findings. Becker (1963) found marijuana users to be "non-compulsive and casual" (p. 44), and the National Institute on Drug Abuse (1980) found that in 1979 only 30 percent of high school seniors using marijuana tried other illicit drugs. Findings from Europe—especially Amsterdam, where marijuana and hashish are legal—confirm the U.S. research showing that a minority of marijuana users experiment with more dangerous drugs (Cohen, 1989).

In research conducted during the 1960s, Kenneth Keniston (1968–1969) identified three types of users: tasters, seekers, and heads. Tasters, the largest group, experimented with drugs casually. Seekers sought intensification of experiences and new forms of awareness. And heads, who were most sharply alienated from American values and included leaders of the hippie movement, promoted the use of psychedelic drugs.

In explaining the spread of heroin use, Hunt and Chambers (1976) developed a disease model consisting of "initiators" and "susceptible communities" and suggested ways to identify and contain the "contagious" individuals. Hunt and Forsland (1980) found that addicts who moved to a Wyoming community from other locations were "not part of a coherent pattern of growing use (as are native users)" (p. 213) and that discontinuity eventually developed between local users and the newcomers because the latter were "not related to the original friendship groups" (p. 214).

More recent research has provided additional evidence that "the most important direct influence on drug use is that of the peer cluster: 'gangs,' best friends, or couples" (Oetting & Beauvais, 1987, p. 133). However, other factors set the stage for involvement in drug-using peer groups. These include the individual's socioeconomic status and neighborhood environment and the influences of family, religion, and school. For example, drug use is more likely when the family is not intact, when the young person has problems in school, or when the family is forced to live in a neighborhood where young people have ready access to drugs and are exposed to deviant role models (Oetting & Beauvais, 1987).

If the individual's social milieu contributes significantly to drug use, will a change in milieu mitigate such use? American soldiers who were addicted to heroin in Vietnam were generally able to kick the habit rather easily when they returned home (Robins, 1973). This shows that people are able to abstain from use of an extremely addicting drug when their social milieu supports nonuse. It is also an example of the phenomenon that drug researcher Charles Winick (1964) terms *maturing out*, that is, the tendency of drug users to decrease their use of drugs of all kinds beginning in their late 20s.

Drug Use and Crime

The nature of drug-related crimes varies with the drug involved. According to the still definitive study by the National Commission on Marihuana and Drug Abuse (1973), "The only crimes which can be directly attributed to marihuana-using behavior are those resulting from the use, possession, or transfer of an illegal substance." Neither marijuana nor low to moderate use of barbiturates is likely to promote violence, "although high dose use of [barbiturates] has been known to cause irritability and unpredictably violent behavior in some individuals" (p. 159). Amphetamine users, in contrast, seem disproportionately involved in violent crimes such as robberies and assaults, and it is possible that these crimes are "directly attributable to acute reactions to the drug" (p. 160).

Heroin and crack are the drugs that are most frequently associated with various kinds of criminal behavior. Heroin and crack addicts can rarely support their habit without resorting to crime. In addition, addicts are "recruited disproportionately from the ranks of those who already have a criminal history" (Wilson, 1977, p. 154; see also Williams, 1992).

Studies of the relationship between addiction and crime note that the crimes committed to support a drug habit tend to be money-seeking crimes like shoplifting, burglary, and prostitution. Although these crimes may provide 40–50 percent of the addict's income for drug purchases, one study estimated that almost half the annual consumption of heroin in New York City is financed by selling the drug itself, along with the equipment needed to inject it (Hudson Institute, cited in Wilson, 1977). All these crimes, considered to be nonviolent in themselves, are often accompanied by violence. "Muggings and armed robberies will be committed regularly by some addicts and occasionally by many; even in burglary, violence may result if the addict is surprised by the victim while ransacking the latter's home or store" (Wilson, 1977, p. 156). The relationship between heroin addiction and crime is supported by evidence that "when the drug users are active in a therapeutic program and presumably not using heroin, criminal activity decreases" (Wilson, 1977, p. 156).

The crack epidemic is also associated with criminal activity. Because crack is produced from large volumes of commercial cocaine, it is expensive and, like heroin, often involves users in the sale of the drug itself or in criminal activities designed to raise money for purchases of the drug. In addition, there is evidence that in some communities use of crack has led to increases in rates of female prostitution and other crimes (Bourgois, 1989; Sterk, 1989; Williams, 1989).

There is a great deal of evidence indicating that crack and cocaine dealers have contributed to the sudden rise in the number of violent deaths and shootings of innocent bystanders in large U.S. cities in the late 1980s and early 1990s (Bourgois,

1989; Williams, 1989). As the crack business becomes more competitive, with more dealers seeking to serve a steady or somewhat decreasing number of customers, we can expect increasing violence in communities where retail drug markets thrive. We can also expect to see continuing use of heavy weaponry, since assault rifles and automatic rifles are readily available to drug dealers and distributors and those who attempt to rob them. (The issue of gun control is discussed in Chapter 7.)

A recent trend in research on drugs and crime is the testing of arrestees for evidence of use of illegal drugs. In 1988 the Department of Justice reported that half to three-fourths of the men arrested for serious crimes in twelve major cities tested positive for recent use of illicit drugs. This finding attracted considerable attention, since in the past law enforcement officials had estimated that only 20 percent of people arrested for serious crimes had used drugs recently (Kerr, 1988). However, it is still not clear that drug use actually causes criminal behavior, although it may facilitate such behavior.

On the other hand, it is evident that there are new patterns of organized crime in the illicit drug trade. New organizations that are not associated with older crime "families" have sprung up in American cities. They frequently resort to extreme violence in controlling local drug dealing. In the 1990s there have been numerous murders and other violent incidents among Dominican, Vietnamese, Chinese, and Colombian participants in the organized branches of the cocaine trade, as well as violent killings among native-born Americans of every description.

Drug Use and AIDS

We saw in Chapter 2 that the primary means by which AIDS is spreading among the heterosexual population is through the sharing of needles and syringes by intravenous drug users. In large cities like New York, AIDS has killed more intravenous drug addicts than homosexuals, the other population most at risk of contracting the disease.

Public health officials were slow to realize the extent of AIDS transmission among intravenous drug users. Hence, they were also slow to initiate educational and other programs that might hinder the spread of the disease in this population. Educational programs focusing on sexual practices are inappropriate for this group; drug treatment programs and efforts to prevent addiction in poor communities are needed (Sullivan, 1987).

Efforts to reach addicts face a number of obstacles. Since their activity is illegal, addicts are reluctant to come forward to be tested for AIDS. Public health workers lack credibility in the eyes of addicts, and attempts to employ ex-addicts in outreach programs encounter resistance from law enforcement personnel. Proposals to give addicts sterile needles on an experimental basis have also been thwarted. The only important test of the effectiveness of a needle exchange program was implemented in New York City in 1988 in the face of strong opposition by groups that believe such programs appear to condone drug use. Proposals for similar programs in Los Angeles, Boston, and Chicago were defeated. By early 1990 it became clear that there was little interest in the New York program, and the experiment was officially ended, though it was continued by volunteers.

Outreach programs also face public opposition, since it is often believed that narcotics addicts "deserve what they get." But perhaps the greatest obstacle is the attitude of the addicts themselves. "Ninety of 100 guys won't come in [for testing]," said one former addict. "They're either too high or else they're trying to score their fix. They don't want to know if they're sick" (quoted in Freedman, 1987, p. B7).

Treatment of Drug Abuse

Efforts to rehabilitate narcotics addicts have been impeded by the notion "once an addict, always an addict." Until recently, statistical evidence supported this notion, and the prospects for returning addicts to normal living were bleak. However, drug

This public-service poster tries to turn a familiar cigarette ad into a powerful warning.

Come to where the Cancer is.

Smoking kills more Americans each year than alcohol, cocaine, crack, heroin, homicide, suicide, car accidents, fires, and AIDS <u>combined</u>.

use spreads through the peer group and may be reversed with a change in social milieu. And drug use does not necessarily follow a predictable course from experimentation to addiction; instead, it encompasses a wide range of behaviors that may include experimentation, occasional use, regular use, and heavy use (Hicks, 1975). There are many complex factors that cause different individuals to fall into different categories of use, and efforts to rehabilitate addicts have not always addressed all of those factors. In the case of crack addiction, for example, until very recently it was thought that the drug was so highly addictive that existing treatment programs and methods could not be effective. However, researchers at the Addiction Research Center in Baltimore have found that crack is less addicting than nicotine but more addicting than alcohol. They found that nine out of ten people who experiment with cigarette smoking become addicted to nicotine. For crack the figure is one out of six, and for alcohol it is one in ten.*

Crack addiction responds to the same treatment that other drugs require, but because it is especially appealing to people who are depressed and do not have strong social support from family and nonaddict friends, it is important to try to remove the crack addict from the social milieu in which the drug is used (Kolata, 1989). This is the basic strategy of therapeutic communities.

Therapeutic Communities   Therapeutic communities are a means of attacking the high relapse rate of addicts who are detoxified and returned to the larger society. They enable individuals to reenter social life gradually and at their own pace. This reduces the shock of moving from a protective institutional environment to the much greater freedom of the outside world.

One of the most highly developed therapeutic community programs is operated

---

*In this connection it is interesting to note that the curves for relapse after cessation of use of tobacco, cocaine, and alcohol are the same. Of the three, nicotine kills the most—some 360,000 Americans a year. (See Figure 5–2.)

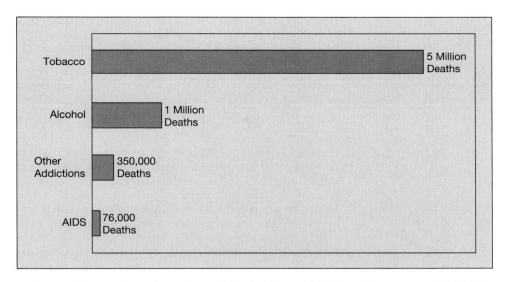

FIGURE 5–2   Estimated number of deaths from addictive substances and AIDS in the United States during the 1980s

Source: Reproduced with the permission of Population Council, from R. T. Ravenholt, "Tobacco's Global Death March," *Population and Development Review* 16, no. 2 (June 1990):237.

by Phoenix House. In the Phoenix program, addicts who have completed their treatment are transferred to a Re-Entry House for gradual reintegration into everyday life. Educational facilities are part of the program and include training in vocational skills and preparation for entry into other educational programs.

The Phoenix House approach rests on two key precepts: that addicts must assume responsibility for their own actions and that treatment should address psychological as well as physical difficulties. Phoenix House relies on ex-addicts, who are often more effective in breaking through the barriers of isolation and hostility. In addition, ex-addicts provide living proof that addiction can be overcome. In operation since 1968, the Phoenix House program has helped many addicts recover permanently.

Methadone Maintenance   Methadone, a synthetic narcotic, has been tested extensively and is now used regularly in treatment programs for heroin addicts. In prescribed amounts it satisfies the addict's physical craving, preventing the agonizing symptoms of withdrawal. Although it does not produce a high, methadone is addicting and therefore offers not a cure but a maintenance treatment for addicts who do not respond to other types of therapy.

Many people, including addicts themselves, believe that methadone keeps addicts dependent on drugs and hence is useful only for a short time while the addict is weaned from heroin. Methadone treatment is sometimes regarded as a form of social control imposed by the dominant culture. (The substance is legally available only through approved programs, which require addicts to report to the treatment center for their daily dosage.) These ambivalent attitudes toward methadone treatment do not seem to deter potential clients. According to one survey, one of the major reasons cited by addicts for not entering treatment earlier was the absence of treatment facilities in their neighborhood (Brown, Benn, & Jansen, 1975).

Narcotic Antagonists   Narcotics users who are weaned from their physical addiction often have a psychological craving for drugs as soon as they return to their normal environment. The need to overcome this problem led scientists to develop *narcotic antagonists*, substances that negate the effects produced by the opiates. By counteracting the positive sensations produced by heroin, the narcotic antagonists help motivated addicts overcome their psychological conditioning to the drug.

SOCIAL POLICY

Social policy addressing drug and alcohol abuse takes two main forms. One consists of control strategies—that is, attempts to help individuals or groups control their own behavior—coupled with efforts to build local institutions (e.g., residential treatment centers) that provide helping services. The other is law enforcement, meaning attempts to tighten the enforcement of existing laws or to enact new laws designed to deal with the problem more effectively. Since control strategies were discussed earlier, in the sections on treatment, this section will focus on law enforcement.

The simplest approach to a problem like drug abuse is to "crack down" on the sale or use of the drug. This was the rationale for Prohibition, in which the manufacture, sale, or transportation of alcoholic beverages was banned by an amendment to the U.S. Constitution. Although Prohibition was repealed long ago, the attitudes that gave rise to this approach are still in evidence. Chronic drinkers are still thrown in jail to "dry out"; people are still arrested for possession of a single marijuana cigarette; drug addicts still receive heavy jail sentences. In many places treatment is limited to incarceration. (Some unintended consequences of this approach are discussed in Box 5–1.)

Repeated arrests of chronic alcoholics merely perpetuate a "revolving door" cycle. Offenders are arrested, processed, released, and then arrested again, some-

BOX 5–1   UNINTENDED CONSEQUENCES: CRACKING DOWN ON DRUGS

When citizens clamor for "crackdowns" on some form of pleasure or some type of substance that is perceived as a social problem, they often demand that legislators ban or prohibit the substance or behavior in question. But along with prohibitions on substances such as alcohol or illicit drugs come some unintended and unwanted consequences. Chief among these is the growth of an underground of lawbreakers who are served by criminal suppliers, most often organized-crime syndicates. An excellent example of this is New York State's experience during the 1970s. In 1973 New York State declared a "war on drugs." The Rockefeller "get tough" law, which prescribed severe mandatory penalties for narcotic drug offenses and for serious offenses involving other drugs (but excluding marijuana), had two purposes: to reduce illegal use of drugs by frightening both users and dealers and to reduce the crimes associated with addiction. However, the law had no appreciable effect on patterns of heroin availability or use. Moreover, it had a detrimental effect on young people. Because it provided mandatory prison terms for adults caught with commercial quantities of illegal drugs, youths below the age of 18 became extremely important in the drug distribution network. Adolescents became professional drug dealers, and recruitment into the illegal drug economy began to occur at very early ages (Williams, 1989; Williams & Kornblum, 1985).

Critics of the national "war on drugs," contend that it is creating similar unintended consequences—more organized crime syndicates to serve the underground drug market and more jail cells for those arrested for selling or using drugs. As drug enforcement increases the pressure on sellers, there is more violence in the streets as different drug organizations defend their selling "turf," the area in which they claim the exclusive right to sell drugs.

None of these unintended consequences of drug prohibitions automatically implies that such prohibitions are wrong; however, it is clear that those consequences need to be anticipated in the formulation of drug policy (Skolnick, 1992). Indeed, in April 1993 two prominent federal judges said that they would no longer preside over drug cases, stating that emphasis on arrests and imprisonment rather than prevention and treatment has been a failure (Treaster, 1993).

times only hours after their previous release. Each such arrest, which involves police, court, and correctional time, is expensive and may actually contribute to the labeling process in which an excessive drinker becomes an alcoholic and behaves accordingly.

In the 1980s there was considerable pressure for legislation intended to reduce the number of automobile accidents caused by drunken driving. In 1984 the Gallup Poll found that 79 percent of Americans favored a national law that would raise the legal drinking age to 21 in all states, since statistics indicate that a large percentage of drunken drivers are under 21. Shortly thereafter, President Reagan signed legislation that would deny some federal highway funds to states in which the drinking age is below 21. Now all states require that a person be 21 or older in order to purchase liquor and beer (other than 3.2 beer in some states).

In addition to attempting to prevent teenagers from driving while drunk, some states have instituted programs in which motorists are stopped for sobriety checks during holiday weekends. Others require first offenders to participate in education programs stressing that alcohol and driving do not mix. Critics of these efforts point out that most drunk drivers are not social drinkers who have overindulged but chronic alcoholics or problem drinkers. They claim that education programs will not change the behavior of these people; the alcohol addiction itself must be treated. On the other hand, groups like Mothers Against Drunk Driving call for strict legal sanctions against people who drink and drive. Both educational programs and law enforcement efforts seem to have had some effect: The number of alcohol-related automobile accident fatalities has decreased markedly, from 46.3 percent of all accidental deaths in 1982 to 39.7 percent in 1990 (Smothers, 1991).

Some of the methods used in drug law enforcement have been challenged on constitutional grounds. In one case a federal appeals court decision freezing the assets of defendants in drug cases was criticized as undermining the right to counsel and the presumption of innocence (Lubasch, 1988). Similarly, the use of undercover agents in schools may be a violation of privacy. The civil rights implications of such techniques have not yet been fully tested in the courts.

Many observers believe that the drug problem can be eased by revising drug laws so that they deal with issues more realistically and consistently. The most insistent demands for reform have focused on marijuana. It is considered illogical to classify marijuana with the far more dangerous hard drugs, and even people who do not favor legalization of marijuana use may support reductions in the penalties for possession and sale of the drug. So far, however, there has not been a major shift in public opinion in favor of legalization of marijuana that would allow lawmakers to seriously consider such legislation.

With regard to hard drugs, some experts advocate revision of the law and, in some cases, legalization of these drugs. One argument for the legalization of heroin is that it would drive down the price of the drug so that addicts would no longer be compelled to engage in crime to support their habit; the British system is cited in support of this position. The British view drug addiction as a disease that requires treatment, and they regulate the distribution of narcotics through physicians and government-run clinics. This system does not give addicts unlimited access to narcotics, but it eases the problem of supply. Those who oppose this approach fear that it might tempt people to experiment with drugs. Moreover, the British system is flawed because many addicts do not wish to register their addiction and prefer to find sources in the illegal drug markets (MacGregor, 1990).

What can be said about legalization at this writing is that more social scientists and law enforcement officials are taking its possibility seriously. Thus, Harvard sociologist Nathan Glazer, a critic of liberal social policies, has stated: "Is it possible to reduce the intensity of the war against drugs, no great success to date, by some degree of legalization? I'm definitely on the side of let's talk about it" (quoted in Roberts, 1990, p. B1). It should be noted, however, that opposition to legalization is very strong in minority communities, where it is often seen as a form of surrender that is likely to entrap even more poor minority people in addiction (Nadelmann, 1992).

The problem of enforcement at the national level is complicated by issues of foreign policy. Through economic and military aid, the United States supports the governments of countries that are major suppliers of illegal drugs, particularly Colombia, Peru, and Bolivia. It has been suggested that the United States should suspend foreign aid to governments that do not cooperate with efforts to stop the flow of drugs into the U.S. market. Other suggestions include imposing trade sanctions on those countries or reducing military assistance to them. The invasion of Panama and the capture of Panamanian dictator Manuel Noriega in December 1989 illustrate the influence of narcotics control efforts on foreign policy.

An issue that has generated a great deal of controversy is the testing of public employees for drug use. Recent appeals court rulings have reversed lower court decisions holding that such testing violates the Fourth Amendment to the Constitution, which protects citizens against "unreasonable searches and seizures." Many private firms are imposing drug (including alcohol) testing on employees in sensitive positions. This trend has become especially prominent since the *Exxon Valdez* oil spill in 1989.

Today drug abuse remains one of the most serious social problems in the United States. At present there is no fully effective means of dealing with it; drug traffickers have succeeded in overcoming every obstacle placed in their way, and the demand for illegal drugs remains high. Some experts believe that there is no solution to the problem; others are convinced that it would be even worse without existing enforcement efforts. The Clinton administration is committed to shifting the emphasis of drug policies away from interdiction of supplies, concentrating instead on education about the dangers of alcohol and drug use. These policies, and the need for more adequate funding of alcohol and drug treatment programs, will be the themes of substance abuse legislation in the mid-1990s.

SUMMARY

1. In sociological contexts, the term *drug* refers to any chemical substance that affects body functions, mood, perception, or consciousness; has a potential for misuse; and may be harmful to the user or to society. Drug abuse is any use of unacceptable drugs, and excessive or inappropriate use of acceptable drugs, so that physical or psychological harm can result.

2. The issue of drug use has objective and subjective dimensions. The objective aspect is the degree to which a given substance causes physiological, psychological, or social problems for the individual or the social group. The subjective aspect involves people's perceptions of the consequences of drug use and how those perceptions result in social action.

3. The word *addiction* is used to describe physical dependence on a drug, in which the body has adjusted to its presence. The word *habituation* is sometimes used to mean psychological dependence on a drug, in which the user needs the drug for the feeling of well-being that it produces.

4. Alcohol use is widely accepted in Western culture, even though its abuse creates many complex problems. There are large numbers of problem drinkers and alcoholics (alcohol addicts) in the United States. It is possible that the tendency to become an alcoholic is an inherited trait.

5. Drinking is heaviest at higher socioeconomic levels, among men, among nonchurchgoers, and in cultures whose members do not normally drink alcoholic beverages with meals. Alcohol is the most widely used drug among youth. Older people are less likely than younger people to drink, but as the proportion of elderly people in the population increases, so does the number of problem drinkers and alcoholics among the elderly.

6. Social problems related to excessive alcohol use include health problems, automobile accidents, criminal conduct, family disorganization, and homelessness.

7. Attempts to help alcoholics overcome their addiction take a variety of forms, including group therapy (e.g., Alcoholics Anonymous), Antabuse programs, and community care and employee assistance programs.

8. The most commonly abused drugs are marijuana, cocaine and its derivative crack, the opiates, the hallucinogens, the amphetamines, and the barbiturates. Of these, by far the most widely used is marijuana.

9. Drug use is largely a matter of opportunity. The younger one is at the time of the first opportunity to try a drug, the more likely one is to eventually try it.

10. It is generally agreed that drug use is a learned social behavior. The user must learn how to use the drug and to identify his or her reaction to it as pleasant. The most important direct influence on drug use is that of the peer group. People can stop using drugs relatively easily if their social milieu does not encourage such use.

11. The drugs that are most frequently associated with criminal behavior are heroin and crack; many addicts cannot hold jobs and must resort to crime to support their habit. Increased use of crack is also associated with criminal activity and with high rates of murder and violence in large cities.

12. The primary means by which AIDS is transmitted among the heterosexual population is through the sharing of needles and syringes by intravenous drug users. Efforts to prevent the spread of the virus in this way face a number of obstacles, including legal barriers and public opposition.

13. Approaches to the rehabilitation of addicts include therapeutic communities, where individuals prepare to reenter the larger society at their own pace; methadone maintenance, in which a synthetic narcotic is used to wean addicts from heroin; and the use of narcotic antagonists, substances that prevent the euphoria produced by opiates.

14. Increased emphasis on law enforcement has not solved the problems associated with abuse of alcohol and other drugs. Many people advocate reform of the law, especially with regard to marijuana use. Some also call for legalization of hard drugs, but this remains a highly controversial issue.

SUGGESTED READINGS

American Academy of Arts and Sciences. *Political Pharmacology: Thinking About Drugs* (Proceedings of the American Academy of Arts and Sciences). Cambridge, MA, Summer 1992. A collection of critical evaluations of U.S. drug policy by a panel of accomplished researchers in the field of substance abuse.

BAYER, RONALD (ED.). *Re-Thinking Drug Policy.* Cambridge, England: Cambridge University Press, 1993. Discusses recent research on the demographics of drug use, trends in alcohol- and drug-related crime, effects on minority communities, and many other central topics in the area of substance use and social policy.

BECKER, HOWARD S. *Outsiders.* New York: Free Press, 1963. The classic treatment of labeling theory.

BROOK, ROBERT C., AND PAUL C. WHITEHEAD. *Drug-Free: Therapeutic Community.* New York: Human Sciences Press, 1981. An evaluation of a therapeutic community for young amphetamine abusers.

COHEN, SIDNEY. *The Substance Abuse Problems.* Binghamton, NY: Haworth Press, 1981. A collection of essays by a former director of the top federal drug-abuse agency; describes alcohol as the most dangerous of all drugs.

MORALES, EDMUNDO. *Cocaine: White Gold Rush in Peru.* Tucson: University of Arizona Press, 1988. A study by a Peruvian sociologist of the enormous impact the North American appetite for cocaine has had on the inhabitants of Andean villages.

PEELE, STANTON. "A Moral Vision of Addiction: How People's Values Determine Whether They Become and Remain Addicts." *Journal of Drug Issues* 17 (1987): 187–215. An analysis of the relationship between people's values and their use or nonuse of drugs.

SCHAFFER, HOWARD, AND MILTON EARL BURGLASS. *Classic Contributions in the Addictions.* New York: Brunner/Mazel, 1981. A group of readings on the theory of addiction treatment.

VAILLANT, GEORGE. *The Natural History of Alcoholism.* Cambridge, MA: Harvard University Press, 1983. The definitive history of alcoholism in the United States and other societies.

WILLIAMS, TERRY. *The Cocaine Kids.* Reading, MA: Addison-Wesley, 1988. A brilliant ethnographic study of the young people who become involved in the cocaine trade in a large American city and its effects on their lives.

Crime and Criminals

Chapter Outline

■ Crimes reported to the police account for about a third of actual offenses and about half of violent crimes.

■ Eighty-three percent of the population aged 12 in 1987 can expect to be victims or intended victims of violent crimes at least once in their lifetimes.

■ Women account for 5.5 percent of the total prison population in the United States.

■ People under 25 account for about 59 percent of all arrests for property crimes.

■ In 1992 more than 13 million violent and property crimes were committed in the United States.

Americans consistently rank crime among the most serious social problems in the United States. Depending on their concerns about such issues as health care or the state of the economy, they may rank these as more serious problems at a given moment. But for many decades crime has been ranked at or very near the top of the list of major social problems. This is why every president feels compelled to propose legislation to combat crime shortly after election, as President Clinton did in the first year of his administration.

It is important to realize, however, that at least some crime has existed in almost all societies. As the French sociologist Émile Durkheim (1950) pointed out, wherever there are people and laws, there are crime and criminals:

> Crime is present . . . in all societies of all types. There is no society that is not confronted with the problem of criminality. Its form changes; the acts thus characterized are not the same everywhere; but, everywhere and always, there have been men who have behaved in such a way as to draw upon themselves penal repression. . . . What is normal, simply, is the existence of criminality. (p. 65)

It is generally agreed that despite some areas of improvement the rate of serious and violent crime has reached alarming proportions in the United States. Indeed, there is much disagreement over whether there have been improvements at all. Measured from 1980 to 1989, there have been decreases in crime rates, but since 1985 the rates for all crimes except burglary have been increasing.

One reason for the disagreement is that it is extremely difficult to measure actual rates of crime. Regular surveys by the Law Enforcement Assistance Administration reveal that the actual rates of violent personal and property crime are several times higher than the official rates presented in the FBI's *Uniform Crime Reports (UCR),* which are based on crimes reported to the police. Many victims do not report crimes to the police because they believe that nothing can be done or that the crime was unimportant. Sample surveys of Americans indicate that crimes reported to the police account for about 33 percent of actual offenses and about 50 percent of violent crimes (Reid, 1991).

Even with a large proportion of crimes going unreported, statistics show a rapid increase in crime in the early 1970s. The crime rate continued to increase in the late 1970s, but in the early 1980s it began to level off. The rate per 100,000 inhabitants actually declined somewhat between 1982 and 1983 but began increasing slowly again after 1984. Since 1985 there has been a steady increase in the absolute number of serious crimes and in the rate of crime per 100,000 inhabitants, which controls for any increase in population size that alone might result in more crime. The number of serious crime offenses reported to the police in 1992 was approximately 14.4 million, of which over half were larceny or theft. Violent crimes, including murder, forcible rape, robbery, and aggravated assault, accounted for 13.5 percent of all known crimes in 1992 (*UCR,* 1993). (See Figures 6–1, 6–2, 6–3, and 6–4.)

Sociologists believe that the dip in crime rates in the 1980s was due largely to the fact that the "baby boom" generation had matured past the crime-prone adolescent and young adult years. But crime rates are also quite sensitive to changes in economic conditions, and the small but appreciable rise in crime rates in recent years may reflect the declining fortunes of certain parts of the United States, especially the older manufacturing centers and some farming communities. Thus, although the deceleration of crime rates since the 1970s is most welcome, the rates remain high.

The extent of the nation's crime problem is measured by a special index called the *crime index*. Developed by the Committee on Uniform Crime Records of the International Association of Chiefs of Police, the crime index collects data on the most serious and most frequently occurring crimes—those that are most likely to come to the attention of the police. These include murder and nonnegligent manslaughter, forcible rape, robbery, aggravated assault, burglary, larceny-theft, motor vehicle theft, and arson. The statistics reported throughout this chapter are taken from the crime index.

Official statistics, of course, do not tell the whole story. It has never been easy, for example, to assess accurately the extent of organized and occupational (white-collar) crime. Exposures of scandals in government and business show that these types of crime are far more widespread and pervasive than is generally realized. Not only is the rate of crime itself extremely high, but fear of crime, especially in large cities, significantly affects the lives of many people. Large numbers of Americans feel unsafe in their homes, neighborhoods, or workplaces. Many have stopped going to places they used to go to at night, and fear of violent crime is widespread.

Sociologists who study the effect of press coverage of crime on public fear of

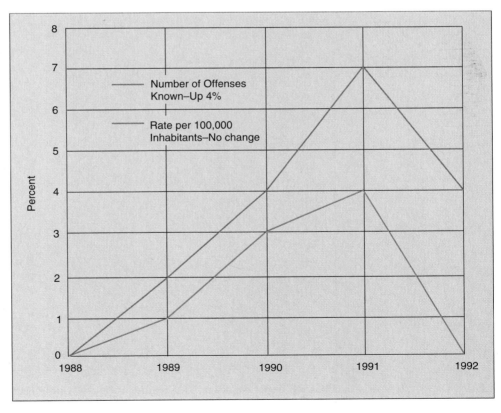

FIGURE 6–1   Crime Index Total (percent change from 1988)

Source: UCR, 1990.

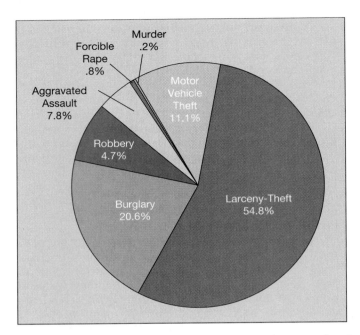

FIGURE 6–2 Crime Index Offenses, 1989 (percent distribution)

Source: UCR, 1990.

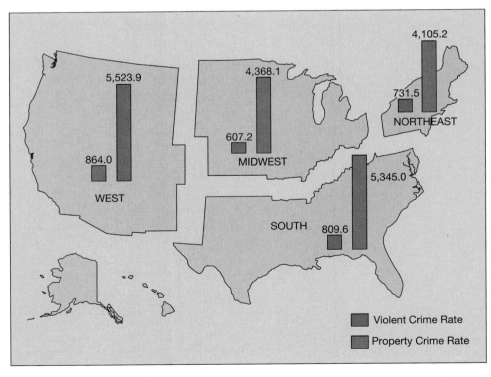

FIGURE 6–3 Regional Violent and Property Crime Rates, 1989 (per 100,000 inhabitants)

Source: UCR, 1990.

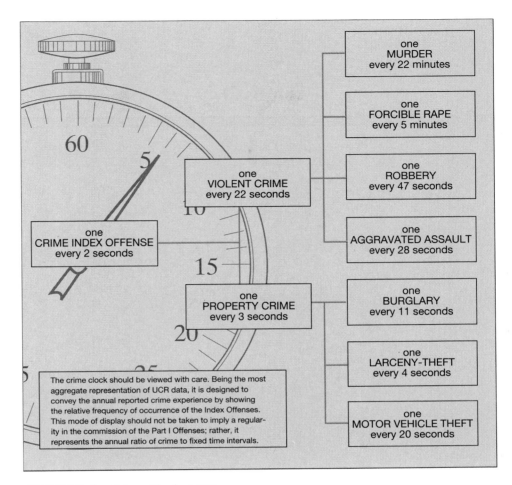

The crime clock should be viewed with care. Being the most aggregate representation of UCR data, it is designed to convey the annual reported crime experience by showing the relative frequency of occurrence of the Index Offenses. This mode of display should not be taken to imply a regularity in the commission of the Part I Offenses; rather, it represents the annual ratio of crime to fixed time intervals.

one CRIME INDEX OFFENSE every 2 seconds

one VIOLENT CRIME every 22 seconds

one PROPERTY CRIME every 3 seconds

one MURDER every 22 minutes

one FORCIBLE RAPE every 5 minutes

one ROBBERY every 47 seconds

one AGGRAVATED ASSAULT every 28 seconds

one BURGLARY every 11 seconds

one LARCENY-THEFT every 4 seconds

one MOTOR VEHICLE THEFT every 20 seconds

FIGURE 6–4   Crime Clock, 1992

Source: UCR, 1993.

crime report that attitudes about safety in one's neighborhood and about going out at night in the city in which one resides vary directly with the rate of index crimes in that city, but that reports of crime in other cities make people feel safe in comparison. The reports of crime that are most closely correlated with fear of crime are those describing sensational murders in one's own city, that is, murders that are reported on the front pages of newspapers and on television. Other murders, even in one's own city, do not have a measurable impact (Heath, 1984; Liska & Baccaglini, 1990). Of course, the crimes that are most likely to generate fear of crime are those that directly affect one's family and friends, even if the crimes are relatively minor compared to murder. (Table 6–1 lists crime rates for selected cities.)

THE NATURE OF CRIME

There is no single, universally agreed-upon definition of crime. In the words of one of the world's foremost historians of crime, the late Sir Leon Radzinowicz, crime

is something that threatens serious harm to the community, or something generally believed to do so, or something committed with evil intent, or something forbidden in the

TABLE 6–1   CRIME RATES, BY TYPE—SELECTED LARGE CITIES: 1991
(OFFENSES KNOWN TO THE POLICE PER 100,000 POPULATION. BASED ON BUREAU OF THE CENSUS ESTIMATED RESIDENT POPULATION AS OF JULY 1.)

CITY RANKED BY POPULATION SIZE, 1990*	Crime index, total	VIOLENT CRIME					PROPERTY CRIME			
		Total	Murder	Forcible rape	Robbery	Aggravated assault	Total	Burglary	Larceny-theft	Motor vehicle theft
New York, NY	9,236	2,318	29.3	39.3	1,340	909	6,918	1,524	3,489	1,904
Los Angeles, CA	9,730	2,526	28.9	55.3	1,118	1,324	7,204	1,615	3,660	1,929
Chicago, IL	(*)	(*)	32.9	(*)	1,557	1,502	8,228	1,858	4,684	1,686
Houston, TX	10,824	1,600	36.5	72.8	833	657	9,225	2,385	4,429	2,411
Philadelphia, PA	6,833	1,406	27.6	56.6	872	450	5,427	1,344	2,560	1,523
San Diego, CA	8,537	1,220	14.7	41.6	470	693	7,317	1,507	3,938	1,872
Detroit, MI	12,264	2,727	59.3	137.7	1,309	1,221	9,536	2,515	4,248	2,774
Dallas, TX	15,066	2,568	48.6	117.5	1,094	1,308	12,497	3,064	6,994	2,439
Phoenix, AZ	9,958	1,106	12.9	48.2	346	698	8,853	2,432	4,753	1,667
San Antonio, TX	12,291	792	21.8	73.0	395	302	11,498	2,609	7,381	1,508
San Jose, CA	5,364	659	6.6	55.7	166	430	4,706	927	3,214	565
Baltimore, MD	11,371	2,544	40.6	93.7	1,440	970	8,827	2,170	5,242	1,416
Indianapolis, IN	7,357	1,445	19.4	114.6	409	902	5,912	1,784	3,059	1,069
San Francisco, CA	9,384	1,645	12.9	54.1	950	629	7,738	1,435	4,692	1,611
Jacksonville, FL	10,331	1,629	18.2	109.6	589	913	8,702	2,588	5,033	1,082
Columbus, OH	10,145	1,131	21.6	101.8	587	421	9,014	2,568	5,165	1,280
Milwaukee, WI	9,044	979	25.6	78.9	668	206	8,065	1,482	4,451	2,133
Memphis, TN	10,184	1,422	27.3	105.3	727	563	8,761	2,674	3,929	2,159
Washington, DC	10,755	2,452	80.1	35.8	1,215	1,121	8,303	2,074	4,869	1,360
Boston, MA	10,837	2,066	19.7	84.9	836	1,126	8,771	1,752	4,669	2,350
Seattle, WA	12,255	1,364	8.1	82.1	519	755	10,891	1,998	7,607	1,286
El Paso, TX	9,630	1,067	9.3	50.3	282	725	8,563	1,727	5,787	1,050
Cleveland, OH	8,945	1,832	34.3	179.1	1,007	612	7,113	1,991	3,037	2,085
New Orleans, LA	10,831	2,190	68.9	60.3	1,192	869	8,640	2,476	4,189	1,975
Nashville-Davidson, TN	8,665	1,575	17.3	101.3	522	934	7,090	2,034	4,298	757
Denver, CO	7,625	1,050	18.4	89.1	341	602	6,575	1,915	3,448	1,213
Austin, TX	11,295	624	10.3	58.0	327	229	10,671	2,437	7,237	997
Fort Worth, TX	16,973	1,950	42.7	96.7	749	1,061	15,023	3,692	8,385	2,946
Oklahoma City, OK	11,073	1,128	12.5	105.3	334	677	9,945	2,634	5,997	1,314
Portland, OR	11,182	1,806	11.8	103.2	606	1,086	9,376	2,113	5,838	1,425
Kansas City, MO	13,198	2,833	30.8	108.9	1,131	1,562	10,366	2,969	5,141	2,256
Long Beach, CA	9,131	2,101	21.4	64.8	929	1,086	7,031	1,802	3,719	1,510
Tucson, AZ	10,401	939	5.8	80.0	214	639	9,462	1,807	6,819	836
St. Louis, MO	16,031	3,520	65.0	85.5	1,324	2,046	12,511	3,350	6,848	2,313
Charlotte, NC	12,643	2,176	28.3	101.6	720	1,326	10,467	2,885	6,905	677

City									
Atlanta, GA	18,953	4,041	50.9	158.3	1,607	2,225	14,912	3,439	8,742	2,732
Virginia Beach, VA	5,859	272	6.8	31.8	128	105	5,587	1,042	4,213	332
Albuquerque, NM	10,284	1,422	13.0	66.4	332	1,010	8,862	2,632	5,602	628
Oakland, CA	12,187	2,496	39.2	121.1	1,035	1,301	9,691	2,329	5,446	1,916
Pittsburgh, PA	8,219	1,153	9.7	80.6	726	337	7,066	1,582	3,476	2,008
Sacramento, CA	10,098	1,299	17.5	58.6	605	618	8,800	2,056	4,739	2,004
Minneapolis, MN	11,282	1,578	17.1	199.3	699	662	9,704	2,408	5,935	1,361
Tulsa, OK	8,887	1,328	11.3	111.7	396	809	7,559	2,353	3,692	1,514
Honolulu, HI	5,959	240	3.4	32.1	100	104	5,718	1,157	4,206	356
Cincinnati, OH	9,722	1,578	14.7	130.2	631	803	8,144	2,312	5,253	579
Miami, FL	18,256	4,191	34.0	64.1	2,304	1,789	14,065	3,396	8,322	2,347
Fresno, CA	12,031	1,274	14.4	78.0	604	579	10,757	2,168	5,406	3,184
Omaha, NE	7,081	956	10.3	61.1	187	698	6,125	1,176	4,437	512
Toledo, OH	9,503	1,038	10.7	124.5	538	365	8,465	1,753	5,284	1,428
Buffalo, NY	9,555	1,835	15.2	96.9	821	901	7,721	2,569	3,804	1,348
Wichita, KS	9,830	872	7.8	92.7	458	313	8,958	2,435	5,579	944
Santa Ana, CA	7,654	1,103	19.7	25.3	649	409	6,552	1,418	3,684	1,449
Mesa, AZ	7,596	698	5.1	52.9	132	508	6,897	1,562	4,452	884
Colorado Springs, CO	7,441	481	8.7	80.2	134	258	6,960	1,341	5,205	414
Tampa, FL	16,286	3,491	19.5	116.6	1,048	2,307	12,795	3,841	6,842	2,113
Newark, NJ	14,806	3,400	31.8	88.2	1,881	1,399	11,406	2,235	4,122	5,049
St. Paul, MN	7,892	990	4.4	103.7	308	574	6,902	1,662	4,396	844
Louisville, KY	6,425	828	15.9	57.9	459	295	5,598	1,846	3,114	638
Anaheim, CA	7,152	714	9.2	40.8	362	303	6,438	1,577	3,717	1,144
Birmingham, AL	12,586	2,565	51.6	103.6	691	1,719	10,021	2,931	5,521	1,568
Arlington, TX	9,480	789	9.7	62.1	262	455	8,692	1,788	5,640	1,264
Norfolk, VA	9,243	1,158	32.4	77.2	577	472	8,084	1,722	5,251	1,111
Corpus Christi, TX	10,443	825	12.2	77.6	226	509	9,618	2,217	6,814	588
St. Petersburg, FL	10,427	2,225	12.7	71.9	767	1,373	8,202	2,144	5,061	998
Rochester, NY	11,196	1,036	27.5	71.4	588	349	10,159	2,572	6,729	859
Jersey City, NJ	9,201	2,011	10.0	42.3	1,123	836	7,190	2,009	2,831	2,350
Anchorage, AK	6,687	712	10.7	112.5	231	357	5,976	1,061	4,249	656
Lexington-Fayette, KY	7,018	794	5.7	72.2	200	516	6,255	1,414	4,437	374
Akron, OH	8,066	1,257	17.8	99.2	442	697	6,809	1,771	4,253	785
Aurora, CO	8,631	1,645	4.8	80.8	248	1,312	6,986	1,432	4,996	558
Baton Rouge, LA	13,118	2,316	24.6	60.3	484	1,747	10,802	2,714	6,807	1,282
Stockton, CA	11,327	1,288	25.5	74.8	693	494	10,039	2,288	5,972	1,780
Raleigh, NC	7,790	833	11.8	56.8	309	456	6,957	1,861	4,675	420
Shreveport, LA	10,098	1,258	25.0	60.0	362	811	8,840	2,269	6,039	531

*The rates for forcible rape, violent crime, and crime index are not shown because the forcible rape figures were not in accordance with national Uniform Crime Reporting guidelines.

Source: *Statistical Abstract*, 1993.

interests of the most powerful sections of society. But there are crimes that elude each of these definitions and there are forms of behavior under each of them that escape the label of crime. The argument that crime is anything forbidden, or punishable, under the criminal law is open to the objection that it is circular. But at least it is clear cut, it refers not to what ought to be but to what is, and it is an essential starting point. (Radzinowicz & King, 1977, p. 17)

According to this argument, a *crime* is any act or omission of an act for which the state can apply sanctions. This is the most frequently used definition of crime and the one we will use in this chapter. However, it should be kept in mind that definitions of crime are subject to changing values and public sentiments; moreover, as we will see shortly, factors such as police discretion play a major role in the interpretation of particular behaviors as crimes.

The *criminal law* in any society prohibits certain acts and prescribes the punishments to be meted out to violators. Confusion frequently arises because although the criminal law prescribes certain rules for living in society, not all violations of social rules are violations of criminal laws. A swimmer's failure to come to the aid of a drowning stranger, for example, would not constitute a criminal act, although it might be considered morally wrong for the swimmer not to have done whatever was possible to save the victim short of risking his or her own life.

Many acts that are regarded as immoral are ignored in the criminal law but are considered civil offenses. Under *civil law*—laws that deal with noncriminal acts in which one individual injures another—the state arbitrates between the aggrieved party and the offender. For example, civil law is involved when a person whose car was destroyed in an accident sues the driver responsible for the accident in order to recover the cost of the car. The driver at fault is not considered a criminal unless he or she can be shown to have broken a criminal law—for instance, to have been driving while intoxicated. Further confusion results from changes in social attitudes, which usually precede changes in the criminal law. In some states, for example, old laws that are still "on the books" continue to define as criminal some acts that are no longer considered wrong by society, such as certain forms of sexual behavior between consenting adults.

Police Discretion

In addition to problems of definition, such as ambiguity about whether or not an act such as loitering is a crime, certain other factors contribute to the difficulty of knowing what crimes are committed in a particular society. A significant factor is the role of police discretion. In practice, the definition of criminality changes according to what the police believe criminal behavior to be. Given the thousands of laws on the books, the police have considerable discretion regarding which laws to ignore, which laws to enforce, and how strongly to enforce them. This discretionary power, in turn, gives them many opportunities to exercise their own concept of lawful behavior in decisions about what citizen complaints merit attention, whom they should arrest, and who should be released.

In an important study of police discretion, Michael K. Brown (1988) compared police activities in two Los Angeles police districts and three smaller suburban towns in the Los Angeles metropolitan region. On the basis of interviews with patrol officers and their supervisors, he concluded that

a police bureaucracy has a significant impact on the behavior of patrolmen. . . . Patrolmen in the two divisions of the LAPD are formalistic and more willing to make an arrest in a variety of incidents than patrolmen in small departments, who are consistently more lenient and less willing to invoke the force of the law in the same circumstances. (p. 275)

When asked whether they would normally arrest disorderly juveniles on their beat, for example, 28 percent of veteran police officers with five years or more experience in the smaller departments said that they would not arrest the offenders, while 65 percent of the LAPD veteran officers said that they would seek to arrest disorderly juveniles. Note that these findings apply to a limited number of communities. They cannot be said to demonstrate that big-city police officers always behave differently than those in smaller towns. They do, however, resemble the findings of other social-scientific studies, which have shown that police discretion can account for important differences in the enforcement of laws from one community to another (Lipskey, 1980).

In a classic study of two groups of adolescents in the same high school, William Chambliss (1973) examined how the biases of the local police affected their treatment of middle- and lower-class delinquents. A group of middle-class boys—the "Saints"—had been truant almost every day of the two-year period during which they were studied. They drove recklessly, drank excessively, and openly cheated on exams. Yet only twice were members of the Saints stopped by police officers; even then, nothing appeared on their school records. The members of the other group, the "Roughnecks," all came from lower-class families. Unlike the Saints, who had cars and could "sow their wild oats" in parts of town where they were not known, the Roughnecks were confined to an area where they could be easily recognized; they therefore developed a reputation for being delinquent.

The demeanor of the two groups of boys differed markedly when they were apprehended by the police. The Saints, who were apologetic, penitent, and generally respectful of middle-class values, were treated as harmless pranksters. The Roughnecks, who were openly hostile and disdainful toward the police, were labeled as deviant. These results demonstrate that factors such as low income, unemployment, or minority status are not the only ones that have a bearing on the commission of juvenile crimes. Although such factors did account for a higher rate of detection and punishment, the rates of actual misbehavior in Chambliss's study were virtually the same for both groups. Differences in the official records of the two groups reflected the discretionary power of the police.

Problems of Accuracy

Another factor that contributes to the problem of determining the level of crime in a society is that police statistics depend on police reports, which, in turn, depend on the level and quality of police personnel in a given area. Since police are assigned to lower-income communities in greater numbers, there is a tendency for police records to show higher crime rates for those communities and lower rates for more affluent areas.

If official data on crime can be shown to be less than fully accurate on a limited scale, it is possible that similar problems undermine the accuracy of national crime statistics. The standard index of criminal activity in the United States is the *UCR*, which supplies racial and economic profiles of people arrested for such common-law crimes as murder, rape, assault, and robbery. Recent data support the long-held assumption that minority group members are more likely than nonminority individuals to be involved in crimes. Yet it must be remembered that *UCR* statistics cite only individuals who are apprehended for their crimes. If, like the Saints in the Chambliss study, adult offenders belonging to middle- and upper-class groups are rarely caught or punished, *UCR*-based data become inaccurate. Because it does not profile those who successfully evade apprehension and prosecution, the *UCR* fails to reveal the entire range of criminal activity in the United States.

Acting on this hypothesis, researchers have attempted to devise more reliable ways of tracking criminal activity. Self-report studies, which ask respondents to report their own criminal involvement through an anonymous questionnaire, have provided alternative data. In a study examining the correlation between race and criminal activity, Michael Hindelang (1978) evaluated the results of various self-report studies. He found that data from such studies did not concur with *UCR* findings. Whereas minority groups have higher crime rates when judged by official data (such as juvenile or criminal court records or the *UCR* index), self-reporting techniques indicate that whites and nonwhites have similar rates of criminal activity. Thus, the idea that race is a factor in criminality is called into question when different standards of measurement are used. On the other hand, some criminologists argue that while self-report studies question the distribution of crime in the population, they do not show significant differences in levels of crime from those shown in the *UCR* (Elliot & Ageton, 1980; Kempf, 1990).

Another attempt to supplement *UCR* data has led to the development of *victimization reports*. These surveys, conducted by the Census Bureau, collect information from a representative sample of crime victims. Comparisons of *UCR* and victimization indexes reveal discrepancies in the data, and depending on which standard is used, different conclusions can be drawn about the correlation between crime and socioeconomic status (Reid, 1993). *UCR* data reflect only crimes that are reported, yet many victims—through fear, ignorance, or alienation—do not file reports. Victimization surveys indicate that this is particularly true in low-income, high-crime areas. Certain crimes—especially sex-related crimes such as rape and child molestation—are underreported, and the statistics are distorted as a result.

The difficulty of finding a reliable index for measuring the impact of socioeconomic status on criminal activity makes it necessary to consider many sources before reaching a conclusion. Thus, after comparing thirty-five separate studies on the subject, one team of researchers hypothesized that social class has no bearing on an individual's likelihood of being involved in criminal activity (Tittle, Villemez, & Smith, 1978). Members of the middle and upper classes have a delinquency rate proportionately equal to that of their lower-class neighbors.

In sum, it appears that the poor, the undereducated, and minority groups have become the victims of selective law enforcement, stereotyping, and misleading statistics. The rich and powerful, on the other hand, have been insulated from these problems. They are so seldom sent to prison that when one of them is finally jailed for fraud, embezzlement, or tax evasion, it makes headlines. Some sociologists, noting the difficulty of obtaining accurate information on the incidence of such crimes, have contended that the upper classes may actually have a higher rate of crime than the lower classes (Pepinsky & Quinney, 1991; Reckless, 1973). It will be helpful to keep these contrasts in mind as we discuss the various types of crime.

TYPES OF CRIME AND CRIMINALS

In this section we will review nine major types of crime and criminals. Seven of these have been classified by sociologists Marshall B. Clinard and Richard Quinney (1973), who categorized criminal behavior according to how large a part criminal activity plays in people's lives, that is, whether or not people see themselves as criminals and the extent to which they commit themselves to a life of crime. To these we add an eighth category, juvenile delinquency, and a ninth, corporate crime. Two forms of illegal activity—occupational and organized crime—will receive more extensive treatment here because their social costs probably exceed those of all the others combined.

Violent Personal Crime

This category of crime includes assault, robbery, and the various types of homicide—acts in which physical injury is inflicted or threatened. The incidence of such crimes is very high. One study concluded that 83 percent of the population aged 12 in 1987 could expect to be victims or intended victims of violent crimes at least once in their lifetime, and 52 percent would be victims of such crimes more than once (U.S. Department of Justice, 1987).

Although robbery occurs most often between strangers, murders are very often a result of violent disputes between friends or relatives. In 1989, 54 out of every 100 murder victims were related to or acquainted with their assailants, and murders initiated by arguments (as opposed to premeditated murders) accounted for 35 percent of all murders committed during that year. Murders and aggravated assaults, therefore, are usually considered unpremeditated acts. The offenders are portrayed in the media as normally law-abiding individuals who are not likely to engage in other criminal activities. Some murders may be "contract murders" that are committed by hired killers and often linked to organized crime. When weapons are involved, guns account for 68.2 percent of murders (*UCR,* 1993). (Violent crimes are discussed more fully in Chapter 7.)

Occasional Property Crime

Crimes of this type include vandalism, check forgery, shoplifting, and some kinds of automobile theft. These crimes are usually unsophisticated in nature, and the offenders lack the skills of the professional criminal. Because occasional offenders commit their crimes at irregular intervals, they are not likely to associate with habitual lawbreakers. Nonprofessional shoplifters, for example, view themselves as respectable law abiders who steal articles from stores only for their own use. They excuse their behavior on the grounds that what they steal has relatively little value and the "victim" is usually a large, impersonal organization that can easily replace the stolen article (Pepinsky & Quinney, 1991; Quinney, 1970).

Neither nonprofessional shoplifters nor nonprofessional check forgers are likely to have a criminal record. Like vandals and car thieves, they usually work alone and are not part of a criminal subculture; they do not seek to earn a living from crime.

Occupational (White-Collar) Crime

The phenomenon of occupational crime was defined and popularized by sociologist Edwin H. Sutherland, first in a 1940 article and then in his 1961 book *White Collar Crime.* Sutherland analyzed the behavior of people who break the law as part of

Shoplifting or "boosting" is one of the most common forms of juvenile crime.

their normal business activity: corporate directors who use their inside knowledge to sell large blocks of stock at tremendous profits; accountants who juggle books to conceal the hundreds of dollars of company funds that they have pocketed; and firms that make false statements about their profits to avoid paying taxes. Such acts tend to be ignored by society. They rarely come to the criminal courts, and even then they are rarely judged as severely as other kinds of criminal activities.

Since Sutherland first described it, the category of occupational crime has also come to include such acts as false advertising, violations of labor laws, price fixing, antitrust violations, and black-market activities.

The occupational offender is far removed from the popular stereotype of a criminal. Few people imagine that a lawyer or stockbroker is likely to engage in illegal activities. Because of their respectable appearance, it is difficult to think of these offenders as criminals. In fact, occupational offenders often consider themselves respectable citizens and do everything possible to avoid being labeled as lawbreakers—even by themselves.

Sutherland's theory of *differential association* asserts that occupational criminality, like other forms of systematic criminal behavior, is learned through frequent direct or indirect association with people who are already engaging in such behavior. (We discuss this theory later in the chapter.) Thus, people who become occupational criminals may do so simply by getting into businesses or occupations in which their colleagues regard certain kinds of crime as the standard way of conducting business.

A good example of occupational crime is the "insider trading" that frequently occurs in the securities industry. Some stockbrokers and major shareholders may be privy to "inside" information about an impending corporate merger or a change in the financial condition of a company that will affect the price of its stock. Brokers who possess such information are prohibited from either profiting from it themselves or selling it to others who may be able to profit from it. Nevertheless, in the 1980s the senior partners of several large brokerage houses were convicted of using inside information to make hundreds of illegal stock transactions worth many millions of dollars (Auletta, 1987).

Embezzlement   *Embezzlement*, or theft from one's employer, is usually committed by otherwise law-abiding people during the course of their employment. Embezzlement occurs at all levels of business, from a clerk stealing petty cash to a vice-president stealing large investment sums. Most cases are not detected, and companies are often unwilling to prosecute for fear of bad publicity. In 1992, 13,700 people were arrested for embezzlement (*UCR*, 1993).

Donald Cressey's book *Other People's Money* (1953) is a classic study of embezzlers. On the basis of interviews with convicted embezzlers, Cressey concluded that three basic conditions are necessary before people will turn to embezzlement. First, they must have a financial problem that they do not want other people to know about. Second, they must have an opportunity to steal. Third, they must be able to find a formula to rationalize the fact that they are committing a criminal act—such as "I'm just borrowing it to tide me over."

Fraud   *Fraud* is obtaining money or property under false pretenses. It can occur at any level of business and in any type of business relationship. A citizen defrauds the government by evading the payment of income taxes; workers defraud their employers by using company property or services for their personal benefit; an industry defrauds the public when its members agree to keep prices artificially high. The cost of fraud may run from a few cents to millions of dollars, and the methods may be as crude as the butcher's thumb on the scale or as sophisticated as the coordinated efforts of dozens of lawyers, executives, and government officials. In 1992 there were 424,600 arrests on charges of fraud (*UCR*, 1993).

Within this category of crime, the incidence of crimes committed by means of computer technology has increased dramatically. Computer crimes are quite diverse, ranging from "data diddling," or changing the data stored in a computer system, to "superzapping," or making unauthorized use of specialized programs to gain access to data stored in a computer system. Estimates of the amount of money stolen through computer crimes range from $100 million to $40 billion a year (Reid, 1991).

The U.S. government estimates the cost of white-collar crimes of all types at $40 billion a year; other estimates range as high as $100 billion, not including the costs of enforcement and court costs (Reid, 1991).

Corporate Crime

Corporate crime includes a wide range of illegal practices by private corporations. Although particular officials in a company may eventually be held responsible for them, these misdeeds often result from the organized activities of many employees. When a corporation illegally dumps toxic wastes into a stream or a landfill, for example, individuals throughout the company, from presidents and vice-presidents to truck drivers and laborers, may be involved. Such crime is extremely difficult to control because the lower-level employees can claim that they were carrying out orders from above, while top officials can deny knowledge of the practice and blame those below them. Law enforcement agencies thus are often frustrated in their efforts to locate guilty individuals and must settle for weaker sanctions against the corporation as a whole, usually in the form of fines and other penalties (French, 1984; Hills, 1987).

Corporate crimes include, but are not limited to, environmental crimes, illegal credit card manipulations, insider trading in financial institutions, intimidation of competitors and employees, illegal labor practices, defrauding of pension plans, falsification of company records, bribery of public officials, and computer crimes. Because it is so often undetected, there are no reliable estimates of the cost of corporate crime to the public (French, 1984; Weston, 1987). On occasion, however, major corporate crimes are exposed.

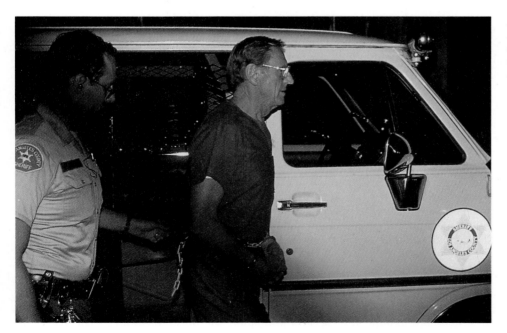

Real estate speculator Charles Keating is shown here in custody for his fraudulent manipulation of savings and loan deposits.

Measured in terms of loss of public and private funds, the single worst example of corporate crime in American history occurred toward the end of the 1980s. It is known as the savings and loan scandal and will cost taxpayers at least $500 billion over the next few years, not to mention the large amounts of unprotected savings lost by individuals. To assess the impact of this scandal one needs to realize that the total value of property reported stolen in other forms of crime each year amounts to about $13.4 billion (of which almost 40 percent is recovered, leaving an annual loss of about $8 billion). During the 1990s the amount paid to recoup the losses in the savings and loan scandal will be over six times greater than the total of all property lost to all other forms of crime over the same period.

Public-Order Crime

In terms of sheer numbers, public-order offenders constitute the largest category of criminals; their activities far outnumber reported crimes of any other type. Public-order offenses include prostitution, gambling, use of illegal substances, drunkenness, vagrancy, disorderly conduct, and traffic violations. Most of these are often called *victimless crimes* because they cause no harm to anyone but the offenders themselves. Society considers them crimes because they violate the order or customs of the community, but some of them, such as gambling and prostitution, are granted a certain amount of tolerance.

Public-order offenders rarely consider themselves criminals or view their actions as crimes. The behavior and activities of prostitutes and drug users, however, tend to isolate and segregate them from other members of society, and these individuals may find themselves drawn into criminal roles.

Conventional Crime

Conventional offenders tend to be young adults who commit robbery, larceny, burglary, and gang theft as a way of life. They usually begin their criminal career in adolescence as members of juvenile gangs, joining other truants from school to vandalize property and fight in the streets. As juvenile offenders they are not organized or skillful enough to avoid arrest and conviction, and by young adulthood they have compiled a police record and may have spent time in prison.

Conventional offenders could be described as semiprofessional, since their techniques are not as sophisticated as those of organized and professional criminals and they move into a criminal life only by degrees. For this reason, their self-concept as criminals develops gradually. By the time they have built up a criminal record, they have usually identified fairly strongly with criminality. The criminal record itself is society's way of defining these offenders as criminals. Once they have been so defined, it is almost impossible for them to reenter the mainstream of society.

Since only a small percentage of conventional crime results in arrest, most offenders in this category are convinced that crime does pay (Plate, 1975). Moreover, the life of a successful criminal has a certain excitement.

Many criminals are in a sense seduced into a life of crime by the excitement they experience in the criminal act itself. Not only the sudden windfall of money but the thrill of getting away with an illegal act and the release of tension after the act has been committed can become part of the reward system for crime (Katz, 1988). Because offenders associate mostly with other criminals, they develop a shared outlook that scorns the benefits of law-abiding behavior.

Organized Crime

The groups that we usually think of as representing organized crime tend to be large and diversified regional or national units. They may organize initially to carry on a particular crime, such as drug trafficking, extortion, prostitution, or gambling.

Later they may seek to control this activity within a given city or neighborhood, destroying or absorbing the competition. Eventually they may expand into other types of crime, protecting their members from arrest through intimidation or bribery of public officials.

Unlike other types of crime, organized crime is a system in which illegal activities are carried out as part of a rational plan devised by a large organization that is attempting to maximize its overall profit. To operate most efficiently, organized crime relies on division of labor in the performance of numerous diverse roles. Within a typical organized crime syndicate in a large metropolitan area, there will be groups in the stolen car and parts business, others in gambling, still others in labor rackets, and in each of these and other businesses there will be specific occupations like enforcer, driver, accountant, lawyer, and so on. Another major feature of organized crime is that the crime syndicate supplies goods and services that a large segment of the public wants but cannot obtain legally. Without the public's desire for gambling or drugs, for example, organized crime's basic means of existence would collapse.

In a controversial book titled *The Underground Empire*, James Mills (1986) describes a worldwide network of drug distributors that is able to operate with relatively little interference by law enforcement agencies because government officials are willing to accept information affecting national security in return for the sanctioning of drug traffic. Whether this is wholly true or not, there can be no doubt that drug trafficking and other organized crime activities bring in hundreds of billions of dollars in annual revenues, and those who control such sums have a great deal of power (Sterling, 1990). In some parts of the world, organized crime threatens the economic and social stability of entire nations, as can be seen in the civil strife caused by violent drug cartels in Colombia and other Latin American nations. In Italy in recent years the consequences of Mafia-related violence and corruption have threatened to create economic and social disaster (Calderone, 1993; Sterling, 1990).

Organized crime gets its huge profits from supplying illegal goods and services to the public. Its major source of profit is illegal gambling in the form of lotteries, "numbers," off-track betting, illegal casinos, and dice games. Much illegal gambling in the United States is controlled by organized crime syndicates operating through elaborate hierarchies. Money is transferred up the hierarchy from the small operator who takes the customer's bet through several other levels until it finally reaches the syndicate's headquarters. This complex system protects the leaders, whose identities remain concealed from those below them. Centralized organization of gambling also increases efficiency, enlarges markets, and provides a systematic way of paying graft to public officials.

Closely related to gambling and a major source of revenue for organized crime is loan sharking, or lending money at interest rates above the legal limit. These rates can be as high as 150 percent a week, and rates of more than 20 percent are common. Profits from gambling operations provide organized crime syndicates with large amounts of cash to lend, and they can ensure repayment by threatening violence. Most of the loans are made to gamblers who need to repay debts, to drug users, and to small businesses that are unable to obtain credit from legitimate sources.

Drug trafficking is organized crime's third major source of revenue. Its direct dealings in narcotics tend to be limited to importation from abroad and wholesale distribution. Lower-level operations are considered too risky and unprofitable and are left to others.

Organized crime uses some of its huge profits to expand into legitimate businesses that serve as useful tax covers and money-laundering operations. When organized crime figures have large amounts of cash from their illegal businesses and also spend lavishly for their personal lifestyles, they need ways of showing their income as legitimate gain so that they do not come under suspicion from IRS investigators and so that they can channel their cash into banks and other investments without attracting undue attention. These businesses also confer a certain amount of respectability and provide another source of profit. Using its ready reserves of cash and threats of force, the syndicate can temporarily lower prices to ruin competitors, employ strong-arm tactics to obtain customers, and generally conduct business outside the law.

Organized crime is also deeply involved in labor racketeering. By infiltrating labor unions, for example, it gains access to union funds; it may also make profitable deals with management. The disappearance (and probable murder) of Jimmy Hoffa, president of the International Brotherhood of Teamsters, in 1975 is believed to have been a result of the union's involvement with various crime "families."

Organized Crime and Corruption Organized crime could not flourish without bribery. By corrupting officials of public and private agencies, organized crime seeks to ensure that laws that would hamper its operations are not passed, or at least not enforced.

Corruption occurs at all levels of government, from police officers to high elected and appointed officials. It is especially effective with individuals in more powerful positions, since they can prevent lower-level personnel from enforcing laws against organized crime activities. If the cooperation of the police chief can be obtained, for example, a police officer who tries to arrest gamblers may be shifted to another assignment or denied a raise or promotion. Other officers will quickly learn from this example.

Professional Crime

Professional criminals are the ones we read about in detective novels or see on television: the expert safecracker with sensitive fingers; the disarming con artist; the customer in a jewelry store who switches diamonds so quickly that the clerk does not notice; the counterfeiters working under bright lights in the basement of a respectable shop. This class of criminals also includes the less glamorous pickpockets, full-time shoplifters and check forgers, truck hijackers, sellers of stolen goods, and blackmailers.

Professional criminals are dedicated to a life of crime; they live by it and pride themselves on their accomplishments. These criminals are seldom caught, and even if they are, they can usually manage to have the charges dropped or a sentence reduced. Meyer Lansky, a particularly successful thief who was also a top figure in a national crime syndicate, spent only three months and sixteen days in jail out of a criminal career that spanned over fifty years (Plate, 1975). These are the cleverest of all criminals, with the most sophisticated working methods.

Professional criminals tend to come from higher social strata than most people who are arrested for criminal activities. They frequently begin as employees in offices, hotels, and restaurants, with criminal life as a sideline. Eventually their criminal careers develop to the point at which they can make a living almost entirely from criminal activities. This phase usually starts at the same age at which conventional criminals are likely to give up crime. As criminologist E. M. Lemert put it, "Unemployment occasioned by old age does not seem to be a problem of con men; age ripens their skills, insights, and wit, and it also increases the confidence they inspire in their victims" (quoted in Quinney, 1979, p. 245). Most professional criminals enjoy long, uninterrupted careers because experience improves their skill at avoiding arrest. They often justify their activities by claiming that they are simply capitalizing on the fact that all people are dishonest and would probably be full-time criminals themselves if they had the ability and opportunity. Many are employed in organized crime operations.

Juvenile Delinquency

Historically, children have been presumed to lack the "criminal intent" to commit willful crimes; hence, juvenile law is designed primarily to protect and redirect young offenders rather than punish them. There is a separate family court system

Arrests in the "war on drugs" often lead to felony convictions for youthful offenders. As a consequence of efforts to lengthen prison terms for people with multiple felony convictions, these early episodes could greatly increase the risk of eventual life imprisonment.

for dealing with juvenile offenders, and their sentencing is limited. Within those limits, however, judges have wide discretion in dealing with youthful offenders and can choose the approach that they feel will be most effective.

In recent years there has been increasing dissatisfaction with the workings of juvenile law (Jacobs, 1989). Some critics contend that law enforcement authorities have too much latitude in interpreting juvenile behavior and that standards differ too greatly from one community to another. In addition, there is evidence that today's young criminals are much more sinister than yesterday's. Claude Brown, a well-known writer on this subject, remarks that the modern juvenile criminal "is so deadly and cynically rational that he is terrifying." Referring to a young man who routinely murders his robbery victims, Brown writes, "I was actually pleased to learn that he was serving a 15-year sentence. It would be comforting to know that this young cynic was doing a 30-year bit" (1984, p. 44).

As noted in the preceding chapter, many young people become involved in drug commerce at the retail level, especially because as juveniles they often run somewhat less risk of incarceration than persons over 18. Involvement in petty sales and other aspects of drug commerce puts juveniles at risk of addiction and, increasingly, of violent death. As the demand for cocaine and crack abates while law enforcement pressure continues, there is an escalation of violence, often involving automatic weapons, among drug dealers and their associates. Thus, in some large American cities the homicide rate among juvenile males has reached record levels.

Teenagers who are arrested on minor sales or possession charges often begin a career in and out of detention centers and jails, where the young person is initiated into the world of professional crime (Sullivan, 1989). Young women who become involved in the drug world and associated illegal hustling often trade sexual services for drugs and thus are recruited into the occupational culture of prostitution. While prostitution may not be considered a serious crime, it places young women at serious risk of violent death or injury and of sterility or death from sexually transmitted diseases.

Among juveniles a very common reason for arrest is "status crimes" such as running away and vagrancy. In 1991 about 135,000 juvenile runaways were arrested in the United States, of whom 56.7 percent were females (*Statistical Abstract,* 1993). This is one of the few types of arrest in which the usual gender distribution is reversed. The reason so many juvenile women are runaways is that they are far more likely than boys to be abused, both sexually and otherwise, in their homes.

CONDITIONS AND CAUSES OF CRIME

In this section we will consider several explanations of crime, beginning with nonsociological explanations and continuing with various sociological approaches based on the theoretical perspectives described in Chapter 1.

Biological Explanations of Crime

A medieval law stated that "if two persons fell under suspicion of crime the uglier or more deformed was to be regarded as more probably guilty" (Ellis, 1914, quoted in Wilson & Herrnstein, 1985, p. 71). This law and others like it illustrate the age-old and deep-seated belief that criminality can be explained in terms of certain physical characteristics of the criminal. An example of this point of view is the theory of crime advanced by an Italian physician, Cesare Lombroso, in the late nineteenth century.

Lombroso was convinced that there is a "criminal man" (or woman), a type of human being who is physically distinct from ordinary human beings. In the course of his examinations of convicts both before and after their deaths, he developed the concept of *criminal atavism*—the notion that criminality is associated with physical characteristics resembling those of primitive humans and lower primates: a sloping forehead, long arms, a primitive brain, and the like. Lombroso believed, in short, that there was such a thing as a "born criminal." Although this explanation was wrong, it served to initiate scientific inquiry into the causes of crime.

In the twentieth century Lombroso's theory and other biologically based explanations of crime have been discredited and supplanted by sociological theories. However, some theorists (e.g., Wilson & Herrnstein, 1985) defend the identification of biological characteristics that appear to be *predisposing factors* in criminal behavior rather than full explanations of such behavior. They believe that certain inherited traits, such as an extra Y chromosome or a particularly athletic physique, may be correlated with a greater than average tendency to engage in criminal behavior.

Research on the possibility of a link between criminality and an extra Y chromosome has consistently found that no such relationship can be demonstrated. Nevertheless, biologists, medical researchers, and some behavioral scientists continue to search for possible genetic causes of crime. New initiatives by the National Academy of Sciences and other prestigious scientific organizations to study the possible biological basis of crime have generated heated controversy and scientific debate. In part this is because biological research on crime usually fails, as sociologist Joan McCord points out, "to look at the social and psychological variables." McCord herself analyzed data from a long-term study of pairs of brothers in the Boston area between 1926 and 1933 and compared the criminal histories of the brothers with each other and with those of subjects from similar backgrounds; she found no evidence for a genetic contribution to criminality. While new efforts to establish genetic or other biological origins of criminality are also likely to fail, most sociologists agree with Troy Duster, who argues that such studies can help because if they properly account for social variables such as racism and class inequality they will counteract the notion of a biological basis for crime in the lower classes or among some racial groups (Horgan, 1993).

Gender and Crime

Since nations began collecting systematic statistics on crime, analysts have realized that men are far more likely than women to commit crimes. Indeed, gender is one of the most obvious correlates of criminality. Although there are significant variations from one society to another, a review of numerous studies of crime in different countries concludes that "males are five to fifty times as likely to be arrested as are females" (Wilson & Herrnstein, 1985, p. 104). As women have gained greater social equality with men in industrialized countries, the ratio of male to female arrests has decreased, but men still lead in most categories of crime. (See Figure 6–5.)

The number of women in U.S. prisons is rising rapidly. Between 1986 and 1991 it almost doubled, increasing from 19,812 to 38,796. Women now account for 5.5 percent of the total prison population (*Statistical Abstract,* 1993). Although the increase in the number of women in prisons may be due to a trend toward more arrests and tougher sentencing of women, some experts believe that increasing economic pressures and the spread of drugs throughout the population are also playing a major role. (The role of drugs in female crime was discussed in Chapter 5.)

The different arrest rates for men and women seem to be a result of different patterns of socialization. In our society men have traditionally been raised to be more aggressive than women, and they have therefore been more likely to commit certain kinds of crime. Women generally have been regarded more protectively by the police and the courts; therefore, they have been less likely to be arrested and, if arrested, less likely to be punished severely, especially if they are wives or mothers. Despite the persistent differences in arrest rates among women and men, with men more than eight times more likely to appear in official crime statistics, in the second half of this century rates of crime by women have increased rapidly. As more women are socialized under conditions of deprivation and abuse, we can expect continued recruitment of those women into lives of street hustling, prostitution, and shoplifting, which, in turn, will account for increasing numbers of arrests of women (Friedman, 1993; Miller, 1986).

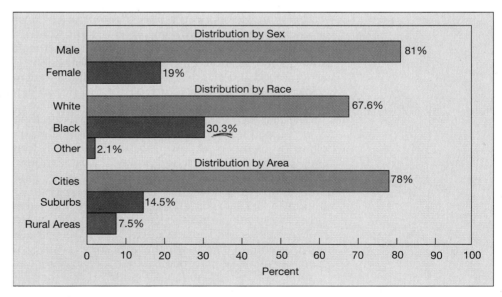

FIGURE 6–5   Total Arrests, 1992, by Sex, Race, and Area

Source: UCR, 1993.

Age and Crime

Criminologists have found age to be more strongly correlated with criminal behavior than any other factor (Wilson & Herrnstein, 1985). The age of the offender is closely related not only to the rate at which crimes are committed but also to the types of crimes committed. Data from several nations, including England, Wales, and France, provide evidence that the correlation between age and crime holds across geographic boundaries (Hirschi & Gottfredson, 1983).

Teenagers and young adults accounted for 44.6 percent of arrests in the United States in 1992, and 29.2 percent of all arrests were of people under 21. A solid majority of arrests for property crimes—58.9 percent—were of persons under 25 (*UCR*, 1993). Although young people may be arrested more than older offenders because the young are less experienced, it is clear that many teenagers and young adults, especially those who become involved in gang activities, are enticed by opportunities to commit various kinds of theft. Automobile and bicycle theft and vandalism are among the major juvenile crimes, although they are by no means limited to the young.

Some criminals give up crime in their late 20s or early 30s, for reasons that are not clear to criminologists (Hirschi & Gottfredson, 1983). Perhaps they marry and find their family life more rewarding than crime. For these individuals, family responsibilities seem to be a more powerful inhibitor of criminal behavior than rehabilitation or coercion. This "maturing out" is a subject of great interest to sociologists. In a study of the criminal careers of juvenile males in three urban communities composed of whites, African Americans, and Latinos, respectively, Mercer Sullivan (1989) found that as the boys in those communities grew older there was an increasingly marked convergence in their tendency to reduce their criminal activity in favor of increased income from legitimate sources. Sullivan attributes this change to their greater maturity, their recognition that sanctions were becoming more severe, and their perception that their opportunities to hold real jobs were better than they had been when they were younger.

Sociological Explanations of Crime

Demographic factors do not offer a complete explanation of crime. They do not, for example, explain why some juveniles and young adults drift into longer-term criminal careers or why some young people never commit crimes. Nor do they tell us why some individuals, such as white-collar criminals, begin breaking laws during adulthood and middle age. Thus, in addition to demographic analyses of crime, sociologists offer at least four types of theories to explain why some people become criminals and others do not.

The first theoretical approach to be discussed in the remainder of this section has developed from conflict theory; it claims that most crime is either a form of rebellion by members of lower social classes or a form of illegal exploitation by some members of the rich and powerful classes. A second approach, derived from the functionalist perspective, explains crime as resulting from the uncertainty about norms of proper conduct that accompanies rapid social change and social disorganization. A third major explanation applies the interactionist perspective to the study of how people drift toward criminal subcultures and become socialized for criminal careers. And in the next chapter we will add a fourth theory of crime, known as control theory, which views crime as a type of economic behavior that is based on criminals' perceptions of the likely consequences of their actions.

Conflict Approaches to the Study of Crime   Conflict theorists identify inequalities of wealth, status, and power as the underlying conditions that produce criminal behavior. Groups in society that are disadvantaged relative to other groups, such as the poor and racial minorities who experience discrimination, are thought to be likely to rebel against their situation. Criminality, in this view, is one way in which disadvantaged individuals act out their rebellion against society (Quinney, 1979).

INEQUALITY AND CRIME. As noted earlier in the chapter, official statistics show a high incidence of crime among members of the lower socioeconomic classes. Those statistics have fueled a sociological debate over the relationship between social class and criminality. Earlier in this century many sociologists believed that people in lower socioeconomic classes were more likely than those in higher classes to commit crimes. In 1978 criminologists Charles R. Tittle, Wayne J. Villemez, and Douglas A. Smith analyzed existing studies of crime and class status to determine whether the inverse relationship between class status and the commission of crime always held. When they examined data from arrest records, they found evidence to support the prevailing view. But when they reviewed data from self-report studies, they found no link between class and crime. On the basis of these results, the investigators concluded that "it is time to shift away from class-based theories to those emphasizing more generic processes" (1978, p. 654).

These findings confirmed the results of a study by William J. Chambliss and Richard H. Nagasawa (1969). On the basis of firsthand observation of juvenile delinquents, the researchers concluded that "official statistics are so misleading that they are virtually useless as indications of actual deviance in the population" (p. 71). They also suggested that the demeanor of different groups, the visibility of the offenses, and the bias of police and courts give rise to official rates of crime and delinquency that are "a complete distortion of the actual incidence" (p. 71).

Cross-cultural research has shown that inequality cannot be viewed as a root cause of crime. Although differences in social class have been correlated with homicide, they are not directly related to property crime or to the overall crime rate: Countries with greater income inequality have less property crime than countries with less inequality (Krohn, 1976). [Note, however, that such studies suffer from methodological problems and their findings should not be viewed as conclusive (Kempf, 1990).]

In many American cities political and community leaders engage in heated debate over whether the police are more prone to arrest members of minority groups or whether minority group members commit more crimes and therefore are arrested more frequently.

RACE AND CRIME.   Every study of crime based on official data shows that blacks are overrepresented among those who are arrested, convicted, and imprisoned for street crimes. According to official statistics, blacks are arrested at higher rates than whites on charges of murder, rape, robbery, and other index crimes.

In any society one can find differences in crime rates among various racial and ethnic groups. Chinese and Japanese Americans have lower crime rates than other Americans; Hungarian immigrants to Sweden have higher crime rates than native Swedes; Scandinavian immigrants to the United States got into less trouble with the police than Americans of Anglo-Saxon descent (Reckless, 1973). In the case of black Americans, however, the differences are pronounced; for example, "if blacks were arrested for robbery at the same rate as are whites, there would be half as many robbers arrested in the United States" (Wilson & Herrnstein, 1985, pp. 461–462).

It is possible that the overrepresentation of blacks in official crime statistics is due to greater surveillance of black communities by the police and to the greater likelihood that blacks who commit crimes will be arrested and imprisoned. One expert has calculated that about 80 percent of the disproportion in the rates of imprisonment of whites and blacks can be attributed to the disproportion in arrest rates (Blumstein, 1982). However, victimization surveys show that police and court bias cannot be the sole cause of the higher rate of reported crime among blacks. Blacks are far more likely than whites to be victims of crime, and it is unlikely that these higher victimization rates are caused by whites entering black neighborhoods in order to commit crimes (Wilson & Herrnstein, 1985).

A more plausible explanation for the high rate of crime among blacks is the disproportionately high percentage of blacks in the lower classes—which, as we saw earlier, are associated with higher crime rates. But economic disadvantage alone cannot fully account for the racial disparity in crime rates. The higher arrest rates for blacks persist even when socioeconomic status is taken into consideration. Moreover, offenders who commit numerous crimes begin to exhibit delinquent behavior early in life, before their outlook has been affected by such factors as inability to find a good job (Wolfgang, Figlio, & Sellin, 1972).

Another possible explanation is isolation in a racial ghetto where members of the community are continually exposed to norms that encourage criminal behavior. Ironically, the evidence to support this view comes from studies of communities that appear to *discourage* criminality among their members: It has been pointed out that oriental Americans living in isolated communities in California have much lower crime rates than the general population (Beach, 1932; Tagaki & Platt, 1978).

Still another factor that is thought to contribute to high rates of crime among blacks is family disorganization, especially the rapid increase in the number of female-headed families. Such families lack male role models with legitimate jobs, leaving open the possibility that children will be influenced by others in the community, including individuals who engage in criminal activities. Such an explanation can be neither proved nor disproved, but it appears to lend support to the anomie and differential-association theories discussed in the following pages.

The Functionalist View: Anomie Theory

Anomie theory, also known as the goals-and-opportunities approach, is favored by many modern scholars, notably Robert K. Merton (1968). Merton argues that a society has both approved goals and approved ways of attaining them. When some members of the society accept the goals (e.g., home ownership) but do not have access to the approved means of attaining them (e.g., earned income), their adherence to the approved norms is likely to be weakened, and they may try to attain the goals by other, socially unacceptable means (e.g., fraud). In other words, criminal behavior occurs when socially approved means are not available for the realization of highly desired goals.

Anomie, the feeling of being adrift that arises from the disparity between goals and means, may vary with nationality, ethnic background, bias, religion, and other social characteristics. Some societies emphasize strict adherence to behavioral norms—this is the case in Japan, for example—and for them the degree of anomie may be fairly low. Others place relatively more emphasis on the attainment of goals and less on their being attained in socially approved ways. Merton maintains that the United States is such a society. Identifying anomie as a basic characteristic of American society, he lists several kinds of adaptations that are common in the United States. One of these, *innovation,* consists of rejecting approved practices while retaining desired goals. This seems to characterize the behavior of certain lower-class gang members, who have adoped socially approved goals but abandoned socially approved methods of attaining them.

This rejection of approved practices occurs widely in groups with the greatest "disjuncture" among goals, norms, and opportunities. In this country it is most often found among those who have the greatest difficulty obtaining a good education or training for high-paying jobs, particularly in disadvantaged minority groups. Higher crime rates among such groups are not automatic, but they can be expected when the goals that people internalize are dictated to them by a society that at the same time erects barriers to the attainment of those goals by approved means. If more attainable goals were set for people in lower socioeconomic classes, presumably there would be less disjuncture between goals and means, and less anomie. For example, if low-cost rental housing were more widely available as a goal, more poor people could see how even low-wage jobs would improve their lives. When only luxury homes are available (and shown as models on television), the poor sense the futility of conventional jobs or other approved means.

Since the initial formulation of the anomie approach, research seems to have provided at least some support for its basic premise, although there are types of crime that it fails to explain adequately, such as assault for purposes other than monetary gain.

This omission is related to the question that is most frequently raised about Merton's theory: Are financial success and material possessions only middle-class goals? Do members of the lower classes have different values and aspirations? Many sociologists believe that people in the lower classes tend to hold two sets of beliefs simultaneously. That is, they share the norms and values of the larger society but are forced to develop standards and expectations of their own so that they can deal realistically with their particular circumstances. (See the discussion of the "lower-class value stretch" in Chapter 8.) For example, people in the lower classes share with the affluent the view that crime is bad, but they find conventional means to attain goals, such as secure jobs, lacking. They may then consider illegal "hustles" as an alternative means to some goals, especially when these crimes seem justified by the behavior of others outside their communities whom they observe buying drugs or sex or other illicit goods and services. It is not surprising, therefore, that studies have supported Merton's view that anomie, rather than poverty itself, is a major cause of crime and delinquency.

Interactionist Approaches: Differential Association and Delinquent Subcultures Interactionist explanations of criminal behavior focus on the processes by which individuals actually internalize the norms that encourage criminality. This internalization results from the everyday interaction that occurs in social groups. Interactionist theories differ in this respect from anomie theory, which sees criminal behavior as resulting from certain aspects of social structure. Two examples of interactionist theories of criminality are Edwin Sutherland's theory of differential association and the subcultural approach to the study of juvenile delinquency.

DIFFERENTIAL ASSOCIATION. Introduced by Sutherland in 1939, the approach known as *differential association,* with some later modifications, still seems to explain the widest range of criminal acts. According to this theory, criminal behavior is a result of a learning process that occurs chiefly within small, intimate groups—family, friends, neighborhood peer groups, and the like. The lessons learned include both the techniques for committing crimes and, more important, the motives for criminal behavior. The law is defined not as a set of rules to be followed but as a hindrance to be avoided or overcome.

Briefly stated, the basic principle of differential association is that "a person becomes delinquent because of the excess of definitions favorable to violation of law over definitions unfavorable to violation of law" (Sutherland & Cressey, 1960, p. 28). People internalize the values of the surrounding culture, and when their environment includes frequent contact with criminal elements and relative isolation from noncriminal elements, they are likely to become delinquent or criminal. The boy whose most admired model is another member of his gang or a successful neighborhood pimp will try to emulate that model and will receive encouragement and approval when he does so successfully.

Although a child usually encounters both criminal and noncriminal behavior patterns, those encounters vary in frequency, duration, priority, and intensity. The concepts of *frequency* and *duration* are self-explanatory. *Priority* means that attitudes learned early in life, whether lawful or criminal, tend to persist in later life, although this tendency has not been fully demonstrated. Intensity refers to the prestige of the model and the strength of the child's emotional ties with the model.

DELINQUENT SUBCULTURES AND CONFLICTING VALUES.   The legal definition of crime ignores the effect of social values in determining which laws are enforced. Although judges and prosecutors use the criminal law to determine the criminality of certain acts, the process of applying the law involves issues of class interest and political power: One group imposes its will on another by enforcing its definition of illegality. For example, authorities are not nearly as anxious to enforce laws against consumer fraud as they are to enforce laws against the use of certain drugs. Consumer fraud is often perpetrated by powerful business interests with strong political influence. The drug user, on the other hand, usually lacks power and public support.

The issue of class interests is especially relevant to the study of delinquent subcultures. Albert K. Cohen (1971), for example, viewed the formation of delinquent gangs as an effort to alleviate the difficulties gang members experience at the bottom of the status ladder. Gang members typically come from working-class homes and find themselves measured, as Cohen put it, with a "middle-class measuring rod" by those who control access to the larger society, including teachers, businesspeople, the police, and public officials. Untrained in such "middle-class virtues" as ambition, ability to defer gratification, self-discipline, and academic skills, and therefore poorly prepared to compete in a middle-class world, they form a subculture whose standards they can meet. This delinquent subculture, which Cohen described as nonutilitarian, malicious, and negativistic, "takes its norms from the larger culture, but turns them upside down. The delinquents consider something right, by the standards of their subculture, precisely because it is wrong by the norms of the larger culture" (1971, p. 28).

Other sociologists do not believe that the formation of delinquent subcultures is a frustrated reaction to exclusion by the dominant culture. Instead, they see delinquency as a product of lower-class culture. A study of street gangs by Walter Miller (1958), for example, identified six "focal concerns" of lower-class culture that often lead to the violation of middle-class social and legal norms. Those concerns are as follows:

1. *Trouble.* Trouble is important to the individual's status in the community, whether it is seen as something to be kept out of or as something to be gotten into. Usually there is less worry about legal or moral questions than about difficulties re-

Through their dress and styles of behavior, these members of a teenage gang in England assert their loyalty to an adolescent sub-culture and their opposition to the norms of conventional adult society.

sulting from the involvement of police, welfare investigators, and other agents of the larger society.

2. *Toughness.* Toughness consists of an emphasis on masculinity, physical strength, and the ability to "take it," coupled with a rejection of art, literature, and anything else that is considered feminine. This is partly a reaction to female-dominated households and the lack of male role models both at home and in school.

3. *Smartness.* In the street sense of the term, smartness denotes the ability to outwit, dupe, or "con" someone. A successful pimp, for example, would be considered "smarter" than a bank clerk.

4. *Excitement.* To relieve the crushing boredom of ghetto life, residents of lower-class communities often seek out situations of danger or excitement such as gambling or high-speed joyrides in automobiles.

5. *Fate.* Fate is a major concern because lower-class citizens frequently feel that important events in life are beyond their control. They often resort to semimagical resources such as "readers and advisers" as a way to change their luck.

6. *Autonomy.* Members of this group are likely to express strong resentment toward any external controls or exercise of coercive authority over their behavior. At the same time, however, they frequently seem to seek out restrictive environments, perhaps even engineering their own committal to mental hospitals or prisons.

More recent research by Gerald Suttles (1970) and Elijah Anderson (1988) on the street corner culture of delinquents and other groups provides evidence of continuity in these values. Anderson, for example, writes that lower-class life has an internal coherence that is seldom appreciated by the casual observer. Both studies show that teenagers and young adults in lower-class street corner groups make careful distinctions based on trust and confidence. They may be labeled as street people by the larger society, but among themselves they continually rank each other according to notions of respect and trust derived from their life on the street.

CONTROLLING CRIME

Efforts by the police, courts, and other agencies to control crime need to be understood as part of the society's much larger system of social control. In its broadest sociological sense, *social control* is the capacity of a social group, which could be an entire society, to regulate itself according to a set of "higher moral principles beyond those of self-interest" (Janowitz, 1978, p. 3). The Ten Commandments are a good example of what is meant by such values as they are translated into norms of everyday life. All of a society's ways of teaching the young to conform to its values and norms (i.e., socialization), together with the ways in which people in a society reward one another for desired behaviors, contribute to social control. But every society also includes members who deviate from its norms, even strongly held norms like the prohibition against murder or thievery. Viewed in terms of the problems created by such deviance, social control can be defined somewhat more narrowly as "all the processes by which people define and respond to deviant behavior" (Black, 1984, p. xi).

Techniques of social control range from informal processes such as gossip, ridicule, advice, and shunning to the formal processes embodied in the actions of the police, courts, corrections officers, and others who work in the criminal-justice system and related systems such as the mental-health and juvenile-justice systems. These formal systems of social control, established by government, are so important and complex, and subject to so much study and debate, that in this chapter we focus on them more than on the informal processes. Nevertheless, it is important to recognize that without the great array of informal controls that exist in every community and society, none of the formal systems would be of much use. If the police and the courts and other formal institutions of social control are at all effective, it is because most people are law abiding and these institutions need deal only with a relatively small minority (which may still be a very large number in absolute terms).

Most formal systems of social control rely on coercion rather than reward. Surely this is true of courts and prisons. But it is not true by definition. Within a prison or other correctional facility a person can be rewarded for behavior that is defined as positive and as having favorable consequences for the individual and for society. The fact that coercion and punishment often far outweigh persuasion and reward reflects the different goals society has incorporated into its institutions of criminal law, that is, police, prosecution, and corrections. As we examine how these formal institutions of social control operate (and sometimes fail to operate), we need to keep in mind that formal efforts to control crime can be classified under four headings: retribution-deterrence, rehabilitation, prevention, and reforms in the criminal-justice system. The latter category includes efforts to improve society's ability to deal with all kinds of crime; it will be discussed in the Social Policy section of the chapter.

Retribution–Deterrence

Retribution and deterrence—"paying back" the guilty for their misdeeds and discouraging them and others from committing similar acts in the future—have historically been the primary focus of efforts to control crime. Only relatively recently has rehabilitation of offenders—attempts to give them the ability and motivation to live in a law-abiding and socially approved manner—gained wide acceptance. The correctional system, however, is still largely punitive. Although retribution no longer follows the "eye for an eye, tooth for a tooth" formula (in which slanderers had their tongues cut out, thieves had their hands amputated, and rapists were castrated), the retributive orientation can be seen in public demands for longer sentences for such crimes as murder or assassination.

The punishments meted out to murderers, forgers, and other offenders are meant to serve several purposes. Besides the often-cited goals of preventing crime and rehabilitating offenders, punishment serves to sustain the morale of those who conform to society's rules. In other words, law-abiding members of society demand that offenders be punished partly to reinforce their own ambivalent feelings about conformity. They believe that if they must make sacrifices to obey the law, someone who does not make such sacrifices should not be allowed to "get away with it." Even those who view criminals as "sick" rather than evil, and call for the "treatment" of offenders to correct an organic or psychological disorder, are essentially demanding retribution.

Some criminologists, such as James Q. Wilson (1977, 1993), have suggested that society needs the firm moral authority derived from stigmatizing and punishing crime. Although Wilson grants that prisoners must "pay their debts" without being deprived of their civil rights after release from prison and without suffering the continued indignities of parole supervision and unemployment, he reaffirms the moral value of stigmatizing crime and those who commit crime:

> *To destigmatize crime would be to lift from it the weight of moral judgment and to make crime simply a particular occupation or avocation which society has chosen to reward less (or perhaps more) than other pursuits. If there is no stigma attached to an activity, then society has no business making it a crime. (1977, p. 230)*

Laws establishing penalties for crimes are promulgated by the states and by the federal government. But concern for the rights of citizens faced with the power of the state to enforce laws and inflict punishment is a prominent feature of the United States Constitution. The Fourth Amendment guarantees protection against "unreasonable searches and seizures"; the Fifth Amendment guarantees that citizens shall not be compelled to testify against themselves or be tried more than once for the same crime (double jeopardy) or be deprived of due process of law; the Sixth Amendment guarantees the right to a public trial by an impartial jury, the right to subpoena and confront witnesses, and the right to legal counsel. The Eighth Amendment prohibits "cruel and unusual punishment" and "excessive" bail or fines.

It is important to note these points because they are at the heart of conflicts about how fairly laws are enforced and how impartially justice is meted out. In the controversy over capital punishment, for example, opponents argue that it has become a form of cruel and unusual punishment. Others argue that because those who are condemned are often unable to afford adequate counsel, they have been deprived of their rights under the Sixth Amendment. Whatever one believes about such controversies, it is clear that the Constitution establishes the basis for protection of individual rights but also leaves much discretion to citizens and lawmakers to establish the ground rules for how justice is to be carried out.

The role of the sociologist in these debates is to help establish a scientific basis for decision making. In the highly controversial area of retribution, this often means attempting to assess the efficacy of punishment, that is, whether it achieves the goal of deterrence for which it is usually established. In the case of capital punishment, there is little or no social-scientific evidence that the death penalty acts as a deterrent. Criminologist Hans Zeisel (1982) has compared murder rates in states that have had the death penalty continuously, states that have had it intermittently, and states that have not had the death penalty at any time. (See Figure 6–6.) He concludes that

> *these curves show with great clarity, first, that the homicide rate fluctuates dramatically over the course of the years; second, that these fluctuations are startlingly similar in all*

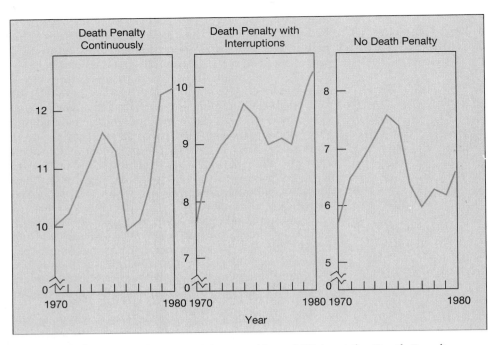

FIGURE 6–6 Homicide Rates in States with and Without the Death Penalty, 1970–1980 (rate per 100,000 population)

Note: States that had the death penalty continuously: Arizona, Arkansas, Connecticut, Florida, Georgia, Montana, Nebraska, Nevada, Oklahoma, Texas, Utah, Virginia. States without the death penalty: Alaska, Hawaii, Iowa, Maine, Michigan, Minnesota, New Jersey, North Dakota, West Virginia, Wisconsin, Washington, D.C. The remainder of the states had the death penalty with interruptions.

Source: From H. Zeisel, *The Limits of Law Enforcement,* 1982, published by the Univeristy of Chicago. Reprinted by permission of the University of Chicago.

> *groups of states and therefore obviously independent of the availability of the death penalty. As if to underscore that independence, the latest surge in the homicide rate begins about the time we began executing again after a decade during which the death penalty was in limbo. (p. 60)*

Zeisel and others also cite the negative effects of the severe anti–drug-dealing and anti–gun-possession laws put into effect in New York during the 1970s. In the years since these laws were passed, there have been significant increases in rates of drug dealing and arrests on drug and gun possession charges, despite much higher penalties for these offenses.

Critics of such findings point out that very often criminals ask themselves before committing a crime, "Will I be punished if I am caught, and how severe will the punishment be?" To find out how certainty and severity of punishment influence criminal behavior, Harold G. Grasmick and George J. Bryjak (1980) conducted a random survey of 400 people in a southwestern city. They found that the more severe people believe the punishment will be, the less likely they are to commit a crime if they perceive the likelihood of arrest to be relatively high. These and similar results have led to efforts to create more fixed sentencing and less ambiguity about penalties in the minds of potential criminals, but to date there is little research that indicates whether such measures have had any effect.

There is, however, a great deal of evidence that the public is increasingly likely to favor retribution independent of deterrence. Data from a 1990 poll show that about 72 percent of Americans favor the death penalty, although far fewer, 59 percent, believe it is a deterrent. The latter figure has decreased slowly over time; in

"Shock camp" or "boot camp" training programs for convicted teenage and young-adult offenders are becoming popular throughout the United States. Such programs have been shown to increase self-esteem, but the question of what lasting skills they impart to inmates remains open.

1981, 63 percent of Americans believed that capital punishment has a deterrent effect. Only 49 percent of African Americans favor the death penalty, and far fewer think it is a deterrent (CBS News/*New York Times* Poll, March 30, 1990). These views probably reflect recent trends in the actual administration of capital punishment, which is increasing in many states and is taking a disproportionate number of black inmates.

Research on the deterrent effects of punishment for crimes other than murder is made extremely difficult by the fact that very few perpetrators of these crimes are actually caught and sentenced. For many decades researchers have been able to show that whatever the punishment, the likelihood of arrest is the greatest deterrent to crime. However, for crimes like robbery and automobile theft, the arrest rate is about 8 percent, and for all index felonies it is only about 12 percent (Zeisel, 1982). These rates are based on crimes reported to the police. Since far more crimes are committed than are known to the police, the actual rates are even lower.

In the case of juvenile crime, although the proportion of teenagers in the population is lower than it was a decade ago, the number of juveniles in various kinds of detention, including prison, has grown to record levels. On any given day about 100,000 adolescents are in detention, of whom 92,000 are in juvenile detention centers and 8,000 in adult prisons (Diesenhouse, 1990). Thus, although the Bush administration called for stricter measures against juvenile crime, many states that previously experimented with strict policies began to shift toward experimentation with rehabilitation programs.

Rehabilitation

The idea of rehabilitating offenders, which has developed only during the past century and a half, rests on the concept of crime as a social aberration and the offender as a social misfit whose aberrant behavior can be modified to conform to society's norms—in other words, "cured." As yet there are no clear guidelines as to the form of rehabilitation that will be most effective with a particular kind of offender. Rehabilitation usually includes varying amounts of counseling, educational and training programs, and work experience. In the past the programs that have had the most success have been those that prepare criminals to enter the world of legitimate work and help them actually secure and hold jobs after incarceration. However, such ambitious programs are unlikely to be implemented on a large scale.

By the 1990s both the ideal and the practice of rehabilitation in prisons and among paroled offenders had reached a low point in what has historically been a cyclical process. Efforts to institute rehabilitation programs often follow efforts to increase the severity of sentencing. When it is shown that longer sentences and harsher punishment do not prevent crime or repeated offenses, society tends to shift toward efforts to rehabilitate criminals (Friedman, 1993; Martin, Sechrest, & Redner, 1981).

Studies of *recidivism*—the probability that a former inmate will break the law after release and be arrested again—have found no conclusive evidence that various approaches to rehabilitation, such as prison counseling programs or outright discharge, are more effective in reducing recidivism rates than more punitive alternatives. All that can be said is that some of the rehabilitation experiments undertaken to date—in particular those that include extensive job training and job placement efforts—have been more successful than others.

In a recent in-depth study of the juvenile-justice system and rehabilitation, sociologist Mark Jacobs (1990) found that professionals in the system—court officials, parole officers, psychologists, correctional administrators, and others—often believe that they must "screw the system" to make it rehabilitate rather than do further harm to juvenile offenders and young "persons in need of supervision." (The latter is a court-designated category of juveniles who are judged by their parents and others to be highly at risk of falling into a criminal subculture; courts can order such children to be placed in foster homes or residential care facilities even if they have committed no crimes.) Jacobs's study showed that rehabilitation is hampered by a maze of organizations and regulations. Juveniles are shuttled from one jurisdiction or program to another and are often the victims of inadequately funded training programs and haphazard supervision by overburdened caseworkers. Given the extreme splintering of the system—family courts, juvenile courts, schools, parents, parole officers, correctional officers, psychologists, and many more—the young offender is often deprived of the rehabilitation to which he or she is entitled. And no coherent set of laws holds anyone in the system accountable for the youth's rehabilitation—no single institution, group, or person can be said to be "at fault." In such a "no-fault" society, Jacobs argues, rehabilitation will remain a distant ideal.

The nature of the prison system itself is a major hindrance to rehabilitative efforts. Prisons remove offenders from virtually all contact with society and its norms and subject them to almost continual contact with people who have committed crimes ranging from murder and petty larceny to homosexual rape and fraud. Often inmates are abused by their guards. A notorious case, probably indicative of more widespread patterns of abuse, was revealed in a 1992 court ruling against 119 former officials and guards at a Georgia prison for women; inmates were able to prove that they had been subjected to sexual abuse and rape over a period of several years (Applebome, 1992).

Within prison walls offenders are punished by being deprived of liberty, autonomy, heterosexual contacts, goods and services, and the security that is normally obtained from participation in ordinary social institutions. At the same time, prisoners create a social order of their own. Adherence to the norms of prison life, which may be necessary for both mental and physical well-being, further separates inmates' goals and motivations from those of the larger society and makes it more difficult for them to benefit from whatever rehabilitative measures are available.

The most common type of rehabilitation program consists of work training. However, prison work is generally menial and unsatisfying, consisting of jobs such as kitchen helper or janitor. The difficulty of rehabilitating offenders in prison has led to various attempts to reform them outside prison walls. This approach seems to have several benefits. Treating offenders without exposing them to all the deficiencies of the prison system not only reduces the antisocial effects of prolonged exposure to a criminal society but also reduces the cost of custodial facilities and personnel. This makes treatment resources more available to those who seem to have the best prospects for rehabilitation. Perhaps the oldest and most widely used system of this kind is the work release program, in which prisoners are allowed to leave the institution for part of the day or week to work at an outside job. Although this type of program was first authorized in Wisconsin in 1913, it has become widely used only since the mid-1950s. Today many states and the federal government have authorized various kinds of work release programs.

Adaptations of the work release approach have also shown some promising results. Among the most innovative of these was the Wildcat experiment sponsored by the Vera Institute of Justice beginning in 1972. In this program ex-addicts and ex-offenders took part in various forms of "supported work"—jobs specifically designed to meet the needs of the chronically unemployed. Instead of being placed individually in unfamiliar jobs, Wildcat workers were given jobs in groups of three to seven and received guidance and evaluation while they worked. Wildcat workers earned more and had more stable jobs than members of a control group and were much less likely to become dependent on welfare. However, the recidivism rate did not follow suit: By the third year of the study, Wildcat group members were more likely than members of the control group to be rearrested (Friedman, 1978). One important lesson from the Wildcat experiment is that supported work is most successful when the individual is also integrated into a new community away from old peer pressures and temptations.

Although the idea of releasing convicted felons into society, even for limited periods, has met with considerable opposition, in general such programs seem to work well. Besides removing convicts from the criminal society within the prison, work release programs reimburse the state for some of the costs of supporting them and also allow the prisoners to support their dependents, thereby helping them stay off the welfare rolls. In addition, a work release program is a practical step toward reintegrating offenders into society, since many of those who successfully complete the program retain their jobs after release. In fact, in a classic study Martinson (1972) found that the most effective single factor in rehabilitating offenders is work—in-prison training for work following release, work during the prison term itself, and above all, job placement and training during probation.

Prevention

The idea of preventing crime and delinquency before they occur is an attractive one, but, like rehabilitation, it is difficult to implement. Aside from the deterrent effect of punishment, crime prevention is customarily defined in three different ways: (1) the sum total of all influences and activities that contribute to the development of a nondeviant personality; (2) attempts to deal with conditions in a person's environment that are believed to lead to crime and delinquency; and (3) specific services or programs designed to prevent further crime and delinquency.

Programs based on the first definition include measures designed to improve the social environment. They encompass such things as improved housing and job opportunities for ghetto dwellers. Although one of their goals may be the reduction of crime and delinquency in the target area, this is rarely their primary goal. Moreover, studies of youths involved in antipoverty programs have not demonstrated a positive correlation between such participation and reduced delinquency rates. The most positive results, however, are found in evaluations of Job Corps and other education, job-training, and social-skills programs in which young people at risk are given a chance to leave their neighborhood peer groups.

The second definition includes efforts based on Sutherland's theory of differential association, such as efforts to reduce children's exposure to the antisocial and/or illegal activities of people around them, to improve their family life, and to create a viable and conforming social order within the community itself. Several projects of this sort have been attempted; some, such as the Chicago Area Project (to be discussed shortly), have had notable success.

The majority of crime prevention programs attempt to work within the third definition—prevention of further delinquency and crime. They include well-established approaches such as parole, probation, and training schools, as well as more experimental programs. It is difficult to compare these approaches with those attempted under the other two definitions, since they deal with quite different sets of circumstances.

An early prevention program, the Chicago Area Project, was established in the mid-1930s in the Chicago slums, where immigrant families were no longer able to control their children because of a weakening social order. The project sought to develop youth welfare programs that would be viable after the project leaders had left. It was assumed that local youths would have more success than outside workers in establishing recreation programs (including summer camping), community improvement campaigns, and programs devoted to teaching and assisting delinquent youngsters and even some adults returning to the community after release from prison. The project not only demonstrated the feasibility of using untrained local youths to establish welfare programs but also indicated a possible decrease in the delinquency rate (Kobrin, 1959). This model has been used successfully in many communities to diminish gang violence.

It is difficult to prove the effectiveness of preventive measures. Although they seem to fail at least as often as they succeed, the difficulty may lie more in the specific kinds of services offered than in the concept of prevention itself. When delinquency prevention seems to fail, there are often signs that there were some beneficial effects, even if they were not of the desired magnitude. It should be kept in mind that most of the programs described here are experimental and have not been attempted on a large scale. Delinquency prevention needs further research and more governmental funding (Hagedorn, 1988; Williams & Kornblum, 1994).

According to Charles Silberman (1980), one of the major problems with programs designed to control juvenile delinquency is that they place too much emphasis on methods of policing, more efficient courts, and improved correctional programs and too little emphasis on community programs that give families the support they need to deal with delinquency:

> If a community development program is to have any chance of success, those in charge must understand that the controls that lead to reduced crime cannot be imposed from the outside; they must emerge from changes in the community itself and in the people who compose it. Hence the emphasis must be on enabling poor people to take charge of their own lives—on helping them gain a sense of competence and worth, a sense of being somebody who matters. (p. 430)

SOCIAL POLICY

Few areas of social policy are as frustrating as anticrime policy. Former U.S. Attorney General Nicholas Katzenbach was dismayed by the quarterly U.S. crime reports and the annual summary published in the *UCR*. "It's bad enough to lose the war on crime," he exploded, "but to lose it five times a year is too much" (quoted in Kamisar, 1993). In their efforts to reduce crime, governments at all levels have experienced the same frustration as the former attorney general. In a few short periods over the past 200 years crime rates have fallen, or at least the rates of some crimes have, but these lulls have been temporary. As crime historian Lawrence M. Friedman points out, crime is far too complicated and diverse, and too firmly embedded in American culture, to be controlled and eliminated. Whenever one kind of crime is reduced, criminals invent others. And social change is constantly at work on the criminal-justice system, producing a recurrent pattern of criminalizing, decriminalizing, and recriminalizing certain behaviors (Friedman, 1993).

President Clinton and Attorney General Janet Reno appear to understand this history of failed wars on crime. In their first round of proposed anticrime legislation, they did not proclaim a great new offensive in the war on crime or make sweeping promises. Their proposals centered on increased funding to enable local law enforcement agencies throughout the nation to hire another 50,000 police officers. They urged stricter measures to control the sale of handguns and to ban the sale of automatic weapons. They also advocated measures to punish corporate crime and attempted to shift the "war on drugs" away from efforts to control the supply coming into the United States to greater emphasis on public education and drug treatment. However, recent crime waves in Florida and California have influenced the Clinton administration to take a tougher stand on anticrime policy, inclusing the "three strikes" approach described later in this section.

Social policies to control crime or punish criminals are not made only at the federal level. States and municipalities often take the lead in promoting new approaches and policies. We will discuss trends and reforms in policies aimed at conventional, occupational, and organized criminals and then examine proposed changes in the juvenile-justice system.

Conventional Crime

In 1992 more than 13 million violent and property crimes were committed in the United States. Of these, only about 21 percent were "cleared" by arrests, and even fewer ended in convictions, making crime an attractive pursuit for many people (*UCR*, 1993). Even the relatively small number of people apprehended presents an almost insurmountable burden for existing correctional systems. Court calendars and prison cells are so overloaded that there is continual pressure to find ways to reduce sentences or to create new forms of corrections. One of the most controversial, yet widespread, strategies is known as *plea bargaining*. In this process the offender

The United States is the world leader in incarceration, with more prisoners per capita than any other nation. A recurring question is whether prisons serve as training ground for criminality or whether they can train individuals for productive roles in the larger society.

agrees to plead guilty to a lesser charge and free the courts from the need to conduct a jury trial. By this means most of those who are convicted of serious crimes receive shortened sentences. Plea bargaining has been criticized for giving mild sentences to dangerous criminals. It has been estimated, however, that if the plea-bargaining process were reduced to even 80 percent of serious crimes, the number of trials would double and put an enormous strain on the court system (Reid, 1993).

The prison system is also experiencing severe strains. By 1990, owing to the increase in drug arrests in many parts of the United States, prison populations had reached record levels (see Figure 6–7). The U.S. rate of imprisonment of 455 people per 100,000 is ten times higher than that of any other nation and far exceeds the imprisonment rate in South Africa, the second highest (Butterfield, 1992). More than 100,000 juveniles are incarcerated on any given day, despite the fact that they account for a smaller proportion of the total population than they did in the 1970s. Adult prison populations have also reached extremely high levels. However, of the more than 4.3 million people in custody in all U.S. correctional systems in 1990 only about 17 percent were in prisons. The majority were under community supervision through probation or parole (*Statistical Abstract,* 1993). (*Probation* is supervision of offenders who have not been sentenced to jail or prison; *parole* is supervision of persons who have been released from prison to community supervision.) And although both probation and parole were originally intended for nonviolent offenders, they are increasingly used for those who have committed felonies, owing to the costs of incarceration and the problems of overcrowding.

Recidivism rates are quite high among felons who are placed on probation. A 1985 study found that 65 percent were rearrested, a situation that indicates the continuing need to develop a greater array of sentencing options while ensuring public safety (Petersilia, 1985; Reid, 1991). Faced with these problems, many states have been seeking alternatives to conventional incarceration and parole. Community corrections, in which the offender provides service to social-welfare agencies or neighborhood associations, is one approach. Another is house arrest and electronic monitoring, described in Box 6–1.

Occupational and Corporate Crime

A variety of legal reforms have been proposed to curb occupational and corporate crime. One approach would be to increase the penalties for such crimes. Frequently a company with a net worth of hundreds of millions of dollars faces a fine of only $50,000, and its executives may be fined only $5,000, upon conviction for fraud or price fixing. Large corporations can regard such penalties as an acceptable risk. One way to increase fines is simply to raise the dollar amount of the penalty for each crime. Another is to make the penalty a fixed percentage of the company's profits.

In the aftermath of the worst scandal in American history, the plundering of

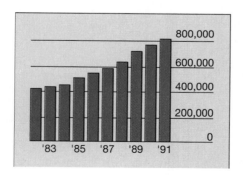

FIGURE 6–7   Population of State and Federal Prisons at the End of Each Year

Source: The Sentencing Project.

Prison overcrowding and budget crises (which make it difficult for states to build new prisons) are contributing to a trend toward greater creativity in the sentencing of convicted offenders. One approach involves greater reliance on house arrest, often with the aid of electronic monitoring devices. Florida's house arrest program, known as community control, is perhaps the best known of these initiatives; it dates from 1983 and includes as many as 5,000 offenders who are "imprisoned" in their homes on any given day (Petersilia, 1988; Reid, 1991).

The offenses for which house arrest is typically used as an alternative to prison include major traffic offenses, property offenses, and drug crimes. More serious and violent crimes, such as sex and weapons offenses, are far less likely to be punished in this way. Also, while such programs are attracting much attention as one solution to the growing problem of prison overcrowding, there are as yet relatively few people in house arrest programs. Illinois, Michigan, and Florida have the largest numbers, although in every case they are a small proportion of the total. But most states have only just begun to experiment with the system, using a very small number of offenders (Schmidt, 1989).

Part of the problem is the fear that dangerous criminals cannot be supervised well enough. This fear appears to be justified: In Chicago in 1990 a convicted car thief who was confined to his apartment lured a man to his home for a drug deal and then shot him to death. It was the first time a prisoner confined at home had been charged with murder (Johnson, 1990).

There is also some question as to whether house arrest is adequate as a form of punishment. Critics may agree that it saves money but question whether it addresses society's need to punish offenders. More liberal critics question the constitutionality of house arrest in that offenders may be deprived of the rights of free speech and assembly without being formally imprisoned. Supporters of the system, on the other hand, point out the benefit to society in that the offender can hold a job and can help pay many of the costs of incarceration and restitution. Moreover, as these systems become more widespread, they may prove to be at least a partial solution to the problem of the negative influence of prison, where so many inmates actually learn to be better criminals or to depend on life behind bars.

hundreds of savings and loan associations, often through illegal financial manipulations, the public is demanding far stiffer penalties against white-collar fraud of this nature. Huge fines have been levied against many of the stock manipulators and real estate swindlers involved in the savings and loan frauds, and numerous companies have been forced into bankruptcy as a result of investigations and fines. It is widely believed that the ten-year prison sentence received by junk bond dealer and stock manipulator Michael Milken is a signal to other white-collar criminals that the era of light sentences is ending.

Another aspect of legal reform involves changing laws to make them less easy to break. For example, complicated tax laws full of alternatives and loopholes may invite cheating. Streamlining the laws might both discourage cheating and make it easier to detect when it does occur. The law could also be reformed to make accomplices in occupational crimes vulnerable to court action so that for each such crime many more corporate employees would face punishment.

Obviously, stronger enforcement must accompany legal reform if it is to be meaningful, and this means more money and personnel for enforcement agencies. To detect more income tax cheating, for example, the IRS must hire more auditors. To detect more white-collar crime, the FBI must devote more resources to investigations in this area. Similarly, once a case against occupational offenders has been won in court, the judge must be willing to invoke the full penalty allowed under the law.

These two approaches—legal reform, particularly tougher penalties, andstronger enforcement—would probably deter much occupational crime. More than mostother types of crime, occupational crime involves calculation, planning, and the weighing of gains against costs. Increasing the costs, as well as the risk of detection, might lead occupational criminals to conclude that honesty is more profitable.

Organized Crime

It is particularly hard to fight organized crime, for several reasons. A major one is the difficulty of obtaining proof of syndicate activities that will be accepted in court. Witnesses rarely come forward; either they fear retaliation or they themselves are too deeply implicated. Since the top levels of the syndicate hierarchy are so well insulated from the other levels, witnesses rarely are able to testify about them. Documentary evidence is equally rare, since the transactions of organized crime are seldom written down. Finally, corruption hinders effective prosecution of organized crime.

Despite these obstacles, in recent years the FBI has made immense progress in its battle against organized crime; today numerous reputed syndicate leaders are under indictment or in jail. Experts credit this breakthrough to a number of factors, of which the most prominent is the fact that the FBI now devotes about one-quarter of its personnel to combating organized crime. Other important factors are the use of undercover agents in long-term investigations, the pooling of resources by agencies that formerly competed with one another, and the granting to the FBI of jurisdiction in narcotics cases. Especially significant has been the use of sophisticated surveillance techniques and computer technology. The witness protection program, in which witnesses are offered new identities, support, and protection in moving to new states away from their organized-crime contacts, has also proven successful in a number of instances. An example is the investigation into the involvement of organized crime in the major air freight robberies depicted in the film *Goodfellas*.

Public-Order and Juvenile-Justice Reforms

Many criminologists and legal authorities agree that there are too many laws making certain behaviors illegal only for children—so-called *status offenses* such as truancy—as well as too many laws addressing nonviolent "victimless crimes" such as adultery, homosexuality, prostitution, and drunkenness. Offenders in both categories account for 40 percent of the caseload in both juvenile and adult courts. In addition, trouble caused by status offenses, or by abuse at home, often causes juveniles to become runaways. When they are apprehended for this offense, they spend even more time in juvenile detention. The large number of arrests of juvenile runaways has led experts such as Edwin M. Schur (1973) to advocate a thorough reform of the concept of juvenile justice that would tolerate a broader range of behaviors and make only specific antisocial acts criminal.

The conservative mood of the nation during the 1980s made such reforms unlikely; instead, the Crime Control Act of 1984 tightened existing laws, relaxed restrictions on police evidence-gathering activity, and allocated more funds to the construction of new prisons and detention facilities. At the same time, there was little effort to decriminalize juvenile status crimes, despite evidence that status offenders do not inevitably go on to commit serious crimes as adults (Silberman, 1980).

By the early 1990s many states had vastly increased their populations of juveniles in criminal detention yet were also experiencing dramatic increases in rates of juvenile crime. In California juvenile crime rose by 10 percent in 1989 despite a juvenile incarceration rate of 556 per 100,000 (compared with a national average of 244). Similar trends were reported in many states that had increased the severity of juvenile sentencing in the 1980s. These poor results led some states, such as Florida and Massachusetts, to launch major new programs to replace traditional prison-type sentencing with community corrections programs.

In addition to proposals directed at law enforcement agencies, some small-scale community-based approaches have been attempted. An example is the House of Umoja in Philadelphia. This program, which combines surrogate family relationships with job opportunities and placement counseling for youths, has virtually eliminated street violence in a ghetto neighborhood. A similar program in Ponce, Puerto Rico, provides a wide range of services to an entire community; one of its achievements has been to cut the delinquency rate in half despite a rapidly growing teenage population (Kornblum & Boggs, 1984). Maryland, New York, and other states are also experimenting with programs that provide intensive home surveillance and counseling for delinquents from high-crime and poverty neighborhoods.

Despite these and other measures, many experts on youth crime agree that the problem remains far from a solution. None of the approaches taken so far has been shown to be successful (Reid, 1993). As a result, public policy toward serious juvenile crime is in a state of considerable confusion, and opinions on what can be done to combat youth crime vary widely. As the rate of juvenile violence rises throughout the nation, policy makers are debating the causes and the proper approaches to this problem. The Department of Justice's position is that the problem is caused by the breakdown of family and community controls and that until these are strengthened there is little that federal funds can accomplish. Members of the Congressional Select Committee on Children argue, however, that the rate of poverty among children has increased to 20 percent at the same time that there have been immense cuts in child welfare services (32 percent), juvenile delinquency prevention programs (55 percent), and drug and mental-health treatment programs (30 percent). Most law enforcement officials believe that without more resources to address joblessness, lack of education, lack of housing and recreational facilities and to provide drug treatment on demand, there will be little overall improvement in the youth crime situation (Diesenhouse, 1990).

Selective Incapacitation

The lack of adequate prison facilities militates against the use of imprisonment as a basic weapon in the fight against crime. However, there may be some value in an approach that tailors sentencing decisions to the individual. In this approach, called *selective incapacitation,* sentences vary according to predictions of the offender's propensity to commit additional crimes (Cohen, 1983). Sentences for the same offense may be quite different, reflecting differences in the offenders' criminal potential. In this way prison facilities are used as efficiently as possible; the worst offenders are kept in prison longer.

An effective policy of selective incapacitation obviously depends on the ability to identify the worst offenders—those who have committed crimes at high rates and are likely to continue to do so. Efforts to identify such criminals are subject to ethical and empirical problems, however, and much additional research will be required to determine what variables can be used to distinguish potential high-rate offenders from the rest of the criminal population. It is not particularly difficult to identify habitual criminals on the basis of previous arrest records. But the problem of predicting which individuals will become habitual offenders remains unsolved.

The Proposed "Three Strikes" Law

As noted earlier, several highly publicized violent crimes in certain areas of the nation—notably Florida, where a number of foreign tourists have been murdered in the past two years, and California, where a 12-year-old girl was kidnapped and killed by a man with an extensive criminal history—have brought public concern about violent crime to the forefront of the national policy agenda. Responding to demands for action at the national level, the Clinton administration has lent its support to a policy that is commonly referred to as "three strikes and you're out." "Three strikes" laws are designed to protect the public against violent criminals by requiring that individuals who have committed three felonies be sentenced to life imprisonment without parole.

The "three strikes" concept has gained popularity throughout the nation because offenders who have been convicted of felonies would presumably be discouraged from committing violent crimes while on probation or parole if they knew that if they were caught and convicted the punishment might be life imprisonment with no possibility of release. However, to date only one state—Washington—has enacted such a law. There, criminals are sentenced to spend life in prison without parole if they are convicted of three felonies from a list of forty-four crimes, most of which involve violence.

Washinton's experience with the new law has revealed some unintended consequences of the "three strikes" approach. Perhaps the most significant of these is the potential for more, rather than less, violence by criminals who feel they have nothing to lose. For example, police officers report that offenders who feel that they have been cornered tend, out of desperation, to engage in greater violence in resisting arrest than would normally be the case.

The "three strikes" approach also has implications that may not be given sufficient thought by voters who favor such a law. For example, small-time criminals who have committed a few robberies that did not involve significant violence could be subject to the same penalty as a vicious predator with a long history of criminal acts. A typical case under consideration in Washington is that of a 35-year-old man who robbed a sandwich shop of $151 by pretending that he was holding a concealed weapon. In a similar incident, a man stole $337 from a vendor by threatening to use a weapon but not actually displaying it. Each of these crimes was the offender's third felony, making him subject to the "three strikes" penalty rather than the normal sentence of one or two years in jail.

Despite the unanticipated consequences of the Washington law and the implications of the "three strikes" approach for offenders who have not committed serious felonies such as rape or aggravated assault, President Clinton has endorsed the policy and incorporated it into a crime bill that was passed by the Senate early in 1994. Recent polls show that the approach is favored by more than 80 percent of Americans, making it likely that a "three strikes" law of some kind will be passed by Congress during the current administration.

SUMMARY

1. The criminal law prohibits certain acts and prescribes punishments to be meted out to offenders. In practice, the definition of criminality changes according to what law enforcement authorities perceive as criminal behavior.

2. Researchers have attempted to find more reliable ways of tracking criminal activity. Self-report studies and victimization surveys provide useful data; both are used to supplement the FBI's *Uniform Crime Reports*.

3. Violent personal crime includes assault, robbery, and the various forms of homicide. Robbery usually occurs between strangers, murder between friends or relatives.

4. Occasional property crimes include vandalism, check forgery, shoplifting, and similar crimes. Offenders are usually unsophisticated and unlikely to have a criminal record.

5. Occupational or white-collar crime is committed by people who break the law as part of their normal business activity. It includes such acts as embezzlement, fraud (including computer crime), and insider trading in the securities industry. Occupational offenders have

a respectable appearance and often consider themselves to be respectable citizens.

6. Corporate crime includes a variety of illegal practices of private corporations, including environmental crimes, insider trading, illegal labor practices, defrauding of pension plans, and the like. Such crime is extremely difficult to control.

7. Public-order offenses include prostitution, drunkenness, vagrancy, and the like. They are often called victimless crimes because they cause harm only to the offender.

8. Conventional criminals commit robbery, burglary, and the like as a way of life, usually beginning their criminal careers as members of juvenile gangs.

9. Organized crime is a system in which illegal activities are carried out as part of a rational plan devised by a large organization for profit. The profits come largely from supplying illegal goods and services to the public.

10. Professional criminals are dedicated to a life of crime and are seldom caught. They include safecrackers, check forgers, and blackmailers.

11. Teenagers and young adults account for almost half of all arrests in the United States. The majority of arrests for property crimes are of persons under 25. In addition, many young people become involved in drug commerce at the retail level. Another common reason for arrests of juveniles, especially young women, is status crimes such as running away and vagrancy.

12. Various explanations of the causes and prevalence of crime have been suggested. They include biological explanations, demographic factors (including gender and age), and sociological explanations based on conflict theory, functionalism, and interactionism.

13. Conflict approaches to the study of crime identify inequalities of wealth, status, and power as the underlying conditions that produce criminal behavior. These inequalities are thought to explain the overrepresentation of blacks in official crime statistics.

14. The functionalist explanation of crime is based on anomie theory, in which crime is considered to be a result of a disparity between approved goals and the means of achieving them.

15. Interactionist explanations include differential association, in which criminal behavior is said to be learned from family and peers, and theories regarding the origin and character of delinquent subcultures.

16. Efforts to control crime take four basic forms: retribution–deterrence, rehabilitation, prevention, and reform of the criminal-justice system. Retribution–deterrence focuses on punishing the criminal and attempting to deter others from committing similar crimes. The idea of rehabilitating offenders rests on the concept of cure; the most successful form of rehabilitation is work release. Programs to prevent crime and delinquency consist of attempts to prevent offenders from committing additional crimes; they include parole, probation, training schools, and more experimental programs.

17. Proposals for reform of the criminal- and juvenile-justice system include imposing harsher and more specific penalties for conventional crimes, increasing the penalties for occupational and corporate crime and improving law enforcement in this area, and repealing laws dealing with status and public-order offenses. Recently there has been increased emphasis on punishment and incapacitation as opposed to rehabilitation of criminals. However, higher rates of imprisonment have had the effect of seriously overcrowding the prison system, leading to proposals of alternative approaches such as community corrections and house arrest.

SUGGESTED READINGS

ALLEN, FRANCIS A. *The Decline of the Rehabilitative Ideal: Penal Policy and Social Purpose.* New Haven, CT: Yale University Press, 1981. An analysis of the reasons for the shift from rehabilitative to retributive philosophies.

CLINARD, MARSHALL B., AND RICHARD QUINNEY. *Criminal Behavior Systems: A Typology,* 2nd ed. Fort Worth, TX: Holt, Rinehart and Winston, 1973. A textbook that describes the subcultures associated with a wide range of criminal occupations.

COLEMAN, JAMES W. *The Criminal Elite.* New York: St. Martin's Press, 1985. An authoritative analysis of crime at high levels of society, with excellent material on white-collar crime.

DATESMAN, SUSAN K., AND FRANK R. SCARPITTI (EDS.). *Women, Crime, and Justice.* New York: Oxford University Press, 1980. A collection of articles on the nature and extent of crime committed by women.

HENRY, STUART. *The Hidden Economy.* London: Martin Robertson, 1978. A study of "fiddling," or pilfering, that describes how those who commit this form of theft rationalize their behavior.

JACOBS, MARK P. *Screwing the System and Making It Work.* Chicago: University of Chicago Press, 1990. A thorough study of why—despite all efforts at reform and rehabilitation—so many professionals in the juvenile-justice system are frustrated by their inability to make the system work.

MILLS, JAMES. *The Underground Empire: Where Crime and Government Embrace.* Garden City, NY: Doubleday, 1986. A controversial report on the worldwide organized-crime network that seeks to demonstrate the links between political regimes in many nations and the influence of organized criminal activity, especially in the narcotics trade.

REID, SUE TITUS. *Crime and Criminology,* 6th ed. Fort Worth, TX: Holt, Rinehart and Winston, 1991. A comprehensive text that covers all the major theories and many of the most recent and important studies in the field of deviance and criminology.

REIMAN, JEFFREY H. *The Rich Get Richer and the Poor Get Prison: Ideology, Class and Criminal Justice.* New York: Wiley, 1979. A radical critique of the criminal-justice system that identifies the process by which the system discriminates between the wealthy and the poor.

WILSON, JAMES Q., AND RICHARD J. HERRNSTEIN. *Crime and Human Nature.* New York: Simon & Schuster, 1985. A thorough, conservatively slanted review of the literature on the causes of crime and its prevention.

Violence

Chapter Outline

- Between 1820 and 1945, human beings killed 59 million other human beings—one every 68 seconds—in wars, murders, quarrels, and skirmishes.
- At least 1 million children are physically abused each year, and many die as a result.
- It is estimated that more than 2 million women are victims of domestic violence each year.
- The rate of death by homicide among white men aged 15–24 is 21.9 per 100,000 population; among black men the rate is 85.6 per 100,000.
- Over 68 percent of the homicides reported in 1992 were committed by people using firearms; over 80 percent of those homicides involved handguns.

Within the space of a week two European tourists are murdered in cold blood in Florida. In North Carolina the father of the nation's most famous basketball player, Michael Jordan, is murdered by two young men with histories of violent crime. A student is shot outside a high school in New York City. In Houston, Los Angeles, and Washington, D.C., there are numerous incidents of random shootings and innocent victims killed by errant bullets. On Long Island a serial killer who preyed on prostitutes is apprehended, but not before he has ended the lives of almost a score of young women. All this lethal violence is only a fraction of that which occurred during a single year, 1993.

The level of deadly violence in the United States is about seventeen times higher than that in England or France or Japan. No other major industrialized nation has homicide rates that come close to those in the United States, and for black men in the United States the chances of living beyond age 40 are worse than in the poorest nations in the world, mainly because of the toll taken by violence. The overall rate of homicide among men aged 15–24 in the United States is about 22 per 100,000; for black men it is about 86 per 100,000. The widespread availability of guns and the

Scenes of extreme violence and its consequences—here, the random shooting of passengers on a Long Island Rail Road commuter train in 1993—have brought the problem of violence in the United States to greater public prominence.

Although we think of ourselves as a peace-loving people, we continually resort to violence in defense of what we consider our vital interests. The American Civil War was among the bloodiest in world history.

contribution of drugs to violence are important factors in this situation, but those who study the problem of violence in America also point to the pervasiveness of violence in our culture. The stability of American institutions may depend on efforts to reduce the level of violence in this nation.

Much violent action is not recognized as such. This is particularly true of violence associated with the rise or expansion of a political party or social movement; most groups try to forget, justify, or disguise their use of violence for these purposes. While extralegal violent acts such as murder, rape, or gang wars elicit public condemnation, other forms of violence are accepted or even praised; this is the case, for example, in most wars. Likewise, in troubled times and in frontier areas, vigilante activities are often approved by the local community as the only available means of maintaining order. In general, violence by or on behalf of the state is less likely to be condemned than violence by private citizens or violent acts in defiance of authority.

Despite the relative stability of its institutions, the United States has witnessed more violent behavior than other Western industrial nations. According to official statistics, approximately 22,540 murders were committed in 1992, as well as 109,062 rapes, 1,126,974 aggravated assaults, and 672,478 robberies (*UCR*, 1993). (See Figure 7–1.) The significance of the problem of violence and the need to find means to control and prevent it are apparent.

THE CONCEPT OF VIOLENCE

The word *violence* has a generally negative connotation; it has been defined as "behavior designed to inflict injury to people or damage to property" (Graham & Gurr, 1969, p. xiv). It may be considered legitimate or illegitimate, depending on who uses it and why and how it is used. Some special uses of violence, particularly in athletic activities like football and hockey, are so socially accepted that they are usually perceived not as violence but as healthy and even character-building behaviors.

Also not generally thought of as violence is *structural violence*, that is, "the

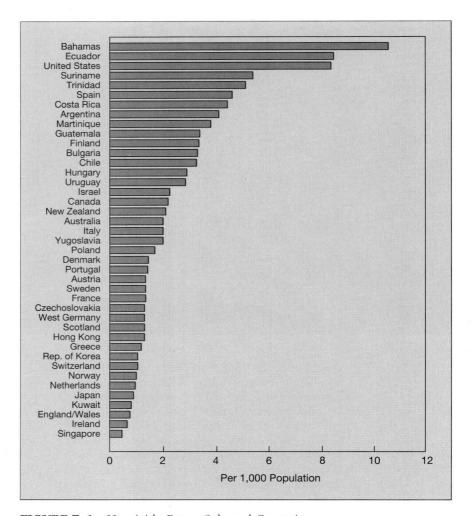

FIGURE 7–1 Homicide Rates, Selected Countries

Source: Reiss & Roth, 1993.

dominance of one group over the other, with subsequent exploitative practices" (Galtung, 1971, p. 124). In such a situation the threat or potential of violence is usually sufficient to keep the dominated group "in its place," but the effect on social relations is very much like that of overt violence. This aspect of violence will not be discussed at length in this chapter, but it should be noted that a dominated group's recognition that it has experienced structural violence may engender overt group violence such as civil disorder and rebellion.

Jerome Skolnick (1969) pointed out that violence "is an ambiguous term whose meaning is established through political processes" (p. 3). What a society classifies as violent is likely to depend largely on who provides the definitions of violence and has the resources to publicize and enforce those definitions. War is a classic example: The actions of one's own side are generally viewed as honorable, while the other side is described as the aggressor and its violent acts are viewed as atrocities. Similarly, within a nation accusations of violent behavior are exchanged by those in power and their relatively powerless adversaries:

Within a given society, political regimes often exaggerate the violence of those challenging established institutions. The term violence *is frequently employed to discredit forms of be-*

havior considered improper, reprehensible, or threatening by specific groups which, in turn, may mask their own violent response with the rhetoric of order or progress. (Skolnick, 1969, p. 4)

Several writers have attempted to justify the use of violence by a colonized people against the colonial regime or by the "have-nots" against the "haves." Frantz Fanon (1968), the Caribbean French psychiatrist whose experiences in the Algerian war made him a revolutionary, spoke of violence as a "cleansing force" that frees the spirit and restores self-esteem; it unifies the people and teaches them to assert themselves against any attempt at tyranny, even by their own leaders. Herbert Marcuse (1964) wrote about the revolutionary potential of people who have been denied full participation in the social life of advanced industrial nations—"the substratum of the outcasts and outsiders, the exploited and persecuted of other races and other colors, the unemployed and the unemployable" (p. 256).

There are, thus, many dimensions to the concept of violence. A useful distinction can be made between *institutional violence*, or violence exercised on behalf of or under the protection of the state, and the *noninstitutional violence* of those who are opposed to established authority. Violence in both of these categories may be either constructive or destructive; but institutional violence is usually presumed to be legitimate until proven otherwise, whereas people who engage in noninstitutional violence are punished. Thus, wars or violent police actions are usually considered legitimate because they are conducted under the aegis of the state; violent protests and demonstrations, revolutionary activity, civil disorders, and violent criminal activity are not. Although this difference is partly a matter of the difference in power between the "ins" and the "outs," it is also based on the traditional idea that the state may do some things that an individual citizen may not do in order to meet its responsibility for protecting the general welfare. It is when the state is seen as using force for purposes contrary to the general welfare that noninstitutional violence—sabotage, terrorism, rebellion, or revolution—is likely to occur.

EXPLANATIONS OF VIOLENCE

The Biological Viewpoint

"No person living today can question the statement that man, *Homo sapiens,* self-proclaimed to represent the pinnacle of evolution, is the most dangerous living species" (Boelkins & Heiser, 1970, p. 15). Between 1820 and 1945, human beings killed 59 million other human beings—one every 68 seconds—in wars, murders, quarrels, and skirmishes (Boelkins & Heiser, 1970). Violence is also commonplace in many American homes. As Steinmetz and Straus (1973) put it, "It would be hard to find a group or institution in American society in which violence is more of an everyday occurrence than it is within the American family" (p. 50).

Is it simply human nature to engage in violence? Since violence among humans is such a common occurrence, some social scientists have argued that human aggressive tendencies are inherent or instinctual. According to this view, only social organization keeps violent tendencies under control. Other experts argue that aggression is natural but violence is not. In an exhaustive review of research on the causes of interpersonal violence, a panel of experts convened by the National Academy of Sciences concluded that there is no solid evidence to support neurological or biological explanations of violent behavior. The panel did note, however, that findings from studies of animals and humans point to several features of the nervous system as possible sources of such explanations and recommended continued research on the subject (Reiss & Roth, 1993). Given the weight of evidence in favor of social and psychological explanations of violent behavior, this recommendation drew considerable criticism from social scientists (Kornblum, 1993).

Frustration–Aggression and Control Theories

Some theorists have argued that violence is a form of aggression that results from frustration. An unfulfilled need produces the frustration, and the frustration is vented in aggression. The strength of the impulses, needs, or wishes that are blocked determines the amount of frustration experienced, which in turn determines the degree of aggression. Failure, lack of affection, and poverty are suggested as possible causes of frustration. The *frustration–aggression theory* has been described as the easiest and most popular explanation of social violence of all kinds, including riots, political turmoil, robberies, and juvenile delinquency (Berkowitz, 1993). The main problems with this theory are that it fails to explain why frustration leads to aggression in some instances and not in others, and that frustration–aggression can be defined so broadly that it can cover almost any conceivable situation.

Related to the frustration–aggression theory is the *control theory,* which states that a person's ability to restrain or control impulsive behavior is correlated with the existence of close relationships with significant others. In this view, people may resort to violence when their attempts to relate to others in their own fashion are frustrated. The fact that violence is significantly more prevalent among ex-convicts, alcoholics, and others who are out of the mainstream of society and estranged from family and friends is also cited as evidence for the control theory. Thus, from the standpoint of control theory, murderers are likely to be "egocentric, impulsive, rebellious, or sadistic persons who cannot control their emotions" (Lunde, 1975, p. 39).

Of course, not all people who fit this description become murderers, nor do all murderers fit this description. One study suggested that there are actually two common personality types among murderers. One is *under*controlled: The person is unable to restrain aggressive impulses, has "never developed internal taboos against lashing out when provoked, and [has] few inhibitions about satisfying . . . acquisitive or sexual desires aggressively." The second is the exact opposite: an *over*controlled person who inhibits aggressive impulses almost completely and for whom "even socially acceptable outlets for aggression, such as swearing or pounding on a table, [are] off-limits" (Lunde, 1975, p. 39). Such people are said to repress their anger or hostility to the breaking point, until they suddenly and unpredictably explode.

It is difficult to demonstrate the validity of the control theory, since most murders and many other violent crimes are spontaneous, and their causes are not always clear. The lack of close relationships could simply be one factor among many that lead to violent behavior. The control theory does, however, suggest one clue to why violent crimes are increasing in frequency. In the past, various social factors—generally accepted moral standards; church membership; smaller, more intimate communities—aided in the development of controlled personalities. As a result of the erosion of these traditional social controls, people feel isolated and are more likely to resort to violence.

Violence as a Subculture

Many sociologists believe that violence is a learned behavior, one that is acquired through the process of socialization. Accordingly, aggressive or violent actions are most likely to occur in a culture or subculture in which violence is accepted or encouraged. Originally devised to explain juvenile gang behavior, the subculture theory has also been seen as the key to violence in general. In this model, members of violent subgroups have a low threshold for provocation, perceiving threats to their integrity in situations that would not be perceived as such by members of the dominant society. The norms of such groups require a combative response to provocation (Felson & Tedeschi, 1993).

In North America hockey is notoriously violent, but most other professional sports also have difficulty controlling the violent behavior of both players and fans.

It has also been suggested that all American males participate to some extent in a subculture of violence; the relatively low rate of violent acts by women is cited as evidence. Eugene C. Bianchi (1974), for example, sees professional football as a metaphor for America's "physical brutality, profit-maximizing commercialism . . . authoritarian-military mentality, and sexism" (p. 842). He notes that school and family join in forming "male children into competitors and achievers" (p. 843).

If violence is a consequence of social learning, frustration is not a prerequisite for violent behavior. Rather, violent habits are acquired through imitation or as a result of reinforcement of aggressive behavior. Along these lines, it has been shown that physically aggressive parents tend to have physically aggressive offspring. In addition, laboratory studies indicate that children who observe adults displaying physical aggression will be more aggressive in their later play activities than children who are not similarly exposed (Bandura, 1986). On the basis of this and other research, Frederick Ilfeld (1970) concluded that

> *physical punishment by parents does not inhibit violence and most likely encourages it. It both frustrates the child and gives him a model to imitate and learn from. The learning of violence through modeling applies to more than just parental behavior. It is also relevant to examples set by the mass media, one's peer or other reference groups, and local and national leaders. (p. 81)*

The subculture theory asserts that aggression is a by-product of a culture that idealizes a tough, "macho" image. This theory developed from analyses of official statistics, which suggest that certain subcultures have higher rates of violent crime than other segments of society. But as we suggested in Chapter 6, the stereotype that most acts of aggression are committed by young, minority males is erroneous because official statistics do not register the actual incidence of crime. Moreover, since the statistics do not reflect the attitudes or ideologies of individual offenders, it is difficult to discover the motives for their crimes. Data collected for the National Commission on the Causes and Prevention of Violence indicated that interpersonal violence received a low rate of approval in all socioeconomic groups (Reiss & Roth, 1993). A study of British men who had been convicted of acts of hostile aggression found that none of the men had committed their crimes in order to protect their reputation or win peer approval. The highest percentage of the crimes sprang from the aggressor's desire to inflict harm on the victim (Berkowitz, 1993).

In sum, people who commit acts of hostile aggression seem to share not an adherence to external subcultural norms but, rather, a similar set of psychological traits that can be found in any social, economic, or ethnic group.

Violence as Rational Choice

Although the implications of violence for human life and society seem wholly irrational, in many instances violent behavior can be interpreted as a rational means of attaining otherwise impossible ends. *Rational-choice theory* looks at all forms of human behavior for evidence of the actor's conscious or unconscious weighing of costs versus benefits (Hechter, 1987). Thus, rational-choice theorists would ask how criminals weight the chance of punishment against the likelihood of gain from breaking the law. Although it would seem that crimes involving terror and bloodshed are highly irrational acts committed by crazed individuals, in fact in many of these situations a rational strategy is at work.

Crimes such as extortion, kidnapping, and blackmail are often accompanied by the threat of violence. They are referred to as *strategic* crimes, however, because the violent act is one move in a complex "game" played by the criminal, the victim, and law enforcement agencies (Laver, 1982). In these "games," the criminals often wish to achieve their goals without resorting to maximum violence, but they must be prepared to use maximum force to convince the authorities that they are serious. To take just one example, "The successful kidnapper is the one who is perfectly prepared to kill the hostage and who can get this point across to his victim" in such a way that the law enforcement agencies involved will agree to meet the kidnapper's demands (Laver, 1982, p. 91).

The rational-choice approach is limited as an explanation of violence, but it is useful in situations in which it is important to understand what the violent actor hopes to gain in a situation. It stresses the importance of communication in cases of kidnapping, siege, and the like. Without communication, the strategic criminal and the authorities cannot reach an agreement that would prevent further violence. An example of such a situation is the standoff between the FBI and David Koresh, the leader of the Branch Davidian cult, which eventually led to the tragic deaths of many cult members in a fire that engulfed their fortified compound near Waco, Texas, in 1993. It is for this reason that the media often play such a crucial role in situations like hijackings, in which hostages are held until the terrorist's demands are met. In fact, the role of the media in violence of all kinds is significant and controversial, as will become clear in the next section.

The Influence of the Mass Media

A major issue in the study of violence is the role of the mass media in communicating or fostering violent attitudes. A survey of television programming conducted by the *Christian Science Monitor* six weeks after the assassination of Senator Robert Kennedy in 1968 found portrayals of 84 killings in 85.5 hours of prime-time evening and Saturday morning programming. The bloodiest evening hours were between 7:30 and 9:00, when the networks estimated that 26.7 million children between the ages of 2 and 17 were watching television (cited in Siegel, 1970). Since the 1970s there have been some changes in programming, and a portion of prime time has been devoted to family viewing. Despite these efforts to address the problem, levels of violence on television remain very high. So-called "action-adventure" programs are standard fare during prime time because they are relatively inexpensive to produce (and therefore more profitable) and because violence is an effective plot device. In addition, there is a great deal of violence in children's programming, especially cartoons.

Since the 1950s, when television viewing became widespread, its impact on young audiences has been the subject of a great deal of research. By the early 1970s it was generally agreed that there is some evidence linking television viewing to short-term aggression, but the debate over its long-term effects continued. In 1982 the National Institute of Mental Health released a report stating that "there is now 'overwhelming' scientific evidence that 'excessive' violence on television leads directly to aggression and violent behavior among teen-agers" (Reinhold, 1982).

Some researchers believe that the effects of television are more subtle. Hartnagel, Teevan, and McIntyre (1975) found that the effect of televised violence on behavior is indirect: "Values and attitudes or perceptions of the world may be substantially affected by television programming which may, in turn, influence behavior" (p. 348). This suggests that young viewers may become calloused by overexposure to violent programming and that, although they may not become violent themselves, they may more readily tolerate violent behavior in others.

Eli Rubinstein (1981) suggests that the problem of media violence may be especially acute for troubled children who already suffer from psychological disturbances that distort their perceptions of reality. He examined the television-viewing habits of ninety-four emotionally disturbed children in a state-operated inpatient facility for children in New York. He found that the behaviors of the children seemed to be related to what they watched on television: They imitated aggressive behavior and pretended to be characters in their favorite TV programs. Although much remains to be learned about the effects of televised violence on troubled children, Rubinstein believes that research must also focus on television's potential for helping this population.

The influence of the mass media, particularly television, in the reporting of protests, demonstrations, civil disorders, and other forms of potentially violent activity is another important issue. There are two questions here: Do the media distort the facts by stressing the violent aspects of news events, and does the presence of media reporters at such events tend to increase the possibility that violence will occur? The answer to both questions may be yes, in some instances. Distortion and provocation are difficult concepts to measure, however, and the matter is far from settled. Gladys Engle Lang and Kurt Lang (1972) have suggested that although the media "both contribute to the appearance of increased frequency and accelerate the cycle of protest," the presence of television and other news media in specific potentially violent situations "probably acts more as a *deterrent of violence* at such events than as an instigator" (pp. 108–109). On the other hand, there is some reason to fear that the extensive publicity given to such events as bomb scares, airplane hijackings, prison riots, and political assassinations may be "contagious," inspiring other attempts to engage in similar behavior. The rash of kidnappings, hijackings, and assassination attempts in recent years has been attributed in part to such media "contagion."

It is an oversimplification, of course, to assume that any portrayal of violence will tempt spectators to act out what they have seen. Both the context of the stimulus and the attitude of the viewer must also be considered. The desire to imitate what is seen on the television or movie screen is likely to depend largely on how it is presented, although we still lack hard evidence on what the relevant variables are. Similarly, the emotional condition of individual viewers will predispose them to react to what they see in different ways. Scenes of a prison riot are likely to evoke quite different reactions from a high school dropout who feels oppressed by "the system" than they would from an ambitious young executive.

Statistically, violent crimes are the least prevalent types of crime. According to the FBI's *Uniform Crime Reports (UCR)* , the violent crimes of murder, robbery, aggravated assault, and forcible rape account for 13.5 percent of all reported crimes; the remainder are property crimes and status offenses. But while violent crime is not the most common type of crime, it is the most frightening. People who return to a burglarized home often report a feeling of revulsion at the thought of strangers handling their personal possessions; the intrusion itself is felt as a defilement. But the defilement of one's body in a violent attack is a far more terrifying prospect. More than any other crime, it threatens one's integrity and sometimes one's life.

In this section we will examine three types of violent crime: homicide, assault, and rape. Later in the chapter we will discuss the violence that occurs in families and the possible links between gangs and violence.

Criminal Homicide

Criminal homicide takes two forms. *Murder* is defined as the unlawful killing of a human being with malice aforethought. *Manslaughter* is unlawful homicide without malice aforethought. In practice, it is often difficult to distinguish between manslaughter and murder. Someone may attack another person without intending to kill, but the attack may result in death. Depending on the circumstances, one case might be judged to be murder and another to be manslaughter. Often the deciding factor is the extent to which the victim is believed to have provoked the assailant.

Paradoxically, most murderers do not have a criminal record. Of course, there are those who use actual or threatened violence as tools in a criminal career, but these are exceptions; as a rule, professional criminals try to keep violence—especially killing—to a "necessary" minimum because of the "heat" it would bring upon them from the law. Most murderers do not see themselves as real criminals, and until the murder occurs, neither does society. Murderers do not conform to any criminal stereotype, and murder does not usually form part of a career of criminal behavior.

Murder does, however, follow certain social and geographic patterns. Reported murders occur most often in large cities. The murder rate for large metropolitan areas is 10 per 100,000 population, compared to 5 per 100,000 in rural counties and cities outside metropolitan areas (*UCR,* 1993). The incidence of murder is unevenly distributed within cities; as Donald T. Lunde (1975) has pointed out, "most city neighborhoods are just as safe as the suburbs" (p. 38). There are also regional differences; for example, murder is more likely to occur in the South, even though it is one of the more rural parts of the country. This seems to be a result of the culture of the region, which tends to legitimize personal violence and the use of weapons.

Most murderers are men, who generally are socialized to be more violent than women and to use guns for recreation or for military purposes; guns are the most common murder weapon. Most murderers are young: In 1992, 55 percent of those arrested for murder were under age 25. The victims are young, too; in 1992, 33.8 percent were between the ages of 20 and 30 (*UCR,* 1993). More than half of all murder victims are members of minority groups. About 90 percent of the time, the killer and the victim are of the same race (*UCR,* 1990).

More significant than the demographic characteristics of murderers and their victims is the relationship between them. Several studies have indicated that this relationship is generally close; often the murderer is a member of the victim's family or an intimate friend. A high proportion of murderers are relatives of their victim, often the husband or wife. Victim studies suggest that there is a great deal of unreported domestic violence and that the majority of violent crimes are committed by family members, friends, or acquaintances (Reid, 1991). One study found that *more than 40 percent of murder victims are killed in residences. . . . More women die in their own bedrooms than anywhere else. One in every five murder victims is a woman who has been killed there by her spouse or lover. Husbands are most vulnerable in the kitchen; that's where wives are apt to pick up knives to finish family arguments.*

The other half of murders involving close relatives include parents killing children, children killing parents, or other close relatives killing each other. These victims usually die in the living room from gunshot wounds. Another 6 percent of murders [are] between more distant relatives. (Lunde, 1975, pp. 35–36)

Most murders occur during a quarrel between two people who know each other well. Both the murderer and the victim may have been drinking, perhaps together, before the event; as noted in Chapter 5, many homicides are alcohol related. Even though many homicides occur during the commission of other crimes, these killings, too, are usually unpremeditated—a thief surprised by a security officer, a bank robber confronted by an armed guard, and so on. In addition, many homicides involve police officers, many of whom are killed in the line of duty. In 1960, 48 law enforcement officials were killed in the states and territories of the United States. This number reached a peak of 134 in 1975 and stood at 61 in 1992 (*UCR,* 1993).

The mentally ill commit murder at the same rate as the general population, but serial killers are almost always psychotic—either paranoid or sexual sadists (Lunde, 1975). These murderers may hear voices commanding them to kill, think they are superhuman or chosen for a special mission, or kill to avert imagined persecution. Sadists may torture before killing and/or mutilate their victims afterward. Unlike most murderers, psychotic killers are seldom acquainted with their victims, who are often representatives of a type or class—rich businessmen, for example, or young middle-class women.

Mass Murders   There is some evidence that mass murders (in which four or more people are killed by the same person in a short time) are becoming more frequent. Although the number of such murders fluctuates from year to year, some of the worst cases of the century have occurred since 1980.

On July 18, 1984, James Oliver Huberty, a recently fired security guard, opened fire in a McDonald's restaurant, killing twenty-one people and injuring twenty others. This was the worst massacre by a single person in a single day in U.S. history. In 1989, Theodore (Ted) Bundy, an articulate and rather charming drifter, was executed for the murder of numerous children and teenagers throughout the United States. These two cases, one a psychotic who murders in a fit of rage, the other a cool but also psychotic individual who organizes a series of killings (and therefore is known as a serial killer), illustrate quite well the types of people who commit mass murders. Generally, a mass murderer like Huberty kills in a fit of spontaneous rage; a serial killer often is highly organized and seeks to perfect a murder technique that will also prevent detection and apprehension. Most serial killers also have deep emotional problems concerning sexuality and describe the act of violence itself as thrilling and compelling (Holmes & DeBurger, 1987; Levin & Fox, 1985; Reid, 1991).

Assault and Robbery

Murder and assault are similar. *Assault* is a threat or attempt to injure. Murder therefore is a form of aggravated assault in which the victim dies. Often an extreme case of assault becomes murder accidentally; it may depend on the weapon used or the speed with which the injured person receives medical attention.

Since murder and assault are similar kinds of crime, most observations concerning murder also apply to assault. However, a person who commits assault is somewhat more likely to have a criminal record than one who commits murder.

Robbery may be defined as taking another person's property by intimidation. It accounts for 37 percent of all reported crimes of violence (*Statistical Abstract,* 1993). (A robbery in which violence was actually used is recorded as an assault.) Unlike murder or assault, robbery usually occurs between strangers; it is also the only major violent crime that is likely to occur between members of different races or classes.

Rape

Forcible rape is the act of forcing sexual intercourse on another person against his or her will. *Statutory rape*, for which the penalties are less severe, is the act of having sexual relations with a man or woman who is below a particular age established by state law. Although most arrests are for statutory rape, forcible rape attracts the most attention.

In the past, forcible rape was an extremely difficult crime to prove. Evidence requirements—the presence of bruises or torn clothing, eyewitnesses, or medical proof of intercourse—were unrealistic. Relatively few rapes occur in front of witnesses, and recent findings indicate that many rapists experience sexual dysfunction—which makes it less likely that rape can be verified by the presence of semen in the victim. Such difficulties discouraged victims from reporting the crime, and those who did press charges often encountered further problems. Defending attorneys sought to discredit the plaintiff's testimony by suggesting that she had provoked or cooperated with her assailant. In some cases the victim's previous sexual behavior was used to imply that she was promiscuous and, hence, not a reliable witness. Women who had suffered from the trauma of rape often found themselves the further victims of unresponsive and even hostile court proceedings. Many victims also feared revenge by the rapist.

These conditions persisted as long as rape was viewed as an exclusively sexual crime. The perpetrator of the "crime of passion" was thought to be driven by overwhelming and uncontrollable desire. Rapists were believed to be different from other people who commit violent crimes. This is only partially true; unlike murderers and those who commit assault, rapists often have a long history of criminal offenses. These offenses, however, tend to be for crimes other than rape (Reiss &

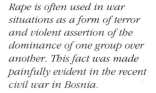

Rape is often used in war situations as a form of terror and violent assertion of the dominance of one group over another. This fact was made painfully evident in the recent civil war in Bosnia.

Roth, 1993). This relatively high rate of criminal involvement suggests that the rapist's motivation may be violent rather than sexual. A team of Massachusetts researchers found that rapists' feelings of anger, need for power, and desire to control the victim are significant factors; sex itself does not seem to motivate them. Rather, sex becomes the means through which the assailant expresses hostility (*Human Behavior,* June 1978).

Defining forcible rape as a crime of violence rather than one of passion helps place it in the proper perspective and invalidates the idea that the victim can initiate the crime by arousing desire in the rapist. It also suggests that women are not the only victims of this crime—men also can be raped, either by other men or by women. The old stereotypes of men as masters and women as objects of desire and domination worked to the disadvantage of both male and female rape victims. The women's movement and changing attitudes have led to a new understanding of this crime. Although rape laws still vary from one state to another, the nationwide trend is to revise existing statutes in favor of the victim. Corroboration by a witness is no longer necessary, and the plaintiff's sexual history is admissible only if it involves previous contact with the accused; moreover, although women are still the most likely victims of rape, men are now entitled to press charges against their attackers.

Rape victims are generally treated with more consideration and sensitivity today than they were in the past. Round-the-clock medical and counseling services are available, and police units staffed with specially trained personnel help victims overcome the trauma of the experience. As a result of these measures, more victims are willing to seek justice. Despite these changes, however, rape remains one of the most underreported of all crimes. According to the FBI, many women are too embarrassed or afraid to report a rape. They feel shamed by the attack and do not want others to know about it. Many also fear that the assailant will attack them again if they report the incident to the police.

Victim studies show that the vast majority of forcible rapes are not reported to the police. A recent study financed by the National Institute on Drug Abuse found that 683,000 adult women were raped in 1990, a figure more than five times higher than the number of rape cases recorded in official reports (Johnston, 1992). The study found that 61 percent of the victims were under 18 and that 22 percent had been raped by strangers. (The latter statistic suggests that family sexual abuse and acquaintance rape account for the majority of rapes.) On the basis of these findings, the researchers estimated that 6.8 million women would say that they had been raped once and 4.7 million that they had been raped more than once. More than 70 percent of the victims said that they were concerned about family members discovering that they had been raped, and about 60 percent said that they worried about being blamed for being raped (Koss & Harvey, 1991).

Date Rape *Date rape,* or *acquaintance rape,* is forcible sex in which the victim is known to the offender. Although the victim has agreed to engage in some form of social interaction with the offender, she has not agreed to have sexual intercourse with him. When a woman is raped on a date, she is much less likely to report the incident than if she were raped by a stranger. Moreover, some people do not consider such incidents to be actual rapes. For example, a survey of junior high school students found that 51 percent of the boys and 41 percent of the girls believed a man has a right to force a woman to kiss him if he has spent a "lot of money" on her (*Dallas Morning News,* May 3, 1988).

Studies have found that between 11 and 25 percent of college women have been in situations in which their boyfriends forced them to have sexual intercourse. As many as 35 percent of male college students report that they have become so sexually aroused on a date that they have forced themselves upon the woman or felt that they were capable of doing so (Malamuth, 1981; Shotland & Goldstein, 1983). Often date rape on college campuses takes the form of gang rapes, usually at parties following heavy drinking or use of other drugs.

The frequency of *reported* date rape began to increase in the late 1980s. Officials at the Santa Monica Rape Treatment Center note that the women involved came from all parts of the nation and that the incidents occurred on all types of college campuses and included "fraternity-party gang rapes, dormitory rape, date rape, stranger rape" (Hendrix, 1988). Until recently, colleges and universities were totally unprepared to respond to such cases, but as the idea of date rape gains acceptance and incidents of such rape are given greater publicity, college administrations are adopting measures designed to prevent such incidents and providing counseling and other resources to victims. In 1993, for example, Antioch College added to a lively debate over issues of consent and coercion in sexual relations by publishing guidelines that require verbal consent at every stage of sexual behavior.

FAMILY VIOLENCE

Child Abuse

Child abuse is a serious problem in the United States. At least 1 million children are physically abused each year, and many die as a result. Because it is such a taboo subject and so often is not reported to the authorities, statistics on child abuse are even more unreliable than data on other crimes. However, a random survey of parents in Boston found that one person in six claimed that his or her child had been a victim of sexual or other abuse, and nearly half of those interviewed claimed to know a child who had been victimized sexually. Fifteen percent of mothers and 6 percent of fathers said that they had been abused as children (Finkelhor & Meyer, 1988). An earlier survey reported significant increases in the incidence of

TABLE 7–1 VIOLENCE AGAINST CHILDREN IN INTACT FAMILIES		

Percentage of households where each type of violence occurred at least once in the past year. Nationwide poll was of two-caretaker households with at least one child 3 to 17 years old at home; 1,146 families were polled in the first survey and 1,428 were polled in the second.

	1975	1985
Slapped or spanked	58.2%	54.9%
Pushed, grabbed, or shoved	31.8	30.7
Threw something	5.4	2.7
Hit or tried to hit with something	13.4	9.7
Kicked, bit, or hit with fist	3.2	1.3
Beat up	1.3	0.6
Threatened with a gun or knife	0.1	0.2
Used gun or knife	0.1	0.2
All violence	63.0	62.0
Severe violence (Last five items)	14.0	10.7
Very severe violence (Last four items)	3.6	1.9

Source: New York Times, November 11, 1985. Copyright © 1985 by the New York Times Company. Reprinted by permission.

child abuse in communities throughout the United States and in other nations as well (Russell, 1984). Only in the last few years has a serious attempt been made to deal with the problem on a national scale—with limited success, as illustrated in Table 7–1.

Child abuse may be defined as a deliberate attack on a child by a parent or other caregiver that results in physical injury. A major obstacle to research on child abuse is concern for the traditional rights of parents; a parent has the right to inflict physical violence on his or her child (Justice & Justice, 1990). According to Suzanne Steinmetz and Murray Straus (1973), "The most universal type of physical violence is corporal punishment by parents. Studies in England and the United States show that between 84 and 97 percent of all parents use physical punishment at some point in their child's life" (p. 50).

If parents are to be responsible for raising and training children, they need to exercise a certain degree of authority, including the right to punish. Our culture strongly defends the right of parents to govern their children as they see fit, and it has traditionally approved of the use of corporal punishment for this purpose ("Spare the rod and spoil the child"). Thus, one of the first court cases in which an outside agency successfully intervened to protect an abused child was the 1866 Mary Ellen case, in which the plaintiff was the Society for the Prevention of Cruelty to Animals.

Increased concern with "children's rights" has changed this picture somewhat. Child labor laws, actions of the Society for the Prevention of Cruelty to Children, and changes in the handling of juvenile delinquents have helped reinforce these rights. However, the rights of parents and the preservation of the family unit are still regarded as primary concerns, even when in any other situation the nature of the injury would warrant criminal investigation and possible prosecution. Indeed, even in some of the worst cases the traditional autonomy of the family unit prevents the authorities from intervening or even learning about the problem. Some researchers estimate that only one case in three is ever discovered (Reiss & Roth, 1993).

According to a study by David Gil (1966), the victims of child abuse appear to be fairly evenly distributed over all age groups and between the sexes, although there are some changes in sex distribution during different stages of childhood and adolescence. At least half the victims in the study had been abused prior to the reported incident. A significant proportion of children seem to invite abuse through provocative behavior, although this plays a much smaller role in explaining attacks on children than the cultural norms discussed earlier. Of all cases of abuse, almost 90 percent were committed by the children's parents, and 14 percent of the mothers who abused their own children had themselves been victims of abuse as children.

A family in which there is child abuse typically has one or more of the following characteristics:

1. There is only one parent.
2. The parent's level of education and socioeconomic status are low.
3. The parent is highly authoritarian.
4. The family includes four or more children and has received some kind of public assistance within a year of the abuse incident.
5. The family changes its place of residence frequently.

Although these characteristics are found in many poor families, it is important to note that any correlation between abuse and poverty is biased by the fact that the behavior of the poor is more likely to be reported in official records than that of members of other classes, who are better equipped to conceal their activities. However, there are some specific problems, such as stress and anxiety, that are particularly prevalent in poor families.

Because studies based on official statistics have an inherent bias against the poor, the findings of a study by Brandt Steele and Carl Pollock (1974) are of interest. For five and a half years the researchers, both psychiatrists, studied sixty families in which significant child abuse had occurred. These families were not chosen by any valid sampling technique and therefore cannot be regarded as statistically representative; they were merely families that happened to come to the attention of the investigators. They did, however, span a wide range of socioeconomic and educational levels, and they included urban, rural, and suburban residents. The information obtained from them led the researchers to conclude that poverty, alcoholism, unemployment, broken marriages, and similar social and demographic factors are less significant than previous studies seemed to indicate. Instead, they found a typical personality pattern among abusive parents: The parent demands a high level of performance from the child at an age when the child is unable to understand what is wanted and unable to comply; and the parent expects to receive from the child a degree of comfort, reassurance, and love that a child would ordinarily receive from a parent. When the expected performance and nurturance are not forthcoming, the parent retaliates the way a small child might, with violence; but in this case the violence is not by the weak against the strong but by the strong parent against the weak, defenseless child.

It is important to note that *in every case studied*, Steele and Pollock found that the abusive parents had themselves been subject to similar unreasonable demands in childhood, and in a few cases they found evidence of the same experience among the grandparents. It seems, therefore, that child abuse could be part of a behavior pattern that is transmitted through the generations in some families and that it might be found to correlate with other aspects of family organization (Wisdom, 1989; Wyatt & Powell, 1988).

Spouse Abuse

On a rainy day in March 1992, Shirley Lowery, a Milwaukee bus driver, was stabbed to death by the man from whom she had fled a few days before. She was attacked as she hurried into the county courthouse to seek an injunction against her former companion, whom she accused of beating and raping her and threatening her life. Like many abusive husbands and boyfriends, her companion could not tolerate the idea of her leaving him. Lying in wait for her in the courthouse hallway, he stabbed her nineteen times with an eight-inch butcher knife.

Instances of violence between spouses have long been acknowledged and even tolerated as part of domestic life. Wives are the most frequent victims of such violence, although cases of battered husbands are sometimes reported. Very often the victims are seriously injured, yet, as with violence directed against children, the traditional autonomy of the family, together with the traditional subordination of women within the family, have made the authorities reluctant to intervene. Only recently has spouse abuse become an issue of social concern, and it is still difficult to assess its frequency and its impact on American family life.

Many researchers believe that spouse abuse is directly related to the high incidence of violence in American families. According to Straus (1977), "There seems to be an implicit, taken-for-granted cultural norm which makes it legitimate for family members to hit each other. In respect to husbands and wives, in effect, this means that the marriage license is also a hitting license (p. 444)." A study of more than 2,100 couples found that 3.8 percent of the husbands had physically assaulted their wives within the previous twelve months (Straus, 1977). The Justice Department estimates that more than 2 million women are victims of domestic violence each year. The vast majority of these women fail to notify the police of the incident, either because they consider it a private matter or because they fear further violence. Each year between 2,000 and 4,000 women are beaten to death by their spouses, and 25 percent of all female suicides are preceded by a history of battering (Reid, 1991).

Even when faced with constant violence, a surprising number of women make no attempt to leave the men who abuse them. Lenore Walker (1977) has suggested that this passivity is a form of fatalism. A pattern of dependency, of "learned helplessness," is established early in many women's lives:

> It seems highly probable that girls, through their socialization in learning the traditional woman's role, also learn that they have little direct control over their lives no matter what they do. . . . They learn that their voluntary responses really don't make that much difference in what happens to them. Thus, it becomes extremely difficult for such women to believe their cognitive actions can change their life situation. (pp. 528–529)

Other experts have described wife abuse as "a complicated and cumulative cycle of tension, belittlement, violence, remorse, and reconciliation that can lead to a paralysis of will and extinction of self-respect" (Erlanger, 1987, p. 1). This "battered women's syndrome," they claim, is a result of the deliberate undermining of a woman's sense of independence and self-worth by a possessive, overly critical man. "There is a sense of being trapped," one victim reports. "You live in terror and your thinking is altered" (quoted in Erlanger, 1987, p. 44).

Recent research has uncovered a high correlation between child abuse and spouse abuse: Between 30 and 40 percent of the time, a man who abuses his wife also abuses his children (Erlanger, 1987). In such situations a battered wife may remain with her husband in an attempt to protect the children. Conversely, the children may try to intervene and defend their mother, thereby causing the father to turn on them.

Elder Abuse

A form of violence that has recently come to public attention is abuse of the elderly by members of their own families, sometimes referred to as "granny bashing." (Abuse of the elderly may take other forms besides outright violence, such as withholding of food, stealing of savings and social security checks, and verbal abuse and threats.) Accurate data on elder abuse are not available, and it is difficult to prove that such violence has occurred. Elderly people bruise easily and fall often, and physicians are not trained to detect abuse in elderly patients. Moreover, because social scientists have only recently begun to study this type of violence, little is known about its causes. It is possible that family members are simply unable to cope with the problems of an aging parent or grandparent yet are unwilling, because of feelings of guilt, to place the parent in a nursing home. As the proportion of elderly people in the population increases, it can be expected that the frequency of elder abuse will also increase.

GANGS, GUNS, AND VIOLENT DEATH

Why is the homicide rate in the United States as much as twenty times the rate in other industrialized nations? (See Figure 7–1.) There is no one answer, but important explanations may be found in an analysis of changing patterns of juvenile violence, the increased firepower available to violent persons, and the inability of American society to agree on appropriate controls over lethal weapons.

In many sensational headlines one reads of brutal violence by juvenile gangs in large cities. In an especially infamous case in New York City, a gang of youths described as a "wolf pack" raped and nearly murdered a female jogger in Central Park. In Los Angeles, the "Crips" and "Bloods" are said to be especially violent gangs engaged in the distribution of crack cocaine. In Chicago and elsewhere, violence is attributed to the activities of armed gangs of various kinds. But in recent years there has been a sudden upsurge of gang activity and gang-related violence in smaller cities and suburban areas. In some instances gangs of skinheads and other groups of teenagers and young adults have perpetrated what are known as hate crimes, often involving violent attacks on homosexuals, Jews, or Asian immigrants. Even more dangerous, however, is the increase in the lethal gang violence associated with the sale and use of crack cocaine in some smaller cities and towns (Eckholm, 1993).

Figure 7–2 shows that homicide arrests among juveniles aged 14 to 17 have risen precipitously since 1983. The teenagers accused of killing an English tourist in northern Florida, for example, had accumulated long histories of arrests for violent criminal acts before age 14. This pattern of early involvement in crime among children from poverty-stricken and socially isolated neighborhoods is a strong signal to society that creative programs to combat poverty and neglect are urgently needed in large and small communities throughout the nation.

Gangs range from the peer groups that hang out on street corners to the well-organized, hierarchical gangs of crime syndicates. Perhaps the most violent gangs are those of organized crime. Their killings are often done by contract killers, professional murderers who kill for a payment. But organized-crime–sponsored murders account for only a small percentage of all murders. Do deaths caused by other types of gangs account for the remainder? This does not seem to be the case.

Juvenile and young-adult gangs often begin as street corner cliques and become incorporated into a larger gang confederation. Such gang organizations are often located in poor, segregated communities, where much of their activity is dedicated to the defense of local territory or turf. But experts on the sociology of gangs are quick to point out that there are many types of juvenile gang structures and many different types of gang activity, not all of which are violent or criminal.

In a thorough study of gang confederations in Milwaukee, John M. Hagedorn (1988) found that while gangs in large cities like Los Angeles, Chicago, and New York have been present more or less continuously for generations, in smaller cities and suburban areas gangs may be a new phenomenon. And simply because a community does not have recognizable gangs does not mean that gangs may not form in the near future. Much depends on relations between teenagers and the police, on the drug trade and its control, and on how young people perceive the need (or lack of it) to defend their turf from other teenagers. Thus, in Milwaukee, although there

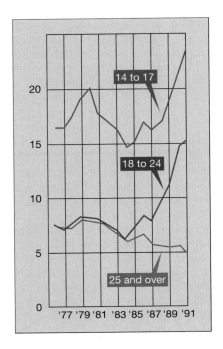

FIGURE 7–2 Homicide Arrests Nationwide per 100,000 People, by Age of Suspect

Source: Eckholm, 1993.

Young members of ethnic groups seeking to adapt to life in American cities often band together in gangs that may engage in violent conflicts with other gangs.

is some fighting, especially as young men strive to gain prestige within the gangs, there is relatively little "gang warfare" or homicide attributable to gang warfare. In Chicago, in contrast, there seems to be far more gang-related homicide, especially among Hispanic gangs.

A large majority of the gang members whom Hagedorn interviewed admitted owning at least one handgun. Hagedorn concludes that the problem of violence and homicide is related more to the increasing availability of guns and the involvement of some gangs in the illegal drug industry than to inherent features of the gangs themselves; this conclusion is shared by most students of gang behavior. Martin Sanchez Jankowsky, one of the nation's foremost authorities on violent gangs, notes that contrary to what some members of the public—and some sociologists—think, gang members typically do not like violence and the risks to personal safety that it entails. But most gang members believe that "if you do not attack, you will be attacked." This worldview implies that much gang violence is premeditated in order to take the opponent by surprise. In addition, Sanchez Jankowski notes, "the injuries incurred as a result of organizational violence [in the gang] become the social cement that creates group bonds in a deviant individualist setting." Overall, he concludes, gang violence "is understood to be the instrument used to achieve objectives that are not achievable in other ways" (1991, p. 177).

Another study of gang activity and involvement in drug dealing supports Hagedorn's conclusions and reinforces the idea that high rates of lethal violence are attributable more to the widespread use of guns than to the presence of gangs themselves. Terry Williams (1989) spent three years following the activities of a mobile drug "crew" in New York. This small and highly entrepreneurial gang was in the retail crack business. Its success depended on discipline: on ensuring that members did not become too high to function in their jobs or so careless that they became victims of violent robberies. Williams, like Hagedorn, documents the widespread and routine possession of handguns, but he also notes the increasing availability of more powerful automatic weapons and submachine guns.

While the crack epidemic is clearly responsible for an increasing number of homicides in poor communities since 1985, the United States had extremely high homicide rates even before the advent of crack; drugs alone therefore do not provide a sufficient explanation. But the availability of easily concealed handguns, together with the traditions of interpersonal violence that date at least from the period of the American frontier, probably accounts for much of the higher levels of deadly violence found in the United States.

Franklin E. Zimring, one of the nation's foremost experts on guns and gun control, reports that the "proportion of all households reporting handgun ownership has increased substantially over a twenty-year period" (1985, p. 138). On the basis of survey research, Zimring estimates that between one-fifth and one-fourth of all American households have one or more handguns. This represents an enormous increase since the late 1950s, when the proportion was probably well below one in ten households. Studies of the relationship between handgun possession and homicide find that when people arm themselves out of fear and a desire for protection there is also an increased risk of fatalities due to accidents involving guns, as well as homicides caused by mistaken recourse to fatal force—as in the tragic case of a Japanese exchange student in New Orleans who was killed when he tried to enter the wrong house in search of a party to which he had been invited (Reiss & Roth, 1993).

SOCIAL POLICY

Researchers at the National Center for Health Statistics report that 4,223 American men between the ages of 15 and 24 were killed in 1987, or 21.9 per 100,000. The rate for black men in the same age group was 85.6 per 100,000. Michigan was the most dangerous state for young black men, with a homicide rate of 232 per 100,000 compared to 155 in California, 139 in the District of Columbia, and 137 in New York. Among young white men the highest rate occurred in California (22 per 100,000), followed by Texas (21), New York (18), and Arizona (17). The safest state for whites was Minnesota (1.9 per 100,000); for blacks it was North Carolina (34.2 per 100,000).

These are alarming statistics, and the American public is clearly justified in its demand that society "do something" about violent crime. However, exactly what should be done is much less clear, as can be seen in the controversies over gun control, media violence, and ways of dealing with family violence.

Gun Control

In recent decades there has been increasing demand for stricter federal supervision of the purchase and sale of firearms, particularly the cheap handguns that are readily available in many areas. However, opponents of gun control legislation, represented primarily by the National Rifle Association (NRA), constitute one of the most powerful interest groups in the nation. The NRA draws much of its strength from areas of the nation where hunting is popular and there is a strong feeling that people need to be able to protect themselves and their families. NRA members claim that gun control measures would violate the "right to bear arms" that is contained in the United States Constitution. This is a strong position and one that most political leaders are unwilling to challenge directly.

The statistics on violence by means of guns—especially handguns—are alarming. Over 68 percent of the homicides reported in 1992 were committed by people using firearms; more than 80 percent of those homicides involved handguns. (See Figure 7–3.) In addition, over 40 percent of robberies and almost 25 percent of aggravated assaults involved the use of a firearm (*UCR*, 1993). The United States leads all other Western nations not only in number of homicides by guns but also in rates of suicide and accident by guns. And about 300 children die in accidental shootings each year.

Opponents of gun control claim that the decision to commit murder has nothing to do with possession of a gun; a killer can stab, strangle, poison, or batter a victim to death. Gun control therefore would make little difference. Although this argument sounds logical, it ignores the lethal potential of guns, which are about five times more likely to kill than knives, the next most commonly used murder weapon. One study found that for every 100 reported knife attacks, an average of 2.4 victims die, whereas for every 100 gun attacks, an average of 12.2 victims die (Gillin & Ochberg, 1970). And since most murders are spontaneous results of passion rather than carefully planned acts, it follows that the easy availability of guns is likely to increase the death rate in criminal assaults. In most cases murders are a result of three factors: impulse, the lethal capacity of the weapon, and the availability of the weapon. Strict gun control would eliminate or at least reduce the latter two factors.

In response to what has come to be perceived as a national epidemic of gunshot injuries and deaths, a majority of Americans now appear to favor strict controls on the sale of handguns. A 1993 Louis Harris survey of 1,250 adults found that for the first time since polling on this issue began, 52 percent of all respondents (61 percent of women) favored a ban on the possession of handguns unless a court has granted an exception. The survey also estimated that nine out of ten Americans support the Brady Bill, which calls for a five-day waiting period before purchase of a handgun and allows local authorities to check the background of the buyer (Barringer, 1993); the bill was passed by Congress and signed by President Clinton in 1993. Proponents of gun control argue that a stronger federal law is needed; they cite countries that have such regulations, such as Japan and England, in which rates of murder by means of guns are very low (Reiss & Roth, 1993).

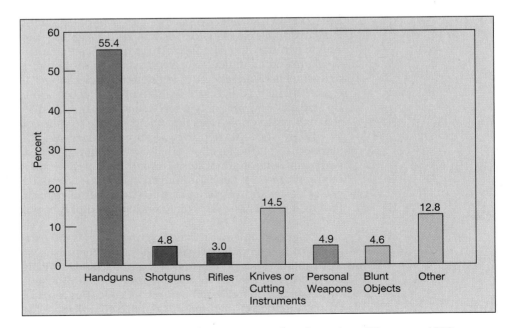

FIGURE 7–3 Percent of Murders Committed with Various Weapons, 1989

Source: UCR, 1990.

James Brady looks on as President Clinton signs the Brady Bill, which requires a five-day waiting period and a background check on individuals who wish to buy handguns.

Not all anti-gun, anti-violence policy is made at the federal level. Throughout the United States communities and voluntary associations are devising ways to reduce the number of guns "on the street." A popular approach that has had surprising results is the "gun buy-back," in which community residents are paid or given gift certificates for local stores if they turn in their guns. Such programs, which are highly publicized, at least give people the feeling that they can do something to help reduce the level of handgun violence.

After some states and cities passed gun control legislation in 1968, studies began to show some evidence that fewer crimes were committed with guns, but such evaluations are hampered by a number of problems in the research: First, it is impossible to know how effective a city's gun control legislation is when guns are so widely available in illegal markets. Second, social scientists can study the effects of policies only when they are significant. In many cases the gun control legislation was rather weak, making it difficult to compare conditions before and after enforcement. Third, assessments of the effects of legislation require longer-term study than is possible in cases in which gun control legislation has been passed only recently. Studies based on statistics covering only a few years have trouble distinguishing effects from mere fluctuations in crime rates that could be due to other causes (Zimring, 1985).

Today the NRA's power seems to be waning as Americans become more alarmed about the level of lethal violence and police departments increasingly side with gun control advocates. Despite NRA opposition, Congress passed legislation banning certain types of automatic weapons, "cop-killer" bullets that can penetrate police vests, and plastic guns that can evade electronic detection. The NRA is also finding it much more difficult to enlist the support of police professional associations and unions.

An important issue related to gun control is the extent to which women who are heads of households will choose to arm themselves with handguns for protection. Since the number of female-headed households is rising rapidly, any increase in the propensity of women to arm themselves could raise the overall level of handgun ownership to 50 million in the next decade. But research shows that women are still far more reluctant than men to purchase handguns; female-headed households are half as likely to have handguns as male-headed households (Zimring, 1985). This suggests that the outcome of the political battle over handguns may eventually depend on how both sides manage to appeal to female voters.

Media Violence

Another way of reducing violence in society might be to deemphasize violence in the media. In 1972 the United States Surgeon General's Study of Television and Social Behavior concluded that

> the causal relationship between televised violence and antisocial behavior is sufficient to warrant appropriate and immediate remedial action. The data on social phenomena such as television and violence and aggressive behavior will never be clear enough for all social scientists to agree on the formulation of a succinct statement of causality. But there comes a time when the data are sufficient to justify action. That time has come. (quoted in Bogart, 1972–1973, p. 521)

It should be possible, through either legislation or voluntary regulation, to reduce the incidence of killings and the reliance on shoot-and-slug formulas, especially in movies and television programming. The media have agreed to devote the first hour of prime-time television—from 8 P.M. to 9 P.M., called the "family hour"—to programming that is considered suitable for family viewing, with the more violent programs being shown at later hours. However, no serious effort has been made to reduce the overall level of televised violence.

Since the early 1970s a team of researchers at the University of Pennsylvania has provided counts of media violence. These counts show that despite the family hour, rates of televised violence have not fallen and in fact have increased steadily. Children's television is even more violent than adult programming (Donnerstain & Linz, 1987; Hirsh, 1987). In addition, changes in the technology of television—particularly the advent of video cassette recorders and cable television—have made it difficult to regulate the amount of televised violence available to the public.

The ready availability of videotapes has become a matter of widespread concern in recent years. Children and teenagers routinely obtain videotapes of movies that feature extreme violence, including dismemberment and sexual mutilation, and watch them without their parents' knowledge. Some organizations have taken a stand against easy access to violent films; they have called for legislation requiring prominent display of Motion Picture Association of America ratings of videotapes and, in some cases, for bans on the sale or rental of certain types of cassettes. To date, however, few states have enacted such requirements. At this writing it is fair to

Although the results of research on the effects of televised violence on viewers are ambiguous, large segments of the American public are increasingly convinced that there is a connection between high levels of televised violence programming and aggressive behavior by viewers of such programs.

say that most attacks on media content are directed against sexuality and against depictions that are thought to legitimate homosexuality and pre- and extramarital sex, rather than against violence.

Dealing with Family Violence

Child abuse is widely recognized as a serious national problem. In recent decades there have been numerous efforts, both by government and by private agencies, to increase public awareness of the problem and to prevent it where possible. The Child Abuse Prevention and Treatment Act was passed by Congress in 1974 to help states and communities organize programs for parents who abuse their children. Also in 1974, the National Institute of Mental Health established a national center in Denver to study the problem more thoroughly and set up a national commission to resolve the complicated legal problems and recommend changes in federal and state laws involving child abuse. Grant programs have also been funded to identify the causes of child abuse and provide treatment through self-help programs and lay therapy. Increasingly, states are requiring social workers and psychologists to report all cases of known or suspected child abuse to child protection authorities in their communities.

In order to break the cycle of abuse, some therapy groups have attempted to teach parenting techniques to mothers and fathers who were abused children themselves. The clinic workers try to supply these parents with alternative outlets for their frustration and anger and encourage them to call for help whenever they feel tempted to strike their children. Parents are also encouraged to seek meaningful relationships with other adults and not to invest their children's behavior with so much significance. C. Henry Kempe, who initiated the first treatment programs for parents at the Denver Child Abuse Center, found that 80 percent of the children could be returned to their parents "without risk of further injury, if their parents received intensive help [while the child lived in a foster home] and if there was a follow-up program after the child went home" (MacLeod, 1974, p. 719). For parents who resist this approach because of previous unfavorable experiences with the mental health system, there is Parents Anonymous. Established in 1970, this organization is similar in many ways to Alcoholics Anonymous. Regular meetings are held during which parents help each other stop mistreating their children.

Like child abuse, spouse abuse has received increased public attention in recent years. This problem is usually dealt with at the local rather than the national level. For example, in the 1970s many municipalities created shelters for battered wives, and others formed crisis intervention teams that attempt to negotiate with or "cool out" couples who are engaging in physical conflict. The need for both shelters and active intervention has not been met on a large scale, however, owing to lack of public funds.

More recently there has been a trend toward efforts to prevent spouse and child abuse by encouraging neighbors, friends, or family members themselves to notify the authorities when they have reason to believe that abuse is likely or is occurring. However, even when the authorities know that abuse is occurring in a particular household, they often are unable to act, especially in cases of child abuse. One problem, as noted earlier, is that there is little agreement on where child protection ends and rights to family privacy begin. Another is the lack of coordination between agencies dealing with spouse and child abuse—the former is treated as a routine police matter and the latter as a concern of child welfare agencies. Increasing cooperation among police investigators, medical professionals, and social workers has therefore become a high priority in many communities.

Race, Poverty, and Violence: The Unfinished Agenda

The links between socioeconomic inequalities and the level of violence in society have been demonstrated in numerous studies. At the end of the 1960s the National Commission on Civil Disorders (the Kerner Commission), after studying rioting in more than 150 cities, warned that the United States was moving toward "two separate societies, one black, one white—separate and unequal." Another commission, the National Commission on the Causes and Prevention of Violence (the Violence Commission), was appointed in 1968 following the assassinations of Dr. Martin Luther King, Jr., and Senator Robert Kennedy. It concluded that violence occurs when groups in a society are denied access to opportunities to obtain a decent living and to participate in the decisions that affect their lives. A third presidential commission, the Commission on Law Enforcement and Administration of Justice (the Katzenbach Commission), also concluded that "the roots of violence and disorder lie deep in the social fabric of American society, in its traditions, inequalities, and conflicts and ineffective governance" (Ball-Rokeach & Short, 1985).

These three major federal studies marked a shift from an emphasis on the psychological disorders underlying violence to a more sociological understanding of the origins of violence. The redress of legitimate grievances and the equitable sharing of the American pie became more important considerations in formulating policy than the search for personality profiles or biological predispositions that would explain violent behavior. The conservative climate of the 1980s did not alter this fundamental shift. Instead, conservative critics of liberal social policies called for increased severity of sentencing and higher rates of incarceration and punishment in lieu of a focus on more equal distribution of wealth and greater integration of the disadvantaged into the nation's economic institutions. While these were far from liberal policies, they did not constitute a challenge to the basic social (rather than psychological) orientation of the 1970s.

BOX 7–1 CURRENT CONTROVERSIES: THE MYTH OF BLACK VIOLENCE

It is widely believed, not only by the public but also by the media and the government, that blacks—especially young black males—are more prone to violence than whites. Official statistics seem to confirm this view: Although blacks make up 13 percent of the population, they account for more than half of those arrested for murder, rape, and nonnegligent manslaughter; this is five times the arrest rate of whites for these crimes. In addition, the victims of violent crime are far more likely to be black. Homicide is the primary cause of death for younger black men as well as for black women under age 40 (FBI, 1990).

Official statistics may be misleading, however. They reflect official attitudes and behavior—particularly the greater likelihood that black offenders will be arrested. Victim surveys provide more accurate information than arrest reports about crimes committed. Thus, while the FBI reported that the proportion of blacks arrested for aggravated assault in 1987 was more than three times greater than the proportion of whites, the National Crime Survey found that the actual proportions were very similar: 32 per 1,000 for blacks and 31 per 1,000 for whites.

If rates of violence are comparable among blacks and whites, why are the consequences of violence, in terms of both imprisonment and death by violence, so much more severe for blacks than for whites? One explanation is the "double standard" of police protection. Police are seven times more likely to charge black teenagers than white teenagers with felonies than to charge white teenagers with similar offenses, and the courts are more likely to imprison black teenagers. More telling, perhaps, is the belief that violent behavior is normal in inner-city black neighborhoods; arrest and imprisonment occur only if violence reaches extreme levels. In cases of domestic violence, for example, law enforcement officials do not intervene until a serious injury or fatality occurs. A similar pattern can be seen in police response to assault and homicide among black males, including gang members (Stark, 1990). One outcome, ironically, is that the life expectancy of males is greater in Bangladesh than in inner-city neighborhoods in the United States (McCord & Freeman, 1990).

The myth of black violence, with its consequences in actual experience, flies in the face of two of the nation's most cherished ideals: equal protection of the laws and social equality. It is further evidence of the need for policies that address the correlation between social inequality and violence rather than stereotyping any particular group as more prone to violence than others.

In the 1990s policy makers with various ideological perspectives once again began debating the issues of crime control that had been raised in the 1960s and 1970s. The primary question was how to diminish rates of crime and violence by increasing the share of the pie available to those at the bottom of the social order. (See Box 7–1, on page 221.) But social scientists are also discovering that they need to develop more varied policy recommendations that also address serious problems of media violence, the targeting of enforcement and rehabilitation programs to communities in greatest need, and the role of educators in combating the epidemic of juvenile violence now claiming so many American lives.

SUMMARY

1. Violence may be considered legitimate or illegitimate, depending on who uses it and why and how it is used. One distinction that is sometimes made is between institutional violence, which is exercised on behalf of or under the protection of the state, and noninstitutional violence, which is exercised by those who are opposed to established authority.

2. Biological explanations of violence are based on the idea that there are instinctive violent or destructive urges in all humans. The frustration–aggression theory holds that an unfulfilled need produces frustration, which is then vented in aggression. A related view is the control theory, in which the ability to control impulsive behavior is correlated with the existence of close relationships with other people.

3. Many sociologists believe that violence is a learned behavior and that violent actions are most likely to occur in a culture or subculture in which violence is accepted. In this theory violent behavior is learned by imitation and is a by-product of a culture that values toughness.

4. Rational-choice theorists have explored the role of violence in so-called strategic crimes such as extortion, kidnapping, and blackmail. In such instances, violent behavior can be interpreted as a rational means of attaining otherwise impossible ends.

5. The role of the mass media in fostering violent attitudes has been a subject of considerable research. The evidence shows that excessive violence on television leads directly to violent behavior among teenagers. It is also thought that the reporting of civil disorders and other forms of violence by the mass media may increase the possibility that further violence will occur.

6. Murder is the unlawful killing of a human being with malice aforethought. Most murderers are young men; more murders occur in cities than in rural areas; and in a large proportion of the cases the relationship between murderer and victim is a close one. Mass murderers are either psychotics who murder in a fit of rage or serial killers who are also psychotic but are cool and well organized.

7. Robbery may be defined as the taking of another person's property by intimidation. It usually occurs between strangers.

8. Forcible rape is the act of forcing sexual intercourse on another person against his or her will. In recent years rapes by offenders who are known to the victim—date or acquaintance rape—have become a matter of concern, especially on college and university campuses.

9. Child abuse, sometimes leading to death, is a serious problem in the United States. Many abusive parents were themselves subjected to abuse in childhood. Spouse abuse is also common and appears to be highly correlated with child abuse.

10. The high rate of homicide in the United States compared to other industrialized nations is sometimes attributed to violence by juvenile gang members, but the available evidence indicates that it is not the presence of gangs per se but the ready availability of guns that accounts for the prevalence of lethal violence in American cities.

11. Policy makers do not agree on what should be done to reduce or eliminate violent crime. Although most Americans favor gun control (i.e., supervision of the purchase and sale of firearms), opponents of such measures are powerful and well organized and until recently have succeeded in preventing the passage of meaningful legislation in this area. There are some signs that the dominance of the gun lobby is weakening, but legislators and the public are still divided on this issue. Efforts to reduce the level of media violence have also met with little success.

12. Family violence is widely recognized as a serious national problem, and there have been numerous efforts to increase public awareness of the problem and to prevent it where possible. There is a need for greater cooperation among police investigators, medical professionals, and social workers who deal with families in which abuse occurs.

13. The relationship between socioeconomic inequality and violence has recently become the focus of analyses of violence and debates over policies directed toward its abatement. Numerous important studies have demonstrated the need for the redress of legitimate grievances and a more equitable sharing of values and resources if the overall level of violence in American society is to be reduced.

SUGGESTED READINGS

ALLEN, JOHN. *Assault with a Deadly Weapon: The Autobiography of a Street Criminal,* eds. Dianne Hall Kelly and Philip Heymann. New York: McGraw-Hill, 1978. A frank account of the life of a street criminal; argues that the criminal-justice system must attempt to rehabilitate communities rather than criminals.

BROWNMILLER, SUSAN. *Against Our Will: Men, Women and Rape.* New York: Simon & Schuster, 1975. A provocative description of the violent aspects of sexual norms and of rape as a form of aggression against women.

COMSTOCK, GEORGE, ET AL. *Television and Human Behavior.* New York: Columbia University Press, 1978. An examination of television's impact on the daily lives of Americans, particularly children.

FANON, FRANTZ. *The Wretched of the Earth.* New York: Grove Press, 1968. A classic analysis by a psychoanalyst of the relationships between colonizers and colonized that sees extreme violence as a common condition of colonialism.

HAGEDORN, JOHN M. *People and Folks: Gangs, Crime, and the Underclass in a Rustbelt City.* Chicago: Lake View Press, 1988. An excellent firsthand account of gangs and gang violence in a medium-sized city.

KRAMER, RITA. *At a Tender Age: Violent Youth and Juvenile Justice.* Fort Worth, TX: Holt, Rinehart and Winston, 1987. A searing account of failures in the criminal-justice system's treatment of violent young people by an author who has marshalled many important facts and brings a decidedly critical and conservative perspective to her observations.

LAVER, MICHAEL. *The Crime Game.* Oxford, England: Martin Robertson, 1982. A readable and useful introduction to the theory of games as applied to crime, with special treatment of bargaining in hostage and other terrorist situations.

PRICE, BARBARA RAFFEL, and NATALIE J. SOKOLOFF. *The Criminal Justice System and Women.* New York: Clark Boardman, 1982. An excellent anthology of research papers and essays about women and crime; includes some fine studies of violence against women and its effects.

REISS, ALBERT J., JR., and JEFFREY A. ROTH (EDS.). *Understanding and Preventing Violence.* Washington, DC: National Academy Press, 1993. A thorough review of recent social-scientific research on the causes of violence, with special emphasis on the possible biological basis of violence; also describes measures that have achieved relative success in controlling or preventing some patterns of interpersonal violence.

Poverty Amid Affluence

Chapter Outline

- The poorest 20 percent of American households received 3.8 percent of all income in 1991.
- Twenty-three percent of all preschool children in the United States are living in poverty.
- The median household income of two-parent families with children was $41,075 in 1991; that of female-headed families with children was $9,413.
- Almost 33 percent of the black population and 28.7 percent of persons of Spanish-speaking descent have incomes below the official poverty level, compared with 11.3 percent of the white population.
- In 1991, only 7,500 low-income public housing units were under construction, compared to almost 127,000 in 1970.

By almost any standard measure, the United States ranks as one of the wealthiest nations in the world. The gross domestic product (GDP)—the total market value of all final goods and services produced within the United States in one year—is over $5 trillion. If we divide the GDP by the total population to derive per capita GDP, a crude but commonly used measure of the comparative wealth of nations, we find that the United States ranks well above most other nations, with a GDP of over $21,000 per person. Other advanced industrial nations, such as France, Germany, and Denmark, fall below this figure by at least $4,000, and the United Kingdom averages only $15,700 (*Statistical Abstract*, 1993).

The decline of the United States as the world's foremost economic power (at least according to some measures) is directly related to disparities in the distribution of the nation's enormous wealth. In our society wealth is concentrated in the hands of a relatively small number of people, while many other Americans can barely make ends meet or are living in poverty. American households have a median income of approximately $30,000; only about 26 percent enjoy incomes above $50,000 (*Statistical Abstract*, 1993). Indeed, we will see in this chapter that the gap between

In many third-world countries poverty is increasing as population growth outstrips economic development.

the rich and the poor has widened in the past decade; that the level of living of most Americans has been declining, with more people falling below the official poverty line; that the concentration of wealth in the hands of a few fortunate people has been increasing; and that policy makers are engaged in an intense debate over how to address the problem of persistent poverty. In the first section of the chapter, we will briefly examine the consequences of the inequality that characterizes American society. Later in the chapter we will explore some theories that attempt to explain the presence of poverty in one of the world's most affluent nations, as well as social policies aimed at reducing or eliminating poverty.

Although this chapter focuses on issues of poverty in the United States, it is important to note that a growing gap between the haves and the have-nots exists throughout the world. One-fifth of the world's people live in the richest nations (including the United States), but their average incomes are fifteen times higher than those of the one-fifth who live in the poorest nations. In the world today there are about 157 billionaires and about 2 million millionaires, but there are approximately 100 million homeless people. Americans spend about $5 billion per year on diets to lower their caloric intake while 400 million people around the world are undernourished to the point of physical deterioration (Durning, 1990). These growing disparities between rich and poor throughout the world have direct effects on the situation of the poor in the United States because many jobs are "exported" to countries where extremely poor workers will accept work at almost any wage. The increase in world poverty also contributes to environmental degradation and problems of political instability and violence, which drain resources that might be used to meet a nation's domestic needs.

But even though people in the world's poorest nations are far poorer than those living below the official poverty line in the United States, it is important to realize that the experience of poverty is based on conditions in one's own society. People feel poor or rich with reference to others around them, not with reference to very poor or very rich people elsewhere in the world. The experience of living in the United States as a teenager in a family for which every penny counts and there is rarely enough money for new clothes or a family car or trips outside town can be as difficult to bear as life in poverty anywhere. That the poor in the United States are relatively better off than the poor in Bangladesh is of little comfort.

THE HAVES AND THE HAVE-NOTS

Although equality of opportunity is a central value of American society, equality of outcome is not. Although Americans believe everyone should have the same opportunity to achieve material well-being, they do not object to inequality in the actual situation of different groups in society. Thus, the middle-class standard of living is the norm that is portrayed over and over again in media representations of American lifestyles. But this image ignores both the handful of extremely rich Americans and the tens of millions who share only minimally in the nation's affluence. To observe inequality and understand its impact, we need only compare a few aspects of the lives led by the affluent and the poor in our society.

The affluent live longer and better, and they can afford the best medical care in the world, the finest education, and the most elegant possessions. In addition, by discreetly influencing politicians, police officers, and other public officials to promote or defend their interests, they can obtain social preference and shape governmental policies. This capacity to purchase both possessions and influence gives the extremely wealthy a potential power that is grossly out of proportion to their numbers.

For the poor, the situation is reversed. Although America's poor people seldom die of starvation and generally have more than the hopelessly poor of the third world, they lead lives of serious deprivation compared not only with the wealthy but with the middle class as well. This relative deprivation profoundly affects the style and quality of their lives. It extends beyond mere distribution of income and includes inequality in education, health care, police protection, job opportunities, legal justice, housing, and many other areas. The poor are more frequently subject to mental illness than other Americans. They require more medical treatment and have longer and more serious illnesses. Their children are more likely to die than those of the more affluent, and their life expectancy is below the national average. They are more likely to become criminals or juvenile delinquents, and they contribute more than their share of illegitimacy, alcoholism, and violence to American society.

The Rich

Economist Paul Samuelson has provided a vivid metaphor for the disparity in the distribution of income in the United States: "If we made an income pyramid out a child's blocks, with each layer portraying $1,000 of income, the peak would be far higher than the Eiffel Tower, but almost all of us would be within a yard of the ground" (quoted in Blumberg, 1980, p. 34). Whatever measure or standard is used, the implications are the same: The rich own more, earn more, and use more—much, much more—and they have been doing so for a long time.

The median net worth of all U.S. families in 1989 was $47,200. The median for families with incomes of less than $10,000 was $2,300, while the median for those with incomes over $50,000 was $185,600 (*Statistical Abstract*, 1993). (Net worth, a frequently used measure of wealth, refers to the value of savings and checking accounts, real estate, automobiles, stocks and bonds and other assets, minus debts.) Surveys by the Federal Reserve Board suggest that 1 percent of all households hold one-third of all personal wealth (cited in the *New York Times,* January 11, 1991). The distribution of income is even more unequal: The wealthiest 20 percent of households received 46.5 percent of all income in 1991, while the poorest 20 percent received 3.8 percent (*Statistical Abstract*, 1993).

The United States has a long history of attempting to redistribute wealth through taxation and other policies. These policies have been instituted for three reasons: (1) The wealthy get more out of the economic system and can afford to pay more taxes; (2) they have a greater investment in the economic system and should pay more to maintain it; and (3) redistributing some income from the rich to the poor is fair and just in a democratic society. It was ideas like these that led to the establishment in the 1930s of President Franklin D. Roosevelt's New Deal, which, together with the Great Society legislation proposed by President Lyndon B. Johnson in the 1960s, created most of this country's welfare institutions and programs. The United States is now considered a *welfare state*, meaning that a significant portion of the GDP is taken by the state to provide certain minimum levels of social welfare for the poor, the aged, the disabled, and others who would not be able to survive under conditions of market competition. In a welfare state, government at all levels attempts to smooth out the effects of recessions and economic booms through such devices as a graduated income tax, public-sector employment, economic incentives for private firms, unemployment insurance, and the transfer of wealth from the rich to the poor.

In creating its welfare state, however, the United States has actually provided more opportunities for the rich to get richer than for the poor to escape from poverty. The opportunities available to the rich have been called *wealthfare*. An outstanding example of wealthfare in action is the across-the-board reduction in personal federal income taxes that resulted from the Economic Recovery Tax Act of 1981. The reductions benefited the rich much more than the poor. For example, a 10 percent reduction for a person with a taxable income of $100,000 amounted to a saving of $13,000; on a taxable income of $10,000, the saving would amount to $300. The Clinton administration's 1993 tax bill has corrected these inequities by increasing the tax rate on individuals making the highest salaries, but the wealthy still enjoy many tax advantages that less affluent people do not share.

In general, the competition for resources—not only income and wealth but what they can buy (health care, comfortable housing, expensive education, etc.)—heavily favors the rich. For example, people in upper-income brackets have many legal ways to avoid taxes. If they purchase real estate, they can obtain substantial tax reductions for mortgage interest payments at the same time that the property is increasing in value. In addition, the wealthy can make tax-free investments that are not available to the less well off. The income from municipal bonds—which are commonly sold in denominations of $5,000—does not have to be reported on tax returns.

Several other aspects of the welfare state's programs have turned out to be wealth-fare, or subsidies for the rich. For example, government import–export policies are designed to protect certain industries, such as textiles or steel, and the jobs of workers in those industries. However, when the government limits imports of a certain product, competition is stifled and consumers must pay the prices demanded by domestic manufacturers. When the government agrees to rescue failing corporations, as it has done with railroads, banks, and aerospace companies, the owners of substantial portions of the corporations' capital are most likely to benefit from such federal subsidies. It can be argued that the poor are relative losers in these situations, since less government money is available for social programs. Similarly, when government revenues are raised through such devices as sales taxes on gasoline, those with less money effectively bear a greater share of the burden because the proportion of tax they pay is higher relative to their smaller incomes than it is for the rich. Such policies are equivalent to subsidies for the wealthy or for the corporations they own, and they place an extra economic burden on the poor (Turner & Starnes, 1976).

Are the Rich a Social Problem?   During the 1992 presidential election campaign, the Democrats seemed to score heavily against their Republican opponents by accusing them of fostering a "public be damned, let me enrich myself" attitude among wealthy Americans. The Democrats pointed to the encouragement the rich receive from the so-called "trickle-down" theory of economics, which states that policies that benefit business or wealthy individuals will stimulate economic activity and thereby create more jobs. Although the Clinton administration has made some very modest gains in correcting the public image of "government for the rich," frequent news stories continually remind us, for example, that the head of Reebok International made $33 million in 1992 or that the CEO of U.S. Surgical drew $15 million, while increasing numbers of low-wage workers saw the value of their earnings diminish even in a period of low inflation (Nasar, 1992). The gains of the rich and the losses of the nonrich during the 1980s are clearly shown in Figure 8–1.

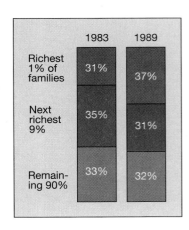

FIGURE 8–1   Share of Total Net Worth of American Families

Source: Federal Reserve.

We will return to this issue in our discussion of corporate power in Chapter 14. Here it is sufficient to point out that although there is no consensus in American society that the rich themselves are a social problem, there is evidence of concern among Americans that the ethic of individual success and enrichment may hamper efforts to develop new policies to address the problems of poverty (Bellah et al., 1985).

The Poor

While the rich are able to take advantage of various ways of improving their situation, the poor face an entirely different set of circumstances. They are part of a society that has the means to greatly alleviate poverty but, instead, has adopted policies that actually increase the percentage of poor people among its members. In the

Since 1975 the poverty rate for children has been higher than that for any other age group.

words of a pastoral letter issued by a committee of Roman Catholic bishops in 1984, "The level of inequality in income and wealth in our society . . . today must be judged morally unacceptable" (quoted in Briggs, 1984). Many social scientists believe that the situation of the poor is likely to become still worse. There are several reasons for this, including technological changes that eliminate certain kinds of jobs, the reluctance of the middle and upper classes to share their wealth with less fortunate members of society, and the general attitude of Americans toward poverty.

Many people believe that the poor are largely to blame for their own poverty. The argument is as follows: "The poor as a class consists of the unemployed, who are responsible for their condition because they will not work. If they could be persuaded to work for a living, or were forced to take jobs, poverty could be eliminated. What we have now is a group of freeloaders who are getting by on welfare." The inaccuracy of this argument is evident when one examines the data on poverty and work.

Out of the 35.7 million people who were classified as living below the official poverty line in 1991, 13.6 million, or 38 percent, were children under 18; another 3.8 million (12.4 percent) were over 65 (*Statistical Abstract,* 1993). Millions more were female heads of households with children under 18 and no husband present, or ill, disabled, or going to school; of the remainder, the majority worked either full or part time in the previous year, but their wages were not sufficient to elevate them above the poverty threshold.

Members of minority groups are especially likely to be included among the poor. The median incomes of minority families range from 57 to 63 percent of the median incomes of white families (*Statistical Abstract,* 1993), while unemployment rates for black and Hispanic workers average about double the rate for white workers. (See Figures 8–2 and 8–3.)

Of enormous significance for the so-called *working poor* is the fact that real wages (i.e., wages measured in constant dollars) have not risen significantly in the past two decades. The median household income (measured in 1991 dollars) was

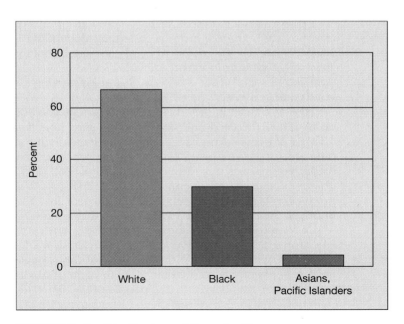

FIGURE 8–2   Distribution of Poor, by Race

Source: Census Bureau, 1992.

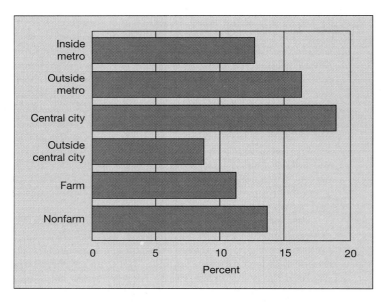

FIGURE 8–3 Poverty Rate, by Area of Residence

Source: Census Bureau, 1992.

$28,803 in 1970. In 1991 it was $30,126, only slightly above the 1970 level (*Statistical Abstract*, 1993).

POVERTY AND SOCIAL CLASS

In every society people are grouped according to their access to the things that are considered valuable in that society. These groupings of people are variously called classes, status groups, factions, or strata, depending on the classification scheme used. Whatever the name, the phenomenon being described is *social stratification*—a pattern in which individuals and groups are assigned to different positions in the social order, positions that enjoy varying amounts of access to desirable goods and services.

The stratification of individuals and groups according to their access to various occupations, incomes, and skills is called *class stratification*. A *social class* is a large number of people who have roughly the same degree of economic well-being; people enter or leave a given class as their economic fortunes change. Marxian social theory emphasizes this form of stratification. For Marx and his followers, the basic classes of society are determined by ownership or nonownership of the means of production of goods and services. The owners are called capitalists, and those who must sell their labor to the capitalists are the workers.

Marx referred to members of capitalist societies who are poor and not in the labor force as the *lumpenproletariat*. This class is made up of people at the margins of society who either have dropped out of the capitalist system of employment or have never been part of it at all. Marx thought of the lumpenproletariat as comprising the criminal underworld, the people of the street, the homeless, and all the other categories that make up the dregs of humanity. He believed that capitalism would always impoverish the working class because the owners of capital would seek to exploit the workers to the fullest extent possible, and as a result the lumpenproletariat would expand and become ever more dangerous to the stability of capitalist societies.

The German sociologist and historian Max Weber was critical of the Marxian perspective. Weber accepted most of the Marxian analysis of economic classes, but he did not believe that capitalism would inevitably cause the expansion of the lumpenproletariat. Moreover, he pointed out that other valued things besides wealth are distributed unequally in modern societies. For example, status (or honor) and power are both highly valued, and their distribution throughout society does not always coincide with the distribution of wealth. People who have made their money recently, for example, are often accorded little honor by capitalists who made their money much earlier.

In their studies of the American system of social stratification, social scientists have developed a synthesis of the Marxian and Weberian approaches. They have devised designations like upper class, upper-middle class, middle class, working class, and poor, which combine the Marxian concept of economic class with the Weberian concept of status.

Sociologists have pointed out that the ways in which we distinguish among these class levels have both *objective* dimensions, which can be measured by quantifiable variables such as income or membership in certain clubs, and *subjective* dimensions, which are the ways in which we evaluate ourselves and others (and the way we feel about people in the various objective classes). Objectively, we base our estimations of social-class position more or less on the Marxian model. Major employers and powerful political leaders are assigned to the upper class. Managers of large firms and relatively wealthy people with successful businesses and professional practices are in the upper-middle class. People who are employed as middle-level managers and lower-paid professionals (e.g., technicians) are in the middle class. People who work in factories or depend on hourly wages are assigned to the working class. People who lack steady work or drift back and forth between legitimate employment and other ways of obtaining income are the poor.

The subjective dimension of social class becomes evident when people are asked to identify the class to which they belong. For example, the proportion of people who classify themselves as poor is considerably lower than the proportion who are so classified by the Census Bureau. (See Table 8–1.) Part of the reason for this is that many poor people have low-paying jobs and hesitate to identify themselves as poor even when they are; they place themselves in the working class. Moreover, as Mary R. Jackman and Robert W. Jackman (1983) have pointed out, re-

TABLE 8–1 DISTRIBUTION OF RESPONSES TO CLASS-IDENTIFICATION QUESTION (FOR TOTAL SAMPLE, BY RACE AND SEX)

	POOR (%)	WORKING (%)	MIDDLE (%)	UPPER-MIDDLE (%)	UPPER (%)	OTHER (%)	NO SOCIAL CLASSES (%)	DON'T KNOW (%)	NOT ASCERTAINED (%)	TOTAL N
Total Sample	7.6	36.6	43.3	8.2	1.0	1.3	0.5	1.5	0.2	1,914
Whites	4.8	35.8	46.4	9.0	1.0	1.1	0.5	1.3	0.2	1,648
Blacks	27.7	41.5	22.1	1.5	1.5	2.6	0.5	2.6	0.0	195
Other*	14.1	39.1	32.8	7.8	0.0	1.6	0.0	3.1	1.6	64
Men	5.4	41.4	40.5	8.5	1.1	1.4	0.9	0.5	0.4	802
Women	9.2	33.1	45.2	8.0	0.9	1.2	0.2	2.2	0.1	1,112

*This category includes Asians, Spanish Americans, and American Indians.

Source: Mary and Robert Jackman, *Class Awareness in the United States,* Table: "Distribution of Responses to Class-Identification Question." By permission of the University of California Press, Berkeley.

spondents who do identify themselves as poor might not do so if the same category were labeled "lower class."

All the categories mentioned earlier are used to discuss the American stratification system, but they contain many problems and are extremely difficult to define scientifically. The designations "middle class" and "working class" are especially problematic. In the 1950s and 1960s, when the gross domestic product doubled each decade, it appeared that the distinctions between the working and middle classes were becoming blurred and meaningless. For a period of about twenty years, it seemed that the United States and Canada were experiencing a convergence in social classes as more and more people shared in the benefits of expanding wealth. Workers—defined in the Marxian sense—were adopting lifestyles that seemed to make them indistinguishable from the middle class of salaried employees and professionals. In that period only the extremes of social stratification were easy to identify: the wealthy at the top and the poor at the bottom. Otherwise, the incomes of most Americans were giving them access to what sociologist David Riesman called the "standard package" of goods and services available in a wealthy society (Riesman, Glazer, & Denney, 1950). That "package" included a home, a car, and such consumer goods as television sets, air conditioners, and washing machines (Blumberg, 1980).

The development of welfare state institutions in the United States from the 1930s to the end of the 1960s supported the notion that the classes were converging toward a generalized level of affluence. The growing strength of labor unions allowed workers to bargain for higher wages and better benefits than ever before. The growth of mass educational institutions made education available to more people and provided training for new jobs and professions. Social-welfare programs like social security, Aid to Families with Dependent Children (AFDC), food stamps, Medicare and Medicaid, affirmative-action programs, youth programs, unemployment insurance, and many other kinds of government support seemed to offer the hope that the degree of inequality in American society would be reduced still further. However, as can readily be seen in Figure 8–1, events of the 1970s and 1980s reversed the trend toward greater affluence for all. This is a subject to which we return in later sections of the chapter.

THE NATURE OF POVERTY

Poverty is a deceptively simple term to define. Certainly the poor have less money than other people. In addition, the money they do have buys them less. The poor must often purchase necessities as soon as they have cash (for example, when a welfare check arrives). They cannot "shop around" for sales or bargains, and they are often victimized by shopkeepers who raise their prices the day welfare checks are delivered. When they buy on credit, the poor must accept higher interest rates because they take longer to pay and are considered poor credit risks. Inflationary price rises affect the poor first, and more severely. The cost of essential consumer goods, ranging from rice and sugar to toilet tissue and soap, may rise suddenly (e.g., when energy costs increase as a result of a crisis in the Middle East), but the wages of the lowest-paid people and government income assistance payments rise slowly if at all.

For most people, poverty simply means not having enough money to buy things that are considered necessary and desirable. Various formal definitions of poverty have been offered, however. John Kenneth Galbraith (1958) stressed the sense of degradation felt by the poor and concluded that "people are poverty stricken when their income, even if adequate for survival, falls markedly behind that of the community" (p. 245). Another study emphasized self-respect and opportunities for social mobility and participation in decision making (Miller et al., 1967). Poverty may mean a condition of near starvation, bare subsistence (the minimum necessary to maintain life), or any standard of living measurably beneath the national average. To deal more effectively with poverty as a social problem, a generally agreed-upon, scientifically based, and more specific definition is needed.

The Poverty Line

Official U.S. government definitions of poverty are based on the calculation of a minimum family "market basket." The U.S. Department of Agriculture regularly prepares estimates of the cost of achieving a minimum level of nutrition, based on average food prices. It is assumed that an average low-income family must spend one-third of its total income on food; thus, by multiplying the family food budget by three the government arrives at a poverty income that can be adjusted for the number of people in the household and for changes in the cost of food. The official, food-based poverty line can also be adjusted to account for the tendency of rural people to supplement their incomes with subsistence agriculture and gardens. The official measure is also corrected each year or even more often for changes in the cost of living as measured by the consumer price index (CPI). In 1991 this inflation-corrected, official poverty line for a family of four was $13,924. By this measure, 35.7 million people, or 14.2 percent of the U.S. population, were below the poverty line.

This official poverty measure was developed in 1965 by Mollie Orshansky, an economist at the Social Security Administration, who reasoned that the only acceptable measure of the adequacy of a person's level of living is food consumption. But although this definition was accepted as the official means of establishing a "poverty line," there has been continuing controversy and debate over definitions of poverty and their implications for social policy. In 1982, during the Reagan administration, a study by the Census Bureau demonstrated that if the noncash benefits provided to the poor by the government—such as food stamps, Medicaid, and housing—are included in the calculation of income, the extent of poverty is much less than is generally believed. Members of the administration therefore argued that social programs aimed at reducing poverty do not take into account the effects of noncash benefits and consistently overstate the rate of poverty in the United States. Thus, in 1985, according to the official food-based definition, there were slightly more than 33 million Americans (14 percent of the population) below the poverty level; but using the Reagan administration's modified definition (in which the value of food stamps, housing subsidies, and medical benefits is factored into the family budget), the number of Americans below the poverty level was 21 million (9.1 percent of the population).

Poverty scholar Patricia Ruggles (1990) has observed that according to official definitions of poverty, a single mother of three who works full time earning $5.00 an hour is not officially poor. Yet her rent, child care costs, and taxes would probably account for 80 percent of her weekly income, leaving her with about $40 a week to pay for food, medical care, clothing, and everything else. According to Ruggles, this anomaly is due to changes in American living standards that have occurred since the official formula for calculating the poverty line was established. When the poverty formula was first developed, such conveniences as telephones and indoor plumbing were not part of Americans' expectations of a minimally adequate level of living. And at that time far fewer children lived with one parent and far fewer women were employed. Child care, a significant expense for most working families (and essential if a single parent is to work), was not the major and necessary expense it is today. With these factors in mind, Ruggles suggests that the official food-price–based estimate of the poverty line should be recalculated at regular intervals on the basis of changing definitions of minimal consumption.

Regardless of how poverty is measured, these calculations are arbitrary. The actual "cost" of living can vary greatly in different social environments. As William P. O'Hare (1983) has written,

> Anyone who lives in a major city knows that if you are trying to support a family of four on [$13,924], you are poor, even if the Government says you are not. The threshold for determining poverty status may be appropriate for some areas of America where the cost of living is low and one can grow some of one's own food, but most poor people live in high-cost urban areas. (p. A21)

The idea that poverty is relative rather than absolute is nothing new. More than thirty years ago Victor Fuchs (1956) proposed that any family may be classified as poor if its income was less than half of the median family income. By this definition, about 20 percent of the population would be considered poor. Contrary to the Orshansky formula or any arbitrary income standard, the use of such a relative standard implied that poverty would exist as long as income distribution remained unequal. And in fact, the proportion of poor people in America has tended to remain stable when measured by the Fuchs formula.

Fuchs

Who Are the Poor?

Since the passage of the Social Security Act (1935), which established federal old-age pensions (social security), unemployment insurance, and aid to dependent children, the nation has made great strides in its effort to combat poverty. Although it remains true that far too many citizens live in poverty, it is not true, as some argue, that programs to combat poverty have had negative effects or no effect at all (Murray, 1984). If we look at Table 8–2, which compares official poverty rates for selected categories of Americans over a period of twenty-seven years, we can see that the most dramatic decrease in

TABLE 8–2 PERCENTAGE OF PERSONS IN POVERTY, BY DEMOGRAPHIC GROUP: 1964, 1983, 1991

DEMOGRAPHIC GROUP*	1964	1983	1991
All	19.0	15.2	14.2
White	14.9	12.1	11.3
Black	49.6	35.7	32.7
Hispanic[†]	—	28.4	28.7
Living with female householder, no husband present	45.9	40.2	39.7
Elderly (65+)	28.5[‡]	14.1	12.4
Children under 18	20.7[‡]	22.2	21.1

*Owing to constraints in the published data, these groups are not mutually exclusive. For example, the category "white" includes all persons living in a household whose head is white. Those whites who are, for example, elderly female household heads will also be included in the other two groups.

[†]Hispanics may be of any race.

[‡]Figures are for 1966 since none were published for 1964 or 1965.

Source: Danziger, S. H., R. H. Haveman, and R. D. Plotnick, 1986, "Antipoverty Policy: Effects on the Poor and the Nonpoor." In S. H. Danziger and D. H. Ewinberg (eds.), *Fighting Poverty: What Works and What Doesn't* (Cambridge, MA: Harvard University Press). Reprinted by permission. Data for 1991 are from *Statistical Abstract,* 1993.

poverty has occurred among the elderly. Much of this decrease is due to the effects of better social security and pension benefits and health-care programs like Medicare and Medicaid. But the table also shows how much poverty remains in American society and how unevenly distributed it is. The poverty rate among American children and the poverty rates for blacks and Hispanics are disproportionately high.

Poverty and Single-Parent Families Twenty-three percent of all preschool childen in the United States are living in poverty. (See Figure 8–4.) The situation is especially severe for children in single-parent families headed by women. The median household income of two-parent families with children was $41,075 in 1991; that of female-headed families with children was only $17,961 (*Statistical Abstract*, 1993).

Black female-headed families are especially likely to be living in poverty; their median income was $9,413 in 1991, compared to $15,513 for white female-headed families (*Statistical Abstract*, 1993). Since less than half of all black families with chil-

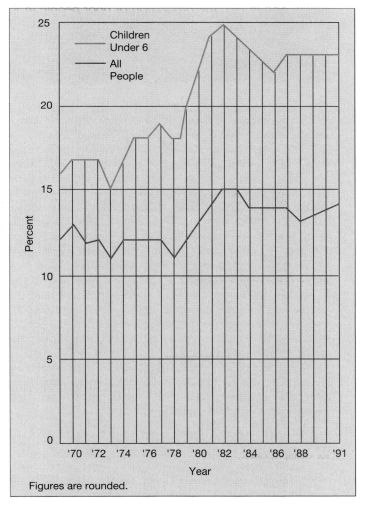

FIGURE 8–4 Percentage of Population Below the Poverty Line, United States, 1970–1991

Source: Data from Census Bureau and National Center for Children in Poverty.

The most common event leading to poverty is the breakup of a couple, which often leaves the woman unable to work because she must care for a young child.

dren have two parents present, it is clear that a large proportion of black children are living in poverty. Almost 50 percent of black and about 40 percent of Hispanic children under age 6 were classified as poor in 1991 (*Statistical Abstract*, 1993).

To a large extent, this situation is due to the severe restrictions placed on female heads of families with regard to employment, primarily because of the need to care for children. Child care is either unavailable or too expensive, and typically the jobs that are available pay too little to make the effort worthwhile. Some women require public assistance until their children are old enough to attend school. Others, lacking skills or education, are forced to depend on welfare as a way of life. Although a large number of welfare mothers would like to work, the lack of facilities for job training and child care confronts them with a double obstacle.

The increase in the number of families headed by one parent is another demographic trend associated with the rise in poverty among children and young people in the United States. Data on young families (those headed by a parent under 30 years of age) shows that from 1973 to 1990 incomes fell by 22 percent for white families, by 28 percent for Hispanic families, and by 48 percent for black families. The increased income insecurity and poverty among young minority families are related to the almost doubling of the number of single-parent families in the same period, to 37 percent of all young families in 1991 (DeParle, 1992).

Children living in poor households experience severe disadvantages in comparison with children from more secure homes. For example, a study of nutrition among poor children concluded that

> *Caloric and nutritive deficiencies in their diet are serious enough to make poor children doze off in school, look fatigued, or suck their thumbs; it is difficult to pay attention when one is hungry. Poor children receive . . . less medical attention than those from more prosperous families; they are hospitalized less often and stay longer when they are admitted; and most poor children never get to see a dentist. And it is clear that poor children are much less likely to receive psychiatric attention for emotional disturbances than those from upper-income groups. The consequence is a tendency to equate emotional upset with lack of intelligence, and this works to weaken the educational opportunities of poor kids. (Seligman, 1968, p. 88)*

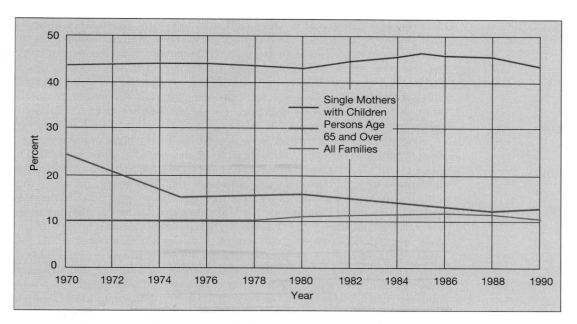

FIGURE 8–5 Percent of Families and Elderly Persons Living Below the Poverty Level

Source: Data from *Statistical Abstract,* 1993

In 1991 the Food Research and Action Center, a nonprofit antihunger group, reported that 5.5 million children under age 12 are hungry in the United States.

Older people also often go hungry. A study released in 1993 by the Urban Institute based on 4,000 interviews with elderly persons in sixteen communities in the United States found that 12 percent of the respondents said that they sometimes go hungry or must choose between paying their rent and eating. In some impoverished central-city communities, however, this figure was as high as 50 percent (Lee, 1993).

Trends in poverty rates over time are illustrated in Figure 8–5.

Poverty and Minority Groups It should be noted that although whites are the largest group among welfare families, blacks and other racial minorities are overrepresented. For example, 32.7 percent of the black population and 28.7 percent of persons of Spanish-speaking descent have incomes below the established poverty level, compared with 11.3 percent of the white population. The median income of white families is $37,783, whereas that of black families is $21,548 and that of Hispanic families is $23,895 (*Statistical Abstract,* 1993).

Several factors are thought to be responsible for the lower earning power of blacks and other minority workers. For one thing, they are less likely to be well educated; among blacks over 25, 32.3 percent have not completed high school (*Statistical Abstract,* 1993). However, in the 1970s and 1980s the gap in educational attainment between whites and blacks narrowed for people under age 25.

The discrimination experienced by blacks, Chicanos, Puerto Ricans, and other minority groups in housing, education, and health care exacerbates the effects of low income. In housing, members of these groups are often forced to pay higher rents and live in dilapidated or deteriorating dwellings. In education, the quality of predominantly minority schools is often inferior to that of predominantly white schools. In these and other areas, the disparity between blacks and whites in terms of both opportunity and treatment is evident. (These problems are discussed more fully in Chapter 9.)

Poverty and Geography Although urban poverty is probably more familiar to most people, a large proportion of poor people live in rural or suburban areas. Rural poverty is not as visible as urban poverty. Separated from the mainstream of urban life, the rural poor are largely hidden on farms, on reservations, in open country, and in small towns and villages. Unemployment rates in rural areas are far above the national average. Largely because of the technological revolution in agriculture and other occupations, poorly educated, unskilled workers have been left with no means of support.

The majority of the rural poor are white, but a high percentage of southern blacks, Native Americans, and Mexican Americans are poor as well. During the 1980s poverty and economic inequality increased among rural Americans owing to downturns in agriculture, mining, and rural manufacturing. Thus, the most recent statistics indicate that people living in rural areas have lower incomes, higher poverty rates, higher unemployment, and lower educational attainment than those living in metropolitan areas (Pollard & O'Hare, 1990). Certain areas that have historically been poor, such as many counties in Appalachia, much of the Mississippi Delta, the arid regions of the Southwest outside the cities and irrigated farming areas, as well as many other rural areas, experienced further declines in the 1980s. Those declines were accompanied by increases in the correlates of poverty: infant mortality, family dissolution, out-migration of the younger and better educated population, and malnutrition (Harrington, 1987).

Among the rural poor are migrant workers who, following the harvest, live in tarpaper shacks with few possessions. The rural poor also include Native Americans on reservations, who lead lives of destitution and regimentation, with decisions made for them by faraway bureaucrats. Other poor populations in rural areas are out-of-work coal miners and small farmers and farm workers who cannot compete with automated production techniques. Attempting to escape poverty, many of the rural poor migrate to urban areas, where they discover that the problems of the countryside are magnified.

In the cities, lack of money is aggravated by higher living costs, overcrowded and inadequate housing, poor nutrition, insufficient medical care, unsanitary health conditions, and other serious problems. The desired jobs are unobtainable, since the demand for unskilled labor has declined drastically. In addition, as businesses move to the suburbs, transportation to work becomes unavailable or too expensive. As a result, rural immigrants frequently end up on the urban welfare rolls.

The Poor on Welfare Americans have an ambivalent attitude toward poverty. We recognize that the poor are not always responsible for their situation, yet those who must turn to public assistance are often pictured as lazy, shiftless, or dishonest. Their private lives are scrutinized, and the constant presence of social workers and welfare investigators in their homes denies them the basic right of privacy. The poor who are on welfare (officially, Aid to Families with Dependent Children) are not free to spend the money they receive as they see fit.

The welfare poor have long been the victims of misconceptions such as the following:

1. Welfare families are loaded with kids—and have more children to get more money.
2. Why work, when you can live it up on welfare?
3. Give them more money and they'll spend it on drink and big cars.
4. Most welfare children are illegitimate.
5. Once on welfare, always on welfare.
6. Welfare people are cheats.
7. Welfare's just a dole, a money handout.
8. The welfare rolls are full of able-bodied loafers (DHHS, 1971).

Space, like all other values we seek, can be scarce for the poor. Like many poor people in rural America, these Native Americans live more of their lives outdoors than more affluent Americans do.

The facts contradict these widely held misconceptions. A study conducted by the Department of Health and Human Services found that

1. Welfare families have an average of 2.2 children. The payment for an additional child is insufficient to cover the cost of rearing another child.
2. In most states payments to a welfare family of four with no other income, excluding payments for special needs, are below the established poverty level.
3. Most welfare families say that if they received any extra money it would be used for essentials. Among welfare mothers, almost half say they would spend the money on extra food.
4. More than half of the children in welfare families are legitimate.
5. Half the families on welfare have been receiving assistance for twenty months or less; two-thirds have been receiving assistance for less than three years.
6. Only about 5 percent of welfare families are found to be ineligible, and less than 0.5 percent of welfare cases are referred for prosecution on fraud charges. Most errors involve honest mistakes by welfare agencies or recipients.
7. Most welfare families are provided with other social services besides financial aid. Among these are health care advice and referrals, counseling on financial and home management, employment counseling, and services to improve housing conditions and enable children to remain in school.
8. Less than 1 percent of welfare recipients are able-bodied unemployed males. These men are required by law to sign up for work or work training in order to remain eligible for benefits. The largest group of working-age adults on welfare are mothers, most of them heads of families (DHHS, 1979).

The Working Poor—"Event Poverty" Perhaps the most pernicious myth about the poor is that they do not share the "work ethic" of the middle class—that they are lazy or shiftless and would much rather be on welfare than work. Many studies have shown that the poor strongly share the work ethic and regret being on welfare. As

A popular stereotype of the poor is that they do no want to work hard. In fact, the poor do much of the work that other members of society consider most exhausting and least attractive. During economic downturns they spend more of their time on unemployment lines looking for new jobs, and they also form lines wherever job training opportunities become available.

Leonard Goodwin (1973) has noted, there are no differences between the poor and the nonpoor in life goals and willingness to work; the differences are that the poor lack confidence in their ability to succeed and accept welfare as a necessity caused by chronic un- or underemployment.

In his thorough studies of the poor in America, David T. Ellwood has found that a majority of the poor are in male-headed families. And for this population "at least 75 percent of income results from earnings. Even among poor female-headed families with children, 40 percent of all income comes from working" (Ellwood & Summers, 1986, p. 83; see also Ellwood, 1988). For these "working poor," poverty is most often caused by an event such as the loss of a job, the death or disability of a spouse, or desertion (Bane, 1986). Moreover, it should be kept in mind that the minimum wage of $4.25 per hour leaves many people well below the poverty line even if they work full time.

CONCOMITANTS OF POVERTY

"Poverty," said George Bernard Shaw, "does not produce unhappiness; it produces degradation." Most Americans take for granted a decent standard of living—especially good health care, decent education and housing, and fair treatment under the law. In this section we will examine the impact of poverty in each of these areas.

Health Care

Compared with the rest of the population, the poor are less healthy by almost every standard. For example, the mortality rates for poor infants are far higher than those for infants in more affluent families, and poor women are much more likely to die in childbirth. Poor women are also far more likely to give birth to their children in a municipal hospital or on the ward of a voluntary hospital. Inadequately housed, fed, and clothed, the poor can expect to be ill more often and to receive less adequate treatment. The health problems of the poor are not limited to physical ailments. Rates of diagnosed psychosis are higher among the poor, and they are more likely to be institutionalized and to receive shock treatment or chemotherapy in lieu of psychotherapy.

Of all the population groups in the United States, the poor are the least likely to have health insurance coverage. David Ellwood's (1988) study of the correlates and consequences of poverty showed that in the mid-1980s over 30 percent of Americans with incomes below the poverty line had no health insurance at all. It is ironic that the poor on welfare qualify for Medicaid, whereas the far larger number of people who become poor because of sudden job loss or separation and divorce are likely to be uninsured. Ellwood notes that policies that deny medical insurance to the working and unemployed poor—such as not requiring employers of part-time workers to pay health benefits—may create an incentive to stay on welfare.

Not only do the poor have unequal access to health services and receive less adequate treatment, but there is evidence that they often view sickness and health differently than middle-class people do. The poor are less likely to identify symptoms for a variety of physical and mental illnesses, and as a result they may seek treatment only after the illness has become serious. When they do see a doctor, the treatment they receive may be cursory (HHS, 1990). Doctors are less likely to advise a poor patient to stay home from work until completely recovered (Eichorn & Ludwig, 1973).

Since the inception of Medicare and Medicaid in 1965, the poor have had greater access to various medical resources. But there are problems with almost all insurance programs: Coverage is often inadequate; it begins only after a specified "deductible" expense level has been reached; and many people do not know exactly what their insurance covers. Accustomed to receiving medical treatment in clinics, the poor continue to visit clinics even though Medicaid would cover many private health services.

Other federal programs have established health-care centers in impoverished communities. But these still are not adequate to solve the health-care problems of the poor. Because most such programs allocate federal funds to match funds provided by a state or local government, they frequently are underfunded precisely where they are needed most. Moreover, each program and agency has different requirements, deadlines, and goals, resulting in a mass of regulations and interminable waiting periods before services are obtained. Finally, these programs do little to solve the overall health problems of the poor, who are victims of malnutrition; higher rates of disease; inadequate housing, sanitation, and rodent control; and even inadequate clothing; as well as less satisfactory medical treatment.

Education

In every respect poor children get less education than those born into more affluent families. They receive fewer years of schooling, have less chance of graduating from high school, and are much less likely to go to college. They are likely to be taught in overcrowded classrooms, often by inexperienced teachers, and to receive little, if any, individual attention. Moreover, most teachers come from a middle-class background and have little training in working with disadvantaged children. They bring to the job the expectation that poor children will read, speak, and behave poorly and perform poorly on tests, and that their parents and home life do not encourage academic achievement. It is not surprising that these expectations become self-fulfilling prophecies.

In recent decades considerable research has been devoted to the question of how effective preschool programs are in counteracting the effects of poverty. A review of that research concluded that children who attended preschool programs had higher intelligence scores at age 6, were less likely to be assigned to special-education classes, were less likely to be held back, and were less likely to drop out or be classified as delinquents (Brooks-Gunn & Hearn, 1982).

A study of children of teenage mothers in Baltimore (Brooks-Gunn & Fursten-berg, 1987) found that maternal welfare status influences schooling in preschool and high school. Among children in preschool programs, those from welfare families make fewer gains. However, if the mother moves off welfare the child is less likely to fail in subsequent years. This finding is especially important in view of the fact that the percentage of children living in poverty increased dramatically in the past decade, so that the population at risk of school failure is higher than ever.

The low educational attainment of poor children tends to perpetuate poverty. In general, the less educated have lower incomes, less secure jobs, and more difficulty improving their economic condition. Children of parents with less than a high school education generally do not do as well in school as children whose parents completed high school. Thus, the cycle in which poverty and education are linked is passed from one generation to the next.

Housing and Homelessness

The poor are likely to live in housing that is overcrowded, infested with vermin, in need of major repairs, lacking basic plumbing facilities, and inadequately heated. More than half of such housing is in rural areas.

Poor people who live in cities are unable to move around and utilize the city's resources but are often forced to move from one bad situation to another because of fire, crime, and other misfortunes. They are isolated and segregated both economically and racially.

Racial segregation increases when middle- and upper-income families leave the city. Cities also lose businesses when more prosperous citizens leave, and consequently their tax revenues decline. This leaves poor residents with fewer jobs and less adequate police protection and other services. Suburban zoning requirements such as minimum lot sizes are designed to attract newcomers who add more in taxes than they require in services. Restrictions on multiple-dwelling structures have the same purpose: to prevent low-income housing from being erected and keep out low-income and minority families.

In the 1980s there was a dramatic increase in the population of homeless individuals in American cities. Homelessness is a particular problem for the poorest groups in society. And "the cause of homelessness is lack of housing" (Kozol, 1988)—not mental illness, drug abuse, teenage pregnancy, or other factors that are often viewed as faults of the poor. This view is supported by statistics. In 1991, only 7,500 low-income public housing units were under construction, compared to almost 127,000 in 1970 (*Statistical Abstract,* 1993).

Rehabilitation of existing structures has been advocated as one solution to the housing problem, one through which the poor "block dweller" need not be uprooted from familiar surroundings. But the cost of rehabilitating antiquated structures in deteriorating neighborhoods is too high, and the potential return on the investment is too low, to appeal to private builders. Because poor families cannot afford rentals or purchase prices that would be profitable to owners and builders, it is extremely difficult to induce private industry to provide low-income housing. Each year, therefore, the lack of housing for the poor becomes more serious—especially during periods of recession.

Justice

As noted in Chapter 6, poor people are more likely than members of the middle and upper classes to be arrested, indicted, convicted, and imprisoned, and are likely to be given longer sentences for the same offenses. Conversely, they are less likely to receive probation, parole, or suspended sentences. Also, adolescents who are poor are more likely to be labeled as juvenile delinquents. Children from affluent families

Most Americans have been led to believe that public housing is a failed social policy, but the vast majority of public housing projects are considered highly successful by their residents.

who commit crimes are likely to be sent to a psychiatrist and left in their parents' custody; poor children who commit crimes are likely to be sent to a correctional institution.

Because of the position of poor people in society, the crimes that they are most likely to commit (property theft and assault) tend to be the ones that are most disapproved of by those who make the laws—members of the middle and upper classes. These crimes also tend to be those that are most visible and widely publicized. Members of the middle and upper-middle classes tend to commit white-collar crimes—embezzlement, price fixing, tax evasion, bribery, and so on. Although crimes like these involve much more money than street crime or property theft, and may even pose a greater threat to social institutions, they tend not to be regarded as serious by the criminal-justice system. Moreover, white-collar crimes are rarely publicized.

Even if they are arrested, prosperous citizens are more likely to be able to afford bail, to know their rights, to be competently defended, and to receive brief sentences. But the indigent defendant who is unable to post bail may be kept in jail for months.

Under the law, every accused person has the right to be represented by counsel, and some cities, counties, and states provide public defenders. But many large cities and a majority of the states lack public-defender services, and in federal courts there are neither paid defenders nor funds to compensate court-appointed counsel, who serve on a voluntary basis. Where public defenders and court-appointed lawyers are provided, they may not have the financial resources or time required for extended investigations.

Inadequate defense is among the reasons that the poor are more likely to be convicted and, if they are, to receive more severe sentences than those who are better off. And poor individuals who have been arrested and convicted are likely to be sentenced to overcrowded jails where few inmates can be truly rehabilitated. Upon release, they bear a stigma that makes it difficult to find or hold a job.

A variety of experiments with an approach known as "supported work" have been attempted in the hope that providing economic opportunities for ex-offenders may help break the link between crime and poverty. In one study (Berk, Lenihan, & Rossi, 1980) the researchers found that when poor prison inmates are released and given economic assistance or job counseling, the rate at which they return to crime decreases. However, in a series of supported-work programs conducted by the Manpower Development Research Corporation (cited in Wilson & Herrnstein, 1985), there was no lasting, significant effect on the criminal activity of ex-convicts or delinquent dropouts. These results may be explained by the fact that so much employment for the poor is low-wage work, which cannot compete with the potential rewards of hustling and crime (Auletta, 1982). Supported-work experiments achieve better results with older men and with poor women who are heads of households.

EXPLANATIONS OF PERSISTENT POVERTY

Structural Explanations

Structural explanations of poverty incorporate elements of both the functionalist and the conflict perspectives described in Chapter 1. They attribute poverty to the functioning of the dominant institutions of society, such as markets and corporations. As these major social structures change, conflicts arise as large numbers of people attempt to adjust to new conditions and new forms of social organization. For example, in a society that is dominated by agrarian production and agricultural markets, the poor tend to be people who lack land or whose land is unsuitable for farming. Or they may be people who have been forced off their land and have come to towns and cities to look for work. In industrial societies the poor tend to be those who have been unable to acquire the skills or knowledge that would enable them to find and keep jobs in factories or other businesses.

During various periods of American history, some groups migrated to the cities in an attempt to escape from an impoverished rural life. Others migrated when they were forced off the land by the mechanization of farming, by the consolidation of farms into larger units, and by the pressure of competition with large agribusinesses. All these changes in the social structure of farming created a class of poor people who were forced to sell their labor for whatever wages they could obtain. Since the Civil War, entire population groups, including U.S.-born blacks and Appalachian whites, with neither land nor marketable skills, have been forced into the cities, where they compete with newly arrived immigrants and other groups for menial, low-paying jobs.

The Marxian structural explanation would add to the causes of poverty just mentioned the case of the impoverished industrial worker. The poor, according to the Marxian view, increasingly are industrial workers who have been displaced from their jobs through the efforts of capitalists to find ever cheaper sources of labor, to automate their production systems and thereby eliminate the need for workers, or to move their factories out of the country altogether. This trend, which is characteristic of all unregulated capitalist societies, creates a "reserve army of unemployed," which, in its desperate search for income of any kind, drives down wages for all workers.

Contemporary social scientists may not all agree with Marx's theory, but they tend to agree that changes in macro-social patterns of growth have a lot to do with increasing poverty. Nobel Prize–winning economist James Tobin, for example, points out that earlier in this century, when U.S. society was undergoing rapid industrialization and urbanization, this "rising economic tide" reduced poverty by increasing employment and providing the revenue needed to invest in education, housing, jobs, and greater income security for the elderly. Now, with slow economic growth, there are fewer "good jobs" to lift people out of poverty and less money to invest in the programs needed to help poor families achieve upward mobility (Tobin, 1994).

Closely related to structural explanations like that offered by Tobin are studies that emphasize the dual market for labor. In studies of the migrations of blacks and other groups to the cities, sociologists have found that there is a dual labor market in which favored groups are given access to the better jobs—those that offer secure employment and good benefits. Other groups, usually minority groups and migrants, are shunted into another segment of the labor market in which the jobs pay extremely poorly and offer no security or benefits (Bonacich, 1976; Piore, 1979; W. J. Wilson, 1987).

Still another structural explanation of poverty maintains that the state, through its efforts to eliminate poverty, actually causes poverty. This explanation has both radical and conservative proponents. The radicals argue that while low wages and unemployment cause a great deal of poverty, the state's welfare and relief programs perpetuate it. This is so, they claim, because the state uses programs like unemployment insurance to prevent rebellions by the poor that might otherwise challenge the existing capitalist order; yet it does not use its power to ensure that all citizens can work for a decent wage (Piven & Cloward, 1972). Arguing in a somewhat similar vein, but from a conservative point of view, George Gilder (1980) claims that poverty in America is generally caused by well-meaning but misguided liberal welfare policies. These policies, he believes, rob unemployed workers of the initiative to develop new, marketable skills and also rob society of capital that should be invested in new businesses that will produce new wealth and new jobs. The high proportion of the poor who work or are actively seeking work constitute a strong argument against this claim.

These structural theories discuss the causes of poverty and the origins of the lower class in terms of the structure of the society in which the poverty occurs. Other theories, to which we now turn, attempt to explain the perpetuation of poverty. They examine the reasons why certain individuals, families, and groups tend to remain poor even in good economic times and in spite of what appear to be ample opportunities for education and personal advancement.

Cultural Explanations

Cultural explanations of poverty are based on the interactionist perspective in sociology. In this view, through the ways in which they are brought up and socialized and through their interactions in everyday life, people become adapted to certain ways of life, including poverty. Those ways of life persist because they become part of a group's culture.

Proponents of the cultural approach argue that a "culture of poverty" arises among people who experience extended periods of economic deprivation. Under these conditions new norms, values, and aspirations emerge. These eventually become independent of the situations that produced them, so that eliminating the problem does not eliminate the behaviors that have been developed to deal with it. The result is a self-sustaining system of values and behaviors that is handed down from one generation to the next.

An influential proponent of the cultural explanation, Oscar Lewis (1968), argues that poverty is a subculture, transcending regional differences and showing "remarkable cross-national similarities in family structure, interpersonal relations, time orientation, value systems, and spending patterns" (p. 4). Lewis accepts structural explanations, such as those discussed earlier, for the causes of poverty and the establishment of the gap between the poor and the well-off. He goes on to state, however, that in learning to adapt to their poverty—that is, in coping with deprivation—people develop cultural forms, language, belief systems, and local institutions that are passed on to their children.

The culture-of-poverty thesis explains poverty as stemming in part from the experience of growing up in an environment of poverty. People who have this experience cannot escape from their environment because their upbringing has prepared them to remain in poverty. The family in the poverty subculture is often female centered and authoritarian. It is characterized by little sheltering and protection in childhood, very little privacy, competition among siblings for limited resources and affection, and early sexual activity.

Lewis argues that a crucial characteristic of the subculture that is formed in this way is "the lack of effective participation and integration of the poor in the major institutions of the larger society" (1968, p. 5). Members of this subculture are likely to feel marginal, helpless, dependent, and inferior; they may be unable to control their impulses or plan for the future. A sense of resignation and fatalism is also likely. These characteristics, Lewis argues, tend to develop in any poor population and are found in both rural and urban locations throughout the world. They enable the poor to cope with the stresses of their situation, but they also prevent them from escaping from it.

The Situational Approach   According to Charles A. Valentine (1968), the "class-distinctive traits" exhibited by the poor do not indicate cultural patterns but, instead, "seem more likely externally imposed conditions or unavoidable matters of situational expediency" (p. 115). The situational approach interprets the behavior of the poor as an adaptation to their environment. Patterns of behavior develop as a response to problems associated with low income and the accompanying economic and social deprivation. The poor have to forgo middle-class values and aspirations, which simply do not apply to their situation. Children react in similar ways because they must make the same adjustments to the same problems that their parents faced.

Valentine divides Lewis's list of poverty culture traits into three categories. The first consists of correlates of poverty: unemployment, underemployment, unskilled work, low-status jobs, meager wages, crowded and deteriorated housing, and lack of education. Valentine regards these as "conditions or symptoms" of poverty rather than as ingrained patterns of response. Behavioral patterns and relationships, the second category of traits, include a harsh childhood, authoritarianism, and little community organization.

Values and attitudes, Valentine's third set of traits, include hostility toward institutions like schools and government, negative feelings about one's place in society, and low levels of expectation and aspiration. With regard to these, Valentine writes, "All these orientations are so strikingly consistent with objective situational facts that it seems hardly necessary to interpret them as ingrained subcultural values. Indeed, for modern Western people these would seem to be almost the inevitable emotional responses to the actual conditions of poverty" (1968, p. 119).

Valentine concludes that Lewis's list of traits does not constitute a separate subsystem of values for the poor. Instead, Valentine proposes a model of a "heterogeneous subsociety with variable, adaptive subcultures." That model includes the following features:

1. The lower-class poor subscribe to norms of the middle class while at the same time showing some distinct subcultural patterns.
2. Those distinctive patterns include not only harmful traits but also healthy and positive ones.

3. The situational and subcultural patterns of the poor have numerous causes that vary from one ethnic or regional group to another.
4. Improving the condition of the lower class will require changes in three areas: increasing the resources available to the poor, altering the social structure, and changing some subcultural patterns.
5. The most likely source of such changes is one or more social movements like the civil rights and antipoverty movements, beginning with the poor and oppressed but affecting the whole society (Valentine, 1968).

The Cultural-Situational Approach Herbert J. Gans (1968) is critical of both the culture-of-poverty and the situational approaches. He finds the situational explanation simplistic. People are not automatons who all react in the same way to a particular stimulus or situation. On the contrary, Gans stresses the heterogeneity of the poor:

> *Some have been poor for generations, others are poor only periodically; some are downwardly mobile; others embrace working-class values; some have become so used to the defense mechanisms they have learned for coping with deprivation that they have difficulty in adapting to new opportunities; and some are beset by physical and emotional illness. (p. 177)*

Gans is critical of the idea that culture is "holistic," that no element of it can be changed unless the entire culture is altered. He argues that behavior results from a combination of cultural and situational influences: "Culture . . . is that mix of behavioral norms and aspirations that causes behavior, maintains present behavior, or encourages future behavior, independently of situational incentives and restraints" (p. 326).

Gans maintains that the ultimate solution to the problem of poverty lies in the discovery of the specific factors that constrain poor people in reacting to new opportunities when these conflict with their present cultural values. He believes that we must examine the kinds of change needed in our economic system, social order, and power structure and in the norms and aspirations of the affluent majority that permit a poor class to exist.

The Adaptation Approach Lee Rainwater (1969), a sociologist who has devoted considerable study to poverty, offers another explanation. Although he admits that a lower-class pattern of behaviors and beliefs exists, he characterizes it differently than other theorists do. He believes that conventional society has somehow imposed its norms on the lower class. Lower-class culture therefore contains some elements that are unique to it and others that it shares with the larger culture.

Rainwater argues that policy should be based on the concept of lower-class culture as an adaptation to relative deprivation—to being so far removed from the average standard of living that one does not have a sense of being part of the society. He advocates "resource equalization strategy," that is, giving the poor enough resources to eliminate this relative deprivation and bring them closer to the average in terms of income and other advantages.

The Value-Stretch Approach Proponents of the culture-of-poverty explanation attribute to the poor a value system characterized by lack of desire to participate in the institutions of the larger society and acceptance of behavior that is considered antisocial by those who are better off. Critics argue that the behavioral differences between the classes are not values but coping mechanisms through which the poor adjust to the realities that prevent them from behaving in more socially desirable ways. Hyman Rodman (1963) has suggested that this phenomenon can be explained by what may be termed the *value-stretch approach*. He agrees that all classes share the general values of society, but he claims that the lower class has an additional set of values. It is not that the lower class rejects majority values or desires less; rather, for the lower class two sets of values exist simultaneously in a hierarchy in which the more desirable values, those that are shared with the larger society, are the least attainable. Rodman therefore argues that the lower class has a wider range of values than the other classes, and he terms this the *lower-class value stretch*. Here is how this double value system works:

> Lower-class persons . . . do not maintain a strong commitment to middle-class values that they cannot attain, and they do not continue to respond to others in a rewarding or punishing way simply on the basis of whether these others are living up to the middle-class values. A change takes place. They come to tolerate and eventually to evaluate favorably certain deviations from the middle-class values. In this way they need not be continually frustrated by their failure to live up to unattainable values. The result is a stretched value system. (p. 209)

Elijah Anderson (1988) has carried Rodman's views further on the basis of his observations of the people who frequent Jelly's, a corner bar and liquor store in a black neighborhood on the South Side of Chicago. "The people I studied," he writes,

> appear not so much to "stretch" a given set of values to meet some general standard as to create their own particular standards of social conduct along variant lines open to them. For example, at Jelly's certain people are esteemed among their immediate peers for being "good" hoodlums. And there are certain wineheads who, even if they had the means to leave the setting, would not be content without socializing with their drinking buddies. (pp. 210–221).

The concept of "value stretch," according to Anderson, does not take into account the "internal coherence and integrity" of low-income groups.

SOCIAL POLICY

As has been evident throughout this chapter, the extent of poverty in the world's most affluent society is a matter of continuing controversy. So is the question of what can be done about poverty. This question is intimately bound up with attitudes toward the poor themselves: Are the poor to blame for their own poverty? Do they avoid work? Would providing more jobs for the poor do any good? One's views on these issues have a lot to do with one's opinions about governmental intervention on behalf of the poor.

Current Social-Welfare Programs

To better understand the debate over the future of our society's social-welfare programs, it will be useful to review the programs that are currently in operation. Current government programs can be divided into four basic categories: human resource development, social insurance, cash income support, and programs that provide income in kind. Human resource development programs are geared toward increasing the employability of the poor by raising their educational and skill levels; they include both formal educational programs in classrooms and on-the-job training programs. One of these is the Job Corps, a residential program that provides remedial education, training in job skills, and guidance and counseling to people between the ages of 14 and 21. The Job Corps has proven to be one of the most successful and cost-effective federal approaches to job training for high school dropouts, who are most difficult to employ and most at risk of becoming chronic welfare recipients. During the Reagan and Bush administrations, conservative critics attempted to cut the program because of its cost, which amounted to more than $19,000 per year per recruit. But after seeing the results of Jobs Corps training (taxes paid by former recruits, reduced expenditures for drug treatment or jail), even Utah Senator Orrin Hatch, usually a staunch critic of federal jobs programs, agreed that the Job Corps more than paid back its costs (Gross, 1992).

Another example of human resource development is Head Start and related programs to compensate for the lack of resources and educational advantages in the home environments of low-income families with preschool children. By the end of the 1980s Head Start, the primary source of high-quality preschool education for poor children in the United States, served only about 400,000 low-income children. Although preschool education is vital if society hopes to give children anything resembling an equal start in the quest for educational achievement, the rate of enrollment of poor children in good preschool programs is less than half the rate of enrollment of children from more affluent homes.

In an extensive study of more than 18,000 preschool students in thirty-six school districts, social scientist and educator Robert E. Slavin found that success after Head Start is greater for children who are able to stay in the program longer and who receive one-on-one tutoring to make sure that they learn to read so that they do not begin to think of themselves as failures at an early age (cited in Chira, 1992). The findings of this research and many other studies that support the lengthening and improvement of Head Start–type preschool and after-school programs have led to heavy lobbying of Congress to expand this successful approach to the learning deficits of children in poor neighborhoods (National Center for Children in Poverty, 1990).

Social-insurance programs are intended to compensate for loss of income, regardless of income level or need. Through unemployment insurance, for example, cash benefits are paid for short periods to insured workers who are involuntarily unemployed. Unemployment insurance was created by the same act of Congress that established the social security system; however, the responsibility for administering unemployment insurance was delegated to the states, which were given broad latitude in setting eligibility standards and levels of benefits. As a result, the amount and duration of unemployment benefits vary greatly from one state to another. In Massachusetts, a worker who is unemployed after paying into the system beyond the minimum period is eligible for benefits of over $200 a week for fifteen weeks. In South Carolina, a worker who has paid into the system is eligible for benefits of only $120 per week for nine weeks (Rosenbaum, 1990).

Other forms of social insurance include workers' compensation programs, which provide wage replacements to insured workers who suffer occupational injuries, and veterans' compensation plans, which issue benefits to disabled veterans to make up for their loss of earning potential. Social security payments to the elderly also fall into this category.

Cash income support programs are provided for unemployable people, those who are not covered by any form of social insurance, and those with special needs. Veterans' pensions fall into this category, as do direct subsidies to families and individuals—that is, public assistance, or welfare.

Income-in-kind programs provide goods and services, such as food, housing, and medical care, to the poor. These programs include public housing and urban renewal; health plans like Medicare and Medicaid (see Chapter 2); and food supplements like the commodity distribution program (which distributes surplus farm products to poor households) and food stamps (which in effect provide discounts on food purchases).

The costs of these programs, together with the persistence of high rates of poverty, have led many Americans to criticize and oppose "welfare." During the 1980s the government's policies in this area were a subject of intense debate. The conservative position, reflected in the programs of the Reagan administration, was that a "safety net" is necessary for the truly "deserving" poor but that too much government assistance to the poor robs them of the initiative they need to survive through their own efforts. Those who argued for various forms of welfare benefits pointed to the harm done by the cuts made during the 1980s, which caused many people to lose their benefits even though they were unable to work. They also sought to defend the welfare system while agreeing that its inefficiency and cost needed to be controlled. Social-policy debates over welfare costs and justifications continue today and often hinge on issues of dependency (Jencks, 1992).

Dependency, Work, and Responsibility

Critics of welfare programs on both the left and the right increasingly agree that welfare policies should not establish disincentives to work, nor should they reward vice or encourage people to regard public funds as a long-term substitute for work (Jencks, 1992). And while there remains a good deal of debate over the degree to which various welfare programs actually do create these negative results, there is also much agreement that welfare payments to families with dependent children ought to encourage recipients to seek job training and employment. This view was incorporated into the 1988 Family Support Act (also known as the welfare reform act), which requires states to oblige welfare recipients with children over a certain age (usually three years) to join a work, education, or job program and provides federal funding to help pay for these opportunities.

Supported by the Clinton administration, this approach to controlling the problem of welfare dependency and the rising costs of welfare support also entails some problems. Training programs require federal and state funding and do not necessarily lead to longer-term employment for trainees. Trainees must have access to care for their children. Finally, the majority of former welfare recipients are hired in public-sector jobs in schools and other agencies. As public budgets are cut, it becomes ever more difficult to secure an adequate number of jobs for former welfare recipients. These problems make the issue of welfare and work an ongoing challenge to policy makers.

In his thorough review of antipoverty policies in the United States and other nations, sociologist W. J. Wilson (1987) notes that the countries that rely least on public assistance (e.g., Sweden and West Germany) emphasize instead such policies as family and housing allowances, child care services, and various types of work incentives. The cornerstone of antipoverty policies in those countries is employment policies—that is, policies that make it easier for adults to manage their work and family lives without undue strain on themselves and their children (Kamerman & Kahn, cited in W. J. Wilson, 1987).

How should the United States address the dependency issue? One answer that is frequently given by social scientists and policy makers is that a serious effort should be made to increase the income of low-wage workers so that the working poor, by far the largest category of poor households, will not be forced to live in poverty. Another, similar approach would be to provide incentives for people on welfare to work if they are able to do so.

As noted earlier in the chapter, a worker who works full time all year at the minimum wage cannot earn enough to keep even a two-person family above the poverty line. To support a family of four, a worker must earn 60 percent more than the minimum wage (Ellwood, 1987). There are a variety of possible approaches to alleviating the problems of people who work at low-wage jobs. Income supplements are one recommended approach; such supplements could include wage subsidies, medical protection, and expansion of the earned income tax credit (EITC).

The EITC was instituted in 1975 as a means of reducing the total tax bill of low-income taxpayers with dependent children. Originally the credit was 10 percent of

BOX 8–1 UNINTENDED CONSEQUENCES: FAMILY SUPPORT POLICIES

Few areas of social policy lead to as many unintended consequences as programs directed at combating poverty. There is, for example, a widespread belief among political leaders and many social scientists that the current child support program, known as Aid to Families with Dependent Children, tends to encourage the breakup of low-income couples because when a male partner with earned income is present in the home the AFDC benefits are either cut off or decreased. Such "family disincentives" were not intended to occur, but many experts believe that they have.

To address this problem, and the related charge that current family support policies encourage dependency on welfare, welfare reform efforts in the past decade have stressed two new initiatives: workfare and the earned income tax credit. These approaches are given even greater prominence in President Clinton's proposed welfare reforms. However, both of these policies may themselves bring about unintended consequences.

"For over twenty years work has been a prominent issue in the national debate over welfare policy. Most Americans seem to agree that adults who are capable of working should if possible contribute to the support of themselves and their dependents" (Wiseman, 1986, p. 1). There are now important workfare programs in Massachusetts, California, Illinois, and New York, and many other states are about to begin similar programs. Among the strongest supporters of workfare are conservative policy makers, who believe in the programs on moral grounds and also because they wish to reduce the cost to government of poverty programs. But wherever they have instituted workfare programs they have also discovered that public support for day-care and after-school care programs must also be increased. Advocates of workfare cannot insist that mothers with dependent children abandon their young ones in order to enter the labor force. Thus, an unintended consequence of workfare has been an increase in bipartisan support for additional public funding of child care programs. Although such programs are not yet adequately funded, there is a new consensus that they must be if workfare is to operate as hoped.

The earned income tax credit (EITC) is another complicated aspect of current welfare reform strategies. In simple terms, it is a program in which the federal government reimburses working people whose income falls below the poverty line despite full-time employment. Since low wages are the chief cause of poverty, the theory behind the EITC is that instead of paying taxes the working poor should be given money by the IRS to compensate for incomes that are below the poverty line. Policy makers and social scientists have advocated increases in the EITC, and in the 1990s it promises to become an increasingly important weapon in the fight against poverty.

But there is a risk associated with greater emphasis on the EITC as a major weapon against poverty. Economists and sociologists point out that there have been many efforts to supplement low wages with public support. While well intentioned, these efforts have often had the unintended effect of encouraging employers to pay low wages. If low-wage employees are going to have their wages supplemented through some reimbursement policy like the EITC, this can be regarded as an indirect subsidy to employers. Thus, critics of the EITC advocate increases in the minimum wage—for example, requiring employers to pay "living wages" to their workers. Since the EITC is only now becoming significant enough to influence the behavior of employers, it is too soon to know whether the critics are correct, but in theory the unintended effects they point out are quite likely to occur.

earned income up to $4,000, with a smaller credit for amounts between $4,000 and $8,000, but in the 1980s it was extended so that somewhat higher incomes become eligible. If the credit exceeds the amount of tax due, an eligible individual can receive a payment from the Internal Revenue Service. In some respects, therefore, the EITC can be viewed as a negative income tax. (See Box 8–1.)

Numerous proposals have been made to modify or extend the EITC. In one approach, a household could designate a principal earner and that person's wages would be subsidized if they were below a specified level; this would increase the reward for working. Another suggestion is to expand the EITC and allow it to vary by family size; this would help protect larger families while encouraging low-income workers with families to return to work. A third approach is to convert the current tax deduction for children into a refundable tax credit.

Single Mothers: A Special Case

Perhaps more than anything else, there is a need to educate the public about social-welfare programs and their recipients. For example, it is widely believed that welfare benefits encourage family dissolution and out-of-wedlock births. In reality, however, since the early 1970s the number of children receiving AFDC benefits has decreased (though not in urban ghettos and other areas of long-term poverty). Moreover, although welfare benefits vary greatly from one state to another, there is little or no correlation between benefit levels and the number of children in female-headed families. Thus, although the precise effects of welfare programs are not clear, most experts agree that modest changes in the welfare system are unlikely to have any effect on the number of children in single-parent homes (Ellwood, 1987).

Another widely held but incorrect assumption is that economic growth and reductions in unemployment will reduce the rate of poverty among female-headed families. In fact, in spite of major variations in economic conditions, the poverty level tends to remain relatively constant for women in this category. When single mothers are asked why they do not seek employment, the primary reason given is "taking care of house/children." This population is unlikely to benefit significantly from increases in available jobs unless there are significant improvements in day care, training, and employment opportunities, as proposed in the 1994 welfare reform legislation.

There are numerous arguments in favor of expecting single mothers to work in order to qualify for welfare payments: Work can lead to greater independence and security for the woman; for children, living in a household where no one is employed may be damaging to motivation. Yet it is impractical to require single mothers to work full time. Some experts therefore recommend that welfare recipients be required to work part time. In addition, they call for major reform of the child-support system so that fathers are held accountable for the support of their children throughout their (the fathers') lives.

In 1988 Congress enacted a welfare reform act that revised the AFDC program to emphasize work, child support, and family benefits. The main thrust of the act was to enable needy children and parents to obtain the education, training, and employment they need to avoid long-term welfare dependency. The law put federal funds and sanctions behind the widely accepted belief that both parents should be responsible for the well-being of their children and that family well-being may be enhanced if mothers work rather than stay at home with their children, provided that adequate child care is available (Institute for Research on Poverty, 1990; Jencks, 1992). President Clinton's promise to "end welfare as we know it" hinges on increased funding for workfare-type programs at the local level.

Poor People's Movements

We have discussed various theories and policies that have been proposed to explain and deal with the social problem of poverty. But what about the poor themselves? In what ways are they involved in the discussions and debates through which national policies are formulated? The poor are not often consulted about their beliefs concerning how society could help them rise out of poverty. When they are moved to protest inferior schools or housing, their voices are not heeded. At times during the 1960s and 1970s, however, a series of poor people's movements disturbed the status quo and forced welfare institutions to pay attention. Led by experienced and vocal organizers like Martin Luther King, Jr., Jesse Jackson, George Wylie, and Fannie Lou Hamer, these movements were instrumental in pressing for local participation in the design and administration of welfare programs (Kotz & Kotz, 1977). The record of societal and governmental response to the voices of the poor leads some observers to conclude that "a placid poor get nothing, but a turbulent poor sometimes get something" (Piven & Cloward, 1972, p. 338).

In recent years a new approach to combating poverty has emerged among the poor themselves. Known as the community development approach, it arose as an alternative to the Reagan administration's strategy of improving the situation of the affluent in the hope that the poor would benefit. Community development involves efforts to marshal resources for economic development—building local industries, restoring abandoned buildings, replacing stores that have been destroyed by riots or fires, and similar projects. Such projects mobilize people in the community, using resources (money and technical skills) provided by outside sources. The Ford Foundation, for example, has endowed a community development corporation that arranges for bank loans and government support for community-level efforts at job creation, skills development, remedial education, and local ownership of business enterprises.

SUMMARY

1. Although the United States ranks among the wealthiest nations in the world, many Americans can barely make ends meet or are living in poverty. During the 1980s the gap between the rich and the poor widened.

2. The United States has a long history of attempting to redistribute wealth through taxation and other policies. In so doing, however, it has actually provided more opportunities for the rich to get richer than for the poor to escape from poverty.

3. More than 35 million people live below the official poverty line. They include children, elderly people, single mothers, ill or disabled individuals, students, and people who work either full or part time but whose incomes are below the poverty level.

4. The stratification of individuals and groups according to occupation, income, and skills is called class stratification. The Marxian view of stratification holds that classes are determined by economic measures. This view has been supplemented by those of Weber and his followers, who pointed out that other valued things besides wealth, such as status and power, are distributed unequally in modern societies. American society can be divided into five main classes: the upper class, the upper-middle class, the middle class, the working class, and the poor.

5. Poverty can be defined in a variety of ways. It can mean a condition of near starvation, bare subsistence, or any standard of living that is measurably below the national average. Official definitions of the poverty line are based on the consumer price index. Alternative measures have been proposed that take into account changing definitions of minimal consumption.

6. A large proportion of the poor are children, and many of those children are living in single-parent families. Blacks and other racial minorities are overrepresented among the poor. Poor people living in rural areas include migrant workers, Native Americans on reservations, and farmers. Many of the poor are on welfare rolls, but many others are working at low-paying jobs.

7. Concomitants of poverty include poor health and unequal access to health services, inadequate education, substandard housing and homelessness, and discrimination in the criminal-justice system.

8. Structural explanations of poverty attribute it to dominant social institutions such as the dual market for labor. The cultural explanation holds that extended economic deprivation creates a "culture of poverty" with its own norms and values. The situational approach interprets the behavior of the poor as an adaptation to their environment. The latter two explanations have been combined to produce the cultural-situational approach, in which the behavior of the poor results from both cultural and situational influences.

9. Current government social-welfare programs are of four types: human resource development, social insurance, cash income support, and programs that provide income in kind. There is a growing consensus both within and outside government that direct payments to the poor can lead to dependency over time.

10. Those who wish to reform the welfare system often call for a system in which welfare recipients would be required to work. Such a system must provide ways for people who are willing and able to work to find jobs. In addition, it is necessary to provide daycare and after-school care programs for the children of single parents.

11. Proposals for alleviating the problems of people who work at low-wage jobs include modifying or extending the earned income tax credit (a means of reducing the total tax bill of low-income taxpayers with dependent children), enabling single mothers to work part time while receiving welfare payments, and reforming the child-support system so that fathers are held accountable for the support of their children. The welfare reform act of 1988 incorporated some of these proposals.

SUGGESTED READINGS

AULETTA, KEN. *The Underclass.* New York: Random House, 1982. A review of major demonstrations and evaluations of antipoverty programs during the late 1970s and early 1980s.

DANZIGER, SHELDON, and DANIEL H. WEINBERG, EDS. *Fighting Poverty: What Works and What Doesn't.* Cambridge, MA: Harvard University Press, 1986. A collection of empirical essays that includes both conservative and liberal views on antipoverty policy together with a dispassionate analysis of the facts about poverty and the effects of past policies. Essential reading in this field.

ELLWOOD, DAVID. *Poor Support.* New York: Basic Books, 1988. An influential study that shows, among other things, that the majority of the poor are hard at work. A book that is likely to have a major impact on social-policy debates in the United States in coming years.

FITCHEN, JANET J. *Poverty in Rural America: A Case Study.* Boulder, CO: Westview Press, 1981. A study of poverty in a rural neighborhood in upstate New York that illustrates how such factors as irregular income and inadequate education interact to perpetuate poverty.

JENCKS, CHRISTOPHER. *Rethinking Social Policy: Race, Poverty, and the Underclass.* Cambridge, MA: Harvard University Press, 1992. An up-to-date critique of the theory of the underclass and a review of progress and setbacks in addressing problems associated with poverty in the United States.

JENCKS, CHRISTOPHER, M. SMITH, H. ACLAND, M. J. BANE, D. COHEN, H. GINTIS, B. HEYNS, and S. MICHELSEN. *Who Gets Ahead? Determinants of Economic Success in America.* New York: Basic Books, 1979. An analysis of the relative effects of such factors as family background, schooling, and race on an individual's status and earnings.

KATZ, MICHAEL B. *The Undeserving Poor: From the War on Poverty to the War on Welfare.* New York: Pantheon, 1990. A history of theories of poverty that has had a significant impact on antipoverty policies in the United States.

KOZOL, JONATHAN. *Rachel and Her Children: Homeless Families in America.* New York: Crown, 1988. A moving study by an author who has lived with the impoverished homeless in New York City. Shows that these families' most pressing problem is not mental illness but the lack of a home where they can raise their children.

LAPHAM, LEWIS H. *Money and Class in America.* New York: Ballantine, 1988. An insider's account of the culture of America's elite upper class. Often bitter and acerbic, this highly critical study pulls no punches.

PIVEN, FRANCES FOX, and RICHARD CLOWARD. *Regulating the Poor: The Functions of Social Welfare.* New York: Vintage, 1971. A powerful and controversial study of the relationships among social-welfare policy, unemployment, and poor people's movements.

STREET, DAVID, GEORGE T. MARTIN, JR., and LAURA KRAMER GORDON. *The Welfare Industry: Functionaries and Recipients in Public Aid.* Newbury Park, CA: Sage, 1979. An essay on urban public assistance that presents the thesis that welfare has become bureaucratized and professionalized but cannot benefit from this condition because it is decentralized among the various states.

WEST, GUIDA. *The National Welfare Rights Movement: The Social Protest of Poor Women.* New York:

Praeger, 1981. A detailed description of the welfare rights movement that shows how it arose and the difficulties it encountered.

WILSON, WILLIAM JULIUS. *The Truly Disadvantaged.* Chicago: University of Chicago Press, 1987. One of the nation's most brilliant sociologists shows that poverty has increased among minority Americans in recent years, largely as a result of major declines in the nation's manufacturing base. Recommends a series of family support and job creation strategies that appeal to conservatives and liberals alike.

Prejudice and Discrimination

Chapter Outline

- In 1992, 19.1 percent of whites aged 25 and over had not completed high school; the comparable figures for blacks and Hispanics were 32.3 percent and 47.4 percent, respectively.
- Sixty-six percent of black and 73 percent of Hispanic children attend predominantly minority schools.
- Research has shown that the average income loss due to discrimination is about $1,400 for black workers and about $1,000 for Mexican Americans.
- Blacks account for 12 percent of the general population, but they make up over 47 percent of the prison population.

American society has a long history of inequality. The first black slaves were brought to what is now the United States in 1619, and by the time the nation gained independence from England in 1776 they numbered about 150,000. Meanwhile, the original inhabitants of the continent, the Native Americans, were being driven from their homes as European settlers pushed westward. In the East, as the industrial revolution gained momentum in the nineteenth century, waves of immigrants arrived to find themselves relegated to the most menial labor and the poorest living conditions. The earlier arrivals fought their way upward in a bitterly competitive society, and the descendants of those who had come earliest defended their position at the top. In the West, the movement for *oriental exclusion* played an important role in the late nineteenth century, when settlers attempted to exclude Asians from the country or from local labor markets in order to reduce the competition for jobs. Later, during World War II, Japanese Americans were interned in camps and their property expropriated.

The scope of discrimination in the United States was the subject of a classic study carried out in the late 1930s and early 1940s by the Swedish economist and social scientist Gunnar Myrdal. Myrdal focused on the situation of blacks in economic and social institutions largely controlled by whites and in a culture torn between the ideal of equality and the reality of discrimination. The position of black Americans as a "poor and suppressed minority" in the land of freedom and opportunity created what Myrdal called the American dilemma. The dilemma was specifically a problem of whites because, as Myrdal put it, "practically all the economic, social, and political power is held by whites" (1962, p. xxv). Myrdal saw reason to hope that white Americans would eventually resolve the problem. He believed that after a long period of relative stagnation, fundamental changes were occurring that would lead to true equality for black and white Americans.

Although the constitutional bases for racial equality were established in the 1860s and 1870s with the ratification of the Thirteenth, Fourteenth, and Fifteenth Amendments, it was not until the mid-twentieth century that the rights guaranteed by these amendments began to be exercised effectively. Starting with Supreme Court decisions affecting specific, small areas of life, black Americans began to work their way toward equality. A major legal breakthrough came in 1954 with the historic decision in *Brown* v. *Board of Education of Topeka* that "separate educational facilities are inherently unequal." The Supreme Court later applied this "separate cannot be equal" doctrine to a wide range of public facilities.

The Civil Rights Act of 1964 was another important step. Unlike the civil rights acts passed in 1957 and 1960, the 1964 act provided a means for fighting discrimination in employment and public accommodations and ways to deny federal funds to local government units that permitted discrimination. There followed a comprehensive Voting Rights Act in 1965 and a federal prohibition against housing discrimination in the Civil Rights Act of 1968. Subsequent "affirmative-action orders" by

This scene from an ethnic neighborhood in a large American city shows how businesses in such neighborhoods may specialize in serving the needs of immigrant people. Some businesses in such communities also flourish by catering to the tastes of outsiders for different foods and consumer goods.

President Lyndon B. Johnson aided the enforcement of these new laws; in addition, the Johnson administration set up new programs, such as Head Start, to counter the effects of discrimination.

But the discrepancy between legal equality and actual inequality remained. The impatience of some American blacks developed into anger, and in August 1964 a riot erupted in Watts, a black section of Los Angeles. By the time the wave of violent protest set off by the Watts riot subsided, it had struck almost every major urban center in the country. In 1967, following especially destructive riots in Newark and Detroit, President Johnson appointed a National Advisory Commission on Civil Disorders to investigate the origins of the disturbances and recommend ways to prevent or control them in the future. The commission's findings suggested that there had been very little change since Myrdal's study. Describing the basic causes of the disorders, the commission stated that

> *The first is surely the continuing exclusion of great numbers of Negroes from the benefits of economic progress through discrimination in employment and education, and their enforced segregated housing and schools. The corrosive and degrading effects of this condition and the attitudes that underlie it are the source of the deepest bitterness and at the center of the problem of racial disorder. (1968, p. 203)*

The commission concluded that "our nation is moving toward two societies, one black, one white—separate and unequal" (p. 1).

Although the situations of other minority groups—Native Americans, Chicanos (Mexican Americans), Hispanic Americans (especially Puerto Ricans and Cubans), Asian Americans, and some white ethnic groups—have received less intensive study, they are similar to that of black Americans. One form of discrimination to which these other groups are particularly vulnerable is harassment at the voting booth, largely owing to their inadequate command of English. The 1975 extension of the Voting Rights Act attempted to alleviate this problem by requiring cities with sizable "language minority" populations to provide bilingual ballots in elections; it also permanently banned the use of literacy tests as a prerequisite for voting.

In recent years there has been a major influx of immigrants from Far Eastern countries—especially Korea, Vietnam, and Cambodia. Their experience has shown that small groups with education, business experience, and some funds, coupled with cultural values that stress family cohesion and extremely hard work, have little difficulty adapting to their new environment (Kim, 1983). On the other hand, large populations that gather in concentrated settlements, as Vietnamese immigrants have done in Texas and California, have been targets of racial hostility. Thus, it appears that the larger a group and the more segregated it is, the more hostility it encounters (Piore, 1979; Portes, 1984).

In the same vein, Stanley Lieberson (1980) argues that when an immigrant group is small, it is relatively easy for it to develop an occupational niche or specialty, as the Greeks and the Chinese have done in the restaurant industry. (He cites a study that showed that 14.8 percent of Greek immigrants were working in the restaurant industry and 9.4 percent of Swedish immigrants were carpenters.) But when an immigrant population grows, it becomes far more difficult for it to retain control of an occupational niche and expand it enough to accommodate newcomers. Later arrivals therefore are more dependent than earlier immigrants on the general labor market.

The situation of immigrant groups highlights the problems of minority status in the United States. But before we can discuss these problems in detail, we must gain a clearer understanding of the meaning of the term *minority* as it is commonly used today.

THE MEANING OF *MINORITY*

Categories of people who do not receive the same treatment as others in the same society are referred to as minorities. But what is a minority? How and why does a minority situation come about? Before we begin to answer these questions, it is important to define three terms that are central to the discussion: racial minorities, ethnic minorities, and assimilation.

Racial minorities are groups of people who share certain inherited characteristics, such as eye folds or brown skin. Many experts believe that the biologically determined racial groups into which humanity is divided—caucasoid, mongoloid, and negroid—are strictly social categories and that the actual hereditary differences among these groups are meaningless (Alland, 1973; Gould, 1981). *Ethnic minorities* are composed of people who may share cultural features such as language, religion, national origin, dietary practices, and a common history and who regard themselves as a distinct group. When members of either a racial or an ethnic minority group take on the characteristics of the mainstream culture by adapting their own unique cultural patterns to those of the majority group, as well as by intermarrying, *assimilation* occurs.

It should be noted that the term *minority* as used here does not refer to a group's numerical strength in the population. This is true even though in most cases minority groups lack both numerical superiority and other means of counteracting unequal treatment.

Wagley and Harris (1958) suggested five characteristics of a minority group:

1. Minorities are subordinate segments of a complex society.
2. Minorities tend to have special physical or cultural traits that are seen as undesirable by the dominant segments of the society.
3. Minorities develop a group consciousness or "we-feeling."
4. Membership in a minority is transmitted by a rule of descent—one is born into it—which can impose the minority status on future generations even if by then the special physical or cultural traits of the minority have disappeared.
5. Members of a minority, whether by choice or by necessity, tend to practice endogamy—that is, to marry within the group. (p. 10)

The characteristics singled out by Wagley and Harris seem most appropriate for a racial or ethnic minority group, especially one that has not yet begun to be assimilated. If oppression and inequality are not too great and assimilation proceeds, some of the minority characteristics will fade: Group consciousness may wane; marriage outside the group may increase; distinctive cultural traits may be abandoned. There is no clear line between totally dominant and totally minority groups; rather, any given group can be placed at some point along a "continuum of minorityness." Various immigrant groups in the United States have moved along this continuum, edging progressively closer to equality and shedding some or all of their distinctive minority characteristics. It should be emphasized, however, that the physical distinctiveness of racial minorities has made the attainment of assimilation and equality much more difficult for them than for other immigrant groups, which are defined largely by cultural traits. Thus, racial minorities have tended to remain minorities much longer than nonracial minorities.

Wagley and Harris's definition is somewhat less accurate for nonracial and nonethnic minority groups. The aged, for example, constitute a minority group in terms of both absolute numbers and the treatment they receive, yet they are not born into such a group. Membership in the homosexual minority is not transmitted from one generation to another. Nevertheless, these groups share the major characteristics of minorities: subordinate status, special traits, and increasingly, group self-awareness.

Subordinate status is the principal characteristic of a minority group. In almost any society the desire for some goods, whether tangible or intangible, exceeds the supply of those goods, and groups within the society are likely to compete for them and for the power to control them. The groups that gain the most power dominate the other groups, controlling their access to the desired goods and often to other goods—social, economic, political, and personal—as well. The dominant group need not be the most numerous; it must merely be able to prevent other groups from effectively challenging its power.

Once established, however, the dominant–subordinate relationship is not fixed for all time. Either through the efforts of the subordinate group itself or as a result of changing legal or economic conditions, power relationships can be altered. We can see in our own society that women are not as subordinate as they were only a decade ago. Similarly, in a few counties in Mississippi where blacks considerably outnumber whites, extensive voter registration has enabled the formerly subordinate blacks to become politically significant. On a broader scale, most of the former colonial areas of Africa and Asia are independent nations, and some nations that formerly lacked influence, such as Japan and China, are now world powers.

Despite these examples of long-term change, it is usually very difficult for members of a subordinate group to attain a share of power and influence. The dominant group naturally wants to protect its privileged position. Among the weapons it uses to do so are prejudice and discrimination.

DEFINING PREJUDICE AND DISCRIMINATION

Discrimination is "the differential treatment of individuals considered to belong to a particular social group" (R. M. Williams, 1947, p. 39). To treat a member of a subordinate group as inferior is to discriminate against that person. Members of the dominant group tend to use one standard of behavior among themselves and a different standard for any member of a subordinate group.

Discrimination is overt behavior. But to justify and explain that behavior to themselves, people tend to rationalize it on the ground that those whom they discriminate against are less worthy of respect or fair treatment than people like themselves—a perspective to which we return later in the chapter. Moreover, people tend to be ethnocentric—to see their own behavioral patterns and belief structures as desirable and natural and those of others as less so. These two tendencies usually result in *prejudice* against the subordinate group—an emotional, rigid attitude toward members of that group (Simpson & Yinger, 1965).

But while prejudices are attitudes, not all attitudes are prejudices. Both share the element of *pre*judgment—the tendency to decide in advance how to think about a situation or event. Unlike other attitudes, however, prejudice involves an emotional investment that strongly resists change. Prejudiced people tend to be so committed to their prejudgments about a particular category of people that even if they are given rational evidence showing that the prejudgment is wrong, they will maintain their prejudice, even defend it strongly, and denounce the evidence.

It is important to note that prejudice need not always involve antipathy. One can be prejudiced in favor of a person or group, with a similar degree of disregard for objective evidence. Prejudice is based on attitude; it is a tendency to think about people in a categorical, predetermined way. Discrimination, on the other hand, is behavior: It is overt unequal treatment of people on the basis of their membership in a particular group. Prejudice and discrimination are closely related, and both are often present in a given situation.

Robert Merton (1949) outlined four possible relationships between prejudice and discrimination: unprejudiced and nondiscriminatory (integration), unprejudiced and discriminatory (institutional discrimination), prejudiced and nondiscriminatory (latent bigotry), and prejudiced and discriminatory (outright bigotry). (See Table 9–1.) Although it is possible to be both completely free of prejudice and completely nondiscriminatory—or, on the other hand, to be a complete bigot—most people fall somewhere between these two extremes. It is possible to be prejudiced against a particular group but not to discriminate against it; it is also possible to discriminate against a particular group but not to be prejudiced against it.

For example, the builders of a new, expensive cooperative apartment house may not be personally prejudiced against Jews, but they may refuse to sell an apartment to a Jewish family—that is, they may discriminate against Jews—out of fear that the presence of Jewish families would make it more difficult to sell the remaining apartments. This is a clear case of institutional discrimination (the lower left cell in Table 9–1). Or the reverse may occur: In a corporation that holds a government contract, and hence is subject to federal equal employment opportunity regulations, the personnel director may be very prejudiced personally against both blacks and women but may hire a black woman as a management trainee—that is, not discriminate against her—in order to comply with the law. This is an example of latent bigotry (the upper right cell).

TABLE 9–1 A TYPOLOGY OF PREJUDICE AND DISCRIMINATION

Prejudice (the Attitude)	Discrimination (the Behavior)	
	Yes	No
Yes	Outright bigotry	Latent bigotry
No	Institutional discrimination	Integration (both psychological and institutional)

Source: Adapted with permission of The Free Press, a Division of Macmillan Inc. from *Social Theory and Social Structure* by Robert K. Merton. Copyright © 1949, 1957 by The Free Press, renewed 1977, 1985 by Robert K. Merton.

Suppose the builders were confronted with a different situation: a black family attempting to buy one of their apartments. They might very well discriminate out of both personal prejudice and concern for profits—a case of outright bigotry (upper left cell). On the other hand, there can be situations in which legal controls prevent latent bigotry from affecting such behaviors as the sale of a house to a black family but cannot prevent social isolation of the family after the sale. These examples point up the difficulty of keeping personal prejudices from leading, sooner or later, to some form of discrimination, particularly if a significant number of people share the same prejudice.

ORIGINS OF PREJUDICE AND DISCRIMINATION

We have said that prejudice and discrimination are weapons used by a dominant group to maintain its dominance. It would be a mistake, however, to see them as always, or even usually, consciously used weapons. Unless the subordinate group mounts a serious challenge to the dominant group, prejudice and discrimination are likely to seem part of the natural order of things. Their origins are numerous and complex, and to explain them it is necessary to consider both the felt needs of individuals and the structural organization of society. Do patterns of prejudice and discrimination result from the aggregation of individual attitudes and behaviors, or are these attributes of individuals shaped by the society of which they are members? In fact, neither argument excludes the other; both are possible. To blame prejudice and discrimination wholly on warped personalities, or wholly on oppressive social structures, is to oversimplify.

Prejudice and Bigotry in the Individual

Frustration–Aggression   At one time or another most human beings feel frustrated. They want something, but because of events or other people they cannot get it. This can lead to feelings of anger and to aggression, which may be expressed in any of several ways. The most obvious way would be to strike at the source of the frustration. But often this is impossible; frustrated individuals do not know the source or are subjectively unable to recognize it or are in a position in which they cannot risk such an action. Whatever the reason, the results are the same: They are unable to vent their anger on the real source of their frustration.

Instead, the aggression is often directed at a safer and more convenient target, usually one that somewhat resembles the real source of the frustration. In other words, the aggression is displaced onto a *scapegoat*. When this displacement is not limited to a particular person but is extended to include all similar people, it may produce a more or less permanent prejudice.

For example, suppose a middle-aged man who has been working for twenty years at the same job is told by his young supervisor that his job will soon be eliminated as a result of automation. The man is understandably angry and frightened. But if he were to vent his aggression on the supervisor he would almost certainly be fired. That evening, as he is telling his woes to friends at the local bar, a young man comes in for a beer. The middle-aged man accuses the youth, and "all you lazy kids," of being a good for nothing and ruining the country, and only the intervention of the bartender prevents him from assaulting the young man.

It is fairly clear that this man has displaced his aggression toward his young supervisor onto all young people. Rather than dealing with the supervisor and the whole range of factors that led to the elimination of his job, he blames the problems of the country on young people; that is, he uses them as a scapegoat. (Frustration–aggression theory is also discussed in Chapter 7.)

Projection Another source of prejudice and discrimination is *projection*. Many people have personal traits that they consider undesirable. They wish to rid themselves of those traits, but they cannot always do it directly—either because they find the effort too difficult or because they are unable to admit to themselves that they possess those traits. They may relieve their tension by attributing the unwanted traits to others, often members of another group. This makes it possible for them to reject and condemn the traits without rejecting and condemning themselves. Since the emotional pressures underlying projection can be very intense, it is difficult to counter them with rational arguments.

An often-cited example of projection is white attitudes toward black sexuality. Historically, many whites saw blacks as extremely promiscuous and uninhibited in their sexual relations, and there was much concern about protecting white women from sexual attacks by black men. Actually, white men enjoyed virtually unlimited sexual access to black women, particularly slaves. White society, however, regarded overt sexuality as unacceptable, and it is likely that white men felt some guilt about their sexual desires and adventures. To alleviate their feelings of guilt, they projected their own lust and sexuality onto black men—a much easier course than admitting the discrepancy between their own values and behavior.

Social Structure

The emotional needs of insecure individuals do not explain why certain groups become objects of prejudice and discrimination. To understand this, we need to look at some larger social processes.

As noted earlier, the demand for more than the available supply of certain goods gives rise, in many societies, to a competitive struggle that usually results in the dominance of one group and the subordination of others (Noel, 1968). Even if the initial competition is for economic goods, the contest is ultimately a struggle for power and, hence, a political process. Once established, political dominance is likely to be reinforced by economic exploitation. Slavery and serfdom are the most

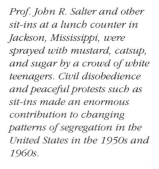

Prof. John R. Salter and other sit-ins at a lunch counter in Jackson, Mississippi, were sprayed with mustard, catsup, and sugar by a crowd of white teenagers. Civil disobedience and peaceful protests such as sit-ins made an enormous contribution to changing patterns of segregation in the United States in the 1950s and 1960s.

obvious forms of exploitation, but "free" workers may also be exploited. Migrant farm workers, illegal aliens, and unorganized clerical and service workers are examples of the latter.

Economic exploitation is one form of discrimination practiced by the dominant group against a subordinate group. Historically, the subordinate group has consisted of unskilled workers. In the case of African Americans, for example, unskilled jobs were plentiful and available (at low wages) before the 1940s. With the development of protective labor legislation (e.g., minimum wage, antidiscrimination, and workers' compensation laws), employers could no longer use the subordinate group as a source of cheap labor. African Americans were systematically denied jobs as white-dominated unions maintained control over skilled jobs and employers sought cheaper unskilled labor by transferring basic manufacturing operations abroad (Bonacich, 1976).

Discrimination can take many other forms. Some of these are practical: Members of the subordinate group may be legally prevented from owning property or voting or may be terrorized into submission, as often happened to strikers early in the labor movement. Some forms of discrimination are symbolic, as when African Americans were refused service in restaurants before the civil rights movement. All are aimed, consciously or unconsciously, at keeping the subordinate people "in their place."

Since members of the dominant group know that they are treating members of the subordinate group as inferiors, they need to justify their behavior. The tendency to rationalize one's own behavior is aided by the tendency to see one's own group as right and worthy and other groups as wrong and unworthy. Members of the dominant group tend to tell themselves that it is right and proper for them to have more—they are smarter, cleverer, and racially superior—and they come to believe that they deserve what they have. Members of the subordinate group, in their view, are lazy, stupid, heathen, biologically inferior, or otherwise unworthy, and therefore they deserve less (or perhaps need less). Thus, the groups in a society that are different from the dominant group, have less power, and are economically useful to the dominant group tend to become the targets of prejudice and discrimination.

Cultural Factors: Norms and Stereotypes

Social Norms   A *social norm* is a commonly accepted standard that specifies the kind of behavior that is appropriate in a given situation. It is relevant to our discussion because, although it does not tell us why prejudice and discrimination begin, it helps explain how and why they are perpetuated.

Social norms are learned in a process that begins almost at birth. Small children soon learn what kind of behavior elicits the approval of their parents and what kind is likely to elicit a rebuke. The same process continues as they encounter other significant adults. Gradually children internalize the values and norms of their society. They receive approval from parents and other adults, and later from their peers, when they behave in socially acceptable ways; they experience disapproval when they do not.

Through this process most children are socialized into the prevailing norms of the society into which they were born. If the society is prejudiced against certain minorities and engages in discriminatory behavior, the children will generally learn those prejudices and behaviors and think they are correct and natural. The original reasons for specific forms of prejudice and discrimination are deeply embedded in the folkways and mores of the society, that is, in the cultural heritage passed on from one generation to the next. Prejudice and discrimination thus acquire a life of their own quite apart from their origins.

The human tendency toward social conformity is also likely to support prejudice and discrimination. Some members of a dominant group may be ambivalent toward the subordinate group and personally feel no prejudice, but if most of the people around them are prejudiced and engage in discriminatory behavior, the ambivalent and indifferent individuals will usually go along. It is easier for them to conform to group norms than to deviate and perhaps bring hostility upon themselves.

Stereotyping   Still another source of prejudice and discrimination is *stereotyping,* or attributing a fixed and usually unfavorable or inaccurate conception to a category of people. Whereas social norms are concerned primarily with behavior and only indirectly with attitudes, stereotyping is basically a matter of attitude.

Usually a stereotype contains some truth, but it is exaggerated, distorted, or somehow taken out of context. Stereotyping has much to do with the way humans normally think. We tend to perceive and understand things in categories, and we apply the same mental process to people. We build up mental pictures of various groups, pictures made from overgeneralized impressions and selected bits of information, and we use these pictures to define all members of a group regardless of their individual differences. Thus, we come to assume that all Native Americans are drunks, all African Americans are lazy, all Puerto Ricans are short, all Italians are gangsters, all Jews are shrewd, all English people are reserved, all Swedes are blond, all Frenchmen are amorous, all old people are senile, and so forth. None of these generalizations will stand up to even perfunctory analysis. Yet many people habitually use such notions in thinking about minority groups. For example, social scientists in the United States believe that young black males are victimized by stereotypes that portray them as violent and swaggering. In studies of the "cool pose" of inner-city black men, Robert Majors finds that this essentially defensive posture is often misinterpreted as a threatening pose, even by black middle-class individuals, and can lead to discrimination and prejudice (cited in Goleman, 1992).

It should be noted that stereotyping is not confined to any particular group, nor is it unique to the United States. Throughout the world it follows well-established patterns based on in-group/out-group distinctions and hostilities (Allen, 1983).

The three approaches just described—psychological, social-structural, and cultural—should not be viewed as mutually exclusive. As Milton Yinger (1987) has pointed out, human problems like racial disharmony are best viewed from all three of these perspectives, not just one.

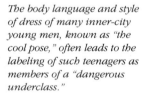

The body language and style of dress of many inner-city young men, known as "the cool pose," often leads to the labeling of such teenagers as members of a "dangerous underclass."

If discrimination is a socially learned behavior of members of dominant groups, designed to support and justify their continued dominance, it is reasonable to expect that it will be built into the structure of society. To members of a society who are socialized to believe that members of certain groups "just are" to be treated as inferiors, it would be perfectly natural to formulate public policies and build public institutions that would discriminate against those groups.

To some extent this is exactly what has happened in the United States. If many blacks, Chicanos, Native Americans, Puerto Ricans, women, and members of other minority groups do not have equal protection of the law in their dealings with public institutions, it is not necessarily because of the conscious prejudices of public officials. Such *institutional discrimination* is an unconscious result of the structure and functioning of the public institutions and policies themselves.

For example, people living near reservations often see Native Americans as lazy and incompetent, unable to exercise initiative or do anything to improve their often deplorable condition. What such people fail to realize is the degree to which this apparent incompetence is a result of the way Native Americans are governed. The ability of Native Americans to handle their own affairs has been hampered by an administrative structure that denies them opportunities to learn new ways of doing things while simultaneously rendering old tribal ways ineffective. As Gary D. Sandefur and Marta Tienda (1988) have written,

> *Native Americans collectively have been victims of discrimination and persecution throughout the history of the development of the United States. The contemporary expression of subjugation and discrimination had changed considerably from the blatant destruction experienced a century ago. . . . Despite substantial increases in educational attainment over the past few decades, many Native Americans remain unprepared to compete in a highly technical and bureaucratized world of work. Consequently, there persist income and employment differentials relative to comparably schooled whites. . . . To the extent that job possibilities on reservations remain limited while large shares of Native Americans reside on them, the prospects for economic parity with whites probably will not be realized. (pp. 8–9)*

It should be noted that Native Americans are by no means a homogeneous group. They have been lumped into a single category ("Indians"), but in fact they constitute a variety of peoples with vastly different cultures. Despite the poverty and hardship they have experienced on segregated reservations and the racism they often experience outside them, many of these groups have succeeded in preserving their traditional identities while adapting to the ways of the larger society.

Since it would be difficult to discuss all categories of institutional discrimination against all minority groups, we will focus on four major categories: education, housing, employment and income, and social justice. But the patterns we will describe apply to other categories as well, such as health care and consumer issues.

Education

An issue that generates a great deal of emotion in the United States is the question of whether black, Puerto Rican, Chicano, and Native American children should attend the same schools as white children. This question underlies such matters as busing to achieve racial balance, quality education for all, and public tax support for private schools.

Americans take public school systems very seriously. Undoubtedly, one reason is that in this country education has generally been seen as the road to social and economic advancement. It is almost an article of faith that American children should get more education than their parents and achieve higher social and economic status. (This subject is discussed in detail in Chapter 13.)

Since the 1940 census, which was the first to ask about educational attainment, the average number of years of school completed by all Americans has increased steadily. In addition, the gap in educational attainment between whites and blacks has narrowed considerably: Before World War II, for example, black men completed three and one-half fewer years of school than white men; by 1988 the difference had been reduced to less than half a year. (See Figure 9–1.)

Despite these gains, it remains true that members of minority groups have less chance of finishing high school or attending college than do whites. In 1992, 19.1 percent of whites aged 25 and over had not completed high school; the comparable figures for blacks and Hispanics were 32.3 percent and 47.4 percent, respectively (*Statistical Abstract,* 1993). Thus, although Figure 9–1 indicates a large gain in educational parity since World War II, large differences remain. The greatest difference is in attainment of a college diploma plus graduate training: In 1992, among Americans aged 25 and over, only 8.3 percent of blacks and 6.3 percent of Hispanics had completed four years of college or more, compared to 14.6 percent of whites (*Statistical Abstract,* 1993).

We have long assumed that higher education leads to higher income. There is no doubt that among people working at this time, the more highly educated usually receive substantially higher salaries than those with little education. Evidence also suggests that even better than a sheepskin (diploma) is a white skin, for minority group members at all levels of education earn less than their nonminority counterparts. (See Table 9–2.) As educational requirements for the labor force increase, it becomes ever more urgent for members of minority groups to enter colleges and universities. Despite recent gains, shown in Table 9–3, minority enrollment rates are lower than they would be under conditions of equality (Evangelauf, 1992).

Desegregation. The most prominent issue with respect to minority education is school desegregation. Desegregation has been a long time in coming. In 1980, twenty-five years after the Supreme Court decision that mandated integration "with

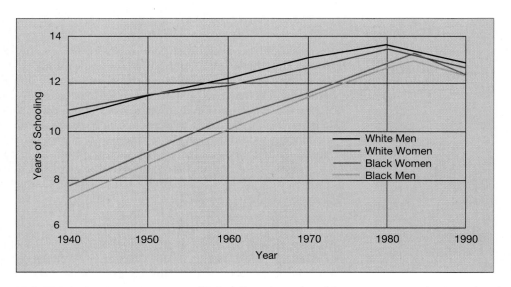

FIGURE 9–1 Average Years of Schooling Completed by Persons Aged 25–29, by Race and Sex, 1940–1990

Source: Data from Farley, Bianchi, & Colasanto, 1979; *Statistical Abstract,* various years.

TABLE 9–2 MEAN INCOME OF HOUSEHOLDS, BY EDUCATION AND RACE AND SPANISH ORIGIN OF HOUSEHOLDER*

	MEAN ANNUAL EARNINGS			
Educational Attainment	All Races	White	Black	Spanish Origin[†]
Elementary School:				
Less than 8 years	$15,579	$16,431	$12,494	$16,279
8 years	17,509	17,816	15,143	17,603
High school:				
1–3 years	21,182	22,759	14,112	19,860
4 years	29,069	30,065	21,139	26,443
College:				
1–3 years	34,677	35,646	26,078	31,367
4 years or more	50,879	51,669	37,700	46,163

*Householder is defined as head of household in census terms.

[†]Persons of Spanish origin may be of any race.

Source: Statistical Abstract, 1990.

all deliberate speed," one-fifth of all black students attended public schools with almost entirely black enrollment and more than half attended schools with 50 percent or more minority enrollment.

De jure segregation—segregation required by law—is now a thing of the past, but de facto segregation, a result of housing patterns, economic patterns, gerrymandered school districts, and other factors, is harder to eradicate. The principal remedy suggested thus far is busing—transporting pupils from their local schools to other schools to achieve a reasonable racial balance in all the schools in a particular area. Despite the fact that about half of all public school pupils are bused daily for purposes other than desegregation (Daniels, 1983), in some communities busing remains an emotional political issue.

TABLE 9–3 1990 RACIAL AND ETHNIC ENROLLMENT AND TWO-YEAR GAINS

	ENROLLMENT	TWO-YEAR GAINS
American Indian	103,000	10.8%
Asian	555,000	11.7
Black	1,223,000	8.2
Hispanic	758,000	11.5
White	10,675,000	3.8
Foreign	397,000	10.0
Total	**13,710,000**	**5.1%**

Source: U.S. Department of Education.

Busing to achieve racial integration has often met with determined resistance in American cities. The scene shown here occurred in Boston where the members of white ethnic communities feared that their children would have to attend schools outside of their own neighborhoods.

The basic arguments for busing are that (1) busing effectively achieves racial balance and (2) minority children (perhaps all children) will receive a better education in racially balanced schools than in racially segregated ones. Both facets of the argument have turned out to be somewhat weaker in practice than in theory. Although the educational achievement of minority children who have been bused to racially integrated schools seems to have improved, the data are inconclusive. And because of "white flight"—movement by white families from areas where busing has been instituted to areas where it has not—busing has not brought about the desired racial balance in many schools. Because American parents usually regard their children's education as extremely important, and because white parents fear that integration will lower educational standards, they may be inclined to leave integrated districts, to send their children to private schools, or to protest vehemently against busing, even though they may not be inclined to discriminate in any other respect.

Washington, D.C., is commonly cited as an example of this situation. After busing was instituted, so many white students moved to the suburbs that in 1970 the school system was 94 percent black. Children were being bused from all-black neighborhoods to schools in other neighborhoods that were rapidly becoming all black. Other cities had similar experiences. In Inglewood, California, for example, minorities constituted 38 percent of the public school enrollment when court-ordered busing was put into effect in 1970; by 1975 minority enrollment was 80 percent, and the busing order was rescinded by the same judge who had ordered it.

In 1966 James Coleman and his colleagues concluded from data on integration and school achievement that desegregation, by exposing minority students to the higher achievements of the middle-class majority, would improve the performance of the former without diminishing that of the latter. Nine years later Coleman reversed himself, stating that in the long run court-ordered desegregation would probably widen the gap between whites and blacks. Recognizing the complexities involved in the phenomenon of "white flight," Coleman pointed out that middle-class whites were fleeing not only lower-class blacks but large, unmanageable, unresponsive school systems. In this regard, it has been pointed out that busing children long distances costs money that might otherwise be used to improve instruction. And it tends to weaken local control and interest in the schools. It is difficult for parents to take an active part in school affairs when the school is not easily accessible.

Busing may also provoke racial tensions within a community, especially when residents' cooperation is not sought prior to the institution of a busing program. Lower-class urban whites, who cannot afford to move to the suburbs, often see attempts to integrate neighborhood schools as a threat to their way of life. For example, in 1975 a federal judge ordered the exchange of some 24,000 students between certain sections of Boston. In effect, blacks were being bused from schools that were overcrowded and inadequate. The Irish and Polish residents of South Boston, who viewed themselves as oppressed ethnic minorities and believed that their community, power, and cultural identity were being threatened, opposed the busing program violently, and it was months before the school system achieved any semblance of order (Buell & DeLuca, 1975). In a survey of white residents of Boston, sociologist Bert Useem (1980) found that the protestors against busing were more likely to have a history of community activity than one of rabble rousing—a fact that helps explain the persistence of Boston's antibusing movement.

As suggested earlier, there is also considerable controversy about whether or not school integration will result in better education. Coleman (cited in Ford, 1975) found that the most important predictors of children's success in school were their backgrounds and social environments; schools had relatively little effect on achievement. In another study, Levitan, Johnston, and Taggart (1975) found that "there is no proof that integration, increased outlays per pupil, more relevant curricula, or any changes have had, or will have, a rapid and significant impact" on improving the school performance of black slum children (p. 93). On the other hand, a statewide survey of Michigan's school system suggested that there was a positive relationship between school services and student achievement (Guthrie et al., 1971). A study of ten communities in various parts of the United States carried out by the U.S. Commission on Civil Rights (1973) found large improvements in the quality of education as a result of school desegregation in all the communities studied. More recent research also indicates that desegregation has had beneficial effects on minority educational attainment but that inequalities of class and disadvantages at home (e.g., lack of a second parent) continue to inhibit academic success (Mare & Winship, 1988). Thus, despite the efforts of numerous experts, the evidence about the effects of desegregation on academic achievement is inconclusive.

It should be noted, however, that educational equality is not the only purpose of school desegregation. Many observers see desegregation as a way for whites and minorities to learn to live with one another on a personal basis. According to this viewpoint, stereotyping and racism are much less likely to occur when people get to know each other as individuals. As David Cohen (1975) has pointed out, desegregation "seems a necessary step toward equality because it is an obvious way to break down racist ideas and institutional arrangements" (p. 37). This point of view is supported by the results of a fifteen-year study of black students educated in predominantly white suburban schools, which found that these students were more likely than students educated in predominantly black city schools to attend largely white colleges, to live and work in racially mixed communities, and to have white friends (Johns Hopkins University, Center for Social Organization of Schools, Rand Corp., cited in the *New York Times,* September 17, 1985).

In the 1980s the central issue related to desegregation was the disparity between the populations of inner cities and suburban rings. When all the school districts in a metropolitan area include both white and black students, it is possible to achieve some degree of integration by transferring students from one district to another. Today, however, "public schools are segregated because blacks and whites live in separate school districts" (Farley, 1984, p. 32). In most large metropolitan areas, white students live in the suburban ring and black students in the inner city. The situation is even more extreme for Hispanic students, who are increasingly concentrated in urban *barrios;* 73 percent of Hispanic students attend predominantly minority public schools (Celis, 1993). When the landmark Supreme Court ruling in *Brown v. Board of Education, Topeka* passed its fortieth anniversary in 1994, Farley and other sociologists who study segregation noted that because of persistent residential segregation, efforts to desegregate the nation's schools have been frustrated.

These facts do not augur well for the future of racial integration in public schools. In the words of Reynolds Farley, a well-known writer on the subject, "Unless there are changes in the current policies that separate city and suburban students into different school districts, the persistence of racial residential segregation will combine with demographic trends to produce schools almost as racially segregated as those which were constitutionally permitted before the 1954 *Brown* decision" (1984, p. 32).

Housing

Housing segregation—the separation and isolation of minority groups into regions, cities, neighborhoods, blocks, and even buildings—has become increasingly prevalent during the past several decades. The major demarcation is between the whites in the suburbs and the blacks and other minority groups in the cities.

A look at some census findings will indicate the extent of white migration from cities to surrounding suburbs. In the 1960s, the white population of the central cities in the Northeast declined by 10 percent. During the same period, the white population of suburban areas of the same cities increased by 15 percent. Between 1970 and 1980 the central cities lost approximately 1 percent of their white population annually and the white populations of both suburban and nonmetropolitan areas increased by 1.2 percent annually. Blacks made inroads into the suburbs during the 1970s: In 1970, only 3.4 percent of the suburban population was black; ten years later, blacks made up 6 percent of that population. These trends continued until the late 1980s, when economic recession began to hit black and other minority communities.

While whites were moving to the suburbs, blacks were moving to the cities in larger numbers. During the 1960s the black population of New York City increased by 38.2 percent. Other cities with black populations of 50,000 or more showed similar gains. Dallas, Los Angeles, Boston, and Detroit experienced net increases of over 20 percent. Although this rate of white migration to the suburbs and black migration to the cities declined during the 1970s and 1980s, a segregated pattern of housing had already become firmly established.

Most of today's housing patterns began to emerge after World War II, when the population began to grow rapidly, accompanied by widespread migration to the cities. At that time the government—primarily through the mortgage programs of the Federal Housing Administration (FHA) and the Veterans Administration (VA)—joined private builders to encourage development of the suburbs as a way to solve the housing shortage. This approach seemed reasonable in view of the American tradition of free enterprise, and in terms of numbers of dwelling units provided, it worked spectacularly well. However, the free-enterprise system created housing only for those who could pay for it, and many members of minority groups could not. Even for those who could, the FHA and VA mortgage requirements, designed to encourage home ownership by families with reasonably dependable earning prospects, presented obstacles.

Not until 1962, when President John F. Kennedy signed a limited antidiscrimination order, did the federal government's housing program make any effort to achieve integration. It would be inaccurate to cite federal housing policy as the only cause of housing discrimination—other factors contributed, including the refusal of some whites to sell their houses to blacks, suburban zoning patterns that tended to keep out poorer families, and the ties among members of minority communities. But it remains true that the officially sanctioned practices and policies of the federal housing agencies from the mid-1930s until 1962 are among the major reasons that American housing is segregated. Moreover, although federal law has prohibited discrimination in the rental, sale, or financing of suburban housing since 1965, this law has been largely unenforced.

In a recent study of trends in residential segregation and poverty in the United States, sociologists Douglas Massey and Nancy Denton (1993) found that although some decrease in housing segregation has occurred in urban regions, the largest cities, including Chicago, Cleveland, Detroit, New York, and St. Louis, have failed to significantly reduce housing segregation. The figures shown in Table 9–4 on page 276 are percentages based on a calculation of how many of each city's African-American residents would have to move out of their segregated neighborhoods to achieve an even distribution of their numbers throughout the city's neighborhoods. Massey and Denton show that poverty, unemployment, homicide, AIDS, and many other problems of urban centers are heightened by the heavy segregation of racially distinct and poor households in physically blighted urban communities. Their research confirms what many other social scientists have shown: Failure to enforce federal laws against housing discrimination continues to produce rates of black segregation that are far higher than those experienced by any other group in U.S. history.

A practice that contributes to high rates of segregation is *racial steering,* in which real estate brokers refuse to show houses outside specific areas to minority buyers. Before the landmark judicial decisions of the 1950s, racial steering was enforced through "restrictive covenants"—agreements among home owners not to sell their property to people who were designated as undesirable. Although restrictive covenants are now illegal, racial and ethnic steering still occurs unofficially in many all-white neighborhoods. Because it operates below the surface, with no written agreements, racial steering is difficult to detect or prevent (Farley, Bianchi, & Colasato, 1979; Farley et al., 1978).

Sociologist Douglas Massey and others who study racial and ethnic segregation assert that more "audit" research is needed to show lawmakers that racial steering and other forms of discrimination exist and that laws against them must be enforced far more rigorously. In audit research, a black or minority couple is sent to real estate agents and shown (or not shown) certain types of housing. Then a white couple is sent to the same agents and the results are compared; this process is repeated many times with different agents to determine whether a systematic pattern of discrimination exists (Massey & Denton, 1993).

The housing problems of another minority group are described by Robert Burnette in *The Tortured Americans* (1971):

> *Until 1961 Indians were excluded from plans for public housing projects. They lived, as many still do, in tarpaper shacks, rickety log houses, ragged tents, abandoned automobile bodies, and hillside caves. When public housing did become available to the Indians, the inevitable corruption that attaches itself like a leech to such projects made a mockery of the program's intentions. (p. 22)*

METROPOLITAN AREA	1970	1980	1990
Northern areas			
Boston	81.2	77.6	68.2
Buffalo	87.0	79.4	81.8
Chicago	91.9	87.8	85.8
Cincinnati	76.8	72.3	75.8
Cleveland	90.8	87.5	85.1
Columbus	81.8	71.4	67.3
Detroit	88.4	86.7	87.6
Gary-Hammond-E. Chicago	91.4	90.6	89.9
Indianapolis	81.7	76.2	74.3
Kansas City	87.4	78.9	72.6
Los Angeles-Long Beach	91.0	81.1	73.1
Milwaukee	90.5	83.9	82.8
New York	81.0	82.0	82.2
Newark	81.4	81.6	82.5
Philadelphia	79.5	78.8	77.2
Pittsburgh	75.0	72.7	71.0
St. Louis	84.7	81.3	77.0
San Francisco-Oakland	80.1	71.7	66.8
Average	84.5	80.1	77.8
Southern areas			
Atlanta	82.1	78.5	67.8
Baltimore	81.9	74.7	71.4
Birmingham	37.8	40.8	71.7
Dallas-Ft. Worth	86.9	77.1	63.1
Greensboro-Winston Salem	65.4	56.0	60.9
Houston	78.1	69.5	66.8
Memphis	75.9	71.6	69.3
Miami	85.1	77.8	71.8
New Orleans	73.1	68.3	68.8
Norfolk-Virginia Beach	75.7	63.1	50.3
Tampa-St. Petersburg	79.9	72.6	69.7
Washington, D.C.	81.1	70.1	66.1
Average	75.3	68.3	66.5

Source: Massey & Denton, 1993.

The problem of inadequate housing on Indian reservations is related to the federal government's long-standing policy of taking Native American children away from their homes to be educated in boarding schools. This had the effect of weakening the Native American family. According to one writer on the subject,

> *Parents who fear they may lose their children may have their self-confidence so undermined that their ability to function successfully as parents is undermined, with the result that they lose their children. When the welfare department removes the children, it also re-*

moves much of the parents' incentive to struggle against the conditions under which they live. (Byler, 1977, p. 8)

Depressed by the destruction of their families and convinced of their powerlessness, some Native American tribes have difficulty developing the patterns of leadership needed to argue their case effectively with the government or to develop their own communities (Tienda & Sandefur, 1988).

Employment and Income

The idea of work as a way to improve one's social status is deeply ingrained in American culture. Although it is no longer as pervasive as it once was, the work ethic still holds that if you really want a job you can find one and that if you work hard you will make money. The corollary to this is the notion that if you are wealthy you deserve your wealth because you worked for it, and if you are poor it is because you are lazy. Thus, one hears the argument that if only blacks and Puerto Ricans and Native Americans would make an effort to find jobs and stick to them, they could improve their lot in life. This view ignores the fact that discrimination is no less prevalent in employment than it is in education and housing.

In some ways discrimination in employment is a direct result of discrimination in education. We have already noted the relationship between income and education. Since today the chances of finding even an entry-level job without a high school diploma are slim, lack of education means that many minority group members will spend their lives underemployed or unemployed (W. J. Wilson, 1987). This, in turn, means a low income, resulting in inferior housing, with the likelihood of a poor education for the next generation, and so on—a cycle of discrimination that is built into the system.

Is there any escape from this situation? What about jobs that do not require much formal education, jobs that one learns mostly through apprenticeship and are represented by many labor unions?

Historically, labor unions have been in the forefront of battles for civil rights, but union locals often resisted minority demands for membership. William Gould (1968) pointed out a basic conflict between the rhetoric of union leadership and established union policies and practices. Unions, like other institutions, are resistant to internal changes or economic sacrifices for the purpose of accommodating the demands of minority workers. There are only so many jobs to go around, and those who have them want to keep them.

This has meant that union-sponsored job-training programs are generally closed to minority workers. Progress in opening apprenticeship and training programs has been slow. For example, the New York City Commission on Human Rights reported that a pattern of exclusion was typical of much of the building construction industry, with the result that nonwhites were effectively barred (cited in Jacobson, 1968). With the exception of the carpenters' and electricians' unions, trade unions in New York City have fought every attempt to open their programs to nonwhites.

Nationally, there has been some improvement in this situation. By 1975 blacks accounted for one-third of new members in trade unions and 12 percent of total union membership. In some unions, notably those of steel and auto workers and state and municipal government employees, blacks accounted for one-third of the total membership (Cameron, 1975). However, these more recently unionized black workers are among the first to be laid off during a recession because of union seniority systems. An indication of this is the fact that although in 1983 blacks accounted for 26 percent of union members, by 1990 this figure had fallen below 24 percent. This negative trend is likely to continue throughout the 1990s (Waldinger & Bailey, 1990).

The overall employment picture is not bright. Current statistics indicate that minority group members hold a disproportionate number of lower-level jobs. Blacks and Hispanics are more likely than whites to be service workers and laborers and less likely to be salespeople and white-collar workers. The effects of occupational discrimination against minorities were translated into dollar terms in a study by Naomi Turner Verdugo and Richard R. Verdugo (1984). Essentially, what the researchers did was to hold other factors, such as education, constant and look closely at differences in the incomes of whites, blacks, and Mexican Americans for the same jobs. They found that the average income loss due to discrimination was $1,399 for black workers and $1,012 for Mexican Americans.

Puerto Ricans also face discrimination in employment. A study by Marta Tienda and Lief Jensen (1988) found that between 1960 and 1980 the income of Puerto Rican families declined. This is not merely a reflection of the problems of nonwhite minorities in general, since the median family income of blacks and other minorities rose during those two decades. (See Table 9–5.) The effect of job discrimination, therefore, is an increasing incidence of poverty and welfare dependency among Puerto Rican families.

The employment problem among minority groups is particularly devastating for young black and Hispanic men. In the absence of legitimate means of getting ahead, many turn to hustling and other forms of illicit activity. In addition, without hope for a steady income, they often find it economically impossible to form stable families. And this situation shows few signs of improving; the employment gap between

TABLE 9–5   EVOLUTION OF MINORITY AND NONMINORITY FAMILY INCOMES, 1959–1984 (MEANS AND MEDIANS IN CONSTANT 1985 DOLLARS)

	BLACKS	MEXICANS	PUERTO RICANS	OTHER HISPANICS	AMERICAN INDIANS	NON-HISPANIC WHITES
Median family income						
1959	$ 9,696	$13,634	$12,345	$15,004	$10,577	$19,812
1969	16,252	18,586	16,181	23,178	18,279	27,934
1979	17,714	20,821	14,988	23,684	23,687	30,057
1984	15,202	18,912	12,282	21,651	NA*	28,564
Mean family income						
1959	$13,360	$17,020	$15,660	$19,326	$12,854	$24,713
1969	20,502	21,988	19,389	27,176	21,020	33,353
1979	22,639	24,497	19,407	28,649	26,206	35,090
1984	20,252	22,780	17,553	27,023	NA*	33,958
Mean family income per capita						
1959	$ 3,879	$ 4,169	$ 4,214	$ 5,567	$ 3,405	$ 7,867
1969	5,966	5,612	5,472	8,064	6,029	10,966
1979	6,892	6,755	5,895	8,921	7,995	12,128
1984	6,522	6,410	5,259	8,751	NA*	12,054
Minority/white per capita ratio						
1959	0.49	0.53	0.54	0.71	0.43	NA†
1969	0.54	0.51	0.50	0.74	0.55	NA†
1979	0.57	0.56	0.49	0.74	0.66	NA†
1984	0.54	0.53	0.44	0.72	NA*	NA†

*Data not available.
†Not applicable.

Source: Sandefur & Tienda, 1988.

young white men and black and Hispanic youths has increased in recent years despite the narrowing of the educational gaps among these groups.

This entire discussion is somewhat deceptive, since it is impossible to look at the employment and income picture of blacks as a monolithic whole. Some black scholars believe that the black job market is really two markets made up of lower-class high school dropouts, on the one hand, and college-educated blacks—a growing and prospering middle class—on the other (Hout, 1984; Kilson, 1981; Wilson, 1988). The black employment crisis, in their view, is a crisis of black youths alone, and particularly of young blacks in the central cities. College-educated blacks are "clearly in the process of 'pulling away' from the black lower strata," according to Martin Kilson (1981, p. 68).

During the 1980s and early 1990s a debate has raged among social scientists who study minorities and poverty in the United States. The issue is whether the concentration of black and Puerto Rican people in inner-city ghettos, where they are isolated from better jobs and educational opportunities, has produced an "underclass," that is, a class of people who are not only poor and undereducated but are being enticed into lives of petty crime and welfare dependency because of their isolation and limited access to legitimate opportunities. Until very recently, the chief proponent of this thesis was one of the nation's leading sociologists, William Julius Wilson. But fearing that the term *underclass* lumps together too many different categories of impoverished people and threatens to become a pejorative label, Wilson and others have abandoned the term even while many other social scientists continue to assert its validity.

Justice

Justice is the final area that we will examine in our attempt to highlight the pervasive nature of institutional discrimination. Two basic assumptions in American law are (1) that justice is blind—that racial, ethnic, economic, or social considerations are irrelevant in the eyes of the law—and (2) that any accused person is considered innocent until proven guilty in a court of law. But do these assumptions apply equally to everyone?

As noted in Chapter 6, minority groups are overrepresented in official arrest records, and it seems probable that in general they are more likely to be arrested and charged with a crime, whether or not they are guilty. The higher arrest rates among minorities are due partly to the higher arrest rates among the poor in general (who, as noted earlier, include a disproportionate number of minority group members), but there is considerable evidence that discrimination plays a role in who gets arrested.

Following arrest, the obstacle of the bail system must be overcome. It is here that the American criminal-justice system may be most discriminatory. To begin with, bail involves money: Those who have it can usually arrange to be released after arrest and await their trial in freedom, subject only to the limitations of the bail agreement. Those who do not have money are punished, in effect, because of the long delay between arrest and trial in many jurisdictions (particularly in big cities). They are compelled to wait in jail—often for months, sometimes for more than a year—until their case comes up. This borders on punishment before conviction and certainly runs counter to the precept of presumed innocence.

One of the few systematic studies of the bail system, the Manhattan Bail Project, found that abuses of the bail system produce even more inequality. Theoretically, bail prevents punishment before conviction and ensures that the accused person will attend the trial. Many judges, however, use bail punitively: They set excessively high bail simply to make it more likely that defendants will be detained. Defendants who cannot obtain the money for bail and must therefore stay in jail are more likely to fare badly in court (Ares, Rankin, & Sturtz, 1963). As Paul Wice (1973) has pointed out,

> *Numerous studies clearly show that detained defendants are far more likely to be found guilty and receive more severe sentences than those released prior to trial. Limited visiting hours, locations remote from the counsel's office, inadequate conference facilities, and censored mail all serve to impede an effective lawyer–client relationship. (p. 23)*

In effect, then, under the current bail system minority defendants are often presumed guilty because they are poor. Other studies have confirmed the widespread misuse of the bail system. For example, the U.S. Commission on Civil Rights (1970) found similar practices with regard to Chicanos in the Southwest:

> *The system of bail in the Southwest frequently is used more severely against Mexican-Americans than against Anglos as a form of discrimination. In certain cases, Mexican-American defendants are faced with excessively high bail. Defendants in other cases are held without any opportunity to put up bail or are purposely confused by local officials about the bail hearing so that they unknowingly forfeit their bail. In one area local farmers put up bail or pay fines for migrant workers and make them work off the amount in a situation resembling peonage or involuntary servitude. (p. 52)*

In his survey, Wice (1973) found that bail is used punitively throughout the nation. The most significant factor affecting the amount of bail set is the seriousness of the charge, despite evidence that this is not directly related to whether or not the defendant will appear for trial. The criterion that is least frequently considered by judges is, paradoxically, the one with the greatest influence on the defendant's ability to pay bail, namely, financial status.

From this evidence it is easy to see why more minority defendants are convicted than are acquitted. Even those who can pay bail can rarely afford a costly defense, and those who are detained have little opportunity to prepare a defense. This inequality in the administration of justice extends to the sentencing process. Though blacks account for only 12 percent of the population, they make up about 47.3 percent of the prison population (*Statistical Abstract,* 1993); whites are much more likely to be released on their own recognizance or given suspended sentences.

SOME CONSEQUENCES OF PREJUDICE AND DISCRIMINATION

The harmful effects of prejudice and discrimination are not limited to minority groups. The lives of members of the dominant group are also stunted by the artificial barriers and warped perceptions that such social divisions create. Here, however, we will consider the effects on the subordinate group, since they are usually more serious.

What happens to people who must live with institutionalized discrimination and the prejudice that accompanies it? There are, of course, effects on the individual personalities of minority group members. And both individuals and groups develop protective reactions against prejudice and discrimination.

First, consider the effects of discrimination on individual personalities. In his ground-breaking work, *Children of Crisis,* Robert Coles (1968) documented some of the effects on the first black children to attend desegregated schools in the South. These children were subjected to blatant discrimination and bitter prejudice, including mob action against them and their parents. For several months Coles observed the children, focusing on how they depicted themselves and their world in drawings. His account of the drawings of one black girl, Ruby, is fascinating. For months

Ruby would never use brown or black except to indicate the ground. However, she distinguished between white and black people.

> *She drew white people larger and more lifelike. Negroes were smaller, their bodies less intact. A white girl we both knew to be her own size appeared several times taller. While Ruby's own face lacked an eye in one drawing, an ear in another, the white girl never lacked any features. Moreover, Ruby drew the white girl's hands and legs carefully, always making sure that they had the proper number of fingers and toes. Not so with her own limbs, or those of any other Negro children she chose (or was asked) to picture. A thumb or forefinger might be missing, or a whole set of toes. The arms were shorter, even absent or truncated.* (p. 47)

At the same time Jimmy, a white classmate, always depicted blacks as somehow related to animals or extremely dirty and dangerous. After about two years of contact with Ruby and other black children in his school in New Orleans, Jimmy grew less fearful of blacks, and the change was reflected in his drawings. Coles concluded that children of each race were conditioned to fear and distrust members of the other race, but that with continuing friendly contact these prejudices were broken down and the children eventually helped change their parents' attitudes as well.

Black separatism is another reaction to discrimination and prejudice. In the 1920s Marcus Garvey espoused an extreme form of separatism. His plan was to seize control of Africa from European colonial powers and build a free United Black Africa to be peopled by New World blacks and like-minded Africans.

The most common reaction against inequality during the past few decades has been public protest. Following the success of the Montgomery bus boycott of 1955 and 1956 (when blacks avoided riding buses until discriminatory seating rules were eliminated), a broad social movement for desegregation emerged. Initially led by Martin Luther King, Jr., the movement was directed against laws that were enforced or created a statutory inequality—that is, an obstruction maintained so as to deny minority groups rights and privileges enjoyed by other Americans. In the 1960s, however, as progress slowed and resistance increased, minority protests sometimes took more violent forms. Feelings of anger, frustration, and rage provoked urban riots across the country. Often the incident that led to a riot was the arrest of a black by white police officers. The police served as visible symbols of the attitudes of the white majority. At no time, however, did a majority of blacks approve of the violent protests (National Advisory Commission on Civil Disorders, 1968).

By the mid-1970s the frequency of riots had diminished considerably. The recession during this period saw both whites and blacks suffering from high unemployment rates and inflation, and expectations of progress were reduced. Moreover, the end of the Vietnam War and the draft caused a general decline in protest movements. There may also have been a sense that riots had reached the limits of their effectiveness and that more deliberate, better organized efforts were necessary. In addition, it is possible, as Frances Piven and Richard Cloward (1972) have theorized, that welfare rolls were increased in response to the riots and that this had the effect of mollifying blacks.

In the 1980s there was no lack of evidence that racism and racial stereotypes persist in the United States. In 1981 a young black man was hanged by members of the Ku Klux Klan in Mobile, Alabama. The purpose of the killing was to enhance the status of the Klan; the murderers believed they could kill a black in Mobile and go free. (As it turned out, they could not; the killers were convicted, and the victim's mother was awarded $7 million in damages.)

A different kind of racism is often experienced by young upper-class blacks. This type of prejudice is considerably more subtle and more difficult to confront than open bigotry. It may take the form of patronizing comments (e.g., "Blacks are not good swimmers because their bodies are less buoyant than those of whites") or simple lack of awareness (e.g., "I never think of you as black"). Blacks are still pre-

Throughout the world, including the United States, there is an alarming resurgence of groups like the Ku Klux Klan, which advocate policies that would maintain the dominance of one race or ethnic group over others.

vented from renting apartments or buying homes in certain neighborhoods, and racist incidents in high schools and colleges are common. In the words of one young black woman, "The old racism seems . . . ever ready to resurface with a vengeance" (Russell, 1987, p. 2).

Recent research by sociologist Joe R. Feagin (1991) in major metropolitan areas also documents the persistence of discrimination and prejudice directed against middle-class blacks in public places. Feagin's black respondents mentioned case after case of white avoidance of blacks, of rejection or extremely poor service in public establishments, of verbal epithets, public harassment, and other threats. Feagin also found, however, that black citizens are increasingly asserting their rights even in embarrassing social situations and demanding redress and apologies from business owners.

The consequences of prejudice can also be seen in the events following the collapse of communism and the easing of the cold war. In many areas these stunning changes also rekindled nationalist passions. The conflicts among different nationality groups in the former Soviet Union, Bosnia, Czechoslovakia, and other nations reminds us again of the fierce power of ethnic and racial sentiments and their ability to violently disrupt political and economic institutions. In the United States, growing tensions among different groups have also caused outbreaks of violence. The FBI reported in 1990 that crimes motivated by racism and bias against minority groups (including homosexuals and religious groups) were becoming more frequent. And sociologist Jack McDevitt found in analyzing 452 cases of crimes motivated by prejudice that the majority (57 percent) involved issues of "turf defense"; that is, they occurred when people walking or driving or working in a neighborhood were attacked for being different from those living there (cited in Goleman, 1990).

SOCIAL POLICY

In response to the demands of blacks and other minority groups for a more equal share in the benefits of the American way of life, various programs have been instituted to alleviate the effects of prejudice and discrimination. In this section we will examine some of the approaches and goals of these programs and evaluate their effectiveness.

Job Training

During the 1960s and early 1970s there was considerable pressure on the government to provide jobs—to act as the "employer of last resort"—as well as to train workers. Programs were established under the Manpower Training and Development Act, the Vocational Education Act of 1963, the Vocational Rehabilitation Program, the Economic Opportunity Act, and the Comprehensive Employment Training Act of 1973. Each of these legislative efforts was drafted to meet a crisis, without much thought regarding how it would relate to the others. In addition, the programs were underfunded and too small in scale to meet the needs of the unemployed.

These problems became more serious during the Reagan administration. Federal job training programs were either eliminated or reduced. The administration hoped that the private sector would take over most of the government's role and encouraged it to do so through tax incentives and the development of partnerships between private organizations and local governments. Many social scientists, on the other hand, emphasized the need for government-sponsored skills training programs and efforts to increase basic literacy as strategies to reduce welfare dependency (Ellwood, 1988; Wilson, 1987).

When social scientists like David Ellwood and Mary Jo Bane assumed prominent roles in the Department of Health and Human Services, they were in a position to argue more effectively for increased funding of training and work opportunities designed to reduce dependence on welfare. The lingering economic recession of the early 1990s reduced revenue from taxes, however, and as a result the ability of government at any level to fund such programs remained quite limited. At the same time, major U.S. corporations were "downsizing," or eliminating as many jobs as possible in order to increase their profitability. This tends to create situations in which more qualified workers compete with less well-trained or experienced ones for a limited number of jobs. Members of minority groups, especially blacks and Puerto Ricans, Mexicans in some states, and Native Americans—all groups that have experienced discrimination in the past—suffer the most severe consequences of these changes. Since welfare reform on a significant scale is dependent on the availability of jobs for people attempting to make the transition from welfare to work, it is difficult to imagine how "workfare" programs can succeed without an improvement in overall economic conditions.

Recent setbacks cannot erase the positive contributions of the programs that were in effect until the early 1980s. Besides those who received job training and secured higher-paying jobs, many people improved their skills in other ways. Some entered counseling programs and went to school and hence were able to keep their jobs; others qualified for high school equivalency diplomas, thereby improving their chances of finding employment.

Affirmative Action

To a large extent, any chance of redressing past institutional discrimination lies in Title VII of the 1964 Civil Rights Act and amendments to that act. This body of federal law, which established the concept of *affirmative action,* prohibits discrimination on the basis of race, color, religion, sex, or national origin in such areas as employment, education, and housing. Institutions that are shown to have engaged in discriminatory practices are required to increase opportunities for women and members of minority groups in a systematic fashion.

The Equal Employment Opportunity Commission (EEOC) was created under Title VII to equalize hiring, compensation, and promotion opportunities in the labor force. The commission attempts to influence businesses to formulate goals (not quotas) for hiring, compensation, and promotion. It also has the power to sue employers, unions, employment agencies, and others through class action lawsuits on behalf of victims of job discrimination.

The power of the EEOC was enhanced in the early 1970s by a series of court decisions that increased its jurisdiction. In *Griggs* v. *Duke Power Company* (1971) the Supreme Court ruled that Title VII "proscribes not only overt discrimination but also practices that are fair in form, but discriminatory in operation." No longer could a company administer preemployment tests that were not job related if their effect was to exclude blacks and other minority group members. In the landmark case of *Robinson* v. *Lorillard Company* (1971), the Court established the precedent of awarding large monetary settlements to those involved in class action discrimination cases.

The affirmative-action mandate of Title VII is also carried out by the Office of Federal Contract Compliance (OFCC), which was created in 1965. The OFCC has the power to cancel, terminate, or suspend government contracts held by companies that practice discrimination and to prohibit them from participating in future government contracts.

The government's affirmative-action mandate applies not only to business and industry but also to educational institutions. In an effort to enable members of minority groups to receive the same educational opportunities as whites, the federal government required schools to establish goals for minority enrollment and, in some cases, set quotas specifying the number of minority students to be admitted each year. These policies met with considerable opposition. Critics, charging that affirmative action is reverse discrimination, focused on the Supreme Court case of Alan Bakke, a white student who was refused admission to the University of California at Davis Medical School even though his grades were higher than those of many black students who were admitted under an affirmative-action program.

The fight against the medical school's program was led by Jewish organizations, which viewed quota systems as a threat to the advancement of Jews in American society. Emphasis on educational achievement had caused the relatively small Jewish population to be overrepresented at institutions of higher education. Many Jews feared that quotas like the one faced by Bakke would limit their access to colleges and universities to roughly the same small proportion as their numbers in the general population.

Those who support affirmative action cite a major difference between discriminatory quotas and affirmative-action policies designed to extend the opportunities available to victims of past discrimination. Describing affirmative action as a societal

More than any other institution in the United States, the military has been successful in developing and carrying out policies of racial and gender integration.

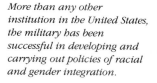

commitment to bringing blacks and other minority groups to a position of equality in the professions, they adamantly deny charges of reverse discrimination. The few whites who lose the opportunity to attend professional schools because of affirmative-action programs are, they argue, victims not of racism but of an effort to eradicate racism from the college and university environment (Steinberg, 1981).

The Supreme Court's decision in the Bakke case straddled these opposing points of view. The medical school's system was struck down, but the Court did not extend its ruling to all preferential admission systems. It held that race could be considered in the admissions process "to advance the diversity of the entering class or to remedy the condition of specific persons who had been discriminated against by the school using the racial instrument" (C. Cohen, 1979, p. 41). In 1984, however, the Court handed down a decision that appeared to be a setback for affirmative action. In *Firefighters Local Union No. 1784* v. *Stotts* it ruled that a seniority system that would cause newly hired black workers to be laid off before white workers who had been employed longer must be allowed to control layoffs because there was no evidence of intent to discriminate against black workers.

Despite the challenges to affirmative action in the 1980s, legislation against racial discrimination remains in force. Indeed, in 1986 the scope of that legislation was expanded in a significant Supreme Court decision: The Court ruled unanimously that Arabs, Jews, and members of other ethnic groups may sue under a post-Civil War law prohibiting discrimination.

Education for Equality

Efforts to achieve greater racial equality in education have focused on two basic policy tools: busing and preschool programs.

Busing   Earlier in the chapter we noted the evidence that busing can succeed if it is carefully planned and carried out. Despite this evidence, the Justice Department has attempted to reduce or eliminate busing plans in some communities. Its views are based on opinion polls that show widespread opposition to busing among Americans who have had little personal experience with racially focused busing. In contrast, a Harris poll of parents whose children had actually been bused for purposes of racial desegregation found that 54 percent believed that the busing experience had been very satisfactory; 33 percent said that it had been partially satisfactory, and only 11 percent said that it had not been satisfactory (cited in Daniels, 1983).

Perhaps the best way to make busing effective would be to bus children from town or city schools to higher-quality suburban schools. Not only would disadvantaged minority children obtain the best possible education, but white flight would no longer be possible. However, in 1974 the Supreme Court ruled in a Detroit case that although the Constitution requires desegregation within a city, it does not require it between city and suburban schools, which are usually in different counties. (In fact, where city and suburban schools are combined in a single county system— as in Charlotte, North Carolina, and Nashville, Tennessee—well-to-do whites could not leave the school system and busing has been successful.)

Research by Gary Orfield (1982) has shown that severe segregation occurs in a relatively small number of states, and often in only one metropolitan area within a state. Yet those are the states with the largest proportions of minority children. There the question arises of how to achieve desegregation in school systems that are predominantly black and Hispanic. According to Orfield, "voluntary" desegregation programs are ineffective. An alternative is the so-called Atlanta Compromise. This arrangement, favored by blacks in that city, involved giving blacks control over the city's school board if they would agree not to pursue a metropolitan-wide desegregation case through the courts. Supporters of this plan claim that once blacks have the authority to address the educational needs of black children, desegregation becomes unnecessary. Such arrangements have failed to win support in other cities, however.

The Impact of Housing Segregation In an influential study titled *American Apartheid*, sociologists Douglas Massey and Nancy Denton (1992) demonstrate that native-born blacks are (and have always been) far more segregated than any other racial or ethnic group in the United States. Persistent patterns of housing discrimination, documented in careful studies by the federal government during the 1980s, show that real estate agents, banks, local governments, and even the federal government have engaged in a variety of discriminatory housing practices or have failed to enforce legislation designed to guarantee freedom of choice in housing decisions. The extremely high rates of racial segregation in U.S. communities are reflected in increasing segregation in public schools (Celis, 1993).

A study released in late 1993 by researchers at the Harvard School of Education (including Gary Orfield) confirms what many observers feared: The lack of vigorous enforcement of antidiscrimination legislation and the increasing segregation of blacks and some Hispanic groups in U.S. cities have resulted in a reversal of the twenty-year trend toward decreasing school segregation (cited in Celis, 1993). These dramatic findings, portrayed in graphic form in Figure 9–2, are likely to stimulate renewed efforts to develop policies to promote desegregation. While few groups wish to resort to busing plans, it is likely that in many cities there will be renewed attempts to bus children to achieve racial integration. (See Box 9–1.) In addition, an increasing number of state courts will hear lawsuits challenging school funding formulas that favor segregated, suburban school districts over districts with higher concentrations of poor, minority residents. At this writing, such suits are pending in more than twenty-five states.

Head Start Recognition of the problems of segregated and unequal schooling is also likely to spur efforts to increase funding for preschool programs. Such programs address the needs of children in communities where segregation and discrimination have produced persistently high rates of school failure. *Head Start* is a blanket term that refers to federally funded preschool programs aimed at preparing disadvan-

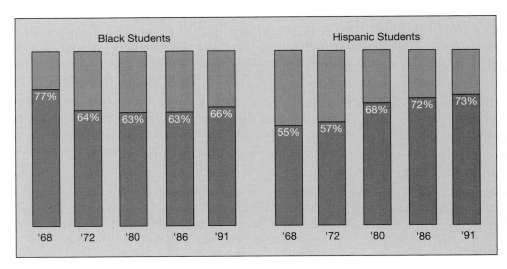

FIGURE 9–2 Percentage of Black and Hispanic Students in Predominantly Minority Schools, 1968–1991

Source: Data from Harvard University School of Education.

BOX 9–1   CURRENT CONTROVERSIES: BUSING

The busing controversy may be on the wane, but it is far from over. Evidence that busing remains a thorny social policy issue is the Supreme Court's 1991 decision to permit the Oklahoma City schools to cease busing children to meet the requirements of a 1972 desegregation order. The Court's ruling, by a vote of 5 to 3, reversed a 1989 decision by a lower federal court to continue requiring the Oklahoma City schools to bus children from segregated schools. The Court ruled that formerly segregated schools may be released from earlier busing orders once they have taken "all practicable steps" to eliminate segregation.

The Court's decision recognizes that schools that comply with desegregation orders may in fact become resegregated. As long as this renewed segregation is due to changing housing patterns rather than to "vestiges of the era of school segregation," remedies such as busing need not remain in effect. The Court did not fully define what it meant by "practicable steps" or "vestiges of . . . school segregation." This ambiguity ensures that lower courts in communities where busing is in effect will continue to hear new challenges to desegregation orders.

In the mid-1980s Oklahoma City stopped busing children in the first through fourth grades. Since that time, a number of schools had become resegregated, and desegregation advocates were demanding the resumption of busing in those grades. Although the original desegregation order was still in effect and would have required busing, the Board of Education argued that the renewed segregation was largely a result of residential segregation, which is due primarily to income differences and personal preferences beyond the control of the school system.

Advocates of desegregation claim that without busing or other measures to move children in segregated neighborhood schools to unsegregated schools, it is difficult to bring about educational integration. For example, in Louisville, Kentucky, where a busing order was in effect for many years, many black parents moved into formerly segregated white neighborhoods to avoid busing. The fear is that without the influence of mandated busing, there will be less pressure to overcome prejudice and discrimination in housing markets, which lead to segregated neighborhoods and, hence, to segregated elementary schools.

Opponents of busing point to cities like Boston and Chicago, where busing orders seem to have stimulated a flight of white residents from the city to avoid busing and mandatory school integration. One reason the Louisville plan worked so well is that the county school system includes suburban areas, so there are fewer communities that can receive families trying to escape desegregation, a situation that did not apply in Chicago and Boston. But whatever local decisions are made as a result of the Court's recent ruling, it is clear that education in desegregated schools is beneficial to minority children later in their lives. Clearly, desegregation through busing or other means (such as the creation of "magnet schools" that draw students from diverse communities) will remain a goal of proponents of equality of opportunity. It will also remain a sore point for those who must live with busing or other desegregation plans (Wells, 1991).

taged children for school. They are quite popular among parents, administrators, and education activists.

At its inception in the 1960s and during its early years, Head Start was a showcase program. Early studies found improvements of 8 to 10 points in the IQs of 480 children in a Head Start program conducted in Baltimore in the summer of 1965 (Levitan, 1968). These immediate, measurable gains in cognitive achievement heralded an enormous expansion of Head Start operations and a push for year-long programs throughout the country. From small beginnings, Head Start grew until it cost several hundred million dollars a year, served approximately 400,000 children, and was widely supported.

The initial goals of Head Start and its early popularity obscured some basic flaws. For one thing, although the concept of early intervention was popular among researchers on child development, and their research did in fact suggest that there is real potential for intellectual improvement through early-childhood training, there

Project Head Start, a preschool enrichment program for disadvantaged children, was begun in the 1960s. Recent evaluations of the achievements of children from some Head Start programs indicate that such programs have lasting beneficial effects that more than justify the expense of the programs.

remain few unchallenged guidelines regarding exactly what is to be taught, how, when, and by whom. It is also argued that Head Start does too little, too late, to be effective. According to this view, the most important period for a child's emotional, social, and intellectual development is the first three years of life, when the child begins to acquire language and learns to manipulate his or her surroundings. Parents, not teachers, therefore are the most important educators, and for intervention to be effective, it must begin during infancy in the child's own home. (These issues are discussed further in Chapter 13.)

Although funds for Head Start were not cut during the 1980s, when many other social programs were scaled back, funding has not been sufficient either to expand the programs or to train and adequately compensate needed personnel. In consequence, of the 2.5 million poor preschool-age children in the United States, only one in five is currently enrolled in Head Start or an equivalent high-quality preschool program. Although an increasing proportion of high-income parents are sending their children to the best preschool programs they can find and afford, low-income parents, whose children are most in need of such programs, are finding them unavailable or fully enrolled. To meet the pressing need for more openings for low-income minority children, foundations and child advocacy groups are demanding large-scale expansion of Head Start programs. The Ford Foundation estimates that Head Start currently costs about $2,400 per year per child and that serving even half of those eligible would cost about $2 billion per year—not an exorbitant sum but one that is likely to be difficult to obtain in a time of decreasing federal revenues and severe budget constraints (Ford Foundation, 1989).

Some Trends and Prospects

What lies ahead for minority groups? Most experts agree that the 1990s will be a decade of struggle for minorities as they try to hold on to past gains in the face of increased racism in American society (as evidenced, for example, in outbreaks of racial violence in Miami and New York or in the problems experienced by Vietnamese immigrants in the Southwest). It will be a decade marked by changing government policies that may have far-reaching implications for minorities, and by upheavals in the leadership of minority institutions themselves.

The Clinton administration is attempting to restore the traditional role of the federal government as initiator and enforcer of programs to guarantee minority rights. Members of the administration believe that the gains made in equal employment opportunity, union organization and representation, voting rights, bilingual education, and Native American affairs were all in jeopardy as government looked to business and to local community groups to correct the problems of poverty and discrimination.

Today minority groups find it difficult, if not impossible, to maintain the foothold they have gained in the job market through affirmative action and equal employment opportunity programs. Government jobs, which make up a sizable portion of minority employment opportunities, are becoming less numerous. When the federal government eliminates functions and departments, the number of blacks and Hispanics with secure public-sector jobs decreases markedly.

The minority employment picture is even more dismal in the private sector. Even when government regulatory commissions are fully funded, discrimination in hiring and employment is more difficult to uncover and correct in the private sector than in the public sector. With only partial funding and a relaxation of regulation and enforcement, it becomes even harder to combat discrimination—the more so as competition among racial groups increases at the lower end of the labor market.

The gains that minority groups have made in union organization and representation are also on shaky ground. Employers are under less pressure to maintain fair labor practices and allow union representation. The United Farm Workers Union (UFW), for example, has found that its very existence is threatened. Made up of Mexican Americans as well as other minority group members, during the 1970s the UFW led the fight for decent pay and working conditions for migrant farm workers. Today they must compete with the Teamsters Union, which is trying to capture union control in the big agricultural valleys of California.

There is also renewed controversy over the efficacy of bilingual education programs. Designed to bridge the cultural gap that Spanish-speaking children experience in English-speaking schools as well as to facilitate learning, bilingual education programs have been sponsored both by the federal Department of Education and by various state departments of education. At present such programs are in danger of being curtailed, if not entirely eliminated.

Native Americans fare no better than members of other minority groups in the areas of education and health care. Operating under a severely restricted budget, the Bureau of Indian Affairs can no longer provide adequate social-welfare services to the thousands of Native Americans who live on reservations. Native Americans also face serious divisions within their own tribes as opposing factions struggle over the issue of how mineral rights on their land should be handled.

Although minority group leaders and policy makers must respond to such problems with new policies and tactics, they will not face a struggle at every turn. Some federal programs in the area of local economic development offer worthwhile opportunities to members of minority groups. By working with the government to develop a range of government-encouraged local business activities, talented black leaders like Franklin Thomas, president of the Ford Foundation, may be taking the most adaptive approach to meeting the chronic needs of all minority groups.

SUMMARY

1. The United States has a long history of inequality. Although much progress has been made toward legal equality as a result of the civil rights movement, inequality remains a significant problem in American society.

2. Racial minorities are made up of people who share certain inherited characteristics. Ethnic minorities consist of people who may share certain cultural features and who regard themselves as a unified group. The principal characteristic of any minority group is subordinate status in society.

3. Discrimination is the differential treatment of individuals on the basis of their perceived membership in a particular social group. It is overt behavior. People rationalize it on the ground that those against whom they discriminate are less worthy of respect or fair treatment than people like themselves. This reasoning results in prejudice against the subordinate group.

4. Prejudice and discrimination have several sources. Among these are individual psychological factors, including frustration–aggression (which involves displacing anger onto a scapegoat) and projection (in which people attribute their own undesirable traits to others). Other factors include social structure (especially economic competition and exploitation) and the norms and stereotypes of a particular culture.

5. Institutional discrimination is discrimination that is built into the structure and form of society itself. In the United States this kind of discrimination is especially evident in the educational system. Here the most prominent issue is school desegregation. Attempts to integrate schools by means of busing have had limited success, partly because of "white flight" to other communities.

6. Another area in which institutional discrimination is evident is housing. Housing segregation is widespread, with the clearest division being between whites in the suburbs and blacks and other minority groups in the cities. Among the causes of housing segregation are federal housing policies and racial steering by real estate agents.

7. Discrimination is also prevalent in employment, often as a direct result of discrimination in education.

Those who lack education are often underemployed or unemployed, which results in low incomes and the likelihood of a poor education for the next generation. Even when their educational levels are similar, however, blacks and members of other minority groups are often paid less than whites.

8. Members of minority groups are more likely than whites to be arrested and charged with a crime. Following arrest, they face discrimination under the bail system, in which those who lack the money to post bail must wait in jail for their cases to come to trial.

9. Prejudice and discrimination have a number of harmful consequences. Among the most destructive is lack of self-esteem among those who are discriminated against. Other reactions are separatism and protest, sometimes leading to riots. There are many indications that racism and racial stereotypes persist, including acts of violence directed against blacks as well as more subtle forms of racism such as patronizing remarks.

10. The gains made by minority groups since the 1960s face major challenges in the 1990s. Affirmative action and equal employment opportunity have been undermined by cutbacks in government funding and hiring. Efforts to increase educational equality through busing and preschool programs have also been criticized, and recent research shows that school segregation has actually increased. Funding for Head Start has not been cut back, but it has not been sufficient either to expand the programs or to train and adequately compensate needed personnel.

SUGGESTED READINGS

FARLEY, REYNOLDS. *Blacks and Whites: Narrowing the Gap?* Cambridge, MA: Harvard University Press, 1984. A thorough and useful demographic analysis of the relative situation of blacks and whites in the United States over the past thirty years.

GLASGOW, DOUGLAS. *The Black Underclass.* San Francisco: Jossey-Bass, 1980. A study of race relations based on comparisons between Watts and numerous other slums.

JAYNES, GERALD DAVID, and ROBIN M. WILLIAMS, JR., EDS. *A Common Destiny: Blacks and American Society.* Washington, DC: National Academy Press, 1989. A thorough analysis of progress toward reversing the legacy of racism and discrimination in the United States, along with a clear discussion of the work

that remains to be done to close the gaps between blacks and whites.

KIM, ILLSOO. *Urban Newcomers: The Koreans.* Princeton, NJ: Princeton University Press, 1983. A fine study of the Korean immigrants in a large American city and their experience in the American economy, as well as their encounters with blacks and other minority groups.

LIEBERSON, STANLEY. *A Piece of the Pie: Blacks and White Immigrants Since 1880.* Berkeley: University of California Press, 1980. This analysis of occupational and residential mobility compares the experience of blacks in America with that of the European white ethnic groups that arrived in great numbers in the early decades of the twentieth century.

MOORE, JOAN, and HARRY PACHON. *Hispanics in the United States*. Englewood Cliffs, NJ: Prentice Hall, 1985. A useful overview of the history of Hispanic people in the United States; details the growth of this population in the twentieth century.

MYRDAL, GUNNAR. *The American Dilemma*. New York: HarperCollins, 1962. A pioneering analysis of American race relations by a Swedish economist and sociologist.

PETTIGREW, THOMAS F., ED. *The Sociology of Race Relations: Reflection and Reform*. New York: Free Press, 1980. A collection of articles about the problem of race relations written at various times from 1895 to the present.

RAINWATER, LEE. *Behind Ghetto Walls: Black Families in a Federal Slum*. Hawthorne, NY: Aldine, 1970. Firsthand accounts of the effects of poverty and racism.

SANDEFUR, GARY D., and MARTA TIENDA, EDS. *Divided Opportunities: Minorities, Poverty, and Social Policy*. New York: Plenum Press, 1988. Excellent comparative data on inequality in American minority groups.

WILSON, WILLIAM J. *The Declining Significance of Race: Blacks and Changing American Institutions*. Chicago: University of Chicago Press, 1978. An influential monograph that analyzes the relationship between class and race, especially in the light of the dual labor market in the United States.

Sex Roles and Inequality

Chapter Outline

- In 1992 the average earnings of women who worked full time were about 75 percent of those of men.
- Women are three times as likely as men to have had interruptions in their work history due to childbearing, child care, illness, disability, and unemployment.
- In school reading books, male central characters are five times as common as female ones.
- In one study, half of the respondents reported that they had been victims of physical harassment on the job.
- Jobs held mainly by women are paid at rates that average 20 percent less than those for equivalent jobs held mainly by men.

In 1990, as American troops and their Arab and European allies prepared for war in the Middle East, the American public was shocked to learn that women in Saudi Arabia are not allowed to drive automobiles. How, Americans asked, could something as basic as the right to move from one place to another by car be denied to half the citizens of a society? The presence of American women soldiers in Saudi Arabia also underlined the deep cultural differences between the two societies.

Few Americans can readily understand how religious beliefs could prevent women from demanding the basic right of mobility. It is no easier for us to accept the norms of Islamic cultures than it is for people of those cultures to accept our ideals of equality and individualism. After all, the idea of gender equality is still fought over in our own society. Many of the gains made by American women in this century came only after a long struggle. And current controversies over date rape, sex-

Carol Moseley Braun, U.S. senator from Illinois, is the only African-American senator and one of the few women in the Senate.

TABLE 10-1 MEDIAN WEEKLY EARNINGS OF FULL-TIME WAGE AND SALARY WORKERS, 1992

OCCUPATION	MEN	WOMEN
Managerial and professional	$777	$562
Technical and sales	519	365
Service occupations	330	248
Precision production	503	336
Operators, laborers	393	279
Farming, forestry, fishing	269	223

Source: Statistical Abstract, 1993.

ual harassment, comparable worth, and wage inequality indicate that gender issues remain a source of vexing social problems in our society.

Over the past several decades women have made many notable gains. They are increasingly entering occupations that were traditionally dominated by men—33.5 percent of mathematical and computer scientists are women, for example, as are 21.4 percent of lawyers and judges. Moreover, the gap between the earnings of men and women is narrowing. In 1992 the median earnings of women who worked full time were about 75 percent of those of men, compared to 66 percent in 1983 (*Statistical Abstract,* 1993). The remaining difference can be explained largely by differences in education and work experiences. A significant obstacle to income equality is the fact that women are three times as likely as men to have had interruptions in their work history owing to childbearing, child care, illness, disability, and unemployment (U.S. Census Bureau, 1987).

Despite the gains of recent decades, sex discrimination and stereotyping continue to limit the opportunities of women. Women are still shunted into the "girl's ghetto": housekeeping; retail trades; insurance; real estate; and service positions such as secretary, receptionist, telephone operator, and clerk. About 59 percent of the working women in the United States are employed in these kinds of jobs (*Time,* December 4, 1989). There were only 6 female senators and 47 female representatives in the U.S. Congress in 1994; and only about 20 percent of state legislators are women. Even when women are in the same professions or occupations as men, their salaries are lower; subtle and persistent discrimination in employment and salaries is still widespread. (Table 10–1 shows the wage gap for selected occupations.)

In the 1970s and early 1980s efforts to combat these inequalities centered on obtaining ratification of the Equal Rights Amendment to the U.S. Constitution. However, by the June 30, 1982, deadline for ratification only thirty-five of the required thirty-eight states had ratified the amendment. The amendment was reintroduced in Congress in 1983, but in the House of Representatives it fell six votes short of the two-thirds majority needed to send it to the states for ratification. Thus, women do not yet have legal assurance of equal rights in American society.

TRADITIONAL SEX ROLES

In Chapter 9 we suggested that prejudice—a predisposition to regard a certain group in a certain way—often becomes the justification for discriminatory behavior. That is, if we believe that a certain group is "inferior" or "different," we can easily defend

The chador, *the traditional dress worn by many Muslim women, is a feature of orthodox Islamic culture that often conflicts with women's desire for greater equality in their society.*

the treatment of members of that group as less than equal. We also suggested that the norms of society are an important source of prejudice and discrimination. If an entire society is prejudiced against a certain group and discriminates against it, such prejudice and discrimination will be accepted as natural and right by most members of that society.

Until fairly recently it was widely accepted that the only desirable roles for a woman were those of wife, mother, and homemaker and that a woman's entire life should revolve around these roles. The roles themselves emphasized that a woman should be nurturing and skilled in the emotional aspects of personal relationships. A man, on the other hand, was expected to be a leader and provider, a highly rational person who would not let emotions get in the way of action. These expectations often caused men to deny their emotions and thus made them less able to enjoy many aspects of life in their families and communities.

Betty Friedan (1963) was among the first contemporary feminists to identify and criticize the traditional view of female roles, which she labeled "the feminine mystique":

> *The feminine mystique says that the highest value and the only commitment for women is the fulfillment of their own femininity. It says that the great mistake of Western culture, through most of its history, has been the undervaluation of this femininity. It says this femininity is so mysterious and intuitive and close to the creation and origin of life that man-made science may never be able to understand it. But however special and different, it is in no way inferior to the nature of man; it may even in certain respects be superior. The mistake, says the mystique, the root of women's troubles in the past, is that women envied men, women tried to be like men, instead of accepting their own nature, which can find fulfillment only in sexual passivity, male domination, and nurturing maternal love. . . . The new mystique makes the housewife-mothers, who never had a chance to be anything else, the model for all women . . . a pattern by which all women must now live or deny their femininity. (p. 43)*

So pervasive was this view, and so thoroughly internalized by both men and women, that Friedan called the dissatisfaction of women with their traditional roles "the problem that has no name."

Today many people think of the traditional roles of women and men as somewhat outdated. At the time that Friedan wrote her book, the traditional roles formed the basis for social behavior. Women were considered too delicate to do "men's work" and therefore were legally denied many career and job opportunities. Men were supposed to "act like a man," to be dominant and unemotional. For women, chastity and fidelity were considered major virtues; for men, promiscuity was considered natural. Women and men were thought to be different and hence were treated differently by social institutions—including the govenment and the legal system. The entire range of social norms and values reflected different standards of behavior for men and women. Few people questioned those standards.

This double standard of behavior is not unique to our society. In many Latin American and Muslim countries, the status of women is far more subordinate than in our own. Few women in those societies have the freedom that men have or are able to pursue careers outside the home. And although women in Eastern European countries have greater equality with men, disparities exist in those countries as well. For example, most of the physicians in the Soviet Union are women, but female physicians receive lower pay than male physicians.

This traditional hierarchy is extremely resistant to change. Women and men are shaped by the culture in which they are raised, so that most adults are thoroughly indoctrinated or socialized for the roles their culture has prescribed for them. Change is suspect because it threatens their identity. Thus, many women oppose attempts to give them equal status with men. It was a women's organization—Stop-ERA, led by Phyllis Schlafly—that led the battle to prevent ratification of the Equal Rights Amendment.

It seems clear that there is considerable variation in the types of behavior that are considered appropriate for men and for women and that to a large extent these behaviors reflect the values of a particular society more than any innate or "natural" qualities. Whereas it was once supposed that behavioral differences between men and women are innate, today we know that these diffeences are largely learned as individuals are socialized into their culture. And although it was once believed that there are universal standards of masculine and feminine behavior, in fact other societies have standards for such behavior that are very different from our own (Richmond-Abbott, 1992).

In the 1950s sex researcher John Money and his colleagues found that the best predictor of a person's sexual identity is not his or her physiological sex but the sex he or she was assigned at birth. Specifically, male children who had been incorrectly identified as female and raised as females, or female children who had been raised as males, identified themselves as members of the other sex even after their true physical sex became known to them (Money et al., 1955). For reasons such as this, many researchers use the term *gender identity* to refer to a person's sexual self-image and to distinguish it from physiological sex.

Several studies have demonstrated how boys and girls in our society are socialized into traditional sex roles. Lisa Serbin and Daniel O'Leary (1975), for example, found that nursery school teachers respond much more to boys' behavior than to girls', tending to reinforce aggression among boys and passivity among girls. Ruth Hartley (1974) found that small boys are taught by their fathers and male peers that they should not be "sissies" and that girls are weak and unimportant. When women are not socialized into a conventional pattern, their behaviors begin to resemble those of men. One need only think of Florence Joyner, or the women who have beaten men in the 1,200-mile Alaskan dog sled race. Women today are far stronger and more athletic than their counterparts of earlier decades and are meeting male standards of physical performance. This suggests that even a woman's "weakness" is largely a reflection of traditional social expectations.

More recent research has placed renewed emphasis on the role of biological factors in determining sex roles. Thus, Alice Rossi (1984) argues that "gender differentiation is not simply a function of socialization. . . . It is grounded in a sex dimorphism that serves the fundamental purpose of reproducing the species. . . . Theories that neglect these characteristics of sex and gender carry a high risk of eventual irrelevance" (p. 1). Rossi considers the biological differences between the sexes to be a major source of "masculine" and "feminine" traits, but she writes that "masculine qualities and feminine qualities do not preclude each other in the same person, although that combination is still not prevalent in American society" (p. 14).

Jan Morris, a respected British author and social commentator who was one of the first people to undergo a sex-change operation, offers the following insight:

> We are told that the social gap between the sexes is narrowing, but I can only report that having, in the second half of the 20th century, experienced life in both roles, there seems to be no aspect of existence, no moment of the day, no contact, no arrangement, no response, which is not different for men and women. . . . I discovered that even now men prefer women to be less able, less talkative, and certainly less self-centered than they are themselves. (quoted in Bleier, 1984, p. 80)

Morris's description of her experience is an apt illustration of the phenomenon that has come to be known as sexism.

THE NATURE OF SEXISM

Sexism is the counterpart of racism and ageism, which are discussed in Chapters 9 and 11, respectively. It may be defined as the "entire range of attitudes, beliefs, policies, laws, and behaviors discriminating against women (or against men) on the basis of their gender" (Safilios-Rothschild, 1974, p. 1). In this section we will describe some of the attitudes and practices that are a part of sexism in our society.

Stereotyping

As we saw in Chapter 9, one source of prejudice and discrimination is stereotyping—attributing a fixed and usually unfavorable and inaccurate conception to a category of people. Stereotypes often make it easier to justify unequal treatment of the stereotyped person or group.

Among the traditional stereotypes about women is the belief that they are naturally passive, domestic, and envious. It is this set of stereotypes that Friedan lumped together and labeled "the feminine mystique." However, Marc Fasteau (1974) has pointed out that there is a "masculine mystique" as well—a set of stereotypes about men that limits their ability to function fully and effectively. The masculine stereotype is that all men are tough, unemotional, and dominant; and however unrealistic and inaccurate this stereotype is, many men (and women) believe it. Many men avoid performing traditionally "female" tasks, such as washing dishes or working as a secretary, for fear that their masculinity will be questioned. And men who might prefer the role of homemaker feel compelled to seek careers in business because they have been socialized to believe that domestic work is not masculine.

Not only does the masculine stereotype limit the freedom of men to engage in any activity or occupation they choose, it also limits their personal relationships. Many men believe that they cannot discuss their feelings with other men. Instead, they tend to be extremely competitive toward other men. They also feel compelled to try to dominate women instead of relating to them as equals (Bem, 1975; Benokraitis & Feagin, 1986; Gould, 1974). (See Chapter 6 for a discussion of the effects of male socialization on crime patterns.)

This scene of pinups decorating the walls of a barbershop illustrates a common form of male stereotyping of women. Are women justified in being offended by such scenes? Are men who claim not to enjoy pinups merely being "politically correct"?

One of the unfortunate effects of stereotypes is that even people who are victimized by them tend to believe that they are true. Thus, many women share attitudes that are prejudicial to women; this causes them to undervalue the work of other women and sets up psychological barriers to their own achievement. Goldberg (1972), for example, found that women value professional work that they think was done by a man more highly than they value the same work if they think it was done by a woman. This holds true even if the professional field has traditionally been reserved for women, as nursing once was. Matina Horner (1970) found that many women were motivated to avoid success, fearing that the more ambitious and successful they became, the less feminine they would be.

More recent data indicate that these attitudes are changing. Aghop Der-Karabetian and Anthony Smith (1977) noted that "women have become more accepting of feminine characteristics not previously considered desirable" (p. 197), implying that women are beginning to view their supposed weaknesses as strengths. In another study, Daniel Bar-Tal and Irene Frieze (1977) suggested that the level of success orientation is related more to one's belief in one's own ability than to lack of motivation based on gender.

The stereotypic notions held by men probably create a greater impediment to equality, however, since men still hold most positions of authority in American society. One survey of 1,500 managers (almost all male) showed that in making personnel decisions managers unconsciously rely on traditional stereotypes about men and women. Thus, managers are much more supportive of men than of women, assuming that men will give their careers top priority whereas women, according to the stereotype, give top priority to their family responsibilities. Managers try harder to retain male employees than they do to retain female employees, and they promote the advancement of men more than that of women. After analyzing these data, the authors of the survey concluded that even a slight managerial bias against women could be translated into a great many unintentional discriminatory acts affecting thousands of career women. The result would be "great personal damage for individuals and costly underutilization of human resources" (Rosen & Jerdee, 1974, p. 58).

In her study of gender and sex roles, sociologist Cynthia Epstein (1988) found that there have been many positive changes in corporations and the professions but that inadvertent and at times open hostility toward women remains a problem in many organizations. The continuing presence of sexism is revealed by the fact that white males still hold about 95 percent of the top management jobs in major corporations (Silver, 1990).

Sexism and Employment

Sexism is perhaps most evident in the employment status of women. Women are concentrated in the lower-status jobs at the low end of the pay scale. The vast majority of retail clerks, typists, and secretaries are women, whereas men account for by far the largest proportions of corporate directors, white-collar administrators, and blue-collar supervisors. It could be claimed that these differences are due to differences in educational attainment. However, as Figure 10–1 shows, this is not the case. For the past several decades men and women have received the same amount of schooling. Although men hold more bachelor's and graduate degrees than women do, more men than women drop out of high school, so that average educational attainment is the same within each group (England & Farkas, 1986; *Statistical Abstract,* 1990).

As mentioned earlier in the chapter, the difference in the average number of years of work experience is a more useful explanation of the income gap between men and women. Various studies (e.g., Corcoran & Duncan, 1979; Mincer & Polachek, 1974; Sandell & Shapiro, 1978) have found that between one-quarter and one-half of the income gap can be accounted for by interruptions in the work histories of women. Corcoran and Duncan (1979) found that the most important factor is the number of years a worker has been with his or her current employer, especially the years during which the employee receives training.

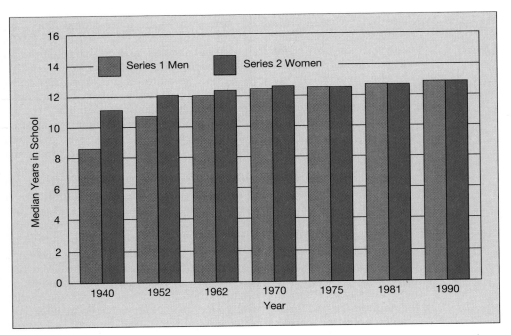

FIGURE 10–1 Median Years of Schooling Completed by Men and Women in the Labor Force

Source: Data from England & Farkas, 1986; *Statistical Abstract,* 1990.

During the 1991 Persian Gulf War women in the armed services demonstrated their ability to perform effectively in combat.

This is not to say that stereotyping does not contribute to the earnings gap. England and associates (1982) studied the income gap from the standpoint of the stereotyping of certain occupations as "male" or "female." Their research showed that "the difference between the median annual earnings of two occupations alike in their skill requirements but one of which is 90 percent female and the other of which is 90 percent male would be $1,360 for women and $2,400 for men." In other words, both men and women suffer wage losses from holding "female" jobs (England & Farkas, 1986). However, because of the far higher percentage of women in such jobs, the net effect is to lower women's earnings relative to men's for reasons other than the skills required for the jobs in question.

This type of pay inequity has given rise to debates over "comparable worth"— the idea that the pay levels of certain jobs should be adjusted so that they reflect the intrinsic value of the job; holders of jobs of comparable value would then be paid at comparable rates. This concept is discussed in more detail in the Social Policy section of the chapter.

Wage and job discrimination are illegal under the Equal Pay Act of 1963 and the Civil Rights Act of 1964, yet they continue to exist. About 3,000 charges of sex discrimination are filed with the Equal Employment Opportunity Commission each year. One way such discrimination works was demonstrated by Levinson (1975) in a study of job inquiries. Levinson selected several classified advertisements in newspapers and defined the jobs advertised as "male" or "female," depending on their present sex composition. Male researchers inquired by telephone about the traditionally female jobs (e.g., secretary), and female researchers inquired about traditionally male jobs (e.g., auto mechanic). Then the procedure was reversed: The researchers of each sex called to inquire about jobs that were considered appropriate for them. Levinson found that in 35 percent of all cases there was clear-cut sex discrimination. Male inquirers for a secretarial job, for example, were told that the job had been filled, whereas subsequent female callers were encouraged to apply. Sometimes the discrimination was more blunt. For example, women callers were

TABLE 10–2 PAY OF WOMEN EMPLOYED FULL TIME, YEAR ROUND AS A PERCENTAGE OF PAY OF MEN FOR SELECTED YEARS

YEAR	WOMEN'S EARNINGS AS A PECENTAGE OF MEN'S
1956	63.3
1960	60.7
1964	59.1
1968	58.5
1972	57.4
1976	60.0
1980	60.5
1983	64.3
1985	65.0
1988	67.8
1990	71.8
1992	75.4

Source: England & Farkas, 1986; updated with data from *Statistical Abstract,* 1993.

told that "we don't hire girls as fuel attendants." Frequently male inquirers for "sex-inappropriate" jobs were encouraged to apply for higher-level management positions, whereas female callers were told to apply for lower-level jobs. Clearly, sex typing of jobs is a major part of sex discrimination.

In sum, there is a significant earnings gap between men and women in the American labor force. This is evident in Table 10–2, which shows women's earnings as a percentage of men's. It can also be seen in Table 10–3, which compares indicators of gender inequality in the United States and selected European nations. Al-

TABLE 10–3 SELECTED INDICATORS OF GENDER INEQUALITY: AUSTRIA, WEST GERMANY, GREAT BRITAIN, AND THE UNITED STATES

INDICATOR	AUSTRIA	WEST GERMANY	GREAT BRITAIN	UNITED STATES
Percent women employed	47.8	49.4	49.9	66.0
Percent women employed full time	35.1	35.0	29.7	49.8
Percent married women employed	42.0	44.8	46.3	59.9
Percent college students who are female	41.1	41.9	37.3	51.7
Women's annual earnings as percent of men's for full time only	71.5	59.9	64.0	61.9

Source: Davis & Robinson, 1991.

though the United States has significantly higher proportions of women, both single and married, in its labor force and enrolled in higher education, it has not achieved greater income equality than the other nations. In fact, the United States lags behind Austria and Great Britain in efforts to increase wage equality (Davis & Robinson, 1991). Between 1950 and 1980 the sex difference in earnings remained remarkably constant, with women's median earnings about 60 percent of men's. Although the sex gap in pay has decreased since 1980—women's earnings now average about 75 percent of men's—there is still a long way to go before full equality is achieved.

Sexual Harassment

Among the most persistent and difficult aspects of sexism is sexual harassment. The tumultuous Senate hearings on the confirmation of Clarence Thomas as a Supreme Court justice focused national attention on the range of behaviors that may be viewed as forms of sexual harassment. The charges leveled against Thomas by Anita Hill, a former employee, included making lewd and suggestive comments, requesting sexual favors, and similar behaviors that are often labeled "flirtation" when they occur outside the workplace. Partly as a result of the Hill–Thomas controversy, and partly as a consequence of women's continual struggle against harassment, people throughout the nation have been drawn into a national debate over the nature and significance of sexual harassment.

The controversy has focused on serious forms of harassment, including date rape, as well as on behaviors that are viewed as annoying if not dangerous. In 1993, for example, the students and faculty of Antioch College in Ohio published a set of written rules that require verbal consent at every stage of sexual intimacy. Although the rules have been the subject of much satire and derision, they represent a model for dealing with a highly sensitive and often taboo subject.

Such episodes are bringing people closer to a consensus about the norms of conduct between men and women. An increasing number of Americans are recognizing that "one person's joke or offhand comment can be another's hostile environment" (Manley, 1987, p. 145). In an attempt to provide a less subjective description of sexual harassment, the Michigan Task Force on Sexual Harassment developed the following definition:

> [Sexual harassment] includes continual or repeated verbal abuse of a sexual nature, including but not limited to graphic commentaries on the victim's body, sexually suggestive objects or postures in the workplace, sexually degrading words used to describe the victim, or propositions of a sexual nature. Sexual harassment also includes the threat or insinuation that lack of sexual submission will adversely affect the victim's employment, wages, standing, or other conditions that affect the victim's livelihood. (Stover & Gillies, 1987, p. 1)

Although sexual harassment has been a common feature of work and community life for well over a century, the problem came under public scrutiny only recently, as a result of court decisions and governmental attempts to punish offenders. Many thousands of complaints of sexual harassment are filed each year in agencies at all levels of government; of these, less than 10 percent are filed by men (Richmond-Abbott, 1992). The formal complaints represent a small fraction of the incidents of harassment that occur in workplaces, schools, community associations, and public settings (MacKinnon, 1979).

As the Hill–Thomas hearings and the Antioch rules suggest, sexual harassment in all its forms is beginning to be defined as a social problem because an increasing number of women are protesting such behaviors. Leaders of the movement against sexual harassment see these behaviors as a way of maintaining women in subordinate social and economic positions. With increasing frequency they are persuading the courts that the supposedly "innocent" pinup or gesture is in reality a form of demeaning harassment.

The Devaluation of Homemaking

A wide variety of laws and statutes are based on the idea that men are breadwinners and women are dependents. For example, a woman automatically receives social security benefits if her husband dies because it is assumed that she is dependent on his wages. For a man to collect benefits if his wife dies, he must prove that he was financially dependent on her. While this provision of the Social Security Act discriminates against men, it also perpetuates the idea that women are not wage earners. At the end of 1975 the Supreme Court revoked another long-standing statute that discriminated against women: It ruled that pregnant women could receive unemployment benefits during the last three months of pregnancy. Previously, statutes in many states had assumed that unemployed women in the final stage of pregnancy were unable to work and therefore were not entitled to unemployment benefits.

Homemakers, who are still predominantly women, suffer the most severe form of economic discrimination. No federal, state, or private insurance agency takes the economic value of homemaking into account. Thus, homemakers cannot obtain private disability insurance even if their spouses would have to hire help if they were disabled; disability insurance policies are written for those who earn wages. And homemakers cannot be enrolled in the social security system in order to qualify for disability benefits, even if they were to pay the required taxes.

The devaluation of the work of homemakers—whose services are not even included in the gross domestic product—results in a number of other inequities. For example, homemakers do not receive full tax credit for the expenses of running a home, even though businesspeople can write off everything from telephone bills to lunches as business expenses. Homemakers are also ineligible for worker's compensation. Perhaps most important, the monetary undervaluation of the work of homemakers results in the undervaluation of the *role* of homemaker. Indeed, Robert Lekachman (1975) has suggested that redefining the household as an economic unit is a prerequisite for sexual equality. In his view, this would encourage members of both sexes to make rational comparisons between home and outside employment. In addition, liberalization of household-expense deductions would facilitate outside employment for both husband and wife.

In a review of research on changing sex roles and housework, sociologist Janet Z. Giele (1988) observes that studies show that women continue to bear the primary responsibility for child care and housework even if they are employed. In the past twenty years men with working wives have begun to take on a greater share of this burden, but inequalities remain. Time budget studies show that when one measures solo time spent with children, fathers average 4.5 hours a week and mothers 19.6 hours, but that men with working wives who themselves support nontraditional sex roles spend significantly more time with their children than do men who lack such ideals. Researchers have also noted that wealth permits working couples to displace housework and child care responsibilities onto hired domestic helpers, which may ease their burden but also serves to increase inequalities of race and class in their communities.

The Women's Movement

The women's movement in the United States was officially founded in 1848, when a Women's Rights Convention held in Seneca, New York, was attended by 300 women and men, many of whom, like Elizabeth Cady Stanton and Lucretia Mott, were active in the abolitionist movement. The Seneca Convention endorsed a platform calling for the right of women to vote, to control their own property, and to obtain custody of their children after divorce. After women won the right to vote in the 1920s, the women's movement receded from public consciousness until the 1960s, a decade characterized by considerable activism and numerous social movements (Richmond-Abbott, 1992).

The resurgence of the movement in the 1960s occurred in a context of widespread social change. In 1963, the year in which Friedan's *The Feminine Mystique* appeared, the President's Commission on the Status of Women published its recommendations for equal opportunity in employment. In 1964 Congress passed the Civil Rights Act, which included a provision—Title VII—that made it illegal to discriminate against women in promotion and hiring. But the Equal Employment Opportunity Commission, established to enforce Title VII, was unwilling to serve as a watchdog for women's rights. As a result, in 1966 a pressure group, the National Organization for Women (NOW), was founded. NOW's stated purpose was "to take action to bring women into full participation in the mainstream of American society *now,* exercising all the privileges and responsibilities thereof in truly equal partnership with men."

Attitudes about gender roles have undergone a major transformation since the resurgence of the women's movement. Although, as we have seen, significant inequalities and double standards continue to exist, they are far less sharply defined than they were earlier in the century. Survey researchers find, for example, that in the 1930s about 75 percent of all Americans disapproved of a woman earning money if she had a husband who was capable of supporting her. By 1978 that proportion had declined to 26 percent. In 1957 as many as 80 percent of respondents to opinion polls agreed that "For a woman to remain unmarried she must be 'sick,' 'neurotic,' or 'immoral.'" By 1978 the proportion who agreed with this idea had fallen to 25 percent (Yankelovich, 1981). Many of these changes in attitudes were due to the impact of the women's movement and the changing nature of women's economic participation.

During the 1970s women's political participation also increased steadily. The National Women's Political Caucus was founded in 1971; as a result of its efforts, 40 percent of the delegates to the 1972 Democratic political convention were women. Continued lobbying by women's political groups resulted in President Carter's appointment of more women to top positions in the government and judiciary than ever before, and in 1981 President Reagan appointed the first woman to serve on the Supreme Court.

In the late 1970s and early 1980s the women's movement encountered increasing opposition, and its momentum slowed. The Equal Rights Amendment failed to obtain ratification by the required number of states. Opposition to more liberal abortion laws was well organized and vocal, and the movement faced severe challenges in several other areas. Nevertheless, reproductive choice remained a dominant theme of the movement, one that could unite women with diverse interests; this was evident in the massive free-choice rally in Washington in 1988, which drew more than 500,000 marchers. With the election of President Clinton in 1992, the movement gained greater influence in Washington.

SOURCES OF SEXISM

We have described some of the causes of the subordination of women from a historical point of view and indicated some of the major inequities that women face in our society. In this section we will discuss in some detail the processes by which American institutions reinforce and perpetuate sexism.

Socialization

In her book *The Second Sex* (1961) the famous French philosopher and sociologist Simone de Beauvoir described how as children women are often socialized for roles in which they are not expected to compete with men in any way. Often, she observed, this means that women are discouraged from studying more challenging subjects like mathematics, science, and philosophy. Instead, they are expected to learn the domestic skills of cooking and running a household and the emotional skills of soothing children's and men's bruised feelings. These observations signal the immense importance of sex-role socialization in forming our attitudes and behavior as men and women.

Socialization is the process whereby we learn to behave according to the norms of our culture. It includes all the formal and informal teaching that occurs in the home and the school, among peers, and through agents of socialization like radio, television, the church, and other institutions (Kornblum, 1991). As Janet Chafetz (1974) has suggested, through socialization people internalize to varying degrees the roles, norms, and values of their culture and subculture. These norms and values become their guides to behavior and shape their deepest beliefs.

Most socialization takes place in the course of interaction with other people; how others react to what we do will eventually influence how we behave. We are also socialized through popular culture—largely through films and books. Socialization may be consciously imposed, as in compulsory education, or it may be subtle and unconscious, conveyed in the nuances of language. According to Eleanor Maccoby and Carol Jacklin (1977), common myths about sex differences, such as "girls are more suggestible than boys" and "boys are more analytical than girls," reinforce sex-role socialization.

A primary agent of socialization in our culture is the family, especially parents. A number of studies have sought to determine how parents socialize their children into traditional sex roles. Michael Lewis (1972), for example, found that parental influences cause differences in the behavior of boys and girls within the first two years of life:

From the earliest age, girl infants are looked at and talked to more than boy infants. For the first six months or so, boy infants have more physical contact than girl infants, but by

Attorney Leslie Abramson, left, questions a witness during the trial of Erik and Lyle Menendez for the murder of their parents. Part of the socialization required for the role of attorney involves learning to be more assertive. Sociologists have found, however, that assertive women are often faulted for being "unfeminine."

the time they are six months old, this reverses and girls get more physical contact and more non-touching contact. . . . The motive appears to be cultural; mothers believe that boys should be more independent than girls and that they should be encouraged to explore and master their world. (p. 56)

Lewis theorized that this tendency of mothers to talk more to their daughters accounts in part for the greater linguistic skills exhibited by women. The lack of physical contact experienced by boys after the age of six months, Lewis suggested, may account for the fact that they tend to be more independent as adults—and also more restricted in the extent to which they are willing to express their feelings.

Education

Education represents a more formal type of socialization. Considering how much time children spend in school, the socialization they receive there inevitably affects how they behave. Several studies have indicated that, by and large, schools reinforce traditional sex-role stereotypes and socialize children into traditional sex roles.

In recent years much emphasis has been placed on ridding the schools of bias against female achievement and increasing gender equality in education. Greater emphasis on girls' and women's sports and efforts to achieve more equal participation in school political activities, newspapers, and many other areas attest to increased concern for sex-role equality. But some major problems remain. For example, women continue to achieve less well than men in math and science, and far fewer women than men are recruited into the ranks of engineers and scientists. Recent studies of the use of computers in schools and enrollment in computer instruction classes demonstrate that males are far more likely than females to be represented in these programs and that parents and teachers tend to think of these important modern tools as the natural domain of male students (Hawkins, 1987).

A recent study by the American Association of University Women found that girls and boys start school with similar levels of skill and confidence but that by the end of high school girls trail boys in science and math. After reviewing more than 100 articles and reports of research conducted during the past ten years, the authors reached several conclusions:

- Teachers pay less attention to girls than to boys.
- Girls lag in math and science scores, and even those who do well in these subjects tend not to choose careers in math and science.
- Reports of sexual harassment of girls are increasing.
- Textbooks still ignore or stereotype women and girls and omit discussion of pressing problems such as sexual abuse.
- Some tests are biased against females and thereby limit their chances of obtaining scholarships.
- Black girls are particularly likely to be ignored or rebuffed in schools. (AAUW, 1992)

Clearly, continued efforts are needed to address these inequalities of socialization if more women are to be attracted to the sciences.

Even when teachers are informed and well intentioned, other parts of the educational system may stymie attempts to eradicate sexist training. For one thing, many textbooks perpetuate stereotypes, myths, and half-truths. Analyses of reading books used in schools have found that they are populated mainly by male characters and that male central characters are five times as common as female ones (Lobban, 1978; Spender & Sarah, 1980). In addition, the books present a caricature of gender roles in adult life. Boys and men are portrayed as active and courageous, girls and women as nurturant, passive, and timid. Perhaps most significant, girls are offered a highly restricted range of images of adult female roles; even witches and queens are for the most part limited to domestic indoor pursuits, in contrast to the adventurous outdoor pursuits available to men.

An especially insidious form of sex segregation occurs during career counseling, which often channels young people into careers on the basis of sex rather than ability. Counselors frequently advocate traditionally female occupations for young women who are qualified and eager to enter so-called male preserves. A girl who is a good math student may be told to go into teaching; a boy with equal skills may be directed toward engineering. One expert has described this situation as follows:

> *Counselors defend such practices on the basis of what youngsters may "realistically" expect to face in the future: marriage, child care, and a lack of opportunity in a number of career fields for females, and the need to support a family at the highest income and status levels possible for males. "Realism," however, has always been an excuse for maintaining the status quo, and it is no different in the case of sex role stereotypes. If, for instance, females do not prepare to enter previously masculine fields, such fields will remain male-dominated, allowing another generation of counselors to assure girls that females can't work in them. In addition, it is questionable whether counselors' notions of more "reality" in fact keep pace with reality. There is undoubtedly a lag between expanding opportunities and changing sex role definitions on the one hand, and counselors' awareness of these phenomena on the other. (Chafetz, 1974, p. 88)*

The Family

While many women report great satisfaction as mothers and homemakers, the traditional role of homemaker often gives a woman a subordinate status within the home, limits her freedom, and leaves her feeling unfulfilled (Richmond-Abbott, 1992). As Robert Bell (1975) has written, "Women are often caught in a vicious circle because of their economic dependence on their husbands and their lack of contact with the work world; and their being tied down to the house restricts, to a great extent, the kind of decisions over which they can claim expertise and, ultimately, control" (pp. 370–371).

Even in many nontraditional marriages in which there is a great degree of equality between husband and wife, the husband often has a more privileged position. One study found that even when both members of a couple are professionals, the woman often is forced into a somewhat subordinate position because it is assumed that the man's career is more important or more likely to be successful than the woman's. As a result, wives in professional pairs are less likely than their husbands to be satisfied with their careers (Giele, 1988).

Many studies indicate that marriage is generally more satisfying to husbands than to wives, who have to make more concessions. In unhappy marriages, wives tend to feel more frustrated than their husbands: Women seek marriage counseling more often than men do and initiate more divorce proceedings. Even among relatively happy marriages, however, women report higher rates of dissatisfaction and depression than men do, and women must make most of the adjustments to make the marriage work. As Jessie Bernard has written, "Because women have to put so many more eggs in the one basket of marriage they have more of a stake in its stability. Because their happiness is more dependent on men's they have to pay more for it" (1974, p. 149).

The psychological consequences of overidentifying with the domestic role were described by Pauline Bart (1974) in her study of depression in middle-aged women. Bart found that, contrary to popular opinion, women become depressed in middle age not because of hormonal changes associated with menopause but, rather, because they find themselves lacking any important function. She found that the lowest rates of depression occur among middle-aged working women, whose jobs keep them occupied and provide satisfaction. Higher rates of depression were found among homemakers whose children had grown up and left home; with fewer people dependent on their domestic role, their identity suffered. Bart found the highest rates of depression among homemakers who had overinvolved or overprotective relationships with their children. For these women, the departure of their children from the household destroyed both their purpose in life and much of their self-esteem.

Overemphasis on the importance of motherhood causes guilt feelings in women who are unfulfilled by the mother role and undoubtedly contributes to depression in middle age. In addition, emphasis on motherhood devalues the father's role in child rearing. Men who share in homemaking activities tend to be ridiculed or ostracized, especially by other men: "Men may downgrade the efforts of other men to contribute to homemaking and pressure them to spend more time and effort on the job or in the peer group" (Lein, 1979, p. 492). Thus, the myth that a woman is best suited to the task of raising a child prevents many women from exercising their capabilities outside the home and many men from exercising theirs inside the home. The result is a sex-based differentiation that keeps women in a subordinate role and prevents members of both sexes from sharing family and work responsibilities (Rotondo, 1983).

Psychiatric Medicine

Psychologists and psychiatrists, most of whom are male, have long held stereotypical notions about women. In the nineteenth century women were viewed as biologically predisposed to hysteria and insanity; "just being female was a disease" (Bleier, 1984, p. 169). In the twentieth century, Bruno Bettelheim, an authority on family life, has stated that "as much as women want to be good scientists and engineers, they want first and foremost to be womanly companions of men and to be mothers." The late renowned psychologist Erik Erikson claimed that a woman has "an 'inner space' destined to bear the offspring of chosen men, and with it, a biological, psychological, and ethical commitment to take care of human infancy" (quoted in Weisstein, 1974, pp. 364–365).

A major survey of psychotherapists (*American Psychologist,* 1975) found that they tend to foster traditional sex roles and are biased in their evaluations of women patients. Among the biases found in the survey were the following:

1. The therapist lacks awareness and sensitivity to the woman client's career, work, and role diversity.
2. The female client's attitude toward childbearing and child rearing is viewed as a necessary index of her emotional maturity.
3. The therapist defers to the husband's needs in the conduct of the wife's treatment.
4. The therapist . . . fosters concepts of women as passive and dependent.
5. The therapist has a double standard for male and female sexual activities. (pp. 1171–1173)

In the two decades since this study was conducted, the number of female therapists has increased significantly, a trend that can be expected to counteract some of the gender biases just described.

Cynthia Epstein (1988) points out that the emphasis in psychoanalysis and psychotherapy on the importance of early childhood experiences in forming personality and attitudes "may account for much of the resistance to the notion that change may occur in adult years and is not linked to early development" (p. 96). Such an attitude may inhibit even highly educated people from examining the gender biases and prejudices in their own behavior.

Language and the Media

The language used in the media (and in textbooks) often reinforces traditional sex-role stereotypes through overreliance on male terms and a tendency to use stereotypic phrases in describing men and women. The use of male pronouns in referring to neutral subjects—"The typical doctor enjoys his leisure"—also implies that women are excluded from an active social life.

While sexism in everyday language is subtle and unconscious, in advertising it is often blatant. One analysis of commercials for children's programs found that almost all narrators were male, more females than males were involved in domestic activities, ten times as many boys as girls were physically active, and every child shown as economically dependent was a girl (Chafetz, 1974).

According to sociologist Barbara Ehrenreich (1992), the importance of sexist themes in advertising, and the way advertisements capitalize on women's anxieties about their appearance, is revealed by the fact that over the past thirty years 1.6 million women have undergone breast enlargement operations, often with dubious medical results.

Typically, far fewer women than men are portrayed in the media as employed, although more than half of all women work outside the home. Few women are shown in executive positions; instead, they play largely decorative roles. Finally, the vast majority of buying decisions are portrayed as being made by men, particularly decisions involving major purchases such as cars.

Recent advertising campaigns have sought to attract the growing population of female executives by presenting successful businesswomen and female scientists endorsing products. But the patterns of sexism in advertising remain strong: "Sex appeal" and sexual stereotypes are still used to sell many products.

Organized Religion

Women attend church more frequently, pray more often, hold firmer beliefs, and cooperate more in church programs than men do; yet organized religion is dominated by men (Mills, 1972). In their theological doctrines and religious hierarchies, churches and synagogues tend to reinforce women's subordinate role. Explicit instructions to do so can be found in the Bible:

> A woman must be a learner, listening quietly and with due submission. I do not permit a woman to be a teacher, nor must woman domineer over man; she should be quiet. For Adam was created first, and Eve afterwards; and it was not Adam who was deceived; it was woman who, yielding to deception, fell into sin. (Timothy 2:11–15)

Historically, organized religion has reinforced many secular traditions and norms, including the traditional view that men are primary and women secondary and that a woman's most important role is procreation. In Judaism, women are required to obey fewer religious precepts than men because less is expected of them. Orthodox Jewish males recite a prayer each morning in which they thank God that they are not women. The Catholic Church still assumes authority over a woman's sexual behavior, forbidding the use of birth control devices because they prevent reproduction.

Most churches bar women from performing the most sacred rituals or attaining the highest administrative posts. The consequences of this practice have been summed up as follows:

> As long as qualified persons are excluded from any ministry by reason of their sex alone, it cannot be said that there is genuine equality of men and women in the church. . . . By this exclusion the church is saying that the sexual differentiation is—for one sex—a crippling defect which no personal qualities of intelligence, character, or leadership can overcome. In fact, by this policy it is effectively teaching that women are not fully human and conditioning people to accept this as unchangeable fact. (Daly, 1970, p. 134)

In recent decades there have been some changes in the status of women in organized religion. The movement to allow women to hold leadership positions in churches and synagogues has had some success: In more liberal denominations (e.g., Episcopalians, Presbyterians, and Reformed Jews), women may be ordained as ministers and rabbis. Within the Catholic Church there are groups of women devoted to changing the norm against female priests, but they encounter severe resistance from traditionalists in the Catholic hierarchy (Farrell, 1991).

Government

The federal government has a long history of discrimination against women (Chafetz, 1974). A 1919 study by the Women's Bureau (a federal bureau created by Congress) found that women were barred from applying for 60 percent of all civil-service positions, notably those involving scientific or other professional work. Women were placed in a separate employment category, and their salaries were limited. The professionals in the Women's Bureau, for example, were required under an act of Congress to receive half the salaries received by men for doing the same work in other federal agencies.

During World War II the pattern of official discrimination continued. Despite the shortage of men, women were barred from most administrative and professional positions. The situation was worse in the armed forces. For example, although the Army had a severe shortage of medical personnel, it refused to commission women doctors. Only an act of Congress forced the Army to change its hiring policies. In the domestic labor force, women were of necessity permitted to enter fields that had previously been closed to them. However, even though the National War Labor Board insisted on a uniform pay scale for both sexes, it left loopholes that effectively discriminated against women; for example, the equal pay provisions did not apply to traditionally female jobs, and industries were permitted to assign different job titles to men and women, even for the same work.

Although discrimination against women has received less overt support from the government in recent years, patterns of discrimination still exist at all levels of government. In state and local government, for example, women face a "glass ceiling" that causes them to be underrepresented in high-level jobs and tends to concentrate them in lower-level, nonexecutive positions. The 1964 Civil Rights Act, which prohibited discrimination on the basis of sex, specifically excluded federal, state, and local governments from its provisions. Thus, women who work for the government are concentrated in clerical or service-type jobs, whereas most administrative posts are held by men. Federal policy toward day-care funding has also discriminated against women. Even though the vast majority of mothers who utilize day care centers could not earn a living without them, federal funding for such centers remains low (Benokraitis & Feagin, 1986). In consequence, increased funding for day care is a major issue in current debates over gender equality and welfare reform.

The Legal System

There are many legal barriers to sexual equality. For example, many state labor laws passed during the late nineteenth and early twentieth centuries set work standards that were designed to protect all workers; they established the maximum hours people could be required to work, the maximum weights they could be required to lift, and so on. The Supreme Court found, however, that such restrictions were unconstitutional with regard to men because they violated constitutional liberties. Women, on the other hand, could still be subject to these restrictions. In its decision in *Lochner* v. *New York* (1908), which upheld a state law limiting the number of hours women factory workers could work, the Court stated that

> *History discloses the fact that woman has always been dependent on man. He has established his control at the outset by superior physical strength, and this control in various forms, with diminishing intensity, has continued to the present. . . . Differentiated by these matters from the other sex, [woman] is properly placed in a class by herself, and legislation designed for her protection may be sustained, even when like legislation is not necessary for men, and could not be sustained.*

This decision in effect legalized and perpetuated state laws that differentiated between men and women. As late as 1965, the EEOC stated that state laws designed to protect women were not discriminatory.

A related issue is sexual harassment on the job. As noted earlier in the chapter, such harassment is widespread and usually intentional. It includes touching and staring at a woman's body, requesting sexual intercourse, and sometimes actual rape. Verbal abuse and derogatory language are common. In one study, half the respondents reported that they had been victims of physical harassment and 70 percent had been subjected to various types of sexual comments or suggestions (MacKinnon, 1979). Although there are legal prohibitions against sexual harassment in the workplace, laws of this type are hard to enforce because it is often difficult to define a particular incident as sexual harassment. Karen Nussbaum, a founder of Nine to Five, a national advocacy organization for working women, notes that another serious problem with existing sexual harassment laws is that a woman who files a complaint may have to endure years of procedures and hearings before she can win a chance at redress (*New York Times*, February 2, 1992).

The problem of legal differentiation between men and women exists in other areas besides employment. Some state educational institutions are permitted to exclude women, either from their student bodies or from their faculties. Many technical high schools admit only boys; many high schools prohibit pregnant or married girls from attending, but permit unmarried fathers or married boys to attend.

Another area in which legal discrimination persists is credit policies. For example, women who are single or widowed often have difficulty obtaining credit because it is assumed that they have no earning potential. The Equal Credit Opportunity Act, passed in 1974, makes it illegal to discriminate against women in many types of credit transactions. However, the law's penalties are weak, and it contains numerous loopholes. For example, wives must *request* that businesses make family credit arrangements in the names of both spouses. Businesses that offer credit are not required to inform women of their legal rights in this area (Benokraitis & Feagin, 1986).

Men also suffer from inequities in family law. In most states husbands are legally obligated to support their wives, regardless of the wife's financial status. Despite efforts to reform divorce laws, alimony is most frequently awarded to wives and only rarely to husbands, even if the wife can support herself. In child custody battles, the father bears a heavier burden of proof that he is a fit parent; custody is routinely given to the mother, and only in cases in which the mother is demonstrably negligent is the father's claim considered seriously.

SOCIAL POLICY

Changes in Child-Rearing Practices

Perhaps the greatest obstacle to equality of the sexes is the "motherhood ethic"—the idea that women are most fulfilled as mothers and that children, particularly young children, require a mother's constant attention if they are to grow up healthy and well adjusted.

It is evident that children need loving, consistent care and attention and the chance to build a relationship with one or two caring adults who are present on a regular basis. However, there is no evidence that those adults must be female. In fact, the absence of male figures can be harmful to a growing and developing child

(Bronfenbrenner, 1981). Many social scientists have found that an important prerequisite for full sexual equality is for fathers to share equally in the process of child rearing (and homemaking in general). This does not mean that all fathers or all mothers must do exactly half the work involved in raising children and keeping house. But political activists who organize efforts to reduce gender-based discrimination argue that society should encourage men to contribute as much to family life as women do.

Several steps could be taken to make it easier for men and women to share domestic tasks. For example, many companies grant maternity leaves to female employees who want to take time off to care for their children. *Parental* leaves would enable men or women who want to take some time to raise a child to do so without losing their jobs. Such a system exists in Sweden, where parents are given a six-month leave upon the birth of a child; the six months can be divided equally between the mother and father (Safilios-Rothschild, 1974).

Another approach would be to upgrade the importance of part-time work by institutionalizing many of the benefits of full-time work, such as unemployment insurance and seniority. This would make it easier for men and women to share the responsibilities of supporting the family and taking care of the home and children.

In 1990 Congress passed a family and medical leave act that would have guaranteed unpaid leave with job security to men and women in firms with fifty or more employees. President Bush vetoed this legislation, reasoning that if companies wanted to establish such a policy they should be encouraged to do so but that it is not the federal government's responsibility to regulate businesses in this way. During his campaign for the presidency Bill Clinton made family leave one of his key campaign promises. As soon as he was elected, Congress again passed the Family Leave Act, and Clinton signed the legislation.

In many instances, however, even such reforms do not go far enough. For men and women who are unwilling or unable to stop working for a long period, and for women who are heads of families, child day care is a necessity. Eight million women with children under the age of 6 are in the labor force. Many more mothers who would work if they could find appropriate day care remain unemployed. The need for day care has increased greatly in recent years as the proportion of single-parent families in American society has risen. (See Chapters 8 and 12.)

There is some controversy over institutional day care for young children. It is well known, for example, that babies and children in large, impersonal residential institutions are often noticeably retarded in many aspects of their development. It has also been noted that communally raised children such as those of the Israeli kibbutzim—although they usually grow up to be well-adjusted adults—tend to be somewhat lacking in imagination and personal ambition. There is little doubt, however, that a well-staffed, well-organized day care center can offer children opportunities and stimuli for exploration and discovery that may be considerably greater than those available at home. Well-trained teachers are alert to developing interests and abilities and know how to encourage them, and there is a greater variety of play equipment than in most private homes.

Although there is no official policy on workplace day care, many companies are finding it in their interests to provide such care. For example, the Stride-Rite Corporation of Cambridge, Massachusetts, has established a day-care center where working parents can bring not only their preschool children but also their aging relatives, who help care for the children. Employees share the costs with an outside foundation set up by the corporation (Teltsch, 1990).

Changes in the Educational Process

To eliminate sexism in education, teachers and school administrators must become more sensitive to their own stereotypes about boys and girls (or men and women) and treat members of both sexes equally—for example, by paying equal attention to male and female students and not assigning tasks according to traditional sex-role stereotypes. One way to counteract the idea that only women take care of children is to attract more male teachers for the lower grades. Another is to eliminate traditional occupational and role stereotypes from the standard curriculum.

During the 1980s progress toward greater equality in education slowed. In 1984, for example, the Supreme Court ruled in *Grove City College* v. *Bell* that legislation prohibiting sex discrimination in education applied only to programs receiving federal aid, not to entire institutions. This ruling had the effect of allowing colleges to bar women from certain courses or to deny them equal athletic opportunities with men. The *Grove City* decision was reversed by an act of Congress in March 1988. Schools and other institutions that accept federal funds are required to end discrimination in all of their programs and activities.

Changes in the Legal System

Many laws and statutes discriminate against women and reinforce prejudices against them. Some states, for example, still require that women be given longer sentences than men for the same crimes, on the assumption that female criminals require more rehabilitation; conversely, many states treat women offenders more leniently than men, on the assumption that women require the state's protection. In Alabama women were excluded from jury duty until 1966, when a federal court ruled that this practice was unconstitutional. However, the Supreme Court has upheld the right of states to keep women from being automatically selected for jury duty: In many states women must volunteer for jury duty or they will not be called.

Title VII of the Civil Rights Act of 1964 forbids discrimination on the basis of sex. However, as we have seen, wage and job discrimination against women remains widespread. Complicated rules for filing discrimination complaints, a huge backlog of cases, lack of enthusiasm in enforcing the act, and loopholes in the act itself have all reduced its effectiveness. Despite these obstacles, in 1988 women in California won a major victory against sex discrimination in employment. In a multi-million–dollar settlement, the State Farm Insurance Company agreed to pay damages and back pay to thousands of women who had been refused jobs as insurance sales agents over a thirteen-year period. The women had been told that a college degree was required for sales agents, even though men who lacked a degree were hired.

One area in which some progress has been made toward greater equality is known as *comparable worth*. The concept of "equal pay for comparable work," rather than "equal pay for equal work," has won some support in recent years. This concept holds that the intrinsic value of different jobs can be measured and that jobs that are found to be of comparable value should receive comparable pay. It is intended to correct the imbalance in earnings caused by the fact that many women hold jobs in relatively low-paying fields. Comparable worth received a major boost in 1983, when a federal judge ordered Washington State to raise the wages of thousands of women employees. Although the decision was appealed, it drew national attention to the fact that jobs held mainly by women are paid at rates that average 20 percent below those for equivalent jobs held mainly by men (Goodman, 1984).

Critics of the comparable-worth concept claim that there is no such thing as an intrinsic value of any job. A job is "worth" what a person is paid for doing it. Discrimination may or may not be present, but many other factors go into determining the wages of all workers. Moreover, comparable worth could turn out to be very costly; in the Washington State case, which was eventually settled out of court, the state increased the salaries of 35,000 employees at a total cost of $482 million. By 1990 the average salary for all jobs in Washington State had increased by 20 percent from the 1986 level as salaries were adjusted to ensure comparable worth. The gap in wages between men and women had been reduced from 20 percent to 5 percent

(Kilborn, 1990). Although advocates of comparable worth hope that this will be an attractive example for other states, the recession of the early 1990s severely hampered prospects for comparable-worth policies.

Reproductive Control

Abortion is one of the most controversial issues in America today. This controversy is basically a conflict over reproductive control. Antiabortion laws were passed in the mid-nineteenth century, when "certain governments and religious groups desired continued population growth to fill growing industries and new farmable territories" (Sanford, McCord, & McGee, 1976, p. 217). Another reason given for the passage of these laws was to protect women against the danger of crude "backstreet" operations. Yet women continued to have abortions, legal or otherwise, and many deaths and injuries resulted. Those who could afford the services of expensive doctors stood a better chance of survival than poorer women, who had to risk highly unsanitary and often degrading conditions.

In the mid-1950s agitation against the existing laws caused a few states to permit abortions under limited circumstances. Women could apply for abortions, but the decisions were made by doctors and hospitals. As a result of bureaucratic red tape and high costs, patients who could afford private physicians were able to benefit most from the reformed laws, while many poorer women continued to have few alternatives to illegal abortions.

In 1970 New York State allowed abortion almost on demand, followed within

Public discussions about sexuality and reproductive control are sure to offend some groups in society. In 1991 the United States Supreme Court upheld the federal government's right to ban abortion advice in health clinics receiving federal funds, but the ruling met with opposition in Congress.

SEX ROLES AND INEQUALITY   **315**

the next two years by Alaska, Hawaii, and Washington State. Many women took advantage of this situation, and mortality and injury rates, as well as the number of illegal abortions, began to drop (Sanford et al., 1976). Responding to the proven success and safety of legal abortions and continued pressure for federal legislation, the Supreme Court affirmed the legality of abortion in 1973.

Abortion has remained highly controversial, however, and many people oppose it adamantly. Right to Life, an organized antiabortion group, is striving to repeal all proabortion laws, with the vigorous support of the Catholic Church. Its members oppose abortion on moral grounds and raise fundamental questions about the nature of human life and the rights of unborn children. It has proposed a constitutional amendment that would permit states to prohibit abortion. In recent years the antiabortion movement has suffered some setbacks due to the Clinton administration's strong support for pro-choice policies. In 1994, for example, the Supreme Court ruled that organizers of violent protests against abortion clinics may be prosecuted under federal racketeering laws. Nevertheless, the movement continues to pursue strategies whose effect is to make it more difficult for women to have abortions (Lewin, 1992).

Related to reproductive control is the availability of sex education and contraception. Clearly, the need for abortion decreases as education and the availability of contraceptive devices increases. Many pregnancies among young women could be prevented by education about birth control. Furstenberg (1979) has noted that schools for the most part "go ignored as sites for pregnancy prevention programs" (p. 157). As Surgeon General Joycelyn Elders pointed out in her 1993 confirmation hearings, sex education in the United States is vague or haphazard. Many poor women have less access to sex education and contraception than other women. As more family planning centers and educational and counseling channels open, more women can educate themselves about contraception and make their own choices with regard to reproductive control. And as the AIDS epidemic continues, many cities are increasing their efforts in the area of sex education.

Social Policy and the Women's Movement

The 1980s were a time of setbacks for the women's movement, especially in the areas of affirmative action, day care, and the politics of equal rights (Faludi, 1991). But the fundamental social changes that created an environment in which the women's movement could flourish are unlikely to be reversed. Women's participation in the labor force is not expected to return to the lower rates that characterized the 1950s and 1960s. Thus, women can be expected to continue to make progress toward occupational parity with men. There are signs of continued progress in other areas, too. More women entering college are planning careers in traditionally male fields such as business, medicine, law, and engineering, and some denominations now ordain women clergy.

In coming years the women's movement is likely to focus on the situation of single-parent families and, within this group, the special needs of low-income female-headed families. With half of all marriages ending in divorce and about one-fourth of all households headed by single parents or unrelated individuals, it is certain that the politics of child care and aid to children will be in the forefront of feminist concerns.

On a global level, what Jessie Bernard (1987) refers to as the Feminist Enlightenment has made significant progress in recent years. Women throughout the world have benefited in many ways, ranging from improved health and education to expanded economic and political opportunities. Much of this pro-gress can be attributed to the role of the United Nations as a platform for issues of concern to women. Throughout the late 1970s and the 1980s women became increasingly skilled at using the UN's information and communication systems effectively.

Changes in Men's Roles

The issues of women's rights have often eclipsed the need for men to examine and change their own sex roles. Inspired by the successes of women, however, many men are exploring the roles that have also limited them in the past, and they are discovering a new freedom in moving toward sex-role egalitarianism. Although the shift in male attitudes appears mainly among younger, educated men in their twenties and thirties (Gelman, 1978), there is reason to believe that sex-role stereotyping among men of all ages is changing. The growing presence of women in the work force is leading to greater egalitarianism as women become breadwinners and men participate more freely in child rearing and housework. Progress in this direction is slow, however; even when they work outside the home, women still do most of the food shopping and cooking (Burros, 1988).

The opening up of fields that have traditionally been "male" or "female" to members of both sexes is likely to remain an important goal of the women's movement and civil rights organizations throughout the United States. Labor shortages in some parts of the nation are also likely to encourage employers to more actively recruit women for nontraditional occupations. But severely restricted state and city budgets will retard these changes in the near term. Clearly, policy initiatives in the area of comparable worth and efforts to combat gender discrimination will continue to occupy legislators at every level of government, but there will surely be increased concern about how to fund these policies. An unintended consequence of these conflicts between desired policies and the ability to make the actual changes is that women continue to shoulder more than their fair share of the burden of domestic responsibilities. (See Box 10–1 on page 318.)

David Williams of the Houston Oilers unintentionally became a feminist hero when he missed an important game in order to be with his wife while she was giving birth to their first child.

"You know how in a new relationship you give and you give," said Marie Benedict, a 35-year-old hotel concierge from La Costa, California, who is in the midst of a divorce. "You try to be superwoman. I worked and I did everything. My husband did nothing."

National survey research shows that the situation is similar for the large majority of working women. Although the burden of trying to be a superwoman was not the main reason Ms. Benedict gave for the failure of her marriage, the stress and unfairness she felt certainly contributed to the couple's problems. The women's movement is dedicated to ending the double standard that specifies that women must bear the majority of domestic responsibilities even if they are full-time workers. In the past thirty years the movement has made a great deal of progress toward ending discriminatory policies that prevent women from entering occupations that were formerly reserved for men, and it has made much progress in changing how women think of themselves—as people who can pursue a career and compete with men, for example—yet the traditional sex roles of domestic life are proving extremely difficult to change.

A 1987 *New York Times* poll found that even though more women are in the workforce and have less time at home, they are still the primary caregivers and meal planners in their households. Ninety percent of the married women who were interviewed reported that they do most or all of the cooking, compared to only 15 percent of the married men. Among married couples, only 18 percent of the men reported that they do most of the food shopping; an additional 6 percent reported that they share responsibility for food shopping (Burros, 1988).

The strength of the norm that requires women to take primary responsibility for the home can be seen in the case of Houston Oilers player David Williams. Williams missed an important game to be with his wife for the birth of their first child. "It was the most unbelievable thing that I've ever seen and I wouldn't have missed it for anything in the world," he said. Team officials threatened to discipline Williams for "wimping out," claiming that showing up for the game was equivalent to going to war. Eventually, however, they were forced to back down in the face of widespread public protest.

From the perspective of social policy, the persistence of the double standard is a fascinating unintended consequence of the women's movement and one that is difficult to resolve through further policies. Greater gender equality in the labor force without concomitant progress toward sharing of domestic roles has increased the stress and fatigue experienced by women. But since the problem lies at the level of the couple and the family, this is an area that does not lend itself to direct policy solutions.

SUMMARY

1. Until fairly recently it was widely accepted that the only desirable roles for a woman were those of wife, mother, and homemaker; men were required to be leaders and providers. Today those roles are viewed as outdated or as representing only some of the roles that may be adopted by people of either sex.

2. The types of behavior that are considered appropriate for men and women reflect the values of a particular society. They are largely learned as a person is socialized into his or her culture.

3. Sexism is the range of attitudes, beliefs, policies, laws, and behaviors that discriminate against the members of one sex. It is based on popular stereotypes about women and men. Sexism is especially evident in employment and contributes to the earnings gap between men and women. It can also be seen in sexual harassment and the devaluation of homemaking. The women's movement has striven to eliminate sexism from American society, and there is evidence that it has had an impact on attitudes about gender roles.

4. The primary source of sexism is socialization, particularly in the family, where children are treated differently on the basis of their sex. More formal socialization occurs in school, where traditional sex-role stereotypes are reinforced. Later the role of homemaker often perpetuates a woman's subordinate status, and even in two-earner marriages the husband may have a more privileged position.

5. Other sources of sexism are psychiatric medicine, which tends to favor traditional sex roles; language and the media, which reinforce stereotypes; organized religion, in which women have a subordinate role; and a legal system that assumes that men are wage earners and women are homemakers.

6. A significant step toward sexual equality would be for fathers to share equally in child rearing and homemaking. This could be encouraged by upgrading part-time work and providing day care for preschool children. Changes are also needed in the educational process so that children of both sexes are treated equally. In 1993 Congress passed the Family Leave Act, which allows employees of either sex to take unpaid leave to care for family members; the legislation was signed by President Clinton.

7. Many laws and statutes discriminate against women and reinforce prejudices against them. Job discrimina-tion on the basis of sex is forbidden by law, but for the most part such laws have not been strongly enforced. Recent efforts to counteract job discrimination have focused on the concept of comparable worth, or measuring the intrinsic value of jobs and paying holders of jobs of comparable value at comparable rates.

8. Another area in which legislation plays an important role is abortion. Abortion laws have been greatly liberalized since the 1950s, but the issue remains highly controversial.

9. In the future the women's movement is likely to focus on such issues as child care and children's aid. In addition, the presence of large numbers of women in the labor force can be expected to produce continued pressure for greater equality between the sexes, although such pressure appears to have the unintended consequence of increasing the total burden of responsibility borne by women.

SUGGESTED READINGS

BERNARD, JESSIE. *The Female World*. New York: Free Press, 1981. A restatement of Bernard's thesis that the female world is essentially separate from the male world, with its own culture, value system, and institutions. Bernard describes the female world as "kin and locale-based" and as adhering to a "love and/or duty ethos."

BLEIER, RUTH. *Science and Gender: A Critique of Biology and Its Theories on Women*. New York: Pergamon Press, 1984. A review, by a feminist biologist, of the sociological and biological literature on gender.

EPSTEIN, CYNTHIA FUCHS. *Deceptive Distinctions*. New York: Basic Books, 1988. A timely review of recent empirical research and theoretical writing about the origins and consequences of gender differences.

GERSON, KATHLEEN. *Hard Choices: How Women Decide About Work, Career, and Motherhood*. Berkeley: University of California Press, 1985. An empirical study based on in-depth interviews with women who experience conflict over how to juggle the demands of careers, relationships, and parenthood.

GOFFMAN, ERVING. *Gender Advertisements*. Cambridge, MA: Harvard University Press, 1979. An analysis of advertising as both a reinforcer and a creator of stereotypical images of men and women.

PASCALL, GILLIAN. *Social Policy: A Feminist Analysis*. London: Tavistock Publications, 1986. A thorough critique of social-welfare policies in Western nations that argues that existing policies often perpetuate sex-based inequalities.

RICHMOND-ABBOTT, MARIE. *Masculine and Feminine*, 2nd ed. New York: McGraw-Hill, 1992. An up-to-date review of research and theory on gender, gender inequalities, and social movements to address women's subordinate status.

RODGERS-ROSE, LA FRANCES, ED. *The Black Woman*. Newbury Park, CA: Sage, 1980. A collection of essays on the experiences of black women in the United States that indicates the variety of attitudes, beliefs, and roles of black women.

ROSSI, ALICE S. "Gender and Parenthood." *American Sociological Review* 49 (1984): 1–19. An important review and synthesis of research on the relationships between biological and social variables in creating gender identities throughout life.

SOKOLOFF, NATALIE J. *Between Money and Love: The Dialectics of Women's Home and Market Work*. New York: Praeger, 1980. An examination of theories explaining the position of women in the labor market in relation to their position in the home.

An Aging Society

Chapter Outline

- The average income of the aged is about 90 percent of that of younger people.
- In 1900 there were 3.1 million Americans over 65; in 1990 there were more than 31 million.
- In 1990 the suicide rate for men aged 65–74 was 32.2 per 100,000, compared to 19.0 for men of all ages.
- There are almost 1.4 million people in nursing homes.
- Over 32 percent of blacks age 65 and over live below the poverty line.
- In 1991 the average monthly social security benefit for retired workers was $629.

Like most other advanced industrial nations, the United States is an aging society. Yet "few Americans realize that their country is in the midst of a demographic revolution that, sooner or later, will affect every individual and every institution in the society" (House Committee on Aging, 1990; Pifer & Bronte, 1986). Before the middle of the next century, the aging of the population will have had an impact at least as great as that of any of the major economic and social transformations of the past, including the massive immigration of the early twentieth century, the post–World War II baby boom, and the large-scale entry of women into the labor force.

The main factors that affect a population's general "youth" or "age" are changes in the fertility rate, the infant mortality rate, and the life expectancy of people at older ages. In social terms, age is one of the major factors that determine groupings and role assignments in a society. How old people are plays a large part in how they feel about themselves and what society expects of them. And the way a society thinks about its aged members depends very much on the value its culture attaches to age as opposed to youth. Our culture places a high value on youth, and consequently it tends to devalue aging because it is associated with changes in physical appearance that detract from the image of youth. This is a feature of most Western cultures, but it is particularly prevalent in American culture.

In our culture, role assignments tend to be based on arbitrarily defined age ranges. One must attend school from age 6 to age 16. One cannot vote until age 18. The law dictates when a person may marry, sign a lease, run for office, and so on—all on the basis of age. Beginning around age 65, people are designated as "old" and encouraged to withdraw from the mainstream of life, regardless of their mental capabilities, motivations, or health. The new status assigned to those who are designated as old is a "roleless" one involving no power, no responsibility, and few rewards (Wood, 1971).

Aging places stress on society as well as on the individual. A major source of structural strain in societies is the long-term failure of social institutions to accommodate the increasing proportion of the population who are elderly. For example, the family has failed to adapt to the presence of older members, and there is considerable strain in the labor force as younger workers find their careers blocked and older ones are forced to leave their jobs before they are ready to do so. The result, according to Matilda White Riley (1987), senior sociologist in the U.S. Office on Aging, is that "human resources in the oldest—and also the youngest—strata are underutilized, and excess burdens of care are imposed upon strata in the middle years" (p. 10).

According to Robert C. Atchley (1978), the social problems associated with certain age groups, especially the very young and the very old, are aggravated by three factors that all have an impact on the roles assigned to people of different ages. Those factors are labeling, the concept of work as the basis of personal value, and economic deprivation. These three factors are inextricably linked, and each reinforces the others. Labeling leads to discrimination against older workers, which reduces their responsibility while still on the job and forces them to retire. Characterized as weak and incompetent, older people often lose their self-confidence and begin to conform to the stereotype. Retirement often removes people from the mainstream of life and diminishes their status and social contacts, consigning still-vital people to a vaguely defined position on the fringe of society. In a world where one's job is the basis of one's worth and acceptance, retired people are relegated to a position of low esteem. People who once described themselves as accountants, salespeople, or secretaries are suddenly and arbitrarily looked upon as noncontributors, a status that reduces both their incomes and their responsibilities.

In the past several decades the economic status of the aged as a group has improved markedly; the average income of older people is about 90 percent of that of younger adults (Palmer & Gould, 1987). The elderly are not a homogeneous group, however, and the situation of those who live alone is not as comfortable as that of couples. The very old (those over 85) and members of minority groups also are less well off than white "young–old" couples. Moreover, although on the whole the elderly are faring much better than they have in the past, this improvement is due largely to public policies designed to alleviate the problems faced by aging individuals. Such policies do not reach the entire older population. Thus, there are still large numbers of older people who experience economic insecurity because of their vulnerability to major costs such as medical expenses that are not fully covered by insurance. We will return to some of these issues later in the chapter.

Much of what we say about the elderly also applies to young people who are not yet in the labor force. Young people in American society frequently are dependent on others for support and lack the power to assert their needs as citizens. In most states, for example, it is unlawful for people under the age of 21 to purchase alcoholic beverages, yet they can be drafted for military service and may vote in national elections. This is not to argue that young people should drink or that the laws should be changed, but it points to the inconsistency in society's treatment of the young as dependent in some cases and as responsible in others.

The problems of different age groups are a vast subject in the social sciences, and it will be necessary in this chapter to dwell primarily on the problems that confront the aged. As our aging society produces an ever-larger population of elderly people, the problems of the elderly become increasingly evident and require more attention from both researchers and policy makers.

PERSPECTIVES ON AGING

Aging as a social problem is often studied from the point of view of one or more of the basic perspectives described in Chapter 1. From the functionalist perspective, for example, aging is a problem because the institutions of modern society are not working well enough to serve the needs of the dependent aged. The extended family, which once allowed elderly people to live out their lives among kin, has been weakened by greater social mobility and a shift to the nuclear family as the basic kinship unit. (See Chapter 12.) The elderly are rendered useless as their roles are replaced by those of other social institutions. As grandparents, for example, older people once played an important role in socializing the young, teaching them the skills, values, and ways of life of their people. Now those functions are performed by schools and colleges, for it is assumed that the elderly cannot understand or master the skills required in today's fast-changing world. Instead, they must be cared for either at home or in institutions such as old-age homes, which remove this burden from the productive members of society.

Interactionists take a different view. They see the term *elderly* operating as a stigmatizing label that suggests that older people are less valuable because they do not conform to the norms of a youth-oriented culture. Interactionists view the elderly as victims of *ageism*—forms of prejudice and discrimination that are directed

Many older people cherish the opportunity to spend time with children and participate in their education.

at them not only by individuals but by entire social institutions. The remedy is to fight ageism in all its forms. (Ageism is discussed more fully later in the chapter.)

Finally, conflict theorists view the problems of the elderly as stemming from older people's lack of power to shape social institutions to meet the needs of people who are no longer in their productive years and have not accumulated the means to preserve their economic and social independence. In this view, the aged need to resist the debilitating effects of labeling and the loss of their roles by banding together in organizations and communities and voting blocs that will assert their need for meaningful lives and adequate social services.

Table 11–1 summarizes the major sociological perspectives on aging.

TABLE 11–1 MAJOR SOCIOLOGICAL PERSPECTIVES ON AGING: A TYPOLOGY OF AGING AS A SOCIAL PROBLEM	
PERSPECTIVE	WHY AGING IS A SOCIAL PROBLEM
Functionalist	Social institutions do not adequately serve people as they grow older (e.g., the family is no longer capable of providing adequate care.
Interactionist	The elderly are stigmatized and are victims of ageism because they do not conform to the norms of a culture emphasizing youthfulness.
Conflict	The problem of the elderly is their relative lack of power; when they organize for political action, they can combat ageism.

Research on the treatment of the elderly in nomadic societies has found that in some situations, especially in times of scarcity or when elderly individuals impede the group's mobility, the elderly may be badly mistreated and even encouraged to die (Cox, 1990). Explorers and anthropologists have also cited instances of mistreatment of the elderly in some tribal societies. But in many settled agrarian societies, the status of adults actually increases with age. In many African and Asian nations, for example, decisions regarding land tenure, kinship, and ceremonial affairs are the province of the aged. In the United States and most Western countries, the productive and cultural roles of the aged have been weakened by industrialization and the migration of family members to cities. In this sense, then, the problems of the aged are part of the larger complex of social changes known as *modernization*.

Modernization has been described as

the transformation of a total society from a relatively rural way of life based on animate power, limited technology, relatively undifferentiated institutions, parochial and traditional outlook and values, toward a predominantly urban way of life based on inanimate sources of power, highly developed scientific technology, highly individual roles, and a cosmopolitan outlook which emphasizes efficiency and progress. (Cogwill, 1974, p. 11)

Thus, many of the problems faced by the aged in America today are social problems that arise from the nature of modern Western society.

Modernization produces far-reaching changes in societies, but clearly the terms *modernization* and *progress* are not equivalent. With modernization come new social problems and, sometimes, new solutions to those problems. Modernization is usually associated with increasing length of life, but this is a positive change only when the quality of life is also enhanced. For many people, however, as the life span increases, so does the pain associated with old age.

Technological and scientific advances have reduced the infant mortality rate and eliminated or provided cures for many formerly fatal diseases. Since many of these advances, such as antiseptics and antibiotics, occurred within a short time (often within this century), record numbers of people began living to old age. As the population of elderly people increased, modern societies all over the globe began to deal with the problem of poverty and illness among their elderly citizens. Pension plans, social security, and medical-care systems had to be developed to address their needs.

From the earliest periods of human prehistory (before written evidence of human civilization appeared) to the present, the average life expectancy of individuals has increased by about forty years. In prehistoric times a person could expect to live into his or her early forties; now life expectancy is approaching 80 in some societies. Great surges in life expectancy occurred with the transition from hunting-and-gathering to agrarian societies, with the development of modern techniques of sanitation and water supply, and with the discovery of the causes of diseases and of antibiotics and techniques for preventing many major diseases. In the past twenty or thirty years, however, there has been a deceleration of the rate of increase in life expectancy (Riley, 1989). There are biological limits to how long humans can live, and although there may be small shifts in life expectancy in the future, we cannot project past advances indefinitely.

We can, however, project increases in the number of elderly people who are alive but unwell. As more people live longer, the proportion with major medical problems increases, as does the need for costly medical care. While most of us wish to live longer lives, the negative side of this wish is that we are likely to suffer longer and more as we do so. For society as a whole, this means an increased need to improve the quality of life for the most elderly among the population and to find ways to care for a growing number of frail and ill elderly (Françoise Cribier, personal communication).

Urbanization, like advances in medical and other technologies, is another major change associated with modernization. The increasing tendency for people to live in cities and for cities and metropolitan regions to dominate the life of modern societies has also affected the lives of the elderly. It has created new jobs for mobile workers who are willing to relocate from rural areas or small towns to large cities, or from the older industrial cities of the North and Midwest to the newer urban centers of the Sunbelt. The resulting migration has led to differing concentrations of elderly and younger people in different parts of the nation. Figure 11–1 illustrates quite dramatically how decreases in employment in rural areas and in the older manufacturing cities have created high concentrations of elderly people in counties throughout the Midwest and Plains states.

In counties with high proportions of elderly residents, such as Smith County, Kansas, there is a need for creative entrepreneurs who are willing to help their elderly neighbors remain independent as long as possible. In many rural counties in the Midwest, a variety of services are provided for elderly people, such as minor home repairs, errands, or monitoring of medical needs. These enable older people

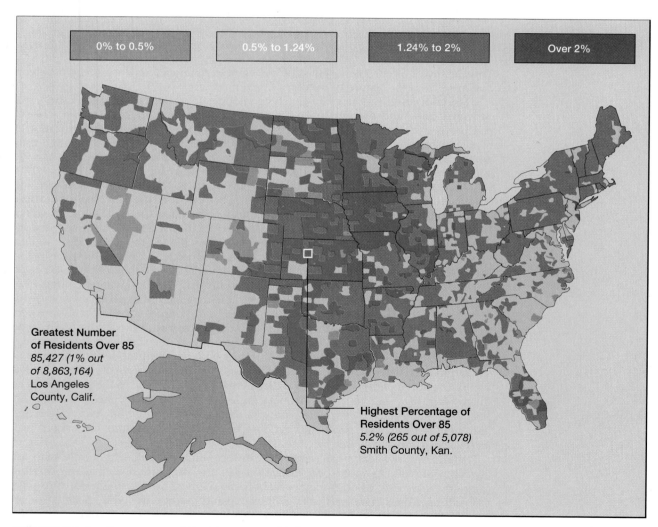

FIGURE 11–1   Percentage of Residents over 85, by County, United States

Source: Data from U.S. Census Bureau.

to live happily on their own and may be harbingers of trends elsewhere in the nation (Barringer, 1993).

Age Stratification

Matilda White Riley and Joan Waring (1976) have described the process of *age stratification*. Age, they point out, operates like race or class in segregating people into different groups or strata. Like the class system, age stratification limits the kinds of roles that the members of each group can hold. Some degree of age stratification seems acceptable and even inevitable. People are attracted to their peers and to those with whom they share common experiences and concerns, and certain activities seem to attract members of particular age groups. However,

> *Many of these age-related differences in access to the good things in life are violations of societal ideas of equity or harmony. They inhibit communication and understanding between generations. They can create a sense of relative deprivation or inadequacy and feelings of hostility with reference to other age strata. (p. 363)*

Age stratification may produce some of the disengagement and retreat that is so common among elderly people in America. Young people who are denied jobs and opportunities to play rewarding roles often react by engaging in deviant behaviors, including crime. Old people may react by becoming dependent or uninvolved or by manifesting the kinds of behavior that are labeled as senile.

Age stratification may also lead to age segregation and conflict. From childhood we are segregated into age groups, classes, and clubs; the retirement community, restricted to people of specified ages, continues this process. In the wake of age segregation come suspicion, mistrust, and hostility. The young lack confidence in their elders; the old often fear the young. Isolation of age groups and intergenerational conflicts are common.

It is possible that many conditions that exist today will be reversed in the future. For example, the middle-aged have traditionally enjoyed an advantaged position relative to the elderly. But that position could be eroded as a result of a combination of factors, including a lower median wage for male heads of households, larger percentages of infants born out of wedlock and children living in female-headed households, and higher educational attainment among individuals currently approaching old age (Riley, 1987). The effect of these trends would be to counteract the "normal" relationship between the old and the middle-aged and perhaps to produce new forms of tension between generations.

Who Are the Elderly?

Anyone over 65 is commonly considered old. Recently, however, social scientists have begun to identify specific groups within the growing population of older people. People between the ages of 65 and 75, who are still inclined to be healthy and active, are called the "young–old." Those over 75, a group that is more likely to require support services, are the "old–old." Those over the age of 85 may be termed the "oldest old." Another group, the "frail elderly," consists of people over 65 who, because of poor health or economic problems, cannot carry out the basic activities of life without help. Assistance to such people may range from full-time nursing care to the delivery of a hot meal each day or help with shopping or cleaning.

Although the oldest elderly people in the U.S. population now number about 3.1 million, or about 10 pecent of those over age 65 (see Figure 11–2 on page 328), projections indicate that this figure is likely to increase to almost 22 percent by the mid–twenty-first century. This will occur because by about 2010 the post–World War

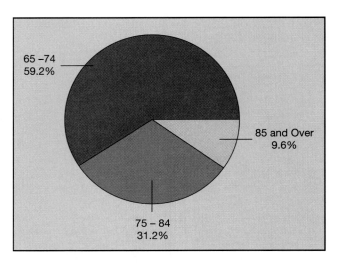

FIGURE 11–2 U.S. Elderly Population: Major Age Categories

Source: Data from Census Bureau, 1989.

II baby boom generation will be entering this age group, and as time goes by, far larger numbers of Americans will be elderly. (See Table 11–2.)

The elderly portion of the American population grows larger in each decade. In 1900 there were 3.1 million Americans over 65; in 1990 there were more than 31 million. More important, the proportion of the population over 65 has tripled, increasing from 4.1 percent in 1900 to 12 percent in 1991, and it is continuing to increase. Demographers in the U.S. Census Bureau estimate that in the next century the elderly will be the fastest growing segment of the population as the huge baby boom generation enters old age. (See Figure 11–3.)

Two-thirds of the elderly live in urban areas, many in central cities. For them, the problems of aging are complicated by the problems of the urban environment: crime, decaying neighborhoods, the shortage of affordable housing, and congestion. (See Chapter 15.)

TABLE 11–2 PERCENT OF TOTAL POPULATION 65+, 1950 TO 2050 (PROJECTED)	
YEAR	PECENTAGE
1950	8.1
1965	9.5
1984	11.8
1995	13.1
2010	13.8
2030	21.2
2050	21.8

Adapted from *Our Aging Society, Paradox and Promise,* Edited by Alan Pifer and Lydia Bronte, by permission of W. W. Norton & Company, Inc. Copyright © 1986 by Carnegie Corporation of New York.

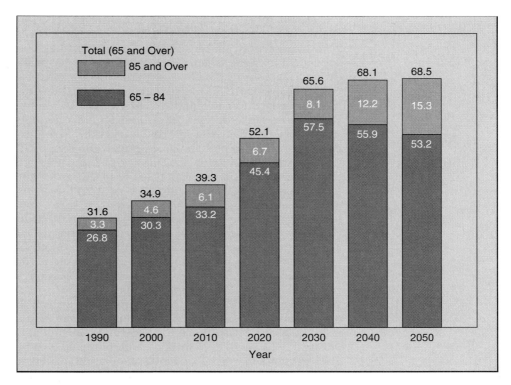

FIGURE 11–3 Projections of the Elderly Population, by Age: 1990–2050 (in millions)

Source: U.S. Census Bureau, 1989.

Although most elderly people live in urban areas, they also represent the highest proportion of the population of small towns. This phenomenon is a result of the patterns of migration that have occurred since World War II, when many people moved from farms to small towns. Many of those people are now elderly. In turn, their children have relocated from small towns to suburbs or cities. Another important pattern of migration is the movement of retired people to the West and South. In some parts of the United States, such as Miami and south Florida and parts of Arizona and southern California, the elderly have become a dominant group and exert considerable political influence. We are likely to see much growth in these areas as the elderly proportion of the population continues to expand.

Ageism

The devaluation of the aged in modern societies has been termed *ageism.* Many attitudes that are prevalent in modern society contribute to ageism. One of these is the inordinate value placed on youthful looks, especially in women (Chernin, 1981; Epstein, 1988). Older adults do not meet the standards of youthful beauty, and many people may be repelled by the appearance of the aged. Another source of ageism is the belief that the old are useless—since they do not work and cannot reproduce, they serve no purpose. Those who do hold jobs are resented for occupying a position that a young person probably needs. Because its roots reach so deeply into the social and psychological fabric of our culture, is extremely difficult to eliminate. Ageism as a social problem is also confounded with sexism. Feminist social scientists ask, with reason, whether ageism would be the problem it is in U.S. society if men outlived women instead of the reverse (Friedan, 1993).

Ageism also prevails in the government. The Administration on Aging, an agency of the Department of Health and Human Services, has low status and limited access to decision makers. When Congress makes budget cuts, programs for the aged are a frequent target. When states and municipalities have to cut their budgets owing to recession or regional depression, they often reduce programs for the aged as well as the poor. The elderly fare no better in business and industry. Although the Age Discrimination in Employment Act of 1967 prohibits discrimination against workers between the ages of 40 and 65, little is done to enforce it. Critics have pointed out that the law itself exhibits ageism, since it does nothing for workers over the age of 65, who probably need protection even more.

Ageism is reflected in the practice of mandatory retirement based on age. This takes a heavy toll on the health, self-respect, social status, and economic security of older people. Retirement isolates the old from the mainstream of American life. The daily social contacts of the working world are gone, and reduced income may bring reduced mobility or prevent participation in social activities. The status of productive worker is replaced by a new status with low prestige and a negative image. Mandatory retirement thus can be considered the most serious and pervasive form of ageism.

Ageism is also present in the health-care system. Although the number of older Americans increases each year, the medical profession is doing little to anticipate or cope with the problems of the elderly.

The mass media play a part in promoting ageism. Just as women and minority groups must contend with negative images in the media, so must old people. Television, which does so much to shape and maintain attitudes, persists in portraying old people as weak in both body and mind and as a burden on their relatives—or else as unnaturally wise or kindhearted. Newspapers and magazines also contain ageist images. An analysis of 265 articles on aging that appeared in a large midwestern newspaper found that instead of featuring older people who were active in their communities, the paper stressed stories about "well-preserved physical culture addicts and 'old timers' reminiscing about the good old days" (Jones, 1977, p. 94). And in a more recent study of changing attitudes toward age and aging, Howard P. Chudacoff (1989) found that only in the past fifty years have newspapers and other communications media begun to stress "age-appropriate behavior." Song lyrics, for example, are increasingly concerned about looking young and not looking old.

The difficulties of the old in our society are mirrored by their higher than average suicide rate. Although declining health, loss of status, and reduced income play a part in suicides by the elderly, lack of relationships with family, friends, and co-workers seems to exert the most consistent influence (Bock, 1972). An analysis of suicides by elderly people in Pinellas County, Florida, over a period of nine years indicated that widowed males were more likely to commit suicide than any other group of old people. Elderly women were more likely to have extended family ties, friends, and club memberships that provided them with social restraints against sui-

TABLE 11–3 SUICIDE RATES, BY AGE AND SEX, 1990 (PER 100,000)		
AGE	MEN	WOMEN
All ages	19.0	4.5
65–74	32.2	6.7
75–84	56.1	6.3
85 and over	65.9	5.4

Source: Data from *Statistical Abstract,* 1993.

cide. Elderly men who enjoyed these kinds of contact were less likely to commit suicide. This finding mirrors the classic finding by Emile Durkheim, one of sociology's founders, that people of any age who lack social attachments are more likely to commit suicide than people with active social lives among families and friends. Table 11–3 compares rates of suicide for men and women over age 65 with rates for the population as a whole.

DIMENSIONS OF THE AGING PROCESS

Physiological Aspects of Aging

Chronological Aging   Chronological aging is the accumulation of years; it is a largely automatic process. We know from our own observations, however, that not everyone ages at the same rate. Some people look and act middle-aged before they leave their 20s, whereas some 50-year-olds radiate the vitality and health that are usually associated with youth.

The dramatic increase in life expectancy and the growing population of older people in America have stimulated interest in the aging process and its causes. The field of study and practice known as *gerontology* has grown. Among other concerns, gerontologists attempt to identify the physical causes and effects of the aging process and to control the factors that diminish the rewards of a long life.

Primary and Secondary Aging   There are two categories within the aging process: primary aging and secondary aging. *Primary aging* is a result of molecular and cellular changes. *Secondary aging* is "an accelerated version of normal aging" (Arehart-Treichel, 1977, p. 38). It is caused by environmental factors: lack of exercise, stress, trauma, poor diet, disease.

The effects of primary aging are seen in all the characteristics that we associate with advancing years: gray hair, wrinkles, susceptibility to disease. As the body ages, its systems degenerate. The brain, for example, loses thousands of cells daily from birth onward. Some of the body's systems, like the skin, are able to regenerate their cells, although they do so less effectively with each passing year. Others, like the kidneys, lack regenerative powers and eventually wear out. More significant, however, is the fact that there is a general decline in the body's immune defenses, which fight off infections like pneumonia. As a result, elderly people often die of diseases that would not usually be fatal to younger people.

Aging is a gradual process; not all of the body's systems age at the same rate. The process of decline usually starts relatively early in life. By the mid-20s the skin begins to lose its elasticity and starts to dry and wrinkle; by 30 the muscles have begun to shrink and decrease in strength. As time passes, the capacity of the lungs is reduced, and less and less air is drawn into the body; circulation slows and the blood supply decreases; bones become brittle and thin; hormonal activity ebbs; and reflexes become slower. Aging is not a disease in itself, but it does increase susceptibility to disease. In old age, therefore, disease becomes chronic rather than episodic.

Some researchers are convinced that each of us carries a personal "timetable" for aging within our cells, a timetable that is controlled by our genes. Others believe that secondary aging factors are also involved. The role of stress is particularly important. One of the most salient age-related changes is the decline in homeostatic capacity—the ability to tolerate stress. This makes older people more susceptible to stress, and it takes them longer to return to normal after being exposed to a stressful situation.

The reduced capacity to cope with stress is a result of primary aging; stress itself is an agent of secondary aging. Together they may be responsible for many of the illnesses that plague the elderly. Older people are confronted by numerous stress-producing situations. Widowhood, the death of friends and family members, and loss of status and productivity are all stressful changes. Studies have demonstrated that such illnesses as leukemia, cancer, and heart disease often strike the elderly in the wake of stress-producing life changes.

There is evidence that many of the effects of aging are neither inevitable nor irreversible. For example, reduced oxygen intake, diminished lung capacity, and slow circulation—and related mental and physical problems—are results not just of age but of the inactivity that comes with it. In one study (Arehart-Triechel, 1977), a group of 70-year-old men participated in a daily exercise program. At the end of a year they had regained the physical-fitness levels of 40-year-olds. Other researchers, studying the effects of vitamin therapy, diet, and hormones on the aging process, are demonstrating that the debilitating conditions associated with age are caused by more than the mere accumulation of years (Riley, 1990).

Psychological Dimensions of Aging

The aging process produces psychological as well as physical effects. Social factors also influence the psychological consequences of age. Self-concept and status are particularly important as aging occurs. One theory views older people as trapped in a shrinking social environment—their world grows smaller and smaller as they leave work, as their friends and family die, and as their mobility decreases; at the same time, their social status changes and they become less influential and less important.

New roles always require some adjustment, but for the elderly this adjustment is complicated because their new roles are poorly defined; there are few role models or reference groups on which they can pattern their behavior. Because of the nebulous quality of their new status, older people become dependent on labels and on the

Some people, such as acclaimed movie actor Katharine Hepburn, are able to perform at extremely high levels of competence even at an advanced age.

opinions of others for their self-definition. In our society the labels applied to the old are consistently negative because they are based on an ethic that equates personal worth with economic productivity (Kuypers & Bengston, 1973; Newman, 1988).

This negative labeling is one of the causes of the psychological difficulties experienced by the aged. The old tend to rely on the image imposed on them, even though that image is a negative one. They internalize it, and eventually their self-image and behavior correspond to the weak, incompetent, useless image that has been forced upon them. It is widely believed, for example, that intellectual ability declines with age. As a consequence, many people are reluctant to place older people in positions of authority or to retrain or reeducate them. Research has shown, however, that this belief is incorrect. Reflexes and responses slow down, but in the absence of organic problems intellectual capacity remains unchanged until very late in life.

False assumptions about the inevitability of the condition known as *senility* account for much of this misunderstanding. Contrary to the widely held belief that one will become senile if one lives long enough, only one of every 100 elderly people can expect to become mentally impaired (Comfort, 1976). "The human brain does not shrink, wilt, perish, or deteriorate with age," says Alex Comfort:

> It normally continues to function well through as many as nine decades. If brain shrinkage or any of the other folkloristic changes were timed by the calendar, Artur Rubenstein at 86 would not have played better than he ever did, nor would Bertrand Russell at 90 have been conducting bitter debates with President Lyndon Johnson. (1976, p. 45)

Negative attitudes about the elderly cause many people to consider an older person senile when in fact that person is merely depressed. In older people, depression causes such symptoms as confusion and loss of certain intellectual abilities. Even elderly people who do become senile do not immediately lose all their capacity for intellectual functioning. Rather, they undergo progressive memory loss. This may be accompanied by gradual decreases in ability to calculate, think abstractly, imagine, speak fluently, or orient oneself in time and space. Eventually this deterioration affects the entire personality, but this is a gradual process (Fisk, 1981).

Recent medical research has provided further evidence that progressive damage and loss of brain function in some elderly people can be traced either to chromosomal loss or damage or to physiological problems such as virus infections (the possible cause of Alzheimer's disease) or exposure to chemical poisons (the possible cause of Parkinson's disease) (Jarvik, 1988). These discoveries could lead to major changes in the diagnosis and treatment of loss of mental faculties in older people. At this writing a controversy is raging over the "suicide machine" that was used to allow a patient with Alzheimer's disease to kill herself even though she was in the early stages of the illness. (See Chapter 2.)

Social and Cultural Dimensions of Aging

The Aged as a Minority Group Social gerontologists frequently refer to the aged as a minority group, pointing out that the elderly exhibit many characteristics of such groups. (See Chapter 9.) Like members of racial and ethnic minority groups, the elderly are victims of prejudice, stereotyping, and discrimination. They are thought to be inflexible, a burden on the young, and incompetent workers. However, some social scientists argue that although the elderly share many of the characteristics of minorities, they are not a true minority group. Unlike traditional minority groups—such as blacks, Native Americans, and Jews—the elderly do not exist as an independent subgroup; everyone has the potential to become old. It has been suggested that it would be more accurate to describe the elderly as a "quasi-minority" (Barron, 1971), reflecting the unique position of the elderly in our society.

The potential power of this quasi-minority is enormous. Not only are the elderly increasing in numbers and as a proportion of the population, but they themselves are changing significantly. As can be seen from the turnout of the elderly at election time, they are a political force to be reckoned with. People over 65 vote at higher rates than the total voting-age population. Thus, as the population grows older, political leaders will be unable to ignore the power wielded by the elderly at the ballot box. In addition, many elderly people remain active in voluntary associations even into their eighties. They play a much larger role in organizational life than most younger people assume (Babchuk et al., 1979).

Myths and Stereotypes About the Elderly Popular culture characterizes old people as senile, lacking in individuality, tranquil, unproductive, conservative, and resistant to change. These beliefs persist despite abundant evidence to the contrary. Many of the myths about older workers, for example, were disproved when they were drawn into the labor force during World War II. Other studies have demonstrated that the elderly are no more difficult to train than the young; in addition, they have a lower than average absentee rate and compare favorably with younger workers in accident rates and productivity.

Some of the most pernicious myths about the elderly are directed against older women. In our society women become devalued much sooner than men; therefore, in old age women tend to have a more negative image than men. Barbara Payne and Frank Whittington (1976) collected and analyzed several major studies about the stereotypes of old age. They found most of those stereotypes to be untrue or based on cultural expectations and social conditioning. Among the topics they considered were the following:

1. *Health.* Older women are portrayed as hypochondriacs and as having more health problems than older men. A number of investigations, including the noted Duke Longitudinal Study of Aging, have shown that there are neither objective nor subjective differences in physical health between men and women. Haug (1981) found that elderly women are more likely than younger women to avoid seeking necessary medical care, and elderly men are more likely than younger men to go to the doctor with a problem.
2. *Marriage.* In a society in which women have traditionally achieved worth only through marriage, widowhood or remaining single are viewed in a very negative light. Older women in particular are characterized as "mateless." This reflects the fact that females tend to outlive males; moreover, older men who want to remarry after the death of a spouse have a greater chance of finding a partner their own age or younger.
3. *Widowhood.* According to a popular stereotype, a widow continues to base her identity on that of her dead husband. This is generally untrue; older women demonstrate a strong sense of personal identity.
4. *The Rocking-Chair Image.* Older women are characterized as grandmotherly types who confine their interests to knitting and rocking by the fireside. A number of studies have shown that there is little difference between the leisure activities of older men and those of older women or between those of people in their middle and later years.

One of the most widely accepted stereotypes about the old is that they are sexually inactive because of both lack of desire and lack of ability. A number of studies have proved that this view is incorrect. Eric Pfeiffer, Adrian Verwoerdt, and Glenn Davis (1972) collected data on the sexual activities of older people and found that while sexual interest and activity tended to decline with age, sex continued to play an important role in the subjects' lives. They also found that elderly men enjoy more sexual interest and activity than elderly women. The principal reason for this distinction is that elderly men are more likely to have a readily available, socially sanctioned, and sexually capable partner.

Many age-related changes in sexual behavior have their antecedents in middle age. Women who have been sexually active throughout their adult lives continue to enjoy sexual activity in old age. Those who have had a less than satisfactory sex life tend to use age as an excuse for avoiding sex (Riley, 1990).

CONCOMITANTS OF AGING

Victimization of the Elderly

The media often portray the old as victims of fraud and violence. Although this kind of reporting may alert the elderly to potential dangers, it also serves to reinforce their image as weak, incompetent, and easy targets. The elderly themselves do not share this view—only 6 percent of people age 65 and older believe that they are "very likely" to be victims of violent crimes (Brown, Flanagan, & McLeod, 1984).

Because many elderly people live in high-crime areas, they run a risk of being victimized. When this does happen, the elderly suffer more than members of other age groups. They are likely to sustain more serious injury during a physical assault and to recover more slowly. Often alone and isolated, old people may lack friends and family members who can provide the emotional support that helps dispel the fear and depression that often follow victimization.

In a study of elderly tenants in public housing, Lawton and Yaffe (1980) found that the social environment of planned housing offers tenants some protection against victimization. Aware of the potential for attack, many tenants shop, do errands, and take walks together. These precautions provide greater security for the participants.

Elderly people are frequent victims of a wide variety of business crimes that prey on their desire for security and comfort. Phony home repair schemes, medical quackery, mail fraud, and schemes to bilk the elderly of their savings abound in nations where there are high proportions of older people living in private homes or apartments. Law enforcement authorities cannot accurately state the amount of loss caused by such swindles, but it is estimated to total hundreds of millions of dollars annually.

Elder Abuse

There is growing awareness in the United States and other aging societies that mental and physical abuse of elderly people is on the rise. (See Chapter 7.) This is especially true in societies where employment opportunities and upward mobility for the working-age population are decreasing. Economic hardship for working-age persons is highly correlated with deteriorating care and even abuse of the elderly, especially the nonaffluent elderly. In recent testimony before Congress it was estimated that there are at least 1.5 million cases of physical abuse of elderly persons in the United States each year, and many experts view this as a conservative estimate because it does not include mental cruelty or severe neglect, which can be as damaging as physical abuse. While much of the elderly abuse reported to authorities occurs in private households, a significant proportion of reported cases occur in nursing homes and other institutional settings.

Health Care and the Aged

Nowadays people either do not encounter the infectious diseases that formerly killed people of all ages or, if they do, they survive them. They live longer, and in their later years their health declines and they become more prone to chronic illnesses, which develop over a long period and are often expensive to treat. Thus, the elderly tend to require increasing amounts of costly medical care, which they may be unable to afford. To complicate matters further, physicians have a tendency to lump together elderly people in a single category, even though an 80-year-old person may be "younger" physiologically and in better health than a 65-year-old person with numerous health problems. Because physicians view older patients largely in terms of chronological age, they often do not provide the same level of care to the elderly that they do to younger patients (Wilkes & Schuchman, 1989).

Many people assumed that with the passage of Medicare and Medicaid the problem of health care for the elderly would be eliminated. But while these programs have alleviated some health-related problems, they have not been completely successful and thousands of elderly people still lack adequate care. The Health Security Act of 1994 is designed to reduce inequalities of access to quality health care for the elderly by asking more affluent elderly people to pay a larger share of their medical costs and by reducing the amount of waste in the present system. At this writing, however, it is not clear what aspects of the reform bill will be passed.

For those who are covered by Medicare and Medicaid, these programs are extremely important. Thirty-five percent of Medicaid expenditures are for the care of elderly people. Medicare covers most hospital costs but only half of physicians' bills; the charges that are not covered can quickly become an enormous financial burden. Moreover, most nursing-home care is not covered, nor are prescription drugs, dental care, hearing aids, eyeglasses, and many other health services. About two-thirds of the elderly have private health insurance in addition to Medicare, but even they can encounter high medical costs if they become seriously ill (Davis, 1986).

Although the problem of medical care for the aged is inextricably linked to the national crisis in health services, some aspects of the problem are unique to the aged. One of these is institutionalization. There are almost 1.4 million people in nursing homes—often not because they require constant attention but because no alternative services are available (*Statistical Abstract,* 1993). Unnecessary institutionalization of the elderly is costly, both in terms of public spending for Medicare and Medicaid and in terms of the negative psychological effects on the occupants.

Economic Discrimination

Older workers are frequent targets of job discrimination. The most common form of discrimination at work is mandatory retirement, a life-altering experience with social, economic, and emotional effects. The practice of mandatory retirement gives companies a tool for cutting labor costs. In a tight economy a company can simply retire its older employees, who earn higher salaries, and replace them with younger workers, who usually are paid less.

Older workers also encounter job discrimination when seeking new employment. The 1967 Age Discrimination in Employment Act is designed to protect workers between 40 and 65 and has not succeeded in eliminating discrimination against those over 65. Employers can no longer advertise for applicants "under 30," but a phrase like "one to three years experience" accomplishes the same goal. When they do obtain interviews, older workers are often rejected as "overqualified," a euphemism for "too old." For these reasons, older unemployed workers remain jobless longer than younger ones.

The social security system has been modified so that the retirement age will increase after the turn of the century. However, the purpose of the change was to reduce financial pressure on the program, not to counteract economic discrimination against the elderly. In fact, it can be argued that public policies toward the aged should be reexamined in light of the improved economic situation of older people today (Palmer & Gould, 1986). A key issue facing American society is how to devise social policies that extend income and medical benefits to the needy elderly while asking those who are affluent to assume a larger share of their own support.

Multiple Jeopardy   To be old, black (or Hispanic or Native American), and female in our society is to experience multiple jeopardy—to face more hardships than one would face if one were in just one or two of these categories.

Although the elderly as a group have fared better economically in recent years

TABLE 11–4 POVERTY BY RACE FOR PERSONS 65 YEARS OR OLDER (IN THOUSANDS)

RACE	TOTAL NUMBER	OVER 65	PERCENT
White	23,747	2,802	10.3
Black	10,242	880	33.8
All races	35,708	3,781	12.4

Source: Statistical Abstract, 1993.

than they did in the past, this is not true of aged blacks. In a report to the House Committee on Aging, the National Caucus and Center on Black Aged (1987) pointed out that elderly blacks are three times as likely to be poor as elderly whites—in fact, over 32 percent of blacks age 65 and over live below the poverty line. (See Table 11–4.) Moreover, their health is poorer than that of whites, and they have fewer contacts with social-service workers. Their old age is a bitter culmination of the discrimination they have suffered all their lives. Most are ineligible for social security because their jobs were menial ones that were not covered by the program. Their health is poor because of inadequate diet and the effects of stressful jobs. In addition, a high percentage of black women live alone.

Figure 11–4 shows that poverty among the elderly is not much worse in the United States than in the United Kingdom, Germany, or Norway, but that compared

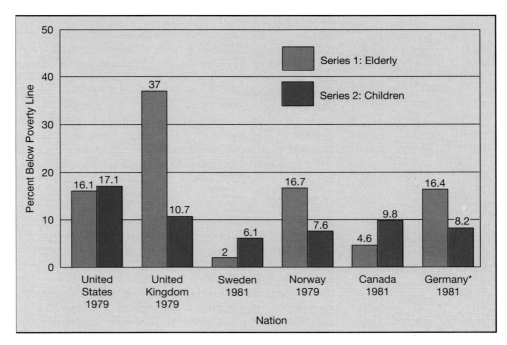

FIGURE 11–4 Comparative Rates of Poverty Using U.S. Poverty Line as Measure

*Former West Germany only.

Source: Adapted from Smeeding, T. M., "Social Thought and Poor Children," Focus, Institute for Research on Poverty, 1990, Vol. 12, No. 3. By permission of the author.

Multiple jeopardy: Many elderly people, especially women and members of minority groups, experience disproportionate levels of poverty and neglect as they become old and frail.

with advanced nations like Sweden or Canada the United States has a long way to go. The figure reveals another, even more ominous situation, however: While poverty among the elderly is not comparatively worse in the United States than in some other nations, the poverty rate among children is higher than in any of those nations. Since poverty among children is associated with a wide range of problems, including poor health, crime, and underachievement in school, it is likely that the effects of childhood poverty will in many cases persist through the entire life cycle, making it more difficult to reduce poverty among the elderly.

Women of all races are disadvantaged in old age. As they move away from the ideal of female attractiveness established by a youth-oriented society, they are increasingly devalued. There are almost 19 million elderly women in America (*Statistical Abstract,* 1993), and many of them have financial problems. Because their salaries were lower than those of men, their pensions and social security benefits are also lower. The social security system gives no credit for homemaking, the principal occupation of most women until recent decades. Older women who want to work suffer the double burdens of age and sex discrimination.

Family Problems

One of the most pervasive myths about the aged is that they are abandoned by their children. In reality, however, the majority of old people who live alone do so voluntarily (Brody, 1978); they often wish to live near their children but not with them. However, many elderly people *do* live with one of their children, and those who do not live with their children see them frequently.

The institutionalized elderly are not typical. They represent a special population who are, on the average, a decade older than most elderly people; in addition, they suffer severe chronic physical or mental ailments. Most of them have outlived their spouse and relatives; many have also outlived their children.

Placing an aged relative in an institution is usually a difficult experience. As Elaine M. Brody (1978) has written,

> *Prior to the institutionalization most families have endured severe personal, social and economic stress in attempting to avoid admission; it is typically the last, not the first resort; and the decision is made reluctantly. The "well" spouse usually is in advanced old age.*

The adult children are approaching or engaged in the aging phase of life with attendant age-related stresses and often are subjected to competing demands from ill spouses or their own children. (p. 21)

The problems of caring for the elderly at home are complicated by the fact that as more people live to an extremely old age, the total family unit ages. People age 65 may have to provide 24-hour care for parents age 90 while experiencing economic and health problems of their own. There may be two generations of elderly people in one family, requiring different degrees of care. Morover, the mobility that is characteristic of Americans may leave parents and their adult children separated by thousands of miles, making home care impossible.

The high divorce rate, the growing number of single-parent families, and the trend toward smaller families also affect the possibilities for home care for the aged. Future generations of old people may lack relatives to care for them, or they may have weak family ties.

Changes in the roles of women also affect how the old are treated. Historically, tending the elderly was the task of daughters or daughters-in-law, who were full-time homemakers. As more women work outside the home, they are less available to care for aged parents. Yet women who work full time are still more likely than men to be expected to care for elderly parents, a situation that can greatly increase the stress and physical burdens experienced by working women.

By the turn of the century the American family will have fewer children but the same number of grandparents and great-grandparents. In addition, there will be multiple patterns of kinship created by divorce and remarriage. In addition to tensions between parents and growing children, there will be tensions between aging parents and adult offspring.

RETIREMENT

Retirement is a fairly recent concept. Before the advent of social security and pension plans, few workers could afford to stop working. As a result, people worked into old age, often modifying the nature of their work to match their diminished strength.

Studies by gerontologists indicate that younger workers foresee retirement before age 65, if possible, but that older workers more often hope to retire later than the conventional age of 65 (Ekerdt, Bosse, & Mogey, 1980). In general, workers would *prefer* to retire earlier but *plan* to retire later. For the most part, this difference is explained by economic factors. If private pension plans and public benefits were improved or a guaranteed minimum income were enacted, people would seek more leisure in their old age. Although these feelings are shared by a majority of the elderly, significant numbers of workers would prefer to continue working as long as possible even if they could be assured of financial security in retirement (Szinovacz et al., 1992).

Even when people have retired from jobs they disliked, they face difficulty in adjusting to their new status. Part of the difficulty lies in the lack of role models and reference groups. As noted earlier in the chapter, this is a problem that all older people must cope with, even the fortunate few who have financial security and good health.

As with any other life experience, different people adjust differently to retirement. One study indicated that about one-third of retired people have difficulty making this adjustment (Atchley, 1978). The most common cause of this difficulty is reduced income. Forty percent of those interviewed cited this reason; another 22 percent mentioned missing their former jobs as the chief problem; 38 percent cited age-related factors such as fears about health or loss of a spouse. The individuals who had the greatest difficulty were those who lacked flexibility and those for whom work was the primary source of satisfaction and self-image. The happiest retirees were those who were able to develop a new hierarchy of values stressing personal relationships, self-development, and leisure activities rather than economic status, power, or position within a company.

Retirement and Leisure

A study conducted by M. Powell Lawton (1978) showed that the later years are likely to be sedentary ones. Lawton's research indicated that sleep and television-viewing outrank traditional leisure activities like sports, gardening, clubs, and other pastimes. The reason for this pattern, in Lawton's view, may be found in the past experience of today's older people. This age cohort was born in an era when the average work week was fifty hours long. Their own working lives began in the period of the forty-eight–hour week, when vacations were rare and holidays were few. Homemakers cared for larger houses and larger families, and they had few labor-saving devices or products. These people had little opportunity to develop an understanding or appreciation of leisure. Moreover, many elderly people are poorly educated, a factor that makes them less likely to enjoy reading or activities that focus on new knowledge or self-improvement. Reduction in income, fear of crime, lack of transportation, and reduced mobility also contribute to the sedentary life of the elderly.

Future generations of retirees will probably be different. Those who have enjoyed affluence, travel, and education are more likely to enjoy retirement. This trend is already evident in the form of retirement communities that offer golf, swimming, and recreational centers. The cohorts that follow these younger retirees, those who came of age in the 1960s and later, to whom leisure and personal growth are as desirable as social status and work, will probably come to retirement with even more interest in and awareness of the uses of free time.

DEATH

Perhaps the most fundamental cause of our negative attitude toward aging is our overwhelming fear of death. To exorcise that fear, we often view people who are about to die as redundant and irrelevant while they are still alive. If those who are about to die are trivialized, death may be seen as meaningless also, and we need not be afraid of it (Jones, 1977).

Death and age have always been closely linked, but today death is almost exclusively the fate of the old. This association has some significant implications:

> Although the old have always died, the dying have not always been old. It is only in very recent decades that death has become primarily the province of the elderly, rather than an event scattered erratically across the life span. . . . Because of the close association between old age and death in modern industrial societies, the individual and social issues relating to death are in many ways individual and social issues of aging. . . . One of the significant reasons that the old are avoided and isolated is their proximity to death. (Kalish, 1976, p. 484)

Social scientists study death in terms of its psychological and social impact. Their research indicates that the old, perhaps because of a natural process of disengagement, have less fear of death than the young. There are also indications that during the process of dying a distinct pattern of feelings and behavior emerges. This *dying trajectory* differs from one person to another and from one situation to another.

The best-known description of the dying trajectory was proposed by Elisabeth Kübler-Ross (1969, 1975). Kübler-Ross believes that the dying process is characterized by five stages: (1) denial and isolation, (2) anger and resentment, (3) bargaining and an attempt to postpone death, (4) depression and a sense of loss, and (5) acceptance. Some social scientists have pointed out that Kübler-Ross's research was done primarily on younger people with terminal illnesses, and that the stages she identified may

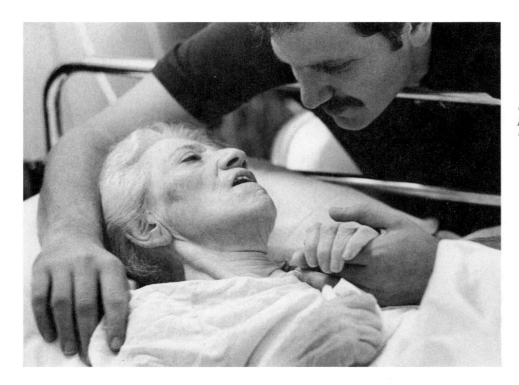

The hospice creates a social environment in which dying persons are treated with dignity and compassion.

not always apply to the elderly—especially the very old, who sometimes claim to be ready for death well before it is clear that they are dying (Retsinas, 1988).

By understanding the dying process, physicians, caretakers, friends, and family members can make the experience easier for the dying person. Being informed of one's true condition has been identified as very important to the terminally ill (Abdellah, 1978). A number of studies suggest, however, that current practices in hospitals and nursing homes offer almost no possibility of a good and meaningful death. Critically ill patients are usually treated as though they were already dead. Their autopsies are planned; they are sometimes kept in hallways or supply closets; their relatives may be approached regarding donation of organs. In contrast, *hospices*—special institutions designed for the terminally ill—are as comfortable and homelike as possible and are staffed by personnel who are trained in working with the dying. A hospice may be a place, a set of services, or both. Hospices increasingly emphasize home health services for the dying, including visiting nurses, on-call physicians, and counselors. Home care enables many people to live their final days in familiar surroundings close to their loved ones.

The underlying problem addressed by the hospice movement is one that was discussed in Chapter 2: Today, because of the availability of life-prolonging medical technologies, people are increasingly faced with choices about how to die. Surveys indicate that most people would prefer to die at home. Being at home with one's family seems to provide a greater chance for "death with dignity"; being institutionalized implies loss of control and individuality.

Federal laws that allow Medicare reimbursement for home hospice care went into effect in 1983. This policy change encouraged more people to choose home care for the dying. In consequence, the number of hospice patients has more than doubled, from 101,000 in the early 1980s to 207,000 in 1992. While this figure indicates the increasing popularity of dying at home, it masks the extreme stress many individuals and families may experience as they attempt to provide round-the-clock care for dying loved ones in their homes (Belkin, 1992).

"Death with dignity" has become a popular phrase as people confront the issues of relegating the old and the terminally ill to institutions and to a life sustained by machines. Often the use of these technologies amounts to prolonging dying rather than maintaining life. Widespread concern about these issues is further evidence of the need for hospices and home health care for the aged.

SOCIAL POLICY

The primary social-policy issues related to the situation of the elderly are housing, health care (including controversies over the "right to die"), and retirement and social security.

Housing

In the 1980s only about 15 percent of Americans age 65 and over lived in housing specifically designated for the elderly. Another 5 percent lived in institutions such as nursing homes. The majority lived in a family setting (usually with a spouse); about 30 percent lived alone. In recent years the percentage living alone has increased rapidly (Carlin & Mansberg, 1987).

Most elderly people who live with their children or other younger relatives do so for financial reasons or because of declining health. Most older people prefer to live in their own homes but near family members. However, as they and their homes age, problems arise that are increasingly difficult to cope with. At the same time, their income tends to decrease and their health-care needs tend to increase, further reducing their ability to live independently.

Despite these problems, most older people want to continue living where they are. Not only do they view it as demeaning to move to a retirement community or an "old folks' home," but their housing choices may be limited by long waiting lists or lack of appropriate housing in a particular area. Among people age 65–74, only about 2 percent are in nursing homes; of those age 75–84, 6 percent are in homes. But among those over 85, 23 percent are in nursing homes, according to federal surveys. Because so many more people in the latter group suffer dementia or physical infirmities, the rapid growth of this group means that an increasing proportion will require nursing-home or comparable care. This, in turn, will require an increase in public funds for such care from the present level of about $20 billion.

In the early 1980s the government's budget cuts curtailed social-welfare pro-

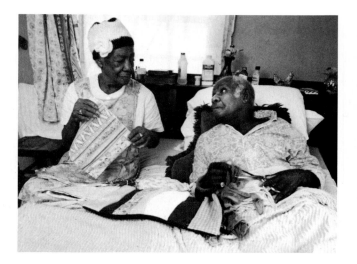

Even after the age of 100, this couple was still actively involved in volunteer work. They continued to live in their own home and enjoyed being near a kinship network that included nine living children and thirty grandchildren.

grams of all kinds. Among the casualties were programs to provide housing for low-income Americans of all ages, as well as federal regulation of the nursing-home industry. At present, therefore, there is no coherent policy regarding housing for the aged, although both the federal and state governments have attempted to promote home care for the frail elderly as an alternative to nursing homes.

Health Care

The problem of providing health care for the aged must be viewed in the context of the rapid expansion of the elderly population. Between 1900 and 1980 the number of Americans over 65 grew eightfold while the population as a whole tripled. By 2030 nearly one-quarter of the U.S. population will be over 65 (Eckholm, 1990). Moreover, more than 3 million elderly people are among the "oldest old"—those over 85—currently the fastest growing age group in the nation. These people are most likely to be mentally or physically impaired and, hence, most in need of care that they cannot afford.

As a result of these trends, Medicare, the federal program that provides health care for the elderly, is in financial trouble. The basic problem is that Medicare payments to doctors, hospitals, and other health-care facilities are increasing at a faster rate than the revenues coming into the fund from payroll taxes (Medicare is part of the social security system). This accounts for the highly controversial proposals currently in Congress that would require elderly people in higher income brackets to pay taxes on the Medicare benefits they receive, to pay for a larger share of their medical care, and to obtain a second opinion before undergoing major surgery. These recommendations are opposed by representatives of the black elderly, who believe that blacks suffer disproportionately from cutbacks in Medicare and Medicaid coverage. They recommend instead that greater emphasis be placed on cost containment and preventive measures (National Caucus and Center on Black Aged, 1987).

Some observers believe that a more comprehensive policy toward health care for the elderly is needed. In the meantime, greater planning and steps to distribute income to living family members so that it is not absorbed by long-term care are becoming a ritual of aging in many families. Many elderly people fear that they will lose all their savings if they are placed in a residential care institution, be it a nursing home or a long-term care facility. Recent changes in the Medicare laws protect an elderly spouse from losing all his or her savings if the other member of the couple is institutionalized. Typically, however, the elderly person lives alone, and it is still common for insurance plans, including Medicare, to insist that an individual's assets be used to pay the costs of nursing home or hospital care above what Medicare will contribute. As a result, many elderly people are creating "living trusts" (not to be confused with the "living wills" discussed in Box 11–1 on page 344) in which they cede ownership of their assets to their children or beneficiaries but retain the right to use those assets to pay for their living expenses. The Clinton health plan proposes to improve Medicare coverage for nursing-home care and to provide incentives for the purchase of long-term care insurance, but it is not yet clear what aspects of those proposals will be approved by Congress.

Retirement and Social Security

The social security system was not designed to be the main source of income for the elderly. It was originally intended as a form of insurance against unexpected reductions in income due to retirement, disability, or the death of a wage-earning spouse. However, the system has become a kind of government-administered public pension plan. Many people do not have pensions, investments, or sufficient savings to support them in retirement, and this, coupled with the practice of mandatory retirement, has made social security the main source of income for the elderly.

Perhaps the greatest flaw in the social security system is that its benefits are too

BOX 11–1 CURRENT CONTROVERSIES: DO WE HAVE A RIGHT TO DIE?

Probably the most controversial doctor in the United States these days is Jack Kevorkian, the so-called "Michigan suicide doctor." It seems that whenever he uses his painless death apparatus to inject a willing patient with a lethal drug he is featured in the national news and either imprisoned or threatened with imprisonment. Kevorkian's actions raise a larger issue for public debate: Do individuals have the right to kill themselves, and do doctors or other medical professionals have the right to allow them to do so or even to assist them? As more people in this and other aging nations endure lingering and painful illnesses after having lived a long life, these questions will be asked with increasing frequency.

The ancient Hippocratic norms of medical practice deny doctors the right to hasten death. But these norms are changing as a growing number of terminally ill patients plead with medical professionals for alternatives to life-prolonging procedures that may actually increase their physical and mental suffering. Faced with the inevitability of death from a terminal illness such as cancer, some individuals would prefer to die in relative comfort at a prescribed time and place, while others would choose to fight the disease to the end in order to cling to life and remain with their loved ones as long as possible. From an ethical standpoint, does the individual have the right to make this decision or should institutions of the state have the right to impose rules that supersede the individual's choice?

Thomas Szasz, himself one of the more controversial critics of mental and medical care in the United States, strongly advocates the right of sui-cide. He is, however, careful to point out the difference between a right to act and the idea that an action should be valued by all. "The right to do X," he writes, "does not mean that doing X is morally meritorious. We have the right to divorce our spouse, vote for a politician we know nothing about, eat until we are obese, or squander our money on lottery tickets." Thus, he argues that the "right to suicide" does not mean that suicide is morally desirable. "It only means that agents of the state have no right or power to interfere, by prohibitions or punishments, with a person's decision to kill himself" (Szasz, 1992, pp. 161–162). In his view, the state and all others who wish to prevent a particular person from killing himself or herself must be content to use persuasion to try to make that person change his or her mind.

Clearly these ideas are extremely controversial. Those who believe in the sanctity of life are quick to argue that for the state to condone assisted suicide or the individual's right to commit suicide by any means is an abdication of the obligation to value human life, be it that of an unborn fetus or an aging, terminally ill individual (Wilson, 1994). Szasz and others who support the right to die admit that Kevorkian is performing a public service by raising the issue for public debate. They also believe that ultimately an individual of any age ought to have access to the drugs or other means that would allow death to be an individual choice, not one that must be assisted by a "death doctor." At this writing, Kevorkian himself has agreed to refrain from assisting suicides until the issue has been resolved.

small for the purpose they must serve. In 1991 the average monthly social security benefit was $629 to retired workers, $609 to disabled workers, and $584 to widows and widowers (*Statistical Abstract*, 1993). This is far from an adequate income.

Social security is financed by fixed wage and payroll taxes based on the first $60,600 of annual income. This means that lower-paid workers pay a higher proportion of their income in social security taxes than higher-paid workers do. Social security benefits, however, are based on the amount of tax paid, not on a percentage of total income. Thus, the poorest workers will remain the poorest after retiring.

Those who want to supplement their social security benefits by continuing to work find that they are confronted with the heaviest tax burden of any age or income group. Until age 65, a person cannot earn more than $8,040 per year without incurring a reduction in social security benefits. For every two dollars earned in excess of that, one dollar in social security is deducted—in effect, a 50 percent tax rate. The earned income is fully liable to both income and social security taxes. Thus, people over 65 who work not only are deprived of a substantial portion of the benefits for which they have already paid but are compelled to continue to pay for it even though they are not permitted to receive it. This inequity is compounded by the fact that nonwage income—such as capital gains or interest on savings—may be earned in any amount without affecting social security benefits. The well-to-do, who are likely to have these kinds of nonwage income, can therefore receive their social security benefits in full while less affluent workers who try to supplement their social security benefits are penalized.

The social security system also discriminates against women. At age 65 a woman is entitled to benefits equal to half of those received by her husband, even if she has never worked outside the home. If she has been employed and has paid social security taxes, she can receive benefits on her own account or through her husband. But she cannot do both. Since most husbands work longer than their wives, most women can collect higher social security payments by drawing from their husbands' accounts.

The most fundamental criticism of the social security system is that it denies that the elderly can and should remain productive. Under current policies large numbers of people are maintained outside the labor force in order to benefit the remaining workers. This is a costly approach, and the costs are increasing as the proportion of older people in the population increases.

Some social scientists call for a radical transformation of public policy toward the elderly. They believe that policy should be based on the idea that people of all ages should have productive roles in society—that society can benefit from the creativity, talent, and motivation of its members throughout their lives. This approach would require far more flexibility in such areas as social security eligibility requirements, employment policies, and private pension arrangements (Morrison, 1986).

SUMMARY

1. The United States is an aging society, and this fact has a major impact on social institutions as well as on the lives of individuals. The social problems of the aged are aggravated by three factors: labeling, the concept of work as the basis of personal value, and economic deprivation.

2. From the functionalist perspective, aging is a social problem because the institutions of modern society are not meeting the needs of the dependent aged. Interactionists believe the elderly are stigmatized because they do not conform to the norms of a youth-oriented culture. Conflict theorists view the problems of the elderly as stemming from older people's lack of power to shape social institutions to meet their needs.

3. Many of the problems faced by the aged in America today arise from the nature of modern Western society, in which the productive and cultural roles of the aged have been disrupted by modernization.

4. Age stratification is the segregation of people into different groups or strata on the basis of their age. It limits the kinds of roles that the members of each group can hold, and it can lead to conflict.

5. The number of aged people in the United States is increasing along with life expectancy, and so is the proportion of the population that is over 65. Two-thirds of the elderly live in urban areas.

6. Ageism is bias against the aged. It arises largely from the belief that the old are useless because they do not work and cannot reproduce, and it is common in government, business, industry, the medical profession, and the media.

7. The aging process can be divided into primary aging and secondary aging. Primary aging is a result of molecular and cellular changes. Secondary aging is an accelerated version of normal aging caused by environmental factors such as stress or poor diet.

8. The psychological difficulties experienced by the aged stem largely from the fact that their new status is poorly defined and they therefore tend to accept the negative labels that are applied to them. For example, it is widely believed that intellectual ability declines with age, but this belief is incorrect. Intellectual capacity remains unchanged until very late in life, and senility affects only 1 percent of elderly people.

9. The aged exhibit many characteristics of minority groups. In particular, they are victims of prejudice, stereotyping, and discrimination. They are also increasingly subject to mental and physical abuse. Among the popular stereotypes about the elderly are the portrayal of older women as hypochondriacs, the negative view of widowhood, the rocking-chair image, and the belief that the old are sexually inactive.

10. The aged are more prone to chronic illness but less able to pay for medical care. Despite the passage of Medicare and Medicaid, many elderly people still lack adequate health care. A major geriatric health issue is unnecessary institutionalization.

11. Older workers often experience economic discrimination, both in the form of mandatory retirement and when they seek new employment. Older women and members of minority groups face additional hardships.

12. Most older people want to live near their children, and many live with them. Many families, however, are ill equipped to care for elderly parents, making institutionalization the only alternative for those who are unable or unwilling to live alone.

13. Workers who retire face difficulty in adjusting to their new status. They lack role models and reference groups; many must also cope with reduced income. For some, leisure is unfamiliar and even threatening.

14. Social scientists have studied the dying trajectory—the pattern of feelings and behavior that emerges during the dying process. They have identified five stages: denial, anger, bargaining, depression, and acceptance. The hospice movement attempts to provide special institutions for the terminally ill as well as home health services for the dying.

15. There is no coherent policy regarding housing for the aged, and existing health-care programs are costly and inadequate. The social security system has also been a target of criticism because it discriminates against women and against elderly people who continue to work, and because the payments are too low to support people without other sources of income. Some social scientists believe that there is a need for a radical transformation of public policy to enable older people to maintain productive roles in society.

SUGGESTED READINGS

GELFLAND, DONALD E., and ALFRED J. KUTZIK, EDS. *Ethnicity and Aging: Theory, Research and Policy.* New York: Springer, 1979. A collection of articles about numerous minority groups; addresses the dilemma of how to reduce inequality without destroying ethnic identification.

HOBMAN, DAVID, ED. *The Impact of Aging.* New York: St. Martin's Press, 1981. A comprehensive survey of the needs of the aged in industrial societies.

HUDSON, ROBERT B., ED. *The Aging in Politics: Process and Policy.* Springfield, IL: Charles C Thomas, 1981. A set of readings that examines the place of the elderly in the political process.

JOHNSON, ELIZABETH S., and JOHN B. WILLIAMSON. *Growing Old: The Social Problems of Aging.* Fort Worth, TX: Holt, Rinehart and Winston, 1980. A discussion of various social problems facing the aged, such as crime, work and retirement, health care, and death and dying.

LOFLAND, LYN H. *The Craft of Dying: The Modern Face of Death.* Newbury Park, CA: Sage, 1979. An analysis of death and dying in modern society from both a historical and a sociological perspective.

National Caucus and Center on Black Aged. *The Status of the Black Elderly in the United States,* a report for the Select Committee on Aging, U.S. House of Representatives, 1987. Documents the relative disadvantage of minority elderly people and shows that they have not gained proportionately from the social-welfare legislation of the past twenty years.

PIFER, ALAN, and LYDIA D. BRONTE. "The Aging Society." *Daedalus* (Winter 1986). Essential reading for anyone who is interested in the consequences of aging in the United States. Includes essays by many of the nation's foremost writers on aging and social policy.

RILEY, MATILDA WHITE. "On the Significance of Age in Sociology." *American Sociological Review 52* (1987): 1–14. A summary essay by the dean of American gerontologists about the social organization of aging and the consequences of aging through the life cycle.

The Changing Family

Chapter Outline

- In 1992, 20 percent of families with earners conformed to the traditional concept of the family, in which the husband worked in the paid labor force while the wife cared for the home.

- In 1991 half as many couples got divorced as married, representing a divorce rate of 4.7 per 1,000 population.

- In 1986 the annual fertility rate in the United States reached the lowest point ever recorded.

- For every 100 unmarried women between the ages of 18 and 24, there are 114 unmarried men; for every 100 unmarried women between the ages of 35 and 44, there are 97 unmarried men.

- Teenage women constitute roughly 25 percent of the population of childbearing age, yet they account for over 45 percent of all illegitimate births.

Do children still chant the old jumprope rhyme, "First comes love, then comes marriage, then comes Mary with the baby carriage"? If so, they are clearly behind the times. As a national news magazine pointed out in an issue devoted to the "state of the American family," a likely sequel to the traditional rhyme is that Mary and John break up two or three years after having the baby. John moves in with Sally and her two boys; the baby stays with Mary, who marries Jack (who is divorced and has three children). Before the baby can understand what is going on, he or she has a family composed of a mother, a father, a stepfather, a stepmother, five stepbrothers and stepsisters, and four sets of grandparents (biological and step).

If this sounds confusing to you, imagine what it takes for young children to make sense of all these relationships. Yet such "confusion" is becoming more normal all the time: About one-third of all children born in the 1980s will probably live with a stepparent before they reach the age of 18 (Kantrowitz & Wingert, 1990; Sweet & Bumpass, 1987). But do these changes mean that the family is on the verge of collapse or that the traditional two-parent family is a thing of the past?

During the 1992 presidential election campaign, the issue of changes in family form and their supposed threat to "family values" was at the center of public debate. Vice-President Dan Quayle and President George Bush appeared to condemn single parenthood and other deviations from the traditional two-parent nuclear family. This did not endear them to the millions of couples who are facing the difficulties of raising children while holding down at least two jobs, and it certainly backfired with single parents who felt slighted by the campaign rhetoric. On the other hand, many social scientists are concerned that the growing numbers of fatherless children and the increase in poverty among children, whatever the causes, promise to produce many other social problems (Popenoe, 1994).

No matter how they view the consequences of change in families, sociologists agree that the family is here to stay as a social institution. They also agree that what Americans understand by "family" is becoming far more diverse. Alongside more traditional two-parent nuclear families, there will be an increasing number of families with one parent or with stepparents, as well as gay and lesbian families. A major question, to which we will turn in the Social Policy section of this chapter, is to what extent laws and other government policies can help people in families of all kinds realize their full potential as human beings.

Many marriages may end in divorce; many children may be raised by one parent or by other relatives; yet society may continue to regard the nuclear family as the norm. In another society an extended-family system might remain the norm despite the frequent breaking up of such families into nuclear units. A social problem arises only when the pressure for change can no longer be accommodated within the lim-

The marriage ceremony represents not only the couple's commitment to each other but also the value placed by society on the family as an institution.

its of the existing social structures or when those who want to maintain those structures fear that they cannot do so. Often these pressures result in changes in the norms themselves. For example, as divorce rates rise, we no longer condemn couples whose marriages are about to break up; instead, we alter our norms regarding marriage. We encourage couples to work out their problems, but if divorce is inevitable, we accept it and sanction another, relatively new norm—remarriage.

As the social institution that organizes intimate relationships among adults and socializes new generations, the family is frequently singled out as the source of many social problems. Functionalist theorists argue that the inability of certain groups, especially the poor and immigrants, to maintain their traditional structures in new societies causes their children to seek alternative relationships—for example, in gangs, criminal groups, or other deviant peer groups. Interactionists study family interaction patterns for clues to why some family members drift toward deviant careers. They often find that certain kinds of families, especially those headed by women or those in which the couple does not marry and conform to conventional norms of family formation, are stigmatized and viewed as the source of social problems like illegitimacy and welfare dependency. For conflict theorists, the family is a source of social problems when the values that are taught within it conflict with those of the larger society. But regardless of their theoretical perspective on the family, sociologists tend to focus on what can be done by other institutions in society, particularly social-welfare institutions, to maintain and reinforce family stability.

In this chapter we will examine various types of problems and policy initiatives related to family structure. But first it is important to gain a clear understanding of the nature of families.

THE NATURE OF FAMILIES

A *kinship unit* is a group of individuals who are related to one another by blood, marriage, or adoption. Within the kinship group there is usually a division of authority, privilege, responsibility, and economic and sex roles. Definitions of kinship differ from one society to another. In some societies the basic kinship group is the

The nuclear family unit consisting of mother, father, and children is common not only in modern industrial nations but in many hunting-and-gathering societies as well. In fact, the traditional Eskimo family kinship system is organized in much the same way as the American nuclear family.

nuclear family—a father, a mother, and their children living apart from other kin (or, increasingly, a single parent and his or her children). In other societies a more common type of kinship group is the *extended family*—parents, children, grandparents, aunts, uncles, and others living together or in very close proximity. In the typical extended family, parents may retain authority over their married sons and daughters, who maintain their nuclear family units within the larger extended-family kinship structure. Increasingly, societies exhibit another type of kinship group, known as the *modified extended family,* in which the individual nuclear families live separately but the extended family remains as a strong kinship organization through a combination of interpersonal attachments among its members and various forms of economic exchanges and mutual aid within the extended-family structure.

The nuclear family is the predominant kinship group in hunting-and-gathering societies and in industrial societies, whereas the extended family is more likely to be found in agrarian societies. However, almost all societies, no matter what their level of economic and political development, are organized around a system of modified extended kinship units within which the nuclear family is a more or less autonomous unit. In societies in which the extended kin system is the dominant family type, married couples generally choose to live within the family network established by either the man's or the woman's kinship group. In societies in which the nuclear family is dominant, newly married couples are expected to set up a household that is relatively independent of both the maternal and the paternal kinship groups while maintaining ties to both extended families.

Industrialization seems to promote the development of smaller family units that are more mobile both geographically and socially: Although extensive ties with relatives may be maintained, the nuclear family becomes the basic familial unit as the extended family loses its major functions. In recent years, however, sociologists have begun to question this basic functionalist hypothesis about changing family structure and form. Functionalist theory proposed that industrialization, the growth of cities, and modern technology and its demands for a highly educated and mobile labor force brought about a decrease in the economic functions of the extended family and an increase in the functions of the nuclear family (Goode, 1959; Parsons, 1943). After years of empirical research on changing family structure in different types of societies, sociologists no longer believe that there is a unilinear trend from extended to nuclear family forms that accompanies industrialization and urbanization. There is evidence from some societies that nuclear families dominated in preindustrial periods and evidence from some industrial societies that extended-family forms persist even with increases in nuclear family organization. Changes in family form and function in the United States and other large contemporary societies suggest that many different family forms are possible and will coexist under different economic and social conditions within a society (Huber & Spitze, 1988).

Regardless of type, all families are characterized by an organization of roles. If the family is to function adequately, its members must perform those roles in ways that are compatible both with the expectations of other family members and with the standards of their society.

Adequate Family Functioning

All families are continually undergoing change because they must constantly adapt to a "family cycle" of development in which the roles of all family members change (Glick & Parke, 1965; McGoldrick & Carter, 1982; Minuchin, 1981). For example, most families go through the stages of early marriage, child rearing, the empty nest, and retirement. During each stage, and in the periods of transition from one stage to the next, the family faces the challenge of maintaining stability and continuity, that is, functioning adequately. Five criteria for adequate family functioning have been suggested (Glasser & Glasser, 1966):

1. *Internal role consistency among family members.* If family members are to contribute to the proper functioning of the family, they must understand what is expected of them and of other family members.
2. *Consistency of family roles and actual role performance.* The requirements that each family is expected to fulfill do not change suddenly, nor is there a severe change in the way family members fulfill their required roles during any particular stage of the family cycle.
3. *Compatibility of family norms with societal norms.* The behavior of family members must conform to societal norms. The limits of society's tolerance of noncomformity vary from one society to another.
4. *Ability to meet the psychological needs of family members.* A family does not function adequately if it is unable to meet the long-term emotional and psychological needs of its members.
5. *Ability of the family group to respond to change.* To maintain itself over a long period, the family must be able to respond to demands for change, whether those demands originate inside or outside the family unit.

All couples argue, but the conflict-habituated relationship is one in which arguments are routine and the couple's home life tends to be tense and unhappy.

Failure to perform any one of these functions could lead to problems within the family. Such failure is usually involuntary, resulting from either external or internal crises. External crises such as war and economic recession disrupt the family from the outside. The absence of a parent during military service changes both that parent's roles and those of the other parent; unemployment of a parent who usually works can be unsettling not only because other family members are likely to be anxious about their unexpected economic insecurity but also because the unemployed parent suffers a loss of self-esteem and/or authority.

Internal crises arise within the family—for example, when a family member suffers from a serious physical or mental disorder. Many families adjust to the need to take on the roles of the handicapped member and the responsibility of caring for him or her. However, this added burden may cause strain between family members. Marital infidelity can be another source of internal crisis, particularly if it is seen as a threat to the family. A major change in the roles of family members may also provoke an internal crisis. For example, a parent who suddenly decides to work outside the home instead of staying home with the children may cause other family members to feel threatened or confused.

These stresses and other interpersonal problems may reduce the family to an "empty shell," one that is held together not so much by feelings of warmth and attraction among its members as by outside pressures. Within the shell, members of the family feel no strong attachment to one another; they neglect mutual obligations and in general keep communication to a minimum.

Some social scientists (e.g., Cline, 1962; Cuber & Haroff, 1965) have distinguished among three types of empty-shell marriages. The first, referred to as the *conflict-habituated relationship,* is characterized by considerable tension and conflict. The husband and wife may quarrel frequently in private yet appear compatible in public. The atmosphere in such a home is usually tense and bitter.

A second type is the *devitalized relationship,* in which the marriage began as "vital"—filled with excitement and mutual gratification—but then drifted toward a state in which the interaction between husband and wife lacks any real interest or excitement. Apathy and boredom are characteristic of such marriages, and serious or violent arguments are rare.

A third type is the *passive-congenial relationship,* in which both partners never expected the marriage to be more than a convenience. They are content with their lives but not actually happy. There is little overt conflict, and the partners may have interests in common. Those interests tend to be insignificant, however, and there is little evidence that either spouse contributes in any meaningful way to the satisfactions of the other.

Several factors contribute to the continuation of these empty-shell marriages. Habit and fear of change play a role, as do economic constraints. In addition, both partners may feel that divorce or separation would be wrong or might harm the children. There is also usually some social pressure to stay together; in many places social life for adults more or less presupposes married couples. Also, some marriage counselors assume that their job is to preserve the marriage, even though their clients might be happier unmarried.

Although about half of all marriages begun during the 1980s and early 1990s will end in divorce, another half will not. Since the breakup of marriages is more often associated with social problems, less attention is devoted to marriages that remain vital throughout the partners' lives. Indeed, with all the stresses and changes that couples must endure, and given the greater acceptance of divorce, it is almost miraculous that so many marriages remain satisfying in that each partner feels fulfilled emotionally, sexually, and socially even with advancing age. Sociologists are only beginning to understand what makes marriages last and remain vital, but clearly economic influences on the married couple are of great importance (Kitson, Benson-Babri, & Roach, 1985).

Effects of Women's Employment

In the traditional concept of the American family, the husband worked in the paid labor force while the wife worked—unpaid—at home. In 1960, about 60 percent of American families still conformed to this model. By 1992, only 20 percent did. (See Table 12–1 on page 356.) What had been accepted as the norm for generations has become an exception. Today almost 68 percent of American women with children under 18 work outside the home (*Statistical Abstract*, 1993).

Many women entered the labor force in order to use the skills they had learned in college and out of a new sense of identity stimulated by the women's movement. Many others found jobs simply because they needed the money. For both groups, the reversals of economic trends that occurred in the late 1970s and early 1990s were major blows. Economic opportunities became less abundant and debt replaced savings. The cost of living outstripped disposable income, and people found themselves working harder than ever just to keep from falling behind. In many cases women were hit hardest by these economic recessions. Often they were single parents, but even working wives experienced severe stress and anxiety. As Katherine Newman found in her extensive interviews of middle-class women, "Having experienced the benefits of middle-class life in their own childhoods, they felt they owed it to their kids to reciprocate across the generations. Downward mobility made it almost impossible to follow through" (1988, p. 215).

Most sociologists agree that the movement of women out of the home and into the labor force is one of the most important social trends of the second half of the twentieth century. It has caused an upheaval in traditional male and female roles within the family as well as in other social institutions as couples struggle to balance the demands of work and family life.

Despite this massive change, attitudes about working mothers have not changed as fast as the statistics. In her study of women who became mothers after the massive movement of American women into the labor force, sociologist Kathleen Gerson (1985) found that most expected or hoped to be able to stay home and care for their young children as their mothers had done. Those whose mothers had been full-time workers expected to be workers themselves and typically welcomed the challenges of work and motherhood. But for all working mothers Gerson found that

TABLE 12–1 FAMILIES WITH EARNERS,* BY TYPE OF FAMILY, 1992

	NUMBER OF FAMILIES (IN THOUSANDS)	PERCENT OF TOTAL FAMILIES WITH EARNERS
Total Families with Earners	44,137	100.0
Married–Couple Families	34,280	77.7
One earner	12,200	28
Husband	8,667	20
Wife	2,801	6
Other family member	732	1
Two or more earners[1]	22,080	50
Husband and wife only	16,225	38
Husband and other family member(s)	1,617	4
Wife and other family member(s)	597	1
Other family members only	158	—
Families Maintained by Women	7,546	17.1
One earner	5,286	12
Two or more earners	2,261	5
Families Maintained by Men	2,311	5.2
One earner	1,462	3
Two or more earners	850	2

*Excludes families in which there is no wage or salary earner or in which the husband, wife, or other person maintaining the family is either self-employed or in the Armed Forces.

[1]Includes other earners, not shown separately.

Source: Data from *Statistical Abstract,* 1993.

inequalities in the workplace, lack of support for their domestic roles (in the form of family sick leave, for example), and lack of support from their spouses made their decision to enter the labor force while their children were young a very difficult (but increasingly necessary) one.

Some studies have shown that family well-being may be enhanced when women work outside the home. Susan Orden and Norman Bradburn (1970) investigated the relationship between perceived marital happiness and the wife's work status. They concluded that if the wife worked outside the home as a matter of choice, the marriage was as happy or happier than it would be if she chose to remain at home; if she worked out of necessity, marital happiness suffered. The relative value of working by choice and remaining at home varied at different stages of the family life cycle: When there were preschool children, happiness was rated as greater if the wife remained at home; when the children were in elementary school, working by choice seemed to produce greater happiness; after the children entered high school, the value of the two choices seemed about equal. However, when the wife worked out of necessity, marital happiness was lower in all cases.

Most evidence does not support the traditional view that women are fulfilled by a domestic role. In an analysis of six national surveys conducted by the University of Michigan and the National Opinion Research Center, James D. Wright (1978) found that the lives of both career women and full-time homemakers include a mixture of satisfactions and problems. Although many working women have a strong sense of independence and enjoy their work, they have more complicated, hectic lives than full-time homemakers, who have more time for themselves but may suffer from boredom, stagnation, and lack of independence and money.

In a more recent study of these issues, Arlie Hochschild (1990) found that women who work have less time for themselves and often think of the work they do in the home as a kind of "second shift." Some women resent the extra work and the time spent juggling the responsibilities of job and home, while others take the situation for granted. In a study of middle-class men's reactions to the problem of the "second shift," Kathleen Gerson (1993) found that many men are beginning to shoulder more of the responsibility for domestic tasks like child care. And recent statistics from the U.S. Census Bureau show that an increasing number of men are becoming "house husbands," at least in the sense that almost one out of five married men is minding preschool children at home (although these statistics do not reflect their feelings about the matter or the quality of their child care). (See Figure 12–1.) A more problematic finding of Gerson's study is that a significant proportion of the men she interviewed were becoming what she calls "autonomous males." They appear to have decided that it is too difficult to adjust to the demand for greater equality or to find wives with more traditional views; instead, they are choosing to avoid lasting relationships in favor of the single life.

Women's Employment and Divorce   Several studies have investigated the relationship of women's employment to marriage and divorce patterns. Heather Ross and Isabel Sawhill (1975) conducted annual interviews of families in which both husband and wife were present in 1968. They found that the higher the wife's annual earnings in 1967, the greater the probability that the couple would separate by 1972. A similar study (Cherlin, 1979, 1992) reported that the higher a woman's actual or potential earnings relative to her husband's, the more likely the couple was to separate. While these correlations are somewhat weak, they suggest that as women gain greater economic independence, couples are more likely to end an unhappy marriage.

The possibility of a connection between women's earnings and divorce is especially controversial in the context of welfare policy. Critics of Aid to Families with Dependent Children, for example, often accuse the program of creating incentives for single parenthood. A series of experiments conducted in Denver and Seattle indicated that providing a guaranteed minimum income to a family increased the family's income. However, because the wife was eligible for payments even if the family broke up, the income support program appeared to encourage separation (Groeneveld, Hannan, & Tuma, 1983; Hannan, Tuma, & Groeneveld, 1977). A reevaluation of these experiments by Glen Cain and Douglas Wissoker (1987–1988) concluded that the destabilizing effect of income maintenance programs had been overstated, primarily because of methodological problems such as failure to account adequately for the effects of job-training programs experienced by the participants at the same time as the income support programs.

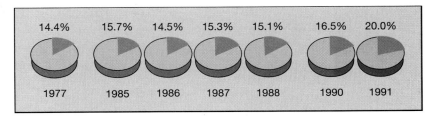

FIGURE 12–1   Percentage of Families in Which Fathers Care for Their Children at Home, 1977–1991

Source: Data from U.S. Census Bureau.

Part-Time Employment Most women with paid jobs are responsible for more than half of the domestic work in their households. These responsibilities have a significant impact on women's work experiences. For example, women may avoid jobs that involve commuting because they need to transport their children to and from school and after-school activities. One result of the conflict between income and family needs is an increase in the proportion of women who work part time.

Some observers believe that the increasing amount of part-time work benefits employers rather than the women who work at such jobs. Part-time work is not well paid and usually does not include fringe benefits. In service industries, it results in a low-paid, floating workforce that is highly advantageous to employers (Perkins, 1983). The employers are, in effect, exploiting the pressure placed on women by the conflicting demands of family responsibilities and economic need.

Family Happiness and Children

Children are believed to bring joy to a household, and the desire to have children is one of the major reasons that couples marry. Yet one study (Campbell, 1975) discovered that young, married, childless couples are the happiest of all marital-status groups. (Single people are the least happy group.) When married couples begin to have children, their reported happiness decreases and feelings of stress rise markedly. Some dissatisfaction is caused by the financial burdens and sacrifices involved in bearing and raising children; some is due to the fact that most young parents have much less time to spend alone together. It is not until the children have left home that married couples regain a state of satisfaction comparable to that which they experienced as newlyweds.

Many couples have decided that children are not necessary for marital happiness, as evidenced by a large decline in the U.S. birthrate (1986 registered the lowest annual fertility rate in American history). Even women who eventually have children are doing so at much later ages; the fertility rate for women 30 to 34 years old has increased significantly. An increasing percentage of women are choosing to spend their twenties "child free." Often the decision to remain childless is not consciously made before marriage but evolves over the years. In a study of fifty-two voluntarily childless wives, J. E. Veevers (1973) found that more than two-thirds remained childless as a result of a series of "temporary" postponements. While they never explicitly rejected motherhood, they repeatedly put off having a baby until a more convenient time—a time that never came.

Some sociologists believe that childless marriages are less stressful and more emotionally satisfying. The study mentioned earlier (Campbell, 1975) revealed that childless husbands over age 30 are more satisfied with their lives, probably because they experience less financial anxiety than fathers of the same age. Childless wives over age 30 report almost the same degree of satisfaction with their lives as mothers of the same age, an indication that many young wives do not regard childbearing as necessary to a woman's role.

The Black Family

A summary of a few important trends in marriage and family patterns for black and white families highlights changes in black–white differences over the past forty years (see Glick, 1981).

■ While blacks have traditionally married at younger ages than whites, whites now marry at much younger ages than blacks. In 1986, 39 percent of white women aged 20–24 were married, compared with 17 percent of black women.

■ On average, black women spend 16 of their expected 73 years of life with a husband; white women spend 34 of an expected 77 years of life married.

- It is estimated that 86 percent of black children and 42 percent of white children will spend some time in a mother-only or other single-parent household (Bumpass, 1984, Table 2).
- The rate at which unmarried black women bear children has declined in recent years; this rate has continued to increase among white women (Jaynes & Williams, 1989, p. 512).

These differences reflect differences in the circumstances surrounding family life for blacks and whites. Chief among these is the reason for the growth in poor families headed by women: Among whites the primary cause is disrupted marriages, while among blacks it is a decrease in marriage rates. In addition, there is evidence that white female-headed households tend to become poor as a result of marital breakup, whereas black female-headed households tend to be formed by women who were poor to begin with (Garfinkel & McLanahan, 1986). Another source of strain on marriages, especially marriages of poor urban minority couples, is the weakening of extended kinship ties as a result of geographic mobility. Lacking adequate social support, the couple is more susceptible to external stresses such as unemployment.

Table 12–2 presents a comparison of the marital-status distributions of blacks and whites. Rows 1 and 2 show the actual distributions; row 3 shows what the marital-status distribution of blacks would be if they had the educational attainment of whites. If black–white differences in marital status were due entirely to differences in educational attainment, the marital statuses of blacks and whites would be the same when differences in education are controlled (i.e., rows 1 and 3 would be identical). Clearly, this is not the case.

TABLE 12–2 MARITAL STATUS OF MEN AND WOMEN AGED 35–44 (IN PERCENT), BY RACE					
SEX AND RACE	NEVER MARRIED	MARRIED ONCE, SPOUSE PRESENT	MARRIED MORE THAN ONCE, SPOUSE PRESENT	SEPARATED, WIDOWED, OR DIVORCED	FIRST MARRIAGES ENDED BY DIVORCE (ESTIMATED)
Men					
White					
(1) Actual marital status	7	66	16	11	29
Black					
(2) Actual marital status	14	49	12	25	42
(3) Assuming white educational attainment	13	51	13	23	40
(4) Assuming white income distribution	9	56	15	20	37
Women					
White					
(1) Actual marital status	5	65	15	15	30
Black					
(2) Actual marital status	13	40	9	38	48
(3) Assuming white educational attainment	12	42	9	37	47

Source: Reprinted with permission from *A Common Density: Blacks and American Society,* © 1989 by The National Academy of Sciences. Published by the National Academy Press, Washington, D.C.

Despite the dramatic rise in single-parent families, especially among African Americans, the extended family is also a thriving institution of African-American life.

Row 4 shows what the marital-status distribution of blacks would be if they had the same incomes as whites. Comparing rows 1 and 4 reveals that controlling for income substantially reduces the disparities between blacks and whites. Thus, we can infer that income is a major factor in explaining black–white differences in the marital status of men: "If, instead of their own income distribution, black men had the income distribution of white men, their marital status distribution would . . . be more like that of white men" (Jaynes & Williams, 1989, p. 530).

In sum, insofar as the black family is distinctive, this is probably a consequence, for the most part, of the special intensity and duration of the poverty and discrimination suffered by African Americans. (See Chapters 8 and 9.) In effect, the problems of the black family are symptomatic of larger social problems. Therefore, we will not undertake a detailed study of the black family as such but will consider the evidence and possible causes of problems among families in general, bearing in mind that some of these occur with particular frequency among poor blacks.

DIVORCE

All but unheard of in the nineteenth century and still rare before World War I, divorce and remarriage have become commonplace in American society. From the early 1930s until the late 1950s, divorce rates in the United States remained fairly constant—about 1.3 per 1,000 population. As late as 1966, the divorce rate was still only 2.5. But in 1991 half as many couples got divorced as married—1.2 million divorces and 2.4 million marriages—representing a divorce rate of 4.7 per 1,000 (*Statistical Abstract,* 1993). Moreover, as Figure 12–2 shows, the divorce *ratio* (the number of currently divorced persons per 1,000 currently married persons who live with their spouses) has more than tripled since 1960. This trend is partially responsible for the significant increase in the proportion of female-headed and single-person households in the population.

The traditional correlations between socioeconomic and educational levels and

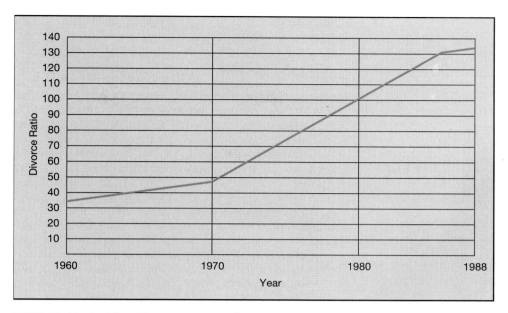

FIGURE 12–2   The Divorce Ratio, 1960–1988

Source: Data from *Statistical Abstract,* 1990.

frequency of divorce are no longer as true as they once were. For example, divorce used to be much more likely among people with a high school education than among people who had completed college, and more frequent among the poor than among members of the middle and upper-middle classes. But in recent years the divorce rate has risen among college-educated couples and people in higher socio-economic groups.

The highest rates of divorce, amounting to about one-third of all divorces, occur in the first three years of marriage. This widely known fact leads many people to believe that having children "cements" a marriage and adds to marital happiness. Sociological research conducted in the 1950s documented this popular belief, but it also demonstrated that the facts are otherwise: Having babies early in a marriage does not make a couple happier and often makes them less happy (Monahan, 1955). In subsequent decades sociologists continued to find that people believe children "cement" marriages while the empirical evidence showed that having children increases the strains on a couple's time, energy, money, and other resources, and that couples who are not happy in their relationship often become less so when babies arrive (Ross & Huber, 1985). One implication of this research is that couples who can plan the arrival of their children have a better marriage and family prognosis than those who cannot.

Stepfamilies

Since most divorced people—especially women with children from a previous marriage—will remarry, married couples with children remain a dominant family pattern in our society. An increasing proportion of these families are stepfamilies. About 19 percent of all white families and 35 percent of all black married-couple families are stepfamilies. Demographer Paul Glick estimates, therefore, that if present trends continue, by the end of the century approximately half of all Americans will be stepchildren, stepparents, or stepsiblings. Although these trends attest to the strength of marriage and family norms, it is also true that combining children in a new family often adds conflict and tension to family life, and this, in turn, is sometimes seen as a cause of the relatively high divorce rate for such marriages (Ahlburg & De Vita, 1992).

Explanations of Trends in Divorce Rates

An examination of all the forces putting pressure on marriage would be beyond the scope of this chapter, but we can point out some of them. Most frequently cited is the change from extended to nuclear families. Another factor is the extent to which functions that were formerly performed by the family have been assumed by outside agencies. Still other factors are the relaxation of attitudes regarding divorce, the reformation of divorce laws so that divorces are easier to obtain, and the growing number of educated women who can earn a living independently of their husbands. (The general change in role expectations for women is discussed in Chapter 10.)

The change to a smaller family unit, coupled with the mobility of many modern families, places more responsibility on a husband and wife for the satisfaction of each other's emotional needs. Where once there were plenty of relatives or long-term neighbors at hand to whom the partners could turn for companionship, today spouses are more dependent on each other.

The decrease in family size has been accompanied by a decrease in family functions. Food production, education, entertainment, and other activities that were once centered in the home are now performed by outside agencies. As Kenneth Keniston has written,

> In earlier times, the collapse of a marriage was far more likely to deprive both spouses of a great deal more than the pleasure of each other's company. Since family members performed so many functions for one another, divorce in the past meant a farmer without a wife to churn the cream into butter or care for him when he was sick, and a mother without a husband to plow the fields and bring her the food to feed their children. Today, when emotional satisfaction is the bond that holds marriages together, the waning of love or the emergence of real incompatibilities and conflicts between husband and wife leave fewer reasons for a marriage to continue. Schools and doctors and counselors and social workers provide their supports whether the family is intact or not. One loses less by divorce today than in earlier times, because marriage provides fewer kinds of sustenance and satisfaction. (1977, p. 21)

Family tensions are also likely to arise in cross-class marriages. Scanzoni (1968) considered such marriages in a study based on interviews with wives in both continuing and dissolved marriages. He found that marriages were much more likely to be dissolved if the partners had significantly different occupational and educational backgrounds. Thus, 43 percent of the divorced women in the study came from white-collar backgrounds and had married the sons of manual or skilled workers; 18 percent were daughters of skilled workers and had married the sons of manual workers. In another 19 percent of the cases the wife came from a lower class than her husband. By contrast, the largest percentage of the women in existing marriages came from the same general occupational background as their husbands. The figures for educational level are similar. These findings imply that people with different backgrounds are likely to have different expectations regarding achievement and behavior in marriage, and that these differences may create significant strains.

Another study of marital stress presents a more refined picture of the effect of class on marriage. Leonard Pearlin (1975) found that inequality in status was not in and of itself a significant cause of stress in marriage. A more important factor was the desire of a partner to improve his or her own status. Those for whom status improvement was not important, or who had married partners of higher status, were relatively undisturbed by the different status of their partners. Those who wanted to improve their own status, however, were more likely to experience marital stress if they married partners of lower status. Pearlin concluded that "status inequality by itself is of little or no consequence. The importance of such inequality to marital problems . . . depends on the meaning and value that are attached to it" (1975, p. 356).

A more recent study (Blumstein & Schwartz, 1983) identified several aspects of married life that appear to increase the likelihood of divorce. Among them are conflicts over the extent to which work intrudes into the relationship, especially in dual-earner families; over the amount of housework performed by the wife; and over the frequent absences of one partner.

Because of the greater social tolerance of divorce, we can expect that partners who might once have resigned themselves to an unhappy marriage, or fought constantly yet stayed together, may now feel more inclined to get a divorce. Women—at least educated women—are better able to earn an adequate living. The increasing acceptance of sexual activity outside of marriage also contributes to the likelihood of divorce. In addition, a child of divorced parents is no longer likely to suffer embarrassment, pity, or discrimination in school. Finally, the chances for remarriage of divorced people, especially men, are fairly high.

The Impact of Divorce

Divorce, even when it is desired by both partners, is almost always accompanied by considerable emotional and financial strain. This is especially true for women, who often have to work and care for children without adequate economic and psychological help from their partners. Because more jobs are open to them, well-educated women are better able to cope with the effects of divorce and in fact may choose not to remarry. Other women have more limited options. Most husbands do not

Raising children is never easy, even for a two-parent family. Single parents often experience even greater strain and role conflict in coping with the demands of work and family life.

continue to support their families after divorce, although they are often legally required at least to pay child support. Divorced mothers therefore are frequently forced into poverty and dependence on public assistance; the leading cause of dependence on welfare (Aid to Families with Dependent Children) is divorce or desertion (Ellwood, 1988). And because it is assumed that divorced people will soon remarry, adequate social supports are not provided to single parents.

There are about 1.2 million divorces in the United States each year. Of these, approximately 50 percent are by couples who have one or more children (Sweet & Bumpass, 1987). The majority of these divorces occur in marriages of less than ten years' duration; as a result, young children, who are most dependent and vulnerable, are especially likely to feel the impact of divorce. Although divorce has become a common event and children of divorced parents may no longer feel the stigma they once experienced, there is no question that in the vast majority of families in which divorce occurs it is an extremely difficult experience for children as well as for adults.

Children may experience divorce as the end of their life as they knew it, as a falling apart and a severe disruption of their existence. They feel fear, anger, depression, and confusion. Often they blame themselves for contributing to their parents' difficulties. Over a longer period children (and, typically, their mothers) experience divorce as a severe diminution in their material well-being; one of the leading causes of poverty among children is the dissolution of their parents' marriage. They may also become "latchkey children," far more responsible for their own care after school and for the care of their siblings than they might have been had there not been a divorce.

Much research focuses on the experience of families with preschool children in the period immediately following a divorce. One study (Hetherington, 1980) found that the lifestyle of such families became "chaotic"—meals were eaten at irregular times, the children's bedtimes were erratic, and so forth. The separated spouses experienced anxiety, occasional depression, and personal disorganization, and the children tended to be bewildered and frightened. Other research has found that children whose parents were divorced were twice as likely as children from intact families to need professional help for an emotional, behavioral, mental, or learning problem (Zill, 1978).

In an important study of the effect of divorce on children, Wallerstein and Blakeslee (1989) tracked sixty families with a total of 131 children for ten to fifteen years after divorce. Although some of the children were better off than they would have been in an unhappy intact family, for most of them the divorce had serious consequences. A significant finding of the study was that many divorced parents are unable to meet the challenges of parenting and instead depend on the children to help them cope with their own problems. The result is an "overburdened child" who must not only handle the normal stresses of childhood but also help a parent avoid depression.

Divorce has a major psychological impact on adults as well. Robert Weiss (1979) observed single parents for several years and identified three common sources of strain: (1) responsibility overload—single parents must make all the decisions and provide for all the needs of their families; (2) task overload—working, housekeeping, and parenting take up so much time that there is none left to meet unexpected demands; and (3) emotional overload—single parents must constantly give emotional support to their children regardless of how they feel themselves. This and other research suggests that the number of parents in the home is not as crucial as the family functioning of the member who is present (Herzog & Sudia, 1973).

Other consequences of divorce that can create problems include the increase in the number of single people in the population, more complicated family relationships when divorced people remarry, and the issue of grandparents' rights to see their grandchildren after a divorce. The basic social problem created by the high divorce rate, however, is that the other institutions of society (e.g., schools and economic institutions) remain geared to the traditional family. Those institutions are under pressure to adapt to the needs of single people and single-parent families—for example, to provide more care for children of working parents, more flexible working hours, and more welfare services.

Cohabiting Couples

Most common among people under the age of 25 and over the age of 65, cohabitation has been increasing at a rate of approximately 15 percent a year for the past decade or more (U.S. Census Bureau, 1988, 1992). Among younger people, living together is most popular among students in "college towns," where they may have more opportunities to experiment with intimate living arrangements (Stein, 1981). There are almost 3 million cohabiting couples in the United States, and this arrangement is even more popular in some Western European nations. Although some cohabiting couples may see living together as a form of trial marriage, others regard it as an alternative to conventional marriage; this is especially true of elderly unmarried couples. Little research has been done on the fate of marriages that occur after a trial period of living together, but the few studies that have been done indicate that they have a slightly lower rate of success over time. Family researcher Eleanor Macklin (1980) suggests that the greater tendency of former cohabiting partners to divorce may be due to a slightly less conventional attitude and less willingness to make commitments, rather than to any aspect of cohabitation itself.

POSTPONEMENT OF MARRIAGE

Postponement of marriage became more common in the decades following World War II as young people chose to concentrate on education and careers. Today American woman are postponing marriage longer than ever before. The median age of women marrying for the first time is 23.9 years. Men also are marrying later than at any time since 1900, with a median age at first marriage of 26.1 years. (See Figure 12–3.) One result of this trend, coupled with the high divorce rate, is that more than one American adult in ten lives alone.

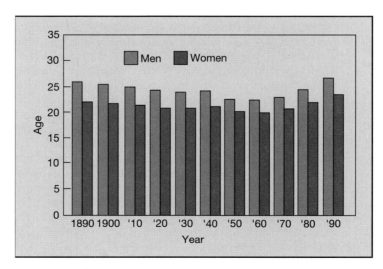

FIGURE 12–3   Median Age of First Marriage for Men and Women

Source: Data from U.S. Census Bureau.

Postponement of marriage has a variety of implications for the family. One result of this trend is a decrease in the average number of children per family—the longer marriage is postponed, the fewer children the couple is likely to have when they eventually do marry. Advances in reproductive technologies and medical care during pregnancy have made it possible for more women to have children while in their forties, and there has been an increase in the number of women who bear their first child late in their reproductive years. Even in such cases, however, the family is likely to have only one or at most two children.

When couples have children relatively late in life, they also become grandparents later, and for a shorter time, than those who marry and have children earlier. (This is especially true for men, who have a shorter life expectancy than women.) Postponement of marriage is also correlated with an increase in the proportion of childless couples, since many people who marry late choose not to have children for personal or economic reasons or because the risk of birth defects increases with the age of the mother.

As a demographic trend, postponement of marriage has a significant effect on the population as a whole. A change of only two years in the median age at first marriage can make a vast difference in the number of married couples in the population in a given year. Moreover, since men tend to marry women who are younger than themselves, women who postpone marriage become caught in a "marriage squeeze": The number of women who would like to marry is greater than the number of available men (Guttentag & Secord, 1983). Thus, for women between the ages of 18 and 24 there are 114 unmarried men for every 100 unmarried women, whereas for women between the ages of 35 and 44 there are 97 unmarried men for every 100 unmarried women (*Statistical Abstract,* 1993).

CHANGING NORMS OF PARENTHOOD

Births to Unmarried Women (Illegitimacy)

Anthropologist Bronislaw Malinowski (1941) suggested that in most primitive societies there is a social dogma stating that "every family must have a father; a woman must marry before she may have children; there must be a male in every household" (p. 202). In other words, it is expected that every child will be provided with a legitimate father who will act as its protector and guardian.

Actually, there are societies in which marriage is not always a social prerequisite for parenthood. In parts of West Africa, for example, a woman may bear a child out of wedlock, and no stigma will be attached to her or to the child as long as the father's identity is reasonably certain. It is not sexual activity out of wedlock that is frowned upon, but promiscuity.

In our society many of the stigmas that were traditionally associated with premarital pregnancy and illegitimacy have been reduced. Relatively few illegitimate children are given up for adoption. Nevertheless, premarital pregnancy is still frowned upon, generally because it indicates that sexual intercourse has occurred out of wedlock; the stigma is removed only if the couple is willing to marry before the child is born. Society still expects children to be provided with two recognized parents, and failure to meet this norm may result in various degrees of social condemnation. One form of condemnation is the legal classification of the child as illegitimate.

It is important to keep this legal aspect in mind when considering the social problem of illegitimacy. Granted that the one-parent family faces special problems—especially in a society in which the nuclear family is the norm—those problems are in themselves no different whether the single parent is unmarried, widowed, or divorced. Many of the distinctive difficulties of the unwed mother and her child, at least in the United States, are a matter of legal status.

The legal consequences of illegitimacy vary greatly from one country to another and, in the United States, from one state to another. In Sweden, Norway, and Denmark illegitimate children are given much the same rights as legitimate ones; however, in many countries, including the United States, the laws discriminate against illegitimate children. Usually the major form of legal discrimination involves the child's right to inherit the father's property. For example, the New York State Court of Appeals has upheld a state law that prevents a child from inheriting from his or her father unless paternity has been established in court within two years of the child's birth and while the father is still living.

Consequences of Illegitimacy   As a result of the relaxation of sexual mores, the increase in premarital sexual activity, and the greater independence of women, more unmarried women are bearing and keeping their children rather than obtaining abortions or giving their children up for adoption. Thus, when we speak of the social problems of illegitimacy we nearly always mean the problems created by the presence of large numbers of single-parent families headed by women who are unable to earn an adequate living for themselves and their children. A mother who gives up her child for adoption ceases to be regarded as a problem, and her child, if adopted, rarely becomes one. Likewise, an unwed mother who is able to support herself and her child, or a married woman who raises an illegitimately conceived child as a member of a legitimate family, arouses little concern. The problem of illegitimacy results from the fact that a lower-class unwed mother who decides to keep her child is likely to be ill equipped to support and care for it. In short, illegitimacy is a social problem to the extent that it contributes to the numbers and hardships of the poor.

Teenage Pregnancy

Most illegitimate children are borne by teenagers. About one million teenage girls become pregnant each year, and over half of them have babies that they do not give up for adoption even though they may still be unmarried at the time of the birth. The problem is particularly severe among black teenagers: Almost one in four black teenage girls gives birth to an illegitimate child before the age of 18 (Hulbert, 1984). Note, however, that rates of childbearing among all low-income youth are very high; the difference in rates of illegitimate births is due to the fact that white teenagers who become pregnant are more likely than black teenagers to marry before the birth of the child.

Teenage women constitute roughly 25 percent of the population of childbearing age, yet they account for over 45 percent of all births to unmarried women (Alan Guttmacher Institute, 1981; Ahlburg & De Vita, 1992). Many of these women are not knowledgeable about the reproductive process and tend not to use contraceptives (Green & Poteteiger, 1978).

A major issue in the United States today is whether young women who become pregnant should be allowed to have abortions and the consequences of this choice. In 1990 the National Institute of Child Health and Human Development reported the results of a study of black teenagers who came to family planning clinics in Baltimore for pregnancy tests. The young women were divided into three groups: those who chose to have an abortion, those who bore the child, and those who turned out not to be pregnant. The groups were followed for two years. The researchers found that 90 percent of the group who had abortions and 79 percent of those whose pregnancy tests were negative graduated from high school or stayed in school. Among those who bore children, 68 percent dropped out of school. The study also found that 4.5 percent of those who chose abortion experienced an adverse psychological effect, compared to 5.5 percent of those who bore children. Opponents of abortion criticized the study, contending that two years was not a long enough period to produce meaningful results and that "post-abortion stress syndrome" often does not show up until five years after the abortion (Holmes, 1990).

Gay and Lesbian Families

In 1988, Madison, Wisconsin, passed an ordinance that enables city employees to take sick leave to care for a domestic partner, regardless of the gender of that partner. In 1989, New York State passed legislation requiring that a gay couple of long standing be considered a family under the state's housing laws. At the same time, San Francisco's city council passed an ordinance that recognized gay couples and unmarried heterosexual couples as families with the same rights as married couples. These laws, which are controversial in many other parts of the nation, are indicators of the importance of homosexual couples and families in some areas.

Most observers of homosexual communities agree that the AIDS epidemic has led homosexual couples to consider longer-term relationships and, in doing so, to desire children of their own. Many homosexual couples consider themselves to be married, and an estimated one-third of lesbians and one-fifth of gay males have children from previous heterosexual marriages (Bell & Weinberg, 1978; Richmond-Abbott, 1992). Moreover, as reproductive technologies become increasingly effective, more lesbian couples are able to have children through artificial insemination. In addition, although laws in many states make it difficult for homosexuals to adopt children, many have succeeded in doing so. As a result, the number of same-sex couples with children is steadily increasing. Little research has been done on children in such families, but the few studies conducted to date offer evidence that love and care, sustained throughout a child's development, offset any difficulty the child may face as a result of the parents' nonconformity (Bell & Weinberg, 1978).

HOMELESS FAMILIES

Although homelessness has been recognized as a serious social problem since the early 1980s, only recently has it become evident that many of the homeless are families—usually mothers living on the streets with their children. A study by Richard B. Freeman and Brian Hall (1986) estimated the total number of homeless family members at 32,000.

The plight of homeless families is illustrated by the case of Laura, a Hispanic woman who lives with her four children in a welfare hotel in New York City. The plaster on the walls in the hotel is covered with a sweet-tasting lead-based paint; Laura's 7-year-old son is suffering from lead poisoning. The bathroom plumbing has overflowed and left a pool of sewage on the floor, and a radiator valve periodically releases a spray of scalding steam. Laura's four-month-old daughter has contracted scabies, a serious skin disease. Laura has taken her children to a clinic, but because she cannot read, she is unable to follow instructions about their care that have been sent to her through the mail. She also was unable to read a request for information from her welfare office, and her welfare payments have been cut off as a result (Kozol, 1988).

A longitudinal study of the homeless population of Minneapolis (Piliavin & Sosin, cited in Institute for Research on Poverty, 1987–1988) found that homelessness is a recurring state, not a permanent one. Within a six-month period, three-fourths of those interviewed had found places to live at least once—either with a friend or relative or in a boardinghouse at the county's expense. Moreover, no fam-

This homeless family having Thanksgiving dinner in the shadow of the Capitol symbolizes the plight of poor families who can no longer afford adequate shelter.

ilies with children were among the long-term homeless (those who remained homeless for over two years).

The families who are most at risk of becoming homeless are those who have experienced a crisis such as divorce or desertion, resulting in a drastic reduction of income and, hence, inability to pay for shelter. Studies have indicated that a large majority of homeless families do not have relatives, parents, or close friends to whom they can turn for support (Committee on Health Care for Homeless People, 1988). In addition, many homeless women with children are victims of family violence and may initially seek refuge in shelters for battered women. This suggests the need for more extensive public programs to provide emergency shelter for adults with children. These and related issues will be discussed more fully in Chapter 15.

REPRODUCTIVE ISSUES

Advances in Reproductive Technology

In England in 1994 a woman who was over 60 and well past menopause gave birth to a child after artificial insemination. The birth immediately became the subject of an immense controversy. As Arthur Caplan (1992), one of the world's foremost students of bioethics, has noted, advances in reproductive technology have created an unprecedented number of moral dilemmas, and those dilemmas are likely to become ever more vexing as reproductive technology becomes ever more powerful.

The possibilities and choices associated with human reproduction have been greatly expanded as a result of technological advances. New reproductive technologies permit women and men to deal with fertility control and childbearing in ways that were never before possible. However, they may also create new problems and raise thorny moral issues both for individuals and for society. We describe several such technologies in this section. Each of them raises moral issues because each to some degree removes reproduction from the control of biology and fate and places reproductive decisions more squarely in the hands of individuals and society.

Amniocentesis   This technique for drawing fluid from the uterus in the first trimester of pregnancy makes possible genetic tests on the fetus, tests that can detect Down syndrome and a few other potentially severe birth defects. Since the risks of these problems increase with a woman's age, amniocentesis allows women in their thirties and early forties to feel more confident about becoming pregnant and enables working women to have healthy children relatively late in their careers. However, the knowledge that one is carrying a fetus that will have severe birth defects or a genetic disease leads to the question of whether to terminate the pregnancy through abortion. Amniocentesis also allows couples to know the sex of their child before birth. Opponents of the technique fear that some couples will abuse that knowledge by choosing to abort a pregnancy when they wish to have a baby of the other sex. The connection between amniocentesis and abortion thus makes the technique controversial even though it is widely used.

Implanted Contraceptives   Opponents of birth control believe that contraception leads to more casual attitudes toward sex and to devaluation of human life. These are similar to arguments regarding abortion, but new contraceptives that can be implanted in a woman's body raise additional issues. These devices have been used in some recent cases in which judges have ordered that women under sentence must prevent themselves from becoming pregnant until they can demonstrate to the court that they are responsible enough to bear children. Such orders have angered women's groups and civil rights organizations as well as traditional opponents of birth control.

Fertility Drugs   Fertility drugs (e.g., Clonapin) allow previously infertile women to become pregnant, but there have been a number of cases in which the drugs have been implicated in multiple pregnancies—triplets, quadruplets, quintuplets, and more. Large multiple pregnancies can be harmful to the mother and greatly increase the risks of premature birth, birth defects, and fetal death. Doctors can use noninvasive sonar (sonograms) to track the development of multiple fetuses; they can even selectively abort fetuses so that the mother need not bear more than one or two babies. Again, the fertility drugs create unanticipated problems that require additional technologies and raise the difficult moral questions of choice and abortion.

Artificial Insemination and In-Utero Implants   To avoid certain reproductive difficulties, doctors can fertilize a woman's ovum with sperm from her husband or from a sperm bank. They can even implant in her uterus an ovum that has been fertilized outside a human body. These techniques allow women without husbands to have children. They also allow infertile couples to have children who carry the genes of at least one of their parents. These methods entail significant moral choices, such as whether to intentionally become a single parent. The procedures also widen the possibilities of surrogacy, currently among the most controversial aspects of reproductive technology.

Surrogacy

Another problem related to reproduction came to prominence in 1987, when a woman who had agreed to bear a child for another couple for a fee attempted instead to claim the baby as her own. Such a situation could not have arisen without recent technological advances in artificial insemination. In this instance, a variety of legal and emotional problems resulted from a procedure that was intended to be a solution to female infertility.

The practice of *surrogacy,* in which a woman is artifically inseminated, receives up to $25,000 to bear the child, and gives up the baby to its natural father, results in the birth of 300 or more babies a year in the United States. However, the practice has implications that extend far beyond the few families who are directly involved. Among the issues generated by surrogacy are the questions of whether a contractual obligation outweighs the rights of a biological parent, whether it is ethical to apply costly reproductive technology when thousands of children are available for adoption, whether surrogacy should be available only to married couples who can pay the fee, and whether the procedure creates a class of "breeder" women who carry and bear children for those who are better off.

Scientists point out that reproductive technologies alleviate the distress felt by infertile couples and could eventually be used to ensure the delivery of healthy babies. Opponents claim that such technologies exploit women, especially lower-class women. In 1988 the New Jersey Supreme Court supported the latter position, ruling that surrogate-motherhood contracts are illegal in that state and that the natural mother is entitled to the custody of her child. But in a 1990 decision a California court denied the request of a surrogate mother for parental rights to the child she had borne for another couple, saying that she had served in a temporary role as a foster parent. Anticipating that surrogacy and in-vitro fertilization would become more common in the future, the judge recommended that all parties to a surrogate agreement undergo psychological evaluation and that all agree from the start that the surrogate mother will have no custody rights (Mydans, 1990).

SOCIAL POLICY

Social policies related to problems of families can be divided into four major categories: divorce law and alimony, efforts to reduce the rate of illegitimacy, programs to assist low-income families, and child care and family support policies.

Divorce Law

In the 1950s and 1960s, as attitudes toward divorce became more liberal, there was growing demand for changes in state divorce laws. Laws that permitted divorce only in extreme cases—adultery, for example—were challenged in many states. Beginning with California in 1970, many states liberalized their divorce laws and moved toward the concept of "no-fault" divorce. No-fault divorce laws allow judges to decide on issues of child custody and division of property without blaming one partner or the other, an approach that eliminates the need to have children testify about parental behavior and thus be dragged into a bitter court battle in addition to the pain they are already suffering. Many states followed California's lead, instituting no-fault laws and allowing couples to petition for divorce under compatible (pre-agreed) terms.

The no-fault approach does not entirely eliminate strife among divorcing couples. There are many instances in which the courts still must adjudicate conflicting claims and settle rancorous custody battles. However, contrary to the claims of critics who believed no-fault policies would lead to an increase in divorce rates, comparative research shows that divorce rates have not increased disproportionately in states with liberal divorce laws compared to those with stricter ones (Cherlin, 1992).

Noncoercive Approaches to Divorce Sociologists who advocate a revival of family values generally seek to develop ways to encourage families to stay together. In doing so they often propose alternatives to policies such as no-fault or consensual divorce. Some pro-marriage sociologists, such as Amitai Etzioni (1993), advocate "supervows," in which a couple include in their marital contract clauses designed to preserve the marriage. An example would be a provision for a six-month waiting period during which the couple would attempt to work things out before one partner seeks a divorce. Another would be an agreement that if one partner wishes to obtain marital therapy or counseling the other partner agrees to do so as well. Through such measures, admittedly not very romantic, couples would at least attach greater value to their marriage vows, and this in turn might help carry them over the inevitable rough spots in their marriage.

Alimony and Child Support   *Alimony*—the money paid by one partner for the support of the other, usually by the husband to the wife—has been closely tied to the concept of fault in divorce proceedings. In the absence of no-fault provisions, the main purpose of a divorce trial has been to fix blame on one party or the other and to make the guilty party (usually the husband) pay a certain amount over and above what he would ordinarily have paid; if the fault rested with the wife, she would receive less than the ordinary amount. However, when a decree of divorce can be granted without the need to punish either partner, alimony can be awarded on the more realistic basis of financial need and ability to provide. Theoretically, this means that it would no longer be unusual for a man to receive alimony from his ex-wife if she has greater earning power, and that a woman with no children would not necessarily be granted alimony from her husband or would receive alimony only temporarily, to give her time to become self-supporting.

The no-fault reforms and reduced alimony settlements have, however, sometimes resulted in unfair treatment of women. The great increase in the number of divorces has sent many women into a job market that cannot absorb them. Some have been forced to seek public assistance, since the courts have little power to compel ex-husbands to contribute to their ex-wives' support (Masnick & Bane, 1980). A related injustice involves the rights to property held in common by the husband and wife. Several states permit the holder of the title to property to keep it. If a woman has allowed her husband to hold in his name assets that belong to both, in the event of divorce she loses any claim to this property and is not compensated for the loss by higher alimony payments (McDonald, 1975).

Children often suffer economically as a result of divorce. In 1989, for example, 9.9 million women were living with children under 21 years of age whose fathers were not living in the household; 58 percent of these women had been awarded child support payments. Of those to whom payments were due in the previous year, only about half received the full amount. Another 24 percent received partial payment, and 25 percent received no payment at all (*Statistical Abstract*, 1993). In view of statistics like these, a high priority of family courts is tracking down ex-husbands who fail to pay for the support of their children. In a 1988 decision the United States Supreme Court ruled that fathers who fail to make child care payments because of financial problems must prove to authorities that they indeed lack adequate funds. And during his 1992 campaign President Clinton pledged to promote tougher policies on enforcement of child support payments.

Efforts to Reduce Illegitimacy

The legal status of illegitimate children has improved somewhat in recent decades. In 1964 the Supreme Court struck down as unconstitutional some laws that discriminated against illegitimate children. In *Levy* v. *Louisiana* (1968) the state of Louisiana had argued that greater rights should be granted to legitimate than to illegitimate offspring, primarily to safeguard the institution of marriage. But the Court decided that such discrimination was not justified because it amounted to punishing one individual for another's behavior. The Court has also declared unconstitutional sections of the Social Security Act that prohibit illegitimate children of a disabled worker from receiving benefits if they were born after the worker became disabled. As a result of these and other decisions, it can be anticipated that the legal position of children born out of wedlock will continue to improve. Indeed, a number of states have discontinued the practice of noting illegitimate status on birth certificates, and at least two have abolished the concept of illegitimacy altogether.

These legal changes do not solve the problem of illegitimacy from society's point of view. As noted earlier, the problem of illegitimacy can be viewed as part of the problem of poverty. At the age of 16, approximately 12 percent of girls from poor households have children, and the percentage increases steadily until by age 19 the majority—about 52 percent—of young women from poor households have given birth. There are no significant racial differences in childbearing among young poor women, but white teenagers are more likely to marry whereas blacks and Hispanics are more likely to become single parents (and, hence, to show up in illegitimacy statistics). This difference can be attributed largely to the problems experienced by young minority men in finding jobs and the income to support a family (Kornblum, 1984).

Many social scientists believe that opportunities to work and learn, especially in combination, are the only practical way to decrease the rate of early childbearing. Policies based on a moral stance against premarital intercourse, such as antiabortion measures and elimination of birth control clinics, have the effect of increasing the rate of illegitimate births, and cutbacks in welfare programs in effect punish children for the actions of their parents.

Assistance to Low-Income Families

Samuel Preston, a well-known sociologist and demographer, has made an eloquent plea for a coherent public policy to assist low-income families with children:

> If we care about our collective future rather than simply about our futures as individuals we are faced with the question of how best to safeguard the human and material resources represented by children. . . . Rather than assuming collective responsibility, as has been done in the case of the elderly, U.S. society has chosen to place almost exclusive responsibility for the care of children on the nuclear family. Marital instability, however, has much reduced the capacity of the family to care for its own children. Hence insisting that families alone care for the young would seem to be an evasion of collective responsibility rather than a conscious decision about the best way to provide for the future. (1984, p. 44)

A variety of measures have been proposed to improve the situation of low-income families with children. They include modification of the earned income tax credit (discussed in Chapter 8); education, employment, and training programs designed to increase the earning capacity of parents; and enactment of a national minimum benefit under the AFDC program. Although continuing federal budget shortfalls will prevent large-scale investment in education and training for low-income parents and their teenage children, such programs are at the top of every family policy analyst's wish list. The success of the Job Corps and of some literacy and community college programs encourages both liberals and conservatives to believe that more training can enhance earning possibilities for low-income people and thereby encourage family cohesion (Berlin & Sum, 1988).

Child Care and Family Support

Both single-parent and dual-earner families must cope with the question of how to provide care for their children while the parents are at work. Two types of social policies would make the choices faced by working parents less difficult (Gerson, 1985). One type consists of employment policies such as paid parental leaves for both men and women. The other consists of the development of a wide range of child care services and facilities. The latter approach could include not only publicly funded programs but also tax incentives to promote day care programs in neighborhoods and workplaces.

The key factors to be considered in developing a child care policy are availability, reliability, quality, and affordability (Bergmann, 1988). Unlike such countries as Sweden and France, the United States has failed to provide high-quality child care facilities at a price that working-class parents can afford. Even middle-class parents have difficulty arranging for reliable care for their children.

Barbara Bergmann (1988) has identified two specific issues that must be addressed if the government becomes seriously involved in the provision of child care: (1) Should the government provide vouchers that parents could use to pay the fees of private child care facilities, or should it provide child care facilities under public management? (2) Should the taxpayers shoulder the whole cost of child care, or should parents be asked to pay some or all of the cost? Bergmann points out that publicly funded and provided child care would be especially helpful for women

---

BOX 12–1   CURRENT CONTROVERSIES: FAMILY SUPPORT AND DAY CARE

Fifty-seven percent of American infants and school-age children have working mothers, and family demographers estimate that the proportion will increase to 80 percent by the year 2000. The rapid increase in the number of working mothers adds to the urgency of the need to find quality child care during working hours. About 50 percent of working mothers report that they are unable to find satisfactory child care (Ford Foundation, 1990). At the same time, deep divisions in government about how best to establish and fund child care present major obstacles to new child care policies.

In 1990 both houses of Congress passed child care legislation; but as the two houses were conferring on a compromise version of the legislation, the Bush administration warned that it would veto the measure because of its cost. The administration favored an approach that would give tax credits and refunds to low-income families that could be used to purchase day-care services. Families who are not poor would be able to deduct $1,000 per year for day-care services for each child under 4. Congress favored a combination of tax credits and vouchers or state guarantees to finance child care. Since about one-third of all day care is provided by religious organizations, this plan would allow for payments to such programs.

In addition to a voucher system, the plan passed by the House of Representatives would greatly expand all-day Head Start programs and would provide additional services for latchkey children in after-school programs. The Senate plan incorporates the tax credit system and the voucher system favored by the House, but not the Head Start initiative. Instead, the Senate plan would create a set of incentive grants to businesses to encourage them to set up day care programs. Democrats in the Senate and the House also want the government to establish standards for day-care, including training of child care workers. Republicans argue that this requirement would create additional bureaucracy.

As many states continue to implement the 1988 Family Support Act, which requires mothers of young children to obtain training and employment as a condition for receiving public assistance, the demand for adequate day-care services for poor families will increase, especially in communities where the existing need is already great. The Ford Foundation and other private philanthropic organizations have also called attention to the urgent need for improvement of existing day-care services. In California, for example, the California Child Care Resource and Referral Network has found that training of new workers in the basics of child development and child care is an extremely high-priority need. There is also a serious problem of frustration and "burnout" among child care workers, many of whom work twelve-hour days with few breaks and have little contact with other practitioners and professionals. The network estimates that "every year some 60 percent of home-based providers [in California] close their operations" (Ford Foundation, 1990, p. 8). The network is seeking to develop a system of peer support, training, and assistance from local resources to improve this situation. Throughout the nation the problem of adequate funding and training of day-care providers and centers is becoming a growing social problem and an ever-greater challenge to policy makers.

who are entering the labor force (e.g., as a result of divorce) and that it would encourage single mothers on welfare to take a first step toward supporting themselves. (See Box 12–1.)

A recent trend in family policy is the establishment of family support centers that offer help to parents and children together. The centers provide a variety of services, including prenatal care, immunizations, day care, classes on child care, literacy tutoring, and teenage groups aimed at pregnancy prevention. Some programs include home visits. The majority of the programs are based in local schools and other community centers, but some states have set up statewide family support programs.

Although there is a great deal of debate over how to fund them, policy makers are approaching agreement on the need for a series of policies to promote family support, expand child care systems, and provide training and job assistance to low-income parents. This growing consensus prompted Marian Wright Edelman, president of the Children's Defense Fund, to observe that "There is finally a real consensus that families need help, and that government has a role to play in providing that help" (quoted in Lewin, 1988, p. A1). Unfortunately, the continuing drain on federal funds caused by the savings and loan bailout, decreasing revenues at the state level, and the recession of the early 1990s is likely to delay large-scale implementation of new family support policies.

SUMMARY

1. A kinship unit is a group of individuals who are related by blood, marriage, or adoption. It may be a nuclear family (a father, a mother, and their children living apart from other kin), an extended family (parents, children, grandparents, and others living together or in close proximity), or a modified extended family (nuclear families living separately but maintaining interpersonal attachments and economic exchanges within the extended family).

2. Families must adapt to a cycle in which the roles of their members change from one stage of development to the next. Adequate family functioning requires internal role consistency among family members, consistency of family roles with actual role performance, compatibility of family norms with societal norms, the ability to meet the psychological needs of family members, and the ability of the family group to respond to change.

3. External or internal crises may reduce the family to an "empty shell" in which family members feel no strong attachment to each other and neglect mutual obligations. Three types of empty-shell marriages are the conflict-habituated relationship, the devitalized relationship, and the passive-congenial relationship.

4. Among the most important social trends of the second half of this century is the movement of women out of the home and into the workforce. As a result of this trend, only about one-fifth of all married couples are supported by the husband alone.

5. Some studies have shown that a wife's job may enhance family well-being. This is especially true if the wife works outside the home as a matter of choice. Other evidence indicates no significant difference in life satisfaction between homemakers and working women. Some women resent their "second shift" of work at home after working at a job, while others take it for granted.

6. When couples have children, their reported happiness decreases owing to the added financial burden and reduced leisure. Many couples have decided that children are not necessary for marital happiness; others are having children at later ages.

7. Although there are certain fairly consistent differences between black and white families—in particular, a larger proportion of poor female-headed families among blacks—most of these differences are probably due to poverty and discrimination.

8. The divorce rate has risen dramatically since the mid-1960s, reflecting severe pressures on the institution of marriage. Among those pressures are the change from extended to nuclear families and the reduction in the number of functions performed by the family. In addition, because of the increased social tolerance of divorce, more couples are willing to get a divorce rather than continue an unhappy marriage.

9. The problems associated with divorce include emotional and financial strain, particularly for women. Divorced mothers frequently are forced to accept public assistance. Children often become bewildered and frightened and may need professional help for emotional and other problems.

10. Postponement of marriage has become common in the United States and has a variety of implications for the family. Among these are fewer children per family, an increase in childlessness, and a shortage of available men for women who wish to marry.

11. Children born to unmarried women (illegitimate children) face discrimination based on their legal status; the major form of legal discrimination involves the right to inherit the father's property. Although the legal status of illegitimate children has improved in recent years, the proportion of illegitimate births has increased, particularly among teenagers. Another sign of changing norms of parenthood is the increasing number of gay and lesbian couples who are raising children, either their own or adopted.

12. The possibilities and choices associated with human reproduction have been greatly expanded as a result of technological advances. However, some of the new technologies raise complex moral issues. For example, numerous legal and emotional problems result from the practice of surrogacy (bearing a child for another couple for a fee).

13. Social policy with respect to divorce has consisted chiefly of reforms in divorce laws. Since 1970 no-fault divorce laws have been adopted in a number of states. These have alleviated some of the problems associated with divorce, but others remain. In particular, the courts are unable to enforce alimony and child support settlements, with the result that many divorced women and their children suffer economic hardship.

14. Illegitimacy is for the most part a problem of poverty and may be addressed through policies intended to alleviate poverty. Many social scientists believe that opportunities to work and learn, especially in combination, are the only practical way to decrease early childbearing.

15. Other areas in which more coherent public policies are needed include assistance to low-income families, expanded child care systems, and job training for low-income parents. Although policy makers have reached a consensus on the need for such programs, continuing drains on federal funds are likely to delay the implementation of new family support policies.

SUGGESTED READINGS

BELLAH, ROBERT N., RICHARD MADSEN, WILLIAM M. SULLIVAN, ANN SWIDLER, and STEVEN M. TIPTON. *Habits of the Heart*. New York: HarperCollins, 1985. A study of the cultural origins of American individualism, with particular emphasis on interviews with American adults about their thoughts and problems when committing themselves to one another and to their communities.

CAPLAN, ARTHUR. *If I Were a Rich Man Could I Buy a Pancreas?: And Other Essays on the Ethics of Health Care*. Bloomington: Indiana University Press, 1992. An up-to-date review of ethical issues in reproductive medicine and other aspects of health care.

CHERLIN, ANDREW. *Marriage, Divorce, Remarriage*, 2nd ed. Cambridge, MA: Harvard University Press, 1992. A highly regarded study of trends in marriage, divorce, and remarriage.

HUTTER, MARK. *The Changing Family: Comparative Perspectives*. New York: Wiley, 1981. An account of the impact of various economic and political forces (e.g., industrialization, urbanization) on family form.

KAMERMAN, SHEILA B. *Parenting in an Unresponsive Society: Managing Work and Family*. New York: Free Press, 1980. A study of working mothers in one-parent, one-earner families and two-parent, two-earner families; presents research on the role problems faced by working mothers and their implications both for them and for the community.

PEPITONE-ROCKWELL, FRAN, ED. *Dual-Career Couples*. Newbury Park, CA: Sage, 1980. A series of articles on the history of research on dual-career couples, issues relevant to the dual-career lifestyle, and the legal position of such couples in the job market.

STAPLES, ROBERT, ED. *The Black Family: Essays and Studies*, 2nd ed. Belmont, CA: Wadsworth, 1978. A collection of articles on various aspects of the black family in America, including historical antecedents, sexuality, and single motherhood.

WEITZMAN, LENORE. *The Divorce Revolution: The Unexpected Social and Economic Consequences for Women and Children in America*. New York: Free Press, 1985. A study of the intended and unintended consequences of social policy that shows how liberalized federal and state divorce laws have often tended to increase the hardships faced by children and women.

Wilson, William J., and Kathryn M. Neckerman. "Poverty and Family Structure: The Widening Gap Between Evidence and Public Policy Issues." In S. H. Danziger and D. H. Weinberg, eds., *Fighting Poverty: What Works and What Doesn't*. Cambridge, MA: Harvard University Press, 1986. Traces the rise in female-headed black families to declining employment rates among black men. Argues, with data, for making the problem of minority unemployment a top policy priority.

Problems of Public Education

Chapter Outline

- Over 99 percent of all children between the ages of 6 and 13 are in school.
- The estimated lifetime earnings of high school graduates are $200,000 higher than those of dropouts.
- In 1992 the average scores on the verbal and mathematical sections of the Scholastic Aptitude Test were 423 and 476, respectively.
- During the 1980s, $1 billion was cut from the Guaranteed Student Loan program.

The United States has been known throughout its history for its emphasis on public education. The nation's founders believed that public education is essential for the maintenance of democratic values, and public schools are thought of as the institution that is largely responsible for extending equality of opportunity (though not equality of result) by preparing new generations of Americans for work and citizenship. In addition, the schools have repeatedly been asked to play a major role in the shaping of American society. In the 1950s, for example, the effort to end racial segregation focused primarily on the school system. When it appeared that the former Soviet Union had taken an early lead over the United States in satellite technology and space research, schools and colleges were urged to put greater emphasis on mathematics, foreign languages, and science. And in the 1990s, as the nation seeks to prepare its young citizens for a technologically demanding future, the schools are under pressure to meet rising expectations in this area.

Education has long been viewed as a tool for solving or alleviating social problems. In fact, the schools are commonly thought of as the social institution responsible for accepting young people from many diverse backgrounds and transforming them into upwardly mobile Americans. How, then, can public education itself be a social problem? The answer, according to many observers, is that the schools are not doing their job, or at least not doing as good a job as they are expected to do. Indeed, public education in the United States is under attack on several fronts. It is criticized for failing to produce competent, educated adults. It is also criticized for failing to reduce or eliminate social inequality.

The "failure" of the American educational system is a complex issue that is defined differently by different groups in society, depending on the goals of the group in question. For example, parents at all social-class levels are demanding that the schools do a better job of preparing students to work and live in a technologically sophisticated society. Parents at lower socioeconomic levels believe that the schools should teach their children the job-related skills they need to improve their social-class position. Various minority groups want schools to prepare their children to compete in American society yet, at the same time, not strip them of their cultural identity—or, in the case of Hispanics, of the language they learn at home. Educational policy makers believe that schools must do more to increase the overall level of student achievement. Many teachers, on the other hand, believe that parents should play a greater role in their children's education.

Are U.S. schools really failing? In all the controversies surrounding public education, there is little agreement even among experts. From a social-scientific viewpoint, part of the problem of knowing whether U.S. schools are truly failing to produce well-educated students lies in the difficulty of conducting comparative research. Comparative studies must "hold constant" social variables such as language and social class, and this is never entirely possible. However, one recent study succeeded in administering standardized tests in different languages and in controlling for social class.

Each time schoolchildren recite the Pledge of Allegiance, they are affirming the values of American citizenship. One of the primary functions of the educational system is to produce citizens who are aware of their rights and responsibilities in a democracy.

Harold W. Stevenson (1992) conducted a comparative study of students in the United States and Asia (China, Japan, and Taiwan). He found that "the test results confirm what has become common knowledge: schoolchildren in Asia perform better academically than do those in the U.S." (p. 71). In mathematics, for example, first graders in U.S. schools did not perform as well as comparable children in Asian schools, although students in some of the better U.S. schools had scores that were similar to those of students in the Asian schools. By the fifth grade, however, the U.S. students had fallen quite far behind their Asian counterparts; students at only one school in the U.S. sample scored as high as students at the worst school in the Asian sample.

Another recent study, which compared schools in the United States and selected European nations, found quite different results (Organization for Economic Cooperation and Development, cited in Celis, 1993). When test scores of U.S. students from sixteen public school systems representing inner-city, suburban, and rural districts were compared to similar sets of scores from schools in sixteen European, Canadian, and Australian systems, the results showed that U.S. students outperformed students in twelve other nations. In math, U.S. students scored ahead of students in only two other nations, but in science they scored in the middle range, along with students in Canada, France, England, Scotland, and Spain. This international study also found that U.S. colleges, especially community colleges, do a better job preparing students for a changing labor market than do institutions of higher education in the other nations studied. And although only

15.5 percent of U.S. college and university degrees are awarded in the sciences, compared to 32 percent in Germany and 26 percent in Japan, far higher proportions of all students attend colleges and universities in the United States than in those nations; hence, the absolute number of science students produced in the United States is high and is continuing to increase.

The United States spends an average of $13,630 per year on each college or university student; comparable averages in other countries range between $6,000 and $7,000 per student (Celis, 1993). While high expenditures per student may be a favorable reflection on U.S. education, the average or poor rating of U.S. students in international comparisons illustrates, according to Education Secretary Richard W. Riley, "why the American habit of being comfortable with just being average comes up short in the new global economic environment" (quoted in Celis, 1993, p. A1) and why the United States needs to press ahead with programs to improve the performance of both schools and students throughout the nation.

The controversy over scholastic achievement scores is another example of how difficult it is to determine whether the schools are actually failing. Since the early 1960s there appears to have been a decline in the verbal and mathematical skills of high school students as measured by the Scholastic Aptitude Test (SAT), a standardized college entrance examination administered to high school students throughout the nation. But there are conflicting opinions on the significance of the drop in mean SAT scores. Many educators believe that the lower scores indicate a decrease in student achievement (and, hence, a decrease in the effectiveness of public schooling). Others, however, argue that the SAT and other standardized tests measure what used to be taught rather than what is currently taught, that they are unimportant or irrelevant, that they may be valid for groups but are not valid for individuals, and so on. This controversy is at the core of the debate over public education and will be discussed more fully later in the chapter.

Not only the goals of education but also the means of achieving them are subjects of heated debate. Should schools be more open to new ideas and teaching methods, or should they focus more on the traditional curriculum—"the basics"? Indeed, what *are* "the basics"? Do they consist simply of reading, writing, and arithmetic, or do they include learning how to get along with others and how to communicate effectively? Are "the basics" the same for all students? These are only some of the fundamental questions that are being asked about public education in the United States today. There are many others. Should more qualified and effective teachers receive merit pay? Should the school year be longer? Should there be a standardized "national" curriculum? There is even some question as to whether education should be a public institution. Perhaps high-quality private schooling should be encouraged by means of a government-sponsored voucher system that would refund to households the amounts they spend on public education through taxes. Such refunds could take the form of "educational vouchers" that could be used to pay for private schooling (Parelius & Parelius, 1987).

The United States has led the world in establishing free public education for its people. Per capita public expenditures on education are higher in the United States than in any other nation. Education is compulsory in the United States; the requirements differ from one state to another, but usually children must attend school until age 16. As a result, over 90 percent of all American children between the ages of 5 and 19 are enrolled in school, and about 75 percent of American adolescents remain in class full time through the final year of secondary school (Kominski, 1987). Moreover, the number of students enrolled in higher education has increased rapidly in this century (Trow, 1966).

So what is wrong? Why is the educational system under attack? How does this impressive record constitute a "failure"? These questions can be answered in different ways, depending on the sociological perspective from which they are viewed.

SOCIOLOGICAL PERSPECTIVES ON EDUCATION

As might be expected, there are vast differences in the analyses of public education offered by sociologists who approach the subject from different theoretical perspectives. Functionalists stress stability and consensus; in their view, education is, or should be, one of several interdependent parts that work together to create a smoothly functioning society whose members all share the same basic values and beliefs. Conflict theorists, on the other hand, focus on the coercive aspects of education; they see society as divided into dominant and subordinate groups, with education being used as a tool to promote the interests of the dominant group while teaching the subordinate groups to accept their situation. Interactionists take still another approach: They examine how expectations of student performance actually determine that performance and can result in labels that shape the student's future. Each of these perspectives gives rise to different approaches to the study of public education.

Functionalist Approaches

From a functionalist perspective, problems in the educational system are a symptom of social disorganization. The educational system is geared to students who come from stable homes and communities. It is not well equipped to handle the problems of students from disorganized homes—for example, homes experiencing divorce or cultural conflict. Such students are often depressed and angry, have trouble concentrating on their schoolwork, and therefore have difficulty achieving in school (Kerckhoff & Campbell, 1977). According to social-disorganization theorists, these students are more likely to join deviant peer groups, such as gangs, that reinforce their negative attitudes toward school.

Also related to functionalism is the theory that the educational problems experienced by various groups stem from deviance from generally accepted norms of achievement. In this view, schools are agents of social control whose tasks are to reinforce society's values and to control deviance through discipline. This perspective can also be applied to the question of whether schools themselves produce deviance by setting unreachable standards for many students. In a study of boys in a British secondary school, for example, the researcher found that working-class students were unable to understand or appreciate the middle-class value orientation of the school. The school, in turn, was unable to modify its bias toward middle-class values and, hence, unable to deal with the working-class students' attitudes. The result was the development of a deviant group of alienated working-class youths (Willis, 1983).

Another functionalist approach focuses on the problems societies face in shaping educational institutions to meet the requirements of changing economies and cultures. Institutional theorists look, for example, at how established bureaucracies in educational institutions militate against decentralization and other types of organizational reform (Hannaway, 1993). Studies of educational institutions often look at how changes in curriculum and other school programs designed for special populations (e.g., underachievers) can best be implemented.

Conflict Approaches

The conflict perspective sees educational problems as stemming from conflicting views of the goals of education. In particular, it stresses the tensions between different groups concerning those goals. The dispute over whether the schools should teach a universal curriculum in a single language or, instead, help preserve the cultural identities of minority students through bilingual education is an example of these tensions.

Conflict theory has two main currents—Marxian and non-Marxian. The Marxian view stresses the goal of reducing social stratification and increasing equality. It argues that schools reflect the values of groups in society that are content with the status quo or favor even less equality. Samuel Bowles, for example, believes that compulsory education in the United States developed to meet the needs of a capitalist economy for skilled and disciplined workers and, while doing so, to justify the unequal social status of workers and capitalists (Bowles & Gintis, 1977). Other investigators (e.g., Jencks et al., 1972) emphasize unequal access to education, especially higher education, and inequalities in the resources available to schools in different states or districts.

The non-Marxian version of the conflict perspective, which is referred to as the *value conflict approach,* focuses on intergroup conflicts that arise out of the desire to maintain or defend a group's status in a particular community. This leads to conflicts over such issues as busing to achieve school desegregation. A case in point is the intense conflict that developed in Boston over efforts to desegregate that city's public schools by means of busing of students. One study of this conflict (Buell, 1982) emphasizes the concept of the "defended neighborhood," a community that actively resists abrupt change. In such a neighborhood, life revolves around the familiar and routine. Only by understanding the beliefs and concerns of the inhabitants, the researchers claim, can the depth of their resistance to a change such as busing be fully understood.

Interactionist Approaches

According to the interactionist perspective, schools label students as "achievers," "underachievers," or "rebels," and those labels follow them throughout their lives. For some students, schools are "factories for failure." A well-known study of ghetto

TABLE 13–1 PERSPECTIVES ON EDUCATION

Basic Perspective	Research Approach	View of Education as a Social Problem	Policy Recommendations
Functionalism	Social disorganization	Schools cannot help students who come from disorganized backgrounds.	Requiring schools to work more closely with parents or guardians, or in some cases take their place.
	Deviant behavior	Problems stem from deviance by some groups from accepted norms of achievement.	Greater discipline, remedial education for nonachieving students.
	Institutional	There are difficulties in shaping educational institutions to meet changing economic or cultural needs.	Allowing schools to adapt to new student populations and new policies such as integration.
Conflict theory	Class conflict	Those with wealth and power attempt to ensure that their children get high-quality education; those with little wealth and power cite evidence that their children are shortchanged.	Channeling adequate resources to the schools to improve the quality of education for the poor and educationally disadvantaged.
	Value conflict	Problems stem from tensions between different groups over the goals of education.	Allowing different groups to achieve their educational goals while also achieving basic competency.
Interactionism	Labeling	Schools label students as "achievers," "underachievers," or "rebels."	Elimination of labeling practices such as ability tracking.

education found, for example, that "a 'slow learner' had no option but to continue to be a slow learner, regardless of performance or potential" (Rist, 1973, p. 93). According to labeling theorists, teachers form expectations about students early in the school year, and in various ways those expectations are communicated to the students themselves. The students tend to perform in ways that meet the teacher's expectations, thereby reinforcing them.

The various perspectives on education as a social problem, and the kinds of policy recommendations generated by each one, are presented in Table 13–1.

EDUCATION: AN INSTITUTION UNDER FIRE

Daniel Bell has stated that "any institution which gains a quasi-monopoly power over the fate of individuals is likely, in a free society, to be subject to quick attack" (1973, p. 410). Such an attack, according to Bell, can be seen in debates over the limitations of intelligence testing and in demands for "open admission" to universities regardless of previous levels of educational achievement. In this section of the chapter we will discuss three areas in which public education is under attack: education's role in achieving greater social equality; the controversy about scholastic achievement test scores; and bureaucratic barriers to educational reform.

Education and Equality: The Issue of Equal Access

It is well known that educational attainment (number of years of school completed) is strongly correlated with socioeconomic status: "Not only does one's education affect occupational and income life chances, but the education of parents has a bearing on the education and socioeconomic position of the offspring" (Lieberson, 1980, p. 124). An egalitarian society has a responsibility to provide equal access to high-quality education for all its citizens. Critics claim that American society has failed to meet this responsibility, particularly in relation to minority groups.

This criticism has become especially sharp as the composition of student popu-

In recent years Native Americans have become increasingly upset over what they perceive as a lack of commitment by the federal government to improving the quality of education on reservations, which are administered by the Federal Bureau of Indian Affairs. Educational attainment among Indians is among the lowest for any minority group in the nation.

lations has changed. Since the 1960s increasing numbers of blacks, Hispanics, and other minority groups have become concentrated in central cities while whites have moved to the suburbs. In some metropolitan areas, as a result, over 90 percent of the students in public schools are black or Hispanic. And since central-city schools often have fewer resources than suburban schools, the quality of education available to black and Hispanic central-city residents tends to be lower than that available to white suburban residents.

Nor are urban minorities the only slighted populations. Native Americans and Alaskan Eskimos have also suffered as a consequence of inadequate education and lack of access to higher-quality educational institutions. Both groups live in remote rural areas, where educational choices are extremely limited. In addition, Native Americans have been forced to depend on reservation schools, which they consider to be of inferior quality (Byler, 1977).

Inequality in access to education is not solely a matter of unequal distribution of resources, however. In a pioneering study, Christopher Jencks (1972) pointed out that blacks receive an average of 10 percent less schooling than whites, and that children from working-class families spend 13 percent less time in school than children from middle-class families. The reasons for these differences are only partly related to inequalities in educational resources and are more directly related to parents' ability to pay for preschool and higher education. Thus,

> Access to low-cost educational services is more equal than access to high-cost services. Elementary and secondary schooling cost relatively little per student, so almost everyone gets them. Preschooling and higher education cost two or three times as much per pupil as regular schooling, so only a fraction of the population has access to them. (Jencks et al., 1972, p. 22)

Black Students   A major factor in the lower educational attainment of blacks compared with whites is the fact that before World War I about 90 percent of all blacks in the United States lived in the southern states (Lieberson, 1980). The South was then (and remains to some extent) less affluent than the North. An analysis prepared by the office of Senator Daniel P. Moynihan, chair of the Senate Finance Committee, shows that southern states and some western ones continue to spend far less per student than school systems in the Northeast and far West. The data in Figure 13–1 (spending per student adjusted by the state's cost of living) show that states like New York and New Jersey spend over twice the amount spent by states like Mississippi and Utah. Since black students are disproportionately concentrated in the deep South, one effect of this difference is that blacks (and poor southern whites) receive only about 70 percent of the amount of schooling received by whites in more advantaged areas of the nation.

In the North, educational opportunities for blacks and whites are more equal, but inequalities between schools located in poor black communities and more affluent white suburbs tend to perpetuate differences in educational attainment. Early in the twentieth century, northern-born blacks were rapidly closing the educational gap between themselves and whites, but the gap widened again after 1915. The reasons for this reversal are complex. According to Stanley Lieberson (1980), an important factor was the competition between black children and the children of European immigrants, who tended to come from better educated families and thus enjoyed an advantage over blacks whose parents had migrated from the South. Another factor, beginning in the Great Depression and continuing to the present, was the higher rate of unemployment among blacks. (The employment status of parents has a great deal to do with the educational attainment of their children because children of lower-income parents are more likely to drop out of school.)

A third factor was segregation:

> Whereas education was seen as a major instrument for assimilating . . . new European groups who were so radically different, policies toward blacks shifted over time as their

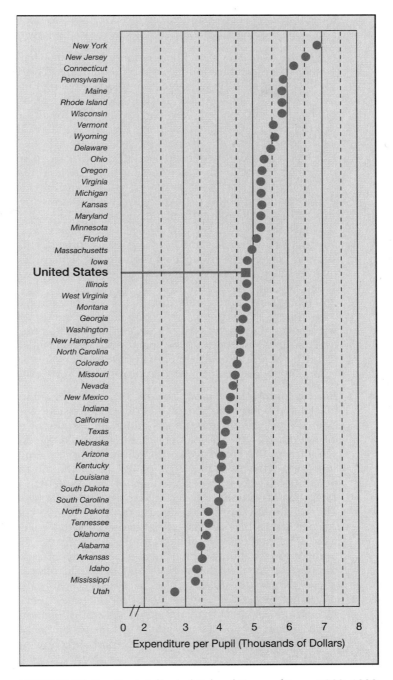

FIGURE 13–1 Cost-Adjusted School Expenditure, 1989–1990

Source: Moynihan, 1992 (data from Educational Testing Service).

presence in many cities increased. The different educational opportunities offered to blacks were accompanied by informal as well as legal steps taken to isolate them from whites in the schools. (Lieberson, 1980, p. 252)

Segregation tends to increase disparities between groups, not only because minority schools, which are usually located in central cities, have fewer resources available to them but also because students in those schools do not learn the values, work habits, and skills they need to compete effectively in the larger society (Orfield, 1991).

Hispanic Students   Another minority group that has faced difficulties in gaining equal access to education is Hispanic Americans. This large group (which accounts for 9 percent of the U.S. population and is growing much faster than the population as a whole) is highly concentrated in metropolitan areas. The educational attainment of Hispanic students is lower than the average for all students. A significant factor in this difference is the fact that many Hispanic students either do not speak English at all or do not speak it well enough to succeed in school. Moreover, Hispanic students, like blacks, have experienced the effects of de facto segregation, a problem that is particularly acute in large metropolitan areas (Orfield, 1986; *Statistical Abstract,* 1993).

Since the late 1960s, a primary goal of education for Hispanic students has been to improve their ability to use English without allowing them to fall behind in other subjects. One technique for achieving this is bilingual/bicultural education, in which students are taught wholly or partly in their native language until they can function adequately in English, and in some cases longer. This approach has received the support of the federal Office of Civil Rights, which requires that schools take "affirmative steps" to correct minority students' deficiencies in the English language in order to receive federal funds.

Bilingual/bicultural education is a subject of intense debate. On one side are those who believe that preserving the language and culture of minority groups is a worthwhile, even necessary, goal of public education. On the other are those who believe that minority students must be "immersed" in English-language instruction if they are to be prepared to compete effectively in American society. Minority parents themselves often disagree on which approach best serves the interests of their children.

Educational Attainment Today   The gap in educational attainment between blacks and whites has narrowed considerably since the turn of the century, mainly as a result of the increase in the minimum amount of education received by almost all Americans. Over 99 percent of all children between the ages of 6 and 13 are in school, and therefore "we can hardly talk about inequality in access to elementary schooling" (Jencks et al., 1972, p. 18). In 1960 almost 44 percent of whites and 76 percent of blacks between the ages of 25 and 29 had not finished high school. By 1985 the proportions had declined to 13 percent of whites and 17 percent of blacks. The same trends apply to college completion. In 1960 only 8.2 percent of whites and 2.8 percent of blacks aged 25–29 had completed college. By 1985 the proportions were 23.2 percent for whites and 16.7 percent for blacks. Considering their extremely low "cultural capital" at the beginning of desegregation, blacks made extraordinary gains in this period, and their rate of gain is now faster than that of whites (Kornblum, 1991).

Rates of school leaving (the dropout rate) remain higher among inner-city blacks and Hispanics than among whites, and alienation from school leads many minority teenagers and young adults to finish their schooling in high school equivalency programs. Despite this serious problem, however, the educational gap between blacks and whites continues to narrow.

It is argued that the higher dropout rates among minority students are caused by the fact that those students do not receive enough help at home. This is known as the cultural-disadvantage argument. Although minority enrollments are higher today than at any time in the past, the parents of these students have less education than the parents of white students and therefore are less able to assist their children.

Although the primary cause of dropping out is poor academic performance, students often drop out of high school because of the difficulties they encounter in trying to cope with school and adult family and work roles at the same time. They may be married and/or pregnant or working at a regular job (this increases the likelihood of dropping out by more than one-third). Whatever the cause, dropping out has a number of serious consequences. Compared to those of high school graduates, the earnings of school dropouts are considerably lower. This disadvantage continues throughout life: The estimated lifetime earnings of high school graduates are $200,000 higher than those of dropouts. Most dropouts believe leaving school before graduating was a poor decision, and an estimated 40 percent eventually return to the educational system (Pallas, 1987).

At the college level, educational attainment for low-income members of minority groups is hindered by lack of financial aid as a result of cutbacks in federally funded student assistance. Cutbacks in federally funded assistance in the 1980s, particularly the emphasis on loans rather than outright grants, put a college education out of reach for many minority students. The disparities in educational attainment between white and minority students are a matter of concern to those who believe that equality of educational attainment is basic to other kinds of social equality. For them, encouraging students to finish high school, developing systems of school financing that provide equal resources for all schools, and ending segregation are important policy goals.

The Great Achievement Controversy

As noted earlier, differences in levels of educational attainment indicate that American society is not providing equal quantities of education to all its citizens. It also appears that the quality of education has fallen. In its report, *A Nation at Risk,* the National Commission on Excellence in Education (1983) cited the decline in the aptitude test scores of high school students between 1965 and 1985 as evidence that schools are failing to maintain high educational standards.

Mean scores on the Scholastic Aptitude Test (SAT), which is taken by about 1 million high school students each year, have been published since the mid-1950s. From the mid-1950s to the mid-1960s, those scores were fairly constant, ranging from 472 to 478 on the verbal-reasoning section of the test and from 495 to 502 on the mathematical-reasoning section. In the second half of the 1960s both scores began to decline. By 1980 the mean verbal score was 424 and the mean mathematical score was 466. The significance of the decline is greater when one takes into consideration the fact that because of changes in the tests it was easier to get higher scores after 1963 than before.

The decline in SAT scores was paralleled by declines in scores on other examinations administered to students in the final high school years, pointing to a general decline in the cognitive achievements of American high school students. Comparable declines have been found in the achievement test scores of students in the upper elementary and early high school years. This apparent decrease in achievement attracted great publicity and became a central concern of educational policy makers at all levels. But should they be concerned?

Scott Menard (1981) conducted a thorough analysis of the outpouring of articles and studies dealing with this issue. The literature offers three basic explanations for the decline in test scores. The first holds that the decline is neither significant nor widespread. There has been a drop of over thirty points in mean SAT scores if the 1955–1965 period is used as a baseline, but if the scores from 1955 to 1975 are used as a baseline, the variation is considerably less than thirty points. Moreover, scores on some standardized tests have risen, including those on the Stanford-Binet (IQ) test and the National Assessment of Educational Progress literacy test.

Another argument against taking the drop in SAT scores too seriously focuses on the question of what is actually being tested. Harnischfeger and Wiley (1976), for example, concluded that tests based on traditional curricula show those curricula to be doing well, and the same can be said for tests based on innovative curricula. A related argument holds that the SAT statistics distort reality and are often misapplied; that is, they are used to evaluate the state of education even though they are not a valid basis for comparing the performance of teachers, schools, districts, or states.

A third set of explanations for the decline in test scores looks to factors other than schooling. Those factors include changes in the tests themselves, changes in the family (e.g., the increase in single-parent families), social changes such as increased drug use and television viewing, and academic changes such as automatic promotion. Menard's analysis uncovered no significant correlations between any of these factors and the test score decline, except that it is possible that a complex set of influences related to birth order, family size, and child spacing (associated with the post–World War II baby boom) had an impact on test scores. Menard concluded that "the available . . . data contradict many suggestions made concerning causes of the test score decline" (1981, p. 204).

In the mid-1980s the decline in SAT scores appeared to end. (See Table 13–2.) However, average scores are still significantly below the levels of the mid-1960s, and many observers continue to call for reform of the educational system, especially in the areas of coursework requirements and academic standards. Indeed, in the opinion of many experts major changes are needed if public schools are to prepare students to function in a rapidly changing society.

Problems of Institutional Change

The primary obstacle to significant changes in the educational system is that educational institutions have a built-in tendency to resist change. To some extent this is a useful quality: Schools tend to conserve society's values and do not yield easily to educational fads. Nevertheless, educational institutions must be able to change in response to changes in other major institutions. Such changes are highly visible, and

TABLE 13–2 AVERAGE SCORES ON THE SCHOLASTIC APTITUDE TEST, 1975–1992

	Total	
	VERBAL	**MATH**
1975	434	472
1976	431	472
1977	429	470
1978	429	468
1979	427	467
1980	424	466
1981	424	466
1982	426	467
1983	425	468
1984	426	471
1985	431	475
1986	431	475
1987	430	476
1988	428	476
1989	427	476
1990	424	476
1991	422	474
1992	423	476

Source: Statistical Abstract, 1993.

several have been mentioned in other parts of this book. The family, for example, has changed dramatically as increasing numbers of women have entered the labor force. Economic institutions also are changing as jobs requiring specialized skills replace jobs that require little training. These and other changes in American society call for adults with skills and outlooks different from those that were typical of their parents' generation. The schools are largely responsible for preparing students for these new adult roles.

The nature of schools themselves is a major barrier to change. Schools have been compared with prisons, mental hospitals, and other institutions in which a large group of involuntary "clients" is serviced by a smaller group of employees (Boocock, 1980). A central problem of such institutions is the maintenance of order and control, a concern that leads to the development of elaborate sets of rules and monitoring systems. Although schools are not *total* institutions in that not all their "clients'" activities take place within their boundaries, they exhibit one of the key traits of total institutions: The administrators tend to place a high priority on maintaining their authority.

Schools as Bureaucracies   Daniel Bell has commented that

> *It is a truism of sociology that the initial patterns of any social system, like the first tracks through a virgin forest, shape its future modes. Traditions become established, routines are set, vested interests develop, innovations either are resisted or must conform to the adaptive patterns laid down at the start, and an aura of legitimacy surrounds the existing ways and becomes in time the conventional wisdom of the institution. (1973, p. 402)*

This aptly describes the situation of education in what Bell calls "postindustrial" society.

Ann Parker Parelius and Robert J. Parelius (1987) have documented the extent of bureaucratization in the American educational system. They point out that increases in bureaucratization are associated with increases in organizational size and complexity. This is certainly true of American school systems. The one-room schoolhouse has become a complex system characterized by an increasingly specialized division of labor. Today's schools have large administrative staffs that include a variety of specialists such as community relations experts and guidance counselors. Even the teachers are specialists—for example, in a certain age group or, at the high school level, in a particular subject area.

Another bureaucratic characteristic of modern school systems is the development of an elaborate hierarchy of authority. (See Figure 13–2 on page 392.) The relationships among people at various levels of the hierarchy have an important effect on educational policy at the district and school levels. In big-city school systems, for example, there may be several administrative layers between the superintendent and the schools themselves. In such cases the superintendent may be unable to control the implementation of policies. A similar situation exists at the classroom level. Teachers have considerable autonomy in how they run their classrooms; if they choose to, they can resist innovation by simply not following the directives of school boards and principals.

From the teacher's point of view, the educational bureaucracy can be a source of severe frustration. One high school English teacher provided the authors with the following description:

> *At 9:30 homeroom ended. We were left with the following: piles of returned books to be sorted for department collection; unredeemed book receipts to be arranged according to new official classes; unclaimed report cards and program cards to be clipped; a roll book in which attendance totals had to be completed. . . . Next we had to go to the transportation office to receive the blank bus and train passes we had requested the day before. For all these things we were given 15 minutes.*

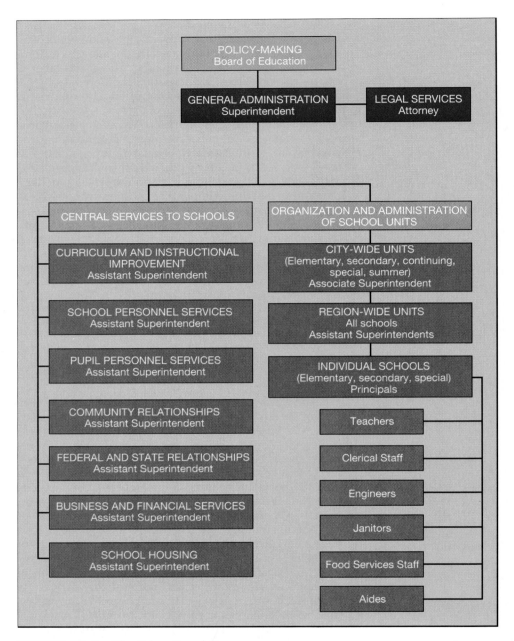

FIGURE 13–2   The Educational Bureaucracy

Source: Reprinted with permission of Macmillan Publishing Company from *Encyclopedia of Education,*
Vol. 8, Lee C. Deighton, Editor in Chief. Copyright © 1971 by Crowell Collier and Macmillan, Inc.

The "Technological Fix"   Much of the pressure for change in the schools has developed out of the typically American belief in the value of technology. The "technological fix," it is widely believed, can solve any problem. Thus, it is commonplace to attempt to apply such techniques as cost accounting, systems analysis, closed-circuit television, and computer technology to educational problems. Although the evidence does not support the notion that technology can solve the problems of public education, some technological initiatives have had positive consequences.

In the forty years since Brown v. Board of Education, *efforts to end racial segregation in schools have not ceased, but neither have they proven to be very successful in the face of persistent residential segregation.*

According to Parelius and Parelius (1987), "students have more and better materials, a greater variety of courses, increased freedom to choose among diverse educational alternatives, and a less authoritarian relationship with teachers and administrators." But at the same time

> there are some important ways in which the school has remained impervious to techno-logical advances. . . . The basic classroom unit of the school has remained fundamentally unchanged. The role structure consisting of one teacher to a room full of students is still with us. . . . The teacher is still concerned with discipline . . . students are still expected to be obedient, punctual, and docile. . . . Blackboard and chalk, paper and pen remain the primary tools. . . . This mode of interaction has successfully resisted change for a long pe-riod of time. (p. 84)

Despite some resistance by teachers, new educational technologies, especially those mediated by computers, are coming into widespread use in U.S. schools. En-trepreneurs like Chris Whittle, whose Whittle Schools invest heavily in computer technologies for their "futuristic" classrooms, believe that these technologies provide a way to increase student learning while decreasing teacher costs. Even if this proves to be true, a major risk associated with this approach is that students in poorer school districts, which cannot afford the new technologies, and students who are not selected for "high-tech" schools will fall even further behind in their educational attainment. If this occurs, the new technologies will not result in improved school-ing but instead will serve to increase the educational inequalities that already pose serious problems for the nation (Blakeslee and Brown, 1990; Weir, 1992).

Intentional Change: Desegregation There are some areas in which public schools have been *required* to change. One of those areas is racial integration—or, more accurately, desegregation. Much of the pressure for change in this area has come from court rulings and legal mandates.

Desegregation effectively began with the Supreme Court's 1954 ruling in *Brown* v. *Board of Education of Topeka, Kansas,* which was based in part on the argument that segregation had negative effects on black students even when their school fa-cilities were equal to those of white students. Black students in segregated schools

Computer-assisted learning is a growing trend in public and private schools, leading some social scientists to question how schools in disadvantaged neighborhoods will be able to afford the new learning technologies.

tended to learn that their schools were inferior and to believe that they themselves were likely to be inferior as well. To avoid the formation of such a negative self-concept, black children should associate with white children as early as possible and should be taught by both white and black teachers.

In the first few years after the *Brown* ruling, desegregation programs were instituted in most of the southern and border states, where schools had been segregated by law. There were some exceptions, however, notably the states of the deep South and the cities of New Orleans and Little Rock, which openly resisted the directives of the courts. By 1967 only 26 percent of the nation's school districts were desegregated (Rist, 1979). In the mid-1960s Congress provided additional impetus for desegregation in the form of the Civil Rights Act of 1964 and the Elementary and Secondary Education Act of 1965. These acts required all state and local agencies that receive federal funds to ensure that "no person shall be excluded from participation, denied any benefits, or subjected to discrimination on the basis of race, color, or national origin."

By the late 1960s most segregation based on state or local law (de jure segregation) had been eliminated, but the problem of de facto segregation remained. The tendency of different neighborhoods to be largely white or largely black resulted in segregated schools because of another traditional characteristic of school systems: the policy of requiring students to attend schools in their own neighborhoods. A number of cities made efforts to reduce de facto segregation, but despite these efforts the proportion of black students attending schools that were all, or nearly all, black continued to increase.

The result of these trends is ironic: Today there is less racial segregation of schools in the South than in other parts of the United States, and the North has become the most heavily segregated region in the country. This has prompted educators to redefine the goals of desegregation. In many schools the focus has shifted to integration, that is, "active efforts aimed at bringing about positive interracial relations within the school" (Levine & Havighurst, 1984, p. 426).

In addition, since the mid-1970s the courts have taken a more active role in monitoring the implementation of desegregation plans (which frequently include districtwide reassignment of students and, hence, busing). They have also required a variety of changes in the instructional methods used by schools, with the goal of improving the quality of education available to minority students. In Boston, for example, a federal judge appointed a new headmaster for South Boston High School. In Detroit, a judge issued a desegregation order that included a requirement that the board of education "design, develop, and institute a comprehensive instructional program for teaching reading and communication skills."

In the past three decades educators have learned a great deal about how to plan and implement desegregation programs. It appears, moreover, that improved curriculum and instruction in the schools will contribute to the success of a desegregation plan (Levine & Havighurst, 1984). On the other hand, critics claim that unless there is a concerted effort to raise the minimum level of mastery expected of students, school desegregation will make little difference in overall educational achievement (Boyer, 1983).

In the 1980s the pace of desegregation slowed, especially in the Northeast. As noted in Chapter 9, there are a number of cities in which the distribution of the white and nonwhite populations places severe limits on the extent to which schools can be desegregated. Recent research by Douglas Massey and Judith Denton (1992) on the persistence of residential segregation suggests that without stronger enforcement of fair-housing laws and other measures to reduce racial segregation, it will be extremely difficult to accelerate the pace of school desegregation. The situation is aggravated by the tendency of middle-class urban residents to enroll their children in private schools. Nevertheless, many school systems throughout the country have adapted successfully to the demand for desegregated public schools.

In 1991 the Supreme Court held that the Oklahoma City schools could be permitted to cease busing children to meet the requirements of a 1972 desegregation order. The Court ruled that school systems could be released from busing orders once they have taken "all practicable steps" to eliminate segregation. Some implications of this ruling are discussed in Box 9–1 in Chapter 9.

School Violence A growing problem in U.S. public schools is theft and violence, whether committed by intruders or by students themselves. A 1978 survey of secondary school students conducted by the National Institute of Education found that 11 percent of students reported having something worth more than a dollar stolen from them in the past month; one-fifth of those thefts involved property worth $10 or more. When students filled out questionnaires anonymously rather than answering questions in face-to-face interviews, the estimates of victimization were about twice as high. In addition, about 36 percent of inner-city junior high and 24 percent of high school teachers reported having been threatened by students (cited in Toby, 1993/1994).

Although this study was conducted almost twenty years ago, the findings remain relevant. Episodes of school violence frequently make the headlines in U.S. cities. Teachers are discouraged, and with reason. Many observers believe that the underlying problem is that the role of the teacher no longer commands automatic respect because students do not care whether their teachers approve of their behavior. When large numbers of students are frustrated and alienated, and their parents are uninvolved in their education, only the most forceful, experienced teachers are able to remain in control of their classes.

Solutions such as installing metal detectors and hiring additional security guards have been attempted, and these measures may help prevent violence by outsiders entering schools, but they do not convey authority to teachers. Educators are searching for ways to empower teachers who are intimidated by violent students. Several possibilities have been suggested, including creating smaller high schools or "schools within schools"; encouraging employers to require high school transcripts; expecting more from students besides mere attendance; and encouraging dropouts to return to school as adults. The latter suggestion is especially attractive because adult high school students often become role models for younger students, and their presence tends to reduce the amount of disorder in the schools they attend (Toby, 1993/1994).

Teacher Professionalism and Unions   Another factor affecting school operations is the increased popularity of teachers' unions. Membership in teachers' trade unions like the National Education Association and the American Federation of Teachers rose dramatically during the 1960s and 1970s—from less than 10 percent of all teachers in the early 1960s to over 30 percent at present. These unions seek to improve the status and material well-being of their members, but they also support a range of policies directed toward reform of the educational system. Among other things, they demand smaller classroom rosters, more resources for the handicapped and slow learners, and more funds for in-service training for teachers. On the other hand, they often oppose certain policies whose goal is to improve the competence and motivation of public school teachers (discussed in the next section). For this reason, critics of the unions claim that they are more interested in maintaining the status quo than in genuine educational reform.

Partly because of the unions' efforts to professionalize teaching and partly as a result of economic factors, there is renewed interest in teaching as a career. A study by the American Council on Education and the Higher Education Research Institute of UCLA found that 8.1 percent of students entering college in 1987 wanted to become elementary or secondary school teachers, compared to 4.7 percent in 1982. (See Figure 13–3.) The increase was attributed to widespread publicity about educational reforms, higher salaries for starting teachers, and awareness of an impending shortage of teachers. These trends have continued in the early 1990s. Education is now the third most popular undergraduate major (after business and the social sci-

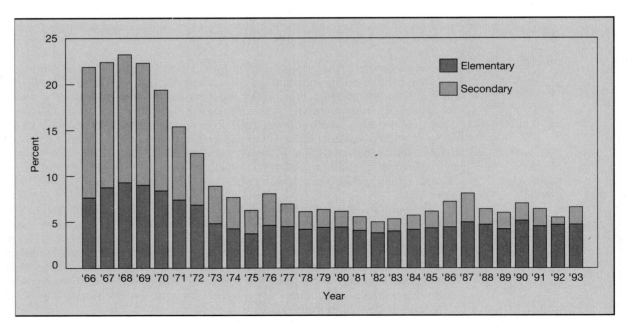

FIGURE 13–3   Freshman Interest in Teaching Careers (percentages by level), 1966–1993

Source: Higher Education Research Institute, UCLA, 1988–1993.

ences), and for the first time in fifteen years enrollments of education majors have been increasing (U.S. Office of Educational Research, 1990).

The public school is the nation's largest educational institution, offering the greatest number of children their basic education. However, as noted earlier in the chapter, public education has been subject to criticism on a number of fronts. The policy recommendations arising out of such criticism take two main forms, depending on whether their proponents take a conservative or a liberal approach to educational policy.

Of all American social institutions, education is most subject to intentional change through social policy. Schools and educational systems are also attractive targets for critics. Those who believe American society has become too secular may advocate prayer in the schools. Others, who believe that the schools have a responsibility to steer children away from the dangers of AIDS or early pregnancy, may advocate more thorough sex education. Still others, who lament the supposed failure of the schools to produce adequately trained students, may come up with schemes to reform the schools. A popular scheme among conservative critics, for example, is a plan to provide parents with "educational vouchers" that would allow them to choose among public and private schools offering all kinds of educational options. The theory is that increased competition among schools to attract students would improve the schools' efficiency or cost effectiveness while stimulating a more open market for educational practices. The main criticism of voucher plans is that they are likely to be used most effectively by more highly educated and affluent parents, leaving the poorer schools to less well equipped parents; this would worsen the existing situation of stratification and inequality in education. Sociologists who study education are often called upon to evaluate this and other policy proposals intended to improve or reform education in the United States.

Michigan is leading the way toward improving the quality of education in poor communities without increasing taxes in affluent communities. In 1994 voters in that state approved a new school funding system based primarily on sales taxes rather than on property taxes. Social scientists will be watching Michigan schools carefully in coming years to see if educational quality improves in poor school districts as a result of this important fiscal change (Celis, 1994).

Educational Conservatism and "Back to Basics"

Educational conservatives believe that the job of schools is to preserve the culture of the past and transmit it to successive generations. This means that schools must concentrate on "essentials"—that is, a set of fundamental subjects and skills—and that all students must be expected to master them. It also means that schools are agencies of social control and as such should stress order, discipline, and obedience.

This point of view has been expressed in a variety of ways since the 1930s, when the debate between "essentialists" and "progressivists" drew national attention. After World War II it was alleged that the schools were failing to safeguard the values of "Americanism"; after the launching of the *Sputnik I* satellite by the former Soviet Union in 1957, American education was blamed for neglecting subjects that were vital to national survival. As one outspoken critic put it, "Instead of offering a four-year program of studies in mathematics, history, foreign languages, and other disciplines, [high schools] encouraged students to divert themselves with ceramics, stagecraft, table decorating, upholstering, and second-year golf" (Rafferty, quoted in Lucas, 1984, p. 41).

The back-to-basics movement found support in the 1983 report of the National Commission on Excellence in Education (*A Nation at Risk*), which called for longer school hours, more homework, and more discipline. It also proposed that teachers receive salary increases based on merit rather than seniority, on the assumption that this would motivate teachers to do a better job in the classroom. The commission recommended that high schools concentrate on what it termed the Five New Basics: English, mathematics, science, social studies, and computer science. It also recommended that schools and colleges adopt more rigorous standards and higher expectations for academic performance, on the theory that students will learn more in a more challenging environment. This recommendation has met with considerable criticism, however. One expert on educational practice sums up the problem as follows:

> The problem is that at least half of all students are making little or no effort to learn, because they don't believe that school satisfies their needs. To make school harder—to increase the length of the school year or the school day, to assign more homework, to require more courses in science and mathematics—is not going to reach those students. It's only going to increase the separation between the half who are already working and the half who are not. (Glasser, quoted in Gough, 1987, p. 656)

Other critics have attacked the commission for using weak arguments and poor data to support simplistic recommendations while ignoring such problems as teenage unemployment, teacher burnout, and high dropout rates and for failing to address the special needs of the poor and minorities (Stedman & Smith, 1985). They have also pointed out that it is extremely difficult to improve the quality of education at the same time that school budgets are being cut back drastically (Finn, 1985; Singer, 1985).

The Fight over National Standards   At the end of the Bush administration, a national conference of governors developed a set of broad educational goals to be achieved by the year 2000. Among those goals were the following: All U.S. students will begin school ready to learn (as a result of Head Start and other preschool programs or simply owing to better health and prenatal care); U.S. students will lead the world in proficiency in math and science; schools will rid themselves of violence; and all citizens will be literate and will possess the skills to compete in a global economy. In the early 1990s, as U.S. students continued to lag behind those of many other nations with advanced educational systems, some reformers went beyond simply setting goals and called for a "national curriculum"—a set of standards, measured by means of standardized exams, that must be met by students in schools throughout the nation.

Opponents of a national curriculum fear that the imposition of standards at a national level will result in a vague set of criteria and goals that could hamper local efforts to achieve educational excellence. The National Congress of Parents and Teachers, which represents local PTAs at the national level, opposes a national curriculum because the idea is untested and raises more questions than it resolves (Celis, 1993).

In an effort to allay some of these fears, the Clinton administration has encouraged the states to develop their own curriculum guidelines and standards. California, Kentucky, South Carolina, and Vermont have already done so, and educators in those states believe that the statewide standards do not prevent local schools from developing innovative educational programs of their own. However, in England, where a national curriculum has been implemented by the government, teachers have staged protests against standardized national exams, claiming that they do not reflect their own educational goals or adequately test students' abilities (Schmidt, 1993). Educators in the United States point to these protests as evidence that a national curriculum will not solve the problems of American education. Thus, the debate over national standards is likely to continue for the foreseeable future.

Humanism and "Open Education"

The liberal view of educational policy is based on the intellectual tradition known as humanism. In this view, the basic aim of education is to promote the maximum self-development of each individual learner, paying specific attention to differences among individuals in terms of interests, needs, abilities, and values. Learning should be as "open" and meaningful as possible, with each learner establishing the goals of his or her own education.

In the United States this approach gave rise to the movement that came to be known as progressivism. Progressivism, which began in the early 1900s and gathered momentum in the 1920s and 1930s, is associated with the educational philosophy of John Dewey. Dewey believed that education should stress the expression of individuality and learning through experience. It should not be imposed from outside but should originate with the needs and interests of the learner. As Dewey defined it, education is "that reconstruction or reorganization of experience which adds to the meaning of experience, and which increases ability to direct the course of subsequent experience" (1916, p. 126).

Dewey's views were central to the development of progressivism, which emphasized vocational training, "daily-living skills," and a "child-centered curriculum." They fell into some disfavor in the post–World War II period, but interest in humanistic education reappeared in the 1960s. In the course of the decade, numerous critiques of mainstream educational thought appeared—books with titles like *How Children Fail* (Holt, 1964), *The Way It Spozed to Be* (Herndon, 1968), *An Empty Spoon* (Decker, 1969), and *Death at an Early Age* (Kozol, 1967). In differing ways, each attacked what its author saw as rigid authoritarianism and systematic suppression of genuine learning in American schools. The basic problem, according to Neil Postman and Charles Weingartner (1969), was that students "are almost never required to make observations, formulate definitions, or perform any intellectual operations that go beyond repeating what someone else says is true" (p. 19). Instead, they learn "how to please the teacher, how to conform to someone else's expectations, and how to locate the 'right answer'" (Lucas, 1984, p. 329).

The outgrowth of this criticism was a call for "open education," or individualized instruction, based on the approach used in British elementary schools. A central feature of that approach involved a change in the arrangement of American classrooms: Rows of desks and chairs were replaced by flexible spaces divided into functional learning areas, and children were free to move from one area to another, choosing their own activities. The goal was independent, self-paced learning. Interest in open education became widespread in the 1970s; it was seen as the best way to make use of children's natural curiosity and to provide them with individualized learning. How-

Interest in the open classroom, in which students work in small groups at their own pace, peaked in the 1970s. Nevertheless, many school districts continue to seek innovative approaches to collaborative learning and group problem solving.

However

individualized child centered. ed. still emphasized in coll. of ed

ever, there is little evidence that open education improved students' intellectual achievement, and it has not proven to be a useful approach at the high school level.

Toward the end of the 1970s the open-education movement faltered. The political climate of the 1980s did not favor humanistic education, viewing it as "soft" and unable to teach students what they really should know (i.e., "the basics"). However, the concept of individualized instruction, though controversial, continues to occupy an important place in the programs of many schools of education. In addition, supporters of this concept remain active at all levels of policy making, calling for greater flexibility in curriculum planning, increased opportunities for educational innovation, and the creation of "alternative schools" within the public educational system. Some versions of the movement for "school-based management" include the aims of liberal school reformers (see Box 13–1).

Preschool Programs

While ideological controversies have swirled around education in elementary and secondary schools, more pragmatic policies have been developed and tested at the preschool level. A case in point is the Perry Preschool Project, a study of 123 black children from low-income families in a neighborhood on the south side of Ypsilanti, Michigan. The children, all of whom had IQs between 60 and 90, were randomly divided into an experimental group that received a high-quality preschool program and a control group that received no preschool program. Information about all the study participants was collected and examined annually from the ages of 3 to 11 and again at the ages of 14, 15, and 19. The information included data on their families; their abilities, attitudes, and accomplishments; their involvement in delinquent and

Dr. James Comer, one of the nation's leading school reformers, advocates far greater involvement of parents, teachers, and students in school decision making.

BOX 13–1 CURRENT CONTROVERSIES: SCHOOL-BASED MANAGEMENT

James Comer, a psychiatrist on the faculty of Yale University, is perhaps the nation's most prominent educational reformer. In part, his powerful influence on educational thinking stems from his own background. He remembers with bitterness his early years as a poor black child in the steel mill neighborhoods of East Chicago, Indiana: "My three friends, with whom I started elementary school—one died at an early age from alcoholism; one spent most of his life in jail, and one has been in and out of mental institutions all of his life. I was the only one to survive whole" (quoted in Schorr, 1988, p. 232). Comer believes his parents made the difference; they were able to act as his advocates in school and knew how to help him through the tough times. His central idea for changing schools that educate children from backgrounds like his is that they must become advocates for those children; they must become "a believer in the kid in the same way my parents were." Comer has developed a sophisticated and proven method for bringing about this important change.

When he began experimenting with school reform in New Haven, Connecticut, in the late 1960s, Comer realized that the students often came from extremely stressed homes and neighborhoods. Often, he believes, "they come to school 'underdeveloped'—socially, emotionally, linguistically, and cognitively—and are thus unable to meet the academic and behavioral expectations of the schools. They withdraw, act up, or act out—and don't learn" (Schorr, 1988, p. 232). Too often they are labeled as slow learners even though their real problem is that they have learning needs that the schools are not prepared to meet. In the face of these problems, the schools often become demoralized in that the teachers become cynical and burned out and the administration places more and more emphasis on rules, regulations, and routine and less and less effort into

seeking new ways to reach the students.

To turn such schools around, Comer advocates paying more attention to child development and basic management of the school. In his model, the school establishes a School Planning and Management Team to organize and maintain the school as a place where child development and learning can take place. On the team are the principal, teachers, parents, and teachers' aides. The goal is to get the parents allied with the school and for all to reach a consensus on what needs to be done for all the children and for individual children. In New Haven this system has produced sensational results—so much so that it has been adopted by the school system of Prince George's County, Maryland, one of the largest urban school districts in the nation.

The movement for school-based management may seem to conflict with the concept of a national curriculum and national educational standards. Indeed, many educators point out that national college placement tests and standardized achievement tests in the lower grades already constitute a set of national standards. Proponents of school-based management like Theodore Sizer, leader of the Coalition of Essential Schools, believe that unless teachers and parents are given more opportunities to work together to realize educational goals, a national curriculum will have little impact on student achievement.

Early in 1994, concerned about the low achievement of students in schools under centralized administrations, the philanthropist Walter Annenberg announced that he was awarding over $120 million to fund local school innovations. The Clinton administration views Annenberg's action as a signal that more work needs to be done to synchronize the efforts of school reformers like Comer and Sizer and those of proponents of national and state educational standards.

criminal behavior; and their patterns of employment and use of welfare assistance. Members of both groups were tested and interviewed; the testers and interviewers were not informed of the group membership of the participants in the study.

The preschool program to which fifty-eight of the children under study were assigned was "an organized educational program directed at the intellectual and social development of young children" (Berrueta-Clement et al., 1984, p. 8). It was staffed by a team of four highly trained teachers. Most of the children participated in the program for two years, at the ages of 3 and 4.

The results of the Perry Project were dramatic. Preschool education improved cognitive performance in early childhood; improved scholastic achievement during the school years; decreased rates of delinquency, crime, use of welfare services, and teenage pregnancy; and increased high school graduation and college enrollment

One of the most important achievements of a good preschool is to help very young children feel comfortable in the classroom environment and to develop social skills such as cooperation, attention, and sharing.

rates. (See Table 13–3.) According to the researchers, "these benefits considered in terms of their economic value make the preschool program a worthwhile investment for society" (p. 1).

Perhaps the most significant outcome of the Perry Project was its effect on educational attainment: Two out of three of the students in the preschool group graduated from high school; the comparable rate for the non–preschool group was one out of two. As noted earlier in the chapter, failure to graduate from high school is a major obstacle to later educational progress and an important factor in many job and vocational-training opportunities.

TABLE 13–3 MAJOR FINDINGS AT AGE 19 IN THE PERRY PRESCHOOL STUDY

CATEGORY	NUMBER RESPONDING	PRESCHOOL GROUP	NO-PRESCHOOL GROUP
Employed	121	50%	32%
High school graduation (or its equivalent)	121	67%	49%
College or vocational training	121	38%	21%
Ever detained or arrested	121	31%	51%
Females only: teen pregnancies, per 100	49	64	117
Functional competence (APL Survey: possible score 40)	109	24.6	21.8
Percent of years in special education	112	16%	28%

Source: From Berrueta-Clement, J. R., Schweinhart, L. J., Barnett, W. S., Epstein, A. S., and Weikart, D. P., 1984, "Changed Lives: The Effects of the Perry Preschool Program on Youths Through Age 19." *Monographs of the High/Scope Educational Research Foundation, 8,* 2. Ypsilanti, MI: High/Scope Press. Reprinted by permission.

The Perry Project is an outstanding example of how social-scientific research can play a vital role in public policy. Despite its desire to cut social spending, the Reagan administration admitted that the Perry results were impressive and justified the continuation of Head Start. Nevertheless, at present only one in five preschool-age children in families below the poverty line attends a high-quality preschool program. The Clinton administration is committed to increasing funding for Head Start and similar preschool programs and would like to ensure that all children have an opportunity to attend preschool programs if their parents wish them to do so.

Open Admissions

Another area of education in which significant policy innovations have been made in recent decades is the public university. In 1970, responding to the charge that many students were being denied equality of educational opportunity by university admissions policies, the City University of New York (CUNY), the nation's third-largest higher-education system, began admitting almost any student with a high school diploma—without changing its requirements for graduation. Many of the new students came from poor and minority communities. The program stimulated a nationwide debate: Would open admissions lead to erosion of the university's academic standards? Did it really increase equality of educational opportunity, and did it significantly benefit black and Hispanic students?

A careful analysis of the open-admissions program (Lavin, Alba, & Silberstein, 1981) found that more white than minority students took advantage of the program and that ethnic segregation among the university's seventeen campuses increased. The overall effect of open admissions, however, was an increase in equality of educational opportunity. "Black open-admissions graduates outnumbered black regular graduates," the authors report, "so that the program more than doubled the number of black students who received a degree of some kind" (p. 271). Moreover,

> *The open-admissions policy has altered forever historic patterns of ethnic access to the University. . . . The thousands of minority students who have entered and graduated from the University since open admissions was inaugurated insure that black and Hispanic students will, in the future, look to the University as a source of opportunity for them.* (pp. 276–277)

In recent years the demands on students entering colleges like those in the CUNY system—demands that they be better prepared in math, science, and English—have prompted a general tightening of admission requirements and an expansion of the remedial courses that many such students are required to take. This new policy is controversial because funds to pay for the added costs are not available at present and because the additional requirements mean that it will take students longer to obtain an undergraduate degree. Whether it represents a retreat from the goals of open admission remains to be determined (Weiss, 1990).

In sum, both the Perry Preschool Project and the CUNY open-admissions program represent major institutional changes that largely succeeded in achieving their goals. They both show that educational institutions can adapt to changed circumstances and that such adaptation can have positive results.

Trends and Prospects

Current trends in educational policy include efforts to improve the quality of public school teaching, lengthening of the school year in some communities, and school-based management. All of these are being discussed within a climate of continued budgetary constraints.

The need to provide more incentives for teachers has received widespread recognition, and teachers' salaries have increased in recent years; the average salary for elementary and secondary school teachers is now $33,100 (*Statistical Abstract,* 1993). There have also been demands that teachers receive higher pay and promotions based on merit, but with few exceptions there has been little progress toward this goal at either the federal or the state level. On the other hand, it is generally agreed that the quality of teachers must be improved, and there has been a great deal of discussion of such issues as improvement of education courses, standardized testing of teachers, and establishment of more rigorous requirements for certification of teachers. It has been suggested that a "master teacher" rank could be created that would recognize and reward outstanding teachers; however, teachers' unions fear that criteria other than ability and dedication might be used in designating master teachers.

A policy that is intended to improve the performance of students is year-round schooling. Long promoted by educators, year-round schedules contain the same number of school days as present schedules, but vacations are shorter and more frequent and can be staggered in order to use school facilities more efficiently. Not only is overcrowding of schools alleviated in this way, but students are likely to learn and retain more when breaks from classroom work are shorter. Several public school systems are considering switching to a year-round schedule. In 1990 the Los Angeles School Board voted to extend the school year to include only thirty vacation days. However, the fiscal crisis in California in the early 1990s prevented this policy from taking effect.

On a more general level, although there has been much debate about the need to devote more resources to public education, the prospects are not bright. As mentioned earlier, federal support for higher education (especially financial aid for students) has been greatly reduced. At the same time, the idea of a voucher system has not generated much support. Some states are investing more in education but face reduced revenues and declining prospects of more federal support for public schools. The costs of the Persian Gulf War and the enormous size of the federal government's budget deficit make it unlikely that funding for public education will be increased.

Throughout this book we have seen many instances of the importance of education in a technologically advanced and rapidly changing society. We have also noted that teaching is becoming more attractive as a career choice among first-year students. But if public education is to meet the challenges facing it, and if young people are to seriously consider teaching as a vocation, increased funding of public education is necessary.

SUMMARY

1. The American educational system is subject to criticism for failing to produce competent, educated adults and for failing to reduce or eliminate inequality.

2. Functionalist theorists believe that problems of public education arise because schools are not equipped to deal with students who come from disorganized homes. Also related to functionalism is the belief that the problems of schooling experienced by certain groups stem from deviance from generally accepted norms of achievement. The institutional approach focuses on the problems societies face in shaping their educational institutions to meet the needs of changing economies and cultures.

3. The conflict perspective sees educational problems as stemming from conflicting views concerning the goals of education. The class conflict approach argues that schools reflect the values of the dominant groups in society. The value conflict approach focuses on intergroup conflicts over such issues as busing.

4. According to labeling theorists, schools attach labels like "achiever" or "rebel" to students and those labels follow them throughout their lives.

5. Because educational attainment is strongly correlated with socioeconomic status, an egalitarian society has a responsibility to provide equal access to education for all its citizens. Although the educational gap between whites and minority groups has narrowed considerably, inequalities of access remain, especially in higher education.

6. The decline in mean SAT scores since the 1960s is a matter of considerable controversy. Many experts argue that the decline in test scores is not significant, but many others have called for major reforms in the educational system, especially in the areas of coursework requirements and academic standards.

7. The American educational system is highly bureaucratized, a fact that acts as a major barrier to educational change. Even the typically American belief in the "technological fix" encounters obstacles in the bureaucratic organization of school systems. Nevertheless, when they have been required to change—for example, to implement desegregation programs—schools have often shown themselves to be surprisingly adaptable.

8. Educational policy recommendations take two main forms. Educational conservatives believe schools should focus on "essentials" or "the basics." They recommend increased attention to academic subjects, more homework and testing, and firmer discipline; some call for a national curriculum and standards. Liberal or "humanist" educators believe schools should promote the maximum self-development of each individual learner. They call for individualized instruction, greater flexibility in curriculum planning, and increased opportunities for educational innovation.

9. At a more pragmatic level, it has been shown that a high-quality preschool program can significantly affect subsequent educational achievement and attainment. As a result, funding for the national Head Start program has been increased. Another major policy innovation is open admissions, meaning that any student with a high school diploma may attend a public university. This approach has not found widespread acceptance, although it appears to have increased equality of educational opportunity at one large university.

10. There is growing recognition of the need to improve the quality of public school teaching, but as yet there has been little progress toward this goal. Policies aimed at improving the performance of students include year-round schooling, and year-round schedules have been instituted in a number of school systems. Meanwhile, federal support for public education has been cut back, and it is unlikely that there will be much action by the federal government to solve the problems of the educational system in the near future.

SUGGESTED READINGS

BERRUETA-CLEMENT, JOHN R., LAWRENCE J. SCHWEINHART, W. STEVEN BARNETT, ANN S. EPSTEIN, and DAVID P. WEIKART. *Changed Lives: The Effects of the Perry Preschool Program on Youths Through Age 19.* Ypsilanti, MI: High/Scope, 1984. A well-documented study of the positive long-term effects of preschool education.

DEWEY, JOHN. *Democracy and Education.* New York: Macmillan, 1916. A classic statement of the role of education in promoting individual growth and secure democratic institutions.

GROSS, BEATRICE, AND RONALD GROSS. *The Great School Debate: Which Way for American Education?* New York: Simon & Schuster, 1985. A useful collection of articles about the major U.S. education reports that have been published in recent years, including analysis of the politics of educational reform from different ideological perspectives. Includes a great deal of resource information for further research.

JENCKS, CHRISTOPHER, MARSHALL SMITH, HENRY ACLAND, MARY JO BANE, DAVID COHEN, HERBERT GINTIS, BARBARA HEYNS, and STEPHEN MICHELSEN. *Inequality: A Reassessment of the Effect of Family and Schooling in America.* New York: Basic Books, 1972. An important study of the consequences of educational attainment for social inequality in the United States.

LIPSITZ, JOAN. *Successful Schools for Young Adolescents.* New Brunswick, NJ: Transaction, 1990. A study of successful middle-grade schools that foster positive social development and academic achievement.

PARELIUS, ANN PARKER, and ROBERT J. PARELIUS. *The Sociology of Education,* 2nd ed. Englewood Cliffs, NJ: Prentice Hall, 1987. A comprehensive text on the sociology of education.

RICHARDSON, JOHN G. (ED.). *Handbook of Theory and Research for the Sociology of Education.* Westport, CT: Greenwood Press, 1986. A collection of original essays and research reviews by thirteen prominent educational sociologists. Includes good material on equality of educational opportunity.

SCHORR, LISBETH B. *Within Our Reach: Breaking the Cycle of Disadvantage.* Garden City, NY: Doubleday Anchor, 1988. A broad analysis of social programs, particularly educational programs, that have had measurable success in helping disadvantaged people gain social mobility.

TROW, MARTIN. "The Second Transformation of American Secondary Education." In Reinhard Bendix and Seymour Martin Lipset (eds.), *Class, Status, and Power: Social Stratification in Comparative Perspective,* 2nd ed. New York: Free Press, 1966. Traces the causes and consequences of the rise of mass public education in America.

MY DADDY
NEEDS HIS
JOB!!

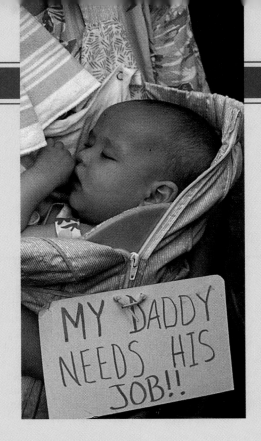

Corporations, Workers, and Consumers

Chapter Outline

- In 1991 the chief executive officers of the top 250 U.S. firms earned an average of $1.3 million in salary and bonuses and another $1.3 million in stock options and other benefits.
- In September 1993 businesses announced job cuts averaging 1,963 a day.
- Forty percent of Americans between the ages of 51 and 61 will have no pension income other than social security when they retire.
- The unemployment rate for minority groups is twice the rate for whites.
- In 1991 almost 10,000 workers were killed on the job and 1.7 million others suffered disabling injuries.

Corporations, workers, and consumers are not social problems, but some of the changes that affect them clearly are. Today the U.S. economy is faced with enormous challenges. Among these are the high level of the federal government's debt, extensive "downsizing" by major corporations, the need to adjust to the end of the cold war, and the ever-growing importance of transnational corporations. With the growth of national and multinational corporations, both workers and consumers seem to be components of a vast, impersonal chain. Employees, of course, are directly affected because they depend on a company not only for their salaries but also for a wide variety of benefits and services ranging from medical and pension plans to psychological satisfaction. But beyond the obviously dependent employees there are many others: the shareholder whose savings are invested in the company; the consumer who relies on the company's product; the worker in a related industry whose job depends on the company's decisions; and the general public whose welfare is affected by the company's interest in conforming to environmental-protection legislation.

The American free-enterprise system has often been perceived as a self-regulating network (Friedman, 1962; Gilder, 1981). Yet many economists argue that some restrictions are necessary just to counterbalance the natural advantages that corporations enjoy because of their size and power (Coleman, 1982). When a business dominates the production or marketing of a particular product, for example, the theoretical checks and balances of the free-enterprise system lose most of their meaning. As the effectiveness of market-imposed guidelines decreases, decisions made within the corporation become more significant. In this context, corporate power refers to the overwhelming ability of large-scale organizations to shape the lives of American citizens as well as others throughout the world. Indeed, William Domhoff (1983) has attempted to show that corporate leaders constitute a "ruling class" that shapes the nation's economic and foreign policies. This is a controversial viewpoint that is continually being debated by sociologists, but there is no doubt that the corporation has an enormous impact on the American worker, and the major multinational corporations probably influence workers throughout the world.

Corporate power is increasingly concentrated in a small number of large-scale private bureaucracies that are insulated from public control. This concentration of power can itself be a social problem when citizens, acting through democratic institutions, are unable to control those bureaucracies. Thus, when plant closings throw thousands of employees out of work; when industrial pollution poisons streams and rivers, killing fish and endangering the health of those who drink the water; when jobs are "exported" to corporate subsidiaries in other countries at the expense of the domestic economy—in these and similar situations corporate power creates social problems.

BIG BUSINESS AND CORPORATE POWER

The United States' shift from an agrarian economy to an industrial one has been accompanied by the concentration of economic power in a relatively few large corporations. Corporations developed out of the burst of commercial and industrial activity that occurred after the Civil War. At first the new companies were dominated by the business magnates who created or controlled them, so-called robber barons like Andrew Carnegie, John D. Rockefeller, and J. P. Morgan. By the first decade of the twentieth century, the already large corporations were becoming still larger through expansion and mergers with other companies. Increasingly complex and sophisticated organizations developed in which effective control of the corporations' operations passed to salaried managers—bureaucrats, in effect—and legal ownership of the corporations was dispersed among thousands or even millions of shareholders.

This pattern still prevails today, and its effects have become more intense as the sheer size and pervasiveness of the modern giant corporation has grown through diversification and concentration of resources. Thus, before it was broken up under a court order in 1983, American Telephone and Telegraph (AT&T) had more than 3 million stockholders and as many employees as the state governments of California, Illinois, Michigan, Ohio, Pennsylvania, and Florida combined. International Telephone and Telegraph Corporation (ITT) has absorbed companies ranging from hotel and car-rental chains to bakeries and publishing firms. Much the same could be said of any number of other huge corporations. Although it has been argued that this is a necessary and beneficial development for a highly complex industrialized society (Galbraith, 1973; Reich, 1991), it also involves problems that will become apparent in the following discussion.

The Shrinking Marketplace

To the American who is bombarded at every turn with advertisements, inducements to buy, and a staggering array of goods and services among which to choose, the concept of a shrinking marketplace is difficult to grasp. Yet while the number and variety of products seem to increase, their sources of production become less numerous. A prime example of this pattern can be seen in the automobile industry. In 1904 there were some thirty-five manufacturers of automobiles in the United States. With the founding of General Motors (GM) in 1908, this situation began to change. Although new companies continued to appear (there were eighty-eight automobile and automobile-related firms in 1921), large corporations like Ford and GM gradually acquired the smaller companies. Although some independents survived until the late 1940s, the trend toward centralization accelerated. Today the automotive industry, perhaps the single most important industry in the country, is dominated by four key corporations—General Motors, Ford, Chrysler, and Toyota—that manufacture more than 90 percent of all automobiles produced in the United States. From these parent corporations have sprung subsidiaries controlling everything from the raw materials used in production to automobile insurance, financing, and maintenance.

This pattern is referred to as the formation of *oligopolies,* that is, markets in which a small number of companies or suppliers control a commodity or service. This trend has accelerated since World War II. Today, as a result, although there are about 250,000 manufacturing corporations in the United States, the top 500 account for the bulk of their sales and profits. These firms are known as the Fortune 500 after the annual summary of their activities that appears in the well-known business magazine *Fortune.*

Since the 1950s the sales and net income of major U.S. corporations have been increasing while employment in those firms has decreased, often through rather drastic reductions in employment. U.S. corporations have been "downsizing" (reducing their workforces) at a dramatic rate for many years, but in the early 1990s that rate accelerated. IBM announced layoffs of more than 20,000 highly skilled employees in the United States and Europe; the telephone companies, General Electric, major defense contractors like Pratt and Whitney, and many other large corporations have continually sought ways to eliminate full-time workers. Total worldwide employment by the Fortune 500 companies declined from 16.2 million in 1979 to 11.8 million in 1992 (*Fortune*, April 19, 1993).

In most cases downsizing is motivated by the need to cut production costs while increasing sales (and thereby increasing shareholders' profits). (See Figure 14–1.) In other instances, changes in personnel policies are motivated by changes in the structure of the corporations themselves caused by the formation and, in many cases, disintegration of conglomerates.

Conglomerates

When federal judge Harold Green ordered the breakup of AT&T in 1983, the era of "Ma Bell" came to an end. The Bell telephone system, which was under the management of AT&T, not only was one of the largest corporations in the world but was, among other things, a quasi-public monopoly. In return for uncontested access to homes in the United States, the Bell system agreed to charge its customers rates established by the Public Service Commission of each state. When the Bell system was broken up into regional operating companies (Pacific Telephone, NYNEX, Southern Bell, etc.), AT&T retained the profitable long-distance service and a number of major operations such as Bell Labs, its research and development division. Almost immediately, new telephone companies such as MCI and Sprint began competing for long-distance business, but the regional telephone companies continued to enjoy a virtual monopoly over access to homes and to charge the rates established by the Public Service Commissions.

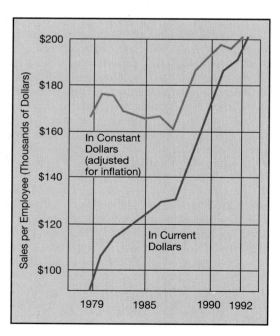

FIGURE 14–1 Sales per Employee, Fortune 500 Companies, 1979–1992

Source: Fortune, April 19, 1993.

The story does not end there, however. With the advent of new interactive communications technologies, in which individuals can receive voice, music, and video information via cable wires or phone lines, new conglomerates are being formed in the information marketplace. The regional Bell companies are seeking to join forces with cable companies and with entertainment corporations like Viacom. These prospective mergers entail some of the most costly corporate changes one can imagine. Billions of investor and corporate dollars are at stake—even though it is not yet clear whether such activities as home shopping and expanded channel capacity will actually produce the vast profits needed to reward investors in the new conglomerates. Regardless of the long-term outcome, the short-term effect of the combination of large communication and entertainment corporations will be to create huge amounts of corporate debt, which will cause them to lay off more workers and seek every possible means of reducing operating costs.

Regardless of the industry in which it occurs, a *conglomerate* is a combination of firms operating in many diverse fields. Among the potential dangers of unsupervised conglomerate mergers are loss of competition (through acquisition of competitors), reciprocity (in which a parent company buys and sells exclusively among its subsidiaries), tacit agreements by conglomerates to respect each other's spheres of activity, and greater corporate secrecy (e.g., when subsidiaries do not issue separate financial statements but are included in those of the conglomerate). Many conglomerates engage in intensive public-relations campaigns. Mobil Oil Company, for example, sponsors cultural events and advertises in newspapers to promote its image as a benevolent force in the economy. Despite the image that conglomerates seek to project, however, they often appear impersonal and are only rarely associated with individuals.

Corporate Raiding   Conglomerate corporations may diminish competition and raise prices to consumers, but the formation of conglomerates can have even more serious consequences. In the 1980s "merger mania" became so widespread that it created a number of major public scandals and problems associated with illegal stock and bond manipulations and rampant corporate raiding.

Conglomerates are often attractive targets for "corporate raiders"—other businesses or rich, powerful individuals (e.g., Carl Icahn or H. Ross Perot) who seek to make large profits simply by acquiring corporations and reorganizing them. An example of this process can be seen in the case of the large communications conglomerate CBS. During the 1980s CBS owned a national television network, one of the nation's largest magazine and book publishing empires, and CBS Records, which included the Columbia and Epic labels (with such stars as Michael Jackson, Bruce Springsteen, and Barbra Streisand). The largest profits for this media conglomerate came from TV and records. During the 1980s, however, the corporation became the target of a series of raids, first by Ted Turner and then by Lawrence Tisch, owner of the Loew's Hotel Corporation and other major real estate properties. Turner first offered to buy CBS and proposed to investors that they buy low-cost and rather risky special CBS investment bonds, which he would create; the bonds promised to yield a profit because Turner would sell off most of the CBS corporations and keep only the lucrative TV properties. The sale of the other parts of the conglomerate (books, magazines, records) would provide immense flows of cash with which to pay back investors in the bonds (known as "junk bonds" in the financial world).

To protect itself from this corporate raid, CBS began selling some of its publishing properties and invited Lawrence Tisch to buy a large share of the company's stocks, in effect taking in a new partner who would help fight off the Turner raid. But eventually Tisch and his allies took control of CBS and themselves sold off major portions of the conglomerate, just as Turner had proposed to do. Thus, Sony of

Japan purchased CBS Records for over $1.5 billion, thereby becoming the largest owner and producer of American music.

During the same period similar raids and junk bond offers were occurring in the case of R.J.R. Nabisco, one of the nation's largest tobacco and food conglomerates, as well as many of the nation's airlines, movie studios, and electronics corporations. The frenzy of corporate raiding and junk bond schemes led to many abuses of financial ethics on Wall Street and in other financial centers. Insider trading (the use of inside knowledge to make illegal purchases of stocks and bonds) and manipulation of corporate records led to the downfall of many major brokerage houses and the imprisonment of stock traders, notably Ivan Boesky and Michael Milken (White, 1991).

It is too early to assess all the consequences of the corporate raiding, stock scandals, and financial failures of the 1980s and early 1990s. The longer-term effects on the American economy are not yet clear, but many analysts worry that the mania for quick profits and high return on investments has deprived many productive companies of the opportunity to develop, with the result that many businesses failed and thousands of jobs were needlessly lost. It also seems clear, as in the case of Sony's purchase of CBS Records, that the corporate raiding of the 1980s further increased the already great power of international corporations at the expense of smaller domestic firms.

Transnational Corporations

Few aspects of corporate power are more controversial than the operations and even the existence of *multinational* or *transnational corporations*. The definition of these entities is extremely broad. David Blake and Robert Walters (1976) have defined them as "economic enterprises that are headquartered in one country and that pursue business activities in one or more foreign countries" (pp. 80–81). In this sense multinationals have existed at least since the international banking houses of the Italian Renaissance. American firms like Singer, United Fruit, and Firestone have had extensive foreign operations—and political influence—since the late nineteenth century. For the most part, however, these were national companies with secondary foreign operations.

The sharp rise in foreign investments and the concentration of financial resources that followed World War II have led to the development of *supra*national corporations. These companies are international organizations that operate across national boundaries, whatever their country of origin may be. The size, wealth, influence, and diversity of operations of these corporations have grown enormously. The annual sales of companies like GM, ITT, and the "Seven Sisters" of the petroleum industry exceed the gross national product of many nations—not just the poorer countries of the third world but highly industrialized countries like Switzerland and South Africa as well. Increasingly, therefore, the term *transnational* is used to emphasize the fact that these corporations operate outside national boundaries almost as if they were nations unto themselves.

For decades the transnational auto companies, such as GM and Ford, have been producing thousands of cars in Europe for sale in the expanding European markets. They have had less success in the growing Asian markets, which are dominated by Japanese manufacturers. Now the Japanese transnational manufacturers, especially Toyota, Nissan, and Honda, are increasing the production of cars in the United States, using Japanese methods and parts. These and other transnational companies seek to create an image of themselves not as Japanese or American but as world companies that are above nationalistic sentiments. Although the transnationals will certainly continue to grow and to account for an increasing share of world production of goods and services, they are widely criticized for often operating outside the control of any nation. The issue of control of transnationals will surely be with us for decades to come. (Table 14–1 lists thirty U.S. firms that earn large proportions of their revenues abroad.)

TABLE 14–1 U.S. FIRMS WITH SIGNIFICANT FOREIGN REVENUES

1991 Rank	Company	Revenue		
		FOREIGN ($MIL)	TOTAL ($MIL)	FOREIGN AS PERCENTAGE OF TOTAL
1	Exxon	78,073	102,847	75.9
2	IBM	40,358	64,792	62.3
3	General Motors	39,083	123,056	31.8
4	Mobil	38,778	56,910	68.1
5	Ford Motor	34,477	88,286	39.1
6	Texaco	24,754	49,648	49.9
7	Chevron	17,180	44,984	38.2
8	E.I. du Pont de Nemours	17,086	38,151	44.8
9	Citicorp	16,848	31,839	52.9
10	Phillip Morris Cos	13,152	48,064	27.4
11	Procter & Gamble	12,327	27,026	45.6
12	Dow Chemical	9,728	18,807	51.7
13	General Electric	8,671	60,236	14.4
14	Xerox	8,590	19,372	44.3
15	Eastman Kodak	8,537	19,419	44.0
16	Digital Equipment	8,325	13,911	59.8
17	Hewlett-Packard	8,104	14,949	54.2
18	United Technologies	8,029	21,262	37.8
19	Coca-Cola	7,401	11,572	64.0
20	American Intl Group	7,322	16,884	43.4
21	Minn Mining & Mfg	6,465	13,340	48.5
22	Amoco	6,372	25,647	24.8
23	Motorola	6,340	11,341	55.9
24	ITT	6,310	20,421	30.9
25	Johnson & Johnson	6,199	12,447	49.8
26	American Tel & Tel	5,442	63,089	8.6
27	American Express	5,162	25,763	20.0
28	JP Morgan & Co	4,975	10,314	48.2
29	Chrysler	4,833	29,370	16.5
30	Goodyear Tire & Rubber	4,676	10,907	42.9

Source: Data from *Forbes,* July 20, 1992.

The Global Factory

Transnational corporations are transforming the world's economy by focusing on rapidly developing markets and on the labor forces in the less developed nations, which have an oversupply of workers in their manufacturing sectors and an undersupply of highly skilled workers with technological training. No longer confined to producing their products in just one country, the transnationals have created a "global factory" that is made possible by two kinds of technology: high-speed transportation and component production (Barnet, 1980). The first enables companies to get raw materials, finished products, communications, and so on from one point to another anywhere in the world. The second divides the production process into component operations that can be carried out anywhere in the world, thereby allowing multinational companies to take advantage of the worldwide supply of cheap labor. For example, U.S. baseball manufacturers send the materials for their product—leather covers, yarn, thread, and cement—to Haiti, where the baseballs are assembled for wages far below those paid for similar work anywhere in the United States.

Critics of U.S. multinationals have been especially vocal in condemning the practice known as "outsourcing"—locating plants that produce goods for American markets in third-world nations where the firm can take advantage of lower wage rates. This practice in effect "exports" manufacturing jobs from the United States to the third world, greatly reducing the number of industrial jobs available for American workers. In recent years, however, a countertrend has become evident: Transnational firms are increasing their investments in the United States. Sony of Japan has purchased CBS Records; the French company Renault owns much of American Motors; Japanese and German automobile manufacturers have opened plants in the United States to assemble their cars, often using parts manufactured abroad. These arrangements are considered preferable to outsourcing because they keep jobs in the United States. But many foreign-based transnationals resist union contracts and the resulting higher wages and benefits.

In addition to engaging in outsourcing, transnational corporations attempt to sell their products in third-world markets. As the populations of those nations increase and their standard of living also rises (albeit much more slowly), they represent a vast untapped source of profits. However, transnationals increasingly produce high-technology products and services intended for markets with much greater buying power than is found in the less developed countries. Accordingly, many observers (e.g., Rohatyn, 1987) argue that it is necessary to develop more buying power in the third world. This, in turn, requires that workers in those nations be paid higher wages. (Table 14–2 compares the wages of General Electric employees in the United States, Singapore, and Mexico.)

The wages of workers in Latin America, Asia, and the Middle East will increase only if the rights of those workers are protected against repression by governments and powerful businesses. Workers must have the right to bargain collectively for wages, pensions, and health and other benefits. The broader rights of citizenship, such as the right to vote and the right of due process under the law, also must be guaranteed if a society's overall standard of living is to increase. Without the right to vote for candidates who support their demands, workers and their families will be unable to make their needs felt without resorting to violence. In sum, it is not enough for transnationals simply to adapt to competitive pressures by shifting their manufactur-

TABLE 14–2 PAY SCALE IN THE MOTOR BUSINESS

Labor costs per hour worked by production employees, at year-end 1987	WAGES	BENEFITS	TOTAL
General Electric Motors in U.S.	$10.92	$5.24	$16.16
Emerson Electric in U.S.*	7.20	2.95	10.15
General Electric Motors in Singapore	1.49	.77	2.26
General Electric Motors and Emerson in Mexico†	.79	.44	1.23

*General Electric's estimate of wages paid by Emerson Electric Company, which G.E. Motors considers its major nonunion competitor.

†Wages and benefits are set by Mexican government.

Source: Glaberson, 1988. Copyright © 1988 by the *New York Times Company.* Reprinted by permission.

As a result of the "outsourcing" of manufacturing jobs and large-scale changes in manufacturing technologies, workers in heavy industries like steel are increasingly frustrated by the lack of new opportunities and the need to deal with government bureaucracies like the unemployment compensation system.

ing operations to low-wage workers. To compete in international markets, they must help those workers improve their standard of living and, thus, their buying power.

Effects on American Workers

For the American worker, the growth of corporate power means that a steadily decreasing number of employers have come to dominate the labor market. This has had several effects. Chief among these is the fact that as unions must cope with increasingly large and centralized corporations, they too tend to become large and centralized, and their leadership tends to become oligopolistic (Edelstein & Warner, 1977).

The decreasing number of employers is also associated with the growing tendency to export capital and jobs overseas, where labor is cheaper and more plentiful. American manufacturing workers have been most seriously affected by this trend. In 1960, over 28 percent of all workers were employed in manufacturing jobs. By 1992, this figure had dropped to 17 percent (*Statistical Abstract,* 1993).

During the 1970s and 1980s U.S. plants, factories, mills, and other industrial facilities suffered for lack of modernization and diversification as capital was diverted abroad. Unable to maintain their competitive edge, many manufacturing facilities closed. Especially hard hit were plants in the nation's older single-industry cities and towns, most of which were located in the manufacturing belt of the Midwest. When rubber mills in Akron and steel mills in Youngstown and the Pittsburgh area shut their doors, the local economies were devastated. With few secondary industries to fall back on, these cities experienced severe economic and social upheavals during the recessions of the mid-1970s and early 1980s. For displaced workers, the situation was equally bleak: According to the Office of Technology Assessment, only 60 percent of the 11 million workers who lost their jobs because of plant shutdowns or relocations from 1979 to 1984 found new jobs in that period (cited in Noble, 1986). The recession in manufacturing, construction, and services beginning in 1990 only made it more certain that many older workers would never recoup the losses of previous years.

The biggest losers in the decline in manufacturing have been industrial towns and cities in the Northeast and Midwest. Manufacturing cities like Gary, Indiana, once the nation's most important producer of steel, have been hit hardest. In the 1970s the Gary steel mills employed almost 28,000 workers in relatively well-paid jobs with good benefits. Today fewer than 8,000 workers are employed in the Gary mills. Nevertheless, modernization of the steel industry, leading to greater efficiency and quality control, may produce a turnaround for cities like Gary. Steel exports are rising, and steel companies' profits are improving. These trends may be too late to help hundreds of communities that lost their industrial base during the last two decades, but for some, such as Gary, they are a welcome sign of better times ahead (Hicks, 1992).

During the 1980s U.S. auto workers also bore much of the brunt of industrial unemployment. As competitive pressures from Japanese and European multinational corporations increased, along with inflation and interest rates, auto plants throughout the nation were shut down. During the 1980s the economic depression in the auto industry—and, by extension, the steel, rubber, and glass industries—was so severe that the executive committee of the United Auto Workers was forced to take an unprecedented position: It recommended that its membership accept significant reductions in wages and benefits in return for agreements from the major auto producers to halt the shutdown of auto plants.

This kind of compromise does not work in every industry. More often, management and labor exhaust all the traditional alternatives and are forced to close down. In some cases plant employees, working with community leaders, take extraordinary measures to avoid a shutdown: They purchase the physical plant, as well as the machinery and materials needed to keep it going, and continue to operate the business under worker ownership and management. Today about 6,000 businesses are operated under employee stock ownership plans, and many jobs have been saved by taking this approach (Roren, 1991).

Employee ownership plans have received widespread press coverage, but only in a minority of cases are they a real solution to the problems of workers. Faced with rapidly changing technology, plant closings and exportation of jobs, and a growing imbalance of power as unions become weaker and large corporations gain strength, workers are increasingly faced with sudden shifts in their economic fortunes. As Figure 14–2 vividly shows, when one uses constant (inflation-adjusted) dollars to measure income, almost all major occupational groups are experiencing falling real wages. Even the finance, insurance, and real estate sector (sometimes called the FIRE sector), which was such a "hot" growth area during the 1980s, has seen falling hourly wages. (Note also that the line for FIRE includes clerical workers as well as the relatively small number who make much higher wages.) Many workers are unable to adjust to these changes and end up in the ranks of the chronically unemployed.

Corporate Power and Wealth

For the owners and top executives of large corporations, the picture is quite different. A few decades ago thirteen families—including the DuPonts, Mellons, and Rockefellers—owned more than 8 percent of the stock of the 200 largest nonfinancial corporations. Half of the large shareholdings in those corporations were directly owned; the rest were in the form of trusts, estates, and family holding companies. One or a few families effectively controlled the voting stock in about 40 percent of these corporations, and the corporations, in turn, controlled half of the remaining corporations (Lundberg, 1968). Today this situation remains largely unchanged: A few wealthy individuals and families control about 40 percent of the private capital in the United States. Moreover, as Table 14–3 on page 418 shows, there are more than twice as many billionaires in the United States as in any other nation.

How is an individual or family able to control a corporation, even by owning only a small portion of the stock? What is the impact of this type of control? Corporations are controlled by their investors—the stockholders—and the investors who own the largest blocks of stock have the most power in the corporation. Thus, a person who owns only 15 percent of a corporation's stock but is the largest stockholder

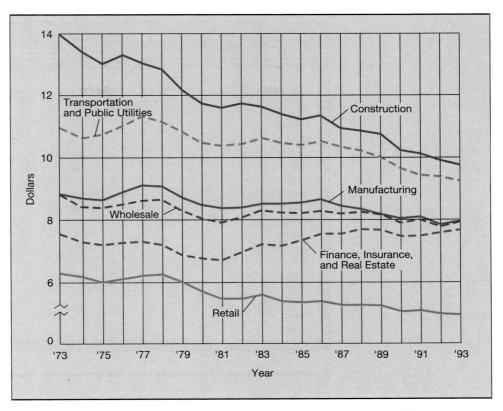

FIGURE 14–2 Average hourly earnings for selected industries. (All figures are for October and are adjusted for inflation)

Source: Data from Bureau of Labor Statistics.

can in effect control the corporation; his or her real power is equal to the corporation's total value because that person's wishes can determine company policy. A large corporation has a significant influence on society—through the advertising it purchases in the media, through the institutions and foundations it supports, through the prices of the goods or services it offers, and so on. By and large, the power of those who control the major corporations is directed not toward redistributing wealth but toward increasing their own income and the corporation's profits.

Another group of very wealthy people are top corporate executives. In 1991 the chief executive officers (CEOs) of the top 250 U.S. firms earned an average of $1.3 million in salary and bonuses and another $1.3 million in stock options and other benefits, for a total of $2.6 million. (See Figure 14–3 on page 418.) In Japan, CEOs earn an average of 20 times what the workers in their companies earn; in Germany, the boss earns 21 times what the average worker earns. In the United States, however, the comparable figure is 160 (Crystal, 1992).

The adverse consequences of the extremely high compensation received by top executives were emphasized in an interview with the late Akio Morita, chairman of the Sony Corporation. According to Morita, American companies

are trapped by their own drive for quick and highly publicized profits, forcing them into a bonus system that has made management itself too expensive. The manager feels he is the one who runs the company, therefore he is the man who makes a profit. But that is not true. Profit is generated through the cooperation of all the people [in the company]. Why should the top management take all the money? (quoted in Mintz, 1986)

TABLE 14–3 NUMBER OF BILLIONAIRES, SELECTED COUNTRIES

COUNTRY	NUMBER OF BILLIONAIRES	COUNTRY	NUMBER OF BILLIONAIRES
Argentina	2	Macau	1
Australia	1	Malaysia	2
Brazil	5	Mexico	8
Canada	10	Netherlands	2
Chile	3	Philippines	1
Columbia	3	Saudi Arabia	6
Denmark	1	Singapore	1
France	9	Spain	3
Germany	44	Sweden	3
Greece	3	Switzerland	7
Hong Kong	8	Taiwan	6
India	1	Thailand	3
Indonesia	2	Turkey	3
Italy	6	United Kingdom	5
Japan	34	United States	101
Korea	3	Venezuela	1
Lebanon	2		

Source: Forbes, July 20, 1992.

High salaries and bonuses for top corporate executives have been justified by reference to the *trickle-down theory.* According to this theory, any increase in the wealth of businesses or individuals will stimulate consumption and thereby increase economic activity and provide jobs and opportunities for the poor and the unemployed (Turner & Starnes, 1976). Critics argue, however, that although some bene-

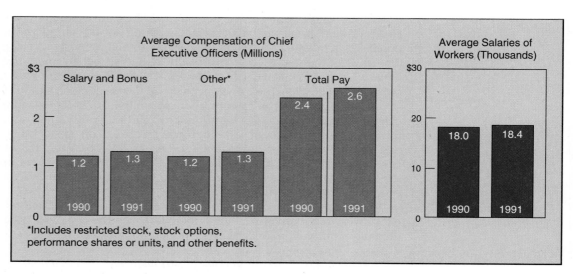

FIGURE 14–3 Average Compensation of Chief Executive Officers (Major U.S. Corporations) and Workers, 1990 and 1991

Source: Data from Crystal, 1992, and Bureau of Labor Statistics.

Most stockholders of major corporations feel that the pressure and responsibility shouldered by the directors of those firms justify their extremely high levels of compensation. However, critics question whether the enormous disparities between executive compensation and worker salaries can be justified.

fits may trickle down to the poor, they do not come close to meeting their real needs and do not in any way justify the pattern and magnitude of executive compensation. Moreover, the proportion of poor families may actually increase as a result of the policies of corporations themselves—for example, efforts to maximize profits by diversifying into more profitable industries and shedding less profitable ones may throw thousands of people out of work, and those workers may never reap any reward from trickle-down wealth. Thus, one study (Hull House, 1984) found that the average income of steelworkers who were laid off in U.S. Steel's plant closings fell by 50 percent over five years.

Trickle down is a version of the eighteenth-century idea that "private vice makes public virtue" (Kornblum, 1991). In other words, the appetites and pleasures of the rich provide work for the poor, which justifies both the pleasures of the rich and the subordinate position of the poor and the working class. Those who desire to improve their position in society are free to do so by working especially hard. As we saw in Chapter 8, however, the available evidence does not support the idea that hard work alone can significantly improve a person's economic status.

WORK IN CORPORATE AMERICA

From Manufacturing to Services

Because people work for so much of their lives, it is important to try to understand the social problems related to work. Later in the chapter we will discuss four of these: unemployment, automation, worker alienation, and occupational safety and health. In this section we will explore four patterns of change in the nature of work in America that have accompanied the shift from a manufacturing-based to a service-based economy.

More White-Collar Workers The impact of the transition from an agricultural economy to an industrial one dominated by large corporations and government organizations can be gauged from a few figures. In 1900, 27 percent of the total labor force consisted of farm workers and 18 percent consisted of white-collar workers. In

1992, a little under 3 percent of the labor force was made up of farming, forestry, and fishing workers, whereas about 58 percent was made up of white-collar workers (*Statistical Abstract,* 1993).

White-collar workers—professional, managerial, clerical, and sales personnel—are the largest occupational category in the nation, surpassing the blue-collar group since 1956. Most of the new white-collar jobs are professional and clerical. The number of clerical personnel has increased by more than 500 percent since 1900 and accounts for about 16 percent of all employed people (*Statistical Abstract,* 1993). Clerical workers now vie with skilled and semiskilled workers as the largest occupational group in the labor force.

The decline in farm employment since the turn of the century has been as dramatic as the rise in white-collar employment. Farm workers—farmers, managers, and farm hands—once the largest occupational category in the United States, are now the smallest category.

Blue-collar workers have witnessed enormous changes in the nature of their work. A declining proportion of the overall labor force, manual workers still constitute a very large segment of the workforce but are employed in a changing array of jobs. The proportion of unskilled laborers has decreased. Similarly, the slight overall net gain shown by service occupations masks some important changes within that category. People employed as private household workers now account for less than 1 percent of the total labor force; in 1900 they accounted for 5 percent of the total. In contrast, the proportion of other service personnel—hotel workers, waiters, barbers—has risen to about 11 percent of all employed people, compared to 4 percent in 1900.

Specialization   As mentioned earlier, there are four broad categories of employment (white-collar, blue-collar, service, and farm workers). Within these categories, of course, there are literally thousands of jobs. The *Dictionary of Occupational Titles,* published by the Department of Labor, lists more than 22,000 jobs—a total that contrasts sharply with the 325 recorded by the 1850 census. The vast difference indicates the increasing specialization of labor and the complexity of its divisions.

Specialization has several important implications. First, lower-echelon workers who were trained only for a single narrow job, and lose that job, may have difficulty finding another like it. Second, these workers often feel that they are merely adjuncts to a machine or a process, with little chance to develop and use more than minor skills or abilities. This feeling often leads to dissatisfaction with work. For high-level managers, the increase in specialization has created problems of worker coordination and cooperation that present them with some of their greatest challenges (Braverman, 1974).

More Low-Paying Jobs   Despite the increase in the total number of jobs in the American economy, average wage and salary income (adjusted for inflation) in most industries declined during the 1980s. One reason for this disturbing trend was the proliferation of low-wage employment. During the 1980s jobs paying poverty-level wages were created at twice the rate that prevailed during the 1960s and 1970s. Although millions of high-wage professional, technical, and managerial jobs were also created, the pace of high-wage job creation was much slower than it had been during the two preceding decades (Bluestone & Harrison, 1987). This trend has continued in the early 1990s, with the result that wages earned by male blue-collar workers declined by 5.9 percent between 1989 and 1993, compared with 2.4 percent for male white-collar workers (Economic Policy Institute, 1993).

One explanation of the growth in low-wage jobs is the expansion of part-time employment, that is, jobs offering less than thirty-five hours of work per week. Such jobs have been created twice as fast as full-time jobs; in 1993, for example, 60 percent of the 172,000 jobs created each month were part time (Economic Policy Institute, 1993). Another explanation is the continued shift of the labor force out of manufacturing and into service jobs. As plants have closed and manufacturing jobs have been exported to less developed countries, displaced workers have been forced to accept jobs in services and trade, which have twice the proportion of low-wage jobs as the manufacturing sector.

Changes in the Age and Sex Composition of the Labor Force The labor force, as defined by the federal government, consists of all people 16 years of age or over (excluding those in institutions*) who worked one hour for pay during one survey week (the employed) plus those who did not work during the survey week, do not have a job, and are actively seeking work (the unemployed). The most significant trends in the labor force are the inclusion of married women and the exclusion of older men.

Older men are being eliminated from the labor force primarily because of educational and occupational obsolescence. As noted in Chapter 11, employers hesitate to keep or hire older men when younger and better trained people are available, usually at lower salaries. Middle-aged women have displaced older men in many clerical and professional jobs, and young high school and college graduates are replacing them in all fields. Whereas 40 percent of males over 65 were in the labor force in 1954, by 1964 only 28 percent were still in the workforce (Baker, 1965), and today only 3 percent of men over age 65 are employed (*Statistical Abstract,* 1993). Meanwhile, more women between the ages of 20 and 64 have entered the labor market, with the first great increase occurring in the 45–54 age group in the 1950s and 1960s. The second major increase occurred between 1965 and 1975 as young women in the 20–34 age group joined the labor force; this younger generation of women was much better educated. Nevertheless, many women in this group had to become secretaries, waitresses, bookkeepers, teachers, retail clerks, and typists—jobs that were traditionally held by women. Although women are employed in greater numbers than ever before, their jobs are vulnerable during economic recessions; and although many women are highly motivated to work, outside employment has not released most married women from household and family tasks. As we saw in Chapters 10 and 12, a married woman typically works many hours at home in addition to holding an outside job.

Problem Aspects of Work

Unemployment Until recently, to be unemployed in America was to be out of the cultural and social mainstream. The economic recessions of the early 1980s and early 1990s, however, made unemployment commonplace. High inflation combined with high interest and mortgage rates and sagging consumer spending threw an increasing number of people out of work, especially in the manufacturing and construction sectors of the economy.

Prolonged joblessness causes serious psychological and social damage. A significant part of today's workforce has been denied not only the benefits of a regular and sufficient income but also the emotional rewards of a steady job: the sense of self-worth that comes from doing a job well and having others value that performance; the sense of community fostered by daily association with colleagues; in sum, the feeling that one is participating in society and contributing to it. The unemployed person, whether involuntarily retired, partially or intermittently out of work, or chronically unemployed, is denied many of these rewards. (For problems of the involuntarily retired person, see Chapter 11.)

*Prisons, asylums, nursing homes.

THE INTERMITTENTLY AND CHRONICALLY UNEMPLOYED   In a competitive society job insecurity is common. Even when the national unemployment rate was low, many people were unemployed for part of the year, and others were underemployed. More serious, however, has been the rise in intermittent and long-term unemployment. The national jobless rate reached 8.5 percent in 1975, the highest it had been since the Great Depression. (See Table 14–4.) After a decline to 6 percent in 1978, the jobless rate rose once more in the early 1980s as recessionary pressures grew. By early 1982 the unemployment rate was 9 percent. Thereafter it declined again, until it fell below 6 percent in 1988, but during the recession of the early 1990s it began to rise again. At this writing it is 6.5 percent.

The recessions affected not only the chronically unemployed—especially women, minority group members, teenagers, the unskilled, and the semiskilled—

TABLE 14–4   UNEMPLOYMENT RATES: UNITED STATES, 1980–1992

	1980	1985	1986	1987	1988	1989	1990	1991	1992
Total	**7.1**	**7.2**	**7.0**	**6.2**	**5.5**	**5.3**	**5.5**	**6.7**	**7.4**
16 to 19 years old	17.8	18.6	18.3	16.9	15.3	15.0	15.5	18.6	20.0
20 to 24 years old	11.5	11.1	10.7	9.7	8.7	8.6	8.8	10.8	11.3
25 to 44 years old	6.0	6.2	6.1	5.4	4.8	4.5	4.8	6.0	6.7
45 to 64 years old	3.7	4.5	4.3	3.8	3.3	3.2	3.5	4.4	5.1
65 years and over	3.1	3.2	3.0	2.5	2.7	2.6	3.0	3.3	3.8
Male	6.9	7.0	6.9	6.2	5.5	5.2	5.6	7.0	7.8
16 to 19 years old	18.3	19.5	19.0	17.8	16.0	15.9	16.3	19.8	21.5
20 to 24 years old	12.5	11.4	11.0	9.9	8.9	8.8	9.1	11.7	12.2
25 to 44 years old	5.6	5.9	6.0	5.3	4.6	4.3	4.8	6.2	6.9
45 to 64 years old	3.5	4.5	4.4	4.0	3.5	3.3	3.7	4.7	5.6
65 years and over	3.1	3.1	3.2	2.6	2.5	2.4	3.0	3.3	3.3
Female	7.4	7.4	7.1	6.2	5.6	5.4	5.4	6.3	6.9
16 to 19 years old	17.2	17.6	17.6	15.9	14.4	14.0	14.7	17.4	18.5
20 to 24 years old	10.4	10.7	10.3	9.4	8.5	8.3	8.5	9.8	10.2
25 to 44 years old	6.4	6.6	6.2	5.5	4.9	4.8	4.9	5.7	6.4
45 to 64 years old	4.0	4.6	4.2	3.5	3.2	3.1	3.2	3.9	4.4
65 years and over	3.1	3.3	2.8	2.4	2.9	2.9	3.1	3.3	4.5
White	6.3	6.2	6.0	5.3	4.7	4.5	4.7	6.0	6.5
16 to 19 years old	15.5	15.7	15.6	14.4	13.1	12.7	13.4	16.4	17.1
20 to 24 years old	9.9	9.2	8.7	8.0	7.1	7.2	7.2	9.2	9.4
Black	14.3	15.1	14.5	13.0	11.7	11.4	11.3	12.4	14.1
16 to 19 years old	38.5	40.2	39.3	34.7	32.4	32.4	31.1	36.3	39.8
20 to 24 years old	23.6	24.5	24.1	21.8	19.6	18.0	19.9	21.6	23.9
Hispanic[a]	10.1	10.5	10.6	8.8	8.2	8.0	8.0	9.9	11.4
16 to 19 years old	22.5	24.3	24.7	22.3	22.0	19.4	19.5	22.9	27.5
20 to 24 years old	12.1	12.6	12.9	10.6	9.8	10.7	9.1	11.6	13.2
Women maintaining families	9.2	10.5	9.9	9.3	8.2	8.1	8.2	9.1	9.9
White	7.3	8.1	7.8	6.8	6.0	6.1	6.3	7.2	7.8
Black	14.0	16.4	15.4	15.4	13.7	13.0	13.1	13.9	14.7
Married men, wife present	4.2	4.3	4.4	3.9	3.3	3.0	3.4	4.4	5.0
White	3.9	4.0	4.0	3.6	3.0	2.8	3.1	4.2	4.7
Black	7.4	8.0	8.0	6.5	5.8	5.8	6.2	6.5	8.3

[a]Persons of Hispanic origin may be of any race.

Source: Statistical Abstract, 1993.

but also highly specialized white-collar employees such as middle-level managers and engineers. Particularly hard hit were academics, especially recent Ph.D.s in the liberal arts and social sciences. Declining enrollments, increased interest in technical and professional training, and a decrease in government grants and private donations, as well as rising costs, contributed to a decline in the number of faculty positions. Some found part-time teaching jobs; others were forced to make a career change. The recessions also cut into the employment of skilled workers in construction, manufacturing, and trade. Most of these trained but jobless workers in business, academia, and skilled blue-collar work were adult men.

Many of the unemployed were young and/or nonwhite. In 1992, for example, 39.8 percent of black teenagers were unemployed, compared to 16.5 percent in 1954 (*Statistical Abstract,* 1993). In general, the unemployment rate for blacks and other minority groups is twice as high as the rate for whites. The chronically unemployed and their children rarely acquire the capacity to break out of the unemployment pattern without some state or federal government help. Many of them are high school dropouts, and their low educational attainment equips them only for low-skilled jobs. These young men and women may not yet have family obligations, but they are nonetheless reluctant to take dead-end jobs as domestics or kitchen workers. (See Chapters 8–10 for fuller discussions of the relationships among discrimination, unemployment, and poverty.)

THE "INVISIBLE" UNEMPLOYED AND THE "DISCOURAGED" WORKER   As stated earlier, the labor force is made up of people age 16 or over (excluding those in institutions) who worked one hour for pay during the survey week plus those who did not work during the survey week, do not have a job, and are actively seeking work. By definition, all other people over the age of 16 are not in the labor force and therefore are not included in government unemployment reports. This definition persistently understates the size of the labor force and the volume of unemployment. For one thing, it excludes unemployed people who, though able and willing to work, did not actively seek work during the survey week. A second factor is the failure of the official data to reflect adequately the underemployment of people with part-time jobs. R. A. Nixon (1968) estimated that a more accurate measure of unemployment would be about double the official rate.

The problem of "invisible" unemployment becomes more serious in recessions, when the average duration of unemployment increases; eventually many people stop looking for jobs altogether because they think it will be impossible to find one. These are known as "discouraged" workers, people who are out of work not because of personal disadvantages such as being too old or too young, untrained or overeducated, but because industries and manufacturers have cut back production and eliminated a large number of jobs. The Bureau of Labor Statistics estimates that the recession of the early 1990s caused about 1 million people to drop out of the labor force in a single year (Rackham, 1991).

CONSEQUENCES OF UNEMPLOYMENT   What are the consequences of being without work? A study of 105 unemployed able-bodied men in Detroit showed that the chief characteristic is extreme isolation (Wilensky, 1966). Half the men in the study could name no close friends, half never visited neighbors, and few belonged to organizations or engaged in organized activities. These findings were in sharp contrast to the social life of an equal-sized sample of employed men. Such data tend to support the thesis that work is necessary if one is to be, in a full sense, "among the living." When work ties are cut, participation in community life declines and the sense of isolation grows. Thus, those with the most tenuous work connections—the retired, the elderly, those who have been squeezed out of the labor market, and those who seldom get into it—are often isolated from their communities and from society at large.

Further studies on the emotional and social effects of long-term unemployment were conducted by D. D. Braginsky and B. M. Braginsky in 1975. This research was

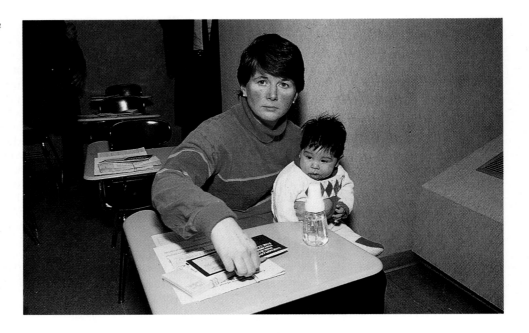

confined to high-status unemployed men who had been thrown out of work in the recession of the mid-1970s. The subjects consisted of two groups, one a control group of employed white-collar men and the other a group of jobless men between the ages of 23 and 59. Almost half of the jobless men were college graduates; many had been engineers and company managers.

The researchers found that such men undergo a "social transformation"; the trauma of unemployment causes a change of attitude that persists even after they are reemployed. Loss of one's job is commonly interpreted as a judgment of incompetence and worthlessness. In the Braginsky study the unemployed men expressed these feelings. Their self-esteem was lowered and they felt alienated from society. They experienced depression, a common reaction to loss. Most suffered deep shame and avoided their friends. Many of those who did find new jobs did not fully recover their self-esteem.

In his study of mental hospitalization and economic downturns and upturns in New York State, Harvey Brenner (1973) demonstrated a high inverse correlation between mental hospital admissions and the unemployment rate. He hypothesized that admissions to mental hospitals increase during economic downturns and decrease during upturns. In testimony before the Joint Economic Committee of Congress in 1976, Brenner presented the following statistics: When the unemployment rate rises by one percentage point, 4.3 percent more men and 2.3 percent more women are admitted to state mental hospitals for the first time; in addition, 4.1 percent more people commit suicide and 5.7 percent more are murdered. Although these correlations are impressive, it cannot be concluded that unemployment is a direct cause of mental illness or suicide. There is evidence, however, that economic troubles are linked to psychological and physiological stress in what has become known as the "pink slip syndrome" (cited in Pines, 1982).

As more and more women have entered the labor force, the consequences of unemployment for women have assumed ever-greater importance. This is particularly true of women who are single parents, who have experienced divorce or separation, and whose families are dependent on their earnings. In a study of the experiences of such women, Katherine S. Newman found that middle-class women who experience divorce "typically have to make do with 29 to 39 percent of the family income they had before divorce" (1988, p. 202). When these women are in the labor force and experience layoffs and unemployment, it is often difficult for them to support their families while looking for new jobs. Typically they had interrupted their careers for marriage and child rearing, and they find themselves less competitive in the labor market than men who have been working more or less continuously. In this regard it is worthwhile to point out that the single greatest cause of women going on "welfare" (Aid to Families with Dependent Children) is the "double jeopardy" situation of loss of spouse and loss of job (Newman, 1988; Reskin & Hartman, 1986).

THE UNDERGROUND ECONOMY   Chronic under- and unemployment has forced millions of Americans to participate in an *underground economy*. This term refers to exchanges of goods and services—both legal and illegal—that are not monitored, recorded, or taxed by government. A dentist, for example, may provide dental care for an out-of-work house painter; in exchange, the patient will paint the dentist's office. Both receive a service that they need, but neither has had to spend money or receive taxable income for the job performed. Less seemly practices, including prostitution and the drug trade, are also part of the underground economy. Young school dropouts are especially likely to enter the underground economy through burglary, prostitution, and drug trafficking (Williams & Kornblum, 1985). It has been estimated that the total value of all transactions in the underground economy throughout the country is about $380 billion per year. (See Figure 14–4.)

The underground economy is a totally untaxed segment of the U.S. economy. Sales are unreported, as are income and the value of the services provided. As a result, millions of dollars in tax revenues are lost. Another major problem arises because people who work in the underground economy, whether they are prostitutes or house cleaners who are paid "under the table," do not receive employee benefits

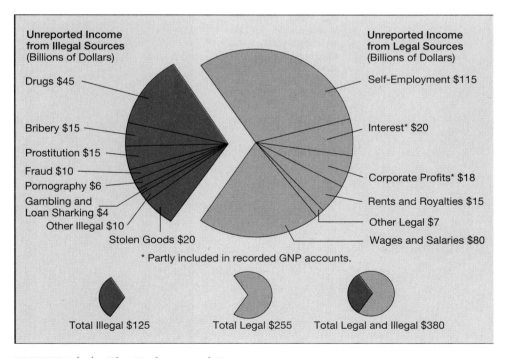

FIGURE 14–4   The Underground Economy

Note: Research on the underground economy is sporadic at best. This chart represents the best available estimates of the extent of unreported transactions in the U.S. economy.

Source: Reprinted from April 5, 1982 issue of *Business Week* by special permission. Copyright © 1982 by McGraw-Hill, Inc.

such as hospitalization insurance or pension plans. When such people require assistance in the form of hospital care, housing, or other social services, the burden falls on already strained municipal and state budgets.

Automation   In the next few decades automation will continue to fundamentally change the character of work in America. Many people fear—not unrealistically—that the principal change will be a reduction in the number of jobs.

AREAS OF AUTOMATION   There have been three major developments in the computer-controlled production methods that are termed *automation*. The first consisted of linking together into a continuous process several production operations that were previously performed separately. In such an integrated system—first developed for the oil-refining and chemicals industries, which require a high degree of control—the product moves from start to finish completely automatically.

Electronic data processing (EDP), which records, stores, and processes information, was the second major development in automation. The most familiar example of EDP is the office computer that handles bookkeeping, accounting, billing, and countless other clerical operations. EDP permits a bank teller to take the dates and sums from a savings passbook and give the customer an instant report of compound interest. On long-distance calls, EDP eliminates the need for an operator by recording the telephone numbers of caller and receiver and checking the time and charges, managing the information more quickly and accurately than an operator could.

The underground economy includes many types of employment and businesses that do not report their transactions or pay taxes. An example is the peddler who buys wholesale merchandise and resells it on the street.

The third development in automation was feedback control computers, or servomechanisms, which compare work actually being done with what should be done and automatically adjust the work process when necessary. A familiar example is the livingroom thermostat, which automatically controls the heating system of a household to maintain a specified temperature. The same principles are employed in a steel mill computer that keeps track of more than 1,000 variables and controls mill operations with a speed and accuracy far beyond any human capability. If the computer finds an error in a product line, it can make the necessary adjustments to correct the error on the next item.

THE IMPACT OF AUTOMATION   What are the effects of such technology? According to sociologist Shoshanna Zuboff (1982), managers and employees whose jobs are controlled through factory computer systems come to believe that their effective "boss" is the computer. In some cases unionized employees have protested the new forms of hidden computer supervision. Workers in the Bell system, for example, blamed computer technology for eroding the family culture of "Ma Bell." They equated the computer with oversupervision, stress, and excessive discipline.

Computer control not only affects workers but also alters the structure of the organization. For one thing, most automated operations require a separate data-processing staff. Computer specialists are different from many of the other people in a factory. They have skills that the others do not understand, and their job is not actually to produce the product but to provide efficient means of producing it. Automation therefore creates a new interdependence between the workers who are directly concerned with the end product and those who are concerned with data processing, whose job is to help accomplish the other workers' goal. People with high status in the organization but no technical expertise must cooperate with technical experts, such as programmers and systems analysts, who have no supervisory authority—a relationship that is unique to modern organizations. Such cooperation is not easy. Because of their lack of computer expertise, managers may insist on a request that is unreasonable from a technical standpoint, using the authority of their position to force the data-processing staff to comply. Conversely, data-processing specialists may use the power provided by their expertise to deny even a reasonable request that is inconvenient. Basically, though, the experts and nonexperts are interdependent, and the organization's structure must reflect this fact.

For people who perform manual work, automation has caused a shift to a different kind of work performance. Jobs increasingly require less physical ability and greater mental ability and concentration. Instead of operating one machine on a production line, workers may have many tasks and responsibilities—monitoring several machines, for example. It is on the higher levels, however, that automation maychange work most dramatically. New hierarchical patterns are emerging, and certain traditional roles of top and middle management are diminishing. As computers are used to run more operations, EDP executives wield more power and top managers in other departments find that their functions and authority are undermined (Zuboff, 1988).

It seems that automation may exacerbate some conditions that produce job dissatisfaction. Work will probably become increasingly demanding and precise. These changes will continue to increase demands by employers for a more highly educated and competent labor force.

Job Satisfaction and Worker Alienation
When people go to work they sacrifice some personal freedom and assume some risk. A job demands that a person put his or her time at another's disposal. It may also mean spending money and time on commuting and enduring physical hazards and discomforts, psychological traumas, boredom, and frustration. In return, workers can expect varying amounts of pay and fringe benefits, job security, meaningful work, opportunities for advancement, flexibility in work time, decent surroundings, and positive interactions with peers and supervisors. Each of these factors affects workers' job satisfaction.

In recent decades there have been many changes in the factors that contribute to job satisfaction. A new generation of workers, raised in the affluence of the 1950s and 1960s and well educated, has brought new ideals to the workplace. Daniel Yankelovich (1978) calls them the New Breed. New Breed workers, while still interested in the traditional concerns of salary and benefits, also place great emphasis on individuality and independence. They are less loyal to their employers and identify less closely with their jobs than their parents did. One of their most cherished values is leisure, the time they can devote to their own personal growth and interests undisturbed by family or job responsibilities. Because of these attitudes, New Breed workers seek jobs that will provide them with opportunities to use their skills fully and still allow time for leisure activities. The concept of *flexitime* or sliding work hours is very appealing to these workers—so appealing, in fact, that one survey showed that many workers are willing to remain in jobs they dislike because their schedules are flexible (Renwick & Lawler, 1978).

A search for psychological satisfactions—not just material ones—characterizes the New Breed. In one survey a group consisting mostly of young workers revealed that they wanted to gain a sense of accomplishment from their jobs, using their knowledge, participating to some extent in decision making, and learning new skills (Rothschild, 1979).

ALIENATION   Marx and other nineteenth-century social critics attacked the assignment of people to activities that have no meaning for them. Factory workers, they charged, are merely part of a productive process, lacking control over either the process or the product. Workers who lose the capacity to express themselves in their work become alienated.

In modern work situations, several elements combine to produce a sense of alienation. The primary source of alienation today is the clash between a person's self-image and the requirements of his or her job. Those who believe that they need the companionship of others may feel stifled by a job that does not allow them to socialize with fellow workers. Some people may be alienated by jobs that offer little opportunity for personal judgment. Others may see themselves as independent and decisive but find that their bosses are constantly and closely supervising them. The symptoms of alienation are not necessarily confined to blue-collar workers. Alienation may occur in any hierarchy that limits autonomy and the chance to use individual skills. Thus, white-collar workers often feel estranged from their employers and the long-term interests of their companies.

Are the causes of alienation different for different types of workers? Are white-collar workers, such as accountants or engineers, affected by the same factors as blue-collar workers, such as assemblers or welders? A study of nearly 800 workers by the Survey Research Center at the University of Michigan (cited in Gruenberg, 1980) found that although intrinsic sources of job satisfaction are important to all workers regardless of their educational background, such external satisfactions as wages and vacation time are more important in determining overall job satisfaction for blue-collar workers than for white-collar employees. This emphasis on what they get out of the job rather than on what they put into it may reflect the low level of job satisfaction felt by most blue-collar workers.

ATTEMPTS TO MAKE WORK MORE SATISFYING   Many jobs are simply dull. For workers who already earn enough to live adequately, additional income cannot always offset the meaninglessness of such jobs. This applies particularly to younger workers, who are likely to be better educated and less concerned than their predecessors about such problems as job security. They particularly resent work that they consider trivial and boring, and they want to control the circumstances of their labor.

Some organizations have tried to enhance job satisfaction. One approach, called "human relations," focuses on the social context of work and seeks to improve communication in the organizational hierarchy. Numerous corporations have conducted surveys in which employees are asked to criticize their jobs. Even when problems cannot feasibly be corrected, tensions seem to be at least temporarily relieved when employees are allowed to let off steam.

Social scientists like Robert Schrank (1978) and Tom Jurevich (1984) have suggested that piecemeal solutions are inadequate. The only way to reduce worker dissatisfaction with jobs that are intrinsically dull, unchallenging, or beneath their abilities is to grant them some of the privileges that already sweeten management and professional positions: flexible schedules, a feeling that their opinions are valued, opportunities to socialize more freely during the workday, and more breaks. However, such changes are unlikely in today's intensely competitive business environment.

Occupational Safety and Health   People have long been concerned about the physical toll exacted by work. Medical writings reveal that even in ancient Rome physicians recognized an unusually high frequency of lung disease among metal workers, miners, and weavers of asbestos cloth. During the Renaissance each craft was known to have its unique maladies. But the industrial revolution created a new wave of deadly occupational hazards. From the beginning, therefore, the American labor movement made safety one of its top priorities, waging a constant battle for better work environments. Yet despite this long history of concern and awareness, occupational health remains a serious problem. In 1991 almost 10,000 workers were killed on the job and 1.7 million workers suffered disabling injuries (*Statistical Abstract,* 1993).

Industrial accidents are only part of the problem. Proponents of occupational health have widened their focus to include illnesses as well as accidents, and they have concentrated on preventing work-related diseases rather than merely treating or compensating workers for them. The situation is grim: At least 100,000 Americans die of job-related diseases each year, and some experts believe that the number may be much higher (Lewin, 1986).

Perhaps the greatest health hazards come from the chemicals industry. Chemicals are involved in the manufacture of almost every product we use. But those chemicals can also produce cancer. Workers who are exposed to certain chemicals

Health scandals and extremely high rates of injury in the meatpacking industry at the turn of the century helped convince Americans of the need for government health and safety regulations. This scene shows a "dressing room" in a meatpacking house in 1882.

have an unusually high rate of malignancies. They frequently suffer from other health problems as well, such as nervous disorders and sterility; their children may suffer from birth defects.

Manufacturers often are unaware of the contents of the substances used in their plants. The only ingredients that must be identified are those that are officially recognized as carcinogens. To complicate matters further, many products are sold under brand names that mask their true contents. There are also cases in which manufacturers are aware of the risks faced by their employees yet deny their existence until they are forced to take action. The battle over levels of cotton dust in the textile and cottonseed oil industries is an example. Constant inhalation of cotton dust causes a respiratory disease called byssinosis, or brown lung. More than 35,000 cotton mill workers have been disabled by it, and many more suffer substantial breathing loss (Hall, 1981–1982). Although byssinosis was first recognized in the eighteenth century, the textile industry attempted to deny its existence. Company doctors and physicians in mill towns diagnosed brown lung as emphysema. It was not until 1968 that it was officially recognized as an occupational illness. A similar situation arose in the case of asbestos. Manufacturers and insurers had known for half a century that asbestos workers were dying prematurely from asbestosis, a lung disorder, but it was not until the mid-1970s that this became public knowledge. Affected workers began to sue the manufacturers for damages.

Occupational health is an issue that is loaded with moral, medical, and economic questions. Industry cites the enormous impact that needed changes will have on the entire economy as the cost of occupational health is passed along to consumers in the form of higher prices. Others argue that compulsory adherence to proposed health regulations will put them out of business or force them to relocate to other countries. Many workers, more fearful of imminent unemployment than of future illness, agree with their employers and take their chances in the workplace. Others, realizing that their interests as consumers and citizens may outweigh their economic stake, join the ranks of consumer activists. That even more workers do not become motivated to question the conditions in which they work and the desirability of what they produce is perhaps attributable in part to the high level of indebtedness among workers, which has resulted from extensive use of consumer credit. Since the relationship between consumers and credit is an important one, we devote the next section of the chapter to this subject.

CONSUMERS AND CREDIT

The United States is a consumer society, one with an economy based on the activities of numerous corporations that depend on the disposable income, or buying power, of consumers. A consumer society requires a large middle and upper class with enough leisure time to enjoy the use of many goods and services that are not strictly necessary (although they may be perceived as such). Americans are proud of their access to an abundance of consumer goods and often contrast that abundance with the scarcities that are frequent in many other nations, especially those in less developed regions.

There are several drawbacks to a consumer-based economy, however. Among these are the dominance of large corporations and franchise operations and the unplanned spread of shopping malls. Smaller businesses find it extremely difficult to compete with better financed, more efficient, highly profitable businesses. Indeed, franchise chains like McDonald's and Burger King have come close to wiping out the Mom and Pop restaurant and the roadside stand, traditional symbols of business independence.

The activities of franchise operations and major corporations like General Motors and IBM are accompanied by massive advertising campaigns. "Early to bed, Early to rise, Advertise, Advertise, Advertise" is the advice of McDonald's former advertising director (Boas & Chain, 1976). The communications media are inundated by advertising messages, so much so that advertising slogans have become part of our everyday conversation. ("Getting there is half the fun," an executive may comment ruefully as she arrives late for a meeting; "Don't leave home without it," a father may say to his son as he hands him an umbrella.) It cannot be denied that advertising plays a crucial role in a consumer society, but some observers are concerned about its effects on other aspects of social life. For example, the growth and development of television and radio stations have been based primarily on the effectiveness of these media as vehicles for advertising, which is their main source of income. To what extent does the dependence of the media on advertisers influence the content of the news and other information they broadcast? These are areas of active social-scientific research (Gans, 1979).

Problems of Debt Entanglement

The effects of a consumer society on other aspects of cultural and social life are a matter of concern to social scientists and others who caution that it leads to excessive materialism, a tendency to judge people by their possessions, and other negative consequences such as waste and planned obsolescence. But perhaps the most serious flaw of a consumer society is the fact that it requires the ready availability of credit. Large-scale production of consumer goods depends on a steady flow of profits, which in turn requires that purchases be made constantly, not just whenever the consumer has a windfall or can accumulate enough through saving—hence the widespread use of consumer credit in the United States.

The rapid diffusion of automated cash machines and credit cards has made spending money and accumulating debt far easier than ever before.

Since the 1950s the United States has been transformed from a cash to a credit society. Outstanding installment debt has grown from $29 billion in 1955 to more than $600 billion today. Although this enormous increase in consumer credit has been a boon to the U.S. economy, it has given rise to a new and pervasive social problem: debt entanglement. From 15 to 20 million Americans are hopelessly entangled in debt (Caplovitz, 1987).

The problem of debt entanglement has received little attention either from social scientists or from policy makers; yet it is a problem of massive proportions. Each year more than 10 million workers have their wages garnisheed to meet their unpaid debts. Many others are sued by their creditors for defaulting on their debts. The problem is particularly severe for low-income unskilled workers, who are predominantly black and Puerto Rican.

During the 1980s total consumer debt doubled; the rate of individual bankruptcies also increased, but it leveled off after the recession of the early 1990s. Recent sociological research on the phenomenon of bankruptcy shows that half of it is due to financial failure on the part of average homeowners, particularly female heads of households. In a study of bankruptcies in the United States (Sullivan, Warren, & Westbrook, 1989), the researchers disproved a number of common myths about individual bankruptcy. Using records of 1,529 consumer bankruptcy filings in three states, they showed that, contrary to the popular notion that many bankruptcies occur among "credit card junkies" who abuse the credit system, such people account for less than 2 percent of bankruptcies. Most people who go bankrupt are homeowners who can no longer pay their debts, often because of family dissolution or medical emergencies. About 10 percent are individuals who invested in risky financial ventures. These bankruptcies, however, account for about 25 percent of the total debt of bankrupt individuals, since often these individuals were quite rich and defaulted on large loans.

The researchers also offered many recommendations for reducing the rate of bankruptcies, including measures to monitor consumer debt/income ratios far more effectively than the consumer credit industry does at present. But by presenting evidence and arguments for regulation of credit markets and consumer debt, they also pointed to the need for more, not less, regulation in the economically more dangerous areas of banking and finance. This is a key point to which we return in the Social Policy section of the chapter.

Possessions and Self-Expression

A consumer society fueled by purchases of goods and services produced by profit-hungry corporations and sold with the aid of elaborate advertising campaigns; a society of debtors often forced into default, with wages garnisheed and mortgages foreclosed—these images suggest a hopelessly materialistic culture pursuing a path that will inevitably lead to its own destruction. Is this a valid picture of American society?

There can be no doubt that material possessions play an important role in most people's lives. As we have seen in this chapter, the corporations that produce and distribute material things significantly influence the lives of workers and consumers. We have noted elsewhere that poverty can be defined in terms of the degree to which a household does or does not possess the things that make life comfortable.

A full discussion of the significance of material possessions for human social life and organization is beyond the scope of this book. It is worth mentioning, however, that emphasis on material objects is not unique to modern societies. As Mihaly Csikszentmihalyi and Eugene Rochberg-Halton (1981) have written,

> The most basic information about ourselves as human beings—the fact that we are human—has been traditionally conveyed to us by the use of artifacts. Civilized people express their identity as humans by wearing clothes, cooking their food and eating with utensils, living in houses, and sleeping in beds. Those people who consider themselves "civ-

ilized" differ from those who are "primitive," mainly in terms of the variety and complexity of the things with which they interact. (p. 92)

These researchers conducted an extensive study of the meaning of possessions in the lives of individuals. Based on open-ended interviews of a socioeconomically stratified sample of families in the Chicago area, the study focused on the interaction between people and the objects in their immediate environment. The researchers found that objects tend to be valued

not because of the material comfort they provide but for the information they convey about the owner and his or her ties to others. . . . A battered toy, an old musical instrument, a homemade quilt provide meaning that is more central to the values of people than any number of expensive appliances or precious metals. (p. 239)

Yet this fact does not change people's behavior: "The habit of acquisition and the addiction to consumption will motivate their expenditure of energy even though these are not the source of their most significant rewards" (p. 239).

It is apparent that material things have immense symbolic value in all cultures and that in complex industrial societies a great deal of effort is devoted to the production and consumption of things. But it is not the things themselves that are central to this situation; it is their symbolic power. As long as material things serve as symbols of the worth of an individual, they will be sought as means of self-expression. If people were to become more aware of the underlying reasons for their attachment to objects, they might devote less energy to the acquisition of consumer goods and more to the attainment of broader cultural and communal goals.

SOCIAL POLICY

Economic policies developed by the states, the federal government, and in some cases private corporations or nonprofit agencies must respond to a number of changes in the United States and the rest of the world. The first, and perhaps most significant, of these is the end of the cold war. With little prospect of war between superpowers, there is much less justification for defense budgets of $280 to $300 billion a year. We will see in Chapter 18 that increased political instability in many parts of the world means that defense and national security remain important concerns and costly government functions. Nevertheless, recent cuts in defense spending make possible a modest increase in spending on social programs.

The second major change in economic affairs is often termed "globalization" and refers to the ever-greater economic interdependence of nations. The passage of the North American Free Trade Agreement (NAFTA) in 1993 is one outcome of this trend. The treaty is intended to move the nations of North America (Canada, the United States, and Mexico) closer to a condition of free trade—that is, trade that is not hampered by tariffs and import or export quotas. Free trade can stimulate economic growth, but it can also have grave consequences for companies and workers in industries that undergo rapid change as a result. For example, Mexican peasants who grow corn fear that they will be wiped out by competition from U.S. agribusinesses, while U.S. auto workers fear that their jobs will be lost to Mexican workers whose wages average less than half of theirs.

Most policy makers and social scientists support free trade and reductions in military spending. They realize, however, that these policies will have many unintended consequences. There is no doubt that large numbers of jobs in defense-related industries will be cut and that higher-wage union jobs are the most vulnerable. It is still too early to judge the full impact of NAFTA, but many observers believe that some U.S.

workers will lose their jobs in the short run as companies move their manufacturing operations south of the Rio Grande in order to benefit from lower wage rates. For this reason, trade unions in the United States and Canada strongly opposed NAFTA.

Most policy makers believe that job training is the primary solution to the problem of worker displacement caused by free trade or by layoffs in the defense industry. However, to date job-training programs have not been very effective. Established in the early 1970s by the federal Trade Adjustment Assistance Act, such programs cost $200 million in 1993 and covered about 30,000 workers. These were workers in manufacturing firms who could show that they had lost their jobs because of the impact of foreign imports or outsourcing. In a study of 1,198 workers in job-training programs in nine states, the U.S. Department of Labor found that only one worker in five was directed into a job that paid at least 80 percent as much as his or her previous job. The study did find that people in the programs were slightly more successful in finding jobs than comparable workers who were not in the programs (cited in Kilborn, 1993).

Other research on job training for younger workers shows that many such programs add thousands of dollars a year to an employee's expected lifetime earnings. That research also shows that white males in the labor force are far more likely to receive such training from private employers than are women and members of minority groups, who depend more heavily on federally sponsored job-training programs (Veum, 1993).

The U.S. government spent $1.1 billion in 1994 on training for unemployed, "dislocated," and "displaced" workers. The Clinton administration's 1995 budget proposes an increase of 31 percent in this sum, and the administration is pledged to making job-training programs more effective. However, the amount of discretionary spending in the federal budget is limited. Figure 14–5 shows that in the proposed 1995 budget only 36 percent of spending is discretionary, and half of that amount continues to be spent on national defense. Mandatory spending for social security, Medicare, and Medicaid, as well as interest on the national debt, accounts for the majority of federal spending and cannot be shifted to other priorities by any politician who wishes to stay in office.

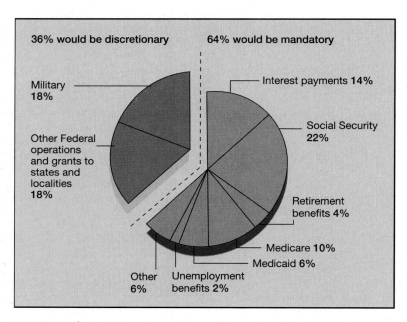

FIGURE 14–5   Major Categories of Spending in Proposed Federal Budget, Fiscal Year 1995

For decades an unemployment rate of 3 to 4 percent was considered normal in a "full-employment" economy, but in recent years the federal government has deemed rates of 5 to 7 percent to be "acceptable." Many writers on economic issues believe that these higher rates are unacceptable in an affluent society. The Clinton administration agrees. It would like to increase funding for job creation in both the public and private sectors through such policies as employment training and the creation of special "empowerment zones" (similar to the "enterprise zones" of the Reagan administration). However, given the federal government's high budget deficit and the Federal Reserve Bank's policy of tightening credit to prevent inflation (a policy that has the effect of discouraging business expansion), the administration is unlikely to be able to implement its desired policies in the near future.

Confidence in the nation's savings institutions is also essential if the U.S. economy is to revive. If funds are to be provided for renewed housing construction and

BOX 14–1 UNINTENDED CONSEQUENCES: THE SAVINGS AND LOAN SCANDAL

From a sociological viewpoint, the failures of many savings and loan institutions (S&Ls) in the late 1980s are a grievous failure of social assessment as well as evidence of greed in high places. This is the conclusion reached by most observers, and it is shared by the majority of citizens. Most Americans believe that the problems of S&Ls are a result of bad management and fraud. In a 1990 survey of public opinion on this issue, for example, the CBS/New York Times Poll found that 63 percent of the sample believed that the crisis was very serious (74 percent of those over age 45), regardless of their political party affiliation (CBS/New York Times Poll, June 2, 1990). When asked, "What do you think is *mainly* responsible for the problems in the savings and loan industry—bad management and fraud by those who run savings and loans, *or* a lack of close supervision by the government?" most respondents indicated that the cause was bad management and fraud, but high proportions also cited lack of regulation or both of these causes. More Democrats than Republicans cited lack of regulation, but the difference was not as great as one might imagine given the emphasis throughout the 1980s on the hypothetical benefits of deregulation.

These poll data confirm what many social scientists believe: The savings and loan crisis is a major public issue and may again convince the public that a balance between government regulation and corporate initiative is legitimate. Increasingly both experts and voters tend to agree that such crises occur when entrepreneurs are given unregulated opportunities for profit. In this instance the unintended consequences of deregulation of the savings and loan industry seem to be largely responsible for the disaster, which will eventually cost U.S. taxpayers more than $500 billion.

In the case of the savings and loans, the directors of these financial institutions were allowed to make risky investments with savings that were insured by the federal government's Federal Deposit Insurance Corporation. Before the 1980s these institutions were tightly regulated and were not allowed to use depositors' federally insured savings to make investments in stocks and bonds and risky commercial real estate deals. But legislation passed during the Reagan administration—along with administrative actions that decreased the number of working federal regulators—encouraged not only unwise investments but much fraud among savings and loan executives (Mayer, 1990; White, 1991). Since few voices were raised in opposition to these steps at the time, social scientists bear part of the blame, although industry executives and political leaders are far more blameworthy in this immense scandal.

One might argue that since business failure is a common feature of the U.S. economy and is protected by bankruptcy laws, the savings and loan debacle is simply a case of poor financial planning and the adversities of real estate markets. According to this argument, business failure is a normal phenomenon and perhaps the savings and loan executives are bearing more than a fair share of blame. However, during the severe recession of the early 1990s, the rate of corporate bankruptcies rose. From January to November 1990 about 55,000 companies declared bankruptcy and defaulted on loans worth more than $65 billion. Since much of that debt is concentrated in the Northeast and in financial and real estate rather than manufacturing industries, economists and sociologists do not see cause for undue alarm, but many do see a need for more, rather than less, monitoring and regulation of the banking and finance industries.

home mortgages and small-business loans, it is necessary for the nation to have a solid banking system, one in which the public has great confidence. That confidence was eroded during the 1980s as a result of the S&L scandal and the growing debt problems of many major banks. Some of this decline in confidence is due to the unintended consequences of public policy (see Box 14–1 on page 435), and it is likely that new policies are needed to strengthen the banking system and restore confidence. Clearly, banking and financial policies will be among the most active areas of public debate during the 1990s.

While debates over the regulation of financial institutions may seem dry and somewhat removed from the problems of workers, it is in this vital area of finance that the potential for job creation and job loss is often found. Anyone concerned with problems in the economy can ill afford to overlook the complications of banking and finance.

SUMMARY

1. Corporate power is increasingly concentrated in a small number of large-scale private bureaucracies. This can be a social problem when citizens, acting through democratic institutions, are unable to control the bureaucracies.

2. In the twentieth century corporations have become increasingly complex and sophisticated organizations controlled by salaried managers (bureaucrats). Among the effects of this trend are the formation (often through corporate raiding) of oligopolies, in which a few companies produce all or most of a given product; the formation of conglomerates through mergers, which combine separate businesses into a single enterprise; and the growth of transnational corporations—international organizations that operate across national boundaries.

3. Transnational corporations are widely criticized for often operating outside the limits of any nation's ability to control their conduct. They have contributed to the emergence of a "global factory" in which the production process is divided into component operations that can be carried out anywhere in the world.

4. For the American worker, the growth of corporate power means a decreasing number of employers and a growing tendency to export capital and jobs overseas. Many U.S. manufacturing facilities have closed, especially in the nation's older cities and towns, creating high rates of unemployment in several major industries. For the owners and top executives of large corporations, on the other hand, increased corporate power translates into increased personal wealth.

5. Work in the United States has undergone major changes in the twentieth century. The greatest change has been the transition from an agricultural economy to an industrial one, with the result that today white-collar workers are the largest occupational category in the nation. Another significant trend is the increasing specialization of labor. The total number of jobs in the American economy has increased steadily, but in the past decade low-wage jobs were created at a much higher rate than high-wage jobs.

6. With respect to the age and sex composition of the labor force, the most significant trend is the inclusion of married women and the exclusion of older men. Older men are being eliminated from the labor force primarily because of educational and occupational obsolescence.

7. In the early 1980s unemployment became commonplace as a result of high inflation combined with high interest and mortgage rates and low consumer spending. In particular, there was a sharp rise in intermittent and long-term unemployment. A disproportionate number of the unemployed are young and/or nonwhite.

8. Official definitions underestimate the size of the labor force and the volume of unemployment. They exclude unemployed people who did not actively seek work during a particular week, and they fail to reflect the underemployment of part-time workers who would like to work full time. Among the consequences of unemployment is a sense of isolation, which produces depression.

9. Chronic under- and unemployment has contributed to the underground ecomony, in which both legal and illegal goods and services are exchanged without the transactions being monitored, recorded, or taxed by government. The total value of these transactions reaches into the hundreds of billions of dollars and results in millions of dollars' worth of losses in tax revenues.

10. Automation has had a variety of effects on work. Managers and employees whose jobs are controlled by computers sometimes feel that the computer is their boss. Computer control can also alter the structure of the organization.

11. The chief sources of job satisfaction, in addition to monetary compensation, are individuality, independence, and a sense of accomplishment. Absence of these factors can lead to dissatisfaction and alienation. Blue-collar workers place more emphasis on external satisfactions than white-collar workers do.

12. The problem of occupational health involves industrial accidents and job-related diseases; perhaps the greatest health hazards are found in the chemicals industry. In some cases manufacturers deny the risks faced by their employees until they are forced to take action by outside agencies.

13. The United States is a consumer society; its economy is based on the activities of numerous corporations that depend on the buying power of consumers. A serious flaw of a consumer society is that it requires the ready availability of credit. The enormous increase in consumer credit has given rise to serious problems of debt entanglement.

14. Economic policies must respond to several major changes in the United States and the rest of the world, of which the most significant are the end of the cold war and the globalization of economic activity. These changes have led to reductions in military spending and the passage of the North American Free Trade Agreement, which in turn have caused large-scale cutbacks in employment. Job-training programs for displaced workers have not proved to be very effective. The Clinton administration proposes to increase spending on such programs and make them more effective, but the amount of public funds available for this purpose is limited.

SUGGESTED READINGS

BARNET, RICHARD J., and RONALD S. MULLER. *Global Reach: The Power of the Multinational Corporations.* New York: Simon & Schuster, 1975. A survey of multinational corporations' involvement in developing and industrialized countries and the impact of their activities on economic problems in the United States.

BENSMAN, DAVID, and ROBERTA LYNCH. *Rusted Dreams: Hard Times in a Steel Community.* New York: McGraw-Hill, 1987. A documentary study of hard times in a famous steel community on the outskirts of Chicago that shows the continuing conflict between workers and corporate managers over who must pay the price of automation and plant closings.

EDWARDS, RICHARD. *Contested Terrain: The Transformation of the Workplace in the 20th Century.* New York: Basic Books, 1979. An attempt to explain the battle between labor and capital over control of the labor process; shows how the nature of work has changed in this century.

JACKALL, ROBERT. *Workers in a Labyrinth: Jobs and Survival in a Bank Bureaucracy.* Montclair, NJ: Allanheld, Osman, 1978. A study of the everyday experiences of clerical workers in large bureaucracies, based on fieldwork in bank branches.

MAYER, MARTIN. *The Greatest-Ever Bank Robbery: The Collapse of the Savings and Loan Industry.* New York: Scribner's, 1990. An objective, though critical, analysis of the savings and loan crisis and its consequences.

NEWMAN, KATHERINE. *Falling from Grace.* New York: Free Press, 1988. A thorough treatment of the experience of sudden unemployment and downward mobility.

RIST, RAY C. (ED.). "Confronting Youth Unemployment in the 1980's: Rhetoric versus Reality." *Children and Youth Services Review,* special issue. New York: Pergamon Press, 1980. A collection of articles on programs, policies, and research dealing with the employment and unemployment situation of youths.

SHAIKEN, HARLEY. *Work Transformed.* Cambridge, MA: MIT Press, 1986. A study of the effects of numerical and other electronic control technologies as applied to American manufacturing. Shows how these developments have revolutionized industrial production, as well as the social transformations they have engendered.

WHYTE, WILLIAM F., and KATHLEEN KING WHYTE. *Making Mondragon.* Ithaca, NY: Cornell I.L.R. Press, 1988. A pathbreaking study of the famous Spanish workers' cooperative system, in which about 20,000 people are employed in more than 100 worker cooperatives.

Urban Problems

Chapter Outline

- 78 percent of the U.S. population resides in urban areas.
- No population group has experienced such persistent residential segregation in urban areas as African Americans.
- The fastest-growing urban communities are on the fringes of metropolitan areas.
- An estimated 78 million Americans are "shelter poor."
- Estimates of the total number of homeless people range from 600,000 to 7 million.

Commenting on the importance of cities and urban issues, Secretary of Housing and Urban Development Henry G. Cisneros notes that "During the 1980's, 90 percent of the national population growth and 87 percent of the employment growth took place within central cities and metropolitan suburbs. Metropolitan areas now contain 78 percent of the total United States population and 83 percent of the household income" (1993, p. 21). Half of all Americans, he observes, reside in the largest thirty-nine metropolitan areas (see Table 15–1), and nearly one-third of the U.S. population inhabits the nation's central cities.

Many of the social problems we have discussed so far—problems of poverty, mental illness, AIDS, drug abuse, violence—are especially serious in the nation's cities. This is not because city people are less moral than rural people but because cities, especially large cities, act as magnets for people who deviate from the norm and seek the company of others like themselves. Often this deviance is what makes cities so fascinating and creative, and it helps explain the attraction of city life for musicians, actors, artists, and people who wish to escape from what they see as the stultifying sameness of rural areas or suburban communities. But the attraction of the city for people who are different and who seek the greater tolerance and anonymity of urban life also increases the concentration in the cities of people who are ill and need help. The legacy of racism and racial and class segregation also leaves the cities with much higher concentrations of poor people than would be expected if these evils were evenly distributed through the population.

At this time a controversy rages over how much responsibility the nation as a whole has for dealing with the problems that are concentrated in the cities. As many cities become de facto poorhouses, they require additional help from states and from the federal government. To better appreciate why this is so and why the policies that have been suggested to address this situation are controversial, it is worthwhile first to step back and consider what we understand by cities and by terms such as *rural* and *urban*.

The distinction between "urban" and "rural" is important in the social sciences because many studies of social problems attempt to determine whether a particular condition is more serious in urban areas or in rural ones. Of course, such attempts raise questions about how one defines the terms *rural* and *urban*. It is not difficult to define them in abstract terms, but such definitions are not readily applicable to the real world. Today there is no longer a clear distinction between rural and urban life. *Urbanism*—a way of life that depends on industry, mass communication, a mobile population, and mass consumer markets—has penetrated even to rural places. For example, whereas the farm once was considered the epitome of rural life, today an increasing proportion of farms are large-scale "agribusinesses" and the small farm is an endangered species. Farming communities are linked to major metropolitan regions by interstate highways, and the residents of those communities watch the same TV shows as people in the densely settled inner cities. In other words, it is not

TABLE 15–1 THE THIRTY LARGEST U.S. CITIES, BY POPULATION (IN THOUSANDS)

RANK	CITY	POPULATION
1	New York, NY	7,323
2	Los Angeles, CA	3,485
3	Chicago, IL	2,784
4	Houston, TX	1,631
5	Philadelphia, PA	1,586
6	San Diego, CA	1,111
7	Detroit, MI	1,028
8	Dallas, TX	1,007
9	Phoenix, AZ	983
10	San Antonio, TX	936
11	San Jose, CA	782
12	Baltimore, MD	736
13	Indianapolis, IN	731
14	San Francisco, CA	724
15	Jacksonville, FL	635
16	Columbus, OH	633
17	Milwaukee, WI	628
18	Memphis, TN	610
19	Washington, DC	607
20	Boston, MA	574
21	Seattle, WA	516
22	El Paso, TX	515
23	Cleveland, OH	506
24	New Orleans, LA	497
25	Nashville, TN	488
26	Denver, CO	468
27	Austin, TX	466
28	Fort Worth, TX	448
29	Oklahoma City, OK	445
30	Portland, OR	437

Source: U.S. Census Bureau, 1990.

a question of whether a place is rural or urban, but of the extent to which urbanism has influenced it.

For the purposes of this chapter, however, some general definitions are needed. Bogue (1969) provides the following definition of *urban* places: "densely settled areas where manufacturing, commerce, administration, and a great variety of specialized services are available. '*Rural* areas' are more sparsely populated and tend to be specialized in agriculture, forestry, or other exploitation of resources" (p. 465). Urban places, thus, are defined largely in terms of population density. There are towns within rural areas that exist to serve rural people, yet we say that the people in those towns are living in urban places. The Bureau of the Census defines *urban populations* as all persons in places of 2,500 inhabitants or more that are incorporated as cities, villages, boroughs, or towns (but excluding persons living in the rural portions of "extended cities" or metropolitan regions). The terms *urbanized area* and *conurbation* refer to a city (or cities) of 50,000 or more inhabitants plus the surrounding *suburbs*—closely settled incorporated or unincorporated places with 2,500 inhabitants or more.

The Census Bureau uses very specific definitions of cities and metropolitan regions; these will be discussed later in the chapter.

THE AMERICAN CITY

Until the nineteenth century the United States was an agrarian country; the few existing cities were scarcely more than market towns. Increasingly efficient transportation and communication and the effects of industrialization caused the bulk of urban growth. Just as technological innovations—such as the use of cast iron in building construction and the invention of the elevator—made it possible for a city to expand vertically, more efficient modes of transportation—such as horse-drawn buses and railroads—made it possible for cities to expand horizontally as well. Railway lines and telegraph wires crossed the continent, tying cities closely to the nation's agricultural heartland. In turn, these improved methods of communication promoted westward expansion and the development of new cities. Many towns were built around railroad lines. Urban growth provided a larger market for agricultural products, which motivated farmers to invent new ways of growing and harvesting crops in order to increase efficiency and minimize expense. The resultant technological advances contributed to the development of the city.

As cities grew, however, the existence of large populations within limited amounts of space began to present special problems. Living in a concentrated community focuses attention on matters of mutual concern and need, concerns that even the individualistic American was unable to ignore. Lighting, fire protection, the care of streets, crime prevention, sewage disposal, water, community health, and marketing facilities all became part of the community consciousness and, hence, the concerns of municipal governments.

Urban Growth and Social Problems

It was not until the twentieth century that adequate water supply and waste disposal systems were finally developed. Before then, cities were notorious for death rates that were substantially higher than those in rural areas, with larger cities suffering higher rates than smaller ones. Writing in 1899, Arnold Weber attributed this "excessive urban mortality . . . to lack of pure air, water, and sunlight, together with uncleanly habits of life induced thereby." He went on to say, however, that there was "no inherent external reason why men should die faster in larger communities than in small hamlets, provided they are not too ignorant, too stupid, or too individualistic to cooperate in the security of common benefits" (1968, p. 348). In fact, innovations in medicine and sanitation did improve the conditions of early urban life.

Management Problems

In general, as cities have grown larger and more crowded, it has become more difficult to manage them. Early American cities were homogeneous and relatively small in both area and population. So few people lived in them that urban problems either could be ignored or were manageable. As cities grew, however, so did their problems. Traffic and transportation facilities were often inadequate; people demanded a variety of municipal services, such as sewage disposal, fire and police protection, and a clean water supply, all of which increased the costs of government. New York was the first city to incorporate police services within the municipal government, a step it took in 1844. Prior to that, cities used a combination of private day policemen and part-time night watchmen. Gradually other public services—fire protection, water, sewage, and the like—were incorporated into the city government.

In the mid-1800s, as cities became more congested, slums began to emerge. These were inhabited mostly by the thousands of immigrants from Ireland, Germany, Italy, and Poland. With the emergence of slums came political machines—local party organizations controlled by professional political "bosses" who dispensed jobs and services (or "patronage") in return for votes and loyalty. The machines drew support from the slum dwellers, the criminal classes, and the fire companies, trafficking in franchises for the new municipal services and setting the stage for the wanton municipal corruption that followed the Civil War. In 1890 Andrew D. White noted that "with very few exceptions, the city governments of the United States are the worst in Christendom—the most expensive, the most inefficient, and the most corrupt" (p. 357).

Antiurban Bias

Perhaps as a result of the congestion and corruption just described, antiurban sentiment became a tradition in American culture. Public sentiment against cities has generally echoed the antiurban bias of Thomas Jefferson, who compared "the mobs of great cities" to sores on the human body.

American literature, particularly in the nineteenth century, extolled the virtues of the self-sufficient farmer in an agricultural paradise, evoking memories of simpler, happier, more innocent times. The city has often been perceived as contrary to the "natural" relationship between the person and the environment. Although the image of a sacred city—Jerusalem or Rome—occasionally appears, it is the image of the sinful city—Sodom and Gomorrah, "Gay Paree"—that predominates. Heresy and vice are associated with the city; virtue and justice live in the country. This is true in literature throughout the world, and it remains a common theme in North America.

In recent years the spread of AIDS and highly addictive drugs like crack have reinforced the negative image of the nation's largest cities, especially New York, Los Angeles, and Miami. It is very likely that the negative view of large central-city areas reflects the continuing legacy of a history of antiurban thought, which is only reinforced by current problems that are concentrated in the cities. To make matters worse, the city is often viewed as a temporary place of settlement, a central place of concentration for immigrants and rural newcomers, the area where one attempts to gain a foothold in society before moving to the suburbs, where there is a bit of greenery and one can visit the city but is not obliged to live there.

Respondents to polls about quality of life and preferred place of residence consistently voice the opinion that life in central cities is less attractive for most people than life in suburbs and small cities (Gallup, 1982; NORC, 1993). One consequence of these negative opinions about central-city life is the continual growth of suburbs and the gradual loss of population in the nation's older cities. As a result, according to Eli Ginzberg, one of the nation's foremost analysts of urban social policy, "The core of urban life has shifted dramatically from the city center to the metropolitan area, with a growing proportion of the population living and working in the suburbs and in the outlying metropolitan areas" (1993, p. 36). But Ginzberg notes that this change can be overstated, since almost one-third of the nation's citizens continue to reside in communities and neighborhoods of the inner city.

The Composition of Urban Populations

The majority of Americans live in large metropolitan areas. There they encounter a very different environment from that provided by small towns or rural communities. Urban life gives rise to subcultures, social institutions, and personality traits that are not found in rural settings (Fischer, 1976); sociologists who study urbanism seek to explain these phenomena. In our discussion of urbanism we will stress the special consequences of life in cities both for individuals and for their communities.

Minority Migration   Today's cities are populated largely by the descendants of rural Americans and immigrants from other countries who came in search of better jobs, higher wages, improved schooling for their children, cultural and political freedom, and a generally higher level of living. The migration to the cities began in colonial times but accelerated in the 1920s, when the drop in foreign immigration forced America's cities to look to the rural heartland for cheap labor. Attracted by the prospect of ready employment in the industrial cities of the Northeast, Midwest, and South, large numbers of rural blacks moved to urban areas. This migration considerably altered settlement conditions in the larger urban communities. Unlike the foreign migrants, who had settled in mixed urban enclaves and begun to intermarry and disperse, the blacks who moved to northern cities settled in neighborhoods that quickly became, and remained, all black. Whereas earlier foreign immigrants gradually increased their incomes and moved out of the immigrant neighborhoods, the black settlements were more permanent, creating cities within cities. The tendency of the wealthy to move to the suburbs had already been established among the cities' white populations, and the urban segregation of blacks increased this tendency. Although today blacks are moving into suburban communities in record numbers, they remain disporportionately represented in the central cities. As a result, the upward mobility of blacks has been severely limited and the precedent set for the increased economic and cultural segregation found in the cities. (See Chapter 9.)

pg. 260

Many U.S. cities have seen a continual influx of foreign immigrants over the past four decades. Miami, Los Angeles, New York, and Houston now have large concentrations of immigrants, many of whom have come from Latin America, the Caribbean, and Asia. At present about 800,000 legal immigrants from these regions are admitted to the United States each year, and an uncounted number of illegal entrants arrive as well. In cities with older segregated ghettos adjacent to newer immigrant neighborhoods, there are increasingly frequent episodes of conflict between the newcomers and residents of the older ghettos. On the other hand, there are also many instances of intergroup cooperation and renewed economic growth in these rapidly changing urban communities (Portes & Rumbaut, 1990; Winnick, 1991). We return to this subject in Chapter 16.

Voluntary and Involuntary Segregation   Residential segregation may take either of two forms: (1) voluntary segregation, in which people choose to live with others similar to themselves (e.g., the ethnic, artistic, or homosexual neighborhoods of large cities), and (2) involuntary segregation, which occurs when various segments of the population (e.g., blacks, Jews, or the aged) are forced by social or economic circumstances to live in specific areas of the city. Although at first most immigrant groups chose to live together in urban enclaves, the situation of urban blacks and other minorities today is largely one of involuntary segregation. Within black neighborhoods there is further segregation according to income. Phoebe Cottingham (1975) found that segregation of families by income within black communities resembles the segregation of whites within white communities.

Throughout American history no population group has experienced such persistent residential segregation in urban areas as African Americans (Massey & Denton, 1992). Although white immigrant groups such as the Irish, Italians, and Poles experienced segregation in earlier periods, only African Americans have experienced high rates of segregation throughout the nation's history. Nor are recent trends encouraging. Table 15–2 shows that the mean racial segregation index for U.S. cities has decreased only slightly over the past twenty years. The younger cities of the West are less segregated than those in the rest of the nation, and smaller cities are less segregated than larger ones; but segregation in the nation's largest cities is a continuing problem (Kasarda, 1993). (The index of segregation indicates the percentage of the black population that would have to move in order for a city to achieve a nonsegregated racial distribution—that is, one in which the probability of a black person living on a given block would be equal to the proportion of blacks in the city as a whole.)

For most city dwellers, residential segregation means a limited choice of lifestyles. This is especially true for minority groups and poor whites—particularly the elderly—and is caused as much by negative self-image as by racial and economic segregation. It is difficult for the poor, the aged, and others to escape from undesirable or dangerous urban areas. As a consequence, these people cannot be described as entirely *voluntary* residents of a particular urban neighborhood. As neighborhoods decline, all people whose daily activities take them into those areas face the hardships brought about by loss of capital and lack of support facilities and community services.

Douglas Massey, the foremost U.S. expert on urban racial segregation, argues that residential segregation of African Americans contributes to unemployment, educational inequality, high rates of criminal victimization, and drug addiction. He advocates much stronger enforcement of the antidiscrimination clauses of the Fair

TABLE 15–2   MEAN MEASURES OF SEGREGATION (INDEX OF DISSIMILARITY): UNITED STATES 1970–1990

	1970	1980	1990
All Cities	63.6	66.8	60.3
Region			
Northeast (12)	63.3	71.3	66.0
Midwest (23)	63.4	70.0	66.0
South (40)	65.9	71.4	64.1
West (25)	60.1	53.8	46.1
Size			
Less than 250,000 (45)	62.1	62.7	56.0
250,000–499,999 (33)	63.6	68.2	61.2
500,000–999,999 (16)	66.5	70.7	64.9
1 million and over (6)	66.2	79.5	75.1
Age[a]			
Pre- 1990 (45)	65.4	71.3	66.6
1900–1940 (40)	62.9	66.3	58.5
1950 and later (15)	59.6	54.3	45.9

[a]City age is defined as the year at which the city achieved 50,000 population size, which is the basis for metropolitan central city status.

Note: The number of cities in each category is shown in parenthesis.

Source: Kasarda, 1993.

Housing Act as a means to attack persistent segregation (Massey & Denton, 1992). We return to this point in the Social Policy section of this chapter.

THEORIES OF URBANISM

The propensity for large numbers of people to live in cities and for urban ways of life to become dominant throughout a society is known as *urbanism*. In rapidly changing regions of the world, such as large portions of Africa and Latin America, cities are growing at even greater rates than they are in North America and Europe. Does life in cities and the spread of urban areas over the globe account for other social problems, such as crime, the breakup of families, and intergroup conflict? Do urban people differ in some fundamental way from those who live in rural areas? Such questions have been the subject of much research and theory and are summarized in the three theories of urbanism to which we now turn.

Wirth's Theory

Several theories of urbanism have been proposed. The oldest and most influential is that of Louis Wirth. Wirth's basic argument is that cities increase the incidence of both social and personality disorders. He described the city as "a relatively large, dense, and permanent settlement of socially heterogeneous individuals" (quoted in Fischer, 1976, p. 29). Borrowing extensively from the teachings of another sociologist, Georg Simmel, Wirth argued that the urban environment literally assaults the city dweller with multiple and intense stimuli. The pressures of this overabundance of stimulation force urban dwellers to adapt in order to maintain their mental equilibrium. Wirth contended that the resultant adaptation has negative effects. The mechanisms that permit the city dweller to withstand the shock of multiple stimuli also cause him or her to become insulated from other people. As a result, the typical city dweller "becomes aloof, brusque, impersonal in his dealings with others, and emotionally buffered in his human relationships" (p. 31). When such withdrawal fails to counter the effects of overstimulation, people experience "psychic overload," which produces irritation and anxiety.

The effects of psychic overload are illustrated in the following remarks by a frustrated urban resident:

> You must understand this is a cramped place. Sometimes it feels like, well, like everything has been put through a trash compactor. Density like this annuls certain clauses in the social contract; it begets those dull, middle-distance stares, a defense mechanism. Some of us don't even acknowledge our next-door neighbors. (Jaynes, 1988, p. 29)

Wirth asserted that this interpersonal estrangement loosens the bonds that unite people. In some cases these bonds are completely severed, and the result is antisocial and alienated behavior. When people are left without emotional support or societal restraint, they begin to act out their fantasies. According to Wirth, this explains the intense creativity and technological advancement, as well as the psychopathic and criminal behavior, that are prevalent in cities. Each extreme is a result of looser social restraints and interpersonal relationships.

Another by-product of city life is the economic process of competition, comparative advantage, and specialization. One result of this process is community differentiation. In most cases this differentiation is most visible in the division of labor, although it exists in other forms as well—for example, in separate districts for businesses, residences, and entertainment. In urban environments people often assume many different roles during an average day, roles that involve social interaction with co-workers, neighbors, close friends, and family. In Wirth's opinion, the very multiplicity of people and places that compete for an unban dweller's time and attention weakens social bonds. As people continue to enter into primary relationships outside the family, the family becomes less important. Since many of these relationships are scattered across the city, neighbors also play a less significant role. According to Wirth, such loosening of social ties produces an alienated condition, or *anomie*, a weakening of the norms that govern acceptable social behavior.

Once the personal approach to preserving societal norms has been weakened, other attempts to control social behavior must be made. Most often, this takes the form of complaints to impersonal government authorities. Wirth believed that such impersonal control can never fully replace the power and moral strength of small primary groups.

Therefore, he considered cities—with their inclination toward individualism, estrangement, stress, and especially social disorganization—as societies in which social relationships are weak. Such weakness may indeed provide more freedom for individuals, but it also leads to social disruption and personality disorders.

Compositionalism

Wirth's theory is not accepted by all urban sociologists. Herbert Gans, among others, has challenged Wirth's ideas about the effects of urbanism on personal behavior. *The Urban Villagers* (1984), Gans's classic study, is a close-up view of life in the Italian neighborhoods of the West End of Boston shortly before those neighborhoods were torn down in the name of "urban renewal." Gans shows that many families were deeply committed to a life that was spent largely within the neighborhood. They were immersed in the life of the Italian-American community and were not at all like the disorganized slum dwellers of Wirthian theory. The forms of deviance found in the neighborhood—gang activity and some organized crime—did not result from social disorganization. Nor were these neighborhoods dominated by impersonal institutions such as housing authorities, as Wirthian theory would predict.

Gans used these findings and those from similar community studies in immigrant neighborhoods to conclude that personal behavior is shaped by the social life of specific neighborhoods and communities, not by the larger social forces described by Wirth under the heading of urbanism. Fischer (1976) calls this a compositional theory of urbanism. The difference between the two theories rests on opposing views of how the city affects the existence of small groups. Compositionalists see the city as a mosaic of social worlds—intimate social circles with their roots in kinship, ethnicity, neighborhoods, occupations, and lifestyles. Whereas Wirth believed that the pressures of the city disrupt these worlds, drawing people away from close associations with family and neighbors, compositionalists believe that these worlds persist undiminished in an urban setting. Gans contends, in fact, that the closeness of these social worlds envelops individuals and protects them from the pressures of city life.

Compositionalists cite economic position, cultural characteristics, and marital and family status as the determinants of personal behavior. The strength of these attributes, rather than the size or density of the community at large, molds a person's social and psychological experience. To a compositionalist, the social-psychological effects of urbanism are meaningless. This, of course, directly contradicts the Wirthian theory, which views cities as having a direct impact on the coherence of small groups.

Subcultural Theory

Fischer's own theory of urbanism agrees with the Wirthian theory in acknowledging that cities produce major social-psychological effects. Fischer, however, believes that these effects occur not because existing social groups break down but because cities foster new ones.

Large cities promote the emergence of diverse subcultures, which in turn add to the enjoyment of urban life for many city people.

Known as the subcultural theory, Fischer's argument suggests that the most socially significant consequence of an urban community is the promotion of diverse subcultures—culturally distinct groups such as college students, Chinese Americans, artists, and homosexuals. In New York's Greenwich Village or San Francisco's Castro district, for example, there are communities of gay men and women who create a local culture of tolerance for homosexuality. In addition, they create institutions of homosexual thought and expression—newspapers, theater, cabarets—in which the norms of the "straight" world are suspended to a degree and other sexual norms are encouraged or discussed. People who are homosexual feel more free to express themselves in such communities and to form close relationships with one another.

In contrast to Wirth, who held that no significant primary social relationships can be achieved in an urban environment, Fischer believes that people in cities live within meaningful social worlds. More important, subculturists contend that large communities attract immigrants precisely because of this distinctively urban phenomenon. In Fischer's view, urbanism intensifies subcultures. This occurs partly through critical mass: A large city is more likely than a small community to attract a sizable proportion of a given subculture. This process operates for artists, academics, bohemians, corporate executives, criminals, and computer programmers as well as for ethnic or racial minority groups.

Subcultural intensification also occurs through multigroup contact. In a densely populated environment subcultures are constantly bumping into one another. Sometimes these groups coexist; in other instances tensions mount. When one subculture finds another annoying, threatening, or both, a common reaction is to embrace one's own social world all the more firmly.

METROPOLITAN GROWTH

The mass migration from the farms to the cities in the nineteenth century has been described as a rural–urban flow. But in the twentieth century, with most of the U.S. population living in or near urban areas, the pattern of flow has changed from rural–urban to intermetropolitan. In 1910 the Bureau of the Census identified twenty-five *metropolitan districts*. This term was designed to assist in the measurement of urban populations, which even then could no longer be contained within the traditional urban political boundaries. These districts varied in size from the largest—New York, with 616,927 acres of land and 6,474,568 people—to the smallest—Portland, Oregon, with a population of 215,048 and a land area of 43,538 acres. Through the metropolitan-district approach, the unity of such urban areas as the Twin Cities of Minnesota, the cities of San Francisco Bay, and the two Kansas Cities along the Missouri–Kansas border was recognized. The importance of the urban clusters around Philadelphia, New York, and Boston also became apparent.

Since 1983 the U.S. Bureau of the Census has defined the urban population according to residence in three categories of urban settlement. The largest of the three, the *consolidated metropolitan statistical area* (CMSA), refers to large metropolitan complexes within which are recognized subcenters that themselves may have large core areas, called *primary metropolitan statistical areas* (PMSAs). Dallas and Fort Worth and the urban areas surrounding them, for example, are classified as a CMSA, but statistics are also published separately for the Dallas and Forth Worth PMSAs. *Metropolitan statistical areas* (MSAs) have a large urban population nucleus (a city of 500,000) and surrounding communities that are closely linked to it through economic and social activities. Indianapolis, Indiana, is an MSA; so is Little Rock–North Little Rock, Arkansas.

How do "metropolitan" and "urban" areas differ? An *urban area* usually contains a large population within a limited area. A *metropolitan area* contains several urban communities, all of which are located in close proximity to one another. For example, the Greater New York Metropolitan Area contains not only New York City but also Long Island, Westchester County, and parts of New Jersey (including Newark) and Connecticut.

Table 15–3 on page 450 shows how many new metropolitan areas have emerged since 1960 as well as the enormous increase in the amount of land in the United States that is included in metropolitan areas. Some of these areas have become socially and economically interrelated, forming urbanized regions or, in some cases, an urban "corridor" such as Boston–New York–Philadelphia–Washington. (Table 15–4 on page 450 lists the fifteen largest metropolitan statistical areas in the United States.) Social scientists often use the term *megalopolis* to refer to these large metropolitan regions (Gottman, 1978).

The development of megalopolitan areas has large-scale effects on the environment and on other parts of the continent. The energy consumed in the major megalopolitan regions of the United States, especially the BosWash (Boston-to-Washington) corridor, contributes enormously to acid rain and other problems in the Northeast and other regions. Air pollution and the demand for shrinking supplies of water in the SanSan (San Diego–San Francisco) megalopolitan strip are reaching emergency proportions at this writing. Development along major auto routes between urban areas within the megalopolitan regions is also a growing problem as urban growth threatens to choke out green space and result in unplanned urban sprawl. In the leading nations of Western Europe, especially Holland, France, Germany, and Denmark, investment in rail transport, high-speed trains, and improved

TABLE 15–3 METROPOLITAN AND NONMETROPOLITAN AREA POPULATION: UNITED STATES, 1960–1990

	1960	1970	1980[a]	1990[a]
Metropolitan areas:				
Number of areas	212	243	268	268
Population (1,000)	112,885	139,480	176,663	197,467
Percent change over previous year shown	—	23.6	—	11.8
Percent of total U.S. population	63.0	68.6	78.0	79.4
Land area, percent of U.S. land area	8.7	10.9	19.0	19.0
Nonmetropolitan areas, population (1,000)	66,438	63,822	49,879	51,243

[a]Areas are as defined December 31, 1992.

Source: Statistical Abstract, 1993.

bus transportation promises to limit the unplanned effects of megalopolitan development, but similar investments in the urban transportation infrastructure have not been made in the United States. On the other hand, as we will see in Chapter 17, the United States has succeeded in implementing air pollution controls that are more stringent than those of European nations, and these controls have had highly positive effects although air pollution remains a serious problem in major urban regions.

TABLE 15–4 THE 15 LARGEST MSAs IN THE UNITED STATES, 1980 AND 1990

Consolidated MSA	1980	1990	Change
New York City area	17,539,532	18,087,251	+ 3.1%
Los Angeles–Anaheim–Riverside	11,497,549	14,531,529	+26.4
Chicago–Gary–Lake County	7,937,290	8,065,633	+ 1.6
San Francisco–Oakland–San Jose	5, 367,900	6,253,311	+16.5
Philadelphia–Wilmington–Trenton	5,680,509	5,899,345	+ 3.9
Detroit–Ann Arbor	4,752,784	4,665,236	− 1.8
Boston–Lawrence–Salem	3,971,792	4,171,643	+ 5.0
Washington–Maryland–Virginia	3,250,921	3,923,574	+20.7
Dallas–Fort Worth	2,930,568	3,885,415	+32.6
Houston–Galveston–Brazoria	3,099,942	3,711,043	+19.7
Miami–Fort Lauderdale	2,643,766	3,192,582	+20.8
Atlanta	2,138,136	2,833,511	+32.5
Cleveland–Akron–Lorain	2,834,062	2,759,823	− 2.6
Seattle–Tacoma	2,093,285	2,559,164	+22.3
San Diego	1,861,846	2,498,016	+34.2

Source: Data from U.S. Census Bureau.

The Transportation Boom

Relatively primitive communication and transportation facilities and the need for defensive fortifications forced ancient and medieval cities to be compact, and the movement of their inhabitants was restricted to a relatively small area. This was also true for cities in the United States throughout most of the nineteenth century, when walking was the chief mode of transportation. After 1870, however, several major advances, beginning with the horse-drawn streetcar, allowed urban residents the luxury of living up to five miles from their place of business. The day of the commuter had dawned. Electric trolley lines and streetcars were introduced in the 1880s and 1890s, extending the commuting distance to about ten miles. When rapid-transit electric trains were introduced around the turn of the century, the distance doubled once again. The movement to the suburbs had begun.

The trend toward suburbanization began in earnest with the introduction of commuter railways. As wealthy third and fourth generation urbanites retreated from the central city, putting ever-larger distances between their residences and their places of business, the separation between low-income and high-income neighborhoods increased markedly. Quick to follow the trend, commercial institutions began their own redistribution process. The first to vacate the central city were convenience-goods and service establishments, the businesses that are most dependent on the type of customer who was rapidly moving to suburbia. As these businesses and various manufacturing concerns were leaving the central city, professional service organizations were moving in, creating a central business district composed of administrative, communications, financial, and other businesses that serviced the entire metropolitan region.

By the 1930s the automobile had made suburban development a major factor in

More efficient forms of transportation, such as horse-drawn buses, made it possible for cities to expand horizontally as well as vertically. This photo shows a New York City street in 1910.

the economic, social, and political life of the United States. Motor vehicle registration increased from 8,000 in 1900 to 26,352,000 in 1930, representing an increase from approximately one automobile for every 10,000 people to one per household (Flink, 1976; Glaab & Brown, 1967). The automobile altered the shape of urban expansion. Whereas previous suburban growth had developed along railroad lines and other public transport systems, the automobile permitted much more dispersed growth. By 1930 urban sprawl was well under way.

The growth of the outlying rings of metropolitan areas occurred so dramatically that by 1930 suburbs were growing two and a half times faster than central cities. In 1910, only 15.7 percent of the total U.S. population lived in the metropolitan areas. Between 1960 and 1965, the growth rate for the United States as a whole was 7.1 percent; the growth rate for nonmetropolitan rings increased by 14.5 percent, markedly faster than the increase within the central cities, which was only 7.9 percent (Glaab & Brown, 1967). And during the 1970s and early 1980s there was a large shift of population from the central cities to the suburbs.

In the 1980s urban growth entered a new stage. On the perimeters of metropolitan areas, large urban clusters emerged, dense and more focused than the conventional suburb. Sometimes referred to as "outer cities," these new developments rival downtown areas in size and surpass them as sources of jobs. An example of this trend is Tysons Corner. Once a crossroads village in rural northern Virginia, Tysons Corner is now a burgeoning business and shopping center on the edge of the Washington, D.C., metropolitan area. Seventy thousand people work in Tysons Corner, but little else happens there; community life and institutions are almost entirely lacking (Stevens, 1987). Nevertheless, urban clusters like Tysons Corner are expanding rapidly in every region of the country, further evidence of the impact of the automobile on metropolitan growth.

The Impact of Suburban Growth

Public policy—especially in the areas of urban renewal and highway construction—has encouraged suburbanization, often to the detriment and/or destruction of central-city neighborhoods. Financial opportunities—particularly Federal Housing Authority or Veterans Administration mortgages—make buying a house more attractive and easier in the suburbs than in the aging residential areas of the central city. Since a large proportion of a mortgage payment is interest and therefore is tax deductible, simple economics makes it expedient for many American families to move to the suburbs.

Federal financing for home ownership—primarily in the suburbs—is much more accessible than funds for rental housing in the city. This has tended to produce increasing social-class segregation, with lower-income minorities concentrated in the cities and more affluent whites in the suburbs. Explicit efforts to add higher-quality rental housing to the stock of inner-city housing have had mixed results. Public housing, almost all of it built before the 1980s, has added about 1.3 million apartment units to the existing stock of lower-cost rental housing, but about 15 percent of those units are troubled by problems of drugs, crime, and violence (Bratt, 1989; Williams & Kornblum, 1994). Except in the very few cases in which careful planning made it possible to achieve successfully integrated projects, public housing policies have merely managed to keep lower-income people in the city, thereby strengthening patterns of segregation. Moreover, it has been almost impossible for the cities to obtain federal funds for mass transportation projects. By encouraging highway construction rather than strengthening mass transportation, government encourages industry to leave the city, thereby eliminating a major portion of the central city's tax base.

The steady growth of suburbs has posed many problems for the older cities, particularly in terms of their internal structure and composition. With the increasing differentiation between central city and suburban ring and the subsequent outflow of population and industry, America's cities face social and economic problems of seemingly insurmountable proportions. As urban history shows, the steady flight to the suburbs by business, industry, and residents—all eager for less expensive and more comfortable quarters—has made renovation and rehabilitation of the central city both difficult and expensive. In many older metropolitan areas, particularly those in the Northeast, the abandonment of urban neighborhoods to the poor, who are ill equipped to move long distances, has led to the proliferation of slums, causing both the economic base and the actual population of the city to decline. Although the suburbs, the nearby towns, and all of their residents belong to the same metropolitan area as the urban centers, they escape responsibility for the financial burdens they place on the cities.

It is important to recognize that suburbs are no longer as homogeneous as they once were (or were thought to be). Long characterized as "bedroom communities," suburbs today mix rural villages with business districts and pockets of poverty and homelessness with areas of middle-class comfort and wealth. Nor are suburbs immune to the problems that are usually associated with cities, such as traffic congestion and lack of affordable housing.

PROBLEMS OF CITIES

Modern cities are constantly undergoing change and restructuring. Economic change is especially significant in urban areas. As new industries are born and old ones die, entire neighborhoods and communities may be lost and new ones created elsewhere. In the 1950s, for example, economic growth in cities like San Francisco, New York, and Seattle was based on seaport industries. But automation in the handling of goods (especially the use of containers and trucks) greatly diminished the need for workers in the ports. Many port cities still serve as transshipment centers, but far fewer workers are needed to perform this function. Some cities have made up for the loss in seaport employment by building major jetports. Still, economic and social change is so rapid that cities are continually racing to adapt and attract new industries. In the meantime they continue to attract newcomers, many of whom bring more than their share of troubles with them.

These major social changes affect urban centers more drastically than they do other communities, and they often create a variety of urban problems. Among these are deconcentration, relocation of manufacturing, and financial problems, all of which are complicated by the division of governmental responsibility between cities and suburbs. These problems will be discussed in this section. Two other serious problems of cities, the lack of affordable housing and the increase in homelessness, are discussed in the next section.

Deconcentration

A primary cause of central-city decay is *deconcentration*: the flight to the suburbs of middle- and upper-middle-class families; the influx of poor minority groups, the chronically unemployed, the aged, and others who tend to be more of a liability than an asset to central-city budgets; the retreat of commerce and industry from the taxing jurisdiction of central cities; the disparity between the requirements of available jobs in the central city and the skills of the resident labor force; and the daily flow into the city of suburban residents, who utilize public facilities without paying for their upkeep. All these circumstances strain the budgets of the central cities at a time when their revenues are decreasing and their public-service obligations have increased substantially.

The decade between 1920 and 1930 was a period of pronounced deconcentration, or suburbanization, in the United States. In subsequent decades the population within the suburban rings increased significantly more than the population of the central cities. By the 1960s suburbanization accounted for almost all growth within metropolitan areas. Today the growth of central cities remains small compared with that of the outer fringes of metropolitan areas. But this does not mean that there is no population change inside the cities. On the contrary, as more affluent households move from inner cities to suburban areas, new populations are constantly arriving, especially from other nations. Thus, although population figures may not show them as growing, the inner cities are in fact subject to major population shifts (Kasarda, 1993).

As people left the cities during the period of most intense suburbanization, business and industry quickly followed. The years from 1954 to 1977 saw the construction of more than 15,000 suburban shopping centers and regional shopping malls, which by 1978 were responsible for more than half of the total annual retail sales in the United States (Kasarda, 1978). From 1975 to 1980 central cities continued to lose population while the suburbs continued to gain new residents, as did nonmetropolitan regions. During that period the cities lost 6.3 million residents, of whom 5 million moved to the suburbs and 1.3 million to nonmetropolitan areas (U.S. Census Bureau, 1981).

The 1990 census confirmed that the fastest-growing urban communities are on the fringes of metropolitan areas. During the 1980s there was a significant shift of jobs and people to the outer counties of metropolitan regions. In New York, for example, the population of the outer counties grew by 13 percent while that of the inner counties grew by just 2 percent. In many metropolitan regions the rapid growth of suburban communities attracts jobs that were formerly located in the urban core. Such shifts—illustrated in Figure 15–1 for the Dallas–Fort Worth metropolitan region—enhance the employment opportunities available to suburban residents, to the detriment of those in the inner cities. Very often this creates further disadvantage for racial minorities in segregated central-city ghettos.

In addition to the movement to the suburbs, there has been a tremendous shift of population from the Snowbelt cities of the North and East to the Sunbelt cities of the South and West—Houston, San Antonio, Phoenix, and others. And as the population has moved, so have jobs—a fact that has added to the problems of the older, larger cities in the northern industrial states. But life is not always sunny in the Sunbelt cities either. In California, for example, severe drought and increasing problems of overpopulation, lack of affordable housing, and earthquakes have tarnished the image of Southern California as the embodiment of the American Dream. Although the large-scale influx of immigrants continues to produce growth in the Los Angeles metropolitan area, it is likely that the region will experience continuing economic problems due to the end of the cold war and the decline in defense production as well as the effects of environmental catastrophes ranging from earthquakes to brush fires and mudslides (Davis, 1990).

Elsewhere in the Sunbelt there are other major urban problems. In their studies of Houston, Joe R. Feagin (1988) and Robert D. Bullard (1988) found that by the end of the 1980s the long period of prosperity in that city, fueled by steady demand for higher-priced oil, had ended. Recession and increasing racial segregation had replaced the upbeat free-enterprise image projected by the city's business leaders. Like many cities in the Southwest and the Northeast, Houston had overbuilt its downtown office centers in anticipation of more white-collar jobs and failed to invest enough of its resources to upgrade schools and health-care facilities in the inner city.

Relocation of Manufacturing

Manufacturers benefit from suburban relocation when they can minimize their transportation and freight costs by locating near suburban highway systems. Accordingly, manufacturing firms have left the inner cities in large numbers. To a certain extent, the departure of manufacturing concerns has been balanced by an influx of new

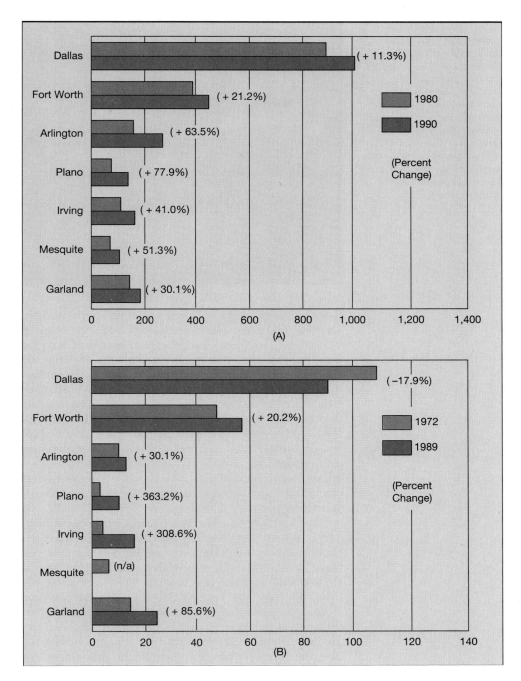

FIGURE 15–1 (A) Population Changes in Dallas, Fort Worth, and Their Suburbs, 1980–1990 (in thousands)
(B) Changes in Manufacturing Employment, 1972–1989 (in thousands)
Source: Copyright © 1991 by the New York Times Company. Reprinted by permission.

Many of the newest urban centers in the United States, such as Silicon Valley in California, have grown as a result of the shift of the economy away from heavy industry toward computers and other forms of "high-tech" manufacturing. The severe recession of the early 1990s showed, however, that even the most economically up-to-date urban regions can suffer during a recession.

types of business establishments offering specialized goods and services. Legal, government, and professional complexes and service organizations such as travel agencies, advertising firms, and brokerage houses all have become more numerous in recent decades. Yet although the percentage of white-collar jobs has increased in the central cities, it has increased much faster in the outlying suburban areas.

Especially dramatic has been the rise of high-tech manufacturing centers like Silicon Valley in California and the Route 128 region near Boston. Among the industries that have found it advantageous to operate in these areas are manufacturers of office and computing machines, communication equipment, electronic components and accessories, and engineering and scientific instruments, as well as computer and data-processing services and research and development labs. These industries are dependent on intensive, sophisticated technical research, and hence the new manufacturing zones are almost always located near major universities such as the Massachusetts Institute of Technology.

High-tech firms have created large numbers of new jobs, especially high-paying jobs in science, engineering, and management. One result is a growing demand for expensive housing in the surrounding communities, which tends to increase the average price of housing in the area and displace lower-income residents (Saxenian, 1985). As the recession of the early 1990s worsened, bankruptcies and layoffs in Silicon Valley and the Route 128 complex became severe as well, demonstrating that these centers of urban economic growth are not immune to the business cycle. Even the gradual recovery from the recession of the early 1990s has not brought strong growth to high-tech manufacturing centers owing to corporate policies calling for deep cuts in employment and continued investment in automation. In consequence, the recovery is proceeding at a fitful pace.

Financial Problems

Property assessments are the primary source of tax revenues for city governments. As a result of the exodus of industry to the suburbs, the real estate tax base of most central cities has been greatly reduced. Population shifts within the boundaries of metropolitan areas have further increased the financial pressures on central cities. Within the larger cities, the increased concentration of low-income groups in the inner cities demands a larger investment in welfare and other social programs. Many cities, fearful of losing residents and businesses to the suburbs, also need to invest in large-scale physical rehabilitation and redevelopment projects.

The economic gap between healthy suburbs and distressed cities has worsened in recent years, despite signs of improvement in some areas. Many urban specialists fear that cities with financial difficulties will channel funds away from essential services such as streets, water and sewage systems, and mass transportation facilities in order to finance their debts and meet operating costs.

Related to the problem of finances is the poor condition of the *infrastructure* (i.e., physical facilities) of many cities. Most American cities grew rapidly after World War II, especially in the 1950s. Large investments were made in public transportation, bridges, and highway systems to serve rapidly growing and increasingly affluent urban populations. But by the 1980s much of this infrastructure had begun to wear out. Estimates made by the federal government in the early 1980s indicated that billions of dollars would be needed to repair and rebuild crumbling city facilities.

In the mid-1980s many observers warned that the decay of the country's roads, bridges, sewers, and rail and water systems had reached alarming proportions. These warnings were reinforced by an increase in the frequency of accidents caused by train derailments and collapsing bridges and overpasses. At the same time, however, the federal budget deficit rose to record levels, precluding large-scale federal investment in infrastructure projects.

In the 1990s we have witnessed numerous natural calamities such as flooding in cities and towns of the Mississippi, Ohio, and Missouri Valleys; earthquakes and brush fires in California; and hurricanes in the Gulf states. These have added to the

The need for extensive infrastructure repair and expansion is brought home vividly to Americans when they see televised reports of tragedies like this bridge collapse.

Large tracts of urban real estate have been devastated when housing has been abandoned because of high crime rates or the inability of poor tenants to make rent payments. Public-private partnerships using federal housing to begin restoration provided these formerly homeless families with their first decent, affordable housing.

burden of financing repair and maintenance of urban infrastructures. Although the Clinton administration sought billions of dollars in additional funding in the 1994 federal budget to help defray the costs of these disasters, those costs are likely to contribute to local, state, and federal budget deficits for years to come.

Government

A major cause of the problems facing cities today is the inequitable distribution of economic resources and costs of public services between the cities and higher levels of government. Of every $100 the U.S. government collects in taxes, it spends about $20 on national defense, $21 on social security, $14 on income security (federal pensions, unemployment insurance, food and nutrition assistance, Aid to Families with Dependent Children, etc.), and $14 on interest on the national debt. Of the remaining $31, it spends about $1 to run the federal government, $7 on health-care services and research (not including Medicare), $2 on transportation (especially highways), and $0.07 on criminal-justice assistance to the states and cities *(Statistical Abstract,* 1993). Although crime and overcrowded prisons are deemed to be major social problems by residents of metropolitan regions, one can see from these figures that very little of the tax revenue collected at the federal level is returned to municipalities to help them cope with these problems. In consequence, suburbs with affluent residents who pay high property taxes can afford adequate protection while inner cities with poorer residents, which have much less revenue from property taxes, must depend on the meager return from federal taxes to tackle their major problems, including not only crime but also poor education, inadequate health care, and others.

Another serious problem related to government is the fact that so many urban social problems extend beyond the jurisdiction of any single local government and often cross state boundaries as well. Such concerns as air and water pollution require control over entire areas, rather than strict observance of municipal boundaries. This is also true for major waterways, mass transit, and water supplies. The situation for recreational facilities, public institutions like libraries and museums, and public services like police and fire protection is less clear. The benefits of all these services are not restricted to a single municipal jurisdiction. On the other hand, they are not equally distributed throughout the entire metropolitan area. Who, then, is to pay how much for these necessary services?

City governments have been forced to bear the financial burden for municipal services even though those services are extensively utilized by suburban residents. Thousands of visitors flock to city museums and parks every day, placing additional burdens on sanitation and public-health facilities and transportation systems, all of which must be paid for out of municipal funds. In this way city residents assume the tax burden for their suburban neighbors. Numerous social scientists have pointed out that regardless of its political boundaries, a metropolitan area is in fact a single economic entity with an integrated labor market, a unified transportation system, and a closely interrelated set of housing markets. Dividing this entity into separate local economies results in inefficiency and duplication of services.

In extreme cases, the discrepancies between municipal boundaries and social needs can have dire consequences. This is illustrated by the case of East St. Louis, Illinois, which has been described as "a textbook case of everything that can go wrong in an American city." Once a prosperous blue-collar town of stockyards and meat-packing plants beside the Mississippi River, East St. Louis is today "a city at rock bottom, a partly inhabited ghost town whose factories and theaters and hotels and auto dealerships and gas stations and half its schools are mostly burned-out shells" (Wilkerson, 1991, p. A16). The causes of this situation include a rapidly declining tax base and the fact that even though East St. Louis borders on St. Louis, it is a separate municipality in another state. The city's finances are in such chaos that trash may go uncollected for days at a time and police officers have had to patrol the city in their own cars when the police cars have broken down.

SHELTER POVERTY, HOMELESSNESS, AND NEIGHBORHOOD DISTRESS

Shelter Poverty

According to a study by Michael E. Stone, a professor of community planning at the University of Massachusetts, more than one-third of all Americans—78 million people—are "shelter poor." This means that they are obliged to pay so much for housing that they no longer have enough money for food, clothing, and medical care (cited in Mariano, 1990). When the official poverty index was originally formulated by Mollie Orshansky (see Chapter 8), it was assumed that the cost of shelter would account for no more than one-fourth of monthly income. However, according to the National Low-Income Housing Information Service, in the past twenty years the number of renters with household incomes below $10,000 has risen from about 6 million to slightly less than 10 million, while the number of apartments renting for $250 a month or less has fallen from about 7 million to about 5.5 million (De-Parle, 1991). The cost of food also absorbs a greater share of the poor family's budget than it did twenty years ago. Social scientists now fear that as a result of the combined effects of rising rent and higher food costs, even more people are living in poverty than is indicated in official statistics. In any case, social scientists now concede that a household paying more than 25 percent of its income for housing is shelter poor and will not have enough income left to pay for other basic needs. (The Stone study indicates that even households that pay less than 25 percent of their income for housing may be shelter poor because they still cannot afford to buy other essentials.) Shelter poverty, it should be noted, also occurs among affluent families when sudden unemployment decreases their income while mortgages and other housing costs remain the same. But shelter poverty is most prevalent among families at or below the poverty line.

As noted in Chapter 8, the majority of America's poor live in substandard, deteriorated housing that has been rejected by people whose incomes allow them to move to better homes. This is especially true of poor members of minority groups, who inhabit substandard housing because they cannot afford anything better and because discrimination keeps them in the slums. As a result, people with higher incomes live in new housing in the suburbs while the poor live in older central-city housing.

Some experts argue that many sections of cities that are severely run down can be rehabilitated. Others claim that this does nothing to solve social problems. The standard procedure in most urban renewal or redevelopment programs involves mass removal of slum housing. To accomplish this, the residents of the area must be removed first. Since most urban renewal projects result in more expensive housing, the residents are for the most part unable to return to their former neighborhoods. Those who can afford to return find that the characteristics that made the neighborhood their own—churches, schools, family, and friends—are no longer there. The majority of those who are dislocated as a result of urban renewal move to nearby areas that will probably be cleared in future renewal projects.

Instead of providing adequate housing at a low cost, most urban renewal drives the poor out of rehabilitated areas because too often the redeveloped housing is for people with high incomes. Low-cost housing for low-income residents has never been financially feasible. Meanwhile, federal public housing policy often ensures the development of a "federal slum." By preventing the working poor from living in the housing projects, the government restricts the projects to the very poor, people on welfare, broken families, and the disabled.

It should be noted that much public housing is far better than the dilapidated, decaying buildings it replaced. However, the problem of segregation of the poor remains; in addition, the quality of the neighborhoods in which the housing projects are located is often substandard. Critics of public housing point out that "even when dwelling units occupied by the poor are not overcrowded, contain their own kitchens and bathrooms, and may even be in somewhat decent repair, they are set in a dismal environment. They are surrounded by abandoned buildings and located on streets that are unsafe and littered with trash" (Salins, 1986, pp. 24–25). A major reason for this situation is that more affluent communities tend to oppose even small additions of low-income housing to their neighborhoods.

Homelessness

A frequent consequence of shelter poverty is homelessness. People who cannot afford rent increases may end up among the growing number of homeless people in the nation's large cities. Moreover, many young families who would have purchased a house a decade ago are forced to stay in rental housing. This development has tended to push rents up and squeeze lower-income people out of the rental market; because of the lack of space in public housing, the result, for many, is homelessness.

Another trend that has contributed to the housing problem is *gentrification,* the return of affluent single people and childless couples to selected central-city neighborhoods. As these new urban residents restore and renovate buildings and upgrade

More affluent urban residents are better able to afford the cost of rehabilitating inner-city housing than poor residents, a fact that contributes to the displacement of low-income families from some neighborhoods.

apartments in decaying neighborhoods, poor residents are forced to seek living space in other parts of the city. If they are unable to find housing that they can afford, they too may end up among the homeless.

We have noted at several points in this book that homelessness has become a major social problem in recent years. As a result of numerous factors, including deinstitutionalization of mental patients, the increasing concentration of poor people in central cities, the lack of low-cost housing, and the displacement of poor families by urban renewal and gentrification, there has been a large and visible increase in the number of homeless people wandering through public places in central cities. The size of the homeless population is extremely difficult to assess. Not only are homeless people virtually impossible to keep track of, but estimates of their numbers tend to reflect the interests of the organizations providing the estimates. Thus, the U.S. Department of Housing and Urban Development estimates the total number of homeless people in the United States at about 300,000; advocacy groups place the total closer to 3 million (Rossi, 1989; Steinbach, 1989).

There have always been homeless groups in the United States: hoboes, unemployed migrants, and the like. For them homelessness was either a chosen lifestyle or a more or less temporary condition. Today's homeless are a more serious problem. Not only is the homeless population larger than ever before, but it includes a much wider range of groups—not only deinstitutionalized mental patients and displaced families but also chronic alcoholics, destitute drug addicts, Vietnam veterans, and unemployed laborers. This large and still-growing population has placed a heavy burden on the public and private shelters and other social services of American cities. In some cities existing shelters and other facilities are woefully inadequate to handle this greatly increased population, and as a result homeless people have sought refuge in bus terminals and train stations. Policies for dealing with homelessness are discussed further in the Social Policy section of the chapter.

Distressed Neighborhoods

As a consequence of the flight of more secure, middle-class people from the central cities over the past twenty years or more, there has been an increase in what social scientists call *neighborhood distress*. In discussing this problem, it is important to note that it is extremely difficult to define precisely what constitutes a neighborhood. The Census Bureau divides urban regions into *census tracts*, relatively homogeneous areas with respect to population, socioeconomic status, and living conditions. Census tracts, which have an average population of 4,000 persons, are equivalent to urban neighborhoods for analytical purposes.

In the largest central cities of the United States, there are slightly over 14,000 census tracts. Analyses of the characteristics of inner-city tracts reveal that there have been sharp increases in the degree of neighborhood distress in many of these tracts. According to social scientists such as John Kasarda, one of the nation's leading analysts of urban social change, as well as other social scientists, neighborhood distress is measured by several characteristics:

- *Poverty*—the rate of poverty in the tract
- *Joblessness*—the proportion of out-of-school males age 16 and older who work less than twenty-six weeks a year
- *Female-headed families*—the proportion of families headed by a female with children under 18
- *Welfare recipiency*—the proportion of families receiving public assistance
- *Teenage school dropouts*—the proportion of persons age 16 to 19 who are not enrolled in school and are not high school graduates (Kasarda, 1993; Ricketts & Sawhill, 1988).

Distressed neighborhoods are not the same as poverty tracts, although the two have much in common. *Poverty tracts* are census tracts in which at least 20 percent of the residents fall below the poverty line; in *extreme poverty tracts* at least 40 percent do so. When the concepts of distressed neighborhoods and poverty tracts are combined, the following definitions emerge (Kasarda, 1993):

■ *Distressed tracts*—census tracts that fall one standard deviation or more (that is, 30 percent or more) below the mean (based on the 1980 census) on all five measures listed earlier (including poverty).

■ *Severely distressed tracts*—census tracts with extremely high rates of teenage school dropouts, causing them to fall one standard deviation above the 1980 national tract average on this measure. (This measure is used in defining severely distressed tracts because completing high school is essential for gaining employment in the nation's rapidly changing economy.)

Table 15–5 indicates that since 1970 there has been a dramatic increase in the number of census tracts in the 100 largest U.S. cities that are classified as poverty tracts or extreme poverty tracts. The increase in distressed tracts has also been significant, but the table indicates that the rate of increase slowed between 1980 and 1990 compared to the previous decade. The growth of severely distressed tracts actually declined very slightly in the same period after rapid growth between 1970 and 1980.

Kasarda's research also shows that there has been an alarming concentration of households living in extreme poverty tracts and distressed tracts in the nation's 100 largest cities. From 1970 to 1990 the number of people living in distressed tracts increased from about 1 million to 5.7 million, or from about 2 percent of the total population of those cities to about 11 percent. Worse still is the growing concentration of minorities in distressed central-city tracts. While 2.2 percent of non-Latino whites live in such areas, 29.7 percent of non-Latino African Americans and 13.2 percent of Latinos live in distressed tracts in the nation's 100 largest cities.

It is difficult to overstate the consequences of this concentration of poor people in distressed neighborhoods. These neighborhoods are likely to be the areas with the highest rates of drug sales and addiction, violent crime, and housing abandonment. Twenty years ago residents of most of the census tracts that

TABLE 15–5 NUMBER OF CENSUS TRACTS, BY POVERTY AND DISTRESS STATUS: 100 LARGEST CENTRAL CITIES, 1970–1990

CENSUS TRACTS	1970	1980	1990
Total number of tracts	12,584	13,777	14,214
(% of city total)	100.0	100.0	100.0
Poverty tracts	3,430	4,713	5,596
(% of city total)	27.3	34.2	39.4
Extreme poverty tracts	751	1,330	1,954
(% of city total)	6.0	9.7	13.7
Distressed tracts	296	1,513	1,850
(% of city total)	2.4	11.0	13.0
Severely distressed tracts	166	562	566
(% of city total)	1.3	4.1	4.0

Source: Data from U.S. Census Bureau, 1990.

are now characterized by poverty and neighborhood distress could find manufacturing jobs nearby. Today the jobs are gone and the economic future of these areas is extremely uncertain. Although there are communities outside central cities that also suffer from high rates of poverty and related social problems, the most important test of policies to address urban social problems will be whether they are able to improve conditions of life in the distressed neighborhoods of the inner cities, for improvements there will result in overall improvements for all residents of urban areas.

SOCIAL POLICY

HUD Secretary Henry Cisneros believes that the secret to renewal in the nation's beleaguered central cities is greater linkage to the growing suburbs. "In the twenty-five metropolitan areas in which suburban incomes rose the fastest, central city incomes also increased," he writes (1993, p. 24). For Cisneros, a former mayor of San Antonio, cities are vital to the nation's economic future, for "Not only are massive amounts of financial and physical capital invested in our cities, but nearly 80 percent of the American people live in metropolitan areas anchored by central cities, and more than 80 percent of the nation's jobs are located in these urban areas" (pp. 25–26).

Cisneros believes that urban social policy must attack the problems of central-city decay through such strategies as the creation of "empowerment zones" in which entrepreneurs who plan to bring new economic activity and jobs to the area receive tax and related benefits from local, state, and federal governments. He also advocates greater funding for programs to aid the shelter poor and homeless, as well as welfare reforms that will put the dependent poor to work rebuilding their communities.

For the present, however, Cisneros must be content to experiment with these policies in the face of persistent federal budget deficits and the Clinton administration's high priorities on health-care reform and deficit reduction. The 1995 federal budget calls for reductions in funds for public housing and low-income housing assistance in favor of emergency housing funds for the homeless. The budget also calls for greater investment in urban infrastructures and postpones large-scale policies to encourage inner-city economic development. But these are decisions based on the difficult choices made necessary by the federal budget deficit, rather than policies based on ideology. The administration believes that improvement in the conditions of life for inner-city residents is essential to the future security of the entire society. And there are sound economic and social reasons for this belief.

Throughout the nation residential land values in cities are significantly higher than in the suburbs, indicating that a central location is desirable to many people. Housing in the central cities, particularly in high-rise apartment complexes, is very expensive. The fact that a central location still has a high economic value is the best evidence that the central city can be restored. Indeed, many urban sociologists view restoration projects in central-city neighborhoods—such as Capitol Hill in Washington, D.C., Old Town and New Town in Chicago, Pioneer Square in Seattle, and Olympic Park in Atlanta—as indications of a revival of central-city life. Others are encouraged by the growth of luxury apartments and condominiums in and around the business districts of urban centers.

However, as noted earlier, the revitalization of neighborhoods by upper-middle-class people is not always beneficial to all concerned. In particular, the poor and the elderly are often victims of this trend as their apartment buildings are converted into condominiums or cooperatives and they come under intense pressure to leave homes and neighborhoods that they can no longer afford. Besides the return of the middle class, therefore, if today's cities are to be fully revitalized some of the businesses that departed for the suburbs will have to return.

To some extent this has happened already. Large regional capitals like New York, Boston, Louisville, Philadelphia, and Baltimore have undergone a transition to new industries based on light manufacturing of high-technology goods and the provision of new services, especially in the areas of finance, insurance, international trade, air freight, and research and development. The influx of new worker populations, often in higher-paying jobs, has stimulated leisure industries in these cities as well.

An example of the kind of redevelopment that is occurring in some urban centers is the Times Square project in New York City. This project has pooled funds from public and private sources to redevelop the Times Square area as a combined entertainment, wholesale marketing, and office complex. The project is controversial, however, because it has the potential to drive up rents in the area, thereby displacing low-income residents. Moreover, the plan calls for the preservation of the historic theaters on Forty-second Street, yet public support of the arts, including the theater, has decreased significantly in recent years. Without such support, it is unlikely that Times Square can be restored to its former glory as an entertainment district. In 1994 the Disney Corporation announced that it would open a major cultural development center in Times Square, a sign of the project's potential for eventual success. Nevertheless, in the view of some critics the Times Square project, like many other urban redevelopment plans, emphasizes the building of structures at the expense of the building of institutions (such as theater companies or musical production organizations) (Kornblum, 1988).

Policies and programs to address urban problems are hampered by state and federal deficits and decreasing tax revenues. The recession of the early 1990s hit urban America particularly hard. Real estate experts believe that the boom in downtown office construction has come to a halt as corporations have scaled back under the pressures of heavy debt, declining revenues, and the need to cut overhead (salaries, rent, contracts, and other expenses). In consequence, by 1993 there were almost 500 million square feet of vacant office space, much of it in newly constructed buildings. This glut of new offices severely strained the ability of banks and insurance companies, which finance office-building construction, to lend capital to other businesses; thus, it contributed to the banking crisis. That crisis, in turn, led to additional layoffs of white-collar workers and executives in the cities. As they lost their jobs and sought employment elsewhere, the revenues of urban governments decreased still further and the plight of the inner-city poor worsened.

Housing

During the 1980s the federal government eliminated or drastically reduced many programs that had provided housing assistance to American families for fifty years. The Reagan administration believed that the forces of supply and demand, operating independently of government incentives and subsidies, would meet the need for moderate- and low-income housing. In effect, this amounted to the lack of a housing policy at the federal level.

At the state and local levels, in contrast, some new initiatives emerged in the late 1980s and early 1990s. Local governments began setting up funds to provide housing assistance to low- and moderate-income families, encouraging private and public partnerships for developing low-cost housing and earmarking certain taxes (e.g., offshore oil taxes or real estate transfer taxes) to finance housing programs. These policies can be seen as part of the increased emphasis of many state governments on economic revitalization.

There is still a need for a strong federal housing policy, however. One reason is that the state and local efforts are uneven; some states, lacking a tradition of

Oliver Sacks, the award-winning psychiatrist and author whose research with the mentally ill was the basis for the movie *Awakenings*, is a firm believer in the need to reopen state mental-hospital wards to shelter the mentally ill homeless who now sleep on city streets, in parks and rail terminals, and in temporary shelters. These troubled people were supposed to be cared for in community mental-health centers, halfway houses, and group homes, but in too many cases they are not. To alleviate their suffering, he proposes making room for them in state hospitals, where they can obtain proper treatment.

On a related front, William J. Bennett, former director of the Bush administration's antidrug programs, advocates the creation of orphanages for children in drug-infested neighborhoods. "We may just have to . . . find some way to get children out of the environment which they're in, to go to orphanages, to go to Boys Town, to expand institutions like that, where they will be raised and nurtured," he declared in a speech to an antidrug organization (quoted in Kosterlitz, 1990, p. 2120).

Many sociologists support Bennett's view. Joyce A. Ladner, for example, has conducted extensive studies of foster care and adoption and notes that "we're seeing increasing numbers of children who are not getting adequate care and for whom adequate care is not an imminent possibility" (quoted in Kosterlitz, 1990, p. 2120). Society, she believes, must cease to believe blindly in an ideal family life that often does not match reality and put more children in group settings that offer safety and stability.

Those who oppose the movement toward reinstitutionalization warn of a return to the era of the "snake pit" and the grim, underfunded, understaffed orphanage. They point out that many mental hospitals and orphanages were shut down because they had become "dumping grounds" for society's most troubled and neglected members. The ideals of community care, patients' rights, and the "mainstreaming" of people with mental disabilities or histories of neglect may be threatened if society again resorts to the "warehousing" of its most problematic citizens. Advocates of community-based care believe that cities and towns need more support in their efforts to add to the insufficient number of small local care programs and facilities. They see the reinstitutionalization movement as a "return to the past."

What is a concerned citizen to think? On the one hand, respected medical professionals such as Sacks advocate a return to institutionalization. On the other hand, many experts continue to hold out hope for community-based care and mainstreaming. Yet these are not necessarily mutually exclusive policies. One could advocate an increase in well-funded and well-staffed orphanages and mental hospitals while at the same time pressing for more community-based facilities. The problem, of course, is that mental hospitals and community care facilities are competing for a dwindling supply of public and private funds. In the area of care for dependent children without parents, for example, the federal government now makes available about $256 million a year, but an estimated $1 billion a year is needed if real progress is to be made toward providing adequate care for needy children. Competing budget demands and the federal budget deficit make it unlikely that such funds will be provided.

government-sponsored social programs, have done little to address the housing problem. In addition, there are problems of competition and lack of coordination among the various public and private agencies involved in housing programs, and in some states there are no reliable data on the amount of housing being created and no means of evaluating housing needs in order to create a consistent housing policy.

Homelessness

In 1987 Congress passed the Stuart B. McKinney Homeless Assistance Act, which allocated hundreds of millions of dollars to house homeless people, and in 1988 the federal government initiated a $2 billion program to create emergency housing for the homeless in states and cities where the need is greatest. Both actions, though clearly necessary, are unlikely to address the long-term problems that have produced a serious lack of adequate housing for the poor. Shelters and temporary quarters need to be augmented; but without increased investment in low- and moderate-income housing, it is likely that gentrification, along with the "normal" calamities of arson and urban blight, will continue to add to the homeless population.

In addition to the need for shelter, there are special needs among the homeless that have only recently been recognized and addressed by policy makers. Foremost among these is the spread of AIDS. It is estimated that between 15 and 20 percent of shelter residents are infected with the AIDS virus and have such symptoms as diarrhea, weight loss, chronic fevers, and pneumonia. Although they account for a small proportion of the homeless population, they present a major problem because they need hospice care and cannot be integrated with the residents of public shelters. A similar situation exists with respect to the mentally ill, as we saw in Chapter 3. (Some experts believe that the mentally ill and homeless children should be cared for in institutions, a controversial proposal that is discussed in Box 15–1.)

Recent estimates by experts on homelessness such as Andrew Cuomo of the Department of Housing and Urban Development have placed the total number of homeless people far higher than the 600,000 estimated during previous administrations. It is now believed that as many as 7 million Americans may have experienced prolonged periods of homelessness in the late 1980s, and that this situation was caused not only by drug abuse and mental illness but also by poverty, racism, and cuts in government spending. According to HUD Secretary Cisneros, "Homelessness has become a structural problem in America: chronic, continuous, large scale, complex" (quoted in DeParle, 1994, p. A1). In an effort to address this massive social problem, the Department of Housing and Urban Development proposes to undertake an aggressive housing development program and to revise the McKinney Act so that services to homeless people would be delivered by nonprofit groups, rather than by federal or local governments (DeParle, 1994). As noted earlier, however, these efforts will be severely hampered by the lack of discretionary funds in the federal budget.

SUMMARY

1. Seventy-eight percent of Americans live and work in urban areas, densely settled areas where manufacturing, commerce, and other services are available. Even in more sparsely populated rural areas, the effects of urbanism are widespread.

2. Most urban growth has been caused by increasingly efficient transportation and communication and the effects of industrialization. Urban growth has stimulated technological advances, but it has also created problems of health and management, as well as a strong antiurban bias among a large proportion of the American public.

3. The population of cities today consists largely of descendants of immigrants from other countries and from rural areas of the United States. Today cities continue to receive large numbers of immigrants from other nations, and conflict between the newcomers and residents of older ghettos is frequent.

4. Residential segregation, both voluntary and involuntary, is common in urban areas. African Americans have experienced the highest and most persistent rates of segregation throughout the nation's history.

5. The three main theories of urbanism are the Wirthian theory, the compositional theory, and the subcultural theory. The Wirthian theory holds that cities increase the incidence of social and personality disorders because city dwellers must adapt to a multitude of intense stimuli. The compositional theory views the city as a mosaic of social worlds that protect individuals from the pressures of city life. The subcultural theory suggests that urban life promotes diverse subcultures.

6. Many urban areas are not single cities but what the Census Bureau terms *metropolitan statistical areas* and *consolidated metropolitan statistical areas*. The core areas of these urban centers are *primary metropolitan statistical areas*. The term *megalopolis* is often applied to a region that contains several metropolitan areas.

7. The growth of metropolitan areas has been associated with the development of new forms of transportation, including the streetcar, commuter railways, and especially the automobile. These hastened the trend toward suburbanization, which was also encouraged by urban renewal and highway construction programs and by federal programs encouraging home ownership.

8. As suburbs have grown, the central cities have decayed. A primary cause of that decay is deconcentration, the flight of middle-class families to the suburbs coupled with the influx of poor minority groups, the unemployed, and the aged to the central cities. Business and industry have also moved to the suburbs; in the cities, manufacturers have been replaced by establishments offering specialized goods and services. Unskilled or semiskilled jobs have been transferred to the suburbs and white-collar jobs in the cities are filled by skilled personnel, leaving unskilled central-city residents with fewer opportunities for employment.

9. The exodus of industry to the suburbs has significantly reduced the real estate tax base of most central cities. At the same time, the increase in the low-income population of the cities creates additional financial burdens. This situation has resulted in serious financial problems for large cities. Related to this problem is the deterioration of the infrastructure, or physical facilities, of many cities, which has been made even worse by natural calamities such as hurricanes, brush fires, and earthquakes. The financial problems of cities are exacerbated by the inequitable distribution of economic resources and costs between the cities and higher levels of government.

10. Housing is a major problem in the central cities. Many urban residents are shelter poor, meaning that they must pay so much for housing that they no longer have enough money for other necessities. Shelter poverty is most prevalent among the poor, who are forced to live in substandard, deteriorated housing. Urban renewal or redevelopment programs involve removing such housing, thereby displacing the poor, and replacing it with housing for people with higher incomes. Housing projects for the poor, on the other hand, quickly turn into slums.

11. *Gentrification,* the renovation of decaying neighborhoods by affluent residents, has also displaced poor city dwellers and added to the homeless population. This large and still-growing population has placed a heavy burden on public and private shelters and other social services in American cities.

12. Over the past twenty years there has been an increase in what social scientists call *neighborhood distress*. Distressed neighborhoods are characterized by high rates of poverty, joblessness, female-headed families, welfare recipiency, and teenage school dropouts. Such areas are also likely to be the ones with the highest rates of drug sales and addiction, violent crime, and housing abandonment.

13. Many of America's oldest cities are undergoing a process of revitalization as members of the upper middle class return, together with new industries. Nevertheless, there is still an urgent need for social policies to improve conditions of life in the inner cities. At present, however, programs designed to encourage economic activity and provide more public housing and services for the homeless cannot be undertaken on a large scale because of high federal budget deficits.

SUGGESTED READINGS

BRADBURY, KATHERINE L., ANTHONY DOWNS, and KENNETH E. SMALL. *Urban Decline and the Future of American Cities.* Washington, DC: Brookings Institution, 1982. An exhaustive comparative study of the nation's 153 largest cities that documents their decline along many dimensions and assesses the potential of public policies for reversing urban decline.

BRATT, RACHEL G. *Rebuilding a Low-Income Housing Policy.* Philadelphia: Temple University Press, 1989. An up-to-date review of U.S. housing policy, its failures and its successes, with recommendations for recommitting the nation to building low-cost housing.

CASTELLS, MANUEL, ED. *High Technology, Space, and Society.* Newbury Park, CA: Sage, 1985. A collection of highly original research studies and essays about how new technologies of communication, production, and transportation are reshaping the American urban landscape.

CISNEROS, HENRY G., ED. *Interwoven Destinies: Cities and the Nation.* New York: W. W. Norton, 1993. A valuable set of essays on urban social problems and likely policy directions in coming years.

FISCHER, CLAUDE S. *The Urban Experience.* Orlando: Harcourt Brace Jovanovich, 1976. A synthesis of research on urban places that defends the subcultural theory and challenges other theories of urban life.

HOWE, MARJORIE, and JAMES YOUNG. *The Faces of Homelessness.* Lexington, MA: D.C. Heath/Lexington Books, 1986. Firsthand observations of the lives of the homeless and of those who seek to remedy their plight. Documents the successes and failures of services intended to help the homeless and those who are at risk of joining their ranks.

LASKA, SHIRLEY BRADWAY, and DAPHNE SPAIN, EDS. *Back to the City: Issues in Neighborhood Renovation.* New York: Pergamon Press, 1980. A collection of articles that attempts to predict population and other changes that will occur in American cities.

LOGAN, JOHN R., and HARVEY L. MOLOTCH. *Urban Fortunes: The Political Economy of Place.* Berkeley: University of California Press, 1987. Views the development of cities in terms of local conflicts over growth and who will benefit from different conceptions of growth.

MOLLENKOPF, JOHN H. *The Contested City.* Princeton, NJ: Princeton University Press, 1983. A study of American urban politics that shows how conflict and politics have helped shape the modern city and its surrounding metropolitan region.

SCARGILL, D. I. *The Form of Cities.* New York: St. Martin's Press, 1980. A text on the organization and physical structure of cities.

SMITH, MICHAEL. *The City and Social Theory.* New York: St. Martin's Press, 1979. An analysis of the writings of five social theorists—Wirth, Freud, Simmel, Roszak, and Sennett—on the dehumanizing aspects of urban life.

WALLACE, SAMUEL E. *The Urban Environment.* Homewood, IL: Dorsey Press, 1980. A study of urban life that focuses on the interrelationships among population, organization, economy, and other factors, and their impact on individuals and society.

WILLIAMS, TERRY, and WILLIAM KORNBLUM. *The Kids Uptown: Struggle and Hope in the Projects.* New York: Putnam, 1994. An in-depth portrait of growing up in public housing and efforts to make such housing safe.

Population
and Immigration

Chapter Outline

- The world's population reached 5.4 billion in 1992.
- If the world's population continues to grow at the current rate, it will double in forty-five years.
- The United States uses about 10,321 kilograms of energy per person per year. The comparable figure for India is 311 kilograms.
- An estimated 500,000 females are missing from China's annual birth statistics.

In many parts of the United States, and in other nations as well, changes in population due to alterations in death or birth rates or patterns of immigration lead to major social problems. In the United States there is a low rate of natural population increase but a high rate of immigration. Immigration thus accounts for much (but by no means all) of the overall growth in the U.S. population. It is often difficult to assimilate new immigrants into American society. The newcomers require special education and health care and other services that may strain already tight municipal budgets. Yet, were it not for immigration, nations like the United States would experience growing labor shortages. Immigration also helps alleviate the effects of severe population pressure in other parts of the world. Indeed, in most nations the problem is not low rates of natural growth but high rates of reproduction and population growth.

THE WORLD POPULATION

Although humanity has flourished for more than 2 million years, the rapid and problematic rise in population that concerns us in this chapter is a feature of the last 300 years. The average population growth rate before 1650 is thought to have been about two-thousandths of a percent per year, and the world's population in that year is estimated to have been 500 million. Thereafter the rates and numbers leap: By 1900 the annual growth rate had reached fully half of 1 percent, and a billion people had been added to the world's population. Between 1900 and 1940 the rate rose to 1 percent; by 1960, to 2 percent. The numerical total reached 2.5 billion in 1950 and 5.4 billion in 1992. (See Figure 16–1.) If the world's population continues to grow at the current rate, it will double in a mere 45 years.

Measures of Population Growth

Before we discuss the significance of these figures, a few definitions are in order. A commonly used measure of population growth is the *crude birthrate*, or the number of births per 1,000 population. A crude birthrate of 20, for example, means that each year a given group of 1,000 people will produce 20 babies. This does not tell us what percentage of the population is of childbearing age, nor how many people can afford to raise children. It also does not tell us how long those 20 babies are likely to live—in particular, whether or not they will live long enough to produce children. Similarly, a crude death rate of 10 indicates only that among a group of 1,000 people 10 will die every year. Again, this figure tells us nothing about the distribution of deaths—whether they occurred among old people or people of childbearing age.

The differential between the (crude) birthrate and the death rate is called the *rate of population growth* or *natural increase* and is usually expressed as a percent.

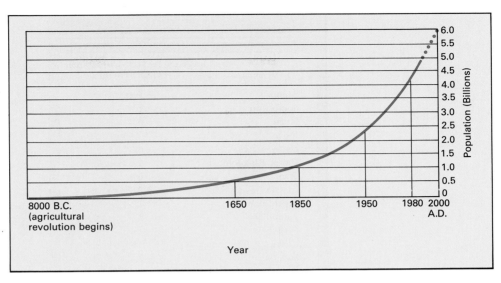

FIGURE 16–1 World Population Growth (8000 B.C. to A.D. 2000)

Source: Jean van der Tak, Carl Haub, and Elaine Murphy, *Population Bulletin,* Vol. 34, No. 5 (December 1979).

(Population growth is also affected by migration to and from the particular unit, a factor that can be discounted for the purposes of this discussion.) In our hypothetical 1,000-person group, in which 20 people were added by birth and 10 removed by death, the total population at the end of the year is 1,010—a rate of growth of 1 percent.

Taken as a whole, the peoples of the world are not reproducing at a higher rate than in the past, but more people are living to the age of fertility and beyond. In effect, more babies are surviving to produce babies themselves. This change is traceable to several causes: enormous advances in sanitation, disease control, and public health; our increased ability to compensate for excessive cold, heat, and other dangers to life in our environment; and our greater power to prevent or quickly counteract the effects of famine, drought, flood, and similar natural disasters.

Most nations have population growth rates of 0.1 to 3.0 percent, with the older, more industrialized nations grouped at the low end and the less developed nations at the high end. (See Table 16–1 on page 474.) If a nation's population growth rate is negative, more people are lost through death than are gained through birth and immigration, and the total population can be expected to decline over time. When a nation's population growth rate is 2 percent or more, as is true for many of the less developed nations, this is considered "explosive" population growth. If it were to continue unabated, such a growth rate would cause the population to double in thirty-five years or less. (A growth rate of 1 percent will cause a population to double in seventy years.) There is, however, new evidence from some sub-Saharan nations of a decline in fertility due to greater availability of contraceptives and increased education of women (Caldwell et al., 1992).

Clearly, all nations must attain population growth rates of less than 1 percent as soon as possible if the world is to avoid the wars, famines, and exhaustion of resources caused by overpopulation. For the less developed nations such low rates are unlikely to occur in the near future. We will see shortly, however, that the experience of the industrialized nations indicates that fertility can be controlled, even without large-scale use of contraception, and that in many of the wealthier nations of the

TABLE 16–1 CHANGES IN POPULATION, SELECTED COUNTRIES

COUNTRY	RATE OF NATURAL INCREASE (PERCENTAGE)
China	1.4
South Korea	1.0
Japan	0.4
India	2.1
United States	0.8
United Kingdom	0.2
France	0.4
Nigeria	2.9
Argentina	1.3
Philippines	2.6
Peru	2.4
Kenya	3.8
Mexico	2.4
Sudan	2.9
Brazil	1.9

Source: Population Reference Bureau, *1990 World Population Data Sheet* (Washington, D.C.: Population Reference Bureau, Inc., 1990).

world fertility rates have actually declined to levels below that required to replace their population (Davis et al., 1987).

Russia seems to be developing an unusual case of potential population decline. In 1990 an average of 2.2 children were born to each woman, but since then this figure has fallen to slightly more than 1.4. In addition, the declining economy and other social problems have led to a dramatic increase in the death rate. In 1994 deaths in Russia exceeded births by nearly 800,000, making Russia the first industrial country to experience a sharp population decrease for reasons other than war, famine, and disease (Specter, 1994).

The Demographic Transition

The figures on world population growth presented earlier reflect a basic fact: Lower death rates are closely associated with the spread of technological change and higher living standards. These constitute part of a process known as the *demographic transition*, in which a population shifts from an original equilibrium in which a high birthrate is more or less canceled out by a high death rate, through a stage in which the birthrate remains high but the death rate declines, to a final equilibrium in which the birth and death rates are lower but the population is much larger. The first stage is characteristic of peasant and primitive populations before large-scale improvement in sanitation, health care, and the like. This is followed by a period characterized by rapid population growth as traditional values regarding family size, together with the lack of birth control techniques, keep the birthrate high while technological advances produce a steady decrease in the death rate, especially for infants. In the final stage, which is characteristic of industrialized societies, values change, the birthrate declines, and rates of natural increase slow.

The demographic transition first occurred in northwestern Europe. During a period of about 100 years in the eighteenth and nineteenth centuries, death rates decreased by about 60 percent while birthrates remained at their traditional high levels. Then, toward the end of the nineteenth century, fertility began a long-term decline. Figure 16–2 illustrates this process in the case of Sweden.

Wherever industrial technology has taken hold on a local level, the third stage of the demographic transition has followed—from northwestern Europe to North America, Australia, and New Zealand, and later through the rest of Europe. Today the populations of Japan, Singapore, Taiwan, Hong Kong, and two or three other such areas have reached the final phase, and they have tended to reach it much more quickly (in about thirty years) than the northern European nations did.

On the other hand, large areas of Asia, Africa, and Latin America remain in the middle phase, with sustained high birthrates and reduced death rates. In this century, and very dramatically since World War II, the amazingly effective adoption of Western methods in medicine and public health on a mass basis, usually involving international aid programs, has resulted in a rapid decline in mortality.

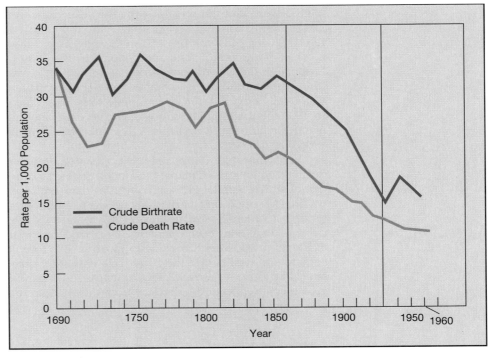

FIGURE 16–2   Crude Birth and Death Rates for Sweden, 1691–1963

Source: Matras, 1973. Courtesy Armand Colin Éditeur, Paris.

Note: This chart exemplifies the classic demographic transition, in which death and birth rates eventually become more or less equal and the rate of population growth stabilizes. Many less developed nations have birth and death rates similar to those in the center of the chart, where crude death rates are declining rapidly and birthrates remain high—a formula for population explosion.

Within a span of about twenty-five years death rates fell from approximately 40 per 1,000 to 20 or less per 1,000. But fertility remains high, often over 40 per 1,000, and the growth rate reaches 3 percent in some places. Adults live longer, and more of the young survive to have children; there are no new frontier lands to draw off excess population. In these societies population growth often outstrips economic and social development; poverty and social unrest are frequent consequences of this situation.

Several nations that are still in the middle phase of the demographic transition border the United States on the south. Among them are the countries of the Caribbean and Central America, Mexico, Haiti, the Dominican Republic, and Puerto Rico. The inhabitants of these nations are simultaneously subject to the stresses of overpopulation and the influence of American popular culture through television and mass consumer markets. Not only are these countries poor, but they are often ruled by violent and repressive regimes—all of which produces migration to the United States. Currently the United States admits about 800,000 immigrants annually, an increase from about 600,000 in the late 1980s and a direct result of the 1986 Immigration and Reform Control Act, which established higher immigration quotas. (The implications of this increase will be discussed later in the chapter.) The United States remains a land of opportunity for immigrants because of its slow rate of growth. Here, except for the "baby boom" during and after World War II, births have outpaced deaths only to a modest degree.

The birthrate in the industrialized nations had begun to drop before the institution of organized family planning programs. The organized programs have certainly accelerated the process, however, especially in the United States: They have made information and contraceptives more widely available; they have worked to repeal laws against the use of contraceptives; and they have influenced opinion in favor of birth control. Thus, in contrast to the 1800 figure of about 55, the crude birthrate in the United States stood at 16 in 1990. In the 1970s the *total fertility rate* (the average number of children born per woman throughout the childbearing years) fell below 2.1, the rate required to maintain the population at the same level. In 1800 the total fertility rate was 7.0, an extremely high rate that reflected the demand for farm labor and the high value placed on having many children (Davis, 1986; Preston, 1986).

In his thorough analysis of low population growth rates in the non-European industrialized nations (Canada, the United States, Japan, Australia, and New Zealand), demographer Samuel Preston concludes that "the recent fall in fertility is related to declining proportions married, increased use of contraception and abortion, and a reduction in family size desires" (1987, p. 44). Of these factors, Preston identifies delay or indefinite postponement of marriage as the most important. He finds, for example, that low fertility came to Japan well before the widespread use of contraception and well before the large-scale entry of women into the labor market. The critical factor was postponement of marriage—Japanese parents were obliging their grown children to delay marriage until they had accumulated the resources to support a child or two.

Rising Expectations

Not only do people in less developed and politically troubled countries look to the United States as a land of opportunity and therefore attempt to migrate here in order to improve their situation, but in the less developed countries (LDCs) themselves there has been considerable improvement in the living standards of a portion of the population. This improvement has led to a state of mind known as "rising expectations," the belief that if conditions have already begun to improve, the trend

In many rural parts of the world, television contributes to the villagers' rising expectations for material well-being.

will continue and a larger portion of the population should be able to share in its benefits.

This process began in the late 1950s and early 1960s, when many LDCs, particularly in sub-Saharan Africa and Southeast Asia, gained independence from the former colonial powers (Geertz, 1963). Turning their attention to efforts to improve the lives of their generally isolated, rural populations, governments embarked on campaigns for favorable terms of trade and direct aid from the developed nations. Ever-greater sums were invested in education, health care, transportation, and communication. These investments ultimately resulted in changing expectations among the populations of the LDCs as newly educated and healthier multitudes were exposed to the media and all the information about culture and standard of living that they convey.

It is important to distinguish between the *standard of living* of a population, which is what people want or expect in the way of material well-being, and the *level of living*, which is what people actually obtain. In many less developed countries and many nations of the former Soviet bloc, there is a wide gap between standard of living and level of living, and this gap produces much frustration and political instability. These problems make economic and social development in the poor regions of the world even more problematic.

Literacy rates are a good indicator of the likelihood that poor and powerless populations may be rapidly gaining a new perspective on their situation. Illiteracy has been decreasing steadily, from an estimated 32.5 percent of the total world population in 1970 to 28 percent in 1980 and about 25 percent in 1990 (U.S. Census Bureau, 1990). These figures, of course, do not show the tremendous disparities in literacy that persist. For example, Cuba enjoys a 96 percent literacy rate and Chile's literacy rate is 93.4 percent, whereas the figure for Egypt is 48.4 percent. India's literacy rate is 48.2 percent, and Pakistan's is 25.6 percent (*Brittanica Book of the Year,* 1992).

While literacy and the wide-ranging awareness that it fosters have increased, mushrooming populations have tended to more than absorb the sums devoted to their well-being, creating a significant lag in the fulfillment of their rising expectations. Per capita energy consumption serves as a good indicator of the quality of life in a population, and by this measure stark disparities among the world's peoples remain: The United States, by far the world's largest consumer of energy, uses about 10,321 kilograms of energy per person per year (expressed in coal equivalent), as compared to France (3,870), Mexico (1,751), the United Kingdom (5,049), Colombia (790), and India (311) (*Statistical Abstract,* 1993). The extremely high U.S. rate reflects the basic nature of American industry, transportation, and housing. The typical middle-class, generally suburban, American lifestyle presumes considerable use of gasoline, as well as the consumption of extremely large quantities of paper, steel, synthetic chemicals, aluminum, and so forth, all of which require high levels of energy for their production.

The fact is that the gaps in living standards between the have and have-not societies have actually widened. In such a situation, rising expectations are associated with a wide spectrum of social problems, including political instability and backwardness, neocolonialism, and terrorism, as well as renewed international migrations by the poor. This is especially true in the heavily indebted nations of Asia, Africa, and Latin America.

THE U.S. POPULATION

Current trends in the U.S. population may be summarized in terms of three striking features: slow growth, population redistribution, and increasing immigration. In 1800 the country's crude birthrate may have been as high as 55, but it soon declined, reaching a low of 18 in the 1930s, before the World War II baby boom. After another low point in the 1970s, the birthrate began rising again. The total fertility rate reached 3.7 between 1955 and 1957 and fell to 1.8 in 1976, well below the 2.1 rate needed for the population to replace itself, assuming current death rates (Hauser, 1980). While fertility among whites alone was even lower than 1.8 during this period, the rate for ethnic and racial minority groups was 2.3 (U.S. Census Bureau, 1980). Present population growth is due mainly to the result of the baby boom—the number of people of reproductive age, who were born just after the war, is now quite high.

Slow population growth means that people's hopes can still be high, and many migrate in search of new opportunities. Recent decades have seen increased migration to the Sunbelt and western states. In 1950, for example, 26 percent of the nation lived in the Northeast and 13 percent lived in the West. By 1990 these percentages had shifted to 20 and 21 percent, respectively. In every area, in addition, there has been movement out of the central cities to the suburbs and beyond. This is true for all races, but much more so for whites, who have left blacks and other minority groups disproportionately represented in the older central cities.

Another significant change in the U.S. population in recent years is the increase in age and income disparities between "old" and "new" ethnic groups. The median incomes of Russian, Polish, and Italian Americans are among the highest in the nation, whereas those of Spanish-speaking groups, especially Puerto Ricans, are the lowest. Conversely, among the "old" ethnic groups the proportion of members under 18 years of age is lowest, while the Spanish-speaking groups have the highest proportion of members under 18 (U.S. Census Bureau, 1990). What this means is that the fastest-growing ethnic minorities in the United States are also among the poorest segments of the population.

Finally, slow growth has been a factor in the dramatic persistence of immigration to the United States. As noted earlier, immigration is the primary source of population growth in the United States, and differences in fertility between old and new ethnic groups have a significant impact on the composition of the population. Immigration also raises a number of complex policy issues, as will become clear later in the chapter.

POPULATION CONTROL

Efforts to control population growth can take any of three basic approaches: (1) Reduce the rate of growth of the population; (2) control fertility so as to achieve a zero rate of population growth; or (3) achieve a negative rate of growth and thus reduce the size of the population. Obviously, all three of these approaches involve reducing the birthrate. However, even when it is agreed that limiting births is necessary, there is much less agreement on how fast and to what extent such limits should be imposed—indeed, on whether or not they should be imposed at all (i.e., whether limits on family size should be voluntary or involuntary). Efforts to limit births raise a number of moral and ethical questions, but the costs of not making such efforts could be catastrophic.

Family Planning

Voluntary efforts to limit births customarily take the form of family planning. Essentially, a family planning program allows couples to have the number of children they want. Although this policy usually entails helping couples limit childbearing, it can also involve helping couples who want children and have been unable to have them. The stress is usually placed on the good of the family—especially the health of the mother and children and the ability to provide education and other desired advantages.

In the United States, the family planning movement owes much to the energy and dedication of a nurse named Margaret Sanger. Sanger hoped to free women from the burdens of unlimited childbearing. In 1916 she opened the nation's first birth control clinic (and was jailed for doing so). Later court decisions permitted physicians to prescribe birth control for health reasons; these were the first in a series of decisions that permitted the sale and advertisement of contraceptive materials and the dissemination of information about birth control. By 1965 some 85 percent of married women in the United States had used some method of birth control (Ehrlich, Ehrlich, & Holdren, 1977).

Table 16–2 shows that over the seventeen-year period from 1965 to 1982, American women learned to practice increasingly more effective forms of birth control. The table shows an astounding increase in sterilization among married women (from 12.4 percent in 1965 to 41 percent in 1982)—usually by means of an operation known as tubal ligation (tying the fallopian tubes so that egg cells cannot descend into the uterus during menses). It also shows a decrease in women's reliance on birth control pills, diaphragms, and the noncontraceptive and more risky methods of rhythm and withdrawal. The rise in voluntary sterilizations

TABLE 16–2   CHANGES IN USE OF BIRTH CONTROL METHODS AMONG MARRIED WOMEN, UNITED STATES

BIRTH CONTROL METHOD	PERCENTAGE OF MARRIED WOMEN AGED 15–44 PRACTICING EACH METHOD, 1965	PERCENTAGE OF MARRIED WOMEN AGED 15–44 PRACTICING EACH METHOD, 1982
Rhythm	10.8	4.7
Withdrawal	5.7	1.7
Condom	22.0	14.4
Foam	3.3	2.9
Douching	5.0	0.2
Diaphragm	9.9	6.7
IUD	1.2	7.1
Pill	23.9	19.8
Sterilization	12.4	41.0
Other	5.8	1.5
Total	**100.0**	**100.0**

Source: Reprinted with permission of the Population Council from Samuel H. Preston, "The decline of fertility in non-European industrialized countries," *Population and Development Review,* Supplement to vol. 12 (1986), 41.

represents both the gradual aging of the population, such that more women are choosing to end their reproductive years, and the desire of many women to be the sole arbiters of their reproductive lives. Increasing numbers of men are also choosing sterilization.

Although it is not stated directly, the "other" figures in the table are a measure of the frequency of abortion as a form of birth control. Note that as women (and their mates) have learned to use more effective birth control techniques, the rate of legal abortions has dropped dramatically. This is indicated by the decrease in the "other" category from 5.8 percent to 1.5 percent, but it is also shown in data from other medically advanced nations. The rate of voluntary abortions is decreasing steadily as women (or couples) choose more effective and less psychologically stressful means of controlling their fertility.

ZPG

In 1968, in response to widespread concern about population growth, an organization known as Zero Population Growth, Inc. (ZPG) was founded. Its goal was to promote an end to population growth as soon as possible through lowered birthrates, both in the United States and in other nations. It would achieve this goal by educating the public about the dangers of uncontrolled population growth and by taking political action to encourage policies favoring reduced population growth.

ZPG has been active in promoting access to birth control and legalized abortion, and it has had a definite effect on attitudes toward family size and population control. However, the organization has encountered some opposition on social and economic grounds. It is argued, for example, that halting population growth would greatly change the age composition of the population, creating a larger proportion of older people and thereby adding to the problems of an already overburdened society. Moreover, a nongrowing population implies a nongrowing economy, and it is often assumed that a continually growing economy is necessary for the maintenance of a high standard of living.

It should be noted that family planning and population control are not synonymous. Family planning has historically dealt with the needs of individuals and families, not those of societies. Kingsley Davis (1971) has pointed out some fundamental weaknesses of the family planning approach as a means of large-scale population control. Chief among these is its basic assumption that the number of children couples want is the number they should have. In a poor country with a growth rate of 3 percent per year, a family of five or six children, which is probably desired by most couples, will be anything but desirable for the economic health of the country—or for the family's own chances of economic betterment. In addition, the strongly medical emphasis of the usual family planning program can limit its large-scale effectiveness, particularly in developing countries, where doctors and nurses are usually scarce.

Population Control in LDCs

In less developed countries, efforts at population control have, in a few rare but instructive cases, made use of compulsory methods of birth control. One such method is sterilization of parents who have had a specified number of children. India adopted such a plan in 1976, with financial incentives to encourage volunteers and, in some states, fines and other penalties for births after the third child (Visaria & Visaria, 1981). In one year more than 8 million sterilizations were performed. As might be expected, this program met with great resistance. Although no one disputed the need to curb the rate of population growth, the Indian government was severely criticized for what was considered a compulsory, rather than a strictly voluntary, policy; in fact, the policy contributed to the defeat of the government of Indira Gandhi.

Many Asian nations have entered the low-growth phase of the demographic transition. In China, however, strict measures designed to discourage couples from having more than one child are highly controversial.

China's population program differs in some important ways from that of any other country. China, whose population is now more than 1 billion, has adopted a one-child-per-family policy for urban dwellers; the goal is a 40 percent reduction in population size by 2050. Couples are strongly urged not to have more than one child unless both parents were only children themselves, and birth control information and material are readily available. At the same time, the bearing and rearing of children are supported through such policies as paid maternity leave, time off for breast-feeding, free nursery care, and all needed medical attention (Ehrlich, Ehrlich, & Holdren, 1977).

This far-reaching policy has already slowed China's population growth significantly, but not without enormous social consequences. Political unrest has increased in the cities, where the policy is far more easily implemented than in the countryside. Far worse, recent studies of the policy's effects indicate that couples are seeking ways to determine the gender of unborn infants so that they can abort female fetuses. The traditional culture of China favors boys over girls to such a degree that many couples believe that they must have a male child at all costs. While no one knows exactly how many female infants are aborted or killed, and some Chinese authorities dispute Western analyses of the situation, the fact remains that the excess of recorded live male births over female births is far greater in China than in any other society. This suggests that various forms of abortion, infanticide, and secret adoptions are occurring. Demographers who have studied the situation closely believe that about half of the estimated 500,000 females missing from the annual birth statistics may have been secretly adopted by foreigners via illicit adoption agencies, but no one knows the fate of the others. Clearly, these are serious, even if unintended, consequences of China's drastic population reduction policy (Johannson & Nygren, 1991).

Nothing as drastic as China's population control policy has ever been attempted before (except in cases of war or genocide), and only a nation with a very authoritarian and highly controlled population can successfully implement such a policy. Thus, for the time being, voluntary birth control seems to be a more realistic—and more desirable—approach to population control in LDCs. Indeed, family planning programs are the primary form of population control in most such countries, sometimes supplemented by other social and economic policies. The main thrust of these programs is the provision of birth control information along with education programs demonstrating the economic benefits of smaller families. Many such programs are directed toward women who have already borne three or more children.

In 1987 the Population Institute, reflecting the views of many professional demographers, recommended a worldwide program of contraception, counseling, and education. Pointing out that "whenever there has been political commitment and where facilities have been available, population rates have come down" (Fornos, quoted in *New York Times*, April 20, 1987), the Institute called upon the United States to take a leadership role in promoting family planning. Nevertheless, the Reagan administration remained firmly opposed to population control policies. During the 1980s the United States greatly reduced its contributions to countries and agencies that conduct family planning programs. Other Western nations have also become less interested in population control as their own fertility rates have declined, and some, including France and some Scandinavian countries, have actually instituted policies that encourage couples to have more children, such as tax deductions for children and subsidies for families with more than two children (Brown, 1990; McIntosh, 1987).

More recently there has been renewed interest in family planning and contraception in Europe and throughout the Western Hemisphere. Research in Kenya and a few other African nations indicates that widespread availability of condoms, as well as increased efforts to educate young women, are resulting in significant reductions in birthrates independently of economic development or urbanization

(Caldwell et al., 1992). On the other hand, the 1994 International Conference on Population and Development, held in Cairo and sponsored by the United Nations, revealed how much division remains over population issues. For example, women's groups in the Arab nations and elsewhere have gone on record as opposing population policies that do not call for more economic opportunities and education for women, while representatives of Catholic nations argue for greater emphasis on economic development and the responsibilities of the rich nations toward the poorer ones (Pope John Paul II, 1991).

IMMIGRATION AND ITS CONSEQUENCES

Throughout the world people from poor nations dream of moving to the richer nations. Most often they do not wish to uproot themselves entirely but hope to be temporary sojourners in the richer nation, working at the better-paying jobs that are said to be available there. If they can save and send money home, they may someday be able to return to a better life in their homeland.

Immigration to the United States has reached levels unmatched since early in this century. But the movement of people from poor to richer lands is occurring elsewhere as well. In Germany and France there has been an influx of people from the poorer nations to the south, especially Turkey and the nations of North Africa. In the Middle East there has been a great movement of temporary workers from Egypt to the richer and underpopulated nations of Saudi Arabia and Kuwait. Before the 1991 war in that region, many of the immigrant workers in these nations were Palestinians or Yemenites. In Japan there are Korean immigrants, and in Australia one finds immigrants from many Asian nations. But the United States leads the world in the number of immigrants entering the country.

It is often said that the United States is a nation of immigrants. Since the earliest days of European settlement, North America has attracted people from all over the world. Some, like the black slaves from Africa, were brought against their will. Many other groups came in search of new opportunities and freedom from oppression. Over two centuries the tides of immigration brought people of different races, different religions, different cultures, and different political views to these shores. This diversity of peoples has become one of the most important aspects of American culture. Tolerance of differences, struggles against racial oppression, arguments about the assimilation of immigrants, the variety of diet and dress and music among Americans—all can be traced to the unique contributions of people of many different national origins and cultures.

But immigration has also contributed to some of the social problems plaguing American society. Beginning with the exclusion of the Native Americans from their original lands, immigration has led to ethnic and racial conflict; competition among nationality groups for a "piece of the pie"; debates about immigration policy, illegal immigration, and the presence of illegal aliens who can be exploited; and the stresses and costs associated with educating and caring for new immigrants. These and other issues can become severe social problems when they are not addressed in a timely fashion. To better understand why this is so, we begin with a summary of the major periods of immigration to the United States.

Immigration to the United States: A Brief History

The Early Colonial Period (to 1790)   During the Colonial period the major population groups in North America other than Native Americans were people from Great Britain, who accounted for 77 percent of the total population. African and native-born slaves of African origin accounted for 19 percent, German immigrants for

4 percent, Irish immigrants for 3 percent, and Dutch immigrants for 2 percent (Bogue, 1984). There were many other immigrant groups in the population, but their numbers were much smaller.

Old Northwest European Migration, 1820–1885 Large-scale immigration to the new nation known as the United States began again in 1820 and was dominated by people from England and other areas of northwestern Europe until about 1885. In this wave of immigrants the largest groups came from northern and western Europe, especially Germany, Ireland, and England. The proportion of immigrants from Ireland reached high levels in the 1840s and 1850s as a result of severe famine and economic catastrophes in Ireland. German immigration reached a peak in the years after 1848, when popular revolutions in Germany failed and many Germans sought asylum or greater political freedom in the United States.

The most significant nonwhite immigrant group during this period was the Chinese, many of whom settled on the West Coast or in the Rocky Mountain states, along with a smaller number of Japanese immigrants. Many of the Chinese immigrants were brought in under labor contracts, having been sought out by labor contractors seeking low-wage workers for the construction of railroads.

The "Intermediate" Migration from Southern and Eastern Europe (1885–1940) As a result of political upheavals in Europe due to the breakup of the Austro-Hungarian and Ottoman Empires, many thousands of people from southern and eastern Europe found their way to the United States. The major immigrant groups during this period were Italians, Poles, Hungarians, Serbians, Croatians, Greeks, and Jews from all of these nations and from Russia. During this period waves of nativist feeling (anti-immigrant or antiforeigner sentiment) swept across sections of the United States. Among other things, nativism gave rise to the oriental exclusion movement, which flourished between 1882 and 1907 and resulted in sporadic violence against Chinese and Japanese Americans and the passage of legislation in some states forbidding further immigration of people from Asia.

At the same time, however, large numbers of Mexican immigrants began streaming into the Southwest, the West, and portions of the Midwest. These immigrants often joined relatives and friends in parts of California and the Southwest where Mexicans had been living long before these regions became part of the United States.

During this period Congress passed the Immigration Act of 1921, which for the first time in American history established quotas and strict controls over the admission of new immigrants, imposing an overall quota of 150,000 per year. Before 1921 there had been no specific limits on immigration to the United States, and well over 20 million immigrants had arrived since the early nineteenth century.

The Post–World War II Refugee Period (to 1968) By the end of World War II, hundreds of thousands of people in European nations had lost their homes and property and many were refugees. Some, like Jews and Roman Catholic activists, were fleeing religious persecution. In 1945 Congress agreed to admit 185,000 immigrants per year, many of whom would be European refugees.

The "New" Immigration (1968–Present) In 1968 Congress again voted to increase immigration quotas, establishing totals of 170,000 per year from the Eastern Hemisphere and 120,000 from the Western Hemisphere. Priority would be given to immigrants who were political or religious refugees or who had close relatives living in the United States. (This is known as the principle of family unification.) In 1980 Congress increased the overall quota to 280,000 per year, not including

The first photo, taken around 1900, shows immigrants waiting to leave Ellis Island after many hours of screening and processing. In an effort to modernize its procedures, the U.S. Immigration and Naturalization Service is testing a new system in which processing will take place before arrival in the United States and each new immigrant will be issued a pass that resembles a credit card.

additional refugees and special categories that might be designated in the future (e.g., the *marielitos,* former political prisoners from Cuba). The increases in immigration quotas in recent decades have given rise to a new pattern of immigration to the United States, with the largest flows of people coming from Asia and Latin America.

Recent Trends in Immigration to the United States

Figure 16–3 shows that since the 1970s the rate of legal immigration to the United States has accelerated. The major cause of this trend has been the gradual liberalization of immigration laws, which have set increasingly larger annual quotas. From an annual total of slightly under 400,000 people in 1970, the United States is now receiving more than 800,000 immigrants each year.

Between 1961 and 1990 approximately 6 million new immigrants came to settle in the United States. Of these, by far the largest share came from Asia (especially China, India, Taiwan, and Korea) and North America (especially Mexico, the Caribbean islands, and Canada). (See Figure 16–4.) In the 1990s an average of almost 800,000 people per year will be admitted, for a total of 8 million during the decade. Although this is an extremely large absolute number, compared to the total U.S. population of over 250 million it represents less than a 3 percent addition over ten years. And this is added to a population that, taken in its entirety, is not growing very much as a result of natural increase.

Even though immigration adds relatively small increments to the U.S. population, it leads to a variety of social problems. One of the outstanding effects of current patterns of immigration is that it is adding significantly to the proportion of racial and ethnic minorities in the nation's population. The 1990 census revealed that the racial and ethnic composition of the population changed more drastically during the 1980s than at any time during this century. In 1980 about one in five Americans claimed African, Asian, Hispanic, or American Indian ancestry. By 1990 that figure had jumped to one in four, with the greatest proportion of the increase caused by the rapid increase in Latino immigration in recent years.

Neither the increase in immigration nor the specific composition of the immigrant population is a social problem in itself. But there are groups within American society that oppose immigration and are hostile toward immigrants, and the resulting conflicts and tensions can be a problem for immigrant groups and for the regions or cities that receive them. More important, not all immigrants arrive in this na-

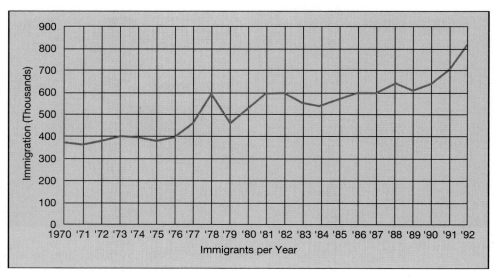

FIGURE 16–3   Legal Immigration to the United States, 1970–1992

Source: Data from *Statistical Abstract,* 1993; U.S. Department of Justice, 1993.

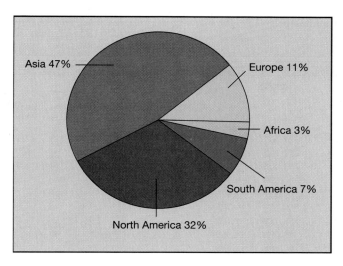

FIGURE 16–4   Sources of Immigration to the United
States (as percent of total)

Source: U.S. Immigration and Naturalization Service, 1990.

tion with legal status. The presence of illegal aliens, or undocumented immigrants, is one of the most severe social problems associated with immigration. In the remainder of this section, therefore, we will consider the social problems caused by the uneven distribution of immigrants in the United States and the special problems of undocumented immigrants.

Urban Concentration of Immigrants

The vast majority of the immigrants who arrive in the United States tend to remain in only a few cities and regions. New York, Los Angeles, Miami, Chicago, and their metropolitan regions are the preferred destinations of almost half of the nation's immigrants. (See Table 16–3 on page 488.) Mexican immigrants tend to congregate in the Southwest and Vietnamese immigrants in Texas, but the major urban centers of the West and East Coasts absorb far more than their proportional share of new immigrants.

   The concentration of new immigrants in a few metropolitan regions greatly adds to the problems of both immigrants and nonimmigrants in those areas. Concentration of immigrants, especially Spanish- and Chinese-speaking newcomers, leads to the formation of large non–English-speaking enclaves where education becomes a problem and the economic and social assimilation of the newcomers may create difficulties for native-born citizens. Increasingly frequent attacks against immigrants and members of minority groups and the rise of "nativist" and anti-immigrant feelings in many parts of the United States are another consequence of the concentration of immigrants in certain localities.

   The phenomenon of *chain migration* is the primary cause of this urban concentration. This term refers to the tendency of immigrants to migrate to areas where they have kin and others from their home communities. While there may be opportunities for them in nearby cities and towns, they often do not move to those places because everyone who shares their culture and language or dialect, and can help them adjust to their new social environment, may be found in the

TABLE 16–3   IMMIGRANTS ADMITTED, BY SELECTED COUNTRY OF BIRTH AND METROPOLITAN AREA OF INTENDED RESIDENCE, 1991

METROPOLITAN AREA OF INTENDED RESIDENCE	TOTAL[a]	MEXICO	PHILIP-PINES	SOVIET UNION	VIET-NAM	HAITI	EL SAL-VADOR	INDIA	DOMINI CAN-REPUBLIC	CHINA: MAIN-LAND
Total[b]	1,827,167	946,167	63,596	56,980	55,307	47,527	47,351	45,064	41,405	33,025
Los Angeles-Long Beach, CA PMSA	257,160	153,918	12,147	877	5,156	55	16,111	2,565	45	3,626
New York, NY PMSA	163,006	3,824	3,421	17,708	786	8,141	1,545	7,368	21,309	8,964
Chicago, IL PMSA	60,590	30,960	2,546	2,641	767	203	280	3,409	63	1,023
San Diego, CA MSA	59,329	47,035	3,548	381	1,683	3	185	193	9	309
Anaheim-Santa Ana, CA PMSA	59,015	40,778	1,526	147	5,366	1	861	783	3	502
Miami-Hialeah, FL PMSA	58,918	5,192	267	370	73	15,996	1,070	243	1,724	152
Houston, TX PMSA	53,690	34,388	673	290	2,518	31	5,294	1,281	79	362
Riverside-San Bernardino, CA PMSA	50,608	42,150	1,324	186	550	6	804	416	15	157
Dallas, TX PMSA	39,352	28,783	275	380	1,177	14	2,145	699	14	210
Washington, DC-MD-VA MSA	36,370	2,807	1,186	423	2,611	339	5,320	1,653	371	742
Fresno, CA MSA	33,033	28,198	157	207	102	3	731	449	—	53
San Francisco, CA PMSA	29,989	7,254	3,702	2,111	1,096	42	1,726	431	9	4,068
San Jose, CA PMSA	28,942	12,233	2,463	471	4,640	3	332	1,774	3	962
Oakland, CA PMSA	24,416	9,093	2,941	368	1,309	5	493	1,391	9	1,667
Boston-Lawrence-Salem-Lowell-Brockton, MA NECMA	21,922	341	306	2,067	1,458	3,240	493	839	1,582	1,083
Phoenix, AZ MSA	21,027	17,184	193	80	623	2	191	144	3	160
Visalia-Tulare-Porterville, CA MSA	17,874	16,874	217	1	4	—	110	71	—	17
Oxnard-Ventura, CA PMSA	17,144	14,961	575	27	148	—	159	123	2	60
Bakersfield, CA MSA	17,008	15,169	516	10	33	—	451	201	1	11
Newark, NJ PMSA	16,909	226	636	689	253	2,035	395	872	529	259

—Represents zero.

[a]Includes other counties, not shown separately.

[b]Includes other metropolitan areas, not shown separately.

Note: The large number of Mexican immigrants in Los Angeles and other areas of Southern California includes hundreds of thousands of people who had resided there for many years but only recently assumed legal immigrant status under the 1986 Immigration and Reform Control Act. The act granted legal status to some 3.6 million immigrants who were residing in the United States without proper documentation at the time of the bill's passage.

Source: Statistical Abstract, 1993.

place of original settlement. Thus, in 1988, 16,341 immigrants from the Dominican Republic settled in New York City, joining many thousands who had arrived there before them. In nearby Philadelphia, in contrast, fewer than 400 Dominicans arrived during the same year.

The uneven distribution of immigrants and their tendency to become concentrated in a few large cities greatly adds to the costs of education and health care in those cities. Since many immigrants arrive without any form of health insurance and do not speak English well enough to qualify for employment, schools and adult education programs are taxed to the maximum in attempting to meet their needs. These expenses of the cities are not usually compensated for by the federal government, even though the entry of immigrants is regulated by federal legislation.

Increased immigration results in the development of new ethnic communities in the cities where immigrants arrive in large numbers. Shown here is "Little Hong Kong" in Flushing, New York, a point of entry for many immigrants from the Far East.

A problem that affects the immigrants in these urban centers is the intense competition and, at times, direct hostility they encounter from nonimmigrants or immigrants who have lived in those cities for long periods. In the case of the Koreans, for example, their propensity to open businesses (especially wig stores, fruit and vegetable stores, and other retail businesses) often leads them to buy stores in segregated minority communities, where they are able to find businesses at a cost they can afford. They thus become a new ethnic and racial group in those communities. Often they encounter anger and hostility from residents who believe that the Koreans are not sensitive to their needs and their local culture (Kim, 1981).

This is a theme explored by the African American filmmaker Spike Lee in his movie *Do the Right Thing*. Elsewhere in the nation, along the Gulf coast of Texas, where Vietnamese shrimp fishermen have come into conflict with native-born fishermen, or in the Southwest, where Mexican immigrants are often discriminated against by earlier settlers, the difficulties of life as a stranger in a strange land are amplified by prejudice and violence.

In response to the hostility they often encounter, children and adolescents in the newcomer groups often form defensive gangs. Those who do not wish to join gangs may be isolated and considered deviant by their peers. But some immigrant groups, notably the Chinese and Koreans, attempt to shelter their children from the problems of urban street life by imposing on them a strict set of values and high expectations for achievement in school (Caplan et al., 1989). Children of Asian immigrants make rapid strides in American schools, often achieving the highest honors in their high schools and on standardized achievement tests. Indeed, the school achievement of Asian Americans is now so high that many of the brightest Asian students have come to believe that they are subject to admission quotas in private universities, an experience exactly analogous to that of high-achieving children of Jewish immigrants two generations ago (Cowan & Cowan, 1989).

Undocumented Immigrants

No one knows with any scientific accuracy how many undocumented immigrants are currently residing in the United States or how many arrive each year. Every year the U.S. Immigration and Naturalization Service (INS) locates more than 1.2 million illegal aliens in the United States and begins deportation proceedings on many of them. The INS estimates that there are approximately 2.7 million illegal immigrants now residing in the United States. By far the largest percentage are people from

The ill-fated Chinese freighter Golden Venture, *shown here after running aground near the mouth of New York harbor, drew worldwide attention to the smuggling of illegal immigrants into the United States. Some of the would-be immigrants drowned as they attempted to make their way to the shore and evade immigration officials.*

Mexico and Central America who have illegally crossed the border between Mexico and the United States, but recent alien arrest statistics suggest that the number of illegal Asian and European immigrants is also increasing. The shocking case of the *Golden Venture*, the ship carrying smuggled Chinese immigrants that ran aground in rough seas off Long Island, brought the black market in illegal immigrant workers to national attention in 1993.

Authorities in New York City estimate that there are as many as 30,000 undocumented immigrants there, a situation that poses some unique problems (Lorch, 1991). Undocumented immigrants are easily exploited by ruthless individuals who know that they cannot readily go to the authorities when they have been victimized. But illegal aliens from China have an especially difficult time. In order to be transported the great distance from China to the United States and to be smuggled into the New York area, many promise to pay as much as $50,000 to professional smuggling rings. Once in New York they often have no means of repaying this debt, and because they cannot qualify for regular work or any social benefits they are at the mercy of the people who brought them into the city. The smugglers often insist that the immigrants work at illegal activities such as collecting gambling debts, or that they work in local restaurants at extremely low wages. If they attempt to leave in search of better opportunities elsewhere, they may be killed. In essence, this practice has created a new form of slavery.

Nor is the situation much easier for illegal immigrants from Mexico and Central America. Often they pay large sums to smugglers, known as coyotes, who attempt to direct them across the border. Very often they are captured and lose both their chance to work in the United States and the hard-earned funds they gave to the smugglers. If they do gain entry into California or Texas and manage to find work, their status is quite precarious, since employers must report them if they are discovered not to have proper documents. Thus, employers who continue to hire them or disregard the evident forgery of their documents also tend to exploit them by paying pitifully low wages and expecting inordinate amounts of work.

It is not clear exactly what effect illegal residents have on the U.S. economy. They may take some jobs away from native-born residents, but they also perform functions that citizens are reluctant to do—"dirty work" or stoop labor on row crops, for example—and they help maintain some industries by accepting lower wages and inferior working conditions. This may hold back progress on wages and working conditions for others, but the survival of such industries stimulates growth in associated services, actually creating more jobs. Indeed, it appears that migrants—who can generally be laid off or discharged more easily than citizens—play a vital, if equivocal, role in many advanced nations, cushioning the native-born population from economic uncertainty (Piore, 1979). And when an increasing proportion of adults are retired—as an estimated 20 percent of U.S. adults will be in 2035—the taxes paid by employed immigrants become extremely important (Rothstein, 1993).

In a study of rural Mexican communities that typically send many immigrants—legal and illegal—to the southwestern United States, Wayne A. Cornelius (1989) found that people in those communities are knowledgeable about changes in U.S. immigration laws and how they affect illegal immigrants' chances of finding work and of being apprehended by the authorities. In his extensive interviews, Cornelius found no evidence that immigrants or likely immigrants were changing their behavior, despite the knowledge that it has become more difficult to gain entry to the United States and to find work of any kind. He did find that more people were planning to become documented temporary farm workers, but he found no decrease in the number who intended to try to immigrate illegally. He also found that more women intended to try to enter the United States, a fact that is confirmed in the statistics of immigration authorities, which show a steady increase in the number of undocumented Mexican women attempting to cross the border. (The special problems of such women are discussed further in Box 16–1.)

Population-related policies in the United States focus mainly on immigration, particularly illegal immigration. Under current immigration laws it is a felony to transport or harbor an illegal immigrant. Until recently it was not against the law to employ such a person. This situation changed in 1986, when Congress passed the Immigration Reform and Control Act. Under the new law employers would be subject to civil penalties ranging from $250 to $10,000 for each illegal alien they hired. With respect to people who are already living in the United States illegally, it is generally agreed that mass deportation is not feasible. Thus, the 1986 law offered legal status to illegal aliens who entered the United States before January 1, 1982, and have lived here continuously ever since. These undocumented aliens may qualify for permanent status (a "green card"), which in turn allows them to

BOX 16–1   UNINTENDED CONSEQUENCES: THE IMMIGRATION MARRIAGE FRAUD AMENDMENTS

Along with the landmark 1986 immigration legislation, Congress also passed a lesser known law, the Immigration Marriage Fraud Amendments, which sought to crack down on marriages that are entered into merely to get around the requirements of immigration laws. The law states that foreigners who marry U.S. citizens will no longer be entitled to immediate permanent resident status (the green card) and speedy processing of their citizenship applications. Instead, it establishes a two-year marital probation period during which the foreign spouse has conditional resident status in the United States. At the end of the probation period the INS must determine whether the marriage is genuine (the couple is still intact, still planning to maintain the marriage, etc.).

Although the law is intended to avoid abuses by people entering into phony marriages, some of its effects have turned out to be far worse than the evils it attempts to correct. In particular, the law places many immigrant women in a situation in which they are virtual prisoners of abusive husbands. The women can neither terminate the marriage nor seek protection against their abusers. Their conditional resident status and lack of access to information and services (owing to limited English skills) prevent them from seeking the help they need. Fearing deportation or the loss of their children, they are helpless against their partners' threats to call the INS if they leave them or report them to the authorities (Jang, 1990).

The exact magnitude of the problem is not known, but in one large city about 1,600 women suffering from domestic violence call the city's crime victims hotline every month. Counselors believe that many of these women have shaky legal status. In one case a woman who had immigrated from Puerto Rico and married a fellow tenant in her rooming house did not file charges against her husband until she had been hospitalized five times over a period of six years for injuries caused by his assaults (Walt, 1990).

Recently Congress passed new legislation intended to remedy this problem. Under the new law battered spouses are not required to remain in abusive marriages for the two-year probation period. "You can't place a spouse in servitude for two years just because they're conditional residents," said an INS spokesperson. Although the new law should provide relief for many immigrant women, it may be difficult for them to demonstrate that they have been subjected to domestic violence or that the marriage was entered into in good faith. Because of lack of awareness of the support services available to them, as well as fear of deportation if the abuse is reported, they may be unable to gather the necessary records of abuse and evidence of a good-faith marriage. Because of these and other technicalities, the effectiveness of the new law may be limited.

begin applying for U.S. citizenship and also allows them to freely leave and reenter the country.

The Immigration Reform and Control Act sought to stem the flow of illegal immigrants from Mexico and elsewhere through a number of reforms in existing laws. The bill passed the employer sanctions just noted. It also sought to discourage illegal immigration by measures that would reduce illegal aliens' chances of finding work in the United States. In particular, it offered legal status to immigrants claiming three months of prior agricultural work, thereby increasing the supply of legal labor for the big farms of Southern California and decreasing the need for more casual, often illegal labor.

In a statement on immigration, the President's Council of Economic Advisors (1990) warned that "as the U.S. economy enters the 1990s concerns are growing about the effects of possible labor shortages on production and wages. Employers in some areas of the country report a shortfall of entry-level workers and are paying wages well above the minimum wage to attract new employees" (p. 193). As this quote indicates, the strongest support for pro-immigration policies is usually found among employers of immigrant labor, especially in agricultural regions and in areas where there is high demand for low-wage labor. But although the Immigration Act of 1990 increased overall quotas, preference in filling the quotas would be given to skilled immigrants.

A highly controversial issue related to immigration is the policy of allowing people who test positive for the HIV virus to enter the United States. The 1990 immigration law ended a tradition of excluding immigrants because of their political and social beliefs or sexual preference. Thus, the decision not to exclude HIV-positive individuals was part of the larger movement to eliminate all civil-rights–related restrictions on immigration. The decision was reversed in 1991 as a result of pressure by conservative members of Congress, but reversed again in 1993.

Although the political climate in which immigration issues are discussed is often troubled with doubts and conflict, with lower-income groups often opposed to increased immigration, the extent to which immigration cuts across racial, ethnic, and social-class lines results in broad-based popular support for pro-immigration policy. The principle of family unification—long a basic element of immigration policy—also explains why immigration legislation has public support. So many people are directly affected or have friends who are affected by efforts to unite families separated by immigration that opposition to the abstract idea of population growth is blunted by human concerns.

SUMMARY

1. A common measure of population growth is the crude birthrate, or the number of births per 1,000 population. The differential between the crude birthrate and the death rate is the rate of population growth, or natural increase. Today more people are living to childbearing age, so that the world population is growing faster than in the past and putting increased pressure on resources and the environment.

2. The demographic transition is a process that consists of three stages: (a) a high birthrate canceled out by a high death rate, (b) a high birthrate coupled with

a declining death rate, and (c) low birth and death rates. The process began in northern Europe in the eighteenth century and has occurred in all areas where industrial technology has taken hold on a local level. Today large areas of Asia, Africa, and Latin America remain in the middle phase of the demographic transition.

3. An unintended effect of population growth coupled with awareness of higher living standards is the "revolution of rising expectations," in which people develop higher expectations regarding their own future and that of their children. Literacy rates serve as an indicator of rising expectations. Although literacy rates have increased in many countries, the gaps in living standards between rich and poor societies have widened.

4. The main trends in the U.S. population are slow growth, population redistribution, and increasing immigration. Among the effects of these trends are the disproportionate representation of minority groups in the older central cities and increased age and income disparities between "old" and "new" ethnic groups.

5. The population of the industrialized nations is growing at a relatively slow rate, and it appears likely that this rate can be maintained through voluntary population control (e.g., family planning). Zero Population Growth, Inc., and other organizations have been active in promoting access to birth control and legalized abortion.

6. In some less developed countries compulsory birth control has been attempted and has met with considerable resistance. In such countries the most effective policies provide not only birth control devices but also economic and social incentives to limit family size.

7. The United States is often described as a nation of immigrants; since the earliest years of European settlement it has attracted people from all over the world. Since the 1970s the rate of legal immigration to the United States has accelerated. The largest numbers of immigrants have come from Asia and North America.

8. A problem related to immigration is the uneven distribution of immigrants among cities and regions within the nation. Almost half of all immigrants settle in New York, Los Angeles, Miami, or Chicago. This greatly adds to the costs of education and health care in those cities.

9. Immigrants in urban centers encounter intense competition and, at times, direct hostility. Their children may form defensive gangs or be isolated by their peers. Some immigrant groups shelter their children from street life and encourage them to achieve in school.

10. Millions of undocumented immigrants are currently residing in the United States, and more arrive each year. Undocumented immigrants are easily exploited by employers and others. Their effect on the U.S. economy is not clear, but it appears that they cushion the native-born population from economic uncertainty.

11. Population-related policies in the United States focus mainly on immigration. It is illegal to transport or employ undocumented immigrants. Illegal aliens who entered the country before 1982 and have lived here continuously ever since may qualify for permanent status. Current quotas on legal immigration give preference to skilled workers; restrictions based on political beliefs or sexual preference have been eliminated. The principle of family unification is a basic element of immigration policy.

SUGGESTED READINGS

BOUVIER, LEON F. *Peaceful Invasions: Immigration and Changing America.* Lanham, MD: University Press of America, 1992. A well-reasoned argument for a moderate U.S. immigration policy for the twenty-first century, in contrast to calls for an open-door policy on one hand or a restrictive policy on the other. The book also offers a concise review of the history of U.S. immigration policy.

BROWN, DAVID L., and JOHN M. WARDELL, EDS. *New Directions in Urban–Rural Migration: The Population Turnaround in Rural America.* Orlando: Academic Press, 1980. A study of the reversal of the traditional pattern of rural–urban migration during the 1970s.

DAVIS, KINGSLEY, ED. *Below Replacement Fertility.* New York: Population Council, 1987. Discusses the problem of lowered fertility in the developed nations; far superior to popular treatments of this complex issue.

EHRLICH, PAUL R., ANNE H. EHRLICH, and JOHN P. HOLDREN. *Ecoscience: Population, Resources, Environment,* 3rd ed. New York: W. H. Freeman, 1977. A highly comprehensive and sophisticated treatment of population and environmental issues throughout the world.

PIORE, MICHAEL J. *Birds of Passage: Migrant Labor and Industrial Societies.* Cambridge, MA: M. I. T. Press, 1979. Argues that the causes of immigration to industrial societies are inherent in the economies of those societies, which demand a continual inflow of cheap labor. Also presents a somewhat critical analysis of the consequences of immigration, both for the immigrants and for the host society.

PORTES, ALEJANDRO, and R. G. RUMBAUT. *Immigrant America: A Portrait*. Berkeley: University of California Press, 1990. An influential empirical study of the distribution of new immigrant groups in U.S. cities, the effects of chain migration to those cities, and the impact of immigration on urban centers such as Miami, Los Angeles, and New York.

WALDINGER, ROGER. *Through the Eye of a Needle*. New York: New York University Press, 1988. A thorough examination of the way immigrant groups attempt to gain a niche in the occupational and business structures of American cities.

Technology and the Environment

Chapter Outline

- A mechanical robot can replace three or more workers.
- Over 98 percent of U.S. households have at least one television set.
- Americans drive their cars almost 2 trillion miles per year, using almost 71 billion gallons of gasoline in the process.
- In urban areas almost half the carbon monoxide in the air comes from motor vehicles.
- Commercial nuclear reactors in the United States discharge 1,615 metric tons of radioactive wastes each year.

The technological and organizational revolutions of the past 200 years are sweeping away social boundaries that were built up over five millennia; in some ways the world has become, as futurist Marshall McLuhan put it, a "global village." Two previous cultural transformations were also based on technological changes, but those transformations occurred at a relatively slower pace. Between the shift from hunting to farming and the shift from villages to urban civilizations based on industrial production and low-cost energy, there were some 5,000 years of social and scientific progress. Today momentous changes are brought about by technology in each new generation, so that science itself seems overwhelmed by the pace and scale of technological change.

The most common view among physical and social scientists with regard to technology is that every major technological innovation has both freed humanity from previous hardships and created new, unanticipated problems. Thus, technology is seen as a two-edged sword. Although most of us benefit immensely from technological progress, technology itself can be viewed as a social problem. In this chapter, therefore, we will look at research and theories about the social impact of technology, as well as particular phases of technological change. Of all the many impacts of the technologies changing our lives every day, probably none has more far-reaching consequences than the impact of technology on the earth's environment. The problems of possible global warming, acid rain, toxic waste disposal, and water and air pollution are direct consequences of technological advances. The way we use energy has an enormous impact on the earth's ecological systems. The technologies of production, climate control, transportation, and agriculture transform the physical shape of the planet and lead to environmental stress. In this chapter, therefore, we will begin by examining how technologies can become social problems and go on to discuss how technologies contribute to problems in the natural environment.

DEFINING TECHNOLOGY

The dictionary definition of *technology* is "the totality of means employed by a people to provide itself with the objects of material culture." In this sense, technology is a way of solving practical problems; indeed, it is often viewed as the application of scientific knowledge to the problems of everyday life. But neither the dictionary definition of technology nor the view of it as applied science places enough emphasis on technology's organizational aspects. Langdon Winner (1977) has provided a useful set of dimensions for understanding the broader meaning of technology:

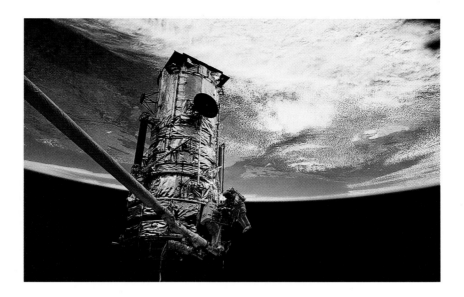

Astronauts Jeffrey A. Hoffman (left) and F. Story Musgrave team up to replace one of two solar array drive electronics units on the Hubble space telescope. The technological exploits of this NASA crew greatly improved the space agency's standing among citizens and lawmakers.

1. Technological tools, instruments, machines, gadgets, which are used in accomplishing a variety of tasks. These material objects are best referred to as apparatus, the physical devices of technical performance.
2. The body of technical skills, procedures, routines—all activities or behaviors that employ a purposive, step-by-step, rational method of doing things.
3. The organizational networks associated with activities and apparatus.

Technological change refers to changes in any or all of the major dimensions of technology listed here. Some technological changes have revolutionary significance in that they alter the basic institutions of society. Thus, the industrial revolution—that is, the development of factories and mass production—has drastically altered the organization of a number of noneconomic institutions, including the family, religion, the military, and science itself.

Not all technological change is revolutionary, however. Some innovations spur minor adjustments in other sectors of society or among small numbers of people. Nor does technological change always consist of a single major invention. Daniel Bell (1973), perhaps the most prominent sociologist in the field of technology and social change, defines technological change as "the combination of all methods [apparatus, skills, organization] for increasing the productivity of labor and capital" (p. 188). This is a valuable definition because it stresses the combination of methods that alter production, rather than single innovations. After all, the technological revolution that took place in American agriculture from the end of the nineteenth century to World War II involved hundreds of major inventions and the skills and organization to support them. The combination of all these factors allowed the United

States to make the transition from an agrarian society to an urban industrial society in less than one century.

TECHNOLOGICAL DUALISM

The phrase "technological dualism" refers to the fact that advances in technology can have both positive and negative impacts. Consider the following examples.

Technology and Jobs Technological innovation is causing drastic and extremely rapid changes in the types of work available to Americans. Between 1975 and 1990, for example, employment in the production of computers increased by about 89 percent. Employment in the production of food and kindred products remained about the same, and employment in textile mill products decreased by about 20 percent (*Statistical Abstract,* 1993). These changes are due to the increasing importance of advanced technology.

At this writing, the unemployment rate in the United States is 6.5 percent, or more than 7 million American workers, most of whom are usually employed, either directly or indirectly, in manufacturing. Many of these workers will never find employment in their original industries because the jobs will have been eliminated through automation. Americans with secure jobs will benefit from the increased productivity of the entire labor force; but the fate of the displaced workers depends heavily on policies and programs that offer opportunities for retraining and further education. Thus, technology has had both positive and negative impacts.

Telecommunications and the Global Village The revolution in telecommunications has already made the United States a single community for some purposes. In 1950, 9 percent of American households had television sets, which were turned on for an average of 4.6 hours a day. In 1992, over 98 percent of U.S. households had at least one television set (*Statistical Abstract,* 1993), which was turned on for an average of about seven hours a day. In 1915 it cost $20.00 to call San Francisco from New York. Today, because of microwave satellite technology, it costs less than $1.00. These new forms of communication make maintaining extended family ties much easier than was the case in earlier decades. And we can all, or almost all, watch the same sporting events or political speeches, and this may strengthen our sense of shared citizenship. But what about literacy? Is the revolution in communication making reading obsolete? The United States publishes more books than ever before, but the reading ability of American children seems to have suffered, partly because of the distraction of television. As more and more television services develop, will earlier traditions of entertainment and urban living be maintained?

In an era when increasing numbers of people are using sophisticated telecommunications technologies to fax their mail and memos, to do library searches, and to communicate via computer terminals throughout the world, there is a growing population of "telecommunications have-nots." People in inner-city ghettos and in remote rural areas who are poor and cannot afford phones, to say nothing of computers, are in danger of being pushed even further toward the margins of society because of their lack of access to telecommunications technologies. In the most rural areas of the nation, telephone companies estimate that as many as 200,000 households are not connected by phone wires. Often the residents of those areas cannot pay the initial installation expenses. Congress and the public service commissions in the states are investigating the problem in the hope of finding a way to subsidize telephone service for poor, remote communities (Johnson, 1991).

Automobility Periodic shortages of gasoline and increasingly frequent traffic jams in metropolitan areas have not cooled America's love affair with the private automobile. Americans drive their cars over 2 trillion miles per year. It takes almost 71 billion gallons of gasoline a year to fuel the American private passenger fleet and almost 56 billion more to fuel our trucks (*Statistical Abstract,* 1993).

Of course, the demand for energy is by no means the only social problem associated with America's dependence on the private automobile. In 1970 motor vehicle accidents resulted in 54,600 deaths. By 1991, because of increased attention to auto safety requirements, the number of deaths had declined to 43,500 (*Statistical Abstract,* 1993). Nevertheless, the amount of harm associated with the automobile remains great: In 1991 the total economic loss due to automobile accidents (including wage loss; property damage; and legal, medical, and funeral expenses) was estimated at $93.8 billion (*Statistical Abstract,* 1993).

CONTROLLING TECHNOLOGY

Some critics of technology are convinced that it has become an autonomous force in society—that it is less and less subject to the control of democratic political institutions. A more hopeful view stresses the problems of social adaptation to technological innovation. In this section we explore these contrasting views of technology.

Autonomous Technology

The theme of technology "run amok" and out of control appears frequently in movies, books, and other fictional works. But these fictional nightmares are based on real experiences. The nuclear accident in the film *The China Syndrome* portrayed almost the same sequence of events that unfolded at about the same time when the nuclear reactor at Three Mile Island near Harrisburg, Pennsylvania, came frighteningly close to a complete meltdown. The computer named Hal that ran the space mission in the film *2001* malfunctioned and had to be taken over by its human crew. This is, of course, a satirical view of computers' domination of human life, but how often do we read about computer mistakes that result in bureaucratic disasters affecting hundreds, perhaps thousands, of people? We depend on machines, which are all too frail and fallible, yet we know that machines do not literally have lives of their own. People make machines and operate them, not vice versa. How can it be, then, that technology has achieved a seeming independence from human control, as many critics argue?

The answer, according to Winner (1977, 1986) and others, is not that individual machines exercise tyranny over human subjects but that the technological order— the complex web connecting the various sectors of technology, such as communication, transportation, energy, manufacturing, and defense—has enmeshed us in a web of dependency. People who live in simple societies meet their basic survival needs with a fairly small number of tools and a simple division of labor. To accomplish such goals as building shelter, gathering and growing food, and warding off enemies, they have evolved a set of tools, which families and other groups manufacture and use as the need arises. The lives of such people are dominated by the need to survive, and technology simply provides the means for doing so. In modern industrial societies, however, most people spend most of their productive hours working to meet the quotas, deadlines, and other goals of large organizations. Each of the corporations, government bureaucracies, and other organizations that together make up the technological order produces goods and services that people want or need. These organizations do so not with a few tools but with a complex array of machines and skills. As a whole, the technological order supplies the basic necessities of life, along with innumerable extras. But in the process much of the life of society has been diverted from meeting the needs of survival to meeting the requirements of technology.

We have seen elsewhere in this book that military technology accounts for the largest single category of expenditure (about 20 percent) in the federal budget. The rout of the Iraqis in the Persian Gulf war of 1991 demonstrated to many Americans that this technology was worth the expense. But amid the euphoria over the allied victory and the evident effectiveness of the weapons systems, many observers asked why the nation could not use its technological knowhow to improve schools and health care and solve other social problems. In attempting to answer this question, Daniel Bell (1991) notes that "smart bombs" and computer-assisted weapons are technologies designed to meet well-defined and very narrow objectives. He warns that "'solutions' to the social problems (if solutions are possible) spring from the different values people hold" (p. 23). Weapons systems and other new technologies are techniques for accomplishing narrow objectives. They cannot solve the far more complex problems of determining values and priorities; allocating scarce resources; and applying our knowledge to solve the problems of complex institutions such as schools, hospitals, and prisons.

Most students of technology agree with Bell that technological systems do not themselves offer solutions to social problems. Langdon Winner, for example, believes that the engineers, the energy czars, and the telecommunications executives of the world—the people who design and direct the large organizations in which technology is embedded—do not know how to lead their nations in a coordinated way: "What we have is an ensemble of actors each of whom has been deluded and anesthetized by the technological milieu that itself possesses a certain logic but which for the most part is a kind of onrushing poorly coordinated muddle" (quoted in Carpenter, 1978, p. 144).

Most writers do not see technology as autonomous. They argue that we have been drawn into the momentum of technological change but are not sure where it is taking us. In the following pages we will discuss this theme as it applies to particular technologies.

Automation

A classic example of the difficulty of understanding the interaction between technology and human values is *automation*, the replacement of workers by a nonhuman means of producing the same product. People may lose jobs because of automation, but does this imply that we should fight automation in the interest of keeping jobs, many of which may be among the dirtiest and most dangerous ones in industrial facilities? On the other hand, the greatly feared displacement of workers by machines may or may not increase productivity and thus create new wealth, which could be channeled into the "higher" work of humans: health care, education, caring for the aged, and so on.

In fact, the stereotypical image of automation, in which a worker is replaced by a mechanical robot, is actually occurring throughout the industrialized world. Each of these machines replaces at least three workers because it can work continuously whereas human workers must be replaced every eight hours. But most robots replace more than three workers, even though they must be tended by highly trained maintenance personnel. Thus, automation increases the productivity of the economy, since a constant or decreasing number of workers can turn out more of a desired product. The question remains, however, as to whether the new wealth generated by higher productivity will be used to benefit the entire society or will be added to that of individuals who are already wealthy.

The direct replacement of workers by machines is the most dramatic and perhaps the most widely held image of automation. Evidence suggests, however, that the contemporary effects of automation as measured by increasing productivity, defined as output per hour of labor, have been much less than the stereotypical image of robots replacing workers would suggest. According to one estimate, productivity due to machines (as opposed to organization) improved at a fairly consistent annual rate of about 2.5 percent between 1919 and 1953 (Solow, 1959, cited in Bell, 1973). In the 1960s the pace of automation increased somewhat, but no major change in that pace occurred in the 1970s. In the 1980s, although the U.S. economy continued to create new jobs, the impact of automation reduced the number of new jobs in the manufacturing sector, especially automobiles and steel. (See Chapter 14.) Ironically, even the robotics industry experienced a slump in the 1980s, largely as a result of cutbacks in spending by automobile manufacturers.

A much more widespread and serious problem than the replacement of workers by machines is the relationship between automation and the exporting of manufacturing jobs from the United States to less developed regions of the world or, within the United States, to parts of the nation where energy and labor costs are lower. The export of manufacturing jobs to such diverse parts of the globe as South Korea, Taiwan, and Central America is possible only as a consequence of modern computer management and satellite communication technology. Today capital can be transferred by telex and computerized banking services to all parts of the world; products can be transported by jet freighters or containerized cargo ships that virtually eliminate pilferage and costly cargo transfers in ports; inventories from plants in different countries can be tracked through computer systems; and skilled jobs can be "deskilled" so that they can be performed by unskilled workers with technological assistance (i.e., automated machinery).

The household is one area of American life that has undergone substantial technological change. It is worth noting here that the adoption of technology by consumers often depends on prior changes in social institutions. Television, for example, is one of numerous information and entertainment technologies that could not have been adopted before more important changes in patterns of work and leisure had been established. When people worked on Saturdays (as they frequently did before World War II) or worked twelve-hour days (as was the case before World War I), and before the advent of household labor-saving devices, it would not have been possible to market such a thing as television, which requires much more leisure than was then available. The late Akio Morita, founder and president of the Sony Corporation, one of the world's leading technological innovators, cited an example that makes the same point about the relationship between institutional change and the effects of automation:

> In 1950, our company marketed a tape recorder. It was of course the first item of its kind in Japan. Our company had developed our own tape and all the components used in the recorder. When we first created this new product, we had a dream of great fortunes to come. It was the result of costly research and development and the concentrated efforts of our engineering staff. We therefore expected that as soon as we put it on the market, it would sell right away. Inventors are always like that. They have the illusion that if they create a new thing, money will come rolling in. But the realities were opposite to our dream. It was a very valuable experience to learn that unless the consumer appreciates the new product, no matter how creative the idea is, it merely ends as a toy or an object of curiosity.

Is Technology Out of Control?

The concept of autonomous technology is a powerful and recurrent one in American social thought. We have emphasized two of the many elements of this concept. The first is the idea that certain kinds of technology are out of control because they are harming people or the environment. Recently this subtheme has gained new prominence as a result of the controversies over pollution, the impact of nuclear technology, modern weaponry, and other issues. Yet concern over the ill effects of techno-logical innovations has a long history. The earliest steam engines used on boats exploded at an alarming rate because engineers could not design effective boiler shells and safety valves. Public outrage led to government-sponsored research on steam technology and safety standards. On the early railroads, defective engineering of trains and bridges exacted a heavy death toll until official action to correct the problem was taken (Florman, 1981). These harmful side effects were resolved through a process of criticism and technological refinement, and optimists argue that similar problems in today's world will be alleviated through the same process.

Despite such well-founded optimism, the technology represented by the nuclear bomb threatens the future of humanity. Although humans have successfully brought under control much of the damage caused by technological innovations, war has proved to be a persistent threat. In the case of nuclear energy, the question is whether we can adapt our social institutions, especially in a global context, to control the possible tragic effects of a technology that also has desirable effects.

The second subtheme of the concept of autonomous technology is that complete control over technology is almost certainly impossible to achieve. The idea that technology bends institutions and cultures to meet the needs of innovation and machine production has its origins in nineteenth- and early twentieth-century thought in the United States and other Western societies that were undergoing rapid industrialization at the time. As industrialization has proceeded, the technological order—which, as mentioned earlier, is the web of interconnected sectors of technology—has increased its influence over society as a whole. Because the body of machines and methods that we have invented has already so thoroughly molded our way of life and our expectations, it is doubtful that in the future we will be able to enhance our control over technology in this second sense.

Whistle-blowers

So many of the proposed solutions to technological problems are themselves new technologies that opportunities for abuse and personal profit through application of these technologies abound. People who see abuses of new technological systems often run grave personal risks when they attempt to expose those abuses. Such individuals are known as "whistle-blowers."

Within any organization, certain ways of doing things, beliefs about the environment in which the group operates, and ideas about how individuals should behave become established. Whistle-blowers challenge some element of this body of procedures, beliefs, and norms in an effort to bring about change. At the least, they must endure snubs or ostracism by fellow workers. At worst, they may be fired or even subjected to physical violence.

The difficulty of succeeding in such a situation can be appreciated by reviewing the experience of Peter Faulkner (1981), an engineer for a private nuclear engineering firm, who in 1974 publicized certain hazardous deficiencies in the design of nuclear power systems. Early in the 1970s Faulkner had become concerned about the fact that many systems that were being marketed contained design flaws that posed grave threats to the public and to the natural environment: "Overconfident engineering, the failure to test nuclear systems fully in intermediate states, and competitive pressures that forced reactor manufacturers to . . . sell first, test later" (pp. 40, 41) contributed to the persistence of these flaws.

Curious about whether his fellow engineers shared his concerns, Faulkner discussed his perceptions with them. From these discussions, he realized that many of them shared his view that poor management had led to the marketing of defective reactors. But most of his colleagues preferred to leave management problems to the executives, even though this resignation of responsibility contributed to the design flaws with which they were already familiar from their daily experience. Senior engineers informed him that utility executives "didn't want management advice—only technical assistance to get them over the next hill."

Frustrated by the indifference of his colleagues, Faulkner made the difficult and costly decision to present articles criticizing the industry to a Senate subcommittee and a scientific institute. Dissemination of critical papers clearly violated the ethics of the nuclear industry and of the engineers within it, but Faulkner acted to further what he considered a higher goal—public safety. Within two weeks he had been interviewed by the company psychiatrist, who wanted to learn whether Faulkner had been motivated by some deep-seated hostility to embarrass his firm. A week later he was fired.

The explosion of the space shuttle *Challenger* in January 1986 is sometimes attributed to a similar situation: failure to listen to whistle-blowers within the company that manufactured the shuttle's solid-fuel booster rockets. It is true that engineers repeatedly warned of the danger of failure of the engine seals in very cold weather, that they were overruled by their superiors, and that when they testified at congressional hearings on the disaster they were either fired or "promoted" to meaningless positions. However, the situation was much more complex than these facts suggest. The pressures to go ahead with the fatal launch were enormous, and subsequent investigations revealed that other aspects of the shuttle program, particularly safety procedures, were seriously deficient. As Charles Perrow (1984) points out in his book *Normal Accidents*, modern technological systems are extremely complex, and despite the best intentions of managers and employees, information is often lost or suppressed as a result of lack of coordination between different parts of the system. The tragic example of the space shuttle aptly illustrates the need for more thorough technology assessment, which will be discussed in the Social Policy section of the chapter.

Bureaucracy and Morality

As noted earlier, technology consists not only of machines but also of procedures and organizations. Today much of the productive activity that occurs in complex societies takes place in large bureaucratic organizations. With their orientation toward specified goals, their division of labor into narrowly defined roles, and their hierarchical authority structures, such organizations are supremely efficient compared to other kinds of groups. But like technology in general, some of the qualities of large organizations that make them so productive and valuable can also cause harm. For example, in a hierarchical system individuals may commit immoral acts because they are not personally responsible for the consequences of those acts, which are carried out under the direction of superiors.

The list of immoral acts committed by people who were carrying out the instructions of superiors in large organizations is long. Writing as London was being pounded by Nazi bombs during World War II, George Orwell (quoted in Milgram, 1974) described the irony of one such situation:

> As I write, highly civilized human beings are flying overhead, trying to kill me. They do not feel any enmity against me as an individual, nor I against them. They are only "doing their duty," as the saying goes. Most of them are kind-hearted law abiding men who would never dream of committing murder in private life. On the other hand, if one of them succeeds in blowing me to pieces with a well-placed bomb, he will never sleep any the worse for it. (pp. 11–12)

Stanley Milgram (1974) called attention to the fact that when an immoral task is divided up among a number of people in a large organization like an air force or a bomb factory, no one person, acting as an individual, actually decides to commit the act, perceives its consequences, or takes responsibility for it. It is easy for each participant to become absorbed in the effort to perform his or her role competently. It is also psychologically easy to reduce guilt with the rationalization that one's duty requires the immoral behavior and that one's superior is responsible in the end.

In a famous series of experiments conducted at Yale University, Milgram studied the conditions under which people forsake the universally shared moral injunction against doing harm to another person in order to obey the instructions of someone in a position of authority. Subjects entered the laboratory assuming that they were to take part in a study of learning and memory. One person was designated a "learner" and the other a "teacher." The experimenter explained that the purpose of the study was to observe the effect of punishment on learning, and then the "learner" was strapped into a chair and electrodes were attached to his wrist. Next the "learner" was told that the task was to learn a list of word pairs and that for every error he would receive an electric shock of progressively greater intensity. The "teacher," who had been present for this interchange, was escorted to another room and seated at the controls of a large shock generator. Each time the "learner" gave a wrong answer, the "teacher" was to flip the next in a series of thirty switches designed to deliver shocks in 15-volt increments, from 15 to 450, starting at the lowest level. (See Figure 17–1a.)

In reality, the "learner" was an actor who received no shock but registered greater discomfort as the supposed intensity of the shocks increased. Grunts gave way to verbal complaints, to demands for release from the experiment, and then to screams. The true purpose of the experiment was to study the behavior of the "teachers." They were affected by the cries and suffering of the "learners"—especially in high-proximity situations—but whenever they hesitated to deliver a shock, the experimenter ordered them to continue. In one form of the experiment, almost two-thirds of the subjects administered the maximum shock of 450 volts. (See Figure 17–1b.) Interviews with these subjects (who had been carefully selected to represent a cross section of society) revealed that they tended to adjust to their task by absorbing themselves in its technical details, transferring responsibility to the experimenter and justifying their actions in the name of scientific truth (Milgram, 1974).

Milgram's experiments generated a great deal of controversy and contributed to the establishment of rules governing federally funded social-science research using human subjects. At the same time, there has not been any significant debate about the implications of his findings for society. Should people be taught that disobedience to authority under some conditions is necessary? This is the situation faced by whistle-blowers, who, as we have just seen, actually overcome their feelings of subservience to technologically oriented bureaucratic hierarchies.

TECHNOLOGY AND INSTITUTIONS

Sociologists who do research on technology and the effects of technological change most often concern themselves with the adaptation of social institutions to changing technology or, conversely, the adaptation of technology to changing social institutions. The best-known statement of these relationships is William F. Ogburn's cultural lag theory, first stated in the 1920s. According to Ogburn, a founder of the study of technology in the United States, "A *cultural lag* occurs when one of two parts of culture which are correlated changes before or in greater degree than the other part does, thereby causing less adjustment between the two parts than existed previously" (1957, p. 167).

A classic example of cultural lag involves the failure of social-welfare legislation over a period of thirty or forty years to adjust to the introduction of new industrial machinery in the United States at the end of the nineteenth century. The frequency of industrial accidents was increasing during that period because operators were not adequately protected from the rapidly moving wheels of the new machines. The loss of life and limb generally meant financial disaster for workers' families because

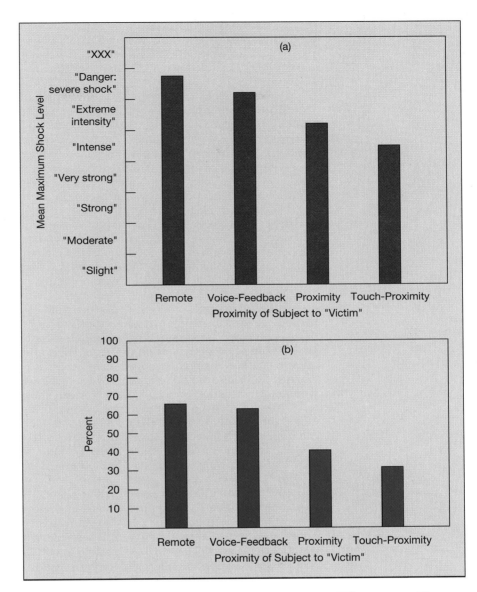

FIGURE 17–1 Results of Milgram's Experiments on Willingness to Obey People in Authority. Part (a) shows the extent to which proximity to the "victim" affected the subject's willingness to administer the maximum shock. Part (b) shows the percentage of obedient subjects under varying degrees of proximity to the "victim." (*Note: The subject is the person administering the shock; the "victim" is an accomplice to the experimenter. The voltage levels indicated in (a) ranged from 15 for "Slight shock" to a maximum of 450 for "XXX." No actual shocks were administered.*)

(*Source:* Data from Milgram, 1974.)

under existing law employers could not easily be held liable. As a result, compensation was meager and slow to come. Only when worker's compensation and employer liability were introduced early in the twentieth century was this maladjustment, which had led to much impoverishment and suffering, finally corrected (Ogburn, 1957).

Typically, social institutions and technology adjust and readjust to one another in a process that approaches equilibrium, unless one or the other alters so radically that a lag develops. In the history of transportation technology, radical changes have occurred relatively often. Witness the impact of the steamboat, the railroad, the automobile, and the airplane. Sometimes mere refinements in existing technology can devastate the social arrangements that had grown up in response to older machines and procedures. This is what happened to the railroad town of Caliente (not its real name) when diesel power replaced steam in the 1940s. A classic study by Cottrell (1951) described the results.

Caliente had been settled at the turn of the century, when the railroad was built, and owed its existence almost entirely to the railroad. When the line was put through, the boiler of a steam engine could withstand high pressures and temperature for only short periods. Roughly every hundred miles a locomotive had to be disconnected from service, and Caliente was located in the middle of the desert for this purpose.

Over the years the community had invested considerable sums in its own future. Railroad workers and others had put their life savings into mortgages; merchants had built stores; and the town had constructed a hospital, a school, and a park. But the diesel engine undermined the economic base of the town, saddling its residents with devalued property and no means of supporting themselves. Diesel engines require much less maintenance and many fewer stops for fuel and water than steam engines do. Thus, the railroad employees living in Caliente either lost their jobs or were transferred; the town had become irrelevant from the point of view of the railroad. In the American free enterprise system, the profitability of the railroad determined the fate of the town. The railroad was under no obligation to cushion the social impact of its move; the state did not offer any assistance; and so the town died.

The construction of interstate highways after World War II had the opposite effect. The width, straightness, and limited access of interstates permit greater traffic flow and higher speeds than are possible on conventional roads. The highways therefore expanded the potential market of retail service businesses located along them. Improved markets, in turn, tend to increase employment in retail and service occupations. The promise of new jobs attracts new residents from areas with less opportunity. Thus, a study of the impact of interstate highways on nonmetropolitan counties between 1950 and 1975 was able to establish an association between highway construction on the one hand and population and economic growth along the interstate corridor on the other (Lichter & Fuguitt, 1980).

Ogburn's theory of cultural lag and other sociological research on adaptation to technological change are often considered examples of *technological determinism,* the crude theory that technological innovation dictates changes in social institutions and culture (Winner, 1977). But Ogburn demonstrated that in many instances cultural change occurs long before technological change. Such "technological lags" are major challenges to modern science and engineering. For example, American culture has come to depend on the availability of relatively cheap fossil fuels. As supplies of such fuels dwindle or become more difficult to secure for political reasons, technological breakthroughs are needed to maintain the supply of low-cost energy. Thus, if physicists and engineers could control the nuclear fusion reaction (in which hydrogen atoms are fused into helium, releasing vast amounts of energy) so that its energy could be captured, Americans might once again have a source of plentiful, cheap fuel.

Fusion research is still in its early stages, however. Upon completion, the most powerful fusion reactor yet designed will be able to generate only about 3 percent as much wattage as the best fission reactors (Bernstein, 1982). If economically feasible fusion reactors are to be built, the nation must invest in the training of additional physicists and technicians, research facilities, and equipment. But because fusion research drains huge sums from the pool of money available for energy research, many critics argue that the federal government should diversify its research grants. They believe that other technologies, such as solar energy, may become much more economical than fusion as researchers solve the problems that contribute to the cost of solar equipment. Public debate of this nature is an important part of the process of overcoming technological lags.

The pressure to discover cheap and efficient routes to the control of nuclear fusion has led scientists to either falsify data or almost entirely neglect the rules of scientific inquiry. This seems to have happened in the late 1980s in the case of two chemists, one in Utah and the other in England, who shocked the scientific world with the announcement that they had discovered a fusion reaction that did not require immense quantities of energy. While the team was garnering lucrative research contracts from firms hoping to profit from the discovery, efforts to replicate their "cold fusion" experiment were made in laboratories throughout the world. None of those efforts was successful. In a study of this scientific scandal, the research physicist Frank Close (1991) warns that the pressure to make discoveries and to bring in profits for universities and research institutes can create the incentive for unscientific manipulations of data or serious lapses in scientific judgment.

The "cold fusion" fiasco illustrates why the norms of science are valuable and need to be protected. In other instances, however, changes in norms and social institutions must occur before advances in technology and its control may be made. One such case, from the history of medicine, has been described by Lewis Thomas (1979). For centuries medicine stumbled along, afflicting the afflicted with "cures" based on little or no insight into human biology:

> *Bleeding, purging, cupping, the administration of infusions of every known metal, every conceivable diet including total fasting, most of these based on the weirdest imaginings about the cause of the disease, concocted out of nothing but thin air—this was the heritage of medicine up until a little over a century ago. (p. 133)*

In the 1830s physicians began to realize that most of these traditional remedies did not work. As this view became accepted, medicine placed greater emphasis on the observation and classification of diseases. The new approach eventually enabled doctors to diagnose and predict the course of most illnesses, even if a cure lay beyond their grasp.

During the 1880s medical research uncovered the role of bacteria and viruses through the application of the scientific method. For the first time in medical history, systematic observation, theorizing, and experimentation made it possible for researchers to compare, replicate, and confirm their findings. Only when the knowledge of disease organisms and their effect on the body had become sufficiently detailed could medical technology produce cures for the major infectious illnesses. By the late 1930s immunizations had been developed for a number of diseases, and sulfa and other "wonder drugs" were being introduced. Today the technological solutions to other health problems still await the achievement of sufficient knowledge by medical science. It is probably only a matter of time before the leading killers in modern society—heart disease and cancer—are defeated. The social ramifications of technological innovation can be extensive, but innovation itself typically depends on a social context that must evolve over a long period.

TECHNOLOGY AND THE NATURAL ENVIRONMENT

In recent decades the American public has begun to worry about the impact of pollution on its air and water (Dunlap & Scarce, 1991). This concern has led to research and speculation about our ability to control the sometimes harmful effects of certain technologies on the natural environment. Barry Commoner (1992), one of the best-known authorities on this subject, has described the fundamental problem in terms of a clash between the speed of change in human civilization and the pace of change in the cycles of the natural environment; he has also noted that most vital natural resources are rapidly being exhausted.

According to Commoner, human civilization has been changing and becoming more complex at an accelerating rate. The ideas, facts, and procedures that make up science and technology at any given time serve as a platform for future progress. A single technological advance such as the wheel, the internal-combustion engine, or the semiconductor may form the basis of an enormous range of inventions. As the ability of humans to exploit the resources of the earth has grown, so has the size of human populations.

These two developments—accelerated technological and scientific change and rapid population growth—are causing pollution and depletion of the natural environment as never before. Natural cycles of purification can absorb only a limited amount of certain artificial substances before ecological damage is done. Water pollution occurs when the ability of streams, rivers, lakes, and oceans to purify themselves is exceeded. When wind, rain, and snow can no longer remove the particles deposited in the air by machines of various kinds, pollution is the result (Commoner, 1971). In these cases the speed at which technology creates pollutants more than exceeds the pace at which nature can absorb them. The spectacular fires and pollution spewing from Kuwait's burning oil wells after the Gulf War were stark reminders of the destructive forces unleashed by humans and the urgent need to control those forces.

Sometimes technologies that seem benign and that we take for granted as part of everyday life have unanticipated consequences. Earlier in this century pesticides and herbicides revolutionized agriculture, making it much more productive. Subsequent research has linked many of these chemicals to the destruction of fish and birds and to certain cancers in humans. Along the same lines, for years we used aerosol containers for purposes ranging from personal hygiene to applying whipped cream to ice cream sundaes. In the mid-1970s the suspicion that a propellant used in aerosol cans was eroding the atmospheric ozone layer, which protects us from harmful radiation, led to the use of different propellants.

Perhaps the central question is, Can we control such harmful effects before it is too late? In many cases the technology exists to control environmental damage, but powerful interests do not wish to shoulder the cost of doing so. Here the problem becomes one of creating a political consensus around a solution. In other cases the technology needed to get us out of jams that earlier inventions have helped put us into does not yet exist. Thus, advanced economies around the world are consuming energy in the form of oil, which is becoming depleted and for which an adequate substitute has not yet been found. Any technological solution to this and other problems will almost inevitably contribute to a whole new generation of crises.

ENVIRONMENTAL STRESS

An investigation of winter fish kills in Wisconsin lakes led to the unexpected conclusion that they were caused by snowmobiles. Heavy snowmobile use on a lake during the winter compacts the snow and makes the ice opaque. This reduces the amount of sunlight reaching underwater plants, which need it for photosynthesis. As the plants' oxygen production declines, they die; and their decomposition consumes considerable amounts of the oxygen left in the water. As a result, the fish are asphyxiated.

As this example suggests, we can best understand environmental stress as the interaction of three systems: the "natural" environment, the technological system,

As recreational vehicles take more people off the roads and onto deserts, dunes, and frozen lakes, the negative environmental impacts also multiply.

and the social system. The fish, ice, oxygen, and plants are all elements of the natural system. The snowmobile is an element of the technological system. The fact that this vehicle is produced, marketed, and used is a product of the social system—as is the fact that no one is held responsible for the fish kills.

Taking a broader perspective, we can define the natural system as containing these elements and their interrelationships: air, water, earth, solar energy, plants, animals, and mineral resources. Our technological system includes electricity-generating facilities, manufacturing processes and plants, various methods for extracting mineral resources, transportation, farming, and the actual consumption and disposal of the products of those processes. Our social system includes attitudes, beliefs and values, and institutional structures. And as with the fish and the snowmobiles, so in larger matters we must look to our social and technological systems for the origins of the problems in the natural system.

Origins of the Problem

Environmental stress refers to what society does to the environment. Examples include discharging substances into the air, water, and soil; producing heat, noise, and radiation; removing plants and animals; and physically transforming the environment through drilling, damming, dredging, mining, pumping, and so on (Ehrlich, Ehrlich, & Holdren, 1977). Environmental stress is not synonymous with pollution, although pollution is perhaps its most familiar form. Webster's dictionary defines *pollution* as "a state of being impure or unclean, or the process of producing that state." Environmental pollution, therefore, refers to "the presence of agents added to

Scientists prepare a test for changes in the atmospheric ozone layer. Depletion of the ozone layer can accelerate the incidence of skin cancer and may be associated with an increase in the earth's average temperature.

the environment by society in kinds and quantities potentially damaging to human welfare or to organisms other than people" (Ehrlich et al., 1977, p. 542).

Four concepts are basic to understanding environmental stress: interdependence, diversity, limits, and complexity (Ophuls, 1977). *Interdependence* literally means that everything is related to, and depends on, everything else; there is no beginning or end to the "web of life." *Diversity* refers to the existence of many different life and life support forms. A basic principle of ecology is that the greater the diversity of species, the greater the probability of survival in any given species. *Limits* are of several kinds. First, there is a finite limit to the growth of any organism. Second, there is a limit to the numbers of a given species that an environment—including other organisms—can support. Finally, there is a finite limit to the amount of materials available in the earth's ecosystem. *Complexity* refers to the intricacy of the relationships that constitute the "web." Because of this complexity, interventions in the environment frequently lead to unanticipated and undesired consequences. DDT, for example, was once repeatedly sprayed over large areas of land to eliminate various disease-carrying or crop-destroying insects. To an impressive degree it succeeded. But DDT is a long-lasting chemical, and its effects are not limited to insects. Much of it washed from farmlands and forests into rivers and oceans, where it was taken up by smaller organisms at the bottom of the food chain. Eventually, as small creatures consumed tiny plants and larger creatures consumed smaller ones, several species of fish-eating birds accumulated so much of the poison that their eggs had thin shells that consistently broke before hatching. The species were in grave danger of extinction, although the users of DDT never intended such a result (Ehrlich & Ehrlich, 1972). Only federal restrictions on the use of DDT prevented the elimination of these bird species.

One of the major difficulties in dealing with environmental stress, therefore, is the number of problems involved and the extent to which they are interrelated. This will become clear as we explore the specific problems and the efforts that have been made to combat them.

Air Pollution

If the atmosphere is not overburdened, natural processes will cleanse it and preserve its composition. Through photosynthesis, for example, green plants combine water with the carbon dioxide that we and other organisms exhale, and produce oxygen and carbohydrates. But these natural processes, like other resources, have limits. They can remove only a limited quantity of harmful substances from the air; and if pollution exceeds their capacity to remove it, the air will become progressively more dangerous to those who breathe it.

Human activities are overtaxing the atmosphere. Although the specific nature of air pollution varies from one locality to another (as a function of geography, climate, and type and concentration of industry), we can identify some of the common components. These include organic compounds (hydrocarbons); oxides of carbon, nitrogen, and sulfur; lead and other metals; and particulate matter (soot, fly ash). In urban areas almost half of the carbon monoxide in the air comes from motor vehicles. The remainder comes from the burning of fossil fuels (oil and coal) in power-generating plants, airplanes, and homes; airborne wastes from manufacturing processes; and municipal trash burning. (See Table 17–1.)

Certain chemical processes frequently render these pollutants more dangerous after they reach the atmosphere. In the presence of sunlight, the emission of hydrocarbons and nitrogen oxides (primarily from cars) produces the photochemical soup called smog that envelops many of our cities; and various oxides combine with water vapor in the atmosphere to produce corrosive acids that eat away the surface of many buildings.

Effects on Human Health   The effects of chronic air pollution are of great significance for human health in the long run. Continued exposure to air pollutants and their accumulation in the body—essentially a slow poisoning process—increase the incidence of such illnesses as bronchitis, emphysema, and lung cancer (Ehrlich & Ehrlich, 1972). Air pollution also causes severe eye, nose, and throat irritations, and poor visibility as a result of smog has been cited as a factor in both automobile and airplane accidents.

TABLE 17–1   AIR POLLUTANT EMISSIONS IN THE UNITED STATES, BY POLLUTANT AND SOURCE

CATEGORY	CARBON MONOXIDE*	SULFUR OXIDES*	VOLATILE ORGANIC COMPOUNDS*	PARTICULATES*	NITROGEN OXIDES*	LEAD†
Transportation	43.5	1.0	5.1	1.6	7.3	1.6
Fuel combustion (stationary sources)	4.7	16.6	0.7	1.9	10.6	0.5
Industrial processes	4.7	3.2	7.9	2.6	0.6	2.2
Solid-waste disposal	2.1	0.2	0.7	0.3	0.1	0.7
Miscellaneous uncontrollable	7.2	0.1	2.6	1.0	0.2	0.0

*Millions of metric tons per year.

†Thousands of metric tons per year.

Source: Statistical Abstract, 1993.

Economic Effects   Air pollution has economic effects as well. Accelerated deterioration of property increases maintenance and cleaning costs; blighted crops mean lost income for farmers and higher food prices for consumers; pollution-caused illnesses erode productivity, reduce workers' earnings, and raise the cost of medical care for everyone. The sulfur emitted from the smokestacks of factories and power plants in the United States would be worth millions of dollars if it could be recovered.

Ecological Effects   Finally, air pollution may have a dangerous long-term effect on the earth's ecosystem. For example, several studies suggest that fluorocarbon gases, commonly used in spray cans and refrigerating systems, may be breaking down the earth's protective ozone layer (Howard & Hanchett, 1975; Yoon, 1994). (The ozone layer surrounds the earth from an altitude of 8 to 30 miles above sea level; it screens out many of the sun's harmful rays.) Fluorocarbon molecules, according to these studies, are not broken down in the earth's lower atmosphere but continue to rise to a much higher altitude. Here they are broken up by high-intensity radiation and begin to chemically destroy ozone molecules. Destruction of the ozone layer would lead to a much higher worldwide incidence of skin cancer and crop failure; there would also be changes in the world's climate.

Concern about ozone depletion was heightened by the finding that the ozone layer above Antarctica decreases by roughly 40 percent each October, shortly after sunlight reappears following the Southern Hemisphere's winter months. The significance of this phenomenon is unclear, but some scientists believe that it may mean that the earth's ozone layer will be depleted more rapidly than expected (Brown et al., 1987).

A particularly troublesome form of air pollution, and one that has attracted increasing attention in recent years, is *acid rain*. This term refers to rainfall that contains large concentrations of sulfur dioxide, which is emitted by utility and industrial plants in many parts of the nation. Acid rain has a highly detrimental effect on forests and lakes, causing severe damage to trees and to fish and other forms of aquatic life and polluting water supplies.

The Global Warming Controversy   Of all the many aspects of pollution and environmental stress, perhaps none alarms scientists and environmental groups as much at present as the possibility of dangerous warming of the planet owing to continued high levels of carbon emissions into the atmosphere. Created primarily by the burning of fuel by humans, the amount of carbon dioxide in the atmosphere is estimated to have increased by 15 to 25 percent since 1800 and is expected—assuming that we do nothing to prevent it—to reach twice the preindustrial level by 2050 (Council on Environmental Quality, 1980).

Each ton of carbon emitted into the air produces 3.7 tons of carbon dioxide. During 1988 about 5.6 billion tons of carbon were produced by the combustion of fossil fuels. The United States was responsible for about one-fifth of this total (Flavin, 1990). Third-world countries burn fossil fuels at far lower rates than industrialized nations, but many of these countries meet their energy needs by burning wood, straw, and similar fuels, which also emit carbon. And as countries such as South Korea become more and more industrialized, they increase their use of fossil fuels. At the same time, the felling and burning of forests in tropical countries adds between 1 and 2 billion tons of carbon emissions to the worldwide total. Growing populations and the associated demand for energy, land, and other resources mean that carbon emissions—and, hence, the amount of carbon dioxide in the atmosphere—are likely to increase for the foreseeable future. Some scientists are concerned that the buildup of carbon dioxide in the atmosphere could produce a "greenhouse effect." That is, the carbon dioxide would trap heat near the earth's surface, raising the average temperature of the atmosphere. Such overheating, even by a few degrees, could melt the polar ice caps, with calamitous results.

Radioactivity The two large explosions that occurred on April 26, 1986, at the nuclear power plant in Chernobyl in the former Soviet Union released a cloud of radioactive gases over central and northern Europe. This cloud caused people in those regions to experience the highest levels of radioactive fallout ever recorded there. Two weeks later minor airborne radioactivity was detected in Tokyo, Washington, and throughout the Northern Hemisphere (Flavin, 1987).

Many environmental scientists fear that the health of people in the former Soviet Union and Europe could be severely affected by this event for decades. Radioactivity is the most dangerous form of air pollution because it is known to increase the probability that people will develop various kinds of cancer. Moreover, in the Chernobyl accident 135,000 people had to be evacuated from populated areas within 20 miles of the plant. Thus, the problems of airborne radioactivity, together with the need to evacuate huge populations in the case of accidents, have raised severe problems for the nuclear power industry throughout the world.

Nor are such problems limited to recent years. Thousands of U.S. military personnel and civilians were exposed to high levels of radiation during the 1950s, when tests of nuclear explosions were conducted. The Clinton administration has adopted a policy of making these events public so that the injured parties may seek compensation and confidence in the government's ability to control hazardous technologies can be restored.

Water Pollution

Water is constantly moving through what is known as the hydrologic cycle. It is found in the atmosphere as vapor; it condenses and falls to the earth as rain, snow, or dew; it percolates underground or runs off the surface as streams, rivers, and finally oceans; it evaporates into the atmosphere as vapor once again; and the cycle continues. While on the ground, water may be absorbed into the roots of plants and, through the leaves, eventually evaporate back into the atmosphere; or it may be drunk from streams by animals or people and evaporated or excreted back into the earth or air. Or it may sink into underground reservoirs and be stored for millions of years.

It is quite possible for water to be used more than once as it passes through a single round of the hydrologic cycle, if it is sufficiently purified between uses by natural or artificial means. However, we render much of our water unfit for reuse through various kinds of pollutants: raw and inadequately treated sewage, oil, synthetic organic chemicals (detergents, pesticides), inorganic chemicals and mineral substances, plant nutrients, radioactivity, and heat. We therefore face a dual crisis with respect to water. The amount available to us could be insufficient for our demands, and what is available could be polluted.

Just as air can cleanse itself if not overburdened, so too can rivers, lakes, and oceans purify themselves naturally. But we have been discharging wastes, directly or indirectly, into our waterways in amounts that prohibit such natural purification. In 1990 some 25 percent of the U.S. population was not served by sewage treatment facilities (*Statistical Abstract*, 1993). The bacteria in untreated sewage render the water unfit for drinking, swimming, and many industrial uses. Finally, the use of oxygen to decompose the waste reduces the life support capacity of the water, with a consequent decline in the number and variety of fish. As the population grows, the problem of waste disposal will become even more acute.

Current farming practices, such as extensive use of nitrate and phosphate fertilizers, also seriously impair water quality. Rain and irrigation cause the runoff of large quantities of these materials into rivers and lakes. The fertilizers work in water much as they do on land, producing algae "blooms"—huge masses of algae that grow very quickly and then die. As with the decomposition of sewage, the decay of these "blooms" consumes oxygen, thereby killing fish and other animals that have high oxygen requirements. As the algae decay, they settle at the bottom of the water, along with various compounds of nitrogen and phosphorus. At one time the bottom of Lake Erie was covered by a layer of muck from 20 to 125 feet thick. Only intensive efforts by environmentalists to stop pollutants from being discharged into the lake and adjoining waterways saved Lake Erie from total destruction.

Long-lasting pesticides and radioactive substances are especially dangerous because they accumulate in the tissues of animals that eat them. One reason this poses such a serious problem is the process known as *biological magnification,* whereby the concentration of a given substance increases as it ascends the food chain. A study of the Columbia River in the western United States revealed that although the radioactivity of the water was insignificant,

> *the radioactivity of the river plankton was 2,000 times greater; the radioactivity of the fish and ducks feeding on the plankton was 15,000 and 40,000 times greater, respectively; the radioactivity of young swallows fed on insects caught by their parents in the river was 500,000 times greater; the radioactivity of the egg yolks of water birds was more than a million times greater. (Curtis & Hogan, 1969)*

Presumably, the radioactive isotopes are released into the river by the nuclear power plant at Hanford, Washington. People who live downriver from such plants ingest and store radioactive isotopes with the water they drink and the fish and other local foods they eat. Because most radioactive substances retain their potency for many years—even centuries—the presence of these isotopes adds significantly to the normal "background" radiation in the environment. This results in a higher incidence of cancer and genetic defects.

Another form of water pollution is thermal pollution. The effluents of many factories and generating plants—especially nuclear power plants—are warmer than the rivers and lakes into which they flow, and when discharged in quantity they may raise the water temperature by as much as ten to thirty degrees Fahrenheit. Such thermal pollution can be ecologically devastating. Because most aquatic animals are cold-blooded, they are at the mercy of the surrounding water temperature. If the temperature rises beyond an organism's capacity for metabolic adjustment, the animal will die. Because larvae and young animals are far more susceptible than mature organisms to death through slight temperature variations, and because rises in temperature also interfere with the spawning and migratory patterns of many organisms, thermal pollution may exterminate some aquatic populations through reproductive failure.

Solid-Waste Disposal

We do not really "consume" most products, despite our reputation as a "consumer society." It is more accurate to say that we buy things, use them, and then throw them away, so that we have several hundred million tons of solid wastes to dispose of every year. These wastes include food, paper, glass, plastic, wood, abandoned cars, cans, metals, paints, dead animals, and a host of other things. The annual cost of disposing of such waste amounts to billions of dollars.

The two principal methods of solid-waste disposal are landfills and incineration. Although landfills are supposed to meet certain sanitary standards, violations are common. Improperly designed municipal incinerators are major contributors to urban air pollution. In addition, many cities use the ocean as a dumping ground. New York City's practice of dumping tons of refuse into the ocean each day has made a "dead sea" out of a large area in the Atlantic (O'Connor & Standford, 1979).

The United States lags behind other industrialized nations in efforts to deal with the problem of solid-waste disposal. The accumulation of garbage in landfills like this site in Alaska is becoming one of the nation's most critical environmental problems.

The large-scale introduction of plastics and other synthetics has produced a new waste disposal problem: While organic substances are eventually decomposed through bacterial action, plastics are generally totally immune to biological decomposition and remain in their original state when they are buried or dumped. If they are burned, they become air pollutants in the form of hydrocarbons and nitrogen oxides.

In the 1980s the waste disposal problem took on new urgency as many landfill sites filled up and fears of groundwater contamination caused many communities to forbid the opening of new sites on their land. In 1987, in a notorious illustration of the seriousness of the problem, a barge filled with garbage from Long Island spent several weeks searching the East Coast for a site that would accept its load of waste.

Toxic Wastes   There is, in addition, the problem of toxic wastes, or residues, from the production of plastics, pesticides, and other products. These residues have typically been buried in ditches or pits. The famous case of Love Canal, near Niagara Falls, arose when toxic residues that had been dumped into the unfinished canal seeped into the surrounding area and contaminated both the soil and the water, creating severe health hazards for local residents. In 1978 Love Canal was declared an environmental disaster area and more than 200 families were evacuated from the neighborhood. In early 1985, after more than six years of litigation, 1,300 former residents of Love Canal were awarded payments totaling $20 million in compensation for health problems (including birth defects and cancers) suffered as a result of the contamination of their neighborhood by toxic wastes. In 1991, thirteen years after the discovery of the contamination and the beginning of cleanup efforts, some houses in the Love Canal area were declared habitable again.

Radioactive Wastes   Nuclear power plants pose a special problem. The fuel in a reactor's core must be replaced periodically. This requires careful planning and handling, because the radioactivity of nuclear fuels increases as they are used. David Lilienthal, the first chairman of the Atomic Energy Commission, described the problem as follows:

> *These huge quantities of radioactive wastes must somehow be removed from the reactors, must—without mishap—be put into containers that will never rupture; then these vast quantities of poisonous stuff must be moved either to a burial ground or to reprocessing plants, handled again, and disposed of, by burial or otherwise, with a risk of human error at every step. (quoted in Curtis & Hogan, 1969, p. 175)*

There are 112 commercial nuclear plants in the United States; they produce 21.7 percent of the power generated in this country. From 1970 to 1987 the amount of radioactive wastes discharged annually from these reactors increased from 67 metric tons to 1,615 metric tons (*Statistical Abstract,* 1993). These wastes have to be safely stored for up to 1,000 years before they become harmless. During that time, any alteration in the seismological conditions of the burial site could disturb the radioactive material and contaminate the area.

Other Hazards

Besides the environmental problems just noted, other threats to our well-being arise from the indiscriminate use of technological knowledge. These include land degradation, noise pollution, chemical hazards, and the undesirable consequences of certain large-scale engineering projects.

Land Degradation   Any local ecosystem, such as a forest, swamp, or prairie, is a complex matrix of interrelated and interacting organisms and processes, one that both supports its own patterns of life and contributes to those of the larger regional, continental, and planetary ecosystems. Serious alteration of a local ecosystem therefore can affect the balance of life in a larger area. Yet through greed and/or igno-

Where to dispose of nuclear waste and how to repair the damage caused by the dumping of toxic chemicals into the environment are becoming critical social problems throughout the industrialized world.

rance of ecological principles, we have diminished or destroyed the capacity of large land areas to support life. We are only beginning to recognize the possible consequences.

Huge deserts can be created by misuse of the environment. By 1952, 23 percent of the earth's total land area was classified as desert or wasteland; by 1984, an estimated 35 percent of the earth's land area was threatened by desertification (Buffey, 1985). Recent research on the expansion of arid lands and deserts shows that overgrazing by domesticated animals, dependence on wood for fuel, and depletion of soil nutrients by crops produce desertification. When natural cycles of drought and wet seasons interact with human overuse, the rate of desertification can increase drastically (Stevens, 1994). It takes from 300 to 1,000 years to produce one inch of topsoil under the most favorable conditions. Many areas of the earth are now losing topsoil at the rate of several inches per year because of management techniques that expose the soil to wind and water erosion. Such irreparable losses are intolerable in view of the world's increased need for arable land.

Noise Pollution Noise is a dysfunctional consequence of technology. It is produced by airplanes, cars, buses, trucks, motorcycles, motorboats, factory machinery, dishwashers, garbage disposals, vacuum cleaners, television, radio, phonographs, air conditioners, jackhammers, bulldozers, and much else. Noise, which can be harmful even when it is not consciously heard, directly affects physical and emotional well-being. Studies have shown that people today suffer from greater hearing losses with increasing age than in the past, and that noise contributes significantly to the tension of daily life, sometimes even precipitating stress-related illnesses such as peptic ulcer and hypertension (Ehrlich & Ehrlich, 1972; Rienow & Rienow, 1967). Noise can also interfere with learning. In one New York City public school, pupils' reading scores improved significantly after the rails of a nearby subway were cushioned with rubber pads and sound-absorbing materials were installed in the classrooms (Goldman, 1982).

Chemicals Pressure to get new products on the market has resulted in the widespread use of various pesticides and herbicides without adequate testing of their long-run cumulative effects. It has also led to the massive use of plastics and other synthetics, which create serious problems of disposal, and untested industrial chemicals such as vinyl chloride gas. (Less than 2 percent of industrial chemicals have been tested for possible side effects.) Moreover, there has been a proliferation in the variety and amount of food additives—chemicals that are used in processing food. Little is known about the long-term effects of continual ingestion of these substances, either alone or in combination.

Large-Scale Engineering Projects Humans have always taken immense pride in their ability to change the face of the earth in ways that are deemed beneficial. However, they frequently fail to anticipate and assess the costs associated with those benefits. Thus, a new dam is hailed both as an engineering masterpiece and because it opens up new lands for agriculture, settlement, and recreation. Less often recognized is that although a dam may permit the controlled distribution of water to desired locations, it also "costs" water loss through evaporation. Moreover, large dams have caused earthquakes because of the tremendous pressure exerted by the billions of gallons of water they store.

Strip mining also poses hazards to the environment. Much of the coal in the United States lies deep within the earth; it must be obtained by means of underground mining. However, there is also a great deal of coal lying close enough to the surface for strip mining, in which the top layers of soil are removed and the coal is excavated. Although strip mining is cheaper and safer than underground mining, it causes much greater harm to the environment. Vast areas of land are denuded of all

This abandoned strip mine site in Arizona calls attention to the environmental impact of large-scale engineering projects.

living things and scarred by huge, ugly trenches. Because the topsoil is removed during the strip-mining process, healthy plant life cannot return for centuries. And because the soil balance is disturbed, water supplies in the area may be irreparably damaged; increased erosion at the mining site can cause both local and distant water sources to become contaminated by sediment, dissolved acids, and other pollutants.

THE UNITED STATES AND THE WORLD ENVIRONMENT

William C. Clark (1989) notes that "Our ability to look back on ourselves from outer space symbolizes the unique perspective we have on our environment and on where we are headed as a species. With this knowledge comes a responsibility not borne by the bacteria: the responsibility to manage the human use of planet earth" (p. 47). Because Americans are among the most wealthy, the most polluting, and the most educated of the earth's peoples, environmental scientists often argue that they bear a large share of the responsibility for wise management of the planet.

The difference in living standards between the United States and most other countries is enormous. In stark contrast to the hunger that prevails in many poor nations, the increased affluence of the United States and other developed countries has made possible a steady increase in per capita consumption of meat and other nutritious foods. In fact, Americans consume, on the average, four times as much food per person as people in poor nations. This is not to say that all Americans are overfed. The poor in the United States, like those in poor countries, are plagued by hunger, malnutrition, and disease (Brown & Postel, 1987).

Not only do most Americans eat much more food than people in most other parts of the world, but the food they eat includes a much larger proportion of meat than of grain. By contrast, three-fourths or more of the food energy in the diet of Asians comes directly from grain (Ehrlich et al., 1977). Vast quantities of grain—one-third of total world production—are fed to livestock in the United States and other developed countries in order to produce meat. It is sometimes claimed that this practice is immoral, because the grain that is fed to livestock in the United States could be used to nourish hungry people elsewhere in the world (Brown & Eckholm, 1974; Brown & Young, 1990).

It is true that the United States exports large amounts of grain to all parts of the world. Some of these exports are part of international aid programs that help alleviate the problem of hunger in the poorer nations; in fact, some of the world's least developed nations depend heavily on such aid. But the fact remains that the developed nations consume a disproportionate share of the world's food resources.

Energy resources and consumption are also distributed unevenly throughout the world. Energy use in the United States amounts to about one-third of the worldwide total. Of that amount, fully 25 percent is burned as fuel for transportation (Ehrlich et al., 1977). Much of the rest is converted into electricity before being distributed to residential, commercial, and industrial users. Like feeding grain to livestock in order to produce meat, converting fuel into electricity is an indirect and costly way of using natural resources (Gibbons, Blair, & Gwin, 1989).

The significance of these facts is twofold. The industrialized nations consume a disproportionate share of total food and energy resources, leaving comparatively little for the majority of the world's population. This is one explanation—though by no means the only one—for the desperate plight of people in the world's least developed nations. The other major effect of the dominant position of the United States in the world economy is that it contributes to environmental problems both at home and abroad. As the world's most industrialized nation, the United States "exports" technologies that can contribute substantially to the environmental problems of other nations. A vivid example is the disaster that occurred in Bhopal, India, in December 1984, in which a deadly gas, methyl isocyanate, escaped from a Union Carbide storage tank, killing more than 2,000 people and injuring about 100,000 others.

In sum, as populations increase in size and affluence, the complexity of social organization, imbalances in energy and food budgets, depletion of resources, and the difficulty of correcting these problems also increase. If the United States is to maintain its position as a world leader, it must take the lead in developing the means of controlling environmental problems.

The United States and other affluent nations can use their resources to help control the growth of the world's population. Through their own aid efforts and through cooperation with agencies of the United Nations and the World Bank, they can help poorer nations develop more adequate and sustainable water supplies. Ecologists estimate that unless continued action is taken, water shortages in arid areas of the world may produce serious regional conflicts and even warfare (Homer-Dixon, Boutwell, & Rathjens, 1993). Areas of growing water shortage are shown in Figure 17–2 on page 522.

SOCIAL POLICY

As is evident from much of the discussion in this chapter, issues of environmental control and restoration often overlap with policies designed to reduce the negative effects of new technologies. The growing fields of technology assessment and risk assessment, for example, contributed to the sensational debates that culminated in the defeat of legislation to fund research and development of a commercial supersonic passenger airplane in the United States (Hall, 1982; Ormes, 1973). Public fears about the effects of sonic booms were not allayed by the results of scientific assessments, and the proposal was defeated. England and France went on to produce a supersonic jet, the Concorde, that so far has proven that sonic boom effects can be controlled. Social policies dealing with technologies and their environmental consequences are extremely controversial—especially when potentially lucrative products are involved—and point up the significance of scientific assessment of the environmental impacts of proposed technologies.

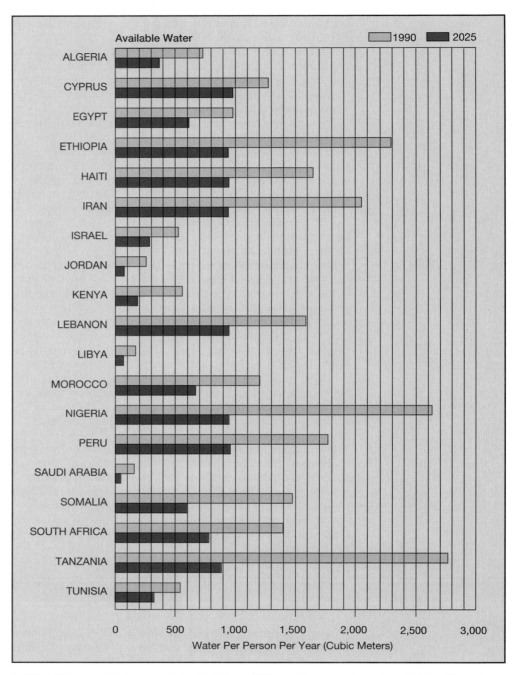

FIGURE 17–2 Estimates of Availability of Water: Various Countries, 1990 and 2025

Source: Homer-Dixon, Boutwell, & Rathjens, 1993.

Futures Studies

Futurists are a heterogeneous group of social analysts who try to describe the society of the future and encourage planning in response to their predictions. Although they differ among themselves on a number of issues, including the degree to which we should be optimistic about bringing technological change under social control, futurists tend to share a number of assumptions. Perhaps the most basic of these is that modern industrial societies are evolving toward a *postindustrial society* (Bell, 1973). The key organizing principle underlying the technology and economy of postindustrial society is the dominance of theoretical knowledge (Naisbitt & Aburdine, 1990).

Many futurists believe that science will become increasingly essential to technological progress, enhancing the power of its practitioners. Some analysts go so far as to predict the emergence of a new class made up of scientists, professionals, and technicians, who will exercise substantial control in postindustrial society because of their monopoly on scientific and technological knowledge. Futurists also predict that postindustrial society will specialize in the production of knowledge rather than goods. Thus, the educational and service sectors will grow more than industries such as mining and manufacturing.

According to some critics, rapid economic and technological change is outpacing the ability of culture and other dimensions of social life to adjust. Daniel Bell (1973), for example, argues that no single morality unites work and home life, a contradiction that threatens industrial society with confusion. Other writers believe that modes of thought that were adaptive in earlier eras are becoming irrelevant in the light of technological progress. People are used to pursuing immediate personal welfare in an environment of scarcity. Given the material bounty to be provided by inventions of the future, a stronger sense of community will be more appropriate in postindustrial society (Bellah et al., 1985).

Appropriate Technology

Appropriate technologists share many of the concerns and assumptions of futurists, but they advocate major changes in technology itself. In most cases appropriate technology is smaller-scale technology. Thus, Amory Lovins (1977, 1986) argues that we need to reexamine our basic way of life and the energy needs that go with it. He favors smaller-scale technological means of meeting our energy needs. Renewable energy sources such as wind and solar energy, which can be harnessed by families and communities, are preferable to other sources such as nuclear power, which is polluting, requires massive amounts of capital, and is controlled by large corporations.

The appropriate technologists are often accused of being utopians who advocate an impractical retreat to a simpler way of life. In answer to the charge of utopianism, they argue that their alternatives sound impractical because most people assume that continued economic and institutional expansion is necessary. A closer examination of social needs would make smaller-scale technology seem more appropriate. Appropriate technologists also point out that they do not oppose all technology, only large-scale technology that has unfavorable social consequences.

Technology Assessment

Technology assessment is a complex area of scientific and political research. Its complexity stems in part from the fact that it requires an interdisciplinary approach if it is to succeed. Physical scientists, social scientists, and policy makers generally speak their own technical languages and have their own perspectives and methods. Often these do not lend themselves to cooperation, and the assessment of a particular technology is limited to a single scientific discipline. Recently, however, a new professional cadre of interdisciplinary scientists has emerged. They are known as "risk professionals" and are skilled in the use of physical and social-scientific methods of assessing and evaluating technological systems (Jasanoff, 1986).

A more fundamental problem in technology assessment is the fact that it is easier to assess the risk of failure in a piece of hardware or a set of mechanisms within a technological system than the risk of failure in the entire system. Thus, in his pathbreaking study of accidents in major technological systems such as air traffic control systems, dams, and nuclear power plants, Charles Perrow (1984) concluded that "the dangerous accidents lie in the system, not in the components" (p. 351).

During the 1980s the pressure for deregulation of many industries resulted in less funding for technology assessment and a greater likelihood of accidents and failures in complex technological systems. This is not to say that there is no justification for deregulation, just that given the expanding risks to people and the environment, the need for better technology assessment and more forceful regulation is increasing.

Environmental Action

The Clean Air Act of 1970 established the Environmental Protection Agency (EPA) and empowered it to set and enforce standards of air quality. The EPA has since been given authority over most matters involving environmental quality.

During the 1980s environmental policy was hampered by the conflicting desires of a society that wished to preserve and improve environmental quality but not to discourage economic growth or distort energy prices. In 1981, as the time for revision of the Clean Air Act approached, the EPA interpreted the law as encouraging *both* economic growth and improved air quality. It proposed less stringent ambient-air standards (e.g., regarding the amount of carbon monoxide that may be emitted by cars and trucks) in an attempt to reach a compromise between the desire for clean air and the need to control energy costs.

In the 1990s issues of environmental quality and regulation have again become popular causes. Under the leadership of Vice-President Albert Gore, a recognized expert on environmental policy, the Clinton administration has taken steps to tighten regulations regarding air pollution, solid-waste disposal, and drainage of wetlands. Such steps are not always popular. For example, after the Mississippi River floods in the summer of 1993, the administration attempted to discourage the rebuilding of some levees and the restoration of some farmland on flood plains, a policy that outraged many residents of the area. In the West, the administration's policies on preserving old-growth timber and restricting grazing on public lands angered many people whose livelihood depended on relatively cheap access to those natural resources. On the other hand, some states, especially California, have become impatient with Congress's reluctance to pass more stringent air-quality legislation and have developed standards of their own. California's air quality standards will require greater control of pollution emissions from gasoline engines and have spurred the development of prototypes of an electrically powered automobile.

An innovative provision of the 1990 Clean Air Act encourages businesses to reduce their smoke emissions below what the law requires. The 1990 act allows companies to "sell" the difference between their emissions and the amount allowable under the law to other companies whose emissions are above the legal limits. Thus, in 1994 a New Jersey utility sold a portion of its "pollution rights" to a Connecticut company. (It was able to do so because Connecticut is downwind of it; therefore, fewer emissions in New Jersey benefit both New Jersey and New York without increasing pollution in Connecticut.) Although they are strongly criticized by environmentalists, these pollution trades may give utilities and manufacturing concerns additonal incentives to reduce their smoke emissions.

In recent years laws regarding the dumping of toxic wastes have been enforced more strictly by government agencies at all levels. There has also been an attempt to cope with the problem of destruction of the earth's ozone shield. Although the depletion of the ozone layer continues, the seriousness of the problem is a matter of debate. Indeed, the difficulty of determining how serious an environmental problem actually is remains a major obstacle in environmental policy making. Nowhere is this situation more evident than in the controversy over "global warming" and policies intended to solve the problem once its severity has been determined. (See Box 17–1.)

BOX 17–1 CURRENT CONTROVERSIES: THE POLITICS OF GLOBAL WARMING

The debate over global warming is both scientific and political in nature. Not only is there disagreement over whether and how much global warming is occurring, but there is even greater debate over what to do about it if it occurs.

The scientific controversy is fairly straightforward; it deals with the precise magnitude of the anticipated change in the earth's average temperature. Estimates of the probable extent of global warming over the next century range from 1.5 to 4.5 degrees Celsius. Even at the lower end of that range, a change of this magnitude could dramatically alter the earth's climate, affecting agriculture, water supplies, and ecosystems and causing severe storms and coastal flooding (Schneider, 1990).

Scientists generally agree that human activities are largely responsible for the huge increase in the levels of carbon dioxide and methane in the earth's atmosphere since the industrial revolution, and that the use of chlorofluorocarbons in aerosol sprays has also contributed to the problem by depleting the atmosphere's ozone layer. They also agree that the result has been to increase the probability of global warming. There is less agreement about the seriousness of the problem and what should be done about the problem.

Policy makers and the public have tended to disbelieve dire predictions of catastrophes like fires and floods resulting from global warming, partly because a number like 1.5 degrees Celsius seems so low. But even those who understand that only a few degrees can mean the difference between an ice age and a habitable planet are divided over what should be done about the situation.

Proposals for dealing with global warming take a variety of forms, all aimed at reducing carbon dioxide emissions both in advanced industrial nations and in less developed countries. Some proposals would require all nations to cut their emissions by 20 percent. Nations that are already more energy efficient than others object to such proposals, believing that they would be unfairly penalized. Third-world countries also object, since their development would be held back by limits on the amount of energy they could use. Some proposals attempt to address this issue by allowing the industrialized nations to maintain their current emission levels while paying for the conversion of less developed countries to more efficient ways of using energy.

A popular proposal would entail issuing "tradable permits" whereby each citizen of the world has the right to emit a certain amount of carbon dioxide. The permits could be traded for cash, food, energy-efficient products, and so forth. In other words, each nation would have a fixed right to emit an amount of carbon dioxide based on its population at the time the agreement was signed.

Critics of such proposals cite the costs of reducing carbon dioxide by 20 percent, which would amount to tens of billions of dollars. But they often fail to cite the benefits—less global warming, less acid rain, less air pollution, lower operating costs for manufactured products, and so forth. For example, one critic, former presidential adviser John Sununu, claims that environmentalists are trying to create a policy "that cuts off our use of coal, oil, and natural gas." Yet no environmental group has made such a proposal; instead, most advocate switching to less polluting energy equipment.

The debate over global warming thus has become highly political, and the controversy will not be resolved easily. There is a need not only for further research by atmospheric scientists to determine the precise extent and consequences of global warming, but also for social-scientific evaluations of its probable impact on societies throughout the world, as well as the likely effects of policies designed to address the problem.

A largely unheralded piece of environmental legislation, the Emergency Planning and Community Right to Know Act (1986), is proving to be an effective tool in local struggles against polluters. In 1991, for example, the town of Baton Rouge, Louisiana, was able to force the American Cyanamid Corporation to reduce its pollution of the region. The community obtained data showing that the company was responsible for at least 25 percent of the 750 million pounds of toxic chemicals poured into the local environment each year. The facts were gathered by the federal Environmental Protection Agency under the mandate provided by the Community Right to Know Act.

There are some loopholes in the act: Small businesses with nine or fewer employees are exempt from the regulations, and large companies that claim to be recycling dangerous chemicals may not be reporting the extent to which they release pollutants into the environment. But despite these obstacles, information gathered under the provisions of the act is increasingly being used by communities to pressure polluters to change their ways—an example of successful environmental policy based on the free flow of information (Schneider, 1991).

The problems of environmental pollution and land degradation are more serious in poor and minority communities than elsewhere. This is true in the United States as well as in third-world nations. A famous example of such problems is the case of Chikpo, India, where local women chained themselves to trees in order to prevent their forest from being cut down by governmental and commercial agencies. Such social movements are having an increasing impact on environmental policies around the globe (Martínez-Alier & Hershberg, 1992). In the United States, the Clinton administration has, for the first time, invoked the 1965 Civil Rights Act on behalf of poor African American residents in Mississippi and Louisiana who have been subjected to far more than their fair share of toxic waste dumping and other pollution hazards such as pesticides. Since state policies are supported in part by federal funds, the Civil Rights Act, which bans discrimination in federally supported projects, may help minority residents gain redress for past harm and greater protection against polluters in the future (Cushman, 1993).

Despite the attention focused on environmental problems in recent years, there is still a need for public education about the state of the environment, how it got that way, and what can be expected to happen in the future. People must be persuaded to change their attitudes and learn that the earth's resources are not limitless. This entails a distinct change in values. Since there are limits to both the amount of goods we can produce and the amount of waste the earth can absorb, we must abandon the concept that "more is better." We must also strive for a relatively equal distribution of our limited supply of life-supporting and life-enhancing goods among all the earth's inhabitants.

SUMMARY

1. Technology has three dimensions: the apparatus, or physical devices, used in accomplishing a variety of tasks; the activities involved in performing those tasks; and the organizational networks associated with activities and apparatus.

2. Advances in technology can have both positive and negative impacts. When technology has adverse side effects, people tend to blame the technology itself, rather than the combination of economic, social, and technical factors.

3. The concept of autonomous technology is a recurrent one in American social thought. One element in this concept is the idea that technology has become independent of human control. Most writers on the subject do not believe this is the case. Instead, they argue that the social order has become interwoven with the technological order to such an extent that it sometimes appears that technology is "out of control."

4. In bureaucratic organizations individuals may commit immoral acts because they are not personally responsible for the consequences of those acts, which are carried out under the direction of superiors. Whistle-blowers are individuals who place their personal moral concerns in opposition to the activities of an organization. They often suffer as a result of their efforts.

5. The best-known statement of the relationship between technology and institutions is Ogburn's cultural lag theory. According to Ogburn, a cultural lag occurs when one of two correlated parts of a culture changes before or in greater degree than the other, thereby causing less adjustment between the two parts than existed previously. Typically, social institutions and technology readily adjust and readjust to each other, but sometimes one or the other changes radically and a lag develops.

6. Environmental stress results from the interaction of the environment, the technological system, and the social system. This interaction produces air and water pollution, problems of solid-waste disposal, and other hazards. A difficulty in dealing with environmental stress is the number of problems involved and the extent to which they are interrelated.

7. Americans consume, on the average, four times as much food per person as people in less developed countries. Energy resources and consumption are also distributed unevenly throughout the world, with energy use in the United States amounting to about one-third of the worldwide total. To satisfy their high standard of living, Americans place enormous stress on the environment. Many observers believe the United States should take the lead in efforts to reverse the effects of environmental stress throughout the world.

8. Futurists try to describe the society of the future and encourage planning in response to their predictions.

They generally agree that industrial societies are evolving toward a postindustrial era in which the key organizing principle is the dominance of theoretical knowledge. Appropriate technologists advocate changes in large-scale technologies that have unfavorable social consequences. Technology assessment and risk assessment use both physical and social-scientific methods in studying the social consequences of existing and proposed technologies.

9. A number of laws designed to control or reduce the harm being done to the environment have been passed since the 1960s, and some progress has been made. The Clinton administration has taken steps to tighten regulations regarding air pollution, solid-waste disposal, and drainage of wetlands; and it has invoked the 1965 Civil Rights Act to combat excessive exposure to pollution hazards in minority communities. However, there is a need for additional public education about the environment and further efforts to change people's attitudes regarding the depletion of the earth's resources.

SUGGESTED READINGS

BROWN, LESTER R., ET AL. *State of the World 1994: A Worldwatch Institute Report on Progress Toward a Sustainable Society.* New York: W. W. Norton, 1994. An annual review of the state of environmental problems throughout the world. Makes chilling reading for anyone who is concerned about the living planet, but also offers clear policy directions.

DA SOLA POOL, ITHIEL. *Technologies of Freedom: On Free Speech in an Electronic Age.* Cambridge, MA: Harvard University Press, 1983. One of the founders of the sociological and political study of technology assesses the consequences of electronic communications for free speech.

ELLUL, JACQUES. *The Technological Society,* trans. John Wilkinson. New York: Knopf, 1964. An examination of "technique" as a basic human response to the environment.

ERIKSON, KAI. *A New Species of Trouble.* New York: W. W. Norton, 1994. A masterful series of case studies of environmental and other disasters affecting poor and minority communities in the United States.

LONG, FRANKLIN A., and ALEXANDRA OLESON, EDS. *Appropriate Technology and Social Values: A Critical Appraisal.* Cambridge, MA: Ballinger, 1980. A collection of essays focusing on the central issues of appropriate technology.

PERROW, CHARLES. *Normal Accidents: Living with High-Risk Technologies.* New York: Basic Books, 1984. A study of the increase in technological risks in modern life and an evaluation of the state of risk assessment.

SCHNAIBERG, ALLAN. *The Environment: From Surplus to Scarcity.* New York: Oxford University Press, 1980. A critical review of existing explanations of environmental problems, with a suggested course of action for avoiding ultimate disaster.

WESTIN, ALAN F. *Whistle-Blowing! Loyalty and Dissent in the Corporation.* New York: McGraw-Hill, 1981. A description of whistle-blowing based on ten case studies.

WINNER, LANGDON. *Autonomous Technology: Technics-out-of-Control as a Theme in Political Thought.* Cambridge, MA: M.I.T. Press, 1977. An examination of attempts to explain technological dynamism; outlines the structure of the technological order and describes its main processes.

War and Terrorism

Chapter Outline

- During World War II almost 17 million soldiers and 35 million civilians were killed.
- It is estimated that between 75,000 and 100,000 Iraqi soldiers died in the Persian Gulf war.
- In 1992 almost 2.2 million veterans were receiving compensation from the U.S. government for war-related disabilities. Of these, 132,000 were totally disabled.
- Between 1975 and 1982, 627,000 Southeast Asians fled their homes to take refuge in the United States.
- A one-megaton bomb striking the ground in downtown Detroit would dig a crater 1,000 feet across and 200 feet deep and would level all buildings within a radius of 1.7 miles.

For a fleeting instant in history, after the fall of the Berlin Wall, the collapse of the Soviet empire, and the sudden end of the cold war, it seemed that the United States and its allies could bring about a new era of world peace. But since then the brutal war in Bosnia, with its nightmare of "ethnic cleansing" and the shelling of civilian populations in Sarajevo and other cities, has become the symbol of a new form of warfare: the regional war based on lingering intergroup hatreds that make the prospects for world peace seem dimmer than ever.

The rapid and successful conclusion of the Persian Gulf war also appeared to presage a new era. But the euphoria brought on by the end of that war was quickly

Oil wells burning out of control in Kuwait at the end of the Iraqi occupation. The Persian Gulf war was notable for the extent to which environmental terrorism was used as a political and social weapon.

dissipated by images of continuing attacks on minority groups within Iraq, notably the Kurds. The U.S. occupation of Somalia provided additional difficult lessons on the limitations of military power. The occupation was intended to end the regional famine caused in part by incessant warfare among bands of armed marauders and warlords. However, some Somalis turned on their rescuers, and the tasks of maintaining peace and rebuilding the Somali economy have proved far more difficult than anyone imagined before the occupation.

Nor did optimism about achieving peace in the Middle East last very long after the Gulf war. Terrorism in the United States, particularly the bombing of the World Trade Center in New York City, and the outbreak of severe violence in Israel and the settlements of the West Bank of the Jordan River threatened to stall progress toward peace in 1994. Threats of similar warfare based on intergroup hostility increased in Georgia and other republics of the former Soviet Union. Instability and violence in Southeast Asia and Africa, caused by overpopulation and environmental stress as well as the difficulty of maintaining national borders, also appeared to increase the prospect that the cold war would be replaced by a worldwide pattern of bloody regional wars in which the United States and the United Nations would be asked to intervene even though their ability to do so effectively is doubtful.

The twentieth century has been called the Century of Total War, both because of the vast increase in the human capacity for waging war and because the possibility of wars involving the entire globe is inherent in the rise of nations with global political ambitions (Aron, 1955). Although the end of the cold war has lessened somewhat the threat of global war and nuclear holocaust, it also seems that the spread of advanced weapons around the globe, the rise of smaller nuclear powers such as Iraq and North Korea, and the worsening of environmental and ethnic problems have increased the threat of wars of all kinds in many parts of the world (Kennedy, 1993). What can be done to reduce the likelihood of war and terrorism? No one can answer this question with certainty. Much may depend on how well individual citizens understand the causes and consequences of war and on how effectively they participate in debates over policies designed to control the arms race and limit the use of force in settling national differences.

In the discussion to follow, we will examine the impact of wars on those who fight them and on civilians, both those back home and those trapped in war zones. We will continue with a survey of some of the theories of war that have been proposed by social scientists and others. The chapter will conclude with a summary of attempts by governments and private citizens to prevent outbreaks of war and terrorism.

THE NATURE OF THE PROBLEM

Direct Effects of War

For those who experience its tragic devastation, war is the most serious social problem one can imagine. Over the centuries warfare has taken millions of lives. According to one estimate (Sorokin, 1937), between 1100 and 1925 about 35 million soldiers were killed in some 862 wars in Europe. Other investigators have calculated that between 1816 and 1965 alone, about 29 million soldiers were killed in 33 major European conflicts (Singer & Small, 1972). And these figures do not include the untold millions of civilians who perished as well. By any standard, the twentieth century has been the deadliest in human history. During World War I, 8 million soldiers and another 1 million civilians died. The casualties of World War II were even higher: Almost 17 million soldiers and 35 million civilians were killed. In the Soviet Union, the generation of men old enough to fight in World War II was decimated. In the Persian Gulf war it is estimated that between 75,000 and 100,000 Iraqi soldiers died, but the impossibility of knowing exact casualty figures is a reminder of how devastating that war was and continues to be for Iraq.

Long after peace is declared, many soldiers bear the scars of their battlefield experience. For every American soldier who died in battle in the major wars of this century, between two and four others received nonfatal wounds (Newspaper Enterprise Association, 1983). Many of the wounded have required medical care for months or years, and many have been so badly injured that they have not been able to hold a job or return to a normal way of life. In 1992 almost 2.2 million veterans were receiving compensation from the U.S. government for war-related disabilities. Of these, 132,000 were totally disabled (*Statistical Abstract,* 1993). The poor are especially likely to be recruited into dangerous military roles. Several studies have shown that during the Vietnam War battle deaths and injuries were more common among lower-class soldiers than among those from the middle or upper classes (Badillo & Curry, 1976; Janowitz, 1978; Zeitlin, Lutterman, & Russell, 1973).

Not all war-related disabilities are physical. War takes a psychological toll as well. During and after World War II, Harvard sociologist Samuel Stouffer and his colleagues (1949) conducted the first major study of war stress. Stouffer found correlations between psychological stress and several types of combat experience. For example, soldiers stationed close to the front lines—who were constantly exposed to the threat of injury or death to themselves and their friends, the hardships of life on the battlefield, the value conflicts involved in killing others, and inability to control their own actions—suffered symptoms of psychological stress to a greater extent than others. In the decades since Stouffer's research was carried out, mental-health experts have identified post-traumatic stress disorder (PTSD) as a common aftereffect of battle. The symptoms of PTSD include feeling generally irritable, depressed, and unhappy and having nightmares and flashbacks of war experiences. One study of Vietnam War veterans found that 36 percent of all men exposed to heavy combat during the war displayed PTSD for an average of ten years after their tour of duty (Kadushin, 1983).

The psychological impact of the Vietnam War may have differed from that of earlier American wars because the Vietnam War was a guerrilla war. The enemy blended in with the civilian population and therefore seemed to be everywhere and nowhere at the same time. These conditions may have been responsible for the unusually high levels of violence against civilians that characterized the Vietnam War, as well as for the mistreatment of prisoners and the use of such weapons as napalm, which killed civilians and the enemy indiscriminately. Soldiers who saw or engaged in these forms of violence suffered from psychological disorders to a greater extent than those who did not (Laufer, Gallops, & Frey-Wouters, 1984).

Indirect Effects of War

In addition to killing and wounding people, war disrupts the lives of the civilians whose homeland has become a battleground. Often it leads to mass migrations of people seeking to escape from danger or persecution or looking for new opportunities. Between 1975 and 1982, for example, 627,000 Southeast Asians fled their homes to take refuge in the United States (*Statistical Abstract,* 1983), and thousands more were accepted by other nations. When refugees arrive in a new country, their problems are not over. As we noted in Chapter 9, they often encounter prejudice, unemployment, and difficulty in adjusting to a new culture.

Another major cause of wartime migration is government policy. During and after World War II, a number of European states forced whole populations to move. During the war, the German government ordered hundreds of thousands of ethnic Germans to move back to Germany from the Eastern European nations that Germany had invaded. After the war, under the terms of the Potsdam Treaty, many more Germans were required to move from various Eastern European nations to areas within the redrawn borders of Germany.

Some of the indirect effects of war are not as easy to calculate as numbers of refugees. For example, it is impossible to measure the economic damage caused by war. Billions of dollars must be diverted from productive uses, first into arms and

Long after ceasefires have been negotiated, the consequences of war are felt among displaced refugees like these Kurdish victims of the 1991 war against Iraq.

then into the effort to repair the damage caused by arms. Even less quantifiable is the impact of war on how people think. World War I left in its wake widespread disillusionment with traditional values. To the men in the trenches, patriotism lost much of its appeal. After the war many people were pessimistic about the future of civilization and felt alienated from their former way of life.

Liberated Kuwait is a good example of the longer-term political and social effects of even a "successful" war. The nation's people remain badly divided in their feelings about the ruling elite, some of whom chose to stay and resist while many more lived in luxury outside the country during the Persian Gulf war. Critics of the elite have called for a more democratic form of government. Similarly, in the former Yugoslavia, uneasy truces cannot heal the hatreds caused by ethnic expulsions and intergroup brutality.

Effects of Nuclear War

In the past 100 years, wars have become less frequent but more intense as military technology has become more lethal. The development of nuclear weapons in the 1940s contributed to peace among the major powers. But the cost of that peace is the threat that if peace breaks down, a war of almost unimaginable destructiveness could ensue. Some idea of the nature of that destruction is provided by accounts of the bombing of Hiroshima, Japan, during World War II.

Thousands of military personnel were exposed to radiation during the testing of nuclear weapons and their effects. These marines were actually miles away from the blast; nevertheless, they were at serious risk owing to radiation fallout.

On the morning of August 6, 1945, as the people of Hiroshima were preparing to go to work, an American aircraft flew over the city. Seconds later a nuclear bomb exploded 2,000 feet above the center of the city. Even though the 12.5-kiloton device was tiny by modern standards, its effect was devastating. The force and heat of the blast annihilated tens of thousands of people almost instantly and delivered a deadly dose of radiation to thousands of others; within three months some 130,000 would be dead. While the explosion and the ensuing firestorm were turning the downtown area into a charred wasteland, a black radioactive rain fell on the injured as they walked through the parts of the city that were still passable. One survivor described these processions of burned victims as follows:

> *They held their arms bent [forward] . . . and their skin—not only on their hands but on their faces and bodies, too—hung down. . . . If there had been only one or two such people . . . perhaps I would not have had such a strong impression. But wherever I walked, I met these people. . . . Many of them died along the road. I can still picture them in my mind—like walking ghosts. They didn't look like people of this world. (quoted in Schell, 1982, p. 41)*

Nuclear bombs more than 1,600 times more powerful than the one that destroyed Hiroshima have now become a standard part of the weapons systems of the major world powers.

The U.S. Office of Technology Assessment (1979) has described the impact that a single nuclear device about eighty times more powerful than the Hiroshima bomb would have on a city like Detroit. A one-megaton bomb striking the ground in downtown Detroit would dig a crater 1,000 feet across and 200 feet deep and would level all buildings within a radius of 1.7 miles. If the attack occurred during the day, when the downtown area would be crowded with workers, more than 200,000 people would be killed within seconds. The number of deaths would double if the bomb were set to explode in the air over the city, although the damage to buildings would be reduced.

Some two-thirds of the energy of a nuclear explosion is converted into heat, which travels away from the blast in a searing flash that lasts for several seconds. In

Detroit, heat from a ground burst could kill and injure about 275,000 people within a distance of about 7.5 miles from "ground zero," the point of the explosion. In addition, fires set by the heat would engulf much of the city, taking still more lives. (See Figure 18–1.)

Besides causing massive physical damage, nuclear blasts release radiation, which in large doses leads to radiation sickness and death within a few weeks. In smaller doses, radiation increases the rate of fatal cancer in the exposed population. Most of the people exposed to the direct radiation of a ground burst in Detroit would already have been killed by the blast. However, the radioactive dust thrown up by the explosion could be blown hundreds of miles downwind into Canada or over Lake Erie to Pittsburgh and beyond. People living within about 100 miles of Detroit who could not be evacuated or housed in fallout shelters would probably receive a fatal dose within the first week.

Even if Detroit were the only city struck by a nuclear attack, the disaster would severely strain the nation's resources. The hospital beds remaining in the Detroit area could serve only about 1 percent of the survivors. Moreover, the several thousand beds in burn centers throughout the nation could accommodate only a tiny portion of the burn victims. Tens of thousands of people would need shelter, food, and other forms of support.

The specter of global nuclear war has lessened since the fall of the Soviet empire. The United States, Russia, and Ukraine have agreed to dismantle or otherwise disable their missiles, but vast destructive nuclear capabilities remain in place around the globe. Even though the threat of nuclear holocaust resulting from the cold war is greatly diminished, the possibility that nuclear bombs will be obtained by nations in unstable areas of the world such as Southeast Asia, North Korea, and the Middle East keep the threat of nuclear war alive. Even a limited nuclear war would create human catastrophes on a scale not hitherto experienced, to say nothing of the environmental damage and destruction such wars would cause for years

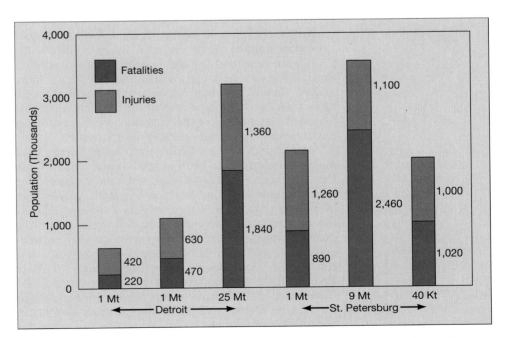

FIGURE 18–1 Anticipated Casualties in the Event of a Nuclear Explosion in Detroit or St. Petersburg

Source: U.S. Office of Technology Assessment, 1979.

afterwards even in regions beyond the boundaries of the original conflict. These concerns suggest that it is premature to celebrate the end of the threat of nuclear war. Experts in the field agree that efforts to control the proliferation of nuclear weapons are as vital today as they ever were.

MILITARY TECHNOLOGY AND THE CONDUCT OF WAR

Throughout human history the actual conduct of war has been closely linked to the nature of existing military technology. The introduction of bronze (and later iron) weapons, the use of horses and chariots in warfare, the invention of gunpowder, and the development of the armored tank are just a few of the technological "improvements" that have affected the nature of warfare and the relative dominance of different human groups.

As the technologies of war have become ever more deadly, the ravages of war have become ever greater. Thus, in the battle of Marathon in 490 B.C. the Athenians killed about 6,400 Persians. Similarly, when rebellious British tribes slaughtered an entire Roman legion in A.D. 62, the casualties totaled less than 7,000. These battles were fought hand to hand with swords, axes, spears, and the like. With the invention of gunpowder in the Middle Ages, it became possible to eliminate large numbers of enemy forces at a distance. From that time on, war became steadily more deadly and involved larger numbers of troops and higher casualties.

In the second half of the nineteenth century, as a result of the industrialization of England and other European nations, the scale and impact of warfare increased dramatically. Although technological advances such as the invention of armor plate and large field cannons increased the firepower of armies, new weaponry did not change the conduct of war as much as did the use of more modern means of transport, especially railroads and steamships, which made possible the movement of enormous numbers of troops to the battlefront. Armies began to count their soldiers by the millions rather than the thousands: "The ideal of every man a soldier, characteristic only of barbarian societies in time past, became almost capable of realization in the technologically most sophisticated countries of the earth" (McNeill, 1982, p. 223).

The advent of tanks and bombs made possible even greater carnage, and the death tolls of modern wars reflect this fact: 10.5 million people died in World War I and another 52 million in World War II. It is estimated that in an all-out nuclear war more than 160 million people would be killed outright and countless millions more would die as a result of the lingering effects of radiation, destruction of the natural environment, and massive social disorganization.

It is important to recognize that changes in the organizational dimension of military technology have been at least as important as advances in military apparatus. (See Chapter 17 for a discussion of the three major dimensions of technology.) A notable example is the introduction of the phalanx by the ancient Greeks. In this form of military organization, foot soldiers were arrayed in ranks in a wedge-shaped formation so that the enemy had only a few targets to strike at. Each row of men in the phalanx was furnished with longer spears than those in front of them, so that several rows could strike at the enemy simultaneously. A phalanx could also defend itself against projectiles by crouching under a "roof" of interlocked shields. When skillfully used, the phalanx was virtually invincible, as can be seen in Alexander the Great's use of this device in conquering the Persian Empire.

A more recent example of change in military organization is the bureaucratization of military administration. Beginning in Europe between 1300 and 1600, taxes were collected on a regular basis for the support of standing armies. In the seventeenth century the Dutch discovered that long hours of repeated drill made armies more efficient in battle and created a strong *esprit de corps*. It soon became evident that "a well-drilled army, responding to a clear chain of command that reached down to every corporal and squad from a monarch claiming to rule by divine right, constituted a more obedient and efficient instrument of policy than had ever been seen on earth before" (McNeill, 1982, p. 117).

One result of the increased efficiency and effectiveness of armies was an increase in the influence of military institutions on social organization. An example from the twentieth century is Japan's development into a war economy before World War II. The entire course of Japan's modernization was guided by the management of the national effort to achieve military power (McNeill, 1982).

During World War II and in subsequent decades, the rate of change in military technology—both apparatus and organization—increased dramatically. As William McNeill (1982) points out,

> *The accelerated pace of weapons improvement that set in from the late 1930s, and the proliferating variety of new possibilities that deliberate invention spawned, meant that all the belligerents realized by the time fighting began that some new secret weapon might tip the balance decisively. Accordingly, scientists, technologists, design engineers, and efficiency experts were summoned to the task of improving existing weapons and inventing new ones on a scale far greater than ever before. (p. 357)*

The outcome of this process of technological advance was the present situation of immense destructive power and, for the first time, the possibility of annihilating the human species.

Controlling Warfare

Despite the increasing scale, sophistication, and destructiveness of modern warfare, there has been some progress toward controlling the conduct of war. As was evident in the United Nations and congressional debates before the Persian Gulf war, there is a body of international law that deals with armed conflicts. It includes a complex set of rules that define the rights and privileges of those who fight and that attempt to protect noncombatants. Underlying this body of law is the ancient concept of the "just war." This doctrine, which developed out of the shared culture of Greek and Roman civilization, has two major branches: justification for going to war *(jus ad bellum)* and justifiable acts in wartime *(jus in bello)*.

Jus in bello is concerned with whether or not a particular war is being fought "justly." It sets limits on the means of violence (e.g., the use of particularly inhumane weapons) and on the injury or damage done to civilians. Table 18–1 on page 538 lists some of the specific actions that have been declared war crimes under international law.

The rules of *jus in bello* are difficult to enforce and are frequently violated. In the Vietnam War, for example, the United States used chemical defoliants that negatively affected human, animal, and plant life. American planes bombed North Vietnamese population centers, and both sides tortured and assassinated civilians. The most notorious American attack on civilians was the massacre of between 175 and 400 noncombatants, including infants, at the hamlet of My Lai in March 1968. For this crime one American officer was convicted and sentenced to life imprisonment, but he was released after serving two years in prison (Beer, 1981).

Further instances of disregard for international law could be seen in the Persian Gulf war. In Kuwait the Iraqi invaders used torture and terrorism. In addition, by pouring crude oil into the Gulf and setting fire to the Kuwaiti oilfields, they added an extremely ominous form of violence, ecoterrorism, to the arsenal of war tactics.

TABLE 18–1   WAR CRIMES

1. Making use of poisoned or otherwise forbidden arms or munitions.
2. Treachery in asking for quarter or simulating sickness or wounds.
3. Maltreatment of corpses.
4. Firing on localities which are undefended and without military significance.
5. Abuse of or firing on a flag of truce.
6. Misuse of the Red Cross or similar emblems.
7. Wearing of civilian clothes by troops to conceal their identity during the commission of combat acts.
8. Improper utilization of privileged (exempt, immune) buildings for military purposes.
9. Poisoning of streams or wells.
10. Pillage.
11. Purposeless destruction.
12. Compelling prisoners of war to engage in prohibited types of labor.
13. Forcing civilians to perform prohibited labor.
14. Violation of surrender terms.
15. Killing or wounding military personnel who have laid down arms, surrendered, or are disabled by wounds or sickness.
16. Assassination, and the hiring of assassins.
17. Ill-treatment of prisoners of war, or of the wounded and sick—including despoiling them of possessions not classifiable as public property.
18. Killing or attacking harmless civilians.
19. Compelling the inhabitants of occupied enemy territory to furnish information about the armed forces of the enemy or his means of defense.
20. Appropriation or destruction of the contents of privileged buildings.
21. Bombardment from the air for the exclusive purpose of terrorizing or attacking civilian populations.
22. Attack on enemy vessels which have indicated their surrender by lowering their flag.
23. Attack or seizure of hospitals and all other violations of the Hague Convention for the Adaptation to Maritime Warfare of the Principles of the Geneva Convention.
24. Unjustified destruction of enemy prizes.
25. Use of enemy uniforms during combat and use of the enemy flag during attack by a belligerent vessel.
26. Attack on individuals supplied with safe-conducts, and other violations of special safeguards provided.
27. Breach of parole.
28. Grave breaches of Article 50 of the Geneva Convention for the Amelioration of the Condition of the Wounded and Sick in Armed Forces in the Field, of 1949, and Article 51 of the Geneva Convention of 1949 Applicable to Armed Forces at Sea: "wilful killing, torture or inhuman treatment, including biological experiments, wilfully causing great suffering or serious injury to body or health, and extensive destruction and appropriation of property not justified by military necessity and carried out unlawfully and wantonly."
29. Grave breaches of the Geneva Convention Relative to the Treatment of Prisoners of War, of 1949, as listed in Article 130: "wilful killing, torture or inhuman treatment, including biological experiments, wilfully causing great suffering or serious injury to body or health, compelling a prisoner of war to serve in the forces of the hostile Power, or wilfully depriving a prisoner of war of the rights of fair and regular trial prescribed" in the Convention.
30. Grave breaches of the Fourth Geneva Convention of 1949, as detailed in Article 147: "wilful killing, torture or inhuman treatment, including biological experiments, wilfully causing great suffering or serious injury to body or health, unlawful deportation or transfer or unlawful confinement of a protected person, compelling a protected person to serve in the forces of a hostile Power, or willfully depriving a protected person of the rights of fair and regular trial prescribed in the present Convention, taking of hostages and extensive destruction and appropriation of property, not justified by military necessity and carried out unlawfully and wantonly." In addition, conspiracy, direct incitement, and attempts to commit, as well as complicity in the commission of crimes against the laws of war are punishable.

Source: Reprinted with permission of Macmillan Publishing Company from *Law Among Nations,* Second Edition, by Gerhard Von Glahn. Copyright © 1970 by Gerhard Von Glahn.

THEORIES ABOUT WAR AND ITS ORIGINS

In the forty-five years since nuclear weapons were developed, war has become a much riskier policy than ever before because local wars fought with conventional weapons could escalate into destruction on a vast scale. Just because the stakes have risen so high, however, does not mean that the chances of a nuclear holocaust are remote. The United States, still the only nation that has even used nuclear bombs in war, has threatened to use nuclear weapons at least eleven times since 1946. Those instances include the Berlin crisis of 1961, the Cuban missile crisis of 1962, and twice during the Vietnam War. Because warfare has become so dangerous and the world's military powers have built up huge stockpiles of both conventional and nuclear arms, many people have begun to study the causes of war in the hope of promoting peace. We turn now to a discussion of some of the theories that have been proposed to account for war.

No single theory can fully explain any given war. Nevertheless, a number of theories have shed light on some of the forces that contribute to war. For the purposes of this discussion, we will not consider rebellions, riots, and other forms of violence that take place within the borders of nations. Instead, we will adopt a narrow definition of war as violent conflict between nations. We consider first the view that human beings are aggressive by nature.

Ethological and Sociobiological Theories

According to some scientists, humans have their primate ancestors to thank, at least in part, for the existence of war. During earlier phases of human evolution, aggressive behavior may have improved the odds of survival and become encoded in the genes of a growing number of individuals. Ethologists and sociobiologists believe that a predisposition to aggression may have been transmitted genetically from one generation to the next. One of the most prominent spokespersons for this view is the ethologist Konrad Lorenz (1968). Like other ethologists, Lorenz has focused his research on the behavior of animals other than humans. From this work he has concluded that aggression is an instinct in humans, as it is in lower animals. Lorenz links

These white-tailed bucks are fighting for dominance over females and grazing territory. Human warfare undoubtedly had origins in biologically based aggression as well, but most social scientists agree that warfare among humans is far too complex to be fully explained by genetics or physiology.

aggression with territoriality. Just as animals defend their nests, burrows, and ranges, humans fight wars to defend their nations. It follows from this explanation that because war results from a natural urge, it is probably inevitable.

Many sociobiologists (scientists who study genetic influences on human behavior) also believe that humans have inherited a predisposition to engage in warfare. However, they are also well aware of the influence exerted by culture. In the view of the noted sociobiologist Edward O. Wilson, learned ways of doing things guide much of human behavior, but genetic tendencies also have a persistent influence. Although aggression may have been adaptive for humans thousands of years ago, Wilson (1975) believes that aggressive tendencies must be controlled if humans are to avoid global suicide.

Lorenz, Wilson, and their followers have been attacked by critics who argue that comparisons of human behavior with that of lower animals are suspect. Among humans, the motivation to fight is a learned response to symbols such as speeches, flags, propaganda, and other stimuli. Thus, human warfare is far more complex than fighting among animals. Moreover, there is no evidence that instinct plays any role in human aggression (Montagu, 1973). In sum, the critics deny that genes influence human behavior in general and warfare in particular; instead, they explain behavior in terms of learned responses.

Clausewitz: War as State Policy

In seeking to account for war in terms of genetically influenced tendencies, Lorenz and Wilson have viewed humans who make war as individuals indpendently motivated by their biological nature. In fact, however, soldiers fight in a social context. Their actions are governed largely by the dictates of military organizations. The freedom of military leaders to direct their armies is constrained by other institutions in society, such as the government, industry, the press, and religious organizations. Finally, even if the leaders of a nation's institutions were to agree among themselves, they would not have a free hand. Political and economic forces that cross national boundaries determine what strategies are available to win a war and whether war itself is a practical tactic in a given situation.

One of the most influential theories of war, proposed in 1832 by the Prussian general and military philosopher Carl von Clausewitz, took into account some of these aspects of the social context of war. During the century before Clausewitz wrote, most of the nations in Europe had been governed by monarchs who had the power to wage war if the use of military force would serve their interests. For this reason, Clausewitz focused on the role of the monarch and described war as an alternative to diplomacy, engaged in for the purpose of gaining land, prestige, and other benefits. According to Clausewitz, war is strictly a means to an end, to be engaged in only if its benefits outweigh its costs. The resources of the whole nation should be mobilized for just one purpose: victory (Rapoport, 1968). Thus, Clausewitz explained war in terms of the rational decisions of monarchs, not in terms of irrational elements of human nature such as a predisposition to aggression.

To support his claim that monarchs were the key actors in wars, Clausewitz adopted a fairly simple view of how societies function. He assumed, for instance, that the job of the military was to serve the monarch, regardless of the ambitions of military leaders. The interests of the military and the monarch were the same. In addition, Clausewitz did not foresee that by the end of the nineteenth century wealthy merchants and industrialists would be able to exert a strong influence on military policy. His functionalist approach to war and politics (i.e., the assumption that the military would always perform its function and serve the monarch) was weakened by the conflict inherent in the rise of powerful elites who could afford to marshall their own armed forces and challenge the power of the monarchy.

In the contemporary world the social control of the armed forces remains a serious problem in many nations. In this regard it is encouraging to note that in Latin America, a region that for decades was dominated by military dictatorships, there has been a drastic decline in the prevalence of military rule. In 1979 at least seven Latin American nations, including Brazil, Argentina, and Chile, were ruled by military dictators; in 1989 there was only one military dictatorship—in Suriname. This situation could change again for the worse owing to the extreme gaps between poor and affluent classes in those nations, but at present civilian control of the military prevails (Brookes, 1991).

Marx and Lenin on War

Early in the twentieth century, N. Lenin built on the ideas of Karl Marx to propose a new theory of war, one that took into account some of the social changes that had transformed European societies since Clausewitz's time. According to Marx, two competing social classes were developing in all industrializing societies. The *bourgeoisie* owned the means of production—that is, land, factories, and other resources needed to produce the necessities of life. The other class, the *proletariat,* sold its labor to the bourgeoisie in return for wages that barely enabled its members to survive. Marx believed that political leaders acted as the agents of the bourgeoisie in their struggle to improve business conditions and keep the proletariat under control.

Marx predicted that as capitalist economies grew, their need for raw materials, labor, and new markets in which to sell finished goods would increase as well. Lenin claimed that the competition among Britain, France, Germany, and other major powers to establish colonies around the world during the nineteenth and early twentieth centuries was evidence that Marx's prediction was correct. Acting in the interests of the bourgeoisie—rather than in those of the monarch or nation, as Clausewitz had argued—the major powers were locked in a fierce competition for colonies. It was this competition that led to World War I, according to Lenin. In essence, the war pitted the national ruling classes against each other; the workers had nothing to gain by taking up arms (Rapoport, 1968). The basis of war, then, is economic competition among national ruling classes. Lenin contended that the violent overthrow of the bourgeoisie by the proletariat would eventually remove this motivation for warfare.

Institutional and International Perspectives

Marx and Lenin believed that economic interests shape most social phenomena, including warfare. A number of social scientists have argued that noneconomic factors must also be considered in trying to account for the existence of war. These explanations can be grouped into two types. The first takes the individual nation as the unit of analysis and looks inside societies at the relationships among institutions such as the military, government, and business. The second group of explanations focuses on institutions and patterns of behavior that cut across national boundaries. According to this perspective, organizations such as the United Nations, as well as international treaties and trade networks, are among the factors that influence the likelihood of war or peace. We will begin with the first set of explanations, looking within nations at the institutional forces that may be responsible for war.

Institutional Forces Within Nations Most social scientists believe that during much of the twentieth century the influence of military leaders on government policy has grown in the United States and many other nations. Many also view that growth as a threat to peace. They maintain that keeping a large, well-equipped military force at the ready makes it easier for political leaders to choose war rather than negotiation as a tactic for handling international conflicts (Barton, 1981). Supporters of military interests, on the other hand, argue that a powerful military discourages other nations from starting wars.

With the rise of aggressive totalitarian societies in Europe during the 1930s, social scientists began to analyze the growing influence of the military on domestic affairs. Harold Lasswell (1941) predicted the rise of "garrison states," in which military leaders impose dictatorial power on society, channel a growing share of the nation's resources into weapons production, and win public support by means of propaganda.

After World War II, a few critics voiced alarm at the newly won power of the military in the United States. In *The Power Elite* (1956), C. Wright Mills argued that by the mid-1950s military leaders were

> *more powerful than they have ever been in the history of the American elite; they have now more means of exercising power in many areas of American life which were previously civilian domains; they now have more connections; and they are now operating in a nation whose elite and whose underlying population have accepted what can only be called a military definition of reality. (p. 198)*

During the war, military officers had met with heads of corporations to coordinate industrial output with military needs. America's political leaders were weak partners in this collaboration because they did not have the expertise to challenge the decisions of corporate and military leaders. Since the war, according to Mills, military institutions had "come to shape much of the economic life of the United States" (p. 222). In effect, the U.S. economy has not returned to its peacetime production patterns. Military and industrial leaders have seen to it that a significant portion of the national budget is allocated to preparation for war.

Although Mills doubted the ability of political leaders to control corporate and military elites, other writers have argued that government officials are indeed a powerful force in defining defense policy. In fact, according to Seymour Melman (1974), the president and top officials of the Pentagon and other federal agencies have the final say in most military decisions that are important to them. Melman has challenged the Marxist explanation of war as a tool used by the rich to solve certain problems of capitalist economies. In his view, managers at the top of the federal government have often made decisions that served their own interests but damaged the economy and the interests of the rich. Pentagon policy during the Vietnam War, for example, resulted in high rates of inflation and diverted money that corporate executives could have invested for other purposes.

Because high government and military officials have so much control over military policy, their values and their beliefs about their nation's rivals are important. For example, in many respects the planning for Operation Desert Shield began after the failed attempt to rescue the hostages held in Iran during the Carter administration. At that time military planners began to develop a more sophisticated approach to desert warfare. They developed the theory of the mobile strike force, and the technologies that would eventually be used against the Iraqis were moved from the laboratory to production lines. The end of the cold war and the perceived Russian threat in Europe allowed planners to view the NATO forces as the nucleus of an army that could be deployed in the Middle East, and that is indeed what happened during the 1991 war. In the thinking of military strategists, therefore, the political and economic climate of the world has become as important as considerations of technology and personnel.

In addition to military, political, and economic elites, there is another actor that affects the likelihood of war: the public. When Clausewitz wrote about warfare, public opinion did not matter much. Monarchs and ministers conducted diplomacy and war without interference from the populace. In the twentieth century, however, many states have become much more democratic. As a result, political leaders must take public opinion into account in setting foreign policy. In some cases public opinion actually favors war. This is especially likely when *nationalism*—the identification of the masses with the idea of nationhood and the exaltation of the nation's culture and interests above those of all other states—is strong. In the early years of this century, powerful nationalistic feelings among the citizens of Germany, a number of Eastern European countries, Great Britain, and other nations helped make peace seem dishonorable and war a feasible option for the leaders of those states.

Today we see renewed nationalism in Eastern Europe, Yugoslavia, the former Soviet Union, and the Middle East as highly dangerous to prospects for world peace. This is so not because of the balance of terror between the United States and the Soviet Union but because the possibility of civil wars and nationalist movements leads to increased fear of terrorism and greater political instability, and the possibility of local wars can draw in the larger nations, as happened in the case of World War I and could happen again in the Middle East.

The International Context of War and Peace So far we have limited our discussion to national institutions and domestic forces that tend to preserve or threaten peace. However, no discussion of the causes of war would be complete without some attention to the international context. The world is made up largely of independent sovereign states, each with its own interests. Because the supply of natural resources, power, prestige, and other valued commodities is limited, nations inevitably compete with one another. There is no central authority powerful enough to resolve all international conflicts peacefully. Nevertheless, a number of forces operate to reduce incentives to make war.

One such force is international cooperation. The League of Nations and later the United Nations are examples of international institutions designed to promote cooperation among nations. A key function of such organizations is the settlement of disputes. The United Nations, for example, has helped restore peace in three wars

A United Nations official visits the Sarajevo airport during the devastating civil war in Bosnia. The rise of nationalism and ethnic conflict throughout the world has placed severe strains on the United Nations' peacekeeping role.

between Israel and the Arabs, in the Korean conflict, in the Greek civil war, in Bosnia, and in a number of other conflicts. It has often failed to resolve clashes involving the superpowers, however. The United States, the former Soviet Union, and other major nations often are unwilling to give up some of their power to arbitrators, especially on issues of vital national interest. Moreover, research on international organizations has cast doubt on their value as peacekeepers in general. Neither membership in the same organization nor a shared voting pattern in the United Nations has been found to be related to peace between nations. In fact, between 1951 and 1962 nations that were members of the same international organizations were more than twice as likely to fight as nonmembers (Russett, 1967). Nevertheless, international organizations succeed in reducing conflict some of the time, and for this reason they are worthwhile. The hope is that they will become more effective as the economic and social costs of war become intolerable.

International trade is another force that tends to promote peace. When influential citizens of two nations benefit economically from peaceful relations, support for war between those nations is diminished. Moreover, trade promotes a common outlook as well as common interests. Trading partners are usually political partners.

Today world trade is dominated by market economies such as those of Japan and the industrialized nations of the West. As the former communist nations of Eastern Europe become market economies and economic development transforms more of the nations of the Pacific Rim into economic competitors of the advanced nations, global competition is likely to increase, making it ever more necessary to have international peacekeeping institutions and effective international law. This is especially true as the renewed influence of nationalism throughout the world threatens to lead to increases in terrorism and instability just as the economic integration of entire continents, exemplified by the European economic union and common market, becomes a real possibility.

TERRORISM: UNDECLARED WAR

During the Persian Gulf war in 1991, the Iraqis sent Scud missiles into civilian neighborhoods of Israel and Saudi Arabia. The allies denounced these attacks as *terrorism,* the use of warlike tactics against nonmilitary populations. Violent terrorist acts—kidnapping, torture, bombings—often are committed by a nation or by a political movement within a nation to call attention to their cause and shake people's faith in the ability of the government to eliminate the movement. The movement may be a revolutionary one that seeks far-reaching change in the government or hopes to gain control over the state. But not all terrorism is revolutionary in nature. The terrorism of cocaine barons in Colombia (known as narco-terrorism) is designed to take revenge on the authorities and to intimidate them into lax enforcement of the law. The terrorism of governments against their own people (known as repressive terrorism or state terrorism) also is not associated with revolutionary movements. But revolutionary terrorism, the most common form, often leads to the other forms. In Peru, for example, a revolutionary terrorist group, Shining Path, opposes the government but also protects cocaine traffickers in return for funds to support the revolutionary movement. In the Middle East, revolutionary Arab terrorist groups have been enlisted by heads of state such as Saddam Hussein and Muammar Quaddafi to conduct repressive terrorist acts.

In recent decades terrorism has become one of the most dangerous threats to world order. In its effects, and sometimes in its causes, terrorism is comparable to more traditional forms of war. It destabilizes governments, preys on innocent victims, and involves large amounts of financial and human resources. Yet unlike war, which openly pits opponents against each other in a recognized trial of strength, terrorism is covert. It seeks to sway the masses through intimidation.

More than any previous terrorist action, the bombing of the World Trade Center in New York City on February 26, 1993, brought the dangers of terrorism to the consciousness of U.S. citizens.

Although random acts of terrorism have occurred throughout history, modern terrorism first appeared in the early nineteenth century, when it was used to promote various revolutionary causes in Europe (Heren, 1978). Recently, however, the incidence of terrorist attacks has risen alarmingly. Bombings, hijackings, the taking of hostages, and the kidnapping of politicians and business leaders have become common perils.

The United States has been relatively free of terrorism. The bombing of the World Trade Center in 1993, the shooting of Jewish students in New York City in 1994, and, some would argue, the terrorism perpetrated by agencies of the U.S. government against the Branch Davidians in Waco, Texas, in 1993 are examples of recent cases of terrorism within the United States. These acts may suggest that terrorism is increasing not only within the United States but around the world. Surely the *potential* for terrorism, due to increases in ethnic and national hostilities around the world, is increasing. On the other hand, in the same year that the World Trade Center bombing took place, the U.S. Department of State reported that acts of terrorism in the world as a whole declined from a total of 567 in 1991 to 361 in 1992, a decrease of 36 percent (Holmes, 1993).

Fluctuations in the number of terrorist acts can be caused by many factors, and especially by events in the more troubled areas of the world. The prospect of lasting peace in the Middle East or a resolution of the conflict in Northern Ireland could produce major decreases in the total number of terrorist acts; conversely, any worsening of conditions in these and similar areas could lead to higher rates of terrorism (Long, 1990; U.S. Congress, 1993).

In addition to its origins in political radicalism, terrorism may spring from various kinds of cults that have much in common despite differing ideologies. According to Kenneth Wooden, author of *The Children of Jonestown* (1981), and Ed Sanders, author of *The Family: The Story of Charles Manson's Dune Buggy Attack Battalion* (1971), the mass murder and suicide of over 900 people in Jonestown, Guyana, and the brutal murders by the Charles Manson cult in California were both linked to the charismatic appeal of a deranged leader whom group members perceived as divinely inspired. The history of David Koresh and the Branch Davidians in Waco follows the same pattern. The more convinced members were of the leader's power, the more isolated they felt from the rest of society. A collective paranoia developed as they perceived themselves to be targets of society's hate. In both cases these feelings led to acts of irrational violence.

As noted earlier, terrorism can be perpetrated by agencies of the state. Earlier in this century Adolph Hitler and Josef Stalin practiced state terrorism, using brutality, fear, and legalized murder on an overwhelming scale to subjugate the masses. The attack and fire that destroyed the Branch Davidian compound suggests that that tragedy may also be considered an episode of state terrorism. Whereas victims of other forms of terrorism may hope to be rescued by government or police forces, victims of state terrorism can have no such hope. Indeed, the extreme nature of state terrorism has led many people to argue that violent rebellion is a justifiable reaction.

There have been numerous instances of state terrorism crossing national boundaries. To take just one example, in April 1986 President Reagan ordered jet fighters to attack the Libyan cities of Tripoli and Bengazi. The raids, in which thirty-seven people were killed and ninety-three wounded, were carried out in retaliation for Libya's alleged sponsorship of the bombing of a discotheque in West Berlin, in which two American servicemen and a Turkish woman were killed and 229 people were wounded. The bombing by French secret service personnel of a Greenpeace vessel in New Zealand is another example of state terrorism (King, 1986).

Terrorism that is carried out by independent agents who are essentially autonomous is known as *transnational terrorism.* This type of terrorism has also become more common in recent decades. Numerous countries have been affected by transnational terrorism, and the number of groups engaging in such acts has increased.

Because of the underground nature of terrorist organizations, it is difficult to understand their methods of operation. Even the beliefs and specific goals of such groups are often obscure, and their dogmas are frequently romanticized blends of older ideologies. Terrorist groups adhere to various forms of separatism, nationalism, fascism, anarchism, Stalinism, and Maoism. Yet terrorist groups are by no means isolated factions operating without the benefit of financial or technological resources. Members of such groups engage in bank robbery, forgery, kidnapping and ransom, and other illegal activities to bring in massive incomes. These incomes, in turn, finance complex strategies.

Despite their ideological differences, there is evidence to suggest a high degree of mutual protection and cooperation among divergent terrorist groups. As Claire Sterling (1978) has pointed out, groups are bound together by shared concerns such as the transport of stolen arms, forgery and theft of documents, cadet training camps, and refuge for members wanted by the law. These concerns tie them to a vast underground network that, owing to its complex organization and strict secrecy, remains beyond the reach of national and international law.

The terrorist recruit is often well educated, young, with an upper-middle- or middle-class background. As individuals, terrorists want to save the world, although their concept of salvation is based on a limited set of inflexible beliefs. The terrorist believes that purity of motive justifies whatever methods are employed. In this detachment from reality, coupled with total willingness to surrender life itself for the cause, terrorists become dehumanized. They see themselves as catalysts, worthless in themselves, through which social change can be accomplished (Hassel, 1977).

In this process the victim, who in the terrorist's mind is merely a pawn in the struggle for societal reform, is stripped of human rights and identity. The terrorist wants to punish society, to force it to accept his or her demands. The terrorist preys on both known and unknown victims, assured that—as representatives of an abhorrent society—the victims are responsible for society's wrongs and unworthy of compassion. Because any society is the combined achievement of thousands of individuals and many generations, the injustice of terrorist thinking is obvious. Terrorists' victims are innocent people whose lives are destroyed by fanatical intolerance.

Those who suffer as a result of terrorist acts can be divided into two groups. The first are random victims, people who are simply in the wrong place at the wrong time. Bombings, hijackings, and the spontaneous seizing of hostages victimize whoever happens to be available. Other members of society are intimidated by the casualness of this kind of terror, and the terrorist hopes that they will pressure their government to meet his or her demands. The other category of victims includes individuals who are singled out because of their prominence. They, too, become dehumanized symbols: All politicians bear the blame for whatever political injustices the terrorist perceives; all businesspeople are held personally responsible for commercial waste and greed. The civilians who have been killed or injured in bombings by terrorist groups as part of the Palestinian-Israeli conflict are an example of the first category; Prime Minister Indira Gandhi of India, who was murdered by Sikh extremists in 1984, is an example of the second.

SOCIAL POLICY

Although stockpiles of nuclear arms in the world's most powerful nations remain high and the possibility of the spread of nuclear arms to less developed nations continues to pose a threat to world peace, for the first time since the development of these terrible weapons there is hope for a reduction in the threat of nuclear war. This hope comes mainly from the progress already made in limiting conventional weapons and from the rapidly changing world situation, particularly the end of forty-five years of "cold" war between the superpowers.

In 1990 the United States, the (then) Soviet Union, and the major nations of Europe agreed to limit the number of tanks, combat planes, artillery pieces, and combat-ready ground forces held by NATO and by the Soviet Union and its former satellites in Eastern Europe. Basically, this pact meant that the Soviet Union began removing its military threat to Europe and that the United States began withdrawing its forces stationed in Europe.

Although it does not address issues related to nuclear weapons, the pact has far-reaching consequences. It allows the United States and Russia to spend less of their federal budgets on weapons of all kinds. It could pave the way toward large-scale reductions in the numbers of nuclear warheads. And it removes from Europe much of the tension created by the superpower confrontation (Gordon 1990). The cooperation between Russia and the NATO powers in negotiating a truce in Bosnia in 1994 is a sign of a new era in Russian-European relations.

Arms Control: A Promise Unfulfilled

The history of disarmament since nuclear weapons were invented consists of a series of limited agreements that have, until very recently, allowed the arms race to continue almost unabated. This is not to say that negotiations to achieve total disarmament have not been attempted. In August 1945, the first resolution passed by the United Nations set up the International Atomic Energy Commission and instructed it to propose plans for the complete elimination of nuclear weapons. Because the Soviet Union had not yet built a bomb, that nation vetoed the commission's proposal, which called for arms control first and prohibition at some time in the future. (Control would permit certain levels of weapons; prohibition would ban them entirely.)

In the early 1950s, France, Great Britain, Canada, the United States, and the Soviet Union again tried to reach a general arms control agreement. In talks that lasted for several years, these nations reached a consensus on several issues, including the date at which total prohibition of nuclear weapons should take effect and how they should inspect one another's defense sites. However, disagreements on issues of arms control and verification led to a deadlock that could not be resolved.

Despite their failure to ban nuclear weapons, the major powers have succeeded in formulating a number of treaties that limit certain weapons and regulate the spread of others. The first of these accords was the Nuclear Test-Ban Treaty, which was signed in 1963. This agreement forbade all nuclear tests under water, in outer space, and on the ground, but it did not prohibit underground tests.

In addition to the test-ban treaty, agreements prohibiting the spread of nuclear weapons to Antarctica, Latin America, Mexico, and outer space were signed between 1959 and 1967. In 1968, the Nuclear Nonproliferation Treaty was ratified by the U.N. General Assembly. This treaty was designed to stop the flow of nuclear weapons to nations that did not already have them. However, the agreement did nothing to slow the production of nuclear weapons by nations that *did* have them.

Since the Nonproliferation Treaty was signed, the United States has entered into a series of negotiations with the former Soviet Union to limit strategic arms, that is, weapons that are considered essential to a nation's offense or defense. Two agreements emerged from the Strategic Arms Limitation Talks (SALT). Under the terms of the SALT I ABM treaty, signed in 1972, each nation might deploy antiballistic missile (ABM) systems at only two sites. (Antiballistic missiles are designed to destroy incoming missiles in the air.) In addition, the two countries froze the production of offensive missile launchers for five years. A second pair of agreements, the SALT II protocols, were reached in 1974. They further limited ABMs and devices designed to launch offensive missiles. Although these protocols were not approved by the Senate, the United States observed them—as did the Soviet Union.

The SALT treaties were flawed in a number of ways. First, they did not bind any nuclear powers except the Soviet Union and the United States. Other nations that possess the bomb, such as France and Great Britain, were not obligated by the terms of these treaties. In addition, the limits on offensive weapons were set above existing levels, thus allowing for continued expansion of both nations' arsenals. Even more detrimental to arms control was the total lack of restrictions on improvements to existing weapons. Both nations were free to build greater accuracy, speed, and range into their missiles. Finally, the agreements did not prevent the two superpowers from developing new weapons such as the cruise missile.

In December 1987 the United States and the Soviet Union signed a treaty to eliminate all shorter- and medium-range nuclear missiles with a range of 300 to 3,400 miles from their arsenals within three years. The treaty also set forth procedures to be followed in eliminating the missiles and rules governing inspection by both sides.

In general, the major powers have abided by the terms of the pacts signed so far. Each of the parties to past agreements has been able to verify that the others were observing the terms of the treaty. Each nation has usually found that compliance with the treaties has served its own interests because compliance eliminates the need to expand the arms race to include the types of weapons limited by the treaty. As a result, treaty violations have been relatively rare (Barton, 1981). Successful arms control negotiations have also reduced the chance that a minor incident will lead to a full-scale war.

But as the wars in the Middle East and Bosnia demonstrate, the arms race will continue as long as nations depend on military strength for security and influence. National leaders are seldom content to maintain military equality with potential enemies. Advances in technology constantly tempt them to build weapons that could provide at least a temporary advantage. Most military experts agree that the performance of the United States' highly sophisticated weapons systems, including computer-guided "smart bombs," infrared sighting systems, the Patriot antimissile missiles, and other arms developed and produced in large quantities during the 1980s, have turned the world toward a new arms race based primarily on the quest for effective conventional weapons.

In the debates that took place in the United States over whether to attack the Iraqi forces in Kuwait, the threat posed by Iraq's nuclear and chemical weapons and the superiority of its armed forces in the Middle East were powerful arguments in favor of quick intervention. The allied victory over Iraq left the Middle East in a highly uncertain state, however, and most military experts believe that arms sales increased in the aftermath of the war.

Another serious problem created by smaller regional wars is the legacy they leave behind in the form of unexploded ammunition and buried land mines. Rich nations such as Kuwait have professional demolition experts to clear the land of thousands of buried mines. Poor nations such as Somalia and Angola must endure unpredictable explosions that take the lives and limbs of thousands of poor farmers. In Afghanistan the Soviets laid 12 million mines during the war in that country in the 1980s. Similar situations exist in Cambodia and many African nations. Since many of the land mines were made in the United States, this nation bears much of the responsibility for establishing better control over the sale of deadly military technology (Donovan, 1994).

Alternatives to the Arms Race

War and the arms race are social problems in themselves, and they leave even greater social problems in their wake, as can be seen in the devastation, poverty, and environmental and political damage in the Middle East after the liberation of Kuwait. If we fail to make progress on these issues of war and the increasing threat of war, the other problems discussed in this book may become footnotes to the history of social conditions "before the war." Yet many proposed solutions to the problem of the arms race seem idealistic in the current political context. One such proposal is renewed pressure by the public for an end to the testing and deployment of nuclear weapons through support for arms control treaties as they have been negotiated in the past. However, the superpowers have tended to word those treaties in such a way as to exclude any new weapons systems that are under development while the agreement is being negotiated (Johansen, 1982).

In most societies the use of violence to resolve conflicts among citizens is held to be not only illegal but also immoral. Hence, violent acts are punished by both legal and moral sanctions. When violence breaks out between nations, however, few such sanctions are available to address it. According to some arms control advocates, the world needs much more effective means of regulating violence and the types of behaviors (e.g., arms buildups) that make violence more destructive when it occurs.

One potential basis for regulation would be agreement among people around the world that the use of military force in international relations is immoral. Johansen (1982) advocates "citizens' diplomacy" to communicate the idea that possession of nuclear weapons is illegitimate. Citizens should work for peace by calling for a nuclear freeze and the elimination of nuclear arms. They should also oppose war by "opposing war taxes, military service, and corporate production of war material" and by teaching schoolchildren the value of peace. A world full of citizens

Stansfield Turner, former director of the Central Intelligence Agency, is worried about the fate of 25,000 nuclear warheads in the former Soviet Union. "We need," he claims, "a new approach to nuclear arms control that takes account of the growing prospect of prolonged civil strife in the Soviet Union." Turner believes that the United States should unilaterally reduce its supply of 25,000 long- and short-range nuclear warheads as a way of reducing overall risk.

What is ominous about this policy recommendation is not so much the idea of a unilateral step toward reduction of nuclear weapons—the United States would still have more than enough nuclear warheads to obliterate much of the world—as the idea that terrorist groups could arm themselves with stolen nuclear warheads. Turner, an expert on international terrorism, does not issue such warnings lightly.

The end of the cold war and the peaceful revolutions in much of Eastern Europe might have been thought to herald a new era of peace in that region. The unanticipated consequence of the decline of totalitarian communism, however, has been to allow previously suppressed minorities to assert their claims for greater autonomy or independence. In many of the former Soviet republics there are minority groups that are asserting independence from the majority (e.g., the Ossetians in Georgia). The situation in former Yugoslavia, where Croats and Serbs vie for control of ethnically mixed areas and ethnic Albanians in the south seek independence, is similar. Czechoslovakia has been divided as a result of schism between Czechs and Slovaks, and in Germany there is growing unrest among East Germans because of their poverty relative to West Germans.

These and other situations of ethnic and nationalistic grievance can easily lead to revolutionary social movements and increases in terrorism (Denitch, 1990). One need only think of the situation in Northern Ireland, where Protestants and Catholics have been waging terrorist war for years, to recognize how volatile the world situation has become and how difficult it is to alleviate these tensions.

One must remember that World War I began around issues of nationalism in southern Europe, in a part of Yugoslavia known as Bosnia, and that World War II saw unprecedented state terrorism unleashed against Jews, gypsies, and other minority groups. So the prospects for peace in a world torn by nationalist strife are not encouraging. Although Stansfield Turner may not have a viable solution to the problem of how to prevent nuclear warheads from falling into the hands of terrorists, he clearly anticipates a rise in terrorism as a result of the new world situation. This is a growing danger to world peace and a new challenge to the United Nations and the community of nations.

who oppose the use of arms on moral grounds would be a more peaceful place, according to this argument.

Other writers have pointed to the lack of a centralized international authority as the root cause of war and the arms race. According to Barton (1981), arms control negotiations are a valid but very limited means of maintaining peace, since there are many situations in which such negotiations are not feasible. Negotiations are especially useful when two nations are nearly equal in power or when both wish to ban a particular weapon. Often, however, nations engaged in conflict are not equal or have no interest in negotiations. The solution, in Barton's opinion, is some form of centralized international government that could dictate and enforce arms control. Enforcement could take "a form analogous to that of domestic police and marshals operating under legal safeguards and the supervision of courts" (p. 221).

In order to be effective, however, a centralized world government would have to command the loyalty of citizens from all or most countries. Otherwise, it would be impossible to enforce the rules. It is hard to imagine that any, let alone most, political regimes would voluntarily place the interests of a central authority above their own. Moreover, nationalistic feelings remain strong around the world. Unwillingness to forgo national interests for the sake of a community of nations has severely limited the ability of the United Nations to resolve conflicts. Thus, although this last alternative would be the most likely to promote peace, it is the least likely to be achieved in the near future.

Dealing with Terrorism

Terrorist acts, especially kidnappings and the holding of hostages, often attract worldwide attention. Indeed, terrorists use violence and drastic actions to attract media attention to their cause as well as to intimidate civilians and show governments that they can exert power. Although public sentiment often favors negotiating with terrorists to win the release of captives, official policies insist that there be no "giving in" to terrorist demands (Bremer, 1988; Clawson, 1988). Policies that have proven somewhat effective include the following: Governments should use boycotts and other measures to put pressure on states that sponsor terrorism; negotiators may promise anything to terrorists but not keep the promises after the captives have been released because promises made under threat are not valid; terrorists should be treated as criminals; the cooperation of journalists and media personnel should be enlisted in order to deprive terrorists of media attention; substantial rewards should be offered for information about and capture of terrorists; and an international campaign against terrorists should be undertaken with the help of a network of experts on the subject.

An informed public that will cooperate with antiterrorist policies is extremely important in combating this social problem. During the 1991 Persian Gulf war, for example, there were predictions of widespread terrorism, especially against air travelers; and although the traffic on commercial flights was drastically reduced because of this fear, the cooperation of the public with searches and stringent antiterrorist measures at airports was credited with preventing more violence than actually occurred.

Although these policies help diminish the spread and effectiveness of terrorism, much larger forces are at work that seem to be increasing the likelihood of terrorism. Among these, the renewed outbreak of intense nationalism in many parts of the world is the most serious. This is discussed further in Box 18–1.

SUMMARY

1. The direct effects of war include extensive death and destruction. In addition, many soldiers suffer lasting physical and psychological injury.

2. Indirect effects of war include disruption of the lives of people whose homeland has become a battleground. War also leads to mass migrations of people seeking to escape persecution or looking for new opportunities. In addition, war causes immeasurable economic damage.

3. The development of nuclear weapons has contributed to peace among the major powers. However, if peace breaks down, a war of unprecedented destructiveness could ensue. The effects of a nuclear war would include not only widespread death and massive physical damage but also radiation sickness and increased rates of fatal cancer. Nuclear warfare would also severely strain the resources of governments, destroy the ability of societies to function, and damage the environment—perhaps irrevocably.

4. Throughout human history the actual conduct of war has been closely linked to the nature of existing military technology. As the technologies of war have become ever more deadly, the ravages of war have become ever greater. Changes in the organizational dimension of military technology have been at least as important as advances in military apparatus.

5. There has been some progress toward controlling the conduct of war. There is a body of international law that deals with armed conflicts, and it includes rules defining the rights and privileges of those who fight and attempts to protect noncombatants. However, these rules are difficult to enforce and are frequently violated.

6. Among the theories that have been proposed to account for war is the view that humans have a predisposition for aggression that has been transmitted genetically from one generation to the next. This view is challenged by those who believe that motivation to fight is a learned response to symbols.

7. According to the nineteenth-century military philosopher Carl von Clausewitz, war was used by monarchs as an alternative to diplomacy as a means of gaining land, prestige, and other benefits. Marx and Lenin, on the other hand, believed that economic competition led national ruling classes (as opposed to workers) to make war on each other.

8. Noneconomic explanations of war are of two basic types: those that look at the relations between institutions within a society and those that focus on relations among nations. In the former category is the belief that a strong, influential military affects the likelihood that a nation will go to war. This view is expressed in Lasswell's prediction of the rise of "garrison states," in which military leaders have dictatorial power, and in Mills's warning of the power of the "industrial-military complex." An opposing view holds that government officials do indeed define military policy. In modern times public opinion has also been an important factor in military policy decisions.

9. Among the forces that operate to reduce incentives to make war are international organizations and international trade. As international economic competition increases, the need for international peacekeeping institutions will also increase.

10. Terrorism has reached alarming proportions in recent decades. Terrorist acts may be spurred by revolutionary fervor, the collective paranoia of followers of a deranged leader, or the attempts of a state to repress its citizens. Transnational terrorism is terrorism by independent agents who are essentially autonomous.

11. Victims of terrorist acts are of two types: random victims and individuals who are singled out because of their prominence. In both cases the victim is dehumanized in the eyes of the terrorist and used as a symbol of political or other injustice.

12. Policies aimed at reducing the buildup of arms have focused on international arms control treaties. These agreements have limited certain weapons and regulated the spread of others. Treaty violations have been relatively rare and have reduced the chance that a minor incident will lead to a full-scale war. However, the arms race will continue as long as nations depend on military strength.

13. Proposed solutions to the problem of the arms race include public pressure for an end to the testing and deployment of nuclear weapons, agreement among people around the world that the use of military force is immoral, and the establishment of a centralized international government that could dictate and enforce arms control. None of these appears likely to come about in the near future.

14. Official policies toward terrorism insist that there be no "giving in" to terrorist demands and that terrorists be treated as criminals. The outbreak of intense nationalism in many parts of the world may lead to an increase in the frequency of terrorist acts.

SUGGESTED READINGS

BEER, FRANCIS A. *Peace Against War: The Ecology of International Violence.* An important study of the social ecology of war, that is, its geographic patterns of incidence, how deadly different kinds of war are, and how the toll taken by war has figured in modern history. Includes an excellent theoretical discussion of the causes of war in human societies.

EVAN, WILLIAM M., and STEPHEN HILGARTNER, EDS. *The Arms Race and Nuclear War.* Englewood Cliffs,

NJ: Prentice Hall, 1987. A comprehensive text on war, the arms race, nuclear peril and its control, and other essential topics in the study of war and peace.

KENNEDY, PAUL. *Preparing for the 21st Century*. New York: Random House, 1993. An assessment of the broad global forces that are affecting rich and poor nations alike and increase (or, in a few cases, decrease) the risk of war between neighboring nations.

LAQUEUR, WALTER. *The Age of Terrorism*. Boston: Little, Brown, 1987. Based on the author's indispensable classic *Terrorism* (1977), this is a history of modern terrorism from its roots in nineteenth-century Europe to the present, with special attention to the critical role of the media.

MCNEILL, WILLIAM H. *The Pursuit of Power: Technology, Armed Force, and Society Since A.D. 1000*. Chicago: University of Chicago Press, 1982. A history of warfare that stresses the importance of social innovations in the conduct of war and in its control.

RUBENSTEIN, RICHARD E. *Alchemists of Revolution: Terrorism in the Modern World*. New York: Basic Books, 1987. The author provides firsthand reports from major terrorist groups throughout the world, including Peru's Shining Path, the Quebec Liberation Front, the Palestinian Liberation Organization, and many others.

acquired immune deficiency syndrome (AIDS) A chronic and fatal disease in which the normal immunological defenses of the body deteriorate, making the sufferer prey to a host of infectious diseases, particularly pneumonia, tuberculosis, and certain forms of cancer.

addiction Physical dependence on a drug.

affirmative action Programs that systematically increase opportunities for women and members of minority groups.

age cohort A group of people who were born in the same period.

ageism The devaluation of the aged and the resultant bias against older people.

age stratification The process by which people are segregated into different groups or strata on the basis of age.

AIDS related complex (ARC) A complex of symptoms that many health scientists believe is indicative of the early stages of AIDS.

alcoholic A person who is addicted to alcohol.

alimony The money paid by one partner for the support of the other after they have obtained a divorce.

amphetamine A drug that has a stimulating effect.

anomie A weakening of the norms that govern acceptable social behavior; a disparity between approved goals and the approved ways of obtaining them.

antagonism An interaction in which one drug negates the effect of another.

appropriate technology A policy perspective that advocates less complex and smaller-scale technological solutions than those offered by large-scale corporate and governmental institutions

asocial sex variance Sexual acts that are strongly disapproved of and are usually committed by one individual or at most a small number of people.

assault An attempt to injure or kill a human being.

assimilation The process by which members of a racial or ethnic minority group take on the characteristics of the mainstream culture by adapting their own cultural patterns to those of the majority group, and by intermarrying.

authority Power that has been routinized within a social organization.

automation Computer-controlled production methods; also, the replacement of workers by a nonhuman means of producing the same product.

baby boom generation That portion of the U.S. population born during the years immediately following World War II.

barbiturate A drug that depresses the central nervous system.

breakdown A condition in which obedience to a set of rules results in no reward or in punishment; a manifestation of social disorganization.

bureaucracy An organization in which activities are divided into precisely defined roles arranged in a hierarchy or chain of command.

civil law Laws that deal with noncriminal acts in which one individual injures another.

class stratification The stratification of individuals and groups according to their access to various occupations, income, and skills; see *social stratification*.

community psychology An approach to the treatment of mental disorders that makes use of easily accessible, locally controlled facilities that can care for people in their own communities.

comparable worth The idea that the pay levels of certain jobs should be adjusted so that they reflect the intrinsic value of the job; holders of jobs of comparable value would then be paid at comparable rates.

computer crimes The illegal manipulation of computer technology to commit robbery, fraud, and other crimes.

conflict-habituated relationship A marriage characterized by considerable tension and conflict.

conglomerate A combination of firms operating in greatly diversified fields.

consolidated metropolitan statistical area (CMSA) The largest urban areas in the United States, consisting of two or more closely linked major cities or primary metropolitan statistical areas, such as Dallas–Fort Worth or New York City–Northern New Jersey–Long Island.

conurbation See *urbanized area.*

conventional crime Crime that is committed by semiprofessional criminals as a way of life.

crime An act or omission of an act for which the state can apply sanctions.

crime index A set of data on the most serious, frequently occurring crimes; murder and nonnegligent manslaughter, forcible rape, robbery, aggravated assault, burglary, larceny-theft, motor vehicle theft, and arson.

criminal law A subdivision of the rules governing society that prohibits certain acts and prescribes punishments to be meted out to violators.

crude birthrate The number of births per 1,000 population.

cultural lag The condition in which one of two correlated parts of a culture changes before or in greater degree than the other, thereby causing less adjustment between the two parts than existed previously.

culture conflict A condition in which people feel trapped by contradictory rules; a manifestation of social disorganization.

debt entanglement The accumulation of large, and frequently unpayable, amounts of personal debt by consumers who have purchased most of what they own by using consumer credit.

deconcentration The situation created by the flight of middle-class families from the central city to the suburbs, together with the influx of poor minority groups, the unemployed, and the aged to those areas.

de facto segregation Segregation that is a result of housing patterns, economic patterns, and other factors.

deinstitutionalization The discharge of patients from mental hospitals directly into the community.

de jure segregation Segregation that is required by law.

demographic transition The process in which a population shifts from an original equilibrium in which a high birthrate is canceled out by a high death rate, through a stage in which the birthrate remains high but the death rate declines, to a final equilibrium in which the birth and death rates are lower but the population is much larger.

dependency ratio The relationship between the number of working people and number of nonworking people in a population.

deviance Behavior that departs from an accepted norm.

devitalized relationship A marriage that began as a vital one but drifted toward a state in which the interaction between husband and wife lacks any real interest or excitement.

differential association An explanation of crime that holds that criminal behavior is a result of a learning process that occurs chiefly within small, intimate groups that value such behavior.

discrimination The differential treatment of individuals who are considered to belong to a particular social group.

domestic network A familial network, especially in regard to black women, consisting of a number of households linked together by ties based on kinship, pseudokinship, and reciprocal personal and economic obligations.

drug A chemical substance that affects bodily function, mood, perception, or consciousness has a potential for misuse; and may be harmful to the user or to society.

drug abuse The use of unacceptable drugs, and excessive or inappropriate use of acceptable drugs, so that physical, psychological, or social harm can result.

drug dependence The compulsion to use a drug, whether the cause is physical or psychological.

dying trajectory The pattern of feelings and behavior that emerges during the process of dying.

educational attainment The number of years of school completed by an individual.

Eichmann effect The feeling of powerlessness to intervene in technological processes directed by bureaucratic institutions.

embezzlement Theft from one's employer.

ethnic minority A minority group composed of people who may share certain cultural features and who regard themselves as a unified group.

extended family A kinship unit that consists of parents, children, grandparents, and other related individuals living together.

flexitime An approach to work hours that allows employees to arrive and depart from the job when they choose, so long as they work during specific core hours and for a certain amount of time per week.

forcible rape The act of forcing sexual intercourse on a woman of legal age.

formication The illusion that insects or snakes are crawling on or in the skin; a paranoid psychosis.

fraud Obtaining money or property under false pretenses.

future shock A general sense of anxiety or confusion about the future and, at times, the present, caused by the constant need to adapt our way of life to new ways of doing things.

futurism A policy perspective that advocates aggressive governmental efforts to prepare for innovation by making adjustments in social institutions.

gay ghetto An area of a city with a large homosexual population and numerous gay institutions.

gender identity A person's sexual self-image, as distinguished from physiological gender.

gentrification The revitalization of urban neighborhoods by professionals and other upper-middle-class people.

gerontology The study of the physical causes and effects of the aging process.

gross national product (GNP) The total market value of all final goods and services produced in the economy in one year.

habituation Psychological dependence on a drug.

halfway house A small residential community, usually under private auspices and most often in an urban area, in which for a period of weeks or months ex-patients are helped to adjust from hospital to normal life.

hallucinogen A drug that distorts the user's perceptions.

health maintenance organization (HMO) A prepaid group practice that provides complete medical services to subscribers in a specific region.

health systems agency (HSA) An agency, financed through government subsidies and business and employee taxes, that plans and administers local health services.

homosexuality A sexual preference for members of one's own sex.

hospice An institution designed for the terminally ill.

human immunodeficiency virus (HIV) The virus that causes acquired immune deficiency syndrome (AIDS).

iatrogenic A medical condition in an individual that is "physician generated," that is, caused by medical treatment, especially by the incorrect administration of medications.

incapacitation A method of controlling crime in which chronic repeat offenders are incarcerated simply to prevent them from committing additional crimes.

incest Sexual relations between individuals who are so closely related that they are forbidden to marry by law or custom.

insider trading The illegal trading of securities based upon "inside" or privileged information that is not known to the public.

institution A more or less stable structure of statuses and roles devoted to meeting the basic needs of people in a society.

institutional coordination The concept that healthcare institutions, particularly those that treat the mentally ill, should be more closely connected and coordinated in their efforts to help their patients.

institutional discrimination Discrimination that occurs as a result of the structure and functioning of public institutions and policies.

institutionalization The process by which the way a social institution works is changed—generally by passing new laws.

institutional violence Violence exercised on behalf of or under the protection of the state.

institution building Efforts to make organizations function more effectively.

juvenile delinquency A violation of the law committed by a person under 18 years of age; usually a status offense.

kinship unit A group of individuals who are related to one another either by bloodlines or by some convention equivalent to marriage.

labeling theory The view that social problems arise because certain groups or individuals, for their own profit, name or label other groups or individuals as demonstrating problems or deviant behavior.

lesbian A female homosexual.

living will A legal or quasi-legal document drawn up by an individual that instructs the family, the physician, and other health-care providers on what course to take should the individual who has written the document become incapacitated and unable to conduct his or her own affairs.

lower-class value stretch Rodman's term for the tendency of the lower class to have a wider range of values than the other classes.

lumpenproleteriat A term taken from the writings of Karl Marx that refers to the poor in a capitalist society who are not part of the labor force, but who are on the margins of the society, often subsisting through criminal and black-market activities.

mainstreaming Educating a handicapped child in an ordinary public-school classroom.

malpractice Physically harmful mistreatment of a patient by a physician.

manslaughter The unlawful killing of a human being without malice aforethought.

Marxian conflict theory The view, based upon the writings of Karl Marx, that social problems and social conflicts arise from the inequitable distribution of wealth and power throughout society.

mass psychosis A condition in which a group of people, possibly under the control of a leader or leaders, behave in a hysterical or irrational way.

Medicaid An assistance program financed from tax revenues and designed to pay for the medical costs of people who cannot afford basic health care.

medical group A group practice, typically consisting of a general practitioner or internist sharing facilities with a number of different specialists.

Medicare A public health insurance program paid for by social security taxes and designed to cover some of the medical expenses of people age 65 and over.

megalopolis See *SCSA*.

mental disorder Psychological or organic problems with the mental functioning of an individual that may require medical treatment but do not require hospitalization.

mental illness Psychological or organic problems with the mental functioning of an individual that are considered serious enough to require hospitalization.

merger The combining of separate businesses into a single enterprise.

metropolitan region An area that contains several urban communities, all of which are located in close proximity to one another.

metropolitan statistical area An urban area in the United States consisting of a medium-sized city or two or more closely linked smaller cities, for example. Indianapolis, Indiana or Little Rock–North Little Rock, Arkansas.

mobility orientation The discrepancy between an individual's aspirations and his or her socioeconomic status.

multinational corporation An economic enterprise that is headquartered in one country and pursues business activities in one or more foreign countries.

murder The unlawful killing of a human being with malice aforethought.

narcotic antagonist A substance that negates the effects produced by opiates.

nationalism Identification of the masses with the nation and the exaltation of its culture and interests above those of all other states.

noninstitutional violence Violence exercised by those who are opposed to established authority.

normlessness A condition in which people have no rules that tell them how to behave; a manifestation of social disorganization.

nuclear family A kinship unit that consists of a father, a mother, and their children living apart from other kin.

occasional property crime Crimes, such as vandalism, check forgery, and shoplifting, that are usually committed by individuals who lack professional criminal skills.

occupational (white-collar) crime Crimes, such as embezzlement, fraud, and price fixing, that are committed in the course of business activity.

oligopoly The control of a commodity or service in a given market by a small number of companies or suppliers.

organized crime A system in which illegal activities are carried out as part of a rational plan devised by a large organization that is attempting to maximize its overall profit.

oriental exclusion The attempt by settlers in the western United States to exclude Asians from the country or from local labor markets in order to reduce the competition for jobs.

outsourcing The location of American manufacturing plants that produce goods for American markets in Third World nations where the manufacturing firm can take advantage of lower wage rates.

parallel pricing The tendency for corporations in a given industry to maintain certain price levels.

passive-congenial relationship A marriage in which both partners are content with their lives and feel adequate but not actually happy.

plea bargaining An arrangement in which an offender agrees to plead guilty to a lesser charge than that of which he or she was originally accused.

political crime Activities, such as treason, sedition, and civil disobedience, that, in the eyes of the state, threaten the existing social order and could do the nation serious harm if unchecked.

pornography The depiction of sexual behavior in such a way as to sexually excite the viewer.

post-industrial society Daniel Bell's term for a society whose organizing principle is the dominance of theoretical knowledge.

power The ability of an individual or group to impose its will on others.

prejudice An emotional, rigid attitude toward members of a particular group that is maintained despite evidence that it is wrong.

price leadership See *parallel pricing*.

primary metropolitan statistical area (PMSA) Urban areas in the United States that consist of one major city and the adjacent, closely linked suburbs, for example, Fort Worth, Texas or New York City.

problem drinker A person whose frequent drinking interferes with his or her health, interpersonal relationships, and economic functioning.

professional crime Crimes, such as safecracking and counterfeiting, that are committed by expert criminals who are dedicated to a life of crime.

professional standards review organization (PSRO) A board of physicians that reviews the treatment given to all Medicare and Medicaid patients.

projection A means of releasing tension that involves attributing one's own undesirable traits to some other individual or group.

pronatalism A term used to describe national policies designed to increase population growth.

prostitution Sexual relations on a promiscuous and mercenary basis with no emotional attachment.

psychotropic drugs Pharmaceutical drugs used in the management of stress, mental disorders, and mental illness.

public-order crime Activities that are considered to be crimes because they violate the order or customs of the community.

racial minority A minority group made up of people who share certain inherited characteristics.

racial steering The deliberate refusal of real estate brokers to show houses to minority buyers outside specific areas.

rate of population growth (natural increase) The differential between the crude birthrate and the death rate.

recidivism The probability that a former inmate will break the law after release and be arrested again.

regressive tax A tax that disproportionately burdens lower- and middle-income earners.

residual deviance Deviance from social conventions that are so completely taken for granted that they are assumed to be part of human nature.

right to die The belief that the terminally ill patient has the right to refuse medical treatment that may be artificially prolonging his or her life.

robbery The act of taking another person's property by intimidation.

role A certain set of behaviors that are expected of and performed by an individual in society on the basis of his or her status or position in society.

roleless role The vaguely defined position of older people on the fringe of society.

rural A term used to describe a sparsely populated area that is specialized in agriculture, forestry, or other exploitation of resources.

safe sex practices Sexual behaviors and techniques, such as monogamy and the use of condoms, that are designed to prevent the transmission of AIDS and other venereal diseases.

saturnalia Periodic "moral holidays," such as Halloween, in which the normal rules of conduct are suspended.

scapegoat A person or group that becomes a target of aggression displaced from the real source of the aggressor's frustration.

secondary deviance A term applied to behavior that elaborates on a deviant act in order to reinforce the role of deviant.

senility dementia A condition of the elderly characterized by a decline in mental capacity.

social disorganization The condition that results when the expectations or rules by which society is organized fail.

social institution The set of folkways, norms, and laws that has grown up around one or more of the major functions of society.

socialization The process by which individuals develop into social beings.

social mobility The movement of an individual from one socioeconomic level to another.

social norm A social standard that specifies the kind of behavior that is appropriate in a given situation.

social pathology A term applied to the "illness" of individuals or social institutions that fail to keep pace with changing conditions and thereby disrupt the healthy operation of the social "organism."

social policy A formal procedure designed to remedy a social problem.

social problem Behavior that departs from established norms and social structures because individual and collective goals are not being achieved; a condition that a significant number of people believe should be remedied through collective action.

social selection hypothesis The hypothesis that social class is a consequence rather than a cause of mental illness and mental disorder, and that people with mental illnesses and disorders gravitate toward the lower socioeconomic levels.

social stratification A pattern in which individuals and groups are assigned to different positions in the social order, with varying amounts of access to the desirable things in the society.

stagflation An economic environment that combines stagnant growth with inflationary prices.

standard consolidated statistical area (SCSA) Two or more SMSAs that have become socially and economically interrelated.

standard metropolitan statistical area (SMSA) A large population nucleus and surrounding communities that are integrated with it economically and socially; according to the Census Bureau, one or more central counties with at least 50,000 inhabitants, plus outlying counties with close economic and social ties to the central counties (e.g., a certain level of commuting).

status offense An act that is illegal if it is performed by a person under 18 years of age.

statutory rape The act of having sexual relations with a woman who is below a particular age established by state law.

stereotyping Attributing a fixed and usually unfavorable or inaccurate conception to a category of people.

sting A law enforcement technique in which people suspected of a criminal activity are given the opportunity to engage in that activity and are subsequently arrested by law enforcement officials.

strategic crime Crimes (such as extortion, kidnapping, and blackmail) in which the threat of violence is used as a strategic ploy in a complex "game" as played out by the criminal, the victim, and the law enforcement agency.

Strategic Defense Initiative (SDI) A futuristic plan for national defense, commonly called "Star Wars," that would prevent nuclear attack upon the United States by utilizing advanced weapons technology in space, such as laser-equipped satellites capable of destroying enemy missiles.

stress Physical or mental tension produced by the demands of environmental factors or by internal (perceived) behavioral requirements.

structural violence The dominance of one group over another, with subsequent exploitive practices.

structured sex variance Sexual behavior that runs counter to prevailing norms and legal statutes but is engaged in by large numbers of people and associated with relatively well-defined roles and social institutions.

suburb A closely settled incorporated or unincorporated place with 2,500 inhabitants or more that forms part of an urbanized area.

supply-side economics The theory that if the side of the economy that supplies goods and services is stimulated, unemployment will decrease and prices will drop.

surrogacy The practice in which a woman, for a monetary fee, is artificially inseminated with the sperm of a man married to another woman who has been unable to bear children. After carrying the child and giving birth, the surrogate mother usually gives custody of the child to the biological father and his wife.

synergism An interaction in which two or more drugs exert a mutual influence on each other to produce an effect much greater than one of them would cause alone.

technology The apparatus, or physical devices, used in accomplishing a variety of tasks, together with the activities involved in performing those tasks and the organizational networks associated with them.

technology assessment A policy perspective that emphasizes the need for scientific study of new technologies in order to anticipate their consequences for the physical and social environment.

tolerated sex variance Sexual acts that are generally disapproved of but either serve a social useful purpose and/or occur so often among a population with such low social visibility that few people are sanctioned for engaging in them.

total fertility rate The average number of children born per woman throughout the childbearing years.

total institution A place where a large number of individuals, cut off from the wider society for an appreciable period, together lead an enclosed, formally administered round of life.

transnational terrorism Terrorism perpetrated by agents who are not affiliated with a recognized government.

trickle-down theory The theory that any measures taken to aid business or wealthy individuals will stimulate economic activity and provide jobs and opportunities for the poor and the unemployed.

underground economy Exchanges of goods and services, both legal and illegal, that are not monitored, recorded, or taxed by government.

urban A term used to describe a densely settled area where manufacturing, commerce, administration, and a great variety of specialized services are available.

urbanism a way of life that depends on heavy industry, mass communication, a mobile population, and other characteristics generally associated with life in urban areas.

urbanized area According to the Census Bureau, a city (or cities) of 50,000 or more inhabitants plus the surrounding suburbs.

urban population According to the Census Bureau, all persons in places of 2,500 inhabitants or more that are incorporated as cities, villages, boroughs, or towns.

value conflict theory The view that social problems and social conflict arise from conditions and actions that are incompatible with normal group values in a society.

victimization report A Census Bureau survey that collects information from a representative sample of crime victims.

victimless crime A crime that causes no physical harm to anyone but the offender; a public-order crime.

violence Behavior designed to inflict physical injury to people or damage to property.

violent personal crime Crimes in which physical injury is inflicted or threatened.

wealthfare The opportunities provided by the government that enable the rich to become richer.

welfare state A state in which a significant proportion of the gross national product is taken by the state to provide minimal social welfare for the poor, the aged, the disabled, and others who would not be able to survive under conditions of market competition.

whistle-blower A person who risks his or her reputation to reveal dangers in technology or the use of technology.

zero population growth The condition that exists when a generation produces only enough children to replace itself.

BIBLIOGRAPHY

AAUW (American Association of University Women), 1992. "How Schools Shortchange Women: The A.A.U.W. Report" (Washington, DC: A.A.U.W. Educational Foundation).

ABDELLAH, F. G., 1978. "Long-term Care Policy Issues: Alternative to Institutional Care," *Annals of the American Academy of Political and Social Science* 438: 28–39.

ABELSON, H., R. COHEN, E. HEATON, and C. SLIDER, 1970. "Public Attitudes toward and Experience with Erotic Materials." In *Technical Reports of the Commission on Obscenity and Pornography,* Vol. 6 (Washington, DC: Government Printing Office).

ADAMS, G., 1987. "The making of an iron triangle." In William M. Evan and Stephen Hilgartner (eds.), *The Arms Race and Nuclear War* (Englewood Cliffs, NJ: Prentice Hall).

ADAMS, S., 1961. "Interaction between Individual Interview Therapy and Treatment Amenability in Older Youth Authority Wards." In *Inquiries Concerning Kinds of Treatments for Kinds of Delinquents* (Sacramento, CA: California Board of Corrections).

AHLBURG, D. A., and C. J. DE VITA, 1992. *New Realities of the American Family* (*Population Bulletin,* vol. 47, no. 2) (Washington, DC: Population Reference Bureau).

Alan Guttmacher Institute, 1981. *Teenage Pregnancy: The Problem That Hasn't Gone Away* (New York: Alan Guttmacher Institute).

ALBRECHT, G. L., 1973. "The Alcoholism Process: A Social Learning Viewpoint." In P. G. Bourne and R. Fox (Eds.), *Alcoholism: Progress in Research and Treatment* (New York: Academic Press).

ALLAND, A., 1973. *Human Diversity* (Garden City, NY: Doubleday.

ALLEN, F. A., 1981. *The Decline of the Rehabilitative Ideal: Penal Policy and Social Purpose* (New Haven, CT: Yale University Press).

ALLEN, I. L., 1983. *The Language of Ethnic Conflict: Social Organization and Lexical Culture* (New York: Columbia University Press).

ALLISON, J. L., 1973. "Poverty and the Administration of Justice in the Criminal Courts." In H. H. Meissner (Ed.), *Poverty in the Affluent Society* (New York: Harper & Row).

ALTMAN, D., 1987. *Aids in the Mind of America* (Garden City, NY: Doubleday Anchor Books).

American Psychiatric Association, 1980. *Diagnostic and Statistical Manual of Mental Disorders,* 3rd ed. (Washington, DC: American Psychiatric Association).

American Psychiatric Association, 1994. *Diagnostic and Statistical Manual of Mental Disorders,* 4th ed. (Washington, DC: Author).

ANDERSON, E., 1988. *A Place on the Corner,* 2nd ed. (Chicago: University of Chicago Press).

ANDERSON, O., 1985. *The American Health Services: A Growth Enterprise since 1875* (Ann Arbor, MI: Health Administration Press).

ANDERSON, O., 1989. *The Health Services Continuum in Democratic States* (Ann Arbor, MI: Health Administration Press).

ANDERSON, R., and O. ANDERSON, 1979. "Trends in the Use of Health Services." In H. E. Freeman, S. Levine, and L. Reeder (Eds.), *Handbook of Medical Sociology,* 3rd ed. (Englewood Cliffs, NJ: Prentice Hall).

ANGRIST, S. S, M. LEFTON, S. DINITIZ, and B. PASAMINICK, 1968. *Women After Treatment: A Study of Former Mental Patients and Their Normal Neighbors* (New York: Appleton-Century-Crofts).

ANTONOVSKY, A., 1974. "Class and the Chance for Life." In L. Rainwater (Ed.), *Inequality and Justice* (Hawthorne, NY: Aldine).

APPLEBOME, P., 1992. "Jailers Charged with Sex Abuse of 119 Women." *New York Times,* November 14, pp. 1, 7.

AREHART-TRIECHEL, J., 1977. "It's Never Too Late to Start Living Longer," *New York Magazine,* April 11, pp. 38–40.

ARES, C. E., A. RANKIN, and H. STURTZ, 1963. "The Manhattan Bail Project," *New York University Law Review* 38: 67–92.

ARON, R., 1955. *The Century of Total War* (Boston: Beacon Press).

ASHLEY, R., 1975. "The Other Side of LSD," *New York Times Magazine,* October 19, pp. 48–50, 59.

ATCHLEY, R. C., 1978. "Aging as a Social Problem: An Overview." In M. N. Seltzer, S. L. Corbett, and R. C. Atchley (Eds.), *Social Problems of the Aging* (Belmont, CA: Wadsworth).

Attorney General's Commission on Pornography, 1986. *Final Report* (Washington, DC: Government Printing Office).

AULETTA, K., 1982. *The Underclass* (New York: Random House).

AULETTA, K., 1987. *Greed and Glory on Wall Street* (New York: Warner Books).

AYALA, V., 1991. "AIDS and the Underclass" (Unpublished doctoral dissertation, City University of New York).

AYALA, V., 1994. "AIDS Patients." In W. Kornblum and C. D. Smith (Eds.), *The Healing Experience: Readings on the Social Context of Health Care* (Englewood Cliffs, NJ: Prentice Hall).

AYERS, B. D., JR., 1993. "Judge's Decision in Custody Case Raises Concerns." *New York Times,* September 9, p. A16.

BABCHUK, N., G. R. PETERS, D. R. HOYT, and M. A. KAISER, 1979. "The Voluntary Associations of the Aged." *Journal of Gerontology* 34: 579–87.

BACHRACH, L. L. 1981. "General Hospital Psychiatry: Overview from a Sociological Perspective," *American Journal of Psychiatry* 138: 879–87.

BADILLO, G. and D. CURRY, 1976. "The Social Incidence of Vietnam Casualties: Social Class or Race?" *Armed Forces and Society* 2: 397–406.

BAHR, H. M., 1968. *Homelessness and Disaffiliation* (New York: Columbia University Press).

BAKER, S. S., 1965. "The Growth and Structure of the Labor Force." *Conference Board Record,* October, pp. 45–54.

BALBUS, I., 1978. "Commodity Form and Legal Form: An Essay on the Relative Autonomy of the Law." In C. E. Reasons and R. M. Rich (eds.), *Sociology of Law: A Conflict Perspective* (Toronto: Butterworths).

BALL-ROKEACH, S., and J. F. SHORT, JR., 1985. "Collective Violence: The Redress of Grievance and Public Policy." In L. A. Curtis (Ed.), *American Violence and Public Policy* (New Haven, CT: Yale University Press).

BANDURA, A., 1986. *Social Foundations of Thought and Action* (Englewood Cliffs, NJ: Prentice Hall).

BANE, M. J., 1986. "Household Composition and Poverty." In S. H. Danziger and D. H. Weinberg (Eds.), *Fighting Poverty: What Works and What Doesn't* (Cambridge, MA: Harvard University Press).

BARBANEL, J., 1987. "Homeless Woman Sent to Hospital under Koch Plan Is Ordered Freed," *New York Times,* November 13, pp. A1, 21.

BARKER, P. R., G. MANDERSCHEID, and I. G. GENDERSHOT, 1992. "Serious Mental Illness and Disability in the Adult Household Population: United States, 1989." IN R. W. MANDERSCHEID and M. A. SONNENSCHEIN (EDS.), *Mental Health, United States, 1992* (Washington, DC: Center for Mental Health Services and National Institute of Mental Health).

BARNET, R. J., 1980. *The Lean Years* (New York: Simon & Schuster).

BARNET, R. J., 1982. "Two Bumbling Giants: The Superpowers' Outdated Policies in a Nuclear World." In J. Wallis (Ed.), *Waging Peace* (New York: Harper & Row).

BARRINGER, F., 1993. "Majority in Poll Back Ban on Handguns." *New York Times,* June 4, p. A14.

BARRINGER, F., 1993. "Polling on Sexual Issues Has Its Drawbacks," *New York Times,* April 25, p. 23.

BARRINGER, F., 1993. "Sex Survey of American Men Finds 1% Are Gay," *New York Times,* April 15, pp. A1, A18.

BARRINGER, F., 1993, "Where Many Elderly Live, Signs of the Future," *New York Times,* March 7, p. L20.

BARRON, M. L. 1971. "The Aged as a Quasi-Minority Group." In E. Sagarin (Eds.), *The Other Minorities* (Lexington, MA: Ginn).

BART, P. B., 1974. "Depression in Middle-aged Women." In V. Gornick and B. K. Moran (Eds.), *Women in Sexist Society* (New York: Basic Books).

BAR-TAL, D., and I. H. FRIEZE, 1977. "Achievement Motivation for Males and Females as Determinant of Attribution for Success and Failure." *Sex Roles: A Journal of Research* 3: 301–13.

BARTON, J. H., 1981. *The Politics of Peace: An Evaluation of Arms Control* (Stanford, CA: Stanford University Press).

BASSUK, E. L., 1984. "The Homelessness Problem," *Scientific American,* July, pp. 40–45.

BAXTER, E., and K. HOPPER, 1981. *Private Lives/Public Spaces: Homeless Adults on the Streets of New York City* (New York: Community Service Society).

BAYER, R., 1986. "AIDS Power, and Reason," *Milbank Quarterly* 64 Suppl. 1: 168–82.

BAYER, R., 1987. *Homosexuality and American Psychiatry: The Politics of Diagnosis,* 2nd ed. (Princeton, NJ: Princeton University Press).

BAYER, R., 1987. "We Must Be Able to Trace Sex Contacts," *Newsday,* April 26, p. 9.

BEACH, W. G., 1932. "Oriental Crime in California," *Stanford University Publications in History, Economics, and Political Science* 3: 404–97.

DE BEAUVOIR, S., 1961. *The Second Sex.* (New York: Bantam).

BECKER, H., 1963. "Becoming a Marijuana User." In *Outsiders: Studies in the Sociology of Deviance* (New York: Free Press).

BECKER, H. S., 1963. *Outsiders: Studies in the Sociology of Deviance* (New York: Free Press).

BECKLEMAN, L., 1978. "When the Cry of the Beaten Child Goes Unheard," *New York Times Magazine,* April 16, p. 85.

BEER, F. A., 1981. *Peace Against War; The Ecology of International Violence* (San Francisco: Freeman).

BELKIN, L., 1992. "Choosing to Die at Home: Dignity Has Its Burdens." *New York Times,* March 2, pp. A1, B4.

BELL, A. P., and M. S. WEINBERG, 1978. *Homosexualities: A Study of Diversity among Men and Women* (New York: Simon & Schuster).

BELL, D., 1973. *The Coming of Post-industrial Society: A Venture in Social Forecasting* (New York: Basic Books).

BELL, D., 1991. "The Myth of the Intelligent Society," *New York Times,* March 16, p. 23.

BELL, R. R., 1971. *Social Deviance* (Homewood, IL: Dorsey Press).

BELL, R. R., 1975. *Marriage and Family Interaction,* 4th ed. (Homewood, IL: Dorsey Press).

BELLAH, R. N., 1985. *Habits of the Heart* (New York: Harper & Row).

BELLAH, R., ET AL., 1985. *Habits of the Heart: Individualism and Commitment in American Life* (Berkeley: University of California Press).

BEM, S. L., 1975. "Androgyny vs. the Tight Little Lives of Fluffy Women and Chesty Men," *Psychology Today,* September, pp. 58–62.

BENJAMIN, H., and R. MASTERS, 1964. *Prostitution and Morality* (New York: Julian Press).

BENNETT, C., B. LEAKE, C. LEWIS, J. FLASKERUD, and A. NYAMATHI, 1993. "AIDS-Related Knowledge, Perceptions, and Behaviors Among Impoverished Minority Women," *American Journal of Public Health* 83, 65–71.

BENOKRAITIS, N. V., and J. R. FEAGIN, 1986. *Modern Sexism Blatant, Subtle and Covert Discrimination* (Englewood Cliffs, NJ: Prentice Hall).

BENSMAN, D., and R. LYNCH, 1987. *Rusted Dreams: Hard Times in a Steel Community* (New York: McGraw-Hill).

BENTLEY, J., 1984. *The Nuclear Freeze Movement* (New York: Franklin Watts).

BERGER, A., and W. SIMON, 1974. "Black Families and the Moynihan Report: A Research Evaluation," *Social Problems* 22: 160–61.

BERGMANN, B., 1988. "A Workable Family Policy," *Dissent,* Winter, pp. 88–93.

BERK, R. A., K. J. LENIHAN, and P. H. ROSSI, 1980. "Crime and Poverty," *American Sociological Review* 45: 766–86.

BERKANOVIC, E., and L. G. REEDER, 1974. "Can Money Buy the Appropriate Use of Services? Some Notes on the Meaning of Utilization Data," *Journal of Health and Social Behavior* 15 (June): 93–99.

BERKOWITZ, L., 1971. "The Study of Urban Violence." In J. C. Davies (Ed.), *When Men Revolt and Why* (New York: Free Press).

BERKOWITZ, L., 1993. *Aggression: Its Causes, Consequences, and Control* (Philadelphia: Temple University Press).

BERLIN, G., and A. SUM, 1988. *Toward a More Perfect Union: Basic Skills, Poor Families, and Our Economic Future.* Occasional Paper No. 3. (New York: Ford Foundation, Project on Social Welfare and the American Future).

BEROWITZ, L., 1978. "Is Criminal Violence Normative Behavior?" *Journal of Research in Crime and Delinquency* 15 (2): 148–61.

BERNARD, J., 1974. "The Paradox of the Happy Marriage." In V. Gornick and B. K. Moran (Eds.), *Women in Sexist Society* (New York: Basic Books).

BERNARD, J., 1987. *The Female World from a Global Perspective* (Bloomington, IN: Indiana University Press).

BERNSTEIN, J., 1982. "Recreating the Power of the Sun," *New York Times Magazine,* January 3, pp. 14–17, 52–53.

BERRUETA-CLEMENT, J. R., L. J. SCHWEINHART, W. S. BARNETT, A. S. EPSTEIN, and D. P. WEIKART, 1984. *Changed Lives: The Effects of the Perry Preschool Program on Youths through Age 19* (Ypsilanti, MI: High/Scope).

BEST, F., 1978. "Preferences on Work-Life Scheduling and Work-Leisure Tradeoffs," *Monthly Labor Review* 101: 31–37.

BIANCHI, E. C., 1974. "The Superbowl Culture of Male Violence," *Christian Century,* September 18, pp. 842–45.

BLACK, D., 1984. *Toward a General Theory of Social Control* (Orlando: Academic Press).

BLAKE, D. H., and R. S. WATERS, 1976. *The Politics of Global Economic Relations* (Englewood Cliffs, NJ: Prentice Hall).

BLAKESLEE, R. N., and D. G. BROWN, 1990. *Integrating Telecommunications into Education* (Englewood Cliffs, NJ: Prentice Hall).

BLAKESLEE, S. 1994 (April 20). "Poor and Black Patients Slighted, Study Says," *New York Times,* p. B9.

BLAU, P., and M. W. MEYER, 1971. *Bureaucracy in Industrial Society,* 2nd ed. (New York: Random House).

BLIER, R., 1984. *Science and Gender: A Critique of Biology and Its Theories on Women* (New York: Pergamon Press).

BLUESTONE, B., and B. HARRISON, 1987. "The Grim Truth about the Job 'Miracle,'" *New York Times,* February 1, p. 3.

BLUMSTEIN, A., 1982. "On the Racial Disproportionality of United States' Prison Population," *Journal of Criminal Law and Criminology* 73: 1259–81.

BLUMBERG, P., 1980. *Inequality in an Age of Decline* (New York: Oxford University Press).

BLUMSTEIN, P., and P. SCHWARTZ, 1983. *American Couples: Money, Work and Sex* (New York: Morrow).

BOAS, M., and S. CHAIN, 1976 *Big Mac: The Unauthorized Story of McDonald's* (New York: New American Library).

BOCK, E. W., 1972. "Aging and Suicide: The Significance of Marital Kinship and Alternative Relations," *Family Coordinator* 21: 71–78.

BOELKINS, R. C., and J. F. HEISER, 1970. "Biological Bases of Aggression." In D. Daniels, M. Gilula, and F. Ochberg (Eds.), *Violence and the Struggle for Existence* (Boston: Little, Brown).

BOGART, L., 1972–1973. "Warning: The Surgeon General Has Determined That TV Violence Is Moderately Dangerous to Your Children's Mental Health," *Public Opinion Quarterly* 36: 491–521.

BOGUE, D., 1969. *Principles of Demography* (New York: Wiley).

BONACICH, E., 1976. "Advanced Capitalism and Black/White Race Relations in the United States: A Split Labor Market Interpretation," *American Sciological Review* 41: 34–51.

BOOCOCK, S. S., 1980. *Sociology of Education: An Introduction* (Boston: Houghton Mifflin).

BOOTH, A., D. R. JOHNSON, and H. M. CHOLDIN, 1977. "Correlates of City Crime Rates: Victimization Surveys Versus Official Statistics," *Social Problems* 25: 187–97.

BOOTH, A., D. R. JOHNSON, and J. EDWARDS, 1980. "In Pursuit of Pathology: The Effects of Human Crowding," *American Sociological Review* 45: 873–78.

BOSK, C. L., 1979. *Forgive and Remember: Managing Medical Failure* (Chicago: University of Chicago Press).

BOULTON, D. 1979. *The Grease Machine: The Inside Story of Lockheed's Dollar Diplomacy* (New York: Harper & Row).

BOWLES, S., and H. GINTIS, 1977. *Schooling in Capitalist America* (New York: Basic Books).

BOYER, E., 1983. *High School* (New York: Harper & Row).

BRADBURY, K. L., A. DOWNS, and K. E. SMALL, 1982. *Urban Decline and the Future of American Cities* (Washington, DC: Brookings Institution).

BRAGINSKY, D. D., and B. M. BRAGINSKY, 1975. "Surplus People: Their Lost Faith in Self and System," *Psychology Today,* August, pp. 68–72.

BRAITHWAITE, J., 1981. "The Myth of Social Class and Criminality Reconsidered," *American Sociological Review* 46: 36–57.

BRATT, R. G., 1989. *Rebuilding a Low-income Housing Policy* (Philadelphia: Temple University Press).

BRAVERMAN, H., 1974. *Labor and Monopoly Capital: The Degradation of Work in the Twentieth Century* (New York: Monthly Review Press).

BREMER, L. P., III, 1988. "Terrorism: Myths and Reality," *Department of State Bulletin,* May, p. 63.

BRENNER, H., 1973. *Mental Illness and the Economy* (Cambridge, MA: Harvard University Press).

BRIGGS, K. A., 1984. "Catholic Bishops Ask Vast Changes in Economy of U.S.," *New York Times,* November 12, p. 1.

BRINKLEY, J., 1986. "Drug Use Held Mostly Stable or Lower," *New York Times,* October 10, p. A14.

BROADHEAD, R. S., and N. J. FACCHINETTI, 1986. "Drug Iatrogenesis and Clinical Pharmacy: The Mutual Fate of a Social Problem and a Professional Movement," *Social Problems* 33, No. 5 (June): 425–36.

BRODY, E., 1978. "The Aging of the Family," *Annals of the American Academy of Political and Social Science* 438: 13–27.

BRONFENBRENNER, U., 1981. "Children and Families," *Society* 18: 38–41.

BROOKES, J., 1991. "Latin American Armies Looking for Work," *New York Times,* March 24, p. E2.

BROOKS, P., 1990. "Taking a Close Look at Women and Health Care," *Blueprint* (United Hospital Fund), Spring/Summer, p. 1.

BROOKS-GUNN, J., and F. F. FURSTENBERG, JR., 1987. "Continuity and Change in the Context of Poverty: Adolescent Mothers and Their Children." In J. J. Gallagher and C. T. Ramey (Eds.), *The Malleability of Children* (Baltimore, MD: Brookes).

BROOKS-GUNN, J., and R. P. HEARN, 1982. "Early Intervention and Developmental Dysfunction: Implications for Pediatrics," *Advanced Pediatrics* 29: 497–527.

BROWN, B. S., G. J. BENN, and D. R. JANSEN, 1975. "Methadone Maintenance: Some Client Opinions," *American Journal of Psychiatry* 132: 623–28.

BROWN, C. 1984. "Manchild in Harlem," *New York Times Magazine,* September 16, pp. 36ff.

BROWN, E. J., T. J. FLANAGAN, and M. McLEOD (EDS.), 1984. *Sourcebook of Criminal Justice Statistics* (Washington, DC: Bureau of Justice Statistics).

BROWN, L. R., 1987. "Analyzing the Demographic Trap." In L. R. Brown et al., *State of the World* (New York: Norton/Worldwatch).

BROWN, L. R., 1990. "The illusion of progress," In L. R. Brown et al. *State of the World 1990: A Worldwatch Institute Report on Progress toward a Sustainable Society* (New York: Norton).

BROWN, L. R., and E. P. ECKHOLM, 1974. *By Bread Alone* (New York: Praeger).

BROWN, L. R., and S. POSTEL, 1987. "Thresholds of change." In L. Brown et al., *State of the World 1987: A Worldwatch Institute Report on Progress toward a Sustainable Society* (New York: Norton).

BROWN, L. R., and J. E. YOUNG, 1990. "Feeding the World in the Nineties." In L. R. Brown et al., *State of the World 1990: A Worldwatch Institute Report on Progress toward a Sustainable Society* (New York: Norton).

BROWN, L. R., et al., 1987. *State of the World* (New York: Norton/Worldwatch).

BROWN, M. K., 1988. *Working the Street: Police Discretion and the Dilemmas of Reform* (New York: Russell Sage).

BROWNELL, S., 1971. "Superintendents of Large City School Systems," In *Encyclopedia of Education.* Vol. 8 (New York: Macmillan).

BRYAN, J. H., 1965. "Apprenticeships in Prostitution," *Social Problems* 12: 278–97.

BRYSON, R. B., J. B. BRYSON, M. H. LICHT, and B. G. LICHT, 1976. "The Professional Pair," *American Psychologist* 31: 10–17.

BUELL, J., and T. DeLUCA, 1975. "On Busing," *Progressive,* April, pp. 26–27.

BULLARD, R. D., 1988. *Invisible Houston: The Black Experience in Boom and Bust* (College Station: Texas A&M Press).

BUMPASS, L. L., 1984. "Children and Marital Disruption: A Replication and Update," *Demography* 21: 71–81.

BURGESS, R. L., and R. L. AKERS, 1966. "A Differential Association-Reinforcement Theory of Criminal Behavior," *Social Problems* 14: 128–47.

BURR, C., 1993. "Homosexuality and Biology," *Atlantic* 27, 47–65.

BURROS, M., 1988. "Women: Out of the House but Not out of the Kitchen," *New York Times,* February 24, pp. A1, C10.

BUTLER, E., 1977. *The Urban Crisis: Problems and Prospects in America* (Santa Monica, CA: Goodyear).

BUTTERFIELD, F., 1992. "Are American Jails Becoming Shelters from the Storm?" *New York Times,* July 19, p. E4.

BYLER, W., 1977. "The Destruction of American Indian Families." In S. Unger (Ed.), *The Destruction of American Indian Families* (New York: Association of American Indian Affairs).

CAIN, G. G., and D. A. WISSOKER, 1987–1988, "Do Income Maintenance Programs Break Up Marriages? A Reevaluation of SIME-DIME," *Focus* 10: 1–15.

CALDERONE, A., 1993. *Men of Dishonor: Inside the Sicilian Mafia* (New York: Morrow).

CALDWELL, J. C., et al., 1992. "Fertility Decline in Africa: A New Type of Transition?" *Population and Development Review* 18, 211–42.

CALLAHAN, D., 1989. *What Kind of Life: The Limits of Medical Progress* (New York: Simon & Schuster).

CALLAHAN, D., 1994. "From Explosion to Implosion: Transforming Healthcare." In W. Kornblum and C. D. Smith (Eds.), *The Healing Experience: Readings on the Social Context of Health Care* (Englewood Cliffs, NJ: Prentice Hall).

CAMERON, J., 1975. "Black America: Still Waiting for Full Membership," *Fortune,* April, p. 172.

CAMPBELL, A., 1975. "The American Way of Mating: Marriage Si, Children Only Maybe," *Psychology Today,* May, pp. 38–43.

CANTOR, D. J., 1970. "A Matter of Right," *The Humanist* 30: 10–12.

CAPLAN, A., 1992. *If I Were a Rich Man Could I Buy a Pancreas?: And Other Essays on the Ethics of Health Care* (Bloomington: Indiana University Press).

CAPLAN, N., et al., (1989. *The Boat People and Achievement in America: A Study of Family Life, Hard Work, and Cultural Values* (Ann Arbor: University of Michigan Press).

CAPLOVITZ, D., 1963. *The Poor Pay More: Consumer Practices of Low Income Families* (New York: Free Press).

CAPLOVITZ, D., 1976. *The Working Addict* (New York: City University of New York, Graduate School and University Center, Metropolitan Drugs and Industry Project).

CAPLOVITZ, D., 1987. Unpublished proposal for research on debt entanglement as a risk factor for mental health (personal communication).

CARLIN, V. F., and R. MANSBERG, 1987. *Where Can Mom Live? A Family Guide to Living Arrangements for Elderly Parents* (Lexington, MA: D. C. Heath/Lexington Books).

CARMODY, D., 1992. "Coverage of Smoking Linked to Tobacco Ads." *New York Times,* January 30, p. D22.

CARPENTER, S. R., 1978. "Review of 'Autonomous Technology: Technics-out-of-Control as a Theme in Political Thought' by Langdon Winner," *Technology and Culture* 19: 142–45.

CELIS, W., 3rd. 1993a. "The Fight over National Standards," *New York Times,* Education Life, August 1, 1993, pp. 14–16.

CELIS, W., 3d. 1993b. "International Report Card Shows U.S. Schools Work." *New York Times,* December 9, pp. A1, A26.

CELIS, W., 3d. 1993. "Study Finds Rising Concentration of

Black and Hispanic Students." *New York Times,* December 14, pp. A1, B6.

CELIS, W., 3d. (1994, March 17). "Michigan Votes for Revolution in Financing Its Public Schools," *New York Times,* pp. A1–A21.

CENSUS BUREAU (U.S. Bureau of the Census), Current Population Report, 1990. *Trends in Income, by Selected Characteristics: 1947 to 1988.* Series P-60, No. 167 (Washington, DC: U.S. Government Printing Office).

CENSUS BUREAU (U.S. Bureau of the Census), Current Population Reports, 1989. *Money Income and Poverty Status in the United States: 1988 (Advance Data from the March 1989 Current Population Survey),* Series P-60, No. 166 (Washington, DC: U.S. Government Printing Office).

CENSUS BUREAU (U.S. Bureau of the Census), Current Population Reports, 1989. *Population Profile of the United States 1989,* Series P-23, No. 159 (Washington, DC: U.S. Government Printing Office).

CENSUS BUREAU (U.S. Bureau of the Census), 1990. *Population Characteristics* (Washington, DC: U.S. Government Printing Office).

U.S. CENSUS BUREAU (U.S. Department of Commerce, Bureau of the Census), 1992 (July). "Income, Poverty, and Wealth in the United States: A Chart Book," *Current Population Reports,* Series P-60, No. 179.

Centers for Disease Control, 1990. *HIV/AIDS Surveillance Report* (Atlanta, GA: Centers for Disease Control).

CHAFETZ, J. S., 1974. *Masculine, Feminine, or Human? An Overview of the Sociology of Sex Roles* (Itasca, IL: Peacock Press).

CHAFETZ, M. E., 1972. *Alcohol and Alcoholism* (Rockville, MD: National Institute on Alcohol Abuse and Alcoholism).

CHAFETZ, M. E., and H. W. DEMONS, JR., 1972. *Alcoholism and Society* (New York: Oxford University Press).

CHAMBLISS, W., 1973. "The Saints and the Roughnecks," *Society* 2: 24–31.

CHAMBLISS, W. J., and R. H. NASAGAWA, 1969. "On the Validity of Official Statistics: A Comparative Study of White, Black, Japanese High-School Boys," *Journal of Research on Crime and Delinquency* 6: 71–77.

CHAPPELL, D., G. GEIS, S. SCHAEFFER, and L. SIEGEL, 1971. "Forcible Rape: A Comparative Study of Offenses Known to the Police in Boston and Los Angeles." In J. H. Henslin (Ed.), *Studies in the Sociology of Sex* (Englewood Cliffs, NJ: Prentice Hall).

CHERLIN, A., 1979. "Work Life and Marital Dissolution." In G. Levinger and O. C. Moles (Eds.), *Divorce and Separation: Context, Causes, and Consequences* (New York: Basic Books).

CHERLIN, A. J., 1981. *Marriage, Divorce, Remarriage* (Cambridge, MA: Harvard University Press).

CHERLIN, A. J., 1992. *Marriage, Divorce, Remarriage,* 2nd ed. (Cambridge, MA: Harvard University Press).

CHERLIN, A. J., R. R. FURSTENBERG, JR., P. L. CHASE-LANSDALE, K. E. KIERNAN, P. K. ROBINS, D. R. MORRISON, and J. O. TEITLER, 1991, June 7. "Longitudinal Studies of Effects of Divorce on Children in Great Britain and the United States." *Science,* pp. 1386–89.

CHERNIN, K, 1981. *The Obsession: Reflections on the Tyranny of Slenderness* (New York: HarperCollins).

CHESLER, P., 1972. *Women and Madness* (New York: Avon).

CHIRA, S., 1992. "New Head Start Studies Raise Question on Help: Should Fewer Get More?" *New York Times,* March 4, p. B6.

CHUDACOFF, H. P., 1989. *How Old Are You?* (Princeton, NJ: Princeton University Press).

CISNEROS, H. G. (ED.), 1993. *Interwoven Destinies: Cities and the Nation* (New York: W. W. Norton).

City University of New York, 1978. *West 42nd Street: "The Bright Light Zone"* (New York: City University of New York, Graduate School and University Center).

CLARK, J. P., and E. P. WENNINGER, 1962. "Socio-economic Class and Area as Correlates of Illegal Behaviour among Juveniles," *American Sociological Review* 27: 826–34.

CLARK, W. C., 1989. "Managing Planet Earth," *Scientific American,* September, p. 47.

CLAWSON, P., 1988. "Terrorism in Decline?" *Orbis* 32: 263–76.

CLAYSON, H., 1992. *Painted Love: Prostitution in French Art of the Impressionist Era* (New Haven, CT: Yale University Press).

CLINARD, M. B., and R. QUINNEY, 1973. *Criminal Behavior Systems: A Typology,* 2nd ed. (New York: Holt, Rinehart & Winston).

CLINE, C., 1962. "Five Variations on the Marriage Theme: Types of Marriage Formation," *Bulletin on Family Development* 3: 10–13.

CLOSE, F., 1991. *Too Hot to Handle* (Princeton, NJ: Princeton University Press).

CLOWARD, R. A., and L. E. OHLIN, 1960. *Delinquency and Opportunity: A Theory of Delinquent Gangs* (New York: Free Press).

COCHRANE, R., and R. M. STAPES, 1981. "Women, Marriage, Employment, and Mental Health," *British Journal of Psychiatry* 139: 373–81.

COCKERHAM, W. C., 1988. "Medical Sociology." In N. J. Smelser (Ed.), *The Handbook of Sociology* (Newbury Park, CA: Sage).

COGWILL, D. O., 1974. "The Aging of Populations and Society," *Annals of the American Academy of Political and Social Science* 415: 1–18.

COHEN, A. K., 1971. *Delinquent Boys* (New York: Free Press).

COHEN, C., 1979. "Why Racial Preference Is Illegal and Immoral," *Commentary* 67 (6): 40–52.

COHEN, D., 1975. "Segregation, Desegregation, and *Brown:* A Twenty-Year Retrospective," *Society* 12 (1): 34–40.

COHEN, J., 1983. "Incapacitation as a Strategy for Crime Control: Possibilities and Pitfalls." In M. Tonry and N. Morris (Eds.), *Crime and Justice: An Annual Review of Research,* Vol. 5 (Chicago: University of Chicago Press).

COHEN, P., 1989. *Cocaine in Amsterdam* (Amsterdam, the Netherlands: University of Amsterdam Center for Criminological Research).

COLEMAN, J. S., 1974. *Power and the Structure of Society* (New York: Norton).

COLEMAN, J. S., 1982. *The Asymmetric Society* (Syracuse, NY: Syracuse University Press).

COLES, R., 1968. *Children of Crisis* (New York: Dell).

COLLINS, G., 1982. "Studies Find Sexual Abuse of Children Widespread," *New York Times,* May 13, pp. C1, C10.

COMFORT, A., 1976. *A Good Age* (New York: Crown).

COMMISSION ON OBSCENITY AND PORNOGRAPHY, 1970. "Patterns of Exposure to Erotic Material," *Report of the Commission* on *Obscenity and Pornography,* Section F (Washington, DC: Government Printing Office).

COMMITTEE ON HEALTH CARE FOR HOMELESS PEOPLE, 1988. *Homelessness, Health, and Human Needs* (Washington, DC: National Academy Press).

COMMONER, B., 1971. *The Closing Circle: Nature, Man, and Technology* (New York: Knopf).

COMMONER, B., 1992. *Making Peace with the Planet* (New York: New Press).

CONRAD, P., and R. KERN (EDS.), 1981. *The Sociology of Health and Illness: Critical Perspectives* (New York: St. Martin's Press).

CORCORAN, M., and G. J. DUNCAN, 1979. "Work History, Labor Force Attachment, and Earnings Differences between the Races and Sexes," *Journal of Human Resources* 14: 3–20.

CORNELIUS, W. A., 1989. "Impact of the 1986 U.S. Immigration Law on Emigration from Rural Mexican Sending Communities," *Population and Development Review* 15: 689–705.

COTTINGHAM, P. H., 1975. "Black Income and Metro-politan Residential Segregation," *Urban Affairs Quarterly* 10: 273–96.

COTTRELL, W. F., 1951. "Death by Dieselization: A Case Study in the Reaction to Technological Change," *American Sociological Review* 16: 358–65.

COUNCIL ON ENVIRONMENTAL QUALITY, 1980. *Environmental Quality* (Washington, DC: U.S. Government Printing Office).

COWAN, N. M., and R. S. COWAN, 1989. *Our Parents' Lives: The Americanization of Eastern European Jews* (New York: Basic Books).

COX, H., 1990. "Roles for Aged Individuals in Post-Industrial Societies," *International Journal of Aging and Human Development* 30, 55–62.

CRESSEY, D. R., 1953. *Other People's Money: A Study in the Social Psychology of Embezzlement* (Montclair, NJ: Patterson Smith).

CRYSTAL, G. S., 1992. *In Search of Excess: The Overcompensation of American Executives* (New York: W. W. Norton).

CUBER, J. F., and P. HAROFF, 1965. *Sex and the Significant Americans* (Baltimore, MD: Penguin Books).

CUMMINGS, J., 1983. "Breakup of Black Family Imperils Gains of Decades," *New York Times,* November 20, pp. 1, 56.

Current Population Reports, 1986. "Child Support and Alimony: 1985: (Washington, DC: U.S. Department of Commerce, Bureau of the Census).

Current Population Reports, 1987a. "Fertility of American Women: June 1986" (Washington, DC: U.S. Department of Commerce, Bureau of the Census).

Current Population Reports, 1987b. "Household and Family Characteristics: March 1986" (Washington, DC: U.S. Department of Commerce, Bureau of the Census).

CURTIS, R., and E. HOGAN, 1969. *Perils of the Peaceful Atom* (New York: Ballantine Books).

CURTIS, W. R., 1986. "The Deinstitutionalization Story," *Public Interest,* No. 85 (Fall): 34–49.

CUSHMAN, J. H., 1993. "U.S. to Weigh Blacks' Complaints About Pollution." *New York Times,* November 19, p. A16.

CZIKSZENTIMIHALYI, M., and E. ROCHBERG-HALTON, 1981. *The Meaning of Things: Domestic Symbols and the Self* (Cambridge, England: Cambridge University Press).

DALY, M., 1970. "Woman and the Catholic Church." In R. Morgan (Ed.), *Sisterhood Is Powerful* (New York: Random House).

DANIELS, L. A., 1983. "In Defense of Busing," *New York Times Magazine,* April 17, 1983, pp. 34 ff.

DANIELS, N., 1985. *Just Health Care* (Cambridge, England: Cambridge University Press).

DANIELS, N., 1987. "Does OSHA Protect Too Much?" In G. Ezorsky (Ed.), *Moral Rights in the Workplace* (Albany, NY: State University of New York Press).

DANK, B. M., 1971. "Coming Out in the Gay World," *Psychiatry* 34: 180–97.

DANZIGER, S. H., R. H. HAVEMAN, and R. D. PLOTNICK, 1986. "Antipoverty Policy: Effects on the Poor and the Nonpoor." In S. H. Danziger and D. H. Weinberg (Eds.), *Fighting Poverty: What Works and What Doesn't* (Cambridge, MA: Harvard University Press).

DAVIDSON, H., 1982. "Practical Problems in Psychiatric Field Surveys," *Acta Psychiatrica Scandinavica* 65, 87–95.

DAVIS, K., 1937. "The Sociology of Prostitution," *American Sociological Review* 2: 744–55.

DAVIS, K., 1971. "Population Policy: Will Current Programs Succeed?" In D. Callahan (Ed.), *American Popular Debate* (Garden City, NY: Doubleday).

DAVIS, K., 1986. "Aging and the Health-Care System: Economic and Structural Issues," *Daedalus,* Winter, pp. 227–46.

DAVIS, K., 1986. "Low Fertility in Evolutionary Perspective." In "Fertility in Industrial Societies," *Population and Development Review,* Suppl. to Vol. 12, pp. 48–65.

DAVIS, K., et al. 1987. "Below-Replacement Fertility in Industrial Societies: Causes, Consequences, Policies," *Population and Development Review,* Suppl. 5 to Vol. 12.

DAVIS, M., 1990. *City of Quartz: Excavating the Future in Los Angeles* (New York: Verso).

DAVIS, N., 1987. "The Prostitute: Developing a Deviant Subculture." In J. H. Henslin (Ed.), *Studies in the Sociology of Sex* (Englewood Cliffs, NJ: Prentice Hall).

DAVIS, N. J., and R. V. ROBINSON, 1991. "Men's and Women's Consciousness of Gender Inequality," *American Sociological Review* 56, 72–84.

DECKARD, B. S., 1979. *The Women's Movement: Political, Socioeconomic, and Psychological Issues* (New York: Harper & Row).

DECKER, S., 1969. *An Empty Spoon* (New York: Harper & Row).

DEJONG, W., C. K. ATKIN, and L. WALLACK, 1992. "A Critical Analysis of 'Moderation' Advertising Sponsored by the Beer Industry: Are 'Responsible Drinking' Commercials Done Responsibly?" *Milbank Quarterly* 70, 661–77.

DENITCH, B., 1990. *The End of the Cold War* (University of Minnesota Press).

DEPARLE, J., 1991. "A Growing Choice: Housing or Food." *New York Times,* December 12, p. 22.

DEPARLE, J., 1992. "Incomes of Young Families Dip 32% in 17 Years, Study Finds." *New York Times,* April 15, p. 27.

DEPARLE, J., 1994. "Report to Clinton Sees Vast Extent of Homelessness." *New York Times,* February 17, pp. A1, A20.

DER-KARABETIAN, A., and A. J. SMITH, 1977. "Sex-role Stereotyping in the U.S.: Is It Changing?" *Sex Roles: A Journal of Research* 3: 193–98.

DesJarlais, D. C., 1987. "Addicts Will Change If They Get the Word," *Newsday,* April 26, p. 8.

Dewey, J., 1916. *Democracy and Education* (New York: Macmillan).

Dial, T. H., et al., 1992. "Training of Mental Health Providers." In R. W. Manderscheid and M. A. Sonnenschein (Eds.), *Mental Health, United States, 1992* (Washington DC: Center for Mental Health Services and National Institute of Mental Health).

Diesenhouse, S., 1990. "A Rising Tide of Violence Leaves More Youths in Jail," *New York Times,* July 8, p. E4.

Dimen, M., 1987. "Brave New World of Love and Death," *Newsday,* April 26, pp. 14–15.

Dobson, A., J. C. Langenbrunner, S. A. Pelovitz, and J. B. Willis, 1986. "The Future of Medicare Policy Reform: Priorities for Research and Demonstrations," *Health Care Financing Review,* Annual Suppl.: 1–7.

Dohrenwend, B. J., and B.*S. Dohrenwend, 1974. "Social Cultural Influences on Psychopathology," *Annual Review of Psychology* 25, 420–34.

Dohrenwend, B. P., and B. S. Dohrenwend, 1969. *Social Status and Psychological Disorder: A Casual Inquiry* (New York: Wiley Interscience).

Dohrenwend, B. P., and B. S. Dohrenwend, 1975. "Sociocultural and Social-psychological Factors in the Genesis of Mental Disorders," *Journal of Health and Social Behavior* 16: 369.

Domhoff, G. W., 1978. *The Powers That Be: Processes of Ruling-Class Domination in America* (New York: Random House).

Domhoff, G. W., 1983. *Who Rules America Now?* (New York: Simon & Schuster).

Donnerstein, E., and D. Linz, 1987. "Sexual Violence and the Media: A Warning." In A. Wells (ed.), *Mass Media and Society* (Lexington, MA: D. C. Heath).

Donovan, W., 1994, "One Leg, One Life at a Time." *New York Times Magazine,* January 23, pp. 26–29.

Dugger, C., 1992. "H.I.V. Incidence Rises Among Black Mothers." *New York Times,* May 1, p. B3.

Dunlap, R. E., and R. Scarce, 1991. "Environmental Problems and Protection," *Public Opinion Quarterly* 55, 651–72.

Durkheim, E., 1950. *Rules of the Sociological Method,* 8th ed., S. A. Solvay and J. H. Mueller (trans.), G. E. G. Catlin (Ed.), (New York: Free Press).

Durning, A. B., 1990. "Ending poverty." In L. Brown (Ed.), *State of the World 1990: A Worldwatch Institute Report on Progress toward a Sustainable Society* (New York: Norton).

Eaton, J. W., and R. J. L. Weil, 1955. *Culture and Mental Disorders* (New York: Free Press).

Eaton, W., 1980. *The Sociology of Mental Disorders* (New York: Praeger).

Eckholm, E., 1990. "An Aging Nation Grapples with Caring for the Frail," *New York Times,* March 27, pp. A1, A18.

Eckholm, E., 1992. "Thorny Issue in Gun Control: Curbing Responsible Owners." *New York Times,* April 3, pp. A1, A15.

Eckholm, E., 1993. "Teen-Age Gangs Are Inflicting Lethal Violence on Small Cities." *New York Times,* January 31, pp. 1, 26.

Economic Policy Institute, 1993 (September). *The Joyless Recovery.*

Edelstein, J. D., and M. A. Warner, 1977. *A Comparative Union Democracy: Organization and Opposition in British and American Unions* (New York: Halsted Press).

Edwards, L. P., 1927. *The Natural History of Revolution* (Chicago: University of Chicago Press).

Ehrenreich, B., 1992. "Stamping Out a Dread Scourge," *Time,* February 17, p. 88.

Ehrenreich, B., and D. English, 1979. *For Her Own Good: 150 Years of the Experts' Advice to Women* (Garden City, NY: Doubleday Anchor Books).

Ehrlich, P. R., and A. Ehrlich, 1972. *Population, Resources, Environment,* 2nd ed. (San Francisco: Freeman).

Ehrlich, P. R., A. H. Ehrlich, and J. P. Holdren, 1977. *Ecoscience: Population, Resources, Environment* (San Francisco: Freeman).

Eichorn, R. L., and E. G. Ludwig, 1973. "Poverty and Health." In H. H. Meissner (Ed.), *Poverty in the Affluent Society* (New York: Harper & Row).

Ekerdt, D. J., R. Bosse, and J. M. Mogey, 1980. "Concurrent Change in Planned and Preferred Age for Retirement," *Journal of Gerontology* 35: 233–40.

Elifson, K. W., and C. Sterk-Elifson, 1992. "Someone to Count On: Homeless Male Drug Users and Their Friendship Relations," *Urban Anthropology* 21, 235–51.

Elifson, K., J. Boles, and M. Sweat, 1993. "Risk Factors Associated with HIV Infection Among Male Prostitutes," *American Journal of Public Health* 82, 79–83.

Elliot, D. S., and S. S. Ageton, 1980. "Reconciling Race and Class Differences in Self-Reported and Official Estimates of Delinquency," *American Sociological Review* 45: 95–110.

Ellis, H., 1914. *The Criminal,* 5th ed. (London: Scott).

Ellul, J., 1964. *The Technological Society* (New York: Knopf).

Ellwood, D. T., 1987. *Divide and Conquer: Responsible Security for America's Poor* (New York: Ford Foundation).

Ellwood, D. T., 1988. *Poor Support: Poverty in the American Family* (New York: Basic Books).

Ellwood, D. T., and L. H. Summers, 1986. "Poverty in America: Is Welfare the Answer or the Problem?" In S. H. Danziger and D. H. Weinberg (Eds.), *Fighting Poverty: What Works and What Doesn't* (Cambridge, MA: Harvard University Press).

England, P., M. Chassie, and L. McCormack, 1982, "Skill Demands and Earnings in Female and Male Occupations," *Sociology and Social Research* 66: 147–68.

England, P., and G. Farkas, 1986. *Households, Employment, and Gender: A Social, Economic and Demographic View* (New York: Aldine de Gruyter).

Epstein, C., 1988. *Deceptive Distinctions* (New Haven, CT: Yale University Press).

Erikson, K. T., 1976. *Everything in Its Path* (New York: Simon & Schuster).

Erlanger, H. S., 1974. "The Empirical Status of the Subculture of Violence Thesis," *Social Problems* 22: 280–92.

Erlanger, H. S., 1987. "A Widening Pattern of Abuse Exemplified in Steinberg Case," *New York Times,* November 8, p. 1.

Etzioni, A., 1993. "How to Make Marriage Matter," *Time,* September 6, p. 76.

EVANGELAUF, J., 1992 (January 22). "Minority-Group Enrollment at Colleges Rose 10% from 1988 to 1990, Reaching Record Levels," *Chronicle of Higher Education.*

FALLOWS, J., 1981. *National Defense* (New York: Random House).

FALUDI, S., 1991. *Backlash: The Undeclared War Against American Women* (New York: Crown).

FAMILY SERVICE AMERICA, 1984. *The State of Families: 1984–85* (New York: Family Service America).

FANON, F., 1968. *The Wretched of the Earth* (New York: Grove Press).

FARIS, R. E. L., and H. W. DUNHAM, 1938. *Mental Disorders in Urban Areas* (Chicago: University of Chicago Press).

FARLEY, R., 1984. *Blacks and Whites: Narrowing the Gap?* (Cambridge, MA: Harvard University Press).

FARLEY, R., et al., 1978. "Chocolate City, Vanilla Suburbs: Will the Trend Toward Racially Separate Communities Continue?" *Social Indicators Research* 6: 439–43.

FARLEY, R., S. BIANCHI, and D. COLASSANTO, 1979. "Barriers to the Racial Integration of Neighborhoods: the Detroit Case," *Annals of the American Academy of Political and Social Sciences* 441: 97–113.

FARNSWORTH, C. H., 1992. "Canadians Defend Care System Against Criticism." *New York Times,* February 17, p. A14.

FARRELL, S., 1991. "Womanchurch," Unpublished doctoral dissertation, City University of New York Graduate School.

FARRELL, W., 1975. *The Liberated Man* (New York: Random House).

FASTEAU, M. F., 1974. *The Male Machine* (New York: McGraw-Hill).

FAULKNER, P., 1981. "Exposing Risks of Nuclear Disaster." In A. F. Westin (Ed.), *Whistle Blowing!* (New York: McGraw-Hill).

FEAGIN, J. R., 1988. *Free Enterprise City: Houston in Political and Economic Perspective* (New Brunswick, NJ: Rutgers University Press).

FEAGIN, J. R., 1991. "The Continuing Significance of Race: Anti-Black Discrimination in Public Places," *American Sociological Review* 56, 101–17.

FEDERAL BUREAU OF INVESTIGATION, 1987. *Crime in the United States* (Uniform Crime Reports) (Washington, DC: Government Printing Office).

FELSON, R. B., and J. T. TEDESCHI, 1993. *Aggression and Violence: Social Interactionist Perspectives* (Washington, DC: American Psychological Association).

FERRENCE, R. G., 1980. "Sex Differences in the Prevalence of Problem Drinking." In O. J. Kalant (Ed.), *Research Advances in Alcohol and Drug Problems, Vol. 5: Alcohol and Drug Problems in Women* (New York: Plenum).

FERRISS, A. L., 1970. "An Indicator of Marriage Dissolution by Marriage Cohort," *Social Forces* 48: 356–65.

FINKELHOR, D., and L. MEYER, 1988. *Nursery Crimes* (Newbury Park, CA: Sage).

FINKELSTEIN, M. M., 1970. "Traffic in Sex-Oriented Materials, Part I: Adult Bookstores in Boston, Massachusetts." In *Technical Reports of the Commission on Obscenity and Pornography,* Vol. 4 (Washington, DC: Government Printing Office).

FINN, C. E., JR., 1985. "The Drive for Excellence: Moving towards a Public Consensus." In B. Gross and R. Gross (Eds.): *The Great School Debate: Which Way for American Education?* (New York: Simon & Schuster).

FISCHER, C. S., 1976. *The Urban Experience* (New York: Harcourt Brace Jovanovich).

FISHER, P., 1972. *The Gay Mystique: The Myth and Reality of Male Homosexuals* (Briarcliff Manor, NY: Stein & Day).

FISK, A. A., 1981. *A New Look at Senility* (Springfield, IL: Charles C. Thomas).

FISKE, E. B., 1987. "Hispanic Pupils' Plight Cited in Study." *New York Times,* July 26, p. 24.

FLAVIN, C., 1987. "Reassessing Nuclear Power." In L. R. Brown et al., *State of the World* (New York: Norton/Worldwatch).

FLAVIN, C., 1990. "Slowing Global Warming." In L. Brown et al., *State of the World 1990: A Worldwatch Institute Report on Progress toward a Sustainable Society* (New York: Norton).

FLINK, J., 1976. *The Automobile and American Culture* (Cambridge, MA: Massachusetts Institute of Technology Press).

FLORMAN, S. C., 1981. "Living with Technology: Tradeoffs in Paradise." *Technology Review* 83 (8): 24–35.

FORD, M. DE G., 1975. "School Integration and Busing: Courts, Busing and White Flight," *The Nation,* July 5, p. 13.

FORD FOUNDATION, Project on Social Welfare and the American Future, 1989. *The Common Good* (New York: Ford Foundation).

FORD FOUNDATION, 1989. *The Ford Foundation Letter* 20, November, 1–3.

FORD FOUNDATION, 1990. "Increasing the Quantity and Quality of Child Care." *Ford Foundation Letter* 121: 1–9.

FREDDI, G., and J. W. BJORKMAN, *Controlling Medical Professionals: The Comparative Politics of Health Governance* (Newbury Park, CA: Sage).

FREEDMAN, S. G., 1987. "New AIDS Battlefield: Addicts' World," *New York Times,* April 8, pp. B1, B7.

FREEMAN, H. E., and O. G. SIMMONS, 1963. *The Mental Patient Comes Home* (New York: Wiley).

FREEMAN, J., 1972. "The Effects of Crowding on Human Performance and Social Behavior." In F. J. McGulgan and P. J. Woods (Eds.), *Contemporary Studies in Psychology* (Englewood Cliffs, NJ: Prentice Hall).

FREEMAN, R. B., and B. HALL, 1986. "Permanent Homelessness in America?" Working Paper No. 2013 (Cambridge, MA: National Bureau of Economic Research).

FRENCH, P. A., 1984. *Collective and Corporate Responsibility* (New York: Columbia University Press).

FREUDENHEIM, M., 1987. "Officials Warn of Gaps in Insurance for Aged," *New York Times,* January 16, p. A10.

FREUDENHEIM, M., 1993. "Many Patients Unhappy with H.M.O.'s." *New York Times,* August 18, p. A14.

FRIEDAN, B., 1963. *The Feminine Mystique* (New York: Dell).

FRIEDAN, B., 1993. *The Fountain of Age* (New York: Simon & Schuster).

FRIEDMAN, L. M., 1984. *Your Time Will Come: The Law of Age Discrimination and Mandatory Retirement* (New York: Russell Sage).

FRIEDMAN, L. M., 1993. *Crime and Punishment in American History* (New York: Basic Books).

FRIEDMAN, L. N., 1978. *The Wildcat Experiment: An Early Test of Supported Work in Drug Abuse Rehabilitation* (Washington, DC: Government Printing Office).

FRIEDMAN, M., 1962. *Capitalism and Freedom* (Chicago: University of Chicago Press).

FRISBIS, W. P., and C. J. CLARKE, 1979. "Technology and Ecological Perspective: Theory and Measurement at the Societal Level," *Social Forces* 58 (2): 591–613.

FUCHS, V., 1956. "Toward a Theory of Poverty." In Task Force on Economic Growth and Opportunity, *The Concept of Poverty* (Washington, DC: U.S. Chamber of Commerce).

FUERBRINGER, J., 1982. "Jobless Rate Rose to 9% for March, Matching Record," *New York Times,* April 3, pp. 1, 20.

FURSTENBERG, E. F., JR., 1979. "The Social Consequences of Teenage Parenthood." In G. B. Spanier (Ed.), *Human Sexuality in a Changing Society* (Minneapolis, MN: Burgess).

GAGNON, J. H., and W. SIMON, 1967. "Introduction: Deviant Behavior and Sexual Deviance.: In J. H. Gagnon and W. Simon (Eds.), *Sexual Deviance* (New York: Harper & Row).

GAGNON, J. H., and W. SIMON, 1973. *Sexual Conduct: The Social Sources of Human Sexuality* (Hawthorne, NY: Aldine).

GALBRAITH, J. K., 1958. *The Affluent Society* (Boston: Houghton Mifflin).

GALBRAITH, J. K., 1971. *The New Industrial State,* 2nd ed. (Boston: Houghton Mifflin).

GALBRAITH, J. K., 1973. "The technostructure and the Corporation in the New Industrial State." In M. Zeitlin (Ed.), *American Society, Inc.* (Chicago: Rand McNally).

GALLAGHER, B. J., III, 1987. *The Sociology of Mental Illness,* 2nd ed. (Englewood Cliffs, NJ: Prentice Hall).

GALLUP, G., 1982. *The Gallup Poll: Public Opinion 1981* (Wilmington, DE: Scholarly Resources).

GALTUNG, J., 1971. "Peace-Thinking." In Lepawsky, Buehrig, and Lasswell (Eds.), *The Search for World Order* (Englewood Cliffs, NJ: Prentice Hall).

GANS, H., 1979. *Deciding What's News* (New York: Pantheon Books).

GANS, H., 1984. *The Urban Villagers,* 2nd ed. (New York: Free Press).

GANS, H. J., 1968. *People and Plans: Essays on Urban Problems and Solutions* (New York: Basic Books).

GARFINKEL, I., and S. S. McLANAHAN, 1986. *Single Mothers and Their Children: A New American Dilemma* (Washington, DC: Urban Institute).

GEERTZ, C., 1963. "The Integrative Revolution." In C. Geertz (Ed.), *Old Societies, New States* (New York: Free Press).

GERSON, K., 1985. *Hard Choices: How Women Decide about Work, Career, and Motherhood* (Berkeley, CA: University of California Press).

GERSON, K., 1993. *No Man's Land: Men's Changing Commitment to Family and Work* (New York: Basic Books).

GIBBONS, J. H., P. D. BLAIR, and H. L. GWIN, 1989. "Strategies for Energy Use," *Scientific American,* September, pp. 136–43.

GIBSON, G., 1983. "Health Services Research," In H. E. Freeman et al., (Eds.), *Applied Sociology* (San Francisco: Jossey-Bass).

GIELE, J. Z., 1988. "Gender and Sex Roles." In N. J. Smelser (Ed.), *The Handbook of Sociology* (Newbury Park, CA: Sage).

GIL, D., 1966. "Child Abuse—A Nationwide Study of Child Abuse and Its Connection with Accident Research." In R. J. Meyers (Ed.), *Childhood Accidental Injury Symposium Proceedings* (Charlottesville, VA: University of Virginia School of Medicine).

GIL, D., 1979. "Violence against Children." In D. G. Gil (Ed.), *Child Abuse and Violence* (New York: AMS Press).

GILDER, G., 1981. *Wealth and Poverty* (New York: Basic Books).

GILLIN, C., and F. OCHBERG, 1970. "Firearms Control and Violence." In D. Daniels, M. Gilula, and F. Ochberg (Eds.), *Violence and the Struggle for Existence* (Boston: Little, Brown).

GINZBERG, E., 1993. "The Changing Urban Scene: 1960–1990 and Beyond." In H. G. Cisneros (ed.), *Interwoven Destinies: Cities and the Nation* (New York: W. W. Norton).

GINZBURG, K. N., 1977. "The 'Meat-Rack': A Study of the Male Homosexual Prostitute." In C. D. Bryant (Ed.), *Sexual Deviancy in Social Context* (New York: New Viewpoints).

GLAAB, C. N., and A. T. BROWN, 1967. *A History of Urban America* (New York: Macmillan).

GLABERESON, W., 1988. "An Uneasy Alliance in Smokestack U.S.A.," *New York Times,* March 13, Sec. 3, p. 1.

GLASSER, P., and L. GLASSER, 1966. "Adequate Family Functioning." In I. M. Cohen (Ed.), *Family Structure Dynamics and Therapy,* Psychiatric Research Report No. 20 (Washington, DC: American Psychiatric Association).

GLASSNER, B., and B. BERG, 1980. "How Jews Avoid Alcohol Problems," *American Sociological Review* 45: 647–64.

GLICK, P. C., 1975. "Some Recent Changes in American Families," *Current Population Reports* (Washington, DC: U.S. Department of Commerce, Bureau of the Census).

GLICK, P. C., 1981. "A Demographic Picture of Black Families." In H. P. McAdoo (Ed.), *Black Families* (Newbury Park, CA: Sage).

GOFFMAN, E., 1961. *Asylums: Essays on the Social Situation of Mental Patients and Other Inmates* (Garden City, NY: Doubleday).

GOLDBERG, P., 1972. "Are Women Prejudiced against Women?" In C. Safilios-Rothschild (Ed.), *Toward a Sociology of Women* (New York: Wiley).

GOLDMAN, A. I., 1982. "Student Scores Rise after Nearby Subway Is Quieted," *New York Times,* April 26, p. 84.

GOLDMAN, H. H., N. ADAMS, and C. TAUBE, 1983. "Deinstitutionalization: The Data Demythologized," *Hospital and Community Psychiatry* 34: 129–34.

GOLDSTEIN, J., and M. GITTER, 1970. "Divorce without Blame," *The Humanist* 30: 12–15.

GOLEMAN, D., 1990. "As Bias Crime Seems to Rise, Scientists Study Roots of Racism," *New York Times,* May 29, pp. C1, C5.

GOLEMAN, D., 1992. "Black Scientists Study the 'Pose' of the Inner City." *New York Times,* April 21, pp. C1, C7.

GOODE, E., and R. R. TROIDEN (EDS.), 1974. *Sexual Deviance and Sexual Deviants* (New York: Morrow).

GOLEMAN, D., 1993. "Mental Disorders Common, but Few Get Treatment, Study Finds. *New York Times,* March 17, p. C13.

GOODE, W. J., 1959. "The Sociology of the Family." In R. Merton, L. Broome, and L. Cottrell (Eds.), *Sociology Today* (New York: Free Press).

GOODMAN, W., 1984. "Equal Pay for 'Comparable Worth'

Growing as Job-Discrimination Issue," *New York Times,* September 4, p. B9.

GOODWIN, L., 1973. *Do the Poor Want to Work?* (Washington, DC: Brookings Institution).

GORDON, M. R., 1990. "Arms Control Catching Up." *New York Times,* October 5, p. A7.

GOTTMANN, J., 1978. "Megalopolitan Systems around the World." In L. S. Bourne and J. W. Simmons (Eds.), *Systems of Cities: Readings on Structure, Growth, and Policy* (New York: Oxford University Press).

GOUGH, P. B., 1987. "The Key to Improving Schools: An Interview with William Glasser," *Phi Delta Kappan,* May, pp. 656–62.

GOULD, R. E., 1974. "Measuring Masculinity by the Size of the Paycheck." In J. H. Pleck and J. Sawyer (Eds.), *Men and Masculinity* (Englewood Cliffs, NJ: Prentice Hall).

GOULD, S. J., 1981. *The Mismeasure of Man* (New York: Norton).

GOULD, W. B., 1968. "Discrimination and the Unions." In J. Larner and I. Howe (Eds.), *Poverty: Views from the Left* (New York: Morrow).

GOVE, W. R., M. HUGHES, and O. R. GALLE, 1979. "Overcrowding in the Home: An Empirical Investigation of Its Possible Consequences," *American Sociological Review* 44: 59–79.

GRAHAM, H. D., and T. R. GURR (Eds.), 1969. *Violence in America: Historical and Comparative Perspectives. A Report to the National Commission on the Causes and Prevention of Violence* (New York: Bantam Books).

GRASSMICK, H. G., and G. J. BRYJAK, 1980. "The Deterrent Effect of Perceived Severity of Punishment," *Social Forces* 59: 417–91.

GREEN, C. P., and K. POTETEIGER, 1978. "Major Problems for Minors," *Society* 15: 8, 10–13.

GREEN, J., and P. S. ARNO, 1990. "The 'medicalization' of AIDS." *Journal of the American Medical Association* 264, 1261–66.

GREENLEY, J. R., 1972. "Alternative Views of the Psychiatrist's Role," *Social Problems* 20: 252–62.

GROB, G. N., 1985. "The Transformation of the Mental Hospital in the United States." *American Behavioral Scientist* 28, No. 5 (May–June): 639–54.

GROENEVELD, L. P., M. T. HANNAN, and N. B. TUMA, 1983. "Marital Stability." In *Final Report of the Seattle-Denver Income Maintenance Experiment, Vol. I: Design and Results* (Menlo Park, CA: SRI International).

GRONFEIN, W., 1985. "Psychotrophic Drugs and the Origins of Deinstitutionalization," *Social Problems* 32, No. 5 (June): 437–54.

GROSS, J., 1992. "Remnant of the War on Poverty, Job Corps Is Still a Quiet Success." *New York Times,* February 17, pp. A1, A14.

GRUENBERG, B., 1980. "The Happy Worker: An Analysis of Educational and Occupational Differences in Determinants of Job Satisfaction," *American Journal of Sociology,* 86: 247–71.

GURR, T. R., 1970. *Why Men Rebel* (Princeton, NJ: Princeton University Press).

GUSFIELD, J. R., 1963. *Symbolic Crusade: Status Politics and the American Temperance Movement* (Urbana, IL: University of Illinois Press).

GUSFIELD, J. R., 1975. "The (F)utility of Knowledge?: The Relation of Social Science to Public Policy toward Drugs," *Annals of the American Academy of Political and Social Sciences* 417: 1–15.

GUSFIELD, J., 1981. *The Culture of Public Problems: Drinking, Driving and the Symbolic Order* (Chicago: University of Chicago Press).

GUTHRIE, J. W., G. B. KLEINDORFER, H. M. LEVIN, and R. T. STOUT, 1971. *Schools and Inequality* (Cambridge, MA: Massachusetts Institute of Technology Press).

GUTTEMACHER, M. S., 1951. *Sex Offenses* (New York: Norton).

GUTTENTAG, M., and P. F. SECORD, 1983. *Too Many Women? The Sex Ratio Question* (Beverly Hills, CA: Sage).

HAGEDORN, J. M., 1988. *People and Folks: Gangs, Crime, and the Underclass in a Rustbelt City* (Chicago: Lake View Press).

HALL, P., 1982. *Great Planning Disasters* (Berkeley, CA: University of California Press).

HALL, R. H., 1981–1982. "The Truth about Brown Lung," *Business and Society Review* 40: 15–20.

HALLEY, R. B., and H. G. VATTER, 1978. "Technology and the Future as History: A Critical Review of Futurism," *Technology and Culture* 19 (1): 53–81.

HALLORAN, E. J., and M. KILEY, 1987. "Nursing Dependency, Diagnosis-Related Groups, and Length of Stay," *Health Care Financing* 8, No. 3 (Spring): 27–36.

HAMPDEN-TURNER, C., 1975. *From Poverty to Dignity* (Garden City, NY: Doubleday Anchor Books).

HANNAN, M. T., N. B. TUMA, and L. P. GROENEVELD, 1977. "Income and Marital Events: Evidence from an Income Maintenance Experiment," *American Journal of Sociology* 82: 1186–1211.

HANNAWAY, J., 1993. "Political Pressure and Decentralization in Institutional Organizations: The Case of School Districts," *Sociology of Education* 3, 147–63.

HANNAY, N. B., and R. E. McGINN, 1981. "The Anatomy of Modern Technology: Prologomenon to an Improved Public Policy for the Social Management of Technology," *Daedalus,* Winter, pp. 25–52.

HARKEY, J., D. L. MILES, and W. A. RUSHING, 1976. "The Relation between Social Class and Functional Status: A New Look at the Drift Hypothesis," *Journal of Health and Social Behavior* 17: 194–204.

HARNISCHFEGER, A., and D. E. WILEY, 1976. "The Marrow of Achievement Test Score Declines," *Educational Technology* 16: 5–14.

HARRINGTON, M., 1987. *The New American Poverty* (New York: Henry Holt).

HARRINGTON, M., 1988. "The First Steps—and a Few Beyond," *Dissent,* Winter, pp. 44–56.

HARRIS, L., 1977. "Gay Is O.K., but . . . ," *The Harris Survey,* July 18, pp. 1–2.

HARRY, J., and W. B. DeVALL, 1978. *The Social Organization of Gay Males* (New York: Praeger).

HARTLEY, R. E., 1974. "Sex Role Pressures and the Socialization of the Male Child." In J. H. Pleck and J. Sawyer (Eds.), *Men and Masculinity* (Englewood Cliffs, NJ: Prentice Hall).

HARTNAGEL, T. F., J. J. TEEVAN, and J. M. McINTYRE, 1975. "Television Violence and Violent Behavior," *Social Forces* 54: 341–51.

HASSEL, C. V., 1977. "Terror: The Crime of the Privileged—An Examination and Prognosis," *Terrorism* 1: 128.

HATTEN, J. M., and R. E. CONNERTON, 1986. "Urban and Rural Hospitals: How Do They Differ?" *Health Care Financing Review* 8, No. 2 (Winter): 77–85.

HAUG, M. R., 1981. "Age and Medical Care Utilization Patterns," *Journal of Gerontology* 36: 103–11.

HAWKINS, J., 1987. "Computers and Girls: Rethinking the Issues." In R. D. Pea and K. Sheingold (Eds.), *Mirrors of Minds: Patterns of Experience in Educational Computing* (Norwood, NJ: Ablex).

HAWLEY, A., 1975. "The Population Explosion." In A. Hawley (Ed.), *Man and Environment* (New York: New York Times).

HEALTH, L., 1984. "Impact of Newspaper Crime Reporting on Fear of Crime," *Journal of Personality and Social Psychology* 47, 263–76.

HECHINGER, F. M., 1985. "Schools and the War on Poverty," *New York Times,* April 23, p. C10.

HECHTER, M., 1987. *The Foundations of Group Solidarity* (Berkeley, CA: University of California Press).

HENDRIX, K., 1988. "Counselors Angry at Weak Response to Rise in Campus Rape." *Tallahassee Democrat (Los Angeles Times),* August 25, p. C5.

HEREN, L., 1978. "Curbing Terrorism," *Atlas World Press Review* 25: 31–33.

HERMAN, J. L., 1981. *Father-Daughter Incest* (Cambridge, MA: Harvard University Press).

HERMAN, J., and L. HIRSCHMAN, 1988. "Father-Daughter Incest," *Signs: Journal of Women in Culture and Society* 2: 735–56.

HERNDON, J., 1968. *The Way It Spozed to Be* (New York: Simon & Schuster).

HERZOG, E., and C. E. SUDIA, 1973. "Children in Fatherless Families." In B. M. Caldwell and N. H. Riccuiti (Eds.). *Review of Child Development Research,* Vol. 3 (Chicago: University of Chicago Press).

HETHERINGTON, E. M., 1980. "Children and Divorce." In R. Henderson (Ed.), *Parent-Child Interaction: Theory, Research, and Prospect* (New York: Academic Press).

HEYL, B. S., 1978. *The Madam as Entrepreneur: Career Management in House Prostitution* (New Brunswick, NJ: Transaction Books).

HHS (U.S. Department of Health and Human Services), Public Health Service, National Institute of Mental Health, 1990. *Research on Children and Adolescents with Mental, Behavioral, and Developmental Disorders* (Rockville, MD: National Institute of Mental Health).

HHS (U.S. Department of Health and Human Services), Public Health Service, 1990. *Healthy People 2000* (Washington, DC: GPO).

HICKS, N., 1975. "Drug Use Called up among Youths," *New York Times,* October 2, p. 22.

HICKS, J. P., 1992. "An Industrial Comeback Story: U.S. Is Competing Again in Steel." *New York Times,* March 31, pp. A1, A19.

HILLKIRK, J., 1990. "Top-dollar CEOs," *USA Today,* April 27, p. 1B.

HILLS, S. L. (ED.), 1987. *Corporate Violence: Injury and Death for Profit* (Totowa, NJ: Rowman & Littlefield).

HILTS, P. J., 1990. "Spread of AIDs by Heterosexuals Remains Slow," *New York Times,* May 1, pp. C1, C12.

HINDELANG, M., 1978. "Race and Involvement in Common Law Personal Crimes," *American Sociological Review* 43: 93–109.

HING, E., 1987. "Use of Nursing Homes by the Elderly: Preliminary Data from the 1985 National Nursing Home Survey," *Advance Data* (U.S. Department of Health and Human Services), May 14.

HIRSCH, K., 1987. "Media Violence and Audience Behavior." In A. Wells (Ed.), *Mass Media and Society* (Lexington, MA: D. C. Heath).

HIRSCHI, T., and M. GOTTFREDSON, 1983. "Age and the Explanation of Crime," *American Journal of Sociology* 89: 552–84.

HIRSCHMAN, C., 1986. "Minorities in the Labor Market." Paper presented at the Conference on Minorities in Poverty, Institute for Research on Poverty.

HOCHSCHILD, A. R., 1990. *The Second Shift* (New York: Avon Books).

HODGSON, T. S., 1992. "Cigarette Smoking and Lifetime Medical Expenditures," *Milbank Quarterly* 70, 81–87.

HOLE, J., and E. LEVINE, 1971. *Rebirth of Feminism* (New York: Quadrangle/New York Times).

HOLLINGSHEAD, A. B., and F. C. REDLICH, 1958. *Social Class and Mental Illness: A Community Study* (New York: Wiley).

HOLMES, R. A., and J. DEBURGER, 1987. *Serial Murder* (Newbury Park, CA: Sage).

HOLMES, S. A., 1990. "Study of Teen-agers Hints Gain for Those Having Abortions," *New York Times,* January 25, p. A21.

HOLMES, S. A., 1993, "U.S. Says Terrorist Attacks Dropped Sharply in 1992." *New York Times,* May 1, p. 4.

HOLT, J., 1965. *How Children Fail* (New York: Dell).

HOMBS, M. E., and M. SNYDER, 1982. *Homelessness in America: A Forced March to Nowhere* (Washington, DC: Community for Creative Non-Violence).

HOMER-DIXON, T. F., J. H. BOUTWELL, and G. W. RATHJENS, 1993. "Environmental Change and Violent Conflict," *Scientific American,* February, pp. 38–45.

HOOKER, E., 1957. "The Adjustment of the Male Overt Homosexual," *Journal of Projective Techniques* 21: 18–31.

HOOKER, E., 1958. "Male Homosexuality and the Rorschach," *Journal of Projective Techniques* 22: 53–54.

HOOKER, E., 1966. "The Homosexual Community." In J. O. Palmer and M. J. Goldstein (Eds.), *Perspectives in Psychopathology: Readings in Abnormal Psychology* (New York: Oxford University Press).

HORGAN, J., 1993. "Genes and Crime," *Scientific American,* February, pp. 24, 26, 29.

HORNER, M., 1970. "Femininity and Successful Achievement: A Basic Inconsistency." In J. M. Bardwick (Ed.), *Feminine Personality and Conflict* (Belmont, CA: Brooks/Cole).

House Committee on Aging, 1990. *Hearings of the Select Committee on Aging of the House of Representatives* (Washington, DC: Government Printing Office).

HOUT, M., 1984. "The Occupational Mobility of Black Men," *American Sociological Review* 49: 308–22.

HOWARD, P. H., and A. HANCHETT, 1975. "Chlorofluorocarbon

Sources of Environmental Contamination," *Science* 189: 217–19.

HOWE, F., 1971. "Sexual Stereotypes Start Early," *Saturday Review,* October 16, pp. 76–77.

HUBER, J., and G. SPITZE, 1988. "Trends in Family Sociology." In N. J. Smelser (Ed.), *The Handbook of Sociology* (Newbury Park, CA: Sage).

HULBERT, A., 1984. "Children as Parents," *New Republic,* September 10, pp. 15–23.

HULL HOUSE ASSOCIATION OF CHICAGO, 1984. Draft report on survey of effects of steel industry layoffs.

HUNT, L. G., and C. D. CHAMBERS, 1976. *The Heroin Epidemic* (Holliswood, NY: Spectrum Books).

HUNT, L. G., and M. A. FORSLAND, 1980. "Epidemiology of Heroin Use in Cheyenne, Wyoming: 1960–1977." In R. Faulkinberry (Ed.), *Drug Problems of the 70's: Solutions for the 80's* (Lafayette, LA: Endac Enterprises/Print Media).

HUNT, M., 1974. *Sexual Behavior in the 1970s* (New York: Dell).

HUNTER, N. D., 1987. "Test Anonymously and Tighten Laws to Prevent Bias," *Newsday,* April 26, p. 10.

ILFIELD, F., 1970. "Environmental Theories of Violence," In D. Daniels, M. Gilula, and F. Ochberg (Eds.), *Violence and the Struggle for Existence* (Boston: Little, Brown).

INSTITUTE OF MEDICINE, Committee on Health Care for Homeless People, 1988. *Homelessness, Health and Human Needs* (Washington, DC: National Academy Press).

INSTITUTE FOR RESEARCH ON POVERTY, 1987–1988. "Tracking the Homeless," *Focus,* Winter, pp. 20–24.

INSTITUTE FOR RESEARCH ON POVERTY, University of Wisconsin–Madison, 1988–1989. "The Family Support Act of 1988." *Focus,* Winter, pp. 15–18.

INSTITUTE ON POVERTY, University of Wisconsin, 1986. "The Relative Well-being of the Elderly and Children: Domestic and International Comparisons," *Focus,* 8, 10–13.

ISAAC, R. J., and V. C. ARMAT, 1990. *Madness in the Streets: How Psychiatry and the Law Abandoned the Mentally Ill* (New York: Free Press).

JACKMAN, M. R., and R. W. JACKMAN, 1983. *"Class Awareness in the United States"* (Berkeley: University of California Press).

JACKMAN, N. R., R. O'TOOLE, and G. GEIS, 1963. "The Self-image of the Prostitute," *Sociological Quarterly* 4: 150–61.

JACKSON, J. K., 1956. "The Adjustment of the Family to Alcoholism," *Marriage and Family Living* 18: 358–70.

JACOBS, M. D., 1990. *Screwing the System and Making It Work* (Chicago: University of Chicago Press).

JACOBSON, J., 1968. "Union Conservatism: A Barrier to Racial Equality." In J. Jacobson (Ed.), *The Negro and the American Labor Movement* (Garden City, NY: Doubleday).

JAMES, J., and J. MEYERDING, 1977. "Early Sexual Experience as a Factor in Prostitution," *Archives of Sexual Behavior* 7: 31–42.

JANG, D., 1990. "Triple Jeopardy: The Plight of Battered Immigrant and Refugee Women." *Immigration Newsletter* 19: 669.

JANOWITZ, M., 1971. *Institution Building in Urban Education* (Chicago: University of Chicago Press).

JANOWITZ, M., 1978. *The Last Half Century: Societal Change and Politics in America* (Chicago: University of Chicago Press).

JARVIK, L., 1988. "Chromosomal Damage and the Etiology of Alzheimer's Disease," *Gerontologist* 28, 739–46.

JASANOFF, S., 1986. *Risk Management and Political Culture* (New York: Russell Sage).

JAYNES, D. J., and R. M. WILLIAMS, JR. (Eds.), 1989. *A Common Destiny: Blacks and American Society* (Washington, DC: National Academy Press).

JAYNES, G., 1988. "Where Are You? A Nameless Man in a Grim World," *New York Times,* February 13, p. 29.

JEFFERSON, T., 1977. *Notes on the State of Virgina,* B. Wishey and W. G. Leuchtenberg (Eds.) (New York: Harper & Row).

JENCKS, C., 1992. *Rethinking Social Policy: Race, Poverty, and the Underclass* (Cambridge, MA: Harvard University Press).

JENCKS, C., M. SMITH, H. ACLAND, M. J. BANE, D. COHEN, H. GINTIS, B. HEYNS, and S. MICHELSON, 1972. *Inequality: A Reassessment of the Effect of Family and Schooling in America* (New York: Basic Books).

JOHANNSON, S., and O. NYGREN, 1991. "The Missing Girls of China: A New Demographic Account," *Population and Development Review* 17, 35–52.

JOHANSEN, R., 1982. "The Failure of Arms Control: Why Government Efforts at Arms Control Have Failed." In J. Wallis (Ed.), *Waging Peace* (New York: Harper & Row).

JOHNSON, A. B., 1990. *Out of Bedlam: The Truth About Deinstitutionalization* (New York: Basic Books).

JOHNSON, D., 1990. "Convict in Home Custody Is Charged in a Killing," *New York Times,* December 2, p. L41.

JOHNSON, D., 1991. "Where Phone Lines Stop, Progress May Pass By," *New York Times,* March 18, p. A12.

JOHNSON, D., 1992. "Survey Shows Number of Rapes Far Higher Than Official Figures," *New York Times,* April 24, p. A14.

JOHNSON, E., 1971. "The Homosexual in Prison," *Social Theory and Practice* 1: 83–92.

JONES, R., 1977. *The Other Generation: The New Power of Older Americans* (Englewood Cliffs, NJ: Prentice Hall).

JULIAN, J., B. M. BUXTON, K. L. RICHARDS-EKEH, and D. C. MOORE, 1981. "Sexual Orientation and Friendship among Female Felons," Paper presented at Pacific Sociological Association Meeting, Portland, Oregon.

JUREVICH, T., 1984. *Chaos on the Shop Floor* (Philadelphia: Temple University Press).

JUSTICE, B., and R. JUSTICE, 1990. *The Abusing Family* (New York: Plenum).

KADUSHIN, C., 1983. "Mental Health and the Interpersonal Environment: A Reexamination of Some Effects of Social Structure on Mental Health." *American Sociological Review* 48: 188–98.

KAGAY, M. R., 1993. "Poll Finds Knowledge About AIDS Increasing." *New York Times,* June 8, p. C5.

KALISH, R. A., 1976. "Death and Dying in a Social Context." In R. H. Binstock and E. Shanas (Eds.), *Handbook of Aging and the Social Sciences* (New York: Van Nostrand-Reinhold).

KAMISAR, Y., 1993. "Why the Bad Guys Keep Winning," *New York Times Book Review,* September 26, pp. 11–12.

KANDEL, D. B., 1991. "The Social Demography of Drug Use," *Milbank Quarterly* 69, 365–414.

KANTROWITZ, B., and P. WINGERT, 1990. "Step by Step," *Newsweek,* Winter/Spring, pp. 24–34.

KASARDA, J., 1978. "Urbanization, Community, and the Metropolitan Problem." In D. Street (Ed.), *Handbook of Contemporary Urban Life* (San Francisco: Jossey-Bass).

KASARDA, J. D., 1985. "Urban Change and Minority Opportunities." In P. E. Peterson (Ed.), *The New Urban Reality* (Washington, DC: Brookings Institution).

KASARDA, J. D., 1993. "Cities as Places Where People Live and Work: Urban Change and Neighborhood Distress." In H. G. Cisneros (Ed.), *Interwoven Destinies: Cities and the Nation* (New York: W. W. Norton).

KASL, S. V., 1981. "The Challenge of Studying the Disease Effects of Stressful Work Conditions," *American Journal of Public Health* 71: 682–84.

KATZ, J., 1988. *Seductions of Crime: Moral and Sensual Attractions in Doing Evil* (New York: Basic Books).

KATZ-ROTHMAN, B., 1982. *In Labor: Women and Power in Pregnancy* (New York: Norton).

KEMPF, K. (ED.), 1990. *Measurement Issues in Criminology* (New York: Springer-Verlag).

KENISTON, K., 1968–1969. "Heads and Seekers: Drugs on Campus, Counter Cultures and American Society," *American Scholar* 38: 97–112.

KENISTON, K., 1977. *All Our Children: the American Family under Pressure* (New York: Harcourt Brace Jovanovich).

KENNAN, G., 1984. "Reflections: Two Letters," *New Yorker,* September 24, pp. 55–80.

KENNEDY, P., 1993. *Preparing for the 21st Century* (New York: Random House).

KEOUGH, C., 1980. *Water Fit To Drink* (Emmaus, PA: Rodale Press).

KERCKHOFF, A. C., and R. T. CAMPBELL, 1977. "Race and Social Status Differences in the Explanation of Educational Ambition," *Social Forces* 55: 701–14.

KERR, P., 1987. "High School Marijuana Use Still Declining, U.S. Survey Shows," *New York Times,* February 24, p. A21.

KERR, P., 1988. "Crime Study Finds Recent Drug Use in Most Arrested," *New York Times,* January 22, pp. A1, B4.

KIHS, P., 1982. "Califano Cites 50% Increase in Heroin Addiction in City," *New York Times,* June 15, pp. B1, B5.

KILBORN, P. T., 1990. "Wage Gap between Sexes Is Cut in Test, But at a Price," *New York Times,* May 31, pp. A1, D22.

KILBORN, P. T., 1993. "U.S. Study Says Job Retraining Is Not Effective." *New York Times,* October 15, p. A1.

KILBOURNE, J., 1991. "Deadly Persuasion: Seven Myths Alcohol Advertisers Want You to Believe," *Media & Values,* Spring-Summer, pp. 10–12.

KILSON, M., 1981. "Black Social Classes and Integrational Poverty," *The Public Interest* 64: 58–78.

KIM, I., 1981. *New Urban Immigrants: The Korean Community in New York* (Princeton, NJ: Princeton University Press).

KIM, I., 1983. *Urban Newcomers: The Koreans* (Princeton, NJ: Princeton University Press).

KING, M., 1986. *Death of the Rainbow Warrior* (New York: Penguin).

KINSEY, A. C., W. B. POMEROY, and C. E. MARTIN, 1948. *Sexual Behavior in the Human Male* (Philadelphia: Saunders).

KINSEY, A. C., W. B. POMEROY, and C. E. MARTIN, 1953. *Sexual Behavior in the Human Female* (Philadelphia: Saunders).

KITSON, G., K. BENSON-BABRI, and M. J. ROACH, 1985. "Who Divorces and Why: A Review," *Journal of Family Issues* 6, 255–94.

KLEIMAN, D., 1987. "The Last Taboo: Case on L. I. Pierces the Silence on Incest," *New York Times,* September 28, pp. A1, B5.

KLEIN, M. W., 1979. "Deinstitutionalization and Diversion of Juvenile Offenders: A Litany of Impediments." In N. Morris and M. Tonry (Eds.), *Crime and Justice* (Chicago: University of Chicago Press).

KLEINER, R. J., and S. PARKER, 1963. "Goal Striving, Social Status, and Mental Disorder," *American Sociological Review* 28: 169–203.

KOBRIN, S., 1959. "The Chicago Area Project—A 25-Year Assessment," *Annals of the American Academy of Political and Social Sciences* 322: 20–29.

KOLATA, G., 1987. "Alcoholism: Genetic Links Grow Clearer," *New York Times,* November 10, pp. C1, C2.

KOLATA, G., 1992. "New Insurance Practice: Dividing Sick from Well." *New York Times,* March 4, pp. A1, A15.

KOMINSKI, R., 1987. "School Enrollment—Social and Economic Characteristics of Students: October 1983," *Current Population Reports* (Washington, DC: U.S. Department of Commerce, Bureau of the Census).

KONNER, M., 1989. "Homosexuality: Who and Why?" *New York Times Magazine,* April 2, pp. 60–61.

KOPSTEIN, A., and J. GFROERER, n.d. "Drug Use Patterns and Demographics of Employed Drug Users: Data from the 1988 National Household on Drug Abuse" (Rockville, MD: National Institute on Drug Abuse).

KORNBLUM, W., 1984. "Lumping the Poor: What *Is* the 'Underclass'?" *Dissent,* Summer, pp. 295–302.

KORNBLUM, W., 1988. "Working the Deuce," *Yale Review,* Fall, 1988.

KORNBLUM, W., 1991. *Sociology in a Changing World* (Fort Worth, TX: Holt, Rinehart and Winston).

KORNBLUM, W., 1991. "Who Is the Underclass?" *Dissent,* Spring.

KORNBLUM, W., 1993. "Following the Action with Violence Research," review of Albert J. Reiss, Jr., and Jeffrey A. Roth (Eds.), *Understanding and Preventing Violence, Contemporary Sociology* 22, 344–46.

KORNBLUM, W., and V. BOGGS, 1984. "New Alternatives for Fighting Crime," *Social Policy* (Winter): 24–28.

KOSS, M. P., and M. R. HARVEY, 1991. *The Rape Victim: Clinical and Community Interventions,* 2nd ed. (Newbury Park, CA: Sage Publications).

KOSTERLITZ, J., 1990. "No Home, No Help," *National Journal,* September 8, p. 2120.

KOTZ, N., 1988. *Wild Blue Yonder: Money, Politics, and the B-1 Bomber* (New York: Pantheon Books).

KOTZ, N., and M. L. KOTZ, 1977. *A Passion for Equality: George A. Wiley and the Movement* (New York: Norton).

KOZOL, J., 1967. *Death at an Early Age* (Boston: Houghton Mifflin).

KOZOL, J., 1988. "The Homeless and Their Children," *New Yorker,* January 25, pp. 65 ff; February 1, pp. 36 ff.

KOZOL, J., 1988. "Pathology and Denial: Distancing the Homeless from Our Lives," *Yale Review,* forthcoming.

KOZOL, J., 1988. *Rachel and Her Children: Homeless Families in America* (New York: Crown).

KRAUS, L. E., and S. STODDARD, 1989. *Chartbook on Disability in the United States* (Washington, DC: U.S. National Institute on Disability and Rehabilitation Research).

KREPS, J., 1977. "The Future of Working Women," *Ms.,* March, pp. 56–57.

KRIEGER, N., and R. APPLEMAN, 1986. *The Politics of AIDS* (Oakland, CA: Frontline Pamphlets).

KRISTOL, I., 1971. "Pornography, Obscenity, and the Case for Censorship," *New York Times Magazine,* March 28, pp. 24–25, 112–16.

KROHN, M. O., 1976. "Inequality, Unemployment and Crime: A Cross-national Analysis," *Sociological Quarterly* 17: 303–13.

KUBLER-ROSS, E., 1969. *On Death and Dying* (New York: Atheneum).

KUBLER-ROSS, E., 1975. *Death: The Final Stage of Growth* (Englewood Cliffs, NJ: Prentice Hall).

KUYPERS, J. A., and V. L. BENGSTON, 1973. "Social Breakdown and Competence," *Human Development* 16: 181–201.

LAKOFF, R., 1975. *Language and Woman's Place* (New York: Harper & Row).

LANE, R., 1976. "Criminal Violence in America: The First Hundred Years," *Annals of the American Academy of Political and Social Science* 423: 1–13.

LANG, G. F., and K. LANG, 1972. "Some Pertinent Questions on Collective Violence and the News Media," *Journal of Social Issues* 28: 93–109.

LASSWELL, H. D., 1936. *Politics: Who Gets What, When, and How?* (New York: McGraw-Hill).

LASSWELL, H. D., 1941. "The Garrison State," *American Journal of Sociology* 46:455–68.

LAVER, M., 1982. *The Crime Game* (Oxford, England: Martin Robertson).

LAVIN, D. E., R. D. ALBA, and R. A. SILBERSTEIN, 1981. *Right Versus Privilege: The Open Admissions Experiment at the City University of New York* (New York: Free Press).

LAWTON, M. P., 1978. "Leisure Activities for the Aged," *Annals of the American Academy of Political and Social Science* 438: 71–79.

LAWTON, M. P., and S. YAFFE, 1980. "Victimization and Fear of Crime in Elderly Public Housing Tenants," *Journal of Gerontology* 35: 768–99.

LEE, F. R., 1993. "Fear of Hunger Stalks Many Elderly." *New York Times,* November 16, p. B4.

LEIGHTON, D. C., et al., 1963. *The Character of Danger* (New York: Basic Books).

LEIN, L., 1979. "Male Participation in Home Life: Impact of Social Supports and Breadwinner Responsibility on the Allocation of Tasks," *Family Coordinator* 28, p. 492.

LEKACHMAN, R., 1975. "On Economic Equality," *Signs: Journal of Women in Culture and Society* 1: 93–102.

LEVIN, J., and J. A. FOX, 1985. *Mass Murder: America's Growing Menace* (Newbury Park, CA: Sage).

LEVINE, D. U., and R. J. HAVIGHURST, 1984. *Society and Education,* 6th ed. (Boston: Allyn & Bacon).

LEVINE, M., 1979. "Gay Ghetto." In M. P. Levine (Ed.), *Gay Men: The Sociology of Male Homosexuality* (New York: Harper & Row).

LEVINE, M., and A. LEVINE, 1970. "The Climate of Social Change." In M. Levine and A. Levine (Eds.), *A Social History of Helping Services: Clinic, Court, School, and Community* (Englewood Cliffs, NJ: Prentice Hall).

LEVINSON, R. M., 1975. "Sex Discrimination and Employment Practices. An Experiment with Unconventional Job Inquiries," *Social Problems* 22: 533–43.

LEVITAN, S. A., 1968. "Head Start: It Is Never Too Early to Fight Poverty." In *Federal Programs for the Development of Human Resources* (Washington, DC: U.S. Congress, Joint Economic Committee, Subcommittee on Economic Progress).

LEVITAN, S. A., W. JOHNSTON, and R. TAGGART, 1975. *Still a Dream* (Cambridge, MA: Harvard University Press).

LEWIN, T., 1986. "A Tragedy That Echoes Still," *New York Times,* March 23, Sec. 3, p. 10.

LEWIN, T., 1988. "Family Support Efforts Aim to Mend Two Generations," *New York Times,* March 8, pp. A1, A12.

LEWIN, T., 1992. "Hurdles Increase for Many Women Seeking Abortions." *New York Times,* March 15, pp. 1, 18.

LEWINE, R. R., D. BURBACH, and H. Y. MELTZER, 1984. "Effect of Diagnostic Criteria on the Ratio of Male to Female Schizophrenic Patients," *American Journal of Psychiatry* 14: 84–87.

LEWIS, M., 1972. "There's No Unisex in the Nursery," *Psychology Today,* May, p. 56.

LEWIS, O., 1968. *The Study of Slum Cultures—Backgrounds for La Vida* (New York: Random House).

LIBMAN, J., 1974. "Prostitution Law in Oregon May End a Double Standard," *Wall Street Journal,* October 18, pp. 1, 30.

LICHTER, D. T., and G. V. FUGUITT, 1980. "Demographic Response to Transportation Innovation: The Case of the Interstate Highway," *Social Forces* 59: 492–511.

LIEBERSON, S., 1980. *A Piece of the Pie: Black and White Immigrants since 1980* (Berkeley: University of California Press).

LIN, H., 1985. "The Development of Software for Ballistic-Missile Defense," *Scientific American,* December, pp. 46–53.

LIPSKEY, M., 1980. *Street Level Bureaucracy: Dilemmas of the Individual in Public Services* (New York: Russell Sage Foundation).

LISKA, A. S., and W. BACCAGLINI, 1990. "Feeling Safe by Comparison: Crime in the Newspapers," *Social Problems* 37, 328–37.

LOBBAN, G., 1978. "The Influence of the School on Sex-role Stereotyping." In J. Chetwynd and O. Hartnett (Eds.), *The Sex Role System* (London: Routledge & Kegan Paul).

LONG, D. E., 1990. *The Anatomy of Terrorism* (New York: Free Press).

LORCH, D., 1991. "Immigrants from China Pay Dearly to Be Slaves," *New York Times,* January 3, pp. B1, B2.

LOVINS, A. B., 1977. *Soft Energy Paths: Toward a Durable Peace* (San Francisco: Friends of the Earth).

LOVINS, A., 1986. *Energy Unbound: A Fable for America's Future* (San Francisco: Sierra Club).

LOWE, M. E., 1985. "In Higher Education, Access Means Success," *New York Student,* March 13–26, p. 8.

LUBASCH, A. H., 1988. "Court Blocks Use of Illicit Assets for Legal Fees," *New York Times,* January 3, p. 28.

LUFT, H. S., 1981. *Health Maintenance Organizations: Dimensions of Performance* (New York: Wiley).

LUNDBERG, F., 1968. *The Rich and the Super-rich* (New York: Bantam Books).

LUNDE, D. T., 1975. "Our Murder Boom," *Psychology Today,* July, pp. 35–42.

MACCOBY, E. E., and C. N. JACKLIN, 1977. "What We Should Know and Don't Know About Sex Differences." In E. S. Morrison and V. Borsage (Eds.), *Human Sexuality: Contemporary Perspectives* (Palo Alto, CA: Mayfield).

MACKINNON, C., 1979. *Sexual Harassment of Working Women* (New Haven, CT: Yale University Press).

MACKLIN, E., 1980. "Nontraditional Family Forms: A Decade of Research," *Journal of Marriage and the Family* 12, 905–22.

MCCORD, C., and H. P. FREEMAN, 1990. "Excess Mortality in Harlem," *New England Journal of Medicine* 322, 173–77.

MCDONALD, S., 1975. "The Alimony Blues: Now Women Sing Them, Too," *New York Times Magazine,* March 16, pp. 60–61, 71–73.

MCEWEN, C., 1980. "Continuities in the Study of Total and Non-total Institutions." In *Annual Review of Sociology* (Newbury Park, CA: Sage).

MACGREGOR, S., 1990. "Could Britain Inherit the American Nightmare?" *British Journal of Addiction* 85, 863–72.

MCINTOSH, C. A., 1987. "Recent Pronatalist Policies in Western Europe," *Population and Development Review,* Suppl. 5 to Vol. 12.

MACKINNON, C. A., 1979. *Sexual Harassment of Working Women* (New Haven, CT: Yale University Press).

MACLEOD, C., 1974. "Legacy of Battering," *The Nation,* June 8, pp. 719–22.

MCNEILL, W. H., 1982. *The Pursuit of Power: Technology, Armed Force, and Society since A.D. 1000* (Chicago: University of Chicago Press).

MALAMUTH, N. M., 1981. "Rape Proclivity among Males," *Journal of Social Issues* 37: 138–57.

MALCOLM, A. H. 1984. "Moral Dilemmas of Mercy Killing: Technologies Require Greater Wisdom," *New York Times,* November 17, p. 9.

MALINOWSKI, B., 1941. *The Sexual Life of Savages in North-Western Melanesia* (New York: Halcyon House).

MANLEY, M., 1987. "Dealing with Sexual Harassment," *Inc,* May, pp. 145–46.

MANN, J., 1987. "Global Trauma," *Newsday,* April 26, pp. 11–12.

MARCUSE, H., 1964. *One-Dimensional Man* (Boston: Beacon Press).

MARE, R. D., and C. W. WINSHIP, 1988. "Patterns of Educational Attainment." In M. Tienda & G. Sandefur, *Divided Opportunities* (New York: Plenum).

MARIANO, A., 1990. "Housing Costs Outpace Income by a Wide Margin," *Washington Post,* August 1, p. E1.

MARSHALL, N., and J. HENDTLASS, 1986. "Drugs & Prostitution," *Journal of Drug Issues* 16, No. 2 (Spring): 237–48.

MARTIN, S. E., L. SECHREST, and R. REDNER (Eds.), 1981. *New Directions in the Rehabilitation of Criminal Offenders.* (Washington, DC: National Academy Press).

MARTÍNEZ-ALIER, J., and E. HERSHBERG, 1992. "Environmentalism and the Poor," *Items* (Social Science Research Council) 46, 1–5.

MARTISON, R., 1972. "Planning for Public Safety," *New Republic,* April 29, pp. 21–23.

MARX, K., 1867. *Capital: A Critique of Political Economy* (Moscow: Foreign Languages Publishing House, 1962).

MARX, K., and F. ENGELS, 1848. *The Communist Manifesto* (Baltimore, MD: Penguin Books, 1969).

MASSNICK, G., and M. J. BANE, 1980. *The Nation's Families: 1960–1990* (Cambridge, MA: Joint Center for Urban Studies of M.I.T. and Harvard University).

MASSEY, D. S., and N. A. DENTON, 1993. *American Apartheid: Segregation and the Making of the Underclass* (Cambridge, MA: Harvard University Press).

MATRAS, J., 1973. *Populations and Societies* (Englewood Cliffs, NJ: Prentice Hall).

MAUER, R., 1990. "Alaskans to Vote on Marijuana Use," *New York Times,* October 25, p. A17.

MAY, M. L., 1986. "The Malpractice Malady," *Social Health Review,* No. 4: 71–75.

MAYER, M., 1990. *The Greatest-ever Bank Robbery: The Collapse of the Savings and Loan Industry* (New York: Scribner's).

MECHANIC, D., 1978. *Medical Sociology,* 2nd ed. (New York: Free Press).

MECHANIC, D., 1986. *From Advocacy to Allocation: The Evolving American Health Care System* (New York: Free Press).

MECHANIC, D., 1990. "Promise Them Everything, Give Them the Streets," *New York Times Book Review,* September 16, p. 9.

MEIER, B., 1990. "Businesses Offering Variant on H.M.O.'s," *New York Times,* May 12, p. 24.

MELMAN, S., 1974. *The Permanent War Economy: American Capitalism in Decline* (New York: Simon & Schuster).

MENARD, S., 1981. "The Test Score Decline: An Analysis of Available Data." In B. E. Mercer and S. C. Hey, *People in Schools* (Cambridge, MA: Schenkman).

MENDELSON, M. A., and D. HAPGOOD, 1978. "The Political Economy of Nursing Homes," In M. M. Seltzer, S. L. Corbett, and R. C. Atchley (Eds.), *Social Problems of the Aging* (Belmont, CA: Wadsworth).

MERTON, R. K., 1968. *Social Theory and Social Structure* (New York: Free Press).

MEYER, J. W., 1985. "Institutional and Organizational Rationalization in the Mental Health System," *American Behavioral Scientist* 28, No. 5 (May–June): 587–600.

MEYERS, F. H. 1970. "Pharmacological Effects of Marijuana." In D. E. Smith (Ed.), *The New Social Drug* (Englewood Cliffs, NJ: Prentice Hall).

MILGRAM, S., 1974. *Obedience to Authority: An Experimental View* (New York: HarperCollins).

MILLER, E. M., 1986. *Street Woman* (Philadelphia: Temple University Press).

MILLER, S. M., M. REIN, P. ROBY, and B. M. GROSS, 1967. "Poverty, Inequaility, and Conflict," *Annals of the American Academy of Political and Social Science,* September, pp. 18–52.

MILLER, W. B., 1958. "Lower Class Culture as a Generating Milieu of Gang Delinquency," *Journal of Social Issues* 14: 5–19.

MILLMAN, M., 1977. *The Unkindest Cut: Life in the Backrooms of Medicine* (New York: William Morrow).

MILLS, C. W., 1956. *The Power Elite* (New York: Oxford University Press).

MILLS, J. 1986. *The Underground Empire: Where Crime and Government Embrace* (Garden City, NY: Doubleday).

MILLS, V. K., 1972. "The Status of Women in American Churches," *Churches and Society* 63: 50–55.

MILNER, C., and R. MILNER, 1973. *Black Players: The Secret World of Black Pimps* (London: Michael Joseph).

MINCER, J., and S. POLACHEK, 1974. "Family Investments in Human Capital: Earnings of Women," *Journal of Political Economy* 82: S76-S108.

MINTZ, M., 1986. "Fruits of Your Labor." In *Bulletin of the "Washington Post" Employees Guild,* July 21.

MIROWSKY, J., 1985. "Depression and Marital Power: An Equity Model," *American Journal of Sociology,* 87, 771–826.

MOLOTSKY, I., 1988. "Senate Votes to Compensate Japanese-American Internees," *New York Times,* April 21, pp. A1, A23.

MONAHAN, T., 1955. "Is Childlessness Related to Family Stability?" *American Sociological Review,* 20, 446–56.

MONEY, J., et al., 1955. "An Examination of Some Basic Sexual Concepts: The Evidence of Human Hermaphroditism," *Bulletin of the Johns Hopkins Hospital* 97: 301–19.

MONTAGU, A., 1973. "The New Litany of 'Innate Depravity,' or Original Sin Revisited." In A. Montagu (Ed.) *Man and Aggression,* 2nd ed. (New York: Oxford University Press).

MOORE, D., 1983. "America's Neglected Elderly," *New York Times,* January 30, Sec. 4 p. 30.

MOORE, J. W., 1978. *Homeboys: Gangs, Drugs and Prison in the Barrios of Los Angeles* (Philadelphia: Temple University Press).

MORRISON, M. H., 1986. "Work and Retirement in the Aging Society," *Daedalus,* Winter, pp. 269–93.

MOYNIHAN, D., 1965. *The Negro Family: The Case for National Action* (Washington, DC: U.S. Department of Labor).

MOYNIHAN, D. P., 1992 (January 3). *Letter to New York.*

MURRAY, C., 1984. *Losing Ground: American Social Policy, 1950–1980* (New York: Basic Books).

MYDANS, S., 1990. "Surrogate Denied Custody of Child," *New York Times,* October 23, p. A14.

MYRDAL, G., 1962. *An American Dilemma* (New York: Harper & Row).

NADELMANN, E. A., 1992. "Thinking Seriously About Alternatives to Drug Prohibition." In *Political Pharmacology: Thinking About Drugs* (Proceedings of the American Academy of Arts and Sciences (Cambridge, MA: American Academy of Arts and Sciences).

NAISBITT, J., and P. ABURDINE, 1990. *Megatrends 2000* (New York: Morrow).

NASAR, S., 1992, "Fed Gives New Evidence of 80's Gains by Richest." *New York Times,* April 21, pp. A1, A17.

NATIONAL ADVISORY COMMISSION ON CIVIL DISORDERS, 1968. *Report of the National Advisory Commission on Civil Disorders* (Washington, DC: Government Printing Office).

NATIONAL CAUCUS AND CENTER ON BLACK AGED, INC., 1987. *The Status of the Black Elderly in the United States,* Report for the Select Committee on Aging, House of Representatives, U.S. Congress (Washington, DC: Government Printing Office).

NATIONAL CENTER FOR CHILDREN IN POVERTY, 1990. *Five Million Children: A Statistical Profile of Our Poorest Young Citizens* (New York: School of Public Health, National Center for Children in Poverty).

NATIONAL CENTER FOR HEALTH STATISTICS, 1990. *Health: U.S., 1989* (Hyattsville, MD: Public Health Service).

NATIONAL CENTER FOR HEALTH STATISTICS, 1992. *Serious Mental Illness and Disability in the Adult Household Population: United States, 1989* (Hyattsville, MD: National Center for Health Statistics, U.S. Department of Health and Human Services).

NATIONAL COMMISSION ON THE CAUSES AND PREVENTION OF VIOLENCE, 1969. *Violent Crime: the Report of the National Commission on the Causes and Prevention of Violence* (New York: Braziller).

NATIONAL COMMISSION ON EXCELLENCE IN EDUCATION, 1983. *A Nation at Risk: the Imperative for Educational Reform* (Washington, DC: Government Printing Office).

NATIONAL COMMISSION ON MARIHUANA AND DRUG ABUSE, 1973. *Drug Use in America: Problem in Perspective,* Second Report (Washington, DC: Government Printing Office).

NATIONAL INSTITUTE ON DRUG ABUSE, 1980. *Highlights from the National Survey on Drug Abuse: 1979* (Washington, DC: Government Printing Office).

NATIONAL OPINION RESEARCH CENTER, 1982. *General Social Survey, 1972–1982* (Chicago: University of Chicago Press).

NATIONAL OPINION RESEARCH CENTER, 1986. *General Social Survey Codebook* (Chicago: University of Chicago Press).

NATIONAL OPINION RESEARCH CENTER, 1987. *General Social Survey Codebook* (Chicago: University of Chicago Press).

NAVY, H., 1970. "The San Francisco Erotic Marketplace." In *Technical Reports of the Commission on Obscenity and Pornography,* Vol. 4 (Washington, DC: Government Printing Office).

NEWMAN, K., 1988. *Falling From Grace* (New York: Free Press).

NEWSPAPER ENTERPRISE ASSOCIATION, 1981. *The World Almanac and Book of Facts: 1983* (New York: Pharas Books).

NIDA (National Institute on Drug Abuse), 1991. *National Household Survey on Drug Abuse: Main Findings 1990* (Rockville, MD: Author).

NIDA (National Institute on Drug Abuse), 1991. *National Household Survey on Drug Abuse: Population Estimates 1990* (Rockville, MD. Author).

NIXON, R. A., 1968. "An Appreciative and Critical Look at Official Unemployment Data." In M. Herman, S. Sadofsky, and B. Rosenberg (Eds.), *Work, Young, and Unemployment* (New York: Crowell).

NOBLE, K. B., 1986. "Study Finds 60% of 11 Million Who Lost Jobs Got New Ones," *New York Times,* February 7, p. 1.

NOBLE, K. R., 1987. "U.S. Appeals Courts, in Four Cases, Back Drug Tests on Public Workers," *New York Times,* May 18, p. A14.

O'CONNOR, J. S., and H. M. STANFORD, 1979. "Chemical Pollutants of the New York Bight." In J. S. O'Connor and H. M. Stanford (Eds.), *Chemical Pollutants of the New York Bight: Priorities for Research* (Boulder, CO: National Oceanic and Atmospheric Administration).

OETTING, E. R., and F. BEAUVAIS, 1987. "Common Elements in Youth Drug Abuse: Peer Clusters and Other Psychosocial Factors," *Journal of Drug Issues* (Spring): 133–51.

OGBURN, W. F., 1957. "Cultural Lag as Theory," *Sociology and Social Research,* 41: 167–74.

O'HARE, W. P., 1983. "Poverty's Bottom Line," *New York Times,* August 19, p. A21.

OPHULS, W., 1977. *Ecology and the Politics of Scarcity* (San Francisco: Freeman).

ORASIN, C., 1983. "Holstering America's Handguns," *New York Times,* September 8, p. 23.

ORDAN, S., and N. BRADBURN, 1970. "Working Women and Marriage Happiness," *American Journal of Sociology* 57: 392–407.

ORFIELD, G., 1982. "Desegregation of Black and Hispanic Students from 1968 to 1980." Paper prepared for the Harvard–M.I.T. Joint Center for Urban Studies.

ORFIELD, G., 1991. *The Closing Door: Conservative Policy and Black Opportunity* (Chicago: University of Chicago Press).

ORFIELD, G., 1986. *The Education of Hispanic Americans: A Challenge for the Future* (Chicago: University of Chicago Press).

ORMES, I., 1973. *Clipped Wings* (London: William Kimber).

OSBORNE, D., 1988. "Toward a Postindustrial Politics," *Dissent,* Winter, pp. 105–13.

OTTEN, A. L., 1984. "The Oldest Old," *Wall Street Journal,* July 30, pp. 1, 13.

PALLAS, A. M. 1987. *School Dropouts in the United States* (Washington, DC: U.S. Department of Education, Office of Educational Research and Improvement).

PALMER, J. L., and S. G. GOULD, 1986. "The Economic Consequences of an Aging Society," *Daedalus,* Winter, pp. 295–323.

PARELIUS, A. P., and R. J. PARELIUS, 1987. *The Sociology of Education,* 2nd ed. (Englewood Cliffs, NJ: Prentice Hall).

PARK, R. E., 1955. "The Natural History of the Newspaper." In *Society: The Collected Papers of Robert Ezra Park, Vol. III* (New York: Free Press).

PARROT, A., and L. BECHHOFER, 1991. *Acquaintance Rape: The Hidden Crime* (New York: Wiley).

PARSONS, T., 1943. "The Kinship System of the Contemporary United States," *American Anthropologist* 45, 22–38.

PAYNE, B., and F. WHITTINGTON, 1976. "Older Women: An Examination of Popular Stereotypes and Research Evidence," *Social Problems* 23: 488–501.

PEAR, R., 1983. "Decline in Health Services for the Poor Is Cited," *New York Times,* January 17, p. A11.

PEAR, R., 1987. "Medical-Care Cost Rose 7.7% in '86, Counter to Trend," *New York Times,* February 9, p. 1.

PEAR, R., 1987. "Women Reduce Lag in Earnings but Disparities with Men Remain," *New York Times,* September 4, pp. A1, A13.

PEAR, R., 1993. "Health Care Costs Up Sharply Again, Posing New Threat." *New York Times,* January 5, p. A1.

PEAR, R., 1993. "White House Plan Would Cover Costs of Mental Illness." *New York Times,* March 16, p. A1.

PEARLIN, L. I., 1975. "Status Inequality and Stress in Marriage," *American Sociological Review* 40: 344–71.

PEELE, S., 1987. "A Moral Vision of Addiction: How People's Values Determine Whether They Become and Remain Addicts," *Journal of Drug Issues* 17, No. 2: 187–215.

PEPINSKY, H. E., and R. QUINNEY, 1991. *Criminology as Peacemaking* (Bloomington: Indiana University Press).

PERKINS, T., 1983. "A New Form of Employment: A Case Study of Women's Part-time Work in Coventry." In M. Evans and C. Ungerson (Eds.), *Sexual Divisions: Patterns and Processes* (London: Tavistock).

PERROW, C., 1984. *Normal Accidents: Living with High Risk Technologies* (New York: Basic Books).

PETERSILIA, J., 1985. *Probation and Felony Offenders* (Washington, DC: U.S. Department of Justice, National Institute of Justice).

PETERSILIA, J., 1988. *House Arrest* (Washington, DC: U.S. Department of Justice, National Institute of Justice).

PFEIFFER, E., A. VERWOERDT, and G. DAVIS, 1972. "Sexual Behavior in Middle Life," *American Journal of Psychiatry* 128 (IU): 1262–67.

PIFER, A., and D. L. BRONTE, 1986. "Introduction: Squaring the Pyramid," *Daedalus,* Winter, pp. 1–11.

PINES, M., 1982. "Recession is Linked to Far-reaching Psychological Harm," *New York Times,* April 6, pp. C1–C2.

PIORE, M. J., 1979. *Birds of Passage* (New York: Cambridge University Press).

PIVEN, F. F., and R. A. CLOWARD, 1972. *Regulating the Poor: The Functions of Public Welfare* (New York: Random House).

PIVEN, F. F., and R. A. CLOWARD, 1977. *Poor People's Movements: Why They Succeed, How They Fail* (New York: Pantheon Books).

PIVEN, F. F., and R. A. CLOWARD, 1982. *The New Class War: Reagan's Attack on the Welfare State and Its Consequences* (New York: Pantheon Books).

PLATE, T., 1975. "Crime Pays." In P. Wickman and P. Whitten (Eds.), *Readings in Criminology* (Lexington, MA: D.C. Heath).

POLLARD, K., and W. P. O'HARE, 1990. *Beyond High School: The Experience of Rural and Urban Youth in the 1980's* (Washington, DC: Population Reference Bureau).

POLLOCK, C., 1987. "Realizing Recycling's Potential." In L. R. Brown et al., *State of the World* (New York: Norton/Worldwatch).

POPE JOHN PAUL II, 1991. "On the Hundredth Anniversary of Rerum Novarum," *Population and Development Review* 17, 553–61.

POPENOE, D., 1994. "Family Decline and Scholarly Optimism," *Family Affairs* 6, 9–10.

PORTES, A., 1984. "The Rise of Ethnicity," *American Sociological Review,* 49: 383–97.

PORTES, A., and R. G. RUMBAUT, 1990. *Immigrant America: A Portrait* (Berkeley: University of California Press).

POSTMAN, N., C. NYSTROM, L. STRATE, and C. WEINGARTNER, 1987. *Myth, Men, and Beer: An Analysis of Beer Commercials on Broadcast Television, 1987* (Falls Church, VA: AAA Foundation for Traffic Safety).

POSTMAN, N., and C. WEINGARTNER, 1969. *Teaching as a Subversive Activity* (New York: Delta).

PRESIDENT'S ADVISORY COMMISSION ON RURAL POVERTY, 1968.

"The People Left Behind," *Employment Service Review,* 5 (3–4): 17–19.

PRESIDENT'S COMMISSION FOR THE STUDY OF ETHICAL PROBLEMS IN MEDICINE AND BIOMEDICAL AND BEHAVIORAL RESEARCH, 1983. *Securing Access to Health Care,* Vol. 1 (Washington, DC: Government Printing Office).

PRESTON, S. H., 1984. "Children and the Elderly in the U.S.," *Scientific American,* December, p. 44.

PRESTON, S. H., 1987. "The Decline of Fertility in Non-European Industrialized Nations," *Population and Development Review,* Suppl. 5 to Vol. 12, pp. 26–47.

PRICE, R. H., 1984. "Research on Mental Health Problems in the Workplace: A State of the Art Review, 1984." Paper delivered at the first Industry–Business Round-table on Alcohol, Drug Abuse, and Mental Disorders at the Worksite.

PRIMM, B. J., 1987. "Black Civic Leaders Must Awaken and Confront the Threat," *Newsday,* April 26, pp. 14–15.

QUINNEY, R., 1970. *The Social Reality of Crime* (Boston: Little, Brown).

QUINNEY, R., 1978. "The Ideology of Law: Notes for a Radical Alternative to Legal Oppression." In C. E. Reasons and R. M. Rich (Ed.), *Sociology of Law: A Conflict Perspective* (Toronto: Butterworths).

QUINNEY, R., 1979. *Criminology,* 2nd ed. (Boston: Little, Brown).

RACKHAM, A., 1991. "Economic Downturn Creates Growth in Ranks of Overqualified or Discouraged Job Seekers," *Los Angeles Business Journal,* January 7, p. 27.

RADZINOWICZ, L. R., and J. KING, 1977. *The Growth of Crime: The International Experience* (New York: Basic Books).

RAIMONDO, LOIS, 1991. "Nurse-midwives Playing Increased Role." *New York Times,* pp. 1, 12.

RAINWATER, L., 1969. "The Problem of Lower-class Culture and Poverty War Strategy." In D. P. Moynihan (Ed.), *On Understanding Poverty* (New York: Basic Books).

RAINWATER, L., 1974. "The Lower Class: Health, Illness, and Medical Institutions." In L. Rainwater (Ed.), *Inequality and Justice* (Hawthorne, NY: Aldine).

RAPOPORT, A., 1968. "Introduction." In Carl von Clausewitz, *On War* (Harmondsworth, England: Penguin Books).

RAVENHOLT, R. T., 1990. "Tobacco's Global Death March," *Population and Development Review* 16: 213–40.

RECKLESS, W. C., 1973. *The Crime Problem,* 5th ed. (Englewood Cliffs, NJ: Prentice Hall).

REGIER, D., 1991. *Psychiatric Disorders in America: The Epidemiological Catchment Area Study* (New York: Free Press).

REGIER, D. A., J. K. MYERS, L. N. ROBINS, and M. KRAMER, 1984. Preliminary Report to the National Institute of Mental Health. Cited in H. M. Schmeck, Jr., "Almost One in 5 May Have Mental Disorder," *New York Times,* October 3, pp. A1, D27.

REICH, R., 1991. *The Work of Nations: Preparing Ourselves for 21st Century Capitalism* (New York: Knopf).

REID, S. T., 1985. *Crime and Criminology,* 4th ed. (New York: Holt, Rinehart & Winston).

REID, S. T., 1991. *Crime and Criminology* (Fort Worth, TX: Holt, Rinehart and Winston).

REID, S. T., 1993. *Criminal Justice,* 3rd ed. (New York: Macmillan).

REINHOLD, R., 1979. "For the Present, Cleveland Is a Sad but Special Case," *New York Times,* December 17, Sec. 4, p. 1.

REINHOLD, R., 1982. "An 'Overwhelming' Violence-TV Tie," *New York Times,* May 6, p. C27.

REINISCH, J. M., 1990. *The Kinsey Institute New Report on Sex* (New York: St. Martin's Press).

REISS, A. J., JR., 1964. "The Social Integration of Queens and Peers" In H. S. Becker (Ed.), *The Other Side: Perspectives on Deviance* (New York: Free Press).

REISS, A. J., JR., and J. A. ROTH (Eds.), 1993. *Understanding and Preventing Violence* (Washington, DC: National Academy Press).

RENWICK, P. A., and E. E. LAWLER, 1978. "What You Really Want from Your Job," *Psychology Today,* May, pp. 53–65, 118.

RESKIN, B., and H. HARTMAN (Eds.), 1986. *Women's Work, Men's Work: Sex Segregation on the Job* (Washington, DC: National Academy of Sciences Press).

RETSINAS, J., 1988. "Are There Stages of Dying?" *Death Studies* 12, 207–16.

RICHMOND-ABBOTT, M., 1992. *Masculine and Feminine,* 2nd ed. (New York: McGraw-Hill).

RICKETTS, E., and E. SAWHILL, 1988. "Defining and Measuring the Underclass," *Journal of Policy Analysis and Management* 7, 38–46.

RIENOW, R., and L. T. RIENOW, 1967. *Moment in the Sun* (New York: Ballantine Books).

RIESMAN, D., N. GLAZER, and R. DENNEY, 1950. *The Lonely Crowd* (New Haven: Yale University Press).

RIESSMAN, C. K., 1983. "Women and Medicalization," *Social Policy* (Summer): 3–18.

RILEY, J. C., 1989. *Sickness, Recovery and Death: A History and Forecast of Ill Health* (Iowa City: University of Iowa Press).

RILEY, M. W., 1987. "On the Significance of Age in Sociology." *American Sociological Review* 52 (February): 1–14.

RILEY, M. W. 1990. "The Influence of Sociological Lives: Personal Reflections." *Annual Review of Sociology,* 16, 1–25.

RILEY, M. W., and J. WARING, 1976. "Age and Aging." In R. K. Merton and R. Nisbet (Eds.), *Contemporary Social Problems,* 4th ed. (New York: Harcourt Brace Jovanovich).

RIST, R. C., 1973. *The Urban School: A Factory for Failure* (Cambridge, MA: M.I.T. Press).

RIST, R. C., 1975. "Pornography as a Social Problem: Reflections on the Relation of Morality and the Law." In R. C. Rist (Ed.), *The Pornography Controversy: Changing Moral Standards in American Life* (New Brunswick, NJ: Transaction Books).

RIST, R. C., 1979. *Desegregated Schools* (New York: Academic Press).

ROBERTS, S., 1990. "On the Question of Legal Drugs, a Vote for Maybe," *New York Times,* January 25, p. B1.

ROBINS, L. N., 1973. *A Follow Up of Vietnam Drug Users* (Washington, DC: Special Action Office for Drug Abuse Prevention).

ROBINS, L. N., et al., 1984. "Lifetime Prevalence of Specific Psychiatric Disorders in Three Sites," *Archives of General Psychiatry* 41: 949–58.

ROBINSON, J. P., 1977. *How Americans Used Time in 1965* (Ann Arbor: University of Michigan, Institute for Social Research).

ROBINSON, J., and G. SMITH, 1971. "The Effectiveness of Correctional Programs," *Crime and Delinquency* 17: 67–80.

RODMAN, H., 1963. "The Lower-class Value Stretch," *Social Forces* 42: 205–15.

ROHATYN, F., 1987. "What Next?" *New York Review of Books,* December 3, pp. 3–5.

ROSECRANCE, R., 1973. *International Relations: Peace or War* (New York: McGraw-Hill).

ROSEN, B., and T. M. JERDEE, 1974. "Sex Stereotyping in the Executive Suite," *Harvard Business Review,* March–April 1974, pp. 45–58.

ROSEN, C., 1991. *Center for Employee Ownership Newsletter.* Spring.

ROSENBAUM, D., 1990. "Unemployment Insurance Aiding Fewer Workers," *New York Times,* December 2, pp. 1, 38.

ROSENHAN, D. L., 1973. "On Being Sane in Insane Places," *Science* 179: 250–58.

ROSETT, A., and D. R. CRESSEY, 1976. *Justice by Consent: Plea Bargains in the American Courthouse* (Philadelphia: Lippincott).

ROSS, C., and J. HUBER. "Hardship and Depression," *Health and Social Behavior* 26, 312–27.

ROSS, C. M., and S. DANZIGER, 1987. "Poverty Rates by State, 1979 and 1985: A Research Note," *Focus* 10, No. 3 (Fall): 1–5.

ROSS, H. L., and I. V. SAWHILL, 1975. *Time of Transition: The Growth of Families Headed by Women* (Washington, DC: Urban Institute).

ROSSI, A. S., 1984. "Gender and Parenthood," *American Sociological Review* 49: 1–19.

ROSSI, P. H., 1989. *Without Shelter: Homelessness in the 1980s* (New York: Priority Press).

ROTHSTEIN, R., 1993. "Immigration Dilemmas," *Dissent,* Fall, pp. 66–71.

RUBINGTON, E., and M. S. WEINBERG (Eds.), 1971. *The Study of Social Problems: Five Perspectives* (New York: Oxford University Press).

RUBINSTEIN, E., 1981. "Violence and the Violent Individual." In J. R. Hays, T. K. Roberts, and K. S. Solway (Eds.), *Proceedings of the Twelfth Annual Symposium, Texas Research Institute of Mental Sciences* (New York: SP Medical and Scientific Books).

RUGGLES, P., 1990. *Drawing the Line: Alternative Poverty Measures and Their Implications* (Washington, DC: Urban Institute).

RUSHING, W., 1969. "Two Patterns in the Relationship Between Social Class and Mental Hospitalization," *American Sociological Review* 34: 533–41.

RUSSELL, D. E. H., 1984. *Sexual Exploitation: Rape, Child Sexual Abuse, and Workplace Harassment* (Newbury Park, CA: Sage).

RUSSELL, D. E. H., 1986. *The Secret Trauma: Incest in the Lives of Girls and Women* (New York: Basic Books).

RUSSELL, K. K., 1987. "Growing Up with Privilege and Prejudice," *New York Times Magazine,* June 14, pp. 22ff.

RUSSETT, B. M., 1967. *International Regions and the International System: A Study in Political Ecology* (Chicago: Rand McNally).

RUZAK, S., 1978. *The Women's Health Movement* (New York: Praeger).

RYAN, W., 1971. *Blaming the Victim* (New York: Random House).

SAFILIOS-ROTHSCHILD, C., 1974. *Women and Social Policy* (Englewood Cliffs, NJ: Prentice Hall).

SAGHIR, M. T., and E. ROBINS, 1973. *Male and Female Homosexuality* (Baltimore, MD: Williams & Wilkins).

SALINS, P. D., 1986. "Toward a Permanent Housing Problem," *Public Interest,* Fall, pp. 22–34.

SANCHEZ JANKOWSKI, M., 1991. *Islands in the Street: Gangs and American Urban Society* (Berkeley: University of California Press).

SANDAY, P. R., 1984. "The Socio-cultural Context of Rape: A Cross-cultural Analysis." In D. E. H. Russell, *Sexual Exploitation* (Newbury Park, CA: Sage).

SANDEFUR, G. T., and M. TIENDA (Eds.), 1988. *Divided Opportunities: Minorities, Poverty, and Social Policy* (New York: Plenum Press).

SANDELL, S. H., and D. SHAPIRO, 1978. "A Re-examination of the Evidence," *Journal of Human Resources* 13: 103–17.

SANDERS, E., 1971. *The Family: The Story of Charles Manson's Dune Buggy Attack Battalion* (New York: Dutton).

SANFORD, W. C., J. MCCORD, and E. A. MCGEE, 1976. "Abortion." In Boston Women's Health Book Collective (Eds.), *Our Bodies, Ourselves* (New York: Simon & Schuster).

SARBIN, T. R., 1972. "Schizophrenia Is a Myth, Born of Metaphor, Meaningless," *Psychology Today* 6: 18–27.

SARTRE, J. P., 1968. "Preface." In F. Fanon, *The Wretched of the Earth* (New York: Grove Press).

SAXENIAN, A., 1985. "Silicon Valley and Route 128: Regional Prototypes or Historic Exceptions?" In M. Castells (Ed.), *High Technology, Space, and Society* (Beverly Hills, CA: Sage).

SCANZONI, J. H., 1968. "A Social System Analysis of Dissolved and Existing Marriage," *Journal of Marriage and the Family* 30: 452–61.

SCANZONI, J. H., 1971. *The Black Family in Modern Society— Patterns of Stability and Security* (Chicago: University of Chicago Press).

SCHEFF, T. J., 1963. "The Role of the Mentally Ill and the Dynamics of Mental Disorder," *Sociometry* 26: 436–53.

SCHELL, J., 1982. *The Fate of the Earth* (New York: Avon Books).

SCHLEGEL, W. S., 1962. "Die Konstitutionbiologischen Grundlagen der Homosexualitat," *Zeitschrift fur Menschliche Verebung, Konstitutionslere* 36: 341–46.

SCHMALZ, J., 1993. "Poll Finds an Even Split on Homosexuality's Cause," *New York Times,* March 5, p. A14.

SCHMIDT, A. K., 1989. *Electronic Monitoring of Offenders Increases," NIJ Reports,* January–February, p. 3.

SCHMIDT, W. E., 1988. "Out-of-Work Michiganders No Longer out of Luck," *New York Times,* March 31, p. A16.

SCHMIDT, W. E., 1993. "Britain Flunks a Test of Its National Curriculum." *New York Times,* Education Life, August 1, 1993, pp. 17–19.

SCHNEIDER, K., 1991. "For Communities, Knowledge of Polluters Is Power," *New York Times,* March 24, p. E5.

SCHNEIDER, S. H., 1990. "Cooling It," *World Monitor,* July, pp. 30–38.

SCHOOR, A. I., 1973. "Housing Policies and Poverty." In H. H.

Meissner (Ed.), *Poverty in the Affluent Society* (New York: Harper & Row).

SCHORR, L. B., 1988. *Within Our Reach: Breaking the Cycle of Disadvantage* (Garden City, NY: Doubleday Anchor).

SCHRANK, R., 1978. "How to Relieve Worker Boredom," *Psychology Today,* July, pp. 79–80.

SCHUR, E., 1969. "Reactions to Deviance: A Critical Assessment," *American Journal of Sociology* 75: 309–22.

SCHUR, E. M., 1973. *Radical Nonintervention: Rethinking the Delinquency Problem* (Englewood Cliffs, NJ: Prentice Hall).

SCHUR, E. M., 1988. *The Americanization of Sex* (Washington, DC: Temple University Press).

SCHULL, A. T., 1988. "Deviance and Social Control." In N. J. Smelser (Ed.), *The Handbook of Sociology* (Newbury Park, CA: Sage).

SELIGMAN, B. B., 1968. *Permanent Poverty* (Chicago: Quadrangle).

SELIGMAN, B. B., 1971. *The Potentates* (New York: Dial Press).

SELKIN, J., 1975. "Rape," *Psychology Today,* January, p. 72.

SERBIN, L. A., and K. D. O'LEARY, 1975. "How Nursery Schools Teach Girls to Shut Up," *Psychology Today,* December, pp. 56–57, 102–3.

SERRIN, W., 1981. "Hard Times for U.S. Labor," *New York Times,* December 25, p. 38.

SERRIN, W., 1982. "In Experiment in Jersey, Workers Buy a Factory," *New York Times,* April 27, pp. B1, B4.

SERRIN, W., 1984. "Experts Say Job Bias against Women Persists," *New York Times,* November 25, pp. 1, 32.

SHAW, C. R., 1931. *The Natural History of a Delinquent Career* (Philadelphia: Albert Saifer).

SHAW, N. S., 1974. *Forced Labor: Maternity Care in the United States* (New York: Pergamon Press).

SHEEHAN, S., 1982. *Is There No Place on Earth for Me?* (New York: Scribner's).

SHERMAN, W., 1980. *Times Square* (New York: Bantam Books).

SHLAY, A. B., and P. H. ROSSI, 1981. "Keeping up the Neighborhood: Estimating Net Effects of Zoning," *American Sociological Review* 46: 703–19.

SHOTLAND, R. L., and L. GOODSTEIN, 1983. "Just Because She Doesn't Want to Doesn't Mean It's Rape: An Experimentally Based Causal Model of the Perception of Rape in a Dating Situation," *Social Psychology Quarterly* 46: 220–32.

SIEGEL, A. E., 1970. "Violence in the Mass Media." In D. Daniels, M. Gilula, and F. Ochberg (Eds.), *Violence and the Struggle for Existence* (Boston: Little, Brown).

SIEGEL, J. S., and C. M. TAEUBER, 1986. "Demographic Perspectives on the Long-lived Society," *Daedalus,* Winter, pp. 77–117.

SILBERMAN, C., 1980. *Criminal Violence, Criminal Justice* (New York: Random House).

SILK, L., 1991. "The Argument over the Banks," *New York Times,* February 8, p. D2.

SILK, L., and D. VOGEL, 1976. *Ethics and Profits* (New York: Simon & Schuster).

SILVER, L., 1990. "Study: Women, Minorities Post Little Corporate Gain," *Washington Post,* August 14, pp. A1, A5.

SILVERMAN, M., and P. R. LEE, 1974. *Pills, Profits and Politics* (Berkeley: University of California Press).

SIMPSON, G. E., and J. M. YINGER, 1965. *Radical and Cultural Minorities: An Analysis of Prejudice and Discrimination* (New York: Harper & Row).

SINGER, I., 1985. "Rhetoric vs. Reality." In B. Gross and R. Gross (Eds.), *The Great School Debate: Which Way for American Education?* (New York: Simon & Schuster).

SINGER, J. D., and M. SMALL, 1972. *The Wages of War, 1816–1965: A Statistical Handbook* (New York: Wiley).

SKERRY, P., 1981. "The Secrets of Success," *The Public Interest* 62: 116–23.

SKOLNICK, J., 1969. *The Politics of Protest* (New York: Simon & Schuster).

SKOLNICK, J. H., 1992. "Rethinking the Drug Problem," *Daedalus* Summer, pp. 133–61.

SKOLNICK, J. H., 1992. "Rethinking the Drug Problem." In *Political Pharmacology: Thinking About Drugs,* Proceedings of the American Academy of Arts and Sciences (Cambridge, MA: American Academy of Arts and Sciences).

SMOTHERS, R., 1991. "Employers Becoming Targets of Suits in the Fight to Halt Drunken Driving." *New York Times,* December 24, p. A10.

SNOW, D. A., S. G. BAKER, and L. ANDERSON, 1986. "The Myth of Pervasive Mental Illness among the Homeless," *Social Problems* 33, No. 5 (June): 407–24.

SNOW, D. A., S. G. BAKER, and L. ANDERSON, 1988. "On the Precariousness of Measuring Insanity in Insane Contexts," *Social Problems* 35, 192–96.

Solidarity, 1982. "How to Put 500,000 Americans back to Work," February, pp. 11ff.

SPECTER, M., 1994 (March 6). "Climb in Russia's Death Rate Sets Off Population Implosion," *New York Times,* pp. 1, 18.

SPECTOR, M., and J. KITSUSE, 1987. *Constructing Social Problems* (Hawthorne, NY: Aldine de Gruyter).

SPENDER, D., and E. SARAH, 1980. *Learning to Lose: Essays on Sexism and Education* (London: Women's Press).

SQUIRE, S., 1987. "Shock Therapy's Return to Respectability," *New York Times Magazine,* November 22, 1987, pp. 78ff.

SROLE, L., T. S. LANGNER, S. T. MICHAEL, P. KIRKPATRICK, M. K. OPLER, and T. A. C. RENNIE, 1978. *Mental Health in the Metropolis: The Midtown Manhattan Study,* rev. ed. (New York: New York University Press).

STACK, C., 1974. *All Our Kin: Strategies for Survival in a Black Community* (New York: Harper Colophon).

STARK, E., 1990. "The Myth of Black Violence," *New York Times,* July 18, p. A21.

STARR, P., 1982. *The Social Transformation of American Medicine* (New York: Basic Books).

Statistical Abstract of the United States, 1983. (Washington, DC: U.S. Bureau of the Census).

Statistical Abstract of the United States, 1987. (Washington, DC: U.S. Bureau of the Census).

STEDMAN, L. C., and M. S. SMITH, 1985. "Weak Arguments, Poor Data, Simplistic Recommendations." In B. Gross and R. Gross (Eds.), *The Great School Debate: Which Way for American Education?* (New York: Simon & Schuster).

STEEL, K., P. M. GERTMAN, C. CRESCENZI, and J. ANDERSON, 1981.

"Iatrogenic Illness on a General Medical Service at a University Hospital," *New England Journal of Medicine* 304: 638–42.

STEELE, B., and C. B. POLLOCK, 1974. "A Psychiatric Study of Parents Who Abuse Infants and Small Children." In R. Helfer and C. Kempe (Eds.), *The Battered Child* (Chicago: University of Chicago Press).

STEELWORKERS RESEARCH PROJECT, 1985. *Chicago Steelworkers: The Cost of Unemployment* (Chicago: Hull House).

STEIN, P., 1981. "The Never Marrieds." In P. Stein (Ed.), *Unmarried Adults in Social Context* (New York: St. Martin's Press).

STEINBERG, S., 1981. *The Ethnic Myth: Race, Ethnicity, and Class in America* (New York: Atheneum).

STEINMETZ, S. K., and M. A. STRAUS, 1973. "The Family as Cradle for Violence," *Society* 10: 50–56.

STENCEL, S., 1973. "Resurgence of Alcoholism," *Editorial Research Reports* 2: 989–1006.

STENCEL, S., 1974. "Homosexual Legal Rights," *Editorial Research Reports* 1: 181–200.

STERK, C., 1987. Unpublished Report to Centers for Disease Control, (personal communication).

STERK, C., 1988. "Cocaine and HIV Positivity," *The Lancet*, May 7, pp. 1052–53.

STERK, C., 1989. "Prostitutes and Their Health," Unpublished doctoral dissertation (Erasmus University, Amsterdam, The Netherlands).

STEINBACH, C. F., 1989. "Shelter-skelter," *National Journal*, April 8, p. 851.

STERLING, C., 1978. "The Terrorist Network." *The Atlantic* 242: 37–47.

STERLING, C., 1990. *Octopus: The Long Reach of the International Sicilian Mafia* (New York: Norton).

STEVENS, W. K., 1987. "Defining the 'Outer City': For Now, Call It Hybrid," *New York Times*, October 12, p. A14.

STEVENS, W. K., 1994. "Threat of Encroaching Deserts May Be More Myth Than Fact." *New York Times*, January 18, pp. C1, C10.

STEVENSON, H. W., 1992. "Learning from Asian Schools," *Scientific American* December, pp. 70–76.

STEWART, G. L., 1972. "On First Being a John," *Urban Life and Culture* 1: 255–74.

STINCHCOMBE, A. L., 1964. *Rebellion in a High School* (New York: Quadrangle/New York Times Books).

STOLL, C. S. (Ed.), 1973. *Sexism: Scientific Debates* (Reading, MA: Addison-Wesley).

STOUFFER, S., et al., 1949. *The American Soldier* (Princeton, NJ: Princeton University Press).

STOVER, P., and Y. GILLES, 1987 (October 27). "Sexual Harassment in the Workplace," conference report, sponsored by Michigan Task Force on Sexual Harassment, Detroit, Michigan.

STRAUS, M. A., 1977. "Wife-Beating: How Common and Why?" *Victimology* 2 (3–4): 443–58.

STRAUS, R., 1971. "Alcohol and Alcoholism." In R. K. Merton and R. Nisbet (Eds.), *Contemporary Social Problems*. 3rd ed. (New York: Harcourt Brace Jovanovich).

STREET, D., ET AL. 1978. *Handbook of Contemporary Urban Life* (San Francisco: Jossey-Bass).

SULLIVAN, M., 1989. *Getting Paid* (Ithaca, NY: Cornell University Press).

SULLIVAN, R., 1987. "AIDS Deaths in New York Are Showing New Pattern," *New York Times*, October 22, p. B1.

SULLIVAN, T. A., E. WARREN, and J. L. WESTBROOK, 1989. *As We Forgive Our Debtors: Bankruptcy and Consumer Credit in America* (New York: Oxford University Press).

SURO, R., 1991. "Where Have All the Jobs Gone? Follow the Crab Grass," *New York Times*, March 3, p. E5.

SUTHERLAND, E. H., 1961. *White Collar Crime* (New York: Holt, Rinehart & Winston).

SUTHERLAND, E. H., and D. R. CRESSEY, 1960. *Principles of Criminology* (Philadelphia: Lippincott).

SUTTLES, G., 1970. *The Social Order of the Slum* (Chicago: University of Chicago Press).

SWEET, J. A., and L. L. BUMPASS, 1987. *American Families and Households* (New York: Russell Sage).

SZASZ, T. S., 1970. "Justice in the Therapeutic State," *Comprehensive Psychiatry* 11: 433–94.

SZASZ, T. S., 1971. *The Myth of Mental Illness: Foundation of a Theory of Mental Illness* (New York: Harper & Row).

SZASZ, T., 1992. "The Fatal Temptation: Drug Prohibition and the Fear of Autonomy," *Daedalus* Summer, pp. 161–65.

TAGAKI, P., and T. PLATT, 1978. "Behind the Gilded Ghetto: An Analysis of Race, Class and Crime in Chinatown," *Crime and Social Justice* 9: 2–25.

TARTER, R. E., and K. L. EDWARDS, 1987. "Vulnerability to Alcohol and Drug Abuse: A Behavior-Genetic View," *Journal of Drug Issues* (Fall–Winter): 67–81.

TELTSCH, K., 1990. "For Younger and Older, Workplace Day Care," *New York Times*, March 10, pp. 1, 8.

TIENDA, M., and I. JENSEN, 1987. "Poverty and Minorities: A Quarter-Century Profile of Color and Socioeconomic Disadvantage." Paper presented at the Conference on Minorities in Poverty, Institute for Research on Poverty.

TITTLE, C. R., W. J. VILLEMEZ, and D. A. SMITH, 1978. "The Myth of Social Class and Criminality: An Empirical Assessment of the Empirical Evidence," *American Sociological Review* 43: 643–56.

THOMAS, L., 1979. *The Medusa and the Snail* (New York: Bantam Books).

THOMAS, R. K., 1966–1967. "Powerless Politics," *New University Thought* 4: 44–53.

THOMAS, W. I., 1923. *The Unadjusted Girl* (Boston: Little, Brown).

THOMAS, W. I., and F. ZNANIECKI, 1922. *The Polish Peasant in Europe and America* (New York: Knopf).

THOMPSON, C., 1973. "'Penis Envy' in Women." In J. B. Miller (Ed.), *Psychoanalysis and Women* (New York: Penguin Books).

TOBIN, J., 1994. "Poverty in Relation to Macroeconomic Trends, Cycles and Policies." In S. H. Danziger and G. Sandefur (Eds.), *Poverty and Public Policy* (Cambridge, MA: Harvard University Press).

TOBY, J., 1993/1994. "Everyday School Violence: How Disorder Fuels It," *American Educator* 17, pp. 4 ff.

TOFFLER, A., 1972. "The Strategy of Social Futurism." In A. Toffler (Ed.), *The Futurists* (New York: Random House).

TONER, R., 1993. "Alliance to Buy Health Care: Bureaucrat or Servant?" *New York Times,* December 5, p. A1.

TREASTER, J. B., 1993. "2 Judges Decline Drug Cases, Protesting Sentencing Rules." *New York Times,* April 17, pp. 1, 27.

Treaster, J.B. (1994, February 1). "Survey Finds Marijuana Use Is Up in High Schools," *New York Times,* pp. A1–A14.

TRIPP, C. A., 1975. *The Homosexual Matrix* (New York: McGraw-Hill).

TROIDEN, R. R., 1987. "Becoming Homosexual." In E. Rubington and M. S. Weinberg (Eds.), *Deviance: The Interactionist Perspective,* 5th ed. (New York: Macmillan).

TROW, M., 1966. "The Second Transformation of American Secondary Education." In R. Bendix and S. M. Lipset (Eds.), *Class, Status, and Power,* 2nd ed. (New York: Free Press).

TURK, A. T., 1978. "Law as a Weapon in Social Conflict." In C. E. Reasons and R. M. Rich (Eds.), *Sociology of Law: A Conflict Perspective* (Toronto: Butterworths).

TURNER, J. H., and C. E. STARNES, 1976. *Inequality: Privilege and Poverty in America* (Pacific Palisades, CA: Goodyear).

TYLER, P. E., 1991. "As the Dust Settles, Attention Turns to New Arms Sales," *New York Times,* March 24, p. E3.

UCR (Federal Bureau of Investigation), 1993. *Crime in the United States (Uniform Crime Reports)* (Washington DC: Government Printing Office).

U.S. BUREAU OF THE CENSUS, 1990. *Census of Population: 1990.* (Washington, DC.)

U.S. COMMISSION ON CIVIL RIGHTS, 1970. *Mexican Americans and the Administration of Justice in the Southwest* (Washington, DC: Government Printing Office).

U.S. COUNCIL OF ECONOMIC ADVISORS ON LABOR SHORTAGES, WORKERS' MOBILITY, AND IMMIGRATION, 1990. *Population and Development Review* 16: 193–98.

U.S. CONGRESS, 1993. *Proliferation Threats of the 1990's: Hearing Before the Committee on Governmental Affairs, United States Senate, One Hundred Third Congress, first session, February 24, 1993* (Washington, DC: Government Printing Office).

U.S. DEPARTMENT OF COMMERCE, INTERNATIONAL TRADE ADMINISTRATION, 1984. *International Direct Investment* (Washington, DC: Government Printing Office).

U.S. DEPARTMENT OF EDUCATION, 1990. *National Goals for Education.* (Washington, DC: Author).

U.S. DEPARTMENT OF HEALTH AND HUMAN SERVICES, 1971. *Welfare Myths vs. Facts* (Washington, DC: Government Printing Office).

U.S. DEPARTMENT OF HEALTH AND HUMAN SERVICES, 1974. *Alcohol and Health* (Rockville, MD: Public Health Service).

U.S. DEPARTMENT OF HEALTH AND HUMAN SERVICES, 1979. *Aid to Families with Dependent Children: A Chartbook* (Washington, DC: Government Printing Office).

U.S. DEPARTMENT OF HEALTH AND HUMAN SERVICES, 1980. *Work and Health: Inseparable in the 80's* (Washington, DC: Government Printing Office).

U.S. DEPARTMENT OF HEALTH AND HUMAN SERVICES, 1982. *Student Drug Use, Attitudes and Beliefs: National Trends 1975–1982* (Rockville, MD: Public Health Service, National Institute on Drug Abuse).

U.S. DEPARTMENT OF HEALTH AND HUMAN SERVICES, 1983a *ADAMHA Data Book* (Rockville, MD: Alcohol, Drug Abuse and Mental Health Administration).

U.S. DEPARTMENT OF HEALTH AND HUMAN SERVICES, 1983b. *Fifth Special Report to the U.S. Congress on Alcohol and Health* (Rockville, MD: National Institute on Alcohol Use and Alcoholism).

U.S. DEPARTMENT OF HOUSING AND URBAN DEVELOPMENT, 1984. *A Report to the Secretary on the Homeless and Emergency Shelters* (Washington, DC: Government Printing Office).

U.S. DEPARTMENT OF JUSTICE, 1978. *The Nation's Toughest Drug Law: Evaluating the New York Experience* (Washington, DC: Law Enforcement Administration, National Institute of Law Enforcement and Criminal Justice).

U.S. DEPARTMENT OF JUSTICE, 1983. *Career Paths in Crime* (Washington, DC: Bureau of Justice Statistics).

U.S. DEPARTMENT OF JUSTICE, 1985. *The Crime of Rape* (Washington, DC: Bureau of Justice Statistics).

U.S. DEPARTMENT OF JUSTICE, 1989. *Probation and Parole, 1988* (Washington, DC: Bureau of Justice Statistics).

U.S. DEPARTMENT OF TRANSPORTATION, National Highway Traffic Safety Administration, 1984. *The 1983 Traffic Fatalities Early Assessment* (Washington, DC: Government Printing Office).

U.S. DEPARTMENT OF STATE, 1971. *Atlas of United States Foreign Relations* (Washington, DC: Government Printing Office).

U.S. DEPARTMENT OF STATE, 1983. *Atlas of United States Foreign Relations* (Washington, DC: Government Printing OFfice).

U.S. OFFICE OF EDUCATIONAL RESEARCH, 1990. *Fall/Winter Bulletin* (Washington, DC: Government Printing Office).

U.S. OFFICE OF TECHNOLOGY ASSESSMENT, 1979. *The Effects of Nuclear War* (Washington, DC: Government Printing Office).

USEEM, B., 1980. "Solitary Model, Breakdown Model, and the Anti-busing Movement," *American Sociological Review* 45: 357–69.

VAILLANT, G. E., 1983. *The Natural History of Alcoholism* (Cambridge, MA: Harvard University Press).

VALENTINE, C. A., 1968. *Culture and Poverty: Critique and Counter-proposals* (Chicago: University of Chicago Press).

VAN DYKE, C. and R. BYCK, 1982. "Cocaine," *Scientific American,* March, pp. 128–41.

VEEVERS, J. E., 1973. "Voluntary Childless Wives: An Exploratory Study," *Sociology and Social Research* 57: 356–66.

VELARDE, A. J., and M. WARLICK, 1973. "Massage Parlors: The Sexuality Business," *Society* 11: 63–64.

VERDUGO, N. T., and R. R. VERDUGO, 1984. "Earnings Differentials among Mexican American, Black, and White Male Workers," *Social Science Quarterly* 65 (2): 417–25.

VERHOVEK, S. H., 1993. "At Issue: Hold a Baby or Hold That Line?" *New York Times,* October 19, pp. A1, B10.

VEUM, J. R., 1993. "Training Among Young Adults: Who, What Kind, and for How Long," *Monthly Labor Review,* August, pp. 27–32.

VON GLAHN, G., 1970. *Law among Nations,* 2nd ed. (New York: Macmillan).

WAGLEY, C., and M. HARRIS, 1958. *Minorities in the New World* (New York: Columbia University Press).

WALD, M. L., 1987. "Battle against Drunken Driving Should Shift Focus, Some Experts Assert," *New York Times,* January 3, p. 5.

WALDINGER, R., and T. BAILEY, 1990. "The Continuing Significance of Race: Racial Conflict and Racial Discrimination in Construction," Unpublished Paper. (Center for Conservation of Human Resources, Columbia University).

WALDO, D., K. LEVIT, and H. LAZENBY, 1986. "National Health Expenditures," *Health Care Financing Review* 8, No. 1 (Fall): 1–10.

WALKER, L., 1977. "Battered Women and Learned Helplessness," *Victimology* 2 (3–4): 525–34.

WALKER, L., 1987. "What Comforts AIDs Families," *New York Times Magazine,* June 21, pp. 16ff.

WALLERSTEIN, J., and S. BLAKESLEE, 1989. *Second Chances: Men, Women and Children a Decade After Divorce* (New York: Ticknor & Fields).

WALT, V., 1990. "Immigrant Abuse: Nowhere to Hide," *Newsday,* December 2, p. 8.

WALTZER, M., 1983. *Spheres of Justice* (New York: Basic Books).

WARR, M., 1985. "Fear of Rape among Urban Women," *Social Problems* 32, 238–50.

WEBER, A., 1968. "Labor Market and Perspectives of the New City," In S. F. Fava (Ed.), *Urbanism in World Perspective: A Reader* (New York: Crowell).

WEINBERG, M. S., and C. J. WILLIAMS, 1980. "Sexual Embourgeoisement?" *American Sociological Review* 45: 333–49.

WEINBERG, S. K., 1955. *Incest Behavior* (New York: Citadel Press).

WEIR, S., 1992 (January). "Electronic Communities of Learners: Fact or Fiction," Working Paper 3–92 (Cambridge, MA: TERC Communication).

WEISS, R. S., 1979. *Going It Alone: The Family Life and Social Situation of the Single Parent* (New York: Basic Books).

WEISS, S., 1990. "CUNY Head Weighs Requiring New General-education Courses," *New York Times,* October 5, pp. B1, B3.

WEISSTEIN, N., 1974. "Psychology Constructs the Female." In V. Gornick and B. K. Moran (Eds.), *Women in Sexist Society* (New York: Basic Books).

WELLS, A. S., 1991. "Asking What Schools Have Done, or Can Do, to Help Desegregation," *New York Times,* January 16, p. B6.

WENNEKER, M. B., J. S. WEISSMAN, and A. M. EPSTEIN, 1990. "The Association of Payer with Utilization of Cardiac Procedures in Massachusetts," *Journal of the American Medical Association* 264, 1255–60.

WERNER, F. E., 1984. "On the Streets: Homelessness Causes and Solutions," *Clearinghouse Review* (National Clearinghouse for Legal Services), May pp. 11–16.

WERTZ, R. W., and D. C. WERTZ, 1979. *Lying-In: A History of Childbirth in America* (New York: Schocken).

WESTIN, A., 1967. *Privacy and Freedom* (New York: Atheneum).

WESTON, R. (Ed.), 1987. *Combating Commercial Crime* (Sidney: Law Book Co.).

WHITE, A. D., 1890–1891. "The Government of American Cities," *Forum* 10, 357–72.

WHITE, I. J., 1991. *The S&L Debacle: Public Policy Lessons for Bank and Thrift Reevaluation* (New York: Oxford University Press).

WHITE HOUSE DOMESTIC POLICY COUNCIL, 1993. *The President's Report to the American People.* New York: Simon & Schuster.

WICE, P. B., 1973. *Bail and Its Reform: A National Survey* (Washington, DC: Government Printing Office).

WILENSKY, H. L., 1966. "Work as a Social Problem." In H. Becker (Ed.), *Social Problems* (New York: Wiley).

WILKERSON, ISABEL, 1991. "Ravaged City on Mississippi Floundering at Rock Bottom," *New York Times,* April 4, pp. A1, A16.

WILKES, M. S., and M. SHUCHMAN, 1989. "What Is Too Old?" *New York Times Magazine,* June 4, pp. 58–60.

WILLIAMS, R. M., JR., 1947. *The Reduction of Intergroup Tensions* (New York: Social Science Research Council).

WILLIAMS, T., 1992. *Crack House* (New York: Addison-Wesley).

WILLIAMS, T. M., and W. KORNBLUM, 1985. *Growing Up Poor* (Boston: D. C. Heath/Lexington Books).

WILLIAMS, T., and W. KORNBLUM, 1994. *The Kids Uptown: Struggle and Hope in Harlem Public Housing Projects* (New York: Putnam).

WILLIAMS, T. M., and W. KORNBLUM, 1991. *Growing Up in Four Harlem Housing Projects,* Report to the MacArthur Foundation. (New York: Center for Social Research, CUNY Graduate School).

WILLIS, P., 1983. "Cultural Production and Theories of Reproduction." In L. Barton and S. Walker (Eds.), *Race, Class and Education* (London: Croom-Helm).

WILSON, E. O., 1975. *Sociobiology: The New Synthesis* (Cambridge, MA: Belknap Press).

WILSON, E. O., 1979. *On Human Nature* (New York: Bantam).

WILSON, J. Q., 1977. *Thinking About Crime* (New York: Vintage Books).

WILSON, J. Q., 1980. "The Changing FBI," *Public Interest* 59: 3–14.

WILSON, J. Q., 1983. "Thinking about Crime: The Debate over Deterrence," *Atlantic Monthly,* September, pp. 72–88.

WILSON, J. Q., 1993. *The Moral Sense* (New York: Free Press).

WILSON, J. Q., 1994. "Abortion: A Moral Issue," *Commentary* Winter, pp. 78–89.

WILSON, J. Q., and R. J. HERRNSTEIN, 1985. *Crime and Human Nature* (New York: Simon & Schuster).

WILSON, W. C., 1971. "Facts Versus Fears: Why Should We Worry about Pornography?" *Annals of the American Academy of Political and Social Sciences* 397: 105–17.

WILSON, W. J., 1978. *Blacks and Changing American Institutions* (Chicago: University of Chicago Press).

WILSON, W. J., 1987. "The Hidden Agenda: How to Help the

Truly Disadvantaged," *University of Chicago Magazine,* Fall, pp. 2–11.

WILSON, W. J., 1987. *The Truly Disadvantaged: The Inner City, the Underclass, and Public Policy* (Chicago: University of Chicago Press).

WINERIP, M., 1988. "Getting the Truth about the Ways of Streetwalkers." *New York Times,* January 15, p. B1.

WINICK, C., 1964. "Life Cycle of an Addict and of Addiction," *U.N. Bulletin on Narcotics* 16: 22–32.

WINICK, C. A., 1970. "A Study of Consumers of Explicitly Sexual Materials: Some Functions Served by Adult Movies." In *Technical Reports of the Commission on Obscenity and Pornography,* Vol. 4 (Washington, DC: Government Printing Office).

WINNER, L., 1977. *Autonomous Technology: Technics-out-of-Control as a Theme in Political Thought* (Cambridge, MA: Massachusetts Institute of Technology Press).

WINNER, L., 1986. *The Whale and the Reactor: A Search for Limits in an Age of High Technology* (Chicago: University of Chicago Press).

WINNICK, L., 1991. *New People in Old Neighborhoods: The Role of New Immigrants in Rejuvenating New York's Communities* (New York: Russell Sage).

WIRTH, L., 1927. "The Ghetto," *American Journal of Sociology,* 23: 57–71.

WISDOM, C. S., 1989. "The Intergenerational Transmission of Violence." In N. A. Weiner and M. E. Wolfgang (Eds.), *Pathways to Criminal Violence* (Newbury Park, CA: Sage).

WISEMAN, M., 1986. "Workfare and Welfare Policy," *Focus* (Institute for Research on Poverty), Fall and Winter, pp. 1–8.

WOFSY, C., 1987. " 'Safe Sex'—Why It's Not a Sure Thing," *Newsday,* April 26, p. 7.

WOLFGANG, M. E., and F. FERRACUTI, 1967. *The Subculture of Violence* (London: Tavistock).

WOLFGANG, M., R. F. FIGLIO, and T. SELLIN, 1972. *Delinquency in a Birth Cohort* (Chicago: University of Chicago Press).

WOMEN'S RIGHTS PROJECT, 1974. *Social Security and Sex Discrimination* (New York: American Civil Liberties Union).

WOOD, V., 1971. "Age-Appropriate Behavior for Older People," *The Gerontologist* 11 (4, P. II): 74–78.

WOODEN, K., 1981. *The Children of Jonestown* (New York: McGraw-Hill).

WORLD BANK, 1987. *World Development Report 1987* (New York: Oxford University Press).

WORLD BANK, 1990. *World Development Report 1990: Poverty* (New York: Oxford University Press).

WRIGHT, J. D., 1978. "Are Working Women Really More Satis-

fied? Evidence from Several National Surveys," *Journal of Marriage and the Family* 37: 301–13.

WYATT, G. E., and G. J. POWELL, 1988. *Lasting Effects of Child Sexual Abuse* (Newbury Park, CA: Sage).

YANICK, R., 1983. "Health Service Administration in Government." In H. E. Freeman et al. (Eds.), *Applied Sociology* (San Francisco: Jossey-Bass).

YANKELOVICH, D., 1978. "New Psychological Contracts at Work," *Psychology Today,* May, pp. 46–50.

YANKELOVICH, D., 1981. *New Rules: Searching for Self-fulfillment in a World Turned Upside Down* (New York: Random House).

YANKELOVICH, SKELLY, & WHITE, INC., 1979. *The General Mills American Family Report, 1976–77: Raising Children in a Changing Society* (Minneapolis, MN: General Mills).

YINGER, M., 1987. "From Several Threads, Stronger Cords," *Oberlin Alumni Magazine,* Spring, pp. 10–13.

YOON, C. K., 1994. "Thinning Ozone Layer Implicated in Decline of Frogs and Toads." *New York Times,* March 1, p. C4.

ZEISEL, H., 1982. *The Limits of Law Enforcement* (Chicago: University of Chicago Press).

ZEITLIN, M., K. LUTTERMAN, and J. RUSSELL, 1973. "Death in Vietnam: Class, Poverty and the Risks of War," *Politics and Society* 3: 397–406.

ZELNIK, M., K. J. YOUNG, and J. F. KANTNER, 1979. "Probabilities of Intercourse and Conception Among U.S. Teenage Women: 1971 and 1976," *Family Planning Perspectives* 11: 177–83.

ZILL, N., 1978. "Divorce, Marital Happiness and the Mental Health of Children: Findings from the FCD National Survey of Children." Paper presented at the NIMH Workshop on Divorce and Children.

ZIMBARDO, P. G., 1972. "Pathology of Imprisonment," *Society* 9 (April): 4–8.

ZIMRING, F. E., 1979. "American Youth Violence: Issues and Trends." In N. Morris and M. Tonry (Eds.), *Crime and Justice* (Chicago: University of Chicago Press).

ZIMRING, F. E., 1985. "Violence and Firearms Policy." In L. A. Curtis (Ed.), *American Violence and Public Policy* (New Haven, CT: Yale University Press).

ZINN, H., 1969. "Violence and Social Change in American History." In T. Rose (Ed.), *Violence in America* (New York: Random House).

ZUBOFF, S., 1982. "Problems of Symbolic Toil," *Dissent,* Winter, pp. 51–62.

ZUBOFF, S., 1988. *In the Age of the Smart Machine* (New York: HarperCollins).

Photo Credits

CHAPTER 1   Reuters/Bettmann, xviii & 1; Misha Erwitt/Sygma, 2; Mulvehill/The Image Works, 10; Regis Bossu/Sygma, 14; Michael Macor/Oakland Tribune/Sygma, 17; Cooper, 19; Jeffrey Markowitz/Sygma, 21; Patrick Forestier/Sygma, 23.

CHAPTER 2   Dan Habib/Impact Visuals, 26 & 27; Steele Perkins/Magnum Photos, Inc., 41; Bob Martin/Vandystadt/Photo Researchers, Inc., 42; Rhoda Sidney, 47; Chris Brown/Saba, 48; Russell D. Curtis/Photo Researchers, Inc., 53.

CHAPTER 3   Four By Five, Inc., 62 & 63; Mary Ellen Mark Library, 65; Greenlar/The Image Works, 68; David M. Grossman/Photo Researchers, Inc., 74; Spencer Grant/Monkmeyer Press, 77; P. Forden/Sygma, 81.

CHAPTER 4   The Image Works, 90 & 91; Andrea Renault/Globe Photos, 92; Daemmrich/The Image Works, 93; Women's Center & Police Department, University of California, Santa Barbara, 98; Brooks Kraft/Sygma, 103; J.L. Atlan/Sygma, 106; Adam Scull/Globe Photos, 109; Jan Halaska/Photo Researchers, Inc., 116.

CHAPTER 5   Reuters/Bettmann, 126 & 127; Burt Glinn/Magnum Photos, Inc., 131; Richard Hutchings/Photo Researchers, Inc., 135; P. Perrin/Sygma, 139; Jan Halaska/Photo Researchers, Inc., 141; Larry Mulvehill/Photo Researchers, Inc., 142.

CHAPTER 6   Spencer Grant/Photo Researchers, Inc., 156 & 157; Smith/Monkmeyer Press, 167; B. Naton/Sygma, 169; John/Chiasson/Gamma-Liaison, Inc., 173; Eric Kroll, 177; Gail Greig/Monkmeyer Press, 181; Michael J. Okoniewski/The Image Works, 185; Jack Spratts/The Image Works, 189.

CHAPTER 7   Dunleavy/San Antonio Express News/Sygma, 196 & 197; Charles Hlavenka/Sygma, 198; Scala/Art Resource, 199; UPI/Bettmann, 203; S. Elbaz/Sygma, 208; Paolini/Sygma, 215; Doug Mills/AP/Wide World Photos, 218; Byron/Monkmeyer Press, 219.

CHAPTER 8   Steve McCurry/Magnum Photos, Inc., 224 & 225; Rameshwar Das/Monkmeyer Press, 226; Nubar Alexanian/Woodfin Camp & Associates, 230; Connie Grosch/Impact Visuals, 238; Alex Webb/Magnum Photos, Inc., 241; Najlah Feanny/Saba, 242; F. Scianna/Magnum Photos, Inc., 245.

CHAPTER 9   Reuters/Bettmann, 258 & 259; John Giordano/Saba, 261; Bettmann, 266; Mark Peterson/Saba, 268; UPI/Bettmann, 272; Gerrit Fokkema, 282; F. Lee Corkran/Sygma, 284; Jacques Chenet/Woodfin Camp & Associates, 288.

CHAPTER 10   Capital Features/The Image Works, 292 & 293; Reuters/Bettmann, 294; Steve McCurry/Magnum Photos, Inc., 296; Hugh Rogers/Monkmeyer Press, 299; Reuters/Bettmann, 301; AP/Wide World Photos, 306; Rhoda Sidney, 315; Rich Kane/Sportschrome, Inc., 317.

CHAPTER 11   Nathan Benn, 320 & 321; Shackman/Monkmeyer Press, 324; John Bryson/Monkmeyer Press, 332; Globe Photos, 338; Ray Ellis/Photo Researchers, Inc., 341; Pernold/RSVP/Action, 342.

CHAPTER 12   Gottlieb/Monkmeyer Press 348 & 349; Conklin/Monkmeyer Press, 351; William Eacon/Photo Researchers, Inc., 352; B. Daemmrich/The Image Works, 354; Karen Kasmauski/Woodfin Camp & Associates, 360; Paula M. Lerner/Woodfin Camp & Associates, 363; Reuters/Bettmann, 369.

CHAPTER 13   Rick Maiman/Sygma, 378 & 379; Bill Bachmann/The Image Works, 381; Jim Carter/Photo Researchers, Inc., 385; Alex Webb/Magnum Photos, Inc., 393; Will & Deni McIntyre/Photo Researchers, Inc., 394; Lawrence Migdale/Photo Researchers, Inc., 399; AP/Wide World Photos, 400; E. Crews/The Image Works, 402.

CHAPTER 14   Renato Rotolo/Gamma-Liaison, Inc., 406 & 407; Andrew Sacks/Time, Inc., 415; Lawrence Migdale/Stock Boston, Inc., 419; Collins/Monkmeyer Press, 424; Tony Savino/The Image Works, 426; Bettmann, 429; Ed Malitsky/Gamma-Liaison, Inc., 431.

CHAPTER 15   Goldberg/Monkmeyer Press, 438 & 439; Craig Aurness/Woodfin Camp & Associates, 448; Culver Pictures, Inc., 451; Robert A. Isaacs/Photo Researchers, Inc., 456; AP/Wide World Photos, 457; C. Vergara/Photo Researchers, Inc., 458; Charles Wenzelberg/AP/Wide World Photos, 458; Alan Carey/The Image Works, 461.

CHAPTER 16   UPI/Tom Salyer/Bettmann, 470 & 471; Raghu Rai/Magnum Photos, Inc., 477; United Nations, 481; Bettmann, 485; Yvonne Hemsey/Gamma-Liaison, Inc., 485; Rafael Macia/Photo Researchers, Inc., 489; Arrigo/Sygma, 490.

CHAPTER 17   Mark Ludak/Impact Visuals, 496 & 497; NASA, 499; Dingo/Photo Researchers, Inc., 511; Saba, 512; Conklin/Monkmeyer Press, 517; Holt Confer/The Image Works, 518; Manzonowicz/Monkmeyer Press, 520.

CHAPTER 18   Reuters/Bettmann, 528 & 529; S. Compoint/Sygma, 530; Reuters/Bettmann, 533; Superstock, 534; Leonard Lee Rue/Monkmeyer Press, 539; Jon Jones/Sygma, 543; Alan Tannenbaum/Sygma, 545.

Name Index

Subject Index

Housing (*cont.*)
   educational segregation as result of, 395
   social policy on, 466
   in suburbs, 452
Houston, 454
Humanism, 398–400
Human resource development programs, 250–51
Hutterites, 75–76
Hydrologic cycle, 515
Hypnosis, 78

Iatrogenic illnesses, 49
IBM (International Business Machines Corporation), 410
Illegal (undocumented) immigrants, 487, 490–93
Illegitimacy, 366–68, 372–73
Illiteracy, 477–78
Immigration and immigrants, 260–62, 472, 483
   to cities, 444
   crime and, 12
   social-disorganization theory on, 9
   social policy on, 492–93
   to United States, 479
      history of, 483–85
      recent trends in, 486–87
      from Southeast Asia, 530, 532
      undocumented, 490–92
      urban concentration of, 487–90
Immigration Marriage Fraud Amendments (U.S., 1986), 492
Immigration Reform and Control Act (U.S., 1986), 476, 492–93
Incapacitation, to prevent crime, 193
Incest, 96
Incinerators, 516
Income, 226, 228 (*see also* Poverty)
   black family and, 360
   discrimination in, 277–79
   disparities between ethnic groups in, 478–79
   education and, 270, 380
   of elderly, 322
   housing segregation by, 444, 452
   from low-paying jobs, 420–21
   poverty line for, 235–36
   for school dropouts, 389
   sex discrimination and, 294, 295, 300–303
   Social Security and, 343–45
   support programs for, 251
   of top corporate executives, 408, 417–19
Income-in-kind programs, 251
Income maintenance programs, 357
India, 481
Indianapolis, 124
Industrial accidents, 508
Industrialization, 409
   as cause of wars, 541
   global warming and, 514–15
   warfare and, 536
Industrial revolution, 498
Inequality, 260–62 (*see also* Discrimination and prejudice;

Poverty; Sex roles and sexism; Social class)
   crime and, 177
   in education, 385–89
   of income, 226–32
   in justice, 244–46
   sexual, 294–95
   of status, in marriage, 362–63
   violence and, 220–22
Infant mortality, 29–30, 32, 33
Informed consent, in social research, 20
Infrastructure, 457
Injuries, 408, 532
Insecticides, 13–14
Insider trading, 168
Institutional discrimination, 264, 269 (*see also* Discrimination and prejudice)
   in education, 269–74
   in employment and income, 277–79
   in housing, 274–77
   in justice, 279–80
Institutional perspective, 9
   on education, 385, 390–97
   on health-care problems, 49–51
   on origins of war, 541–44
Institutional violence, 201
Institutions, 7
   in gay subculture, 105–6
   in health care system, 31
   technology and, 506–9
   for treatment of mental illness, 80–85
Insurance:
   health, 31–33, 36–40, 53, 243
   for homemakers, 304
   malpractice, 36
   mental illness covered by, 80, 88
   workers' compensation, 508
Integration of education, 393–95
Interactionist perspective, 11–13
   on aging, 322–23
   on crime, 179–82
   cultural explanations of poverty in, 248–49
   on education, 384–85
   on family, 351
   on health-care problems, 51–52
   labeling theory in, 12–13
   on mental illness, 66
   on sex-related social problems, 119
International Conference on Population and Development (Cairo, 1994), 483
International trade, 433–34, 544
In-utero implants, 370
Iraq, 502, 530–32, 538, 549
Ireland, 550
Irish-Americans, 135
Irish immigrants, 484
Islam, 294
Italian-Americans, 135
ITT, 409

Japan, 476, 533–34, 538
Japanese-Americans, 260, 484
Jews, 134, 135, 284
Job Corps, 250
Job satisfaction, 427–29
Job training programs, 283, 434

Jonestown (Guyana), mass murder-suicide in, 546
Judaism, 298
Junk bonds, 411
Jury duty, 314
Justice:
   discrimination in, 279–80
   poverty and, 244–46
   sexism in, 312, 314–15
Just war doctrine, 538
Juvenile delinquency, 172–74, 192–93
   interactionist perspective on, 179–82
   programs for prevention of, 187–88
   punishment for, 185
   rehabilitation for, 186
   social class and, 177

Kerner Commission (National Advisory Commission on Civil Disorders), 220–21, 261
Kidnapping, 204
Kinsey Institute, 94
Kinship units, 351–53
Korean immigrants, 489–90
Ku Klux Klan, 281
Kuwait, 510, 533, 538, 549

Labeling perspective, 12–13
   on aging, 322–23, 332
   on education, 384–85
   on homosexuality, 100, 101
   mental illness and, 68, 70–72, 82
   on prostitution, 107
Labor (*see* Employment; Workers)
Labor force, 421, 423
Labor unions, 172, 234
   employment discrimination and, 277
   for teachers, 396–97
   United Farm Workers, 289
   wage reductions and, 416
Land degradation, 518–19
Landfills, 516
Language:
   bilingual education and, 289
   of Hispanic students, 388
   sex stereotypes in, 310
Law enforcement:
   Constitution and, 183
   corruption in, organized crime and, 172
   discrimination in, 279–80
   of drug laws, 152–53
   juvenile delinquency and, 173
   for occupational crimes, 191
Lawyers, 245–46
League of Nations, 543
Legal issues (*see also* Legislation)
   abortion, 315–16
   conduct of war, 538
   criminal and civil law, 164
   divorce, 371–72
   gay and lesbian families, 368
   gun control, 216–18
   homelessness, 85
   homosexuality, 119–21
   illegitimacy, 366–67, 372–73
   pornography, 117, 122–24

prostitution, 107, 121–22
in rape prosecutions, 208, 209
right to die, 43–44
sexism as, 311–12
surrogacy, 371
in testing for drug use, 154
undocumented immigrants, 490–92
Legal system (*see* Justice)
Legislation (*see also* Legal issues)
on abortion, 40, 315
on age discrimination, 329, 336
on alcohol and drug abuse, 139, 152
anticrime, 158, 189, 192
bank deregulation, 435
on child abuse, 220
on child care and family support, 374
on civil rights, 260–61, 283, 285, 305,
526
on definitions of death, 43
on environment, 23, 524, 525
on equal pay, 301
on family leave time, 313
on gun control, 217, 218
on handicapped, 56–57
on health-care reform, 52, 54–56
on homelessness, 466
on homosexuality, 119–20
on immigration, 476, 484, 492–93
on job training programs, 283
labor, 267
Medicare and Medicaid, 37
on mental health, 83, 86
on occupational crime, 191
on retraining displaced workers, 434
sexism in, 314
Social Security, 236, 251
on taxes, 228–29
welfare reform, 252, 254
workers' compensation, 508
Leisure, 339–40
Lesbianism, 99, 104–5, 120, 368
Less developed countries (LDCs), 476–78,
481–83
Levy v. *Louisiana* (U.S., 1968), 372
Liberals, 21
Libya, 546
Life expectancy, 28–29, 32, 325
Lifestyles, 51
Literacy, 477–78, 500
Living wills, 44, 58
Loan sharking, 171
Local governments:
care of mentally ill by, 86–88
finances of, 456–59
Lochner v. *New York* (U.S., 1908), 311
Longitudinal surveys, 18
Los Angeles, 164–65, 261
Louisville (Kentucky), 287
Love Canal (New York), 517
Lower-class value stretch, 249–50
Low-paying jobs, 420–21
LSD (lysergic acid diethylamide), 143
Lumpenproletariat, 232, 233
Lynchings, 281

Mainstreaming, 56
Malpractice, medical, 36, 51
Manslaughter, 206

Manufacturing (*see* Production)
Marijuana, 128–30, 142, 146–47
crime and, 148
decriminalization of, 13
legalization of, 153
participant observation on effects of,
18–19
Marriage (*see also* Family)
cohabitation as alternative to, 365
divorce and, 360–65, 371–72
empty-shell, 354–55
happiness in, children and, 358
homosexuality and, 102
illegitimacy and, 372–73
as immigration fraud, 492
postponement of, 365–66, 476
sex roles in, 308–9
shift in responsibilities in, 318
spouse abuse in, 212–13, 220
stereotypes of elderly regarding, 334
Marxism, 10–11, 232, 233, 246, 384
Massage parlors, 109
Mass media (*see* Media)
Mass murders, 207
"Mass psychosis," 65
Masturbation, 95
Materialism, 431, 432
Maternity and paternity leaves, 313
Media:
ageism in, 330
sex stereotypes in, 310
social problems covered by, 22
violence and, 204–5, 219–20
Medicaid, 33, 37, 39, 243, 335–36, 343
Medical model of mental illness, 67,
78–79
Medical sociology, 31, 48, 52–53
Medicare, 37, 39, 243, 335–36, 341, 343
Megalopolises, 449–50
Men:
childrearing responsibilities of, 313
crimes committed by, 175
homicides among, 198, 216
as customers of prostitutes, 113, 122
discrimination in legal system against,
312
elderly, sexuality of, 334
family life of:
divorce and, 371–72
as house husbands, 357
postponement of marriage by, 366
spouse abuse by and of, 212–13
widowhood and, 330
homosexuality among, 99
in labor force, 421
media portrayals of, 310
mental illness among, 77
as prostitutes, 107–9, 112
sex roles of, 296–98, 317
sex stereotyping of, 298, 299
sexual harassment claims by, 303
violence by, 203
Mental disorders, distinguished from
mental illness, 64
Mental hospitals, 82, 424
deinstitutionalization of patients from,
83–87
homelessness and, 466

Mental illness, 64–66
classifications of, 69–70
definitions of, 66–69
diagnoses of, 70–72
homosexuality seen as, 100
inequality and conflict in incidence in,
72–73
poverty and, 242–43
race and sex in incidence of, 76–78
reinstitutionalization of former mental
patients, 466
senility, 332
sexism and, 308–9
social class and, 73–75
social policy and, 86–88
in soldiers and veterans, 532
treatment and care of:
deinstitutionalization and, 83–85
institutions for, 80–83
methods of, 78–79
unemployment and, 423–24
urban life and, 75
Mentally ill chemical abusers (MICA), 65
Mercy killing (euthanasia), 44, 344
Mergers, 411–12
Methadone, 151
Metropolitan areas, 449–50
Metropolitan statistical areas (MSAs), 449
Mexican-Americans, 484
Mexican immigrants, 491–92
Michigan Task Force on Sexual
Harassment, 303
Middle class, 234
Midtown Manhattan Study, 74, 75
Migrant workers, 240
Migration:
to cities, 444
of elderly, 328
war-caused, 532
Military technology:
conduct of war and, 536–38
nuclear, 533–36
spending on, 433, 502
Minimum wage, 242, 252, 253
Minneapolis, 124
Minority groups (*see also* Blacks; Discrimination and prejudice)
crime rates among, 165
definitions of, 262–63
in distressed neighborhoods, 463
education of, 386–88, 403
elderly among, 336
elderly as, 333
fertility rates of, 478
handicapped as, 43
immigrants as, 486
institutional discrimination against, 269
in medical schools, 50
migration to cities of, 444
poverty among, 231, 239
prostitution among, 111–12
segregation of, 444–46
in Soviet Union, 550
unemployment among, 408, 423
Mobil Oil Company, 411
Modernization, 325
Modified nuclear families, 352
Montgomery bus boycott, 281

Moral issues (*see also* Ethical issues)
  technology and, 505–6
Mothers Against Drunk Driving, 153
Movements:
  of poor people, 254–55
  women's movement, 304–5, 316
Multinational corporations, 412–15
Murders, 161, 167, 206–7 (*see also* Homicides)
  capital punishment for, 183–85
My Lai massacre, 538

Narcotics (*see also* Drug abuse)
  antagonists against, 152
  dealing in, 171
National Academy of Sciences (NAS), 86, 87
National Advisory Commission on Civil Disorders (Kerner Commission), 220–21, 261
National Advisory Council on Alcohol Abuse and Alcoholism, 139
National Commission on AIDS, 58
National Commission on the Causes and Prevention of Violence, 203–4, 221
National Commission on Excellence in Education, 389, 397–98
National Commission on Law Enforcement and Administration of Justice (Katzenbach Commission), 221
National Commission on Marihuana and Drug Abuse, 148
National Congress of Parents and Teachers, 398
National Environmental Policy Act (U.S., 1972), 23
National Institute on Alcohol Abuse and Alcoholism, 139
National Institute on Drug Abuse, 130, 144, 147
National Institute of Mental Health (NIMH), 64, 66, 72, 79, 205, 220
National Institutes of Health (NIH), 42
Nationalism, 543, 550
National Organization for Women (NOW), 305
National Rifle Association (NRA), 216, 218
National Women's Political Caucus, 305
Native Americans, 135, 260, 386
  discrimination against, 269, 275–77, 289
Nativism, 484
Natural disasters, 3, 457–59
"Natural history" of social problems, 22–24
Neighborhood distress, 462–64
Net worth, 228
Neurosis, 70
New York, City of, 449
  gay ghetto in, 105
  immigration to, 488
    undocumented, 491
  ocean dumping by, 516
  redevelopment of, 465

NIMBY (Not In My Back Yard) phenomenon, 87
"No-fault" divorce, 371
Noise pollution, 519
Noninstitutional violence, 201
Nonwhites (*see also* Blacks; Minority groups)
  infant mortality of, 32
  life expectancy of, 32
  unemployment among, 423
Norms, 267–68, 296, 353, 447
North American Free Trade Agreement (NAFTA; 1993), 433–34
Nuclear families, 352–53
Nuclear Nonproliferation Treaty (1968), 548
Nuclear power, 501, 504–5, 508–9
  radioactive wastes from, 516, 518
Nuclear Test-Ban Treaty (1963), 548
Nuclear testing, 515
Nuclear war, 533–36
Nuclear weapons, 504, 530, 539, 547–51
Nursing homes, 39, 336, 343
Nutrition, 235, 520–21

Observation (in sociological research), 18–19
Occupational (white-collar) crimes, 167–69, 190–91
Occupational safety and health, 429–30
  workers' compensation for, 508
Ocean dumping, 516
Office of Federal Contract Compliance (OFCC), 284
Oklahoma City, 287, 395
Old people (*see* Aged and aging)
Oligopolies, 409
Open admissions, 403
"Open education," 398–400
Opium addiction, 131
Oral intercourse, 95
Organizations:
  impact of automation on, 427
  whistle blowers in, 504–5
Organized crime, 123, 170–72, 192, 214
  in drug trade, 149
Orphanages, 466
Outsourcing, 414
Ozone layer, 510, 514, 524

Paraphyllic rapism (acquaintance rape; date rape), 97, 209–10
Parental leaves, 313
Parents Anonymous, 220
Participant observation, 18
Part-time employment, 313, 358, 421
Passive-congenial relationships, 354–55
Peer groups, 12
Pensions, 2, 408
People's Temple, 546
Perry Preschool Project, 400–403
Persian Gulf war, 502, 510, 530, 531, 533, 538, 542, 544, 549, 551
Peru, 544
Pesticides, 516
Pharmacists, 49
Phobias (fears), 65
Phoenix House, 151

Physical health care, 28–31
  abortion and, 367–68
  ageism in, 329
  AIDS crisis in, 44–48
    drug use and, 149–50
    homosexuality and, 104, 106, 121
    prostitution and, 114–15
    sexual behavior and, 93–94
  class issues in, 48–49
  costs of, 33–36
  for disabled and handicapped, 42–43
  effects of alcohol abuse on, 136–37
  for elderly, 335–36, 343
  family planning and, 479–80
  hospices for, 341
  impact of immigrants on, 488
  impact of nuclear war on, 535
  inadequate protection of, 36–40
  institutional perspective on, 49–51
  interactionist perspective on, 51–52
  occupational safety and health and, 429–30
  physical illness misdiagnosed as mental illness, 64
  poverty and, 242–43
  reproductive control in, 315–16
  reproductive technology and, 369–71
  right to die issue in, 344
  social policy issues in, 52–59
  technology and, 509
  unequal access to, 31–33
  for veterans, 532
  for women, 40–42
Physicians, 35–36
  control over numbers of, 50
  illnesses caused by, 49
  malpractice litigation against, 51
  psychiatrists, 68, 78, 79
Physiological aspects of aging, 330–31
Pimps, 112–14
Plea bargaining, 189–90
Poles, 15
Police:
  blacks and, 178, 221
  corruption of, 172
  discretion of, 164–65
  prostitution laws enforced by, 122
Political science, 6
Pollution, 510–12
  of air, 513–15
  from burning oil wells, 510
  social policy on, 524
  solid-waste disposal and, 516–18
  of water, 515–16
Poor people:
  geography and, 240
  handicapped as, 43
  health care for, 37, 39, 48–49
  housing for, 460–61
  among minority groups, 239
  movements of, 254–55
  poverty line to measure, 235–36
  self-identification as, 233–34
  single-parent families, 237–39
  as subculture, 247–50
  trickle-down theory on, 418–19
  on welfare, 240–41
  working poor, 241–42

United States (*see also* Federal
    government)
  AIDS in, 44
  alcohol consumption in, 132
  arms control and, 547–49
  child abuse in, 211
  child care policy in, 374–75
  consumer debt in, 432
  crime in, 158–61, 189
    homicides, 213
    violent, 198–99
  drug enforcement and foreign policy
    of, 154, 171
  economy of, 408
  expenditures on health care in, 33
  gender inequality in, 302–3
  history of discrimination in, 260–62
  immigration to, 472, 476, 483
    history of, 483–85
    recent trends in, 486–87
    social policy on, 492–93
    from Southeast Asia, 530, 532
    undocumented, 490–92
    urban concentration of, 487–90
  net worth of families in, 228
  population of, 478–79
    age demographics of, 322
    birthrates, 358
    divorce rates in, 360
    elderly in, 325–30, 343
    fertility rates in, 350
    infant mortality in, 29–30
    life expectancy in, 28–30
    social policy on, 482, 492–93
  poverty among elderly in, 336–37
  public education in, 380–82
  Soviet Union and, 550
  spending by, 459
  terrorism in, 545
  urbanization of, 442
  use of nuclear weapons threatened by,
    539
  in Vietnam War, 538
  wealth and poverty in, 226–27
  world environment and, 520–21
Urban areas, 440–43
  aged and aging in, 326–27, 328
  air pollution in, 498, 513
  bias against, 443
  combat zones in, 116, 123
  distressed neighborhoods in,
    462–64
  education in, 273–74, 285, 386
  gang violence in, 213–16
  growth of, 449–50
  homelessness and shelter poverty in,
    460–62
  homicides in, 206
  immigrants in, 487–90
  mental illness and, 73, 75–76
  migration to, 246
  migration to suburbs from, 274
  physicians in, 36
  populations in, 443–46
  poverty and housing in, 240, 244
  problems of, 453
    deconcentration, 453–54
    financial, 456–59

  government as, 459–60
  relocation of manufacturing from,
    454–56
  racial rioting in, 261
  social policy on, 464–67
  suburbs and, 452–53
  theories of urbanism, 446–49
  transportation in and to, 451–52
Urbanism, 440–42
  theories of, 446–49
Urbanization, 326

Valium, 79
Value-conflict perspective, 11, 384
Values:
  in criminal behavior, 180–82
  expressed in schools, 383
  functionalist perspective on, 7, 8
  in immigrant communities, 490
  of poverty subculture, 248–50
Value-stretch approach, 249–50
Vera Institute of Justice, 20, 187
Veterans, 530, 532
Victimization reports, 166
Victimless crimes, 170, 192
Victims:
  elderly as, 334–35
  of Hiroshima bombing, 534
  immigrants as, 491
  of murder, 206–7
  of rape, 209
  of terrorism, 547
Vietnam War, 532, 538, 542
Violence, 198–201 (*see also* Crime)
  criminal, 166–67, 206, 213–16
    assaults and robberies, 207–8
    homicides, 206–7
    rape, 97, 186, 208–10
  explanations of, 201–5
  in family, 210–13
    in immigrant families, 492
  international, alternatives to,
    549–51
  riots, 281
  in schools, 395–96
  social policy on, 216–22
  terrorism, 544–47, 551
Voting, 3, 261, 333
Voting Rights Acts (U.S., 1965; 1975),
  260, 261
Voyeurism, 97

Wars, 200, 201, 530–31
  control over, 538
  direct effects of, 531–32
  indirect effects of, 532–33
  nuclear, effects of, 533–36
  social policy on, 547–51
  technology of, 536–38
  terrorism and, 544–47
  theories on, 539–44
Washington, D. C., 272
Waste disposal, 516–18
Water pollution, 515–16
Watts riot, 261
Wealthfare, 228, 229
Wealthy people, 228–30, 416
Weapons (*see also* Wars)

  arms control and disarmament,
    547–49
  government spending on, 502
  gun control, 216–18
  nuclear, 533–36, 539
  technology of, 536–38
  used by gangs, 216
Webster v. *Reproductive Health Services*
    (U.S., 1990), 40
Welfare, 234, 240–41, 250–52
  AFDC (Aid to Families with Dependent
    Children), 254, 357, 364
  as disincentive to work, 252
  to low-income families with children,
    373
  poverty perpetuated by, 247
  preschool programs and, 244
  unemployed women on, 425
Welfare states, 228
Whistle blowers, 504–5
White-collar (occupational) crimes,
  167–69, 190–91
White-collar workers, 419–20, 423, 428
Whites:
  black sexuality viewed by, 266
  homicides among, 198
  migration to suburbs by, 274
  open admissions and, 403
  political power of, 260
  school desegregation resisted by,
    271–73
  violence among, 221
Whittle Schools, 393
Widowhood, 330, 334
Wildcat Experiment, 20, 187
Witness protection program, 192
Women (*see also* Sex roles and sexism)
  alcohol consumption by, 134
  crimes committed by, 175
  discrimination against, 294–95
    in employment, 300–303
    sexual harassment as, 303–4
  elderly:
    discrimination against, 337–38
    Social Security for, 345
    stereotypes of, 333–34
  family life of:
    alimony and child support for,
      372
    in black family, 358–59
    care for elderly by, 339
    employment and, 355–58
    illegitimate births to, 350, 366–68
    impact of divorce on, 364–65
    postponement of marriage by, 366
    reproductive issues and, 369–71
    single-parent families headed by,
      237–39, 254
    spouse abuse and, 212–13, 220
    widowhood and, 330
  family planning and, 479–80
  guns owned by, 218
  health care for, 40–42
  as immigrants, 492
  juvenile delinquency among, 173
  in labor force, 421
    unemployment among, 424–25
  mental illness among, 76–78

as minority group, 263
missing from China's population, 472, 482
sex-related social problems involving:
  incest, 96
  lesbianism, 99, 104–5
  pornography, 116
  prostitution, 107–15
  rape, 97, 208–10
sex roles of, 295–98
status offenses among, 173–74
as victims of domestic violence, 198
voting rights for, 3
Women Against Pornography, 116
Women's Bureau, 311
Women's movement, 304–5, 316
Workers, 408, 419–21 (*see also* Employment)
automation and, 426–27, 502–3
displaced, 500
dual labor market for, 247
effects of large corporations on, 415–16

employee assistance programs for, 141
exploitation of, 267
health problems of, 33
job satisfaction and alienation of, 427–29
job training programs for, 283
Marx on, 9–10
in mental hospitals, 81
occupational safety and health of, 429–30
retirement pensions for, 2
social policy on, 433–36
for transnational corporations, 414–15
undocumented immigrants as, 491–93
unemployment and, 421–26
women as, 294
Workers' compensation, 508
Workfare programs, 253, 283
Working class, 234
Working poor, 231–32, 241–42, 252–54

Work-release programs, 187
World War I, 531, 533, 536, 541, 550
World War II, 531, 532, 536, 538, 542, 550

Xanax (drug), 79

Young people (*see also* Children; Juvenile delinquency)
crimes committed by, 176
delinquency among, 172–74
dependency of, 323
drinking among, 136
gang violence by, 213–16
illegitimate children borne by, 367–68
patterns of drug use among, 144–45
status offenses by, 192
Yugoslavia, 533, 550

Zero Population Growth, Inc. (ZPG), 480–81